PALMER'S MANUAL

of Trees, Shrubs & Climbers

Stanley J Palmer

CONTENTS

LANCEWOOD PUBLISHING

AUSTRALIA

First published 1974
Modified edition 1984
Fully revised edition 1990
Reprinted twice in 1992
Revised and in full colour 1994
Reprinted 1997, 2001, 2003

Published by
Lancewood Publishing, P O Box 1105, Runaway Bay,
Queensland 4216 Australia

Written and edited by Stanley J Palmer
Project management: Stylus Publishing Services Ltd
Design and production: Barbara Nielsen (cover and colour pages), Alison Dench (text)

Printed through Condor Production Ltd, Hong Kong

ISBN 0 646 19362 7

PREFACE

'The land produced vegetation; plants bearing seed according to their kinds and trees bearing fruit with seed in it according to their kinds. And God saw that it was good.'

To believe the Genesis account that an all-powerful creator simply called everything into being requires a certain measure of faith which some may not claim to have. But by whichever means the earth's vegetation did come into being, everyone would have to agree that it is good!

Quite frankly, I would find it more difficult by far to accept that such diversity, utility and sheer beauty could originate in any other way than by the infinite wisdom and creativity of one whose objective was to prepare a perfect habitation for humanity.

But what amazes me even more is that, although mankind spoiled much of what was once perfect, the one who planted the very first garden, in an even greater demonstration of love and kindness, visited this planet and endured the humiliation of the first Easter.

The world races towards the 21st century. Ever increasing demands on natural resources and many kinds of pollution threaten our way of life and peaceful existence. Fortunately there are places of beauty and tranquility preserved for our enjoyment, and nature always responds quickly to any attempt we may make to improve our surroundings.

Every effort put into our gardens is rewarded with a feeling of satisfaction and well-being. It enhances property values, and makes a valuable contribution to the regeneration of a world in which people are healthier, happier and more contented.

This book introduces and explains how to grow an ever increasing range of good plant material with a desire that people everywhere may enjoy even more the incomparable delights of beautiful gardens.

Stanley J Palmer

HOW TO USE THIS BOOK

Palmer's Manual includes a comprehensive cross section of genus, species and cultivars grown and offered by production nurseries in New Zealand and temperate Australia. Whether you're new to the wonderful world of gardening or a connoisseur in search of something rare, the book is designed to make a very complex subject as simple as possible. While some species may not be easy to obtain, the bulk of those featured should be obtainable from most garden centres or retail nurseries.

Plant names

Although it may be hard for average gardeners to pronounce or remember botanical names, if common names were the only terms by which plants were known, the world of horticulture would be in utter confusion. Universally accepted botanical names are given to plants so they can be readily identified when spoken or written about in any part of the world.

Plants can be classified at four main levels, for example:

> Family: Proteaceae
> Genus: Telopea
> Species: speciosissima
> Cultivar: 'Fireglow'

The **family** name is the order or family to which the genus belongs. In the example given it is Proteaceae, a large family embracing plants from many parts of the world, particularly South Africa with beautiful Leucospermums and Leucadendrons and Australia with Banksias, Dryandras and numerous other popular shrubs.

A **genus** is a group of species, sometimes only one, usually of similar structure, and which may be supposed to have arisen from a common ancestor. The generic name Telopea is derived from the Greek *telopos* meaning 'seen from afar'.

A **species** is a single distinct kind of plant with certain distinguishing features often referred to in the specific name, eg, speciosissima meaning 'most beautiful'.

A **cultivar** is a plant sufficiently different from others of its kind to warrant a separate name such as Telopea speciosissima 'Fireglow'. Cultivar names appear between single quotes.

The meaning or derivation of most scientific names appears throughout. **Common names** usually reflect countries of origin, shape or style of flower or leaf or a fancied resemblance to other plants, birds or animals. Many different plants may share a similar common name.

Tree and shrub dimensions

Many variables such as climate, soil, exposure, feeding, pruning, sources of propagation material, condition at planting time and so on, make it impossible to be precise when giving ultimate dimensions of any plant.

Measurements stated throughout are intended only as a rough guide to what may reasonably be expected over a period of five to 10 years. In all cases height is given first, followed by width.

Cross references

Throughout text pages, the bold numbers printed at the end of many descriptions refer to the page on which that variety is illustrated.

Numbers alongside each caption of an illustration refer to the page on which that variety is described.

Plant selection guide

This guide is useful when you need subjects for specific purposes. It may be flowering shrubs of a particular colour, plants for ground cover, perhaps winter flowering trees or a plant for a container. Under various headings you'll find varieties to cover many situations arising in average gardens.

GARDENING BY SYMBOLS

The system of cultural symbols used throughout this book (see below) is designed to help you choose at a glance the correct plants for your particular garden conditions.

Quite often where one set of symbols has to cover several species with differing cultural requirements, the symbols refer either to the majority or the most popular. It is important that you also refer to the information given in the introduction to the genus, or within the description of each species or cultivar. In many cases a particular species may be tolerant of conditions far less favorable that the symbols indicate.

KEY TO SYMBOLS

Sunlight

⬜ Prefers maximum sunshine.

◐ Prefers filtered sunlight such as the dappled shade offered by deciduous trees, or a location which avoids the hottest midday or summer sun.

● Prefers total shade, such as under tall, dense trees, between buildings, in entrance ways, or beneath a roof.

⊖ Quite indifferent, growing happily in any of the above conditions.

Temperature

🌡 Prefers high temperatures, or a location free of frost.

🌡 Tolerant of light to medium frost, or happy under average conditions.

🌡 Hardy to all frost or prefers low temperature.

Exposure to wind

🍃 Tolerant of constant strong winds other than coastal ones.

Requires or prefers protection.

Quite indifferent, or tolerant of any but unreasonable conditions.

Tolerant of coastal exposure.

Moisture

💧 Grows in wet, boggy or poorly drained soil, or needs adequate moisture.

💧 Grows happily under normal or average garden conditions.

💧 Dry conditions essential, or requires perfect drainage.

Soil texture

Grows in light, loose or free soil such as stony, peaty, sandy or volcanic.

Tolerates or requires heavy or clay soils.

Grows under normal or average garden conditions.

Soil chemistry
Relative acidity or alkalinity as measured by the pH scale is an important element in growing plants, especially those requiring specific soil reaction. 'Neutral' soils have a pH of 7. 'Acid' soils have a pH below 7. 'Alkaline' soils have a pH above 7.

Most genus have neither symbol, because they grow happily in the neutral to slightly acid conditions prevailing in a majority of garden soils.

pH7 Requires acid or lime-free conditions.

pH7 Prefers alkaline soil or applications of lime.

TREES AND SHRUBS

ABELIA

A genus of about 15 species of shrubs from China, Japan, Himalayas and Mexico named for Dr Clarke Abel, physician to Lord Amherst's embassy to China in 1817. Easily grown shrubs of considerable garden merit, they seem happy in average garden soils and delight in moist warm climates. Plant in full sun or semi-shade in shrub borders, as dividers, barriers, screens, hedges, individual specimens or in groups. Regular trimming maintains good form and encourages lush new growth and flower. Pests don't seem to bother them.

Caprifoliaceae. *All evergreen.*

Abelia 'Edward Goucher'
Small lilac-mauve bell flowers with orange throat and showy red calyces during summer, produced with the freedom of A grandiflora. Hybrid of A grandiflora × A schumannii. Worthwhile flowering shrub. 1.2 × 1.2m.

Abelia × grandiflora
Glossy Abelia
Usually grown as a clipped hedge. Ovate, 25mm leaves at first dark green and very glossy, mature bronzy red. Masses of white flushed pink, 1cm bell-shaped flowers appear on untrimmed plants. As a hedge, it forms a dense living wall within two years. Soft tip growth is a pleasure to trim. Grandiflora — large flowered. For a hedge one to two metres high, plant between 30 and 45cm apart. 2 × 1.5m.

Abelia × grandiflora 'Francis Mason'
New Zealand raised cultivar with ovate, 3cm leaves richly variegated yellow and green with distinct bronzy hue as they first appear on reddish brown, gracefully arching stems. Funnel shaped, 12mm light pink flower clusters appear spring through summer and when the blossoms fall, rosy sepals provide further colour into autumn. An attractive dwarf shrub for adaptability, form, foliage and flower. Annual heavy pruning encourages healthy growth and greater flower masses. 1.30 × 1.30m.   **9**

ABIES

A genus of about 50 species of coniferous trees widely distributed in the mountainous regions of central and southern Europe, Asia from the Himalayas northwards, Japan and North America, named from Latin *abies*, a fir tree. Abies or Firs have similar features to Piceas or Spruce and may be distinguished by the 'live leaf' test. Fir leaves break off cleanly if pulled, while Spruce come off with a little bark.

Most Abies grow naturally in cool, moist, alpine areas and prefer being cultivated in a similar environment. But except for very hot or dry areas, they do succeed in more temperate gardens. As they grow very slowly, consider them in home landscaping as lawn specimens, rock gardens, containers or bonsai.

Pinaceae. *All evergreen.*

Abies balsamea 'Hudsonia'
Dwarf Balsam Fir
Low, prostrate form of the North American species. Short, dense branches. Short, broadly flattened, dark-green leaves, blue green beneath, balsam scent when crushed. Extremely hardy. Good in rock gardens. 30 × 30cm.

Abies concolor
Colorado Fir, White Fir
North American species forming a tall, narrow, pyramidal specimen with smooth grey bark, spreading branches in whorls to ground level and glabrous young shoots. Linear, 4–6cm, ascending leaves, sparsely arranged and curved sideways like a scythe, green to glaucous blue on both surfaces. Cylindrical cones tapering to a point, green tinged purple, brown when mature. Concolor — same colour throughout. 12 × 5m.

Abies grandis
Giant Fir, Vancouver Fir
From an area from Vancouver Islands, northern California, east to Montana, an immense tree of 75–100 metres with two metre bole. Bark smooth on younger trees, blistered with resinous knobs, becoming ridged and greyish brown with age. Small, rounded, resinous winter buds. Leaves 2–5cm long by 2–3mm wide, glossy green, with two white lines beneath, nasty odour

when crushed. Cylindrical 7–10cm cones, tapering both ends, green maturing brown. Ideal specimen or shade tree for acreage gardens. Grandis — big, showy. 18 × 8m.

Abies mariesii
Maries Fir
Japanese species. Mature specimen to 30m with 1m trunk and smooth, pale grey bark becoming lighter with age. Lower branches decurving, higher ones more erect. Winter buds resinous and downy, young shoots reddish brown. Glossy, dark green, 1.5–2.5cm leaves with two white bands beneath. Cones to 10cm, violet-purple at first, brown when mature. Named for 19th century botanist Charles Maries. 5 × 3m.

Abies nordmanniana
Caucasian Fir
Vigorous, densely foliaged fir from western Caucasus with stately, columnar form and tiers of horizontal branches to ground level. Non-resinous, pale brown winter buds. Glossy, dark-green leaves to 3cm × 2mm, with silvery white, stomatal bands beneath. Serves well as long term container plant with adequate water. Named for A von Nordmann, 19th century Professor of Zoology, Odessa and Helsingfors. 4 × 2m.

Abies pinsapo
Spanish Fir, Hedgehog Fir
From the mountains of southern Spain at altitudes of 1100–1200m, growing slowly to 30m in dense, pyramidal form with 1m trunk and tiers of ascending branches. Ovoid, resinous winter buds, young shoots cinnamon brown, smooth and glabrous. Stiff, deep-green, 10–15 × 2–3mm leaves radiate at right angles around branches. Cylindrical, 10–15cm, deep reddish brown cones. Maintains symmetrical pyramidal form and reasonable dimensions for years. 2 × 1m.

Abies procera
Noble Fir
From Washington and Oregon States. Fast growing, slender conical tree to 70m, with tiers of slightly decurving branches to ground level on 1.5m trunk with thick, deeply fissured, light brown bark. Young shoots covered in rusty brown down. Leaves blue-green to greyish green, 25–35 × 15mm. Cylindrical cones to 25cm, purplish green, maturing brown. For acreage gardens or containers. Procera — tall. 9 × 4m.

ABUTILON

A genus of about 150 species of perennial herbs, soft-wooded shrubs and other plants mostly from tropical and subtropical America, Asia, Africa and Australia named from the Arabic for a species of Mallow. Abutilon flowers have a fancied resemblance to the common name — Chinese Lantern. In mixed borders, or some shady corner, with heavy annual pruning, Abutilon produces an almost constant supply of attractive blooms highly valued for floral art, especially during winter. Suitable for large pots or containers. Grows in any reasonable garden conditions, hardy in most temperate climates.

Malvaceae. *All evergreen.*

Abutilon hybridum
Chinese Lantern
Fast growing, somewhat rangy shrub with deep green or variegated, palmate, 3–5 lobed leaves, and masses of pendent, 3–4cm lantern shaped flowers in shades of red, orange, pink, yellow and white through spring and summer. 1.5 × 1.5m.　**9**

Abutilon vitifolium
Soft wooded Chilean species. Palmate, 15cm leaves with 3–7, pointed and toothed lobes, dull green, covered with felt-like tomentum. Wide open, 7cm, pale lilac blue flowers, sometimes deeper, produced in clusters in the upper leaf axils. Hardy anywhere with good drainage. Vitifolium — with leaves like those of the grapevine. 4 × 2.5m.

ACACIA

A genus in excess of 1000 species, mainly from dry tropical to temperate regions of the world, with about 700 found only in Australia. Name is derived from the Greek, *akis* meaning a sharp point or thorn, with particular reference to a thorny Egyptian species. Wattle is said to have arisen from an earlier generation of settlers who used slender sticks from some species to construct shelters. Relatively few find a consistent following in ornamental gardens, but careful evaluation and selection over many years has revealed a number of reliable species of considerable garden merit.

Acacias adapt to varying conditions but are at their best in poor or stony soil with good drainage and full sun. Those from Australia's dry inland areas are particularly drought resistant. Light pruning after flowering retains a shapely bush and prolongs life. They get along better without excessive fertilizer. Staking until stems are strong enough to be self-supporting is essential. Profuse winter blooming, intense golden colour, landscaping adaptability and trouble-free performance.

Mimosaceae. *All evergreen.*

Acacia baileyana
Cootamundra Wattle, Golden Wattle
Possibly the most popular Acacia cultivated in Australasia. Wide-spreading small tree, outer branchlets gracefully pendulous. Feathery, blue-grey to silver-blue, bipinnate foliage. Fluffy, golden yellow, globular flowers in dense racemes smother the tree in winter. Named for Frederick M. Bailey, 19th–20th century Australian botanist and author. New South Wales. 6 × 4m.

Acacia baileyana 'Ngaroto Gold'
Golden Leaf Wattle
Similar foliage and flower to A baileyana, but after blooming, new growth appears in tones of lime-yellow to golden yellow. Syn A Baileyana 'Aurea'. 6 × 4m.

Acacia baileyana 'Purpurea'
Purple Leaf Wattle
Similar to A baileyana with added feature of lavender to purple-tinted new growth. Outstanding foliage and flower. Prune after flower for stronger growth and better foliage colour. 5 × 3.5m.

Acacia cardiophylla
Wyalong Wattle
Finely divided, feathery and fern-like, bipinnate leaves, soft grey- green in colour. Long arching branches draped in spring with masses of fluffy flower balls. One of the most dainty-foliaged Acacias. New South Wales. 3 × 2.5m.　**9**

Acacia drummondii
Drummond Wattle
Dwarf to small, open shrub, glaucous, bipinnate leaves with up to three pairs of 10 × 2mm flat pinnules or leaflets. Bright golden yellow, rod-shaped, 10–25mm flower heads appear at branch ends winter through spring. Prefers partial shade, summer moisture and pruning after flowering. Named for James Drummond, first 18th–19th century State botanist in Western Australia. 1.30 × 1.30m.

Acacia floribunda
Sallow Wattle
Gracefully spreading, open form with 5–12cm × 12mm leaves or phyllodes, deep green, thin and finely veined, tapering to a fine, curving point. Pale yellow, fragrant flowers in long cylindrical rods or fingers in great abundance spring and early summer. Common name refers to willow-like habit. Floribunda — with many flowers. Queensland, New South Wales, Victoria. 4 × 3m.

Acacia iteaphylla
Port Lincoln Wattle
Ornamental, shrub with numerous angular, ascending or pendulous, glaucous branches. New growth flushed purple-pink. Narrow-lanceolate, 6–10 × 1cm, blue-green phyllodes with silvery sheen and curved point. Small, globular, fragrant, lemon-yellow flowers in axillary racemes appear profusely late autumn through spring. South Australia. Iteaphylla — willow-like leaves. 3 × 4m.

Acacia longifolia
Sydney Golden Wattle
Normally seen as a rounded billowy shrub with narrow-elliptcal phyllodes up to 15 × 3cm, often curved, bright green and with numerous veins. Deep bright yellow flowers in 6cm rods or fingers spring and early summer. Fast grower, flourishes in sandy soils, tolerates salt and a good soil binder near the coast. Consistent coastal breezes tend to encourage prostrate form. Excellent fast screen known to have attained 4m in 18 months. Eastern States, South Australia and Tasmania. 5 × 4m.

Acacia melanoxylon
Blackwood
From areas of high rainfall, thriving in moist gullies. Prized for beautifully marked timber. Forms a dense, round-headed tree with oblanceolate, dull-green phyllodes to 15 × 3cm, straight or curved and with prominent longitudinal veins. Racemes of pale yellow, 1cm, globular flowers appear winter and early spring. Hardy shade or shelter tree in areas of high rainfall. New South Wales, Victoria, South Australia and Tasmania. Melanoxylon — black wood. 30 × 15m.

Acacia podalyriifolia
Mount Morgan Wattle
Forms an open rounded head with smooth, greyish brown bark. Silvery, grey-green, ovate to elliptic, 4 × 3cm phyllodes, soft and satiny to the touch. Beautiful, rich golden, 1cm, globular flowers in large terminal or axillary racemes. Amongst the earliest Wattles to bloom, commencing late autumn and continuing for many weeks. Outstanding tree for gardens where frosts are not too severe. Podalyriifolia — with leaves like Podalyria. Queensland, New South Wales. 5 × 3.5m.　**9**

Acacia pravissima
Alpine Wattle
Upright growth habit, slender, drooping branches. Blue-grey to dull green, irregularly deltoid to cuneate phyllodes like short knife blades densely set along slender branches, become gold-tipped in winter. Bright golden yellow, 5mm flowers in crowded axillary racemes up to 10cm long through spring and early summer. Pravissima — twisted. Victoria, New South Wales. 3 × 2.5m.

Acacia rubida
Red-Stemmed Wattle
Varies from a spreading shrub to small erect tree with angular branchlets. Young shoots reddish brown, bipinnate juvenile leaves which may persist for some years. Green to blue-green, lanceolate phyllodes to 18 × 2cm, straight or slightly curved and with prominent midrib. Stems and foliage become conspicuously reddened during winter. Pale to bright yellow, globular flowers in loose racemes in winter through spring. Eastern States. Rubida — red. 6 × 5m.

Acacia sophorae
Coastal Wattle
Hardy coastal species forming a somewhat spreading bush with elliptic to oblong elliptic, 8–12 × 2–3cm, light green phyllodes with up to five prominent longtitudinal veins. Yellow, rod-like, 3cm flower heads appear winter through spring. Hardy to frost, salt and salt-laden winds and adaptable to varying soils and climates. Valuable for coastal erosion control or reclamation. Eastern States, Sophorae — resembling the genus Sophora. 3 × 4m.

Acacia verticillata 'Rewa'
Rice's Wattle, Prickly Moses
Ornamental shrub with linear, 1–2cm, dark green, awl-shaped, sharply pointed phyllodes in whorls of six and with a pungent odour. In early spring masses of 15mm, rod-like, lemon-yellow blossoms appear. Grows almost anywhere forming a handsome rounded shrub with branches gracefully pendant at the tips. Verticillata — having whorls. Syn A riceana. New South Wales, Victoria and Tasmania. Evergreen. 2.5 × 2m.

A genus of about 150 species of trees and shrubs from eastern and western northern hemisphere, named from the Latin *acer*, sharp, because the hard wood was used in Roman spear shafts. Maples are valued for foliage, colourful young growth and brilliant autumn shades, decorative stems and diverse form.

Generally, maples grow in average, well drained, lime-free garden soil with their roots cool and moist in summer. Ornamental A palmatum cultivars must have deeply worked, loamy soil, conditioned with peat moss and sand, sheltered from hot, drying winds to prevent young foliage burning. The Dissectum or Weeping Maples especially, need filtered sunlight, shelter, staking and training from an early age. Mulching with peat moss or granulated bark and regular deep watering helps maintain desired soil conditions. Most species are less demanding.

Use Japanese maples against fences or walls, in patios, entryways or as small lawn specimens. Attractive in groups of selected species where varying sizes can be spaced effectively. Use under trees or amongst Rhododendrons, Azaleas or Ferns. Weeping Maples are perfect beside pools or boulders, in containers or as Bonsai. Most Western species are large trees for park and, acreage gardens.
Aceraceae. *All listed Acers deciduous.*

Acer buergerianum
Trident Maple, Three Toothed Maple
China and Japan. Erect, forming rounded, spreading crown. Trident-shaped leaves, 7–8cm long with three shallow, forward pointing, triangular lobes. Spring growth coppery red, leaves deep green and glossy through summer, turning vivid red, apricot or yellow in autumn. Forms a rounded crown with low spreading branches. Stake and trim for high branching. Decorative and useful shade for patios, and bonsai. 7 × 5m.

Acer campestre
Field Maple, Hedge Maple
From southern Europe, Turkey to Iran. Medium sized, round-headed tree, hardy, strong growing, often used for tall rustic shelter. Leaves 10cm long with 3–5 rounded lobes, clear yellow in autumn, often flushed red. Campestre — of fields. 10 × 5m.

Acer cappadocicum
Coliseum Maple
From Caucasus, Asia Minor to Himalayas. Broad, 7–15cm, glabrous leaves with 5–7 triangular, slender pointed lobes on 10–20cm petioles, rich butter-yellow in autumn. Erect, slender habit, tolerant of dry conditions. Cappadocicum — of Cappadocia. 8 × 5m.

Acer cappadocicum 'Aureum'
Golden Coliseum Maple
Ornamental cultivar with bright red new growth. Leaves coppery red at first, then golden yellow for many weeks, then light green, then creamy-yellow and red in autumn. 7 × 5m.   **10**

Acer cappadocicum 'Rubrum'
Red Coliseum Maple
Similar to above but with blood red spring foliage, becoming dark green through summer, yellow and red in autumn. Forms a compact rounded crown. 7 × 5m.

Acer caudatifolium
Taiwan Maple
Strong vigorous Taiwanese native with open branch pattern, brilliant red branchlets and attractive greyish-green bark with silvery white stripes. Large, three-lobed leaves at first bright red as they unfold, deep green and glossy through summer, brilliant fiery-orange red in autumn. Protect from heavy frost and strong wind. Keep moist in dry periods. Syn Acer morrisonensis. Caudatifolium — with caudate leaves. 6 × 5m.

Acer circinatum
Vine Maple
Native to moist forests and stream banks in coastal mountains of western North America where, shaded by larger trees, is inclined to sprawl, a characteristic for exploiting in shady garden areas or as an espalier on cool walls where its stems make intricate winter patterns. In full sun it loses its vine-likeness to form a single-trunked specimen. Leaves to 15 × 15cm, 5–10 lobed, light green, turning orange scarlet or yellow in autumn. Tiny clusters of reddish purple flowers in late spring, followed by pairs of winged fruit not unlike small red bow ties hidden amongst the foliage. Circinatum — coiled. 5 × 4m.

Acer circinatum 'Little Gem'
Little Gem Vine Maple
Delightful petite cultivar, a compact, rounded mound with tiny, maple-like, light green leaves, changing in autumn to shades of orange and crimson. Perfect for flower borders, rock gardens or containers. 1 × 1m.

Acer davidii
David's Maple
Native to central China. Handsome tree with erect, open spreading form and distinctive shiny green bark striped silvery white, effective when bare in winter. Bronze tinted new growth, leaves ovate to ovate-oblong, 8–20cm long, glossy green, embossed with deep red veins, turning bright yellow, red, orange and purple in autumn. Clusters of showy, greenish yellow flowers in spring, followed in autumn by green, winged fruits suffused red. Introduced from Yunnan by l'Abbe David, 19th century French missionary and botanist who collected many plants in China and after whom it is named. 8 × 5m.

Above: Abelia x grandiflora 'Francis Mason' **6**

Above and below: Abutilon hybridum *Chinese Lantern* **7**

Above: Acacia podalyriifolia *Mount Morgan Wattle* **7**
Below: Acacia cardiophylla *Wyalong Wattle* **7**

Above: Acer cappadocicum 'Aureum' **8**

Above: Acer palmatum 'Chishio' **14**
Below: A p dissectum 'Atropurpureum' **14**

Above: Acer palmatum dissectum 'Filigree' **14**
Below: Acer palmatum 'Roseo Marginatum' **15**

Below: Acer pseudoplatanus 'Brilliantissimum' **15**

Above: Adenandra uniflora **17**

Above: Agapanthus orientalis blue **18**
Below: Agapanthus orientalis white **18**

Below: Aesculus x carnea *Pink Horse Chestnut* **17**

Above: Adenandra fragrans **17**
Below: Anigozanthus 'Bush Nugget' **25**

Above: Agonis flexuosa 'Variegata' *Variegated Willow Myrtle* **19**

Above: Agapetes serpens *Flame Heath* **18**
Below: Actinodium cunninghamii *Swamp Daisy Albany Daisy* **17**

Above: Agave americana 'Marginata' **19**
Below: Alyogyne huegelii *Desert Rose Lilac Hibiscus* **25**

Acer davidii grosseri 'Hersii'
Smaller growing than A davidii, valued for grey-green and white, striped and marbled bark. Leaves ovate-cordate, 5–12cm long, dark green, either tri-lobed or unlobed. Rich autumn colour. From China. 5 × 4m.

Acer griseum
Paper Bark Maple
Excellent Chinese native small tree with tidy, erect, spreading form and unusual cinnamon-brown bark peeling in thin, papery flakes. Leaves comprise three soft-green segments, the central leaflet ovate-lanceolate, 4–7cm long with coarsely toothed margins. Fiery-red autumn colours. Showy red winged fruits early summer. Griseum — grey. 6 × 5m.

Acer hookeri
Himalayan Maple
From Himalayas, Sikkim, Bhutan. Forms a fine, somewhat erect specimen with drooping side shoots. Young shoots bright red and branches smooth, reddish brown. Leaves oblong-ovate, 10–15cm long, rich coppery bronze and glossy in spring, bright green through summer, orange-red in autumn. Requires shelter from heavy frost and strong wind. Named after Sir Joseph Dalton Hooker 19–20th century botanist and author, at one time director of the Royal Botanic Gardens, Kew. Deciduous. 6 × 4m.

Acer japonicum
Full Moon Maple
This Japanese species forms a small tree not unlike the better known Acer palmatum but with stocky growth, thicker stems and larger foliage. Leaves almost round, 5–12cm across with 7–13 lobes, soft green in summer, crimson red in autumn. Red winged flowers appear in delicate drooping clusters with the young foliage. All forms of A japonica prefer moist, well-drained soil sheltered from cold winds. 3 × 2m.

Acer japonicum 'Aconitifolium'
Fern Leaf Maple
Amongst the most beautiful of maple foliage. Leaves 20cm across, deeply cut almost to the centre into seven or more lobes, each irregularly toothed and serrated. Foliage green through summer, gradually changing through crimson to glorious shades of orange, yellow and red, this most vivid display of garden colour persisting well into winter. Aconitifolium — foliage like Aconite. 2 × 1.5m.

Acer japonicum 'Aureum'
Golden Full Moon Maple
Slow growing form with compact habit. Broad, fan-shaped leaves pale gold as they appear in spring becoming chartreuse yellow through summer. Provide light shade and shelter from strong wind. 3 × 2m.

Acer japonicum 'Vitifolium'
Grape Leaf Maple
Beautiful, vigorous, multi branched form. Leaves fan-shaped or grapevine-like with 10–12 distinct lobes, becoming brilliantly coloured through autumn. Vitifolium — vine-like leaves. 3 × 2m.

Acer macrophyllum
Oregon Maple, Big Leaf Maple
From western North America, a substantial tree to 30m with 1m trunk and sturdy, glabrous branches. Large, 30cm, lustrous dark-green, leaves, paler and finely pubescent beneath with 3–5 deeply cut lobes either entire or with irregularly dentate margins. Bright orange autumn colours. Fragrant yellow flowers in pendulous racemes followed by hairy, red 4–5cm samaras. Macrophyllum — large leaves. 10 × 5m.

Acer negundo
Box Elder Maple
Hardy, North American maple thriving almost anywhere. Leaves pinnate with 3–7, green, ovate, coarsely serrated leaflets. Virtually no autumn colour. Silky sprays of yellowish flowers followed by winged seed pods. Noted for rapid development, hardiness and the provision of rapid screen or shade. The following cultivars are preferred. 9 × 7m.

Acer negundo 'Elegans'
Golden Box Elder
Leaves slightly larger than the Silver Box Elder, green margined golden yellow. Remove immediately any naturally reverting shoots with plain green leaves which may appear in variegated forms of Acer negundo. 6 × 4.5m.

Acer negundo 'Flamingo'
Beautiful cultivar, with vivid carmine pink and white spring growth, gradually changing to white and green flushed soft pink. Autumn shades red and pink. 5 × 4m.

Acer negundo 'Kelly's Gold'
Choice selection with yellow branchlets, golden-yellow new spring leaves, lime green through summer, changing to pale yellow in autumn. 5 × 4m.

Acer negundo 'Variegatum'
Silver Box Elder
Attractive greyish green foliage irregularly edged silvery cream, flushed rose-pink when young. 6 × 4.5m.

Acer negundo 'Violaceum'
Young shoots purple maroon with a whitish bloom, leaves maturing deep green. Striking, bright burgundy, long flower tassels early spring. Vigorous, hardy, erect grower. 6 × 5m.

Acer palmatum
Japanese Maple
Native to Japan and Korea. Forms a round-headed, open airy tree with slender green and red branchlets. Young spring growth reddish. Soft green, 5–10cm, palmate leaves with 5–11 deep lobes, becoming yellow, orange and red in autumn. Perfect against walls, in patios, as a specimen, for containers or Bonzai. Scores of magnificent cultivars have arisen from this species. Palmatum — like a hand with outspread fingers. 5 × 4m.

Acer palmatum 'Asahi Zuru'
Rising Sun Maple
Forms a small round-headed, bushy tree with distinctive variegated foliage. New leaves vivid pink and white at first, later adding a touch of green. Three-toned effect continues through summer and autumn. Requires partial shade and shelter from wind. 3 × 2.5m.

Acer palmatum 'Atropurpureum'
Purple Japanese Maple
Leaves rich crimson in spring, dark to bronze purple through summer and bright scarlet in autumn. Deep purple stems. Atro — dark. 2.5 × 2m.

Acer palmatum 'Aureum'
Golden Japanese Maple
Erect, bushy grower with characteristic palmate leaves, bright yellow with a tinge of pink at first, lime green through summer, becoming pale yellow in autumn. Aureum — ornamented with gold. 4.5 × 4m.

Acer palmatum 'Beni Komachi'
Beautiful Little Red Girl
Forms a bushy shrub with fine, deeply lobed leaves, bright crimson at first, becoming greenish red with crimson margins through summer, vivid scarlet in autumn. Ideal in shrub or flower borders. 2 × 1.5m.

Acer palmatum 'Beni Schichihenge'
Erect, bushy grower with fresh green, palmate leaves dramatically edged in tones of salmon pink to orange. 2 × 1.5m.

Acer palmatum 'Bloodgood'
Grows strongly into a rounded bush with blackish red stems and deep red foliage through spring and summer turning brilliant crimson in autumn. Showy red seed capsule in early summer. 4 × 3m.

Acer palmatum 'Burgundy Lace'
Small erect, rounded maple with striking, deep burgundy wine leaves heavily serrated, fringed, turning scarlet in autumn. 3 × 2.5m.

Acer palmatum 'Butterfly'
Delightfully petite, erect and vase-shaped bush with small, elegant, deeply lobed, bluish green leaves margined creamy white, delicately suffused pink. The pink toning fades through summer, but reappears with autumn, intensifying to brilliant crimson prior to falling. 3 × 1.3m.

Acer palmatum 'Chishio'
Dwarf Japanese Maple
Numerous twiggy branchlets of this slow-growing, bushy maple burst forth in spring with a blaze of small, flame pink leaves. At the height of its brilliance Chishio would rival the finest flowering shrub. Among the choicest dwarf shrubs and because of its size can be easily located away from strong burning winds. 1.30 × 1m.   **10**

Acer palmatum 'Coonara Pygmy'
An Australian cultivar forming a dense, rounded, twiggy shrub with small, palmate, bright green leaves which become brilliant orange to flame in autumn. Excellent for small gardens, containers or bonsai. 1 × 1m.

Acer palmatum 'Crippsii'
Bronze Japanese Maple
Rare, slow-growing maple with erect, vase-shaped, compact habit. Small, finely serrated, deep green foliage with curled margins. 2 × 1m.

Acer palmatum dissectum
Weeping Maple
Graceful branches, first horizontal then weeping to the ground, clothed with rich green, delicate, finely cut, almost fern-like leaves. Dwarf growth habit, slow maturing, continually increasing in beauty throughout their long life. Locate beside pools, by rocks or against a feature wall. Weeping Maples are exclusive shrubs, the choice of discerning gardeners. Dissectum — deeply cut or divided into segments. 1 × 1.5m.

Acer palmatum dissectum 'Atropurpureum'
Similar gracefully pendulous branch pattern combined with lacy, finely cut foliage in shades of rich purple. Outstanding cultivar. 1 × 1.5m.   **10**

Acer palmatum dissectum 'Crimson Queen'
Fine selected weeping Maple with scarlet-red stems. Long, finely dissected, deep reddish-purple leaves. Retains leaf colour throughout summer, turning fiery scarlet in autumn. 1 × 1.5m.

Acer palmatum dissectum 'Filigree'
Filigree Lace Maple
Unique, finely cut and serrated, lacy foliage, pastel green with minute creamy yellow specks. Colour intensifies through summer, becoming rich golden yellow in autumn. Extremely choice maple. 1 × 1.5m.   **10**

Acer palmatum dissectum 'Inaba Shidare'
Vigorous, gracefully pendulous form, intense dark purple, deeply serrated foliage, retaining good colour through summer. 1 × 1.5m.

Acer palmatum dissectum 'Lion Heart'
Strong, vigorous grower, branches erect at first, then spreading and cascading to form a dome-shaped bush. Deep maroon-red foliage. 3 × 3m.

Acer palmatum dissectum 'Ornatum Variegatum'
Distinct variegated weeping maple with delicate lacy leaves intricately and finely divided and sub-divided, bronzy green with markings of pink and cream. Colour somewhat muted through summer but richly hued in autumn. Ornatum — ornamental or showy. 1 × 1.5m.

Acer palmatum dissectum 'Palmatifidium'
Eagle Claw Maple
Leaves less finely cut at the margins than other dissectum forms, bright emerald green through spring and summer changing to gold, orange and crimson in autumn. Strong grower, soon forming an elegant large shrub with cascading branches. 2.5 × 2m.

Acer palmatum dissectum 'Red Dragon'
Outstanding, vigorous weeping maple with gracefully pendulous branches clothed with deep purple-red, finely dissected foliage. Retains its colour through spring and summer, becoming rich fiery scarlet in autumn. 1 × 1.5.

Acer palmatum dissectum 'Red Filigree Lace'
Red Filigree Lace
Finely dissected, lacy, thread-like leaves in deep purple-red almost maroon colouring. Vigorous grower. 1 × 1.5m.

Acer palmatum dissectum 'Rubrifolium'
Finely dissected foliage, bronzy-rust-red through spring, becoming coppery green through summer, golden yellow tinted rich scarlet in autumn. Strong reliable grower. 1 × 1.5m.

Acer palmatum dissectum 'Seiryu'
Upright Lace Leaf Maple
Upright growth habit with branches arising at steep angles to slowly form a broad outline. intricately dissected bright green foliage clothing gracefully pendulous branches. Autumn colours soft yellow to gold, with orange and red tints. 3 × 2.5m.

Acer palmatum dissectum 'Viridis'
Green Weeping Maple
Intricate and delicate soft fresh green, feathery spring foliage becomes deeper green through summer, golden yellow and orange in autumn. 1 × 1m.

Acer palmatum 'Fireglow'
Erect grower with deep purple-red palmate leaves which keep their colour through summer, turning intense scarlet and crimson in autumn. 3 × 2.5m.

Acer palmatum 'Hagoromo'
Japanese Angel Tree
Forms a dense bushy shrub with multi stems. Finely cut, feathery palmate leaves, deep green with a distinctive sheen, turning to delicate shades of pale yellow and orange in autumn. 2 × 2m.

Acer palmatum 'Higasayama'
Mount Higasa Maple
Outstanding maple, leaves deeply lobed, distinctively curved and twisted, creamy white with green central zone, margined rose pink, becoming orange and red during autumn. 3 × 2.5m.

Acer palmatum 'Inazuma'
Thunder Maple
Distinctive, palmate, deeply divided and sharply serrated leaves, rich purple-red in spring, bronzy green during summer, crimson in autumn. 3.5 × 2.5m.

Acer palmatum 'Kamagata'
Curved Leaf Maple
Very dwarf compact grower with delicate appearance. Small, fine-lobed leaves, bright green with a purple hue, turning brilliant orange-yellow in autumn. 1 × 1m.

Acer palmatum 'Katsura'
Wig Maple
Treasured small maple with striking spring growth in pale yellow, suffused light golden orange with deeper margins. Leaves green through summer turning yellow, orange and red in autumn. 2.5 × 2m.

Acer palmatum Linearifolium 'Atropurpureum'
Upright vase-shaped growth habit and long, narrow, strap-like lobed leaves. Young shoots purple red, changing to bronze-green and crimson in autumn. 3 × 2.5m.

Acer palmatum 'O'Kagami'
Mirror Maple
A small robust tree with intense bright red spring growth, deepening to shiny black-purple in summer with glossy, oiled sheen. Fiery scarlet and red autumn shades. 4 × 3m.

Acer palmatum 'Osakasuki'
Attractive seven lobed bright green young foliage, rich green through summer, colouring in autumn to fiery orange or crimson scarlet. Considered the most brilliant Japanese maple for autumn colour. 2.5 × 2m.

Acer palmatum 'Roseo Marginatum'
Tricolor Maple
Small, deeply cut, 5–7 lobed leaves, green and white, delicately margined rose pink. Dense, upright vase form, attractive through all seasons. 2 × 1.5m. **10**

Acer palmatum 'Samurai-Aka'
Distinctive new maroon shoots unfurl to creamy yellow leaves veined in green and overtoned bronze red. Striking and most unusual. 2 × 1.5m.

Acer palmatum 'Sango Kaku'
Coral Bark Maple
Valuable maple for year-round effects. Spring foliage soft lime-green margined red, mid green through summer, turning soft canary yellow in autumn. Conspicuous and attractive vivid coral-red younger stems and twigs, appearing like lacquered canes. A distinct winter feature quite unequalled in other species. Syn Acer palmatum 'Senkaki'. Syn A palmatum 'Seigan'. 3 × 2.5m.

Acer palmatum 'Shaina'
Dense, compact, erect growing sport of Acer palmatum 'Bloodwood'. Spring foliage bright red becoming deep maroon red during summer and intensifying with autumn. 1.75 × 1m.

Acer palmatum 'Shigitatsu Sawa'
Reticulatum Maple
A maple with delicate subtle charm. Pale lime-green leaves with reticulated deep green veins, becoming deeper green during summer, with the addition of red hues in autumn. Shelter and semi-shade preferable. 3 × 2m.

Acer palmatum 'Shindeshojo'
Ruby Leaf Maple
New shoots vibrant, deep ruby red, maturing mid summer to bronzy green with a blending of orange pink, changing to bright orange and red in autumn. Slow growing, bushy habit. 2 × 2m.

Acer palmatum 'Sumingashi'
Large, deeply divided leaves with seven lobes, bright crimson-red in spring, deepening to purplish crimson or maroon in summer and glowing crimson scarlet in autumn. Forms a rounded head with almost black stems. 3 × 2.5m.

Acer palmatum 'Trompenburg'
Distinctive glossy, palmate leaves with up to nine lobes with rolled margins. Spring colour rich deep-purple persisting for many weeks, then changing late summer to reddish green and bright crimson in autumn. Erect, round-headed form. 4 × 2.5m.

Acer palmatum 'Ukigumo'
Floating Cloud Maple
Small, slow growing, erect and bushy form with unusual, light-green leaves freckled with pink and white giving soft and subtle pastel toning, the pink shading more prominent spring and autumn. 2 × 1.5m.

Acer palmatum 'Ukon'
Green Twig Maple
Upright grower with lime-green bark. Attractive soft yellow spring foliage turns lime green, deepens to fresh green in summer and deep golden yellow in autumn. 3 × 2.5m.

Acer palmatum 'Villa Taranto'
Neat, small rounded form with palmate leaves deeply and intricately cut in delicate lacy pattern. Unique leaf colours, light green suffused light red, becoming soft golden yellow in autumn. 2.5 × 2m.

Acer platanoides
Norway Maple
Northern Europe to Caucasus. Strong grower with spreading rounded head. Huge, five-lobed, palmate leaves to 20cm across, deep green, paler beneath, turning vivid gold in autumn. Ornamental shade tree for larger gardens tolerating varying soils and climates, except hot, dry areas. Platanoides — resembling Platanus or plane tree. 9 × 6m.

Acer platanoides 'Columnare'
Norway Column Maple
Large erect form of columnar habit, slower growing and narrower than A platanoides, with dark green, heavy textured leaves. 9 × 3m.

Acer platanoides 'Crimson King'
Crimson Norway Maple
Crimson leaved, slow growing form. Large five-lobed leaves 15cm or more across, shiny, dark coppery-red at first, changing to purple-red in summer and yellowish-purple in autumn. A fine lawn specimen or avenue tree but needs adequate space to display its individuality. Highly rated by garden connoisseurs for foliage and form. 6 × 4.5m.

Acer platanoides 'Drummondii'
Slow-growing tree with striking, light green foliage margined white. Prune any branches which may revert to green. Hardy, but performs better with shelter. 5 × 4m.

Acer platanoides 'Emerald Queen'
Faster growing, wind tolerant, medium grower. Branches erect forming a rounded crown, densely clothed with leathery, glossy, dark green leaves. Golden yellow autumn colour. 7 × 5m.

Acer platanoides 'Nigrum'
Purple Norway Maple
Distinctive deep purple, palmate foliage throughout summer. Upright, round-headed form. 7 × 5m

Acer pseudoplatanus
Sycamore Maple
Native of Europe and western Asia. Large, five-lobed, palmate leaves.Conspicuous long clusters of winged yellowish flowers in spring. A grand old spreading tree from central Europe, rather large for average gardens but useful where rapid growth and hardiness to cold and wind or sea breeze is desired. Pseudoplatanus — bark reminiscent of the Platanus or plane tree. 12 × 9m.

Acer pseudoplatanus 'Brilliantissimum'
Extremely rare and beautiful form, spectacular in spring when young growths appear in glorious shades of coral pink. Leaves become yellowish green and deep green at maturity. Rather slow growing. Locate where strong winds will not burn delicate young leaves. 3 × 2m. **10**

Acer pseudoplatanus 'Eastwoodhill'
Choice and beautiful dwarf growing form from the famous Eastwoodhill estate at Gisborne, New Zealand. Young growths rich salmon pink changing to yellowish green, leaves velvety purple beneath. Possibly a hybrid from A 'Brilliantissimum' × A purpureum. 3 × 2m.

Acer pseudoplatanus 'Leopoldii'
Most attractive foliage, yellowish pink at first, later green speckled and splashed yellow and pink. 6 × 4m.

Acer pseudoplatanus 'Prinz Handjery'
Small, slow growing form of the Sycamore with a close resemblance to 'Brilliant-issimum'. Young growths pinkish cream, leaves tinted purple on the undersides. Very hardy and quite wind tolerant. 5 × 4m.

Acer pseudoplatanus 'Purpureum'
Purple Sycamore
Large, picturesque tree with purplish-green leaves, conspicuously rich purple-red beneath, particularly effective when shimmering in the wind. Upper leaf surface changes to bronzy-green when mature. 6 × 4m.

Acer pseudoplatanus 'Worlei'
Golden Sycamore
Rich golden-yellow, almost orange young leaves, becoming yellow or lime green through summer and yellow in autumn. Forms a compact, rounded crown. 6 × 4m.

Acer rubrum
Red Maple, Canadian Maple
From eastern North America. Beautiful trees particularly suited to cooler areas and moist soils. Palmate, 5–10cm leaves on long petioles with three to five triangular lobes, shining dark green above, paler beneath, turning rich red and scarlet in autumn. Fairly rapid grower with neat, rounded form, reddish twigs, branchlets, buds and quite showy flowers in clusters, followed by red winged seeds. 10 × 5m.

Acer rubrum 'October Glory'
Excellent cultivar, similar to above but selected for its handsome, lustrous leaves which turn brilliant crimson in autumn and persist into winter. 10 × 5m.

Acer saccharinum
Silver Maple
Native to eastern United States. Rapid grower with open form and semi-pendulous branches and silvery grey bark except on oldest wood. Leaves with five deep lobes, 7–15cm wide, light green above, silvery beneath, creating delightful effects when ruffled by the wind. Intense autumn colours of scarlet, orange and yellow especially in colder regions. Saccharinum — sugary. 15 × 12m.

Acer saccharum
Sugar Maple
Native to eastern North America, the source of Maple sugar. Moderate growth rate with a framework of stout upward sweeping branches to form a fairly compact crown. Leaves 7–15cm across with three to five lobes, green above paler beneath, breaking

into a riot of spectacular colour in cold winter areas — deep red, scarlet, orange and yellow. Merits extensive planting wherever space permits specimens of this calibre. Saccharum — sugary. 15 × 12m.

Acer wilsoni
Small species from south western China. Palmate leaves, mostly with three lobes, occasionally with two small basal lobes. Green bark, striated with lighter green streaks. Spring leaves bright shrimp pink to coral pink, maturing soft pale green. 6 × 4m.

A small genus of two or three species of trees and shrubs from New Guinea and New Zealand, named from what is possibly an anagram of the Maori name. Grows in any reasonable soil with good drainage, in sun or semi-shade and protection from strong winds or heavy frost. Moderate pruning after flowering will maintain good form and size.
    Cunoniaceae.

Ackama rosaefolia
Makamaka
First discovered in the Hokianga district in 1826 thriving along banks of streams or forest margins.
    Among the more attractive of smaller New Zealand native trees. Handsome foliage unequally pinnate, 8–25cm long with up to ten pairs and a single terminal leaflet. Distinct reddish tinge on leaf undersides and veins is effective especially when ruffled in the breeze. Young shoots covered with light brown tomentum. Small, creamy flowers in multi-branched panicles to 15cm long appear in great profusion late spring. Rosaefolia — leaves resembling the rose. Evergreen. 5 × 4m.

The genus of about five Australian endemic species, named after *Acmene*, a nymph, is the subject of major botanical revision which includes Sysygium, Eugenia and Waterhousea. Acmena smithii is widely grown in temperate regions as a specimen or screen tree, progressing quickly under soil and climatic extremes and resisting pests and diseases. Plant in reasonable, deeply worked soil with good

drainage in full sun or partial shade. Frost may affect young growth, but without permanent damage. Feed spring and autumn with balanced fertilizer and water frequently during dry periods.
    Myrtaceae.

Acmena smithii
Lilly Pilly, Monkey Apple
Australian native extensively distributed in rainforests and streamsides from Cape York Peninsula, Northern Territory to eastern Victoria.
    Forms a small to medium tree with light brown bark. Attractive, glossy new growth varies from pink through bronze. Leaves lanceolate or ovate, up to 10cm long, deep green, glossy and firmly textured. Multitudes of small, greenish white flowers smother the tree late spring, followed in winter by impressive clusters of succulent, globular, 10–15mm, edible fruit in colours of white, lavender or lavender pink. Popular choice for hedges or screens as low as 1.5m. Train and trim from an early age. Untrimmed will soon reach up to 8m. Plant between 60cm and 2m apart in hedgerows depending on the ultimate height desired. Evergreen. 7 × 5m.

A genus of two species of hardy perennial herbs found in marshy places of Europe, Asia and north America named from the Greek *kore*, a pupil, in allusion to the ophthalmic properties of the plant. Acorus calamus is closely related to Anthurium. Commonly known as sweet flag and usually found naturalized in or along the edges of pools or streams. The rhizome or root contains spicy, camphorous oil once used medicinally. Candied rhizomes were an old-time confection. Plant rhizomes mid spring in shallow water or waterlogged margins of pools or streams in heavy loam and an open, sunny location. If space is limited or when it is necessary to prevent more delicate plants being overrun, divide the clumps each spring to maintain control.
    Araceae. *All evergreen.*

Acorus calamus
Sweet Flag, Calamus
From north and central Europe, temperate Asia and North America. Striking, robust, water or marsh-loving, perennial herbs up to 2m high, growing from stout, pinkish, horizontal rhizomes. Bold, grass-green, linear, iris-like leaves to 1.5m long by 3cm

wide with parallel veins and prominent midrib, arranged in flat, shingled fans. Leaves aromatic when bruised. Unattractive flower in the form of a 5–10cm cylindrical spadix densely covered with minute, greenish-yellow flowers during summer. 2 × 2m.

Acorus calamus 'Variegatus'
Variegated Sweet Flag
Attractive variegated form of above. Leaves deep green with a broad, linear, creamy-yellow band. 2 × 2.

ACTINODIUM

A genus of two species of dwarf shrubs from south Western Australia named from the Greek a*ctinos*, ray or spokes of a wheel and *oides*, like, in allusion to the flower formation. Grows naturally in moist soils with perfect drainage. Plant to avoid midday sun during summer in deeply worked, free-draining soil conditions with course sand and peat moss. Mulch freely, water deeply but infrequently during dry periods. Feed sparingly with low-phosphorus fertilizer. Prune lightly after flowering. Suitable for containers. May be short lived but worth a try.
Myrtaceae.

Actinodium cunninghamii
Swamp Daisy, Albany Daisy
Pleasing dwarf shrub with numerous erect stems from ground level. Small, 5mm, linear-terete leaves pressed closely to the stem. Daisy-like, 4cm, flower heads with central cluster of pink or red petals surrounded by white sepals spring and summer. Excellent for picking. Named after 19th century botanist Alan Cunningham. Evergreen. 75 × 50cm. **12**

ADENANDRA

A genus of about eighteen species of small shrubs from South Africa named from the Greek *aden*, a gland and *andros*, man, referring to prominent staminal glands. They grow freely on rocky mountain sides and sea cliffs.
Plant in deeply worked, free-draining, dry and stony soil, conditioned with peat moss and sand in an open, sunny situation. Feed sparingly with low-phosphorus fertilizer. Tolerates considerable

drought and frost once established. Excellent in borders, rock gardens, banks or where they can be admired at close range.
Rutaceae. *All evergreen.*

Adenandra fragrans
Rose China Flower
Beautiful erect branching shrub with oblong to oblanceolate, deep green, 2cm, aromatic leaves. Fragrant, 2cm, bright pink, starry, five-petalled flowers in flat-topped clusters through spring and summer. Fragrans — fragrant. 1 × 1m. **11**

Adenandra uniflora
China Flower
Found mostly on rocky mountainsides and sea cliffs around Cape Peninsula. Forms a dense twiggy plant with erect, wiry stems and 1cm, oblong to lanceolate, yellowy-green leaves. Through spring and summer the plant is a total mass of 2cm, wide open, china-white flowers tinged pale pink like delicate porcelain. Irresistible. Uniflora — one flowered. 60cm × 1m. **11**

AESCULUS

A genus of about fifteen hardy species of deciduous trees from Europe, North America and Asia named from the Latin *aesculus* — winter oak. It is said that Aesculus seeds were fed to horses by the Turks in the mid 16th century as a cure for stomach disorders, hence the term *Horse Chestnut*. Others say the semi-circular mark left by fallen leaves resembles a horse's hoof.
They are bold-foliaged trees, with showy heads of flowers, some producing large spiny fruits containing nuts which look like chestnuts or conkers but which are quite inedible. Prefers rich, moist, soil conditions, freedom from constant severe winds but tolerant of low light conditions and pollution. Perfect lawn specimen for summer shade, street or avenue planting, acreage gardens, farms or parks.
Hippocastanaceae. *All deciduous.*

Aesculus × carnea
Pink Horse Chestnut
Beautiful tree with rounded form bearing hundreds of deep pink flowers in 20cm plumes early summer. Large dark green leaves divided fanwise into five cuneate-obovate, 15cm leaflets. Hybrid from A hippocastanum × A pavia. Carnea — flesh-coloured flowers. 7 × 6m. **11**

Aesculus × carnea 'Briotii'
Red Horse Chestnut
More compact and deeper coloured form with bold, handsome leaves and rosy-red flowers in erect 22cm clusters appearing after new leaves unfold in spring. Does not produce fruit. Compound leaves with five spreading, heavily veined leaflets. 6 × 5m.

Aesculus flava
Yellow Buckeye
North American species growing over 25m with smooth brown bark and non-resinous winter buds. Leaves palmate with up to seven obovate to ovate, 10–18 × 3–8cm leaflets with prominent, pubescent veins. Yellow flowers in 18cm panicles through summer. Flava — pure yellow. 12 × 8m.

Aesculus hippocastanum
Common Horse Chestnut
Magnificent flowering tree introduced to Europe from Istanbul in 1576. Forms a stately tree with tall, domed crown, heavy twisted trunk and greyish-brown bark, ribbed and fluted with age, peeling in thin flakes. Robust twigs with prominent oval, reddish brown buds set in pairs, the outer scales covered in winter with sticky resin, possibly to discourage insect attack. Bold, palmate, heavily veined leaves with 5–7 obovate, 25cm leaflets. Conical, 30cm panicles massed at branch ends, crowded with white flowers tinged red and yellow in late spring giving the appearance of a decorated Christmas tree. Flowers followed by spiky, green husks containing two polished, reddish-brown seeds. Amongst the more beautiful flowering trees. Hippocastanum — Latin name for horse chestnut. 15 × 10m.

Aesculus indica
Indian Horse Chestnut
Magnificent large tree from north west Himalayas. Large palmate leaves with 5–9, oblong-lanceolate, 22cm leaflets. Impressive, 36cm panicles of frilly white flowers, each with a central blotch of yellow, tinged rose appear early summer. Merits planting wherever space permits. Indica — Indian. 20 × 15m.

Aesculus pavia
Dwarf Red Buckeye
Showy, smaller species from southern United States. Palmate leaves with 5–7 oblong, lanceolate or narrowly elliptic leaflets and 25cm panicles of crimson and yellow flowers elegantly displayed above new spring foliage. Syn Aesculus splendens. Pavia — named for Petrus Pavius, 17th century Dutch botanist. 4 × 3m.

AGAPANTHUS

A genus of about ten species of South African perennial herbs with rhizomatous roots named from the Greek *agape*, love and *anthos*, a flower. Agapanthus are valuable landscaping plants. In warmer climates many hardy species become naturalized in open fields or gullies. Handsome leaves, elegant flowers, neat clean appearance and willingness to perform makes them ideal for backgrounds, bank cover, lining driveways and container plants.

Grows in any reasonable conditions in sun or semi-shade. Hardy to frost and cold weather, but water freely during dry spells. Leave undisturbed until obviously overcrowded as they seem to bloom better when root-bound. Stock doesn't seem to damage plants naturalized in open fields.

Liliaceae. *All evergreen.*

Agapanthus orientalis
The best known species and most commonly planted form, found naturally in South Africa's eastern Cape regions. Dark green, curving, strap-like leaves to 60 × 5cm arise from ground level. Sturdy 1.5m stems crowned with rounded, 20cm heads or umbels containing a hundred or more bright medium blue, trumpet-shaped, 4–5cm flowers, borne profusely late spring through summer. Also a white flowered form. 1.3 × 1m.   **11**

Agapanthus orientalis 'Peter Pan'
Outstanding, free-blooming dwarf cultivar. Foliage clumps grow only 20 to 30cm high. Blue flower clusters appear during summer on 30 to 45cm stems. Use in rockeries or work them in with dwarf shrubs or perennials. 45 × 30cm.

AGAPETES

A genus of about 95 species of evergreen, low-growing, sometimes epiphytic shrubs from south east Asia named from the Greek *agapetos*, beloved, desirable, descriptive of many cultivated species. Along with such plants as Kalmia, Pieris and Rhododendron, they belong to the Erica family and need similar cool, acidic soil conditions. Plant in semi-shade in loose, deeply worked, free-draining, organically enriched, moisture-retentive acid soil. Mulch freely, keep moist and maintain high humidity during summer. Syn Pentapterygium.

Ericaceae. *All evergreen.*

Agapetes buxifolia
Interesting species from Bhutan. Forms a small to medium shrub with spreading branches covered with soft, fine hair. Leaves elliptic-oblong to ovate-oblong to 30 × 12mm, crenate towards the pointed apex, wedge-shaped near the base, bright glossy green and leathery. Bright orange-red, waxy, 25mm, tubular flowers borne singly or in pairs in leaf axils through spring, followed by white fruit. Protect from frost. Buxifolia — box-leaved. 1.3 × 1.3m.

Agapetes hosseana 'Scarlet Elf'
Native of Thailand and lower Burma where it was first discovered growing as an epiphyte with swollen tuberous rootstock at elevations of about 1200m. Forms a compact spreading shrub with long arching, pendulous branches, covered with short, fine white hairs. Leaves obovate to elliptic to 45 × 25mm, glabrous, bronzy green, margins entire, prominent midrib near the base. Bright red, cylindrical or tubular, 22mm flowers without conspicuous veins, but with contrasting shallow reflexed green lobes and green calyx flushed purple-red, borne in axillary groups of 2–5 towards the ends of branchlets, spring through mid-summer, followed by white fruit. Excellent plant for rockery, border, container or hanging basket in frost-protected locations. Syn P Red Elf. 60 × 90cm.

Agapetes serpens
Flame Heath
Charming semi-epiphytic shrub from the Himalayas, with long, slender, densely hairy, arching stems arising from a tuberous root. Lanceolate to oblong, 12mm leaves, shining, coppery red when young, maturing glossy bronze green, flushed red near the tips. Flowers produced freely in the form of 3–4cm, five angled, inflated, vivid scarlet tubes with reddish calyx, hanging loosely in pairs beneath each arching stem, appearing like miniature Japanese lanterns. Blooming may commence any time from winter, continuing through summer. Plant in a special corner reserved for garden treasures or even a hanging basket. Serpens — creeping. 1 × 1m.   **12**

Agapetes smithiana
Impressive dwarf shrub from Bhutan and Assam. Branches covered in short, rust-brown bristles. Spirally arranged leaves, elliptic to obovate, to 30 × 15mm, leathery, shallowly veined and slightly convex above, almost glaucous beneath, margins indistinctly toothed and with short, protruding bristle-like glands. Tubular to urn-shaped, 14mm yellow flowers with small angular lobes, set in a greenish yellow calyx, borne singly or in clusters up to five from mature leaf axils through late summer. Good for hanging baskets. 50 × 75cm.

AGATHIS

A genus of about twenty species of tall coniferous trees from the Philippines, Indonesia, Polynesia, Australia and New Zealand, named from the Greek *agathis*, ball of thread, alluding to globular female cones. The New Zealand species, although naturally confined to the northern half of the North Island, is known to succeed in sub-zero temperatures without damage. Grows in almost any reasonable soil with good drainage and adequate water. Tolerant of windy situations.

Araucariaceae

Agathis australis
New Zealand Kauri
Erect, slender-pyramidal form and blue-grey bark. Young leaves lanceolate, 6–12cm long, bronze-green, leathery and smooth, becoming narrow and shorter on mature trees. Although a forest tree of immense proportions, the Kauri grows so slowly that after three or four decades, it may still be less than 10m high. Merits extensive planting. Australis — southern. Evergreen. 6 × 2.5m.

AGAVE

A genus of more than 300 species of rosette forming plants with succulent leaves from north and south America, mostly Mexico, named from the Greek *agavos* — admirable, referring to the handsome appearance of the plant in bloom. The term Century Plant alludes to many years of growth before producing its first and only flower stalk prior to wilting and dying. A new crop of youngsters then arises from the base.

Agaves flourish naturally in poor, hot and dry areas against seemingly impossible conditions. Apart from maximum sunlight, they have no special demands. With adequate space for unhindered development of their bold tapering leaves, Agaves create garden drama difficult to achieve with other species. Great for

scree, rock or feature gardens, simulated desert areas, large banks. Allow adequate space from walkways to avoid contact with their aggressive leaf-tip spines.
Agavaceae. *All evergreen.*

Agave americana
Century Plant
Interesting feature plant from Mexico in the form of a large, open, trunkless rosette of spreading, broad, thick and succulent, grey-green leaves to 2m × 25cm, margined with sharp brown hooks and a long shiny point. Americana — of North or South America. 2 × 2m.

Agave americana 'Marginata'
Identical to americana in form and structure, but with a broad band of gold along the leaf margins. 2 × 2m.   **12**

Agave americana 'Medio Picta'
Broad band of yellow down centre of each leaf rather than along the margins. 2 × 2m.

Agave attenuata
Smaller species, also from Mexico, with light green to grey green leaves to 70cm long, soft and downy in texture and without spines. Forms a perfect rosette, sometimes two or three, with a tendency to lie to one side rather than grow erect, a trait which can be exploited by careful placement. Attenuata — narrowing to a point. 1 × 1m.

Agave filifera
From eastern Mexico, a petite plant which forms a rosette of narrow, stiff, bright green leaves 20–25cm long, light to dark green or purplish with white leaf margins which split into loose filaments. Filifera — thread bearing. Excellent landscaping plant on a smaller scale. 50 × 50cm.

Agave victoriae-reginae
Delightful dwarf rosette with numerous dark green, thick, fleshy, leaves about 15 × 5cm, narrowly outlined white. Perfect form and leaf design, a most decorative plant for feature gardens containers. Named in honour of Queen Victoria. 30 × 25cm.

AGONIS

A genus of about ten species of West Australian trees and shrubs named from the Greek *agonis*, without angles. Agonis have subtle charm and make a worthwhile contribution to contemporary landscaping. They grow quickly, resist drought and harsh, arid or coastal conditions and are suited to heavy or poor soils provided frequent deep watering is given until established.
Myrtaceae. *All evergreen.*

Agonis flexuosa
Willow Myrtle, Willow Peppermint
Forms a neat specimen with single trunk and willowy branches almost to the ground. Young growth silky pink, branchlets quite pendulous. Narrow-elliptic, willow-like leaves to 15cm × 15mm, bronzy green when mature. Strong fragrance from crushed leaves suggests the name Willow Peppermint. White, 1cm flowers in showy axillary clusters of about ten appear spring and early summer, followed by woody, globular, 5mm seed capsules. Flexuosa — tortuous or zigzag, referring to angular branchlets. 5 × 4m.

Agonis flexuosa 'Nana'
Dwarf, somewhat spreading form with typical A. flexuosa foliage and attractive coppery pink new shoots through most of the year. Crushed leaves give off eucalyptus fragrance. Open, sunny aspect. 1 × 1m.

Agonis flexuosa 'Variegata'
Variegated Willow Myrtle
Rare and beautiful shrub with slender, gracefully drooping stems and foliage striped green and cream with pink markings. Prefers semi-shade, protection from strong winds and regular watering during dry periods. 2.5 × 2m.   **12**

Agonis juniperina
Juniper Myrtle
Upright shrub or small tree with gracefully drooping branchlets densely clothed with small, 5–10mm, soft green, very narrow pointed leaves. Terminal clusters of small white flowers with brown centres appear in great masses during autumn and again late spring. Flower-sprays last well when cut. Benefits from annual trimming. Juniperina — juniper-like. 5 × 4m.

Agonis juniperina 'Florists Star'
Dense masses of starry white myrtle flowers produced on graceful, fine-foliaged branches during winter and early spring. Useful landscaping plant and excellent cut flower. 3 × 2m.

Agonis linearifolia
Forms an erect, branched medium shrub with narrow-oblanceolate leaves to 25mm. Small white axillary flowers in clusters appear winter through early summer, followed by fused clusters of small, globular seed capsules. Linearifolia — with linear leaves. 3 × 2.5m.

AILANTHUS

A genus of about five species of tall deciduous trees from China, named from the Latin *ailanto*, Sky Tree. Essentially a tree for larger areas but worth planting for shade, autumn foliage and highly coloured samaras or winged seeds. Grows rapidly when young, slowing down after 10–15 years. Prune back regularly for size control. Watch for seedlings or suckers which may appear in great profusion, a reason for declaring it a noxious weed and banning its propagation in some countries.
Simaroubaceae.

Ailanthus altissima
Tree of Heaven
Chinese native, grown in many of the world's big cities because of its resistance to smog, insect pests and diseases. Rapid grower with immense pinnate leaves to 70cm long divided into 11–14, lanceolate or ovate, 8–12cm leaflets with entire margins. Terminal panicles of inconspicuous, whitish green flowers with a disagreeable odour, followed by showy clusters of orange to reddish brown winged fruit in late summer, valued for dried arrangements. Syn A glandulosa. Altissima — very tall. Deciduous. 15 × 10m.

ALBIZIA

A genus of about 150 species of trees and shrubs from Asia, Africa and Australia named after Filippo degli Albizzi, Italian naturalist who introduced the Silk Tree to cultivation in 1749. Albizia julibrissin, possibly the best known species flourishes in temperate climates of both hemispheres. Regarded as one of the showiest trees especially when seen from above where its ferny foliage and silky flowers may be fully appreciated.
Hardy in sub zero temperatures. Plant in deeply worked, well drained, moisture-retentive soil. Staking, tying and removal of lateral growths will train the tree to a magnificent, single trunk shade canopy. Revels in hot dry areas once established.
Mimosaceae.

Albizia julibrissin
Silk Tree, Nemu Tree, Pink Mimosa
Originally from southern Asia, Iran to Japan. Graceful, rich green bipinnate leaves to

30cm long with hundreds of 15mm leaflets which fold up at night. During summer, rounded, fluffy brushes of pink stamens like the fuzz of silk appear in great masses above the leaf canopy. Leaf fall reveals picturesque pattern of bare branches. Perfect shade or screen for outdoor living areas. Julibrissin — from the native name. Deciduous. 5 × 4.

Albizzia julibrissen 'Red Silk'
Choice selected form of the Silk Tree bearing a profusion of carmine-red silky flowers. Deciduous. 5 × 4m

Albizzia lopantha
Plume Albizia
Rapid grower from Western Australia often used as shelter in warmer regions. Ferny, bipinnate leaves to 30cm with hundreds of tiny leaflets. White to cream, 8cm spikes of wattle-like flowers in winter. Plants grown from seed on site early spring can attain a height of 2.5m before the following winter. Ideal for short term shelter or screening. Prolific seed crops can become somewhat of a pest in light soils. Evergreen. 12 × 8m.

ALECTRYON

A genus of about 16 species of medium evergreen trees distributed throughout the Pacific from Hawaii, New Guinea, Australia and New Zealand named from the Greek *alektryon*, cock, a possible reference to the comb-like protrusion on the fruit of some species. Of the two New Zealand species, only Titoki is commonly cultivated. Unsuitable for exposed situations. Plant in medium to heavy loam with good drainage. Recommended as a worthwhile ornamental.

Sapindaceae.

Alectryon excelsus
Titoki, New Zealand Oak
New Zealand native forming a spreading tree with almost black bark. Young shoots covered with rust-coloured pubescence. Pinnate leaves to 30cm with up to six pairs of ovate-lanceolate, glossy, deep green leaflets to 10 × 5cm. Sprays of woolly, rust-red flowers early summer, followed by shiny, jet-black seeds protruding from a scarlet, fleshy aril. Excelsum — tall. Evergreen. 7 × 4m.

ALNUS

A genus of about 35 species of deciduous trees from the Northern hemisphere, often growing beside lakes or rivers, named from the Latin *alnus*, the alder. Alder wood has been used extensively in the past in the manufacture of farm footware, charcoal for gunpowder, wood turning and tanning. An interesting display of pendulous, tassel-like, greenish yellow male flower catkins appear in clusters before the leaves. Club-shaped, female flowers develop into small woody cones after pollination, quite decorative on bare branches and valued for floral art.

Alders grow in moist or marshy soils, conditions which facilitate the development of ball-shaped nodules on the roots, designed to take nitrogen from the air for nourishment. Especially in cooler climates, alder is an ideal shade tree for moist lawn areas, swampy ground or alongside rivers or streams for beauty and erosion control.

Betulaceae. *All deciduous except A jorullensis.*

Alnus cordata
Italian Alder
From southern Italy and Corsica. Medium to large tree, quite erect when young, developing a cone-shaped head. Young shoots reddish brown and sticky. Leaves lustrous deep green, broadly ovate to rounded, 8–12cm, tough, leathery, smooth and pliable with fine-toothed margins and prominent veins. Cordata — heart shaped. 12 × 8m.

Alnus glutinosa
Black Alder, Common Alder
From Europe to Caucasus and Siberia and North Africa. Forms a medium tree with narrow-pyramidal outline and brownish-black bark. Young shoots very sticky. Leaves lustrous dark green, paler beneath, broadly ovate to orbicular, 5–10cm across. Bark and seed cones black. Glutinosa — sticky or gluey. 8 × 6m.

Alnus incana
Grey Alder
From Europe, Caucasus, Asia. Medium tree with smooth, pale grey bark and downy grey shoots. Leaves broadly ovate with rounded base, variously lobed, wrinkled by irregular lines and veins, green above, greyish-white and downy beneath. Incana — hoary or grey. 12 × 8m.

Alnus incana 'Aurea'
Golden Alder
Excellent cultivar with yellow shoots and branches maturing orange-red, leaves yellow, felted beneath. Showy, orange-red catkins. 10 × 8m.

Alnus jorullensis
Evergreen Alder
From Mexico and Central America. Medium tree with papery, pale grey bark and distinct horizontal rings around the trunk. Leaves oblong-elliptic, 5–10cm long, short tapered, mid green, yellowish and pubescent beneath, margins irregularly toothed except the base. Roots notoriously invasive. Locate well away from drains, driveways, or paths. Evergreen. 6 × 4m.

Alnus rubra
Red Alder, Oregon Alder
From western North America. Medium to large tree with slender pyramidal outline and slightly pendulous branches. Buds distinctly red and sticky, bursting into 10–15cm catkins before the leaves in spring. Leaves ovate to elliptic to 15cm, margins shallow lobed or coarsely serrate, glabrous dark green above, blue-grey beneath with reddish-brown pubescence. Rubra — red. 10 × 6m.

Alnus viridis
Green Alder
From Central Europe. Medium to large shrub forming a clump of several erect, hazel-like stems with sticky shoots. Leaves to 6 × 5cm, ovate with abruptly acute apex and rounded base, irregularly serrated margins, matt green above, paler and glossy beneath. Viridis — green. 2.5 × 1.5m.

ALOYSIA

A genus of about 35 species of aromatic shrubs from Central America named after Maria Louisa, 18th–19th century princess of Parma. Only Aloysia citriodora with strongly lemon-scented leaves seems to be in general cultivation, favoured for culinary purposes, potpourri and sachets.

Plant in deeply worked, moisture retentive, well-drained soil in full sun. Grows straggly and woody if left to itself. Prune heavily early spring, apply general fertilizer for lush growth and pinch growing tips frequently.

Verbenaceae.

Above: Ardisia crispa *Coral Berry* **26**

Above: Araucaria heterophylla *Norfolk Island Pine* **26**
Below: Azalea 'Ben Morrison' **29**

Above: Astartea 'Winter Pink' **28**
Below: Aucuba japonica 'Crotonoides' *Spotted Laurel* **28**

22

Above: Azalea 'Blue Danube' **30**

Above: Azalea 'Gerhard Nicholai' **30**

Above: Azalea 'Eureka' **30**
Below: Azalea 'Chiara' **30**

Above: Azalea 'Gretel' **30**
Below: Azalea 'Mardi Gras' **31**

Above: Azalea 'Janet Rhea' **31**

Above: Azalea 'Bridal Bouquet' **30**
Below: Azalea 'Gay Paree' **30**

Above: Azalea 'Pax' **31**
Below: Azalea 'Lorna' **31**

Above and below: Azalea 'Rosa Belton' **32**

Aloysia triphylla
Lemon Verbena
A twiggy, deciduous shrub from Argentina and Chile. Leaves usually in whorls of three, lanceolate, 7–10 × 2cm, rough surfaced and with refreshing lemon fragrance. Small, 5mm, white to pale purple flowers in terminal, 15cm panicles can be picked for indoors. Could never be described as handsome, but an old fashioned favourite for an out of the way corner. Syn Lippia citriodora. Triphylla — leaves in threes. Deciduous. 2 × 1.5m.

ALYOGYNE

A genus of four Australian endemic species of flowering shrubs related to Hibiscus, named from the Greek *alytos*, undivided and *gyne*, female, referring to the style. Valued for rapid growth and wealth of bloom. The listed species is hardy and adaptable, growing in either light or heavy, deeply worked, free-draining soil in sun or partial shade, sheltered from strong wind. Tends to become straggly if not pruned heavily after flowering for growth renewal.
Malvaceae.

Alyogyne huegelii
Desert Rose, Lilac Hibiscus
From South Australia to Western Australia. Medium, spreading shrub sparsely covered with rough hairs. Bright green, thick textured leaves to 8cm, palmately divided into five deep lobes, margins irregularly toothed and curled. Flowers 7–10cm wide, single Hibiscus-like, with five petals, appearing singly from leaf axils spring through autumn. Colours vary from lilac blue to deep purple. There are also white and yellow forms. Huegelli — after 19th century Austrian botanist, Karl von Hugel. Evergreen. 1.5 × 1m. **12**

AMELANCHIER

A genus of 25 species of small trees and shrubs from North America, Europe and Asia, named from the French *amelanchier*, for A ovalis. The species listed grows naturally near moist woodlands or riverbanks and prefers to be grown in lime-free, deeply worked, free-draining, moisture retentive soil conditioned with peat moss, humus and sharp sand. Grows in full or partial sun, but autumn colours

more intense in full sun. Mulch freely and water regularly during dry periods. Hardy to sub-zero temperatures.
Rosaceae.

Amelanchier canadensis
Shad Bush
From eastern North America. Neat shrub or small tree with erect, glabrous, grey branchlets. Leaves elliptic with rounded base, thin textured, 5 × 2.5cm, margins finely toothed, woolly on both surfaces when young, remaining so beneath. Impressive, rich golden yellow to russet red autumn foliage, followed by picturesque winter branch pattern. Along with new leaves, great quantities of lacy, white, 25mm flowers in erect 6cm racemes appear in spring. This 'fairy-light' effect is dramatic even if for just a few days. Under certain conditions purple-black, sweet, edible berries about the size of currants follow. Canadensis — of Canada or North America. Deciduous. 4 × 3m.

ANIGOZANTHUS

A genus of eleven Australian endemic species from south west Western Australia, named from the Greek *anoigo*, to open and *anthos*, a flower — the petals of these curious flowers flare open almost to the base. Hybridists in Western Australia and Victoria have bred and released hybrids of superior quality which perform under diverse climatic conditions. They come in many compact, colourful, disease resistant and floriferous varieties. Anigozanthus need deeply worked, free-draining, gravelly soil and full sun. Keep reasonably moist as plants get established and hand-weed rather than cultivate deeply to avoid root damage. Feed sparingly at planting time and after an annual clean-up.
Haemodoraceae. *All evergreen.*

Anigozanthus 'Bush Dawn'
Bright yellow flowers tinted lime on 1.5m branched stems during summer. Long flowering season. Good for cutting.

Anigozanthus 'Bush Emerald'
Red stem and ovary and emerald green perianth on 70cm stems through winter and spring. Garden specimen or cut flowers.

Anigozanthus 'Bush Nugget'
Reddish stem and ovary with yellow flower on 50 to 80cm branched stems early spring and summer. Good colour. Excellent landscaping or cut flower plant. **11**

Anigozanthus 'Bush Ranger'
Bright red flowers on 50cm branched stems through spring and summer. Exceptional flowering qualities. Splendid in the garden or containers.

ANOPTERUS

A small Australian endemic genus of two species, attractive small trees or shrubs named from the Greek *ano*, upward and *pteron*, wing referring to the upward facing seed wing. The name is easily confused with *Anopteris*, a genus of ferns. The listed species grows slowly but otherwise thrives in deeply worked, organically enriched, free-draining soil. Mulch freely, apply balanced fertilizer spring and autumn, water regularly during dry periods. Prefers semi shade. Prune annually to preserve good form.
Escalloniaceae.

Anopterus glandulosus
Tasmanian Laurel
Tall shrub from moist lowland and mountain forests of Tasmania. Dark green, leathery, glossy, oblanceolate, 6–18 × 2–5cm leaves with bluntly serrated margins. Bell-shaped, 2cm, pure white fragrant flowers in erect, 15cm spikes not unlike Lily of the Valley spring and summer. Glandulosus — gland-ular. Evergreen. 2 × 1m.

ARAUCARIA

A genus of about twenty species of evergreen, coniferous trees from South America and south west Pacific, named for Arauco Indians of central Chile who live in the native territory of Araucaria araucana. All species form tall, columnar or narrow pyramidal trees with wide-spreading branches in whorls. Essentially trees for public areas or acreage gardens in avenues or isolation with plenty of space for full development.
Plant in average soil with good drainage and stake until established. Norfolk Island Pine is especially suited to coastal planting, withstanding strong, salt laden winds.
Araucariaceae. *All evergreen.*

Araucaria araucana
Monkey Puzzle
From Central Chile. Stately specimen tree of erect, symmetrical outline. Branches at

first horizontal, mostly in whorls of five. With maturity, upper branches more ascending, lower ones more pendulous. Stiff, leathery, bright green, glossy, triangular-ovate, 3–5cm, sharply pointed, and spirally arranged leaves densely cover all branches. Araucana — also in reference to the Arauco area in Chile. 8 × 5m.

Araucaria cunninghamii
Hoop Pine
From New South Wales, Queensland and Papua New Guinea. Resembles Norfolk Island Pine but distinguished by long horizontal, upswept branches with foliage bunched or tufted towards the tips. Juvenile leaves, needle-like and flattened, 15mm long with spiny, recurved points. Adult foliage dark green, broader, overlapping and with incurved points. While found mostly by coastal waterways, it thrives in warm inland areas and is highly drought resistant. Named after 19th century botanist, Alan Cunningham. 10 × 5m.

Araucaria heterophylla
Norfolk Island Pine
Native to Norfolk Island. Stately, erect, narrow-pyramidal outline to 60m with branches of equal length and evenly spaced in, starlike, horizontal whorls. Light green, awl-shaped, 5–10mm juvenile leaves, soft, flattened and incurved. Adult leaves 4–6mm, closely overlapping, lanceolate to ovate-triangular, blunt incurved apex. Used extensively in contemporary landscaping, in containers and for coastal planting. Heterophylla — diversely leafed. 10 × 5m.   **21**

ARBUTUS

A genus of 14 species of evergreen shrubs or small trees from north and central America, south and western Europe and Asia Minor named from the Latin *arbuteus*, strawberry tree. Valued for beauty of foliage, flower and fruit, for tolerance of considerable heat or cold, coastal conditions, industrial pollution and other adverse situations.

Plant in deeply worked, organically enriched, well-drained, moisture retentive, lime-free soil in full sun or partial shade. Shelter from strong winds, mulch freely and keep moist during dry periods until established. Watch and spray for thrips and aphids. Resists coastal gales and unusually lime tolerant for ericaceous plants. Specimen, screen or background, attractive both trained or left unpruned.

Ericaceae. *All evergreen.*

Arbutus × andrachnoides
Natural hybrid from A unedo × A andrachne. Forms a large shrub with impressive deep red branches. Leaves elliptic or lanceolate, to 10cm long, glabrous, dark green above, light green and pubescent beneath and serrated margins. Ivory-white flowers in pendent panicles and occasional rounded, reddish, 1cm fruit, somewhat smoother than A unedo, late autumn and winter. Andrachnoides — resembling andrachne. 3 × 2m.

Arbutus unedo
Strawberry Tree
Native of southern Europe to Asia Minor. Large shrub or small tree with reddish stems and glabrous, 10cm, oblong to obovate, glossy, dark green foliage. Flowers 1cm, white or pink tinted, pitcher-shaped or like Lily of the Valley in crowded terminal panicles and scarlet strawberry-like fruit during autumn and winter, edible in small quantities. 5 × 3m.

Arbutus unedo 'Rubra'
Salmon pink to red flowers borne profusely followed by heavy clusters of orange-red strawberry-like fruit. 3 × 2m.

ARCTOSTAPHYLOS

A genus of about fifty species of evergreen shrubs native to the western regions of United States named from the Greek *arktos*, a bear and *staphule*, bunch of grapes from which the term Bearberry applied to some species is derived. They come in varying forms from prostrate shrubs to small trees. Related to Rhododendron, they need similar soil conditions — deeply worked, free-draining, acid soil conditioned with peat moss and located in full sun. Give occasional deep watering during dry periods. Frequent tip pinching during growth period will control size.

Ericaceae.

Arctostaphylos nevadensis
Pine Mat Manzanita
Prostrate species from California and Nevada. Roots freely where branches touch ground, often forming mats. Young shoots grey and pubescent, inclined to be sticky, mature stems deep brownish-red. Variable leaves, narrowly lanceolate to broadly obovate, 2–3cm long, light green, with distinct short tip. Erect racemes of white to pink urn or bell-shaped flowers in spring and early summer, then rounded, dark brown fruit. Nevadensis — of Sierra Nevada. Manzanita — Indian name. Evergreen. 15 × 60cm

ARDISIA

A genus of about 250 species of tropical or warm temperate trees and shrubs, named from the Greek *ardis*, a point referring to pointed anthers. From the world's subtropical areas but mostly East Indies, Japan and Korea, six extending to Australia. The few species cultivated are valued for an almost constant display of polished red berries borne on a tidy dwarf shrub. Plant in shade or semi-shade in moisture retentive, rich, well-drained soil conditioned with peat moss or leaf mould. Water frequently during dry periods. Feed with a balanced dry or liquid fertilizer spring and autumn. Excellent container plant.

Myrsinaceae.

Ardisia crispa
Coral Berry
From Indonesia, Philippines, India, China and Japan. Choice dwarf berry shrub with glossy, deep green, elliptic-lanceolate, thin, leathery, 6–12cm leaves with shallow crenate, rolled margins, lighter green and felted beneath. Clusters of small pink or white flowers late spring, followed by crowded bunches of polished red 5–8mm berries which remain on the plant for months during autumn and winter. Often grown indoors, but thrives in warm shady areas outside with good drainage. Crispa — finely wavy, referring to leaf margins. Evergreen. 75 × 60cm.   **21**

ARISTOTELIA

A genus of about five species of trees and shrubs found in Australia, New Zealand, New Hebrides and South America named after Greek philosopher Aristotle. Grows in almost any reasonable soil or climate. May be deciduous in colder climates. Excellent fast growing tree for backgrounds, or to provide light-shade for other plants.

Elaeocarpaceae

Aristotelia serrata
Wineberry, Makomako
New Zealand native widely distributed throughout the three main islands. Small tree with upright growth habit. Reddish branchlets on young shoots, becoming darker with maturity. Leaves broadly ovate to ovate, to 12 × 8cm, medium green above, purplish

beneath with margins deeply and sharply serrated. Beautiful in spring as leaves appear and branches are smothered with panicles of rosy coloured flowers followed by 5mm, dark red fruit if male and female flowers (on separate trees) are present. Seed-grown plants variable in flower colour. Serrata — serrated leaves. Evergreen. 5 × 3m.

ARTHROPODIUM

A genus of about twelve species of perennial herbs with fleshy, rhizomatous roots from Australia, New Guinea, New Caledonia and New Zealand named from the Greek *arthron*, joint and *pous*, foot, referring to jointed pedicels or flower stalks. Builds up an impressive clump of straplike leaves and masses of white flower clusters, excellent for borders or rock gardens and cut blooms. Grows in sun or shade, on the coast or beneath large trees. At its best mass-planted on semi-shady banks. Will survive light frost.
Liliaceae.

Arthropodium cirrhatum
New Zealand Rock Lily, Reinga Lily
Found naturally on shady banks from North Cape to Marlborough Sounds. Forms a bold clump of flax-like, lanceolate, deep green, curving, 45–60 × 5–6cm leaves, paler beneath. Scapes or stems to 90cm long arise from the base bearing panicles of starry, white flowers about 20mm across with a hint of mauve at the base of the petals from which appear two woolly anthers with curved, white and yellow tails. Cirrhatum — with cirrhi or curls. Evergreen. 75 × 75cm.

ASCARINA

A genus of about ten species of small trees and shrubs from New Zealand, Polynesia and Malaysia. Plant in good garden soil with adequate moisture, in sun or shade. Prune to preserve good form either as a bushy shrub or single-stemmed specimen.
Chloronthaceae.

Ascarina lucida
Hutu
New Zealand endemic species, found in lowland and lower mountain forests of the three main islands, but especially in west coast forests of the south island. Forms a closely branched framework of slender, dark purplish-red stems. Distinctive elliptic to obovate leaves to 7 × 4cm, glossy, bright green above, paler beneath and coarsely serrated margins. Slender, pendulous, green flower spikes borne at the ends of branchlets spring and early summer. Contrasting glossy foliage against purplish stems a feature. Specimen or background planting. Lucida — bright, shining or clear. Evergreen. 3 × 2m.

ASCLEPIAS

A genus of over 100 species of perennial herbs and shrubs named after Asklepios, Greek god of medicine. The listed species is grown mainly for the fascination of observing the life cycle of the beautiful Monarch butterfly. Grow in full sun, average soil conditions with good drainage and protect from frost.
Asclepiadaceae.

Asclepias physocarpa
Swan Plant
Every garden or home where children live should have at least one Swan Plant if for no other reason than to see nature work miracles with Monarch butterflies which have a voracious appetite and quickly devour every leaf. Then there are the curious inflated, silvery-green seed pods resembling swans which can be floated in a dish of water. Physocarpa — *physa*, a bladder and *karpos*, fruit. Evergreen. 1 × 1m.

ASPARAGUS

A genus of about 300 species of perennial herbs, shrubs or climbers widely distributed throughout the Old World, named from the Latin *asparagus*. The genus includes the popular culinary Asparagus officinalis from eastern Mediterranean regions which has been enjoyed for over 2000 years. Besides its traditional use as a pot or hanging plant, the listed species is utilized in landscaping as ground cover because of its resistance to dry conditions, its wealth of rich green foliage and the way its inoffensive hooked prickles repel both animals and vandals.

Thick, fleshy, tuberous roots may aid resistance to drought, but to maintain lush green foliage all year, keep watered during dry spells, feed in spring with a complete fertilizer, and remove old shoots. Use in containers on decks or patios, hanging plants, climbers on trellis or mass plant for ground or bank cover or wall spiller. Keeps greener in semi-shade but grows in full sun in average garden conditions and considerable range of temperatures.
Liliaceae.

Asparagus densiflorus 'Sprengeri'
South African native with arching or drooping, somewhat spiny stems to 1.5m long densely clothed with shiny, bright green, needlelike, 20mm leaves, more correctly known as cladophyll. Small white flowers succeeded by attractive, 1cm, bright-red fruit. Densiflorus — densely flowered. Sprengeri — for Carl L Sprenger, 19th century German nurseryman. Evergreen.

ASPLENIUM

A genus of about 700 species of terrestrial or epiphytic ferns from all over the world named from the Greek *splen*, the spleen, a reference to the medicinal capability this plant was once thought to possess. Reasonably hardy, best in semi or full shade, planted in deeply worked, moisture-retentive soil with peat moss and sand.

Provide good drainage in winter and water when dry. Ferns play a vital part in landscaping. Use individually amongst shade loving flowering plants such as Azaleas, dwarf Rhododendrons, or mass plant for effective ground cover in shady locations.
Polypodiaceae. *All evergreen.*

Asplenium bulbiferum
Hen and Chicken Fern, Mother Spleenwort
Widely distributed through eastern Australian States, South Australia and New Zealand. Terrestrial or epiphytic fern found in moist gullies and rainforests. Triangular, finely cut, fresh green, bipinnate or tripinnate fronds over a metre long, arch gracefully from the base in neat, rosette or fountain form. Multitudes of sori, baby plants, appear on the upper leaf surface which can be detached and grown on in humid conditions. Container grown plants keep healthier if the bulbils are removed. Bulbiferum — bulb bearing refers to the young plantlets. 90 × 90cm.

Asplenium bulbiferum 'Maori Princess'
Larger growing form with bright green glossy leaves, fronds with typical bulbils, wider and less indented than above, eventually reaching 1.5m in length. Hybrid from A bulbiferum × A oblongifolium. 1 × 1m.

ASTARTEA

A genus of about five species of low-growing shrubs mainly from Western Australia, closely related to Baeckea and named after *Astarte*, Phoenician goddess of fertility. Cultivated species have proved adaptable to varying conditions such as waterlogging and extended drought. Deeply worked, free draining soil is recommended and little or no fertilizer. Encourage dense growth and more flowers by light pruning after flowering.
Myrtaceae. *All evergreen.*

Astartea fascicularis
Small spreading shrub from Western Australia. Narrow, flat or three-sided, 5cm, heath-like leaves clustered in bundles on flexible, gracefully arching branches. The whole plant is studded from winter through autumn with 1cm, five-petalled flowers, white with a touch of pale pink at the base. Quite hardy to frost. Fascicularis — in bundles. 1 × 1.5m.

Astartea 'Winter Pink'
Australian hybrid from Astartea clavulata × Baeckea astartioides. Forms a dense shrub with 4mm leaves in whorls and great masses of deep pink, 1cm flowers carried on erect branches from autumn through winter when garden colour is scarce. Excellent for picking. 60 × 70cm.   **21**

ASTELIA

A genus of twenty-five species of evergreen, perennial herbs, from Australasia, Polynesia, Mauritius and Falkland Island named from the Greek *a*, without and *stele*, a pillar, without stem or trunk. Astelias are admired for their highly ornamental, evergreen foliage displayed in crowded rosettes. Naturally, they're found on the bush floor, growing on rotten logs, in coastal rock crevices or perched in the forks of trees. They grow from short, thick rhizomatous roots with numerous linear, curving, swordlike leaves crowded at the base, often completely covered with silky hairs or scurfy scales. Sometimes called *Bush Flax* or *Perching Lilies*. Panicles of flowers and fruit are somewhat inconspicuous.
Plant in cool, fertile, deeply worked, moisture retentive, free-draining soil conditioned with peat moss, preferably

in semi-shade. Be certain not to bury their crowns when planting. Soil falling amongst the leaves may cause the plant to rot. Protect from frost, strong wind and the hottest midday sun. Mulch freely and keep moist during dry periods. Most effective when grouped.
Liliaceae. *All evergreen.*

Astelia banksii
Wharawhara
New Zealand coastal terrestrial species found north of latitude 38° thriving on coastal cliffs, with numerous curving silvery-green, linear leaves to 1.5m × 4.5cm, covered with peeling scales above, white felted beneath and recurved margins. Panicles of fragrant, pale green flowers tinted ivory on 50cm stems followed on female plants by ovoid fruit, greenish-white at first, distinct magenta-purple when mature. Tolerant of coastal extremes and most ornamental. Banksii — after Sir Joseph Banks. 1.3 × 1.3m.

Astelia chathamica 'Silver Spear'
Possibly the most popular plant of this type. 'Silver Spear' is a selected form of the endangered Chatham Island Astelia. A most ornamental, clump-forming plant with spikey, erect habit and silvery-green, phormium or sword-like leaves with silver-satin appearance. Originally discovered and developed in the New Plymouth nurseries of Duncan and Davies. Plants not propagated from the original clone, may vary considerably from the true 'Silver Spear'. Dramatic plant for many landscaping situations and excellent for floral art. 1.3 × 1.3m.

ASTERISCUS

A genus of four species of perennial and annual herbs or shrubs from the Mediterranean, Cape Verde Islands and Canary Islands, named from the Greek *asteriskos*, a little star. The listed species, found amongst maritime rocks along western Mediterranean and Canary Island coastlines is admired for good form, and a profusion of brilliant flowers which present a blaze of gold over handsome foliage. A hardy, easily grown plant suited to warm, frost-free areas such as dry rockery pockets, garden beds or borders in deeply worked, free-draining, sandy or gravelly soil in full sun. Feed and mulch in spring and water occasionally in dry periods. Excellent for coastal gardens and in containers.
Compositae.

Asteriscus maritimus
Gold Coin
Tufty, shrubby plant with ascending, woody, multi-branched, hairy stems. Leaves oblanceolate to spathulate, grey-green, covered with long hairs. Brilliant yellow, daisy-like, 3–4cm flowers with broad central zone of numerous orange-yellow disc florets, surrounded by 30 ray florets with fine-toothed margins, borne on long stems spring through autumn and at other times of the year. Each flower lasts for about two weeks in fine weather. Inter-plant with blue-flowered plants for dramatic effects. Syn Odontospermum 'Gold Coin'. Evergreen. 30 × 60cm.

AUCUBA

A genus of three or four species of dioecious shrubs and small trees from east Asia, Aucuba being the latinized version of the Japanese name. The Japanese species and cultivars have a reputation for very ornamental foliage, colourful berries and the ability to withstand adverse growing conditions including drought, salt laden winds and pollution. The male and female flowers are produced on separate plants and both need to be planted in close proximity for berry production.
Best in shade or semi-shade but tolerant of considerable sunlight. Plant in deeply worked, well drained soil. They resist dryness, but respond to occasional deep watering and feeding with balanced fertilizer in spring and autumn. Periodic pruning and thinning will preserve shape, size and vigour. Renew tired plants by cutting almost to ground level.
Cornaceae. *All evergreen.*

Aucuba japonica
Japanese Laurel
From southern Japan, Taiwan and China. A bushy shrub with elliptic to narrow-ovate, clean, polished, leathery leaves, about 15cm long, coarsely toothed and deep green without variegation. Panicles of olive green, starry flowers when pollinated, produce shiny red, 12mm, bead-like berries through the winter, untouched by birds. 1.5 × 1m.

Aucuba japonica 'Crotonoides'
Spotted Laurel
Female plant with large, leathery, glossy green leaves splashed and spotted golden yellow. Attractive waxy red berries. 1.5 × 1m.   **21**

Aucuba japonica 'Forest Green'
A superior form, selected for its larger, rich green foliage and heavy crops of bright red, 2cm fruit. Female. 1.5 × 1m.

Aucuba japonica 'Golden King'
Leathery, serrated leaves more heavily splashed with gold than crotonoides. Colours better when grown in shade. Male. 1.5 × 1m.

Aucuba japonica 'Jungle Girl'
Resembles 'Forest Green' but with a little yellow spotting on the foliage. Female. 1.5 × 1m.

Aucuba japonica 'Mr Goldstrike'
Similar to crotonoides but with smaller golden flecks. Male. 1.5 × 1m.

Aucuba japonica 'Picturata'
Large showy leaves with central broad splash of brilliant gold, edges deep green splashed yellow. Prefers more shade than crotonoides for colour intensity and prevention of leafscorch. Fruits well if pollinated. Female. 1.5 × 1m.

Aucuba japonica 'Sulphur'
Large, mid green deeply serrated leaves with broad irregular margins of creamy-sulphur. Slower growing and more compact. Female. 1 × 1m.

AULAX

A genus of three dioecious species from South Africa named from the Greek *aulax* — furrow. Distinct female and male flowers on separate plants. Easy to grow, reasonably hardy to frost and quite drought resistant. Plant in deeply worked, free-draining soil with sand and peat moss. Water deeply and infrequently during prolonged dry periods.
Proteaceae.

Aulax cancellata
Upright grower with reddish stems and curved, 5–10cm, needle or pine-like leaves closely arranged on erect stems. New shoots reddish. Female plant usually smaller and more compact than the male. Yellow flower heads appear feathery but quite bristly to the touch. Bracts retained after flowering, enclose seeds to form 3–4cm 'cones', yellow or green, shaded dark crimson. Male flowers comprised of similar yellow tufts surrounded by contrasting reddish young growth. Syn Aulax pinifolia. Cancellata — cross-barred or latticed. Evergreen. 1.5 × 1m.

AZALEA
(EVERGREEN)

Azaleas really belong to the Rhododendron genus of 700–800 species, but as they've been known by this name for centuries and have a distinctive character and appearance, Azaleas are featured in this book under their own heading and grouped as 'evergreen' or 'deciduous'. Azalea is named from the Greek *azaleos*, dry, in allusion to the arid habitat of some species. Virtually all evergreen Azaleas have Asiatic origin. Hybridists in Japan, Europe and USA have provided hundreds of colourful and free-flowering shrubs to adorn gardens in wide-ranging climatic conditions of both hemispheres.

Evergreen Azaleas are not necessarily evergreen in the usual sense, but have what is known as dimorphic leaves — of two dissimilar shapes or forms. At flowering time, or soon after, new spring leaves appear along the stems which in autumn often turn yellow prior to falling. Then in early summer, smaller, thicker, darker and more leathery leaves emerge, crowded towards the tip of each branch. Often they turn bronze or reddish through winter and are usually shed the following spring although some cultivars may retain them for 2–3 years.

They're easy to grow in average, lime-free, slightly acid to neutral, free-draining soil conditioned with peat moss, sand or scoria. Excessive alkalinity may be corrected with aluminium sulphate. Some Azaleas revel in sunshine and provide brilliant floral displays in semi-tropical climates. Others are inclined to suffer burn to either foliage or flower and require filtered sunlight. However, maximum exposure to sun encourages compact growth, ripening and hardening of the stems for optimum flower production.
Ericaceae.

Evergreen Azaleas
Cultivars bred in USA include hybrids from Black Acres, Gable, Girard, Glenn Dale, Greenwood, Harris, Kerrigan, Linwood, Morrison, North Tisbury, Nuccio, Robin Hill and Rutherford. Satsuki hybrids and Kurumes are from Japan while Kaempferi and Vuykiana hybrids originated in Holland.

Many of the cultivars marked 'Indica', sometimes referred to as Belgian Indian Azaleas probably arose from R indicum and R simsii crosses, bred in Belgium during the 19th century and subsequently in other countries.

In the following descriptions, terms such as 'single' or 'double' are familiar to most gardeners. A flower described as 'hose-in-hose' simply means that it appears as a tube within a tube.

Flowering seasons vary according to climatic conditions, and are mentioned only as a rough guide — **Early** — winter through early spring. **Mid season** — late winter through mid spring. **Late** — late spring through summer. Height and width dimensions in centimetres are meant only as a rough guide as growing conditions are so variable.

Azalea 'Advent Bells'
Bright rosy-red, large semi-double, early to mid season. Compact, free-flowering. Indica. 75 × 75cm.

Azalea 'Alaska'
White flared and speckled light green in the throat, medium to large semi-double, mid season. Compact, spreading growth. Rutherford. 80 × 120cm.

Azalea 'Albert Elizabeth'
White with broad, rosy-red margin, lime green throat, large semi-double to peony, frilled, mid season. Rounded upright form. Indica. 80 × 100cm.

Azalea 'Alexander'
Bright red toned orange, medium single, late. Prostrate grower for ground cover, banks or wall spiller. North Tisbury. 25 × 100cm.

Azalea 'All Glory'
Vivid salmon pink to cerise, small single, mid season. Compact, rounded grower. Kurume. 90 × 90cm.

Azalea 'Anna Kehr'
Deep rose pink, medium double, mid season. Rounded, compact growth. Kehr. 75 × 90cm.

Azalea 'Ben Morrison'
Rosy salmon pink flaring to ruby red in the throat, margined white, medium single, early to mid season. Compact rounded form. Vigorous. Morrison. 100 × 100cm.   **21**

Azalea 'Betty Ann Voss'
Light rose pink, medium to large hose-in-hose like a rosebud, mid season. Dwarf compact grower. Robin Hill. 60 × 60cm.

Azalea 'Bit of Sunshine'
Soft light red, medium, single to hose-in-hose, mid season. Dense, compact grower. Kurume. 70cm.

Azalea 'Blue Danube'
Light violet to purple, medium single, mid season. Deep green foliage, erect spreading growth. Vuykiana. 90 × 120cm.   **22**

Azalea 'Border Gem'
Rose pink, medium single, mid season. Compact, dense grower. Girard. 75 × 75cm.

Azalea 'Bridal Bouquet'
Pure white, medium fully double, mid season. Fresh green foliage, compact form. Indica. 75 × 75cm.   **23**

Azalea 'Butterfly'
Pure white, small to medium hose-in-hose, mid season. Compact bushy growth. Kurume. 60 × 60cm.

Azalea 'Carnival Clown'
Purple-violet flushed red, large single ruffled, early to mid season.. Compact rounded form. Nuccio. 100 × 100cm.

Azalea 'Cayuga'
Pink with distinctive white throat, medium single to hose-in-hose, mid season. Compact, mounding form. Greenwood. 75 × 90cm.

Azalea 'Charlie'
Vivid rosy red, large double ruffled, early to mid season. Compact low spreader. German. 70 × 70cm

Azalea 'Chiara'
Clear pink, large ruffled single, mid season. Free flowering, dense compact growth. Girard. 75 × 75cm.   **22**

Azalea 'Chinzan'
Vivid pink with darker blotch, medium single, late. Compact growth, deep green foliage. Satsuki. 50 × 50cm.

Azalea 'Cliff's Choice'
Pale coral pink with deeper margins, medium semi-double hose-in-hose, mid season. Upright, rounded form. Indica. 100 × 120cm.

Azalea 'Comte de Keratone'
Soft warm pink, deeper pink veins, petals flecked white at edges with deeper maroon throat, double, mid season. Indica. 75 × 75cm.

Azalea 'Comtesse de Kerchovi'
Clear salmon pink, lightly shaded white at petal tips, large double, wavy petals, early to mid season. Low, spreading compact. Indica. 75 × 90cm.

Azalea 'Daishuhai'
Salmon red with white throat, bicolour, large single, mid season. Low spreading growth. Satsuki. 60 × 60cm.

Azalea 'Debonaire'
Delicate soft pink on outer edges, centre shading to almost white, lemon green ray in the throat, medium single. Compact bush. Black Acres. 90 × 90cm.

Azalea 'Dorothy Gish'
Deep pink, medium frilled hose-in-hose, early to mid season. Dwarf compact form. Indica. 40 × 40cm.

Azalea 'Dr Glaser'
Deepest red, large ruffled double, mid season. Rich green foliage tinged reddish purple in winter. Low spreading form. Indica. 75 × 75cm.

Azalea 'Eikan'
Creamy white with splashes of salmon pink, and yellow, medium single, mid to late. Low sprawling habit. Satsuki. 60 × 90cm.

Azalea 'Ellamere'
Tangerine or orange-red, large ruffled semi-double, early. Low compact form. Indica. 75 × 90cm.

Azalea 'Ellie Harris'
Light pink, semi-double hose-in-hose, early to mid. Compact, heavy flowered. Harris. 100 × 100cm.

Azalea 'Elsa Kaerger'
Vibrant, deep-orange red, large frilled fully double, early. Compact grower. Indica. 75 × 75cm.

Azalea 'Eros'
Deep pink, fading lighter and small dark blotch, medium single, late. Low spreading form. Glen Dale. 75 × 90cm.

Azalea 'Eureka'
Deep rose pink with a broad white margin, medium to large double, early to mid season. Dense, low rounded form. Indica. 60 × 75cm.   **22**

Azalea 'Fascination'
Pale pink bordered red, large single, mid to late. Low compact growth. Harris. 75 × 75cm.

Azalea 'Festive'
White with purplish red stripes, medium single, early. Erect spreading grower. Glen Dale. 130 × 100cm.

Azalea 'Fielder's White'
Pure white with lime green throat, medium single, slight fragrance, early to mid season. Old reliable favourite. Large vigorous bush. Indica. 1.5 × 1.5m.

Azalea 'Frosted Orange'
White with prominent reddish orange border, large single, late. Low compact grower. Harris. 75 × 90cm.

Azalea 'Fuji-no-Tsuki'
Delicate, clear mauve with lighter throat, large single, mid season. Low compact bush. Indica. 50 × 75cm.

Azalea 'Gaiety'
Brilliant pink with a silky sheen, large single, mid season. Deep green foliage, low spreading growth. Glenn Dale. 60 × 90cm.

Azalea 'Gay Paree'
Pure white margined cyclamen or violet-red, large semi-double hose-in-hose, mid season. Deep green foliage, compact rounded growth. Kerrigan. 75 × 100cm.   **23**

Azalea 'Gerhard Nicholai'
Glowing cyclamen pink, large ruffled semi-double, mid season. Compact bushy grower. Indica. 75 × 100cm.   **22**

Azalea 'Girard's Crimson'
Crimson with deeper red blotch, medium single, mid season. Free flowering. Girard. 100 × 100cm

Azalea 'Glacier'
White with faint green overlay, medium single, early to mid season. Vigorous growth, glossy foliage. Glen Dale. 150 × 100cm.

Azalea 'Great Expectations'
Vivid reddish orange, medium double, mid season. Spreading growth, suitable for ground cover, basket or container. Kehr. 60 × 90cm.

Azalea 'Greenwood Orange'
Reddish orange, medium double, mid season. Open, upright growth. Greenwood. 75 × 75cm.

Azalea 'Gretel'
Pure white margined florescent china rose-pink, large double, early to mid season. Low compact form. Indica. 50 × 75cm.   **22**

Azalea 'Gumpo'
Dwarf, compact, low growing plants with closely tufted foliage. Medium to large, frilled single blooms mid to late spring. In

shades of pale pink, mid pink, salmon pink, and white. Satsuki. 30 × 75cm.

Azalea 'Happy Days'
Light purple, double, hose-in-hose, mid season. Low compact grower. Indica. 50 × 75cm.

Azalea 'Hardy Gardenia'
Pure white, semi-double hose-in-hose, mid to late season. Forms a low mound. Linwood. 45 × 45cm.

Azalea 'Hearthglow'
Deep yellowish pink, strong reddish orange central flush, medium double, mid season. Strong growth. Black Acres. 120 × 100cm.

Azalea 'Helen Fox'
Pale red irregularly margined white, large single, early to mid season. Upright, compact grower. Glen Dale. 90 × 90cm.

Azalea 'Hinode Giri'
Bright cerise crimson, small single, mid season. Rounded compact bush. Hardy, free-flowering. Kurume. 120 × 150cm.

Azalea 'Issho-no-Haru'
White, washed lavender, occasionally streaked bright magenta, large single, late. Compact grower. Satsuki. 75 × 75cm.

Azalea 'Janet Rhea'
Purple-red with irregular white border, medium semi-double, mid season. Compact growth. Linwood. 75 × 75cm.   **23**

Azalea 'Jeanne Weeks'
Light pink, semi-double hose-in-hose like rosebuds, mid season. Compact, low habit. Robin Hill. 50 × 90cm.

Azalea 'Jewel Box'
Glowing rose pink, small to medium hose-in-hose, mid season. Compact growth. Kurume. 75 × 75cm.

Azalea 'Joan Garrett'
Salmon pink with reddish flare, very large 10–15cm single, mid season. Compact spreading form. Harris. 90 × 120cm

Azalea 'Joseph Hill'
Brick red, small single, late. Low growing, spreading form. North Tisbury. 30 × 90cm.

Azalea 'Kirin'
Deep rose pink shaded silvery rose, small semi-double hose-in-hose, mid season. Petite, compact plant becomes a total mass of bloom. Syn 'Coral Bells'. Kurume. 75 × 75cm.

Azalea 'Kocho no Mai'
Deep lavender mauve to purple with paler throat, small, semi-double hose-in-hose, mid season. Sturdy compact bushy plant. Syn 'Butterfly Dance'. Kurume. 90 × 100cm.

Azalea 'Little Red Riding Hood'
Intense crimson orange, small single, mid season. Vigorous compact grower. Kurume. 90 × 100cm.

Azalea 'Lorna'
Deep pink, medium double hose-in-hose, mid season. Spreading, compact grower. Gable. 90 × 100cm.   **23**

Azalea 'Lucy'
Deep rose pink, large ruffled double, early to mid season. Low-spreading, bushy grower. Indica. 60 × 75cm.

Azalea 'Mardi Gras'
Red centre shading to rose pink and margined white, semi-double, mid season. Compact grower. Indica. 60 × 75cm.   **22**

Azalea 'Melody'
Bright rosy red with deeper spots in the throat, medium semi-double hose-in-hose, mid season. Dense, compact grower. Indica. 75 × 75cm.

Azalea 'Miss Jane'
White central zone bordered purplish pink, medium double, mid season. Compact grower. Black Acres. 50 × 90cm.

Azalea 'Mission Bells'
Crimson red, large ruffled double, mid season. Low bushy growth. Indica. 75 × 90cm.

Azalea 'Mrs Alfred Sanders'
Bright cerise red, large ruffled double, mid season. Low compact grower, ideal tub plant. Indica. 50 × 75cm.

Azalea 'Mrs Gerard Kint'
Coral pink to orange margined white, small to medium single, mid to late season. Compact grower, small leaves, prolific bloomer. Indica. 40 × 60cm.

Azalea 'My Fair Lady'
Bright rose pink and white bicolour, medium double, mid season. Compact form. Indica. 60 × 60cm.

Azalea 'Nancy of Robin Hill'
Soft salmon pink with small pink flare, medium double hose-in-hose, late. Low compact growth. Robin Hill. 75 × 75cm.

Azalea 'Nuccio's Jewel Box'
Bright rose pink, medium semi-double hose-in hose, early to mid season. Compact spreading form, good winter foliage colour. Nuccio. 75 × 100cm.

Azalea 'Only One Earth'
Vibrant rosy carmine, medium semi-double hose-in-hose, mid season. Compact rounded form. Indica. 90 × 90cm.

Azalea 'Orchid Beauty'
Vivid purplish red, medium double hose-in-hose, mid season. Compact form. 40 × 90cm.

Azalea 'Pacific Twilight'
Deep lavender violet, large frilled double, early to mid season. Bright green foliage, erect spreading growth. Indica. 90 × 100cm.

Azalea 'Pastel Petticoat'
Light lavender lilac, medium double, early to mid season. Open layered form, aptly named. Indica. 75 × 90cm.

Azalea 'Paul Schaeme'
Bright red, medium to large double, early to mid season. Low, rounded compact grower. Indica. 50 × 60cm.

Azalea 'Pax'
Pure white, frilled double, mid season. Dwarf compact grower. One of the best whites. Indica. 60 × 60cm.   **23**

Azalea 'Peach Kirin'
Peach pink, small semi-double hose-in-hose, early to mid season. Dwarf compact form, becomes a total mass of bloom. Kurume. 75 × 75cm.

Azalea 'Pearl Bradford'
Light purple pink, blotched purplish red, medium single, very late. Low moulding form, dense foliage. Glenn Dale. 60 × 75cm.

Azalea 'Pink Cloud'
Light purplish pink, medium double, mid to late season. Strong spreading form. Greenwood. 120 × 150cm.

Azalea 'Pink Ice'
Pale pink becoming silvery white flushed lilac, medium to large double, early to mid season. Deep green foliage, compact growth. Indica. 60 × 90cm.

Azalea 'Pink Pancake'
Pink flushed salmon and flared red, small to medium wavy single, late. Low prostrate spreader, excellent ground cover. North Tisbury. 25 × 90cm.

Azalea 'Pink Ruffles'
Clear two-toned pink, margined white, medium ruffled double, early to mid season. Compact grower. Indica. 75 × 75cm.

Azalea 'Princess Maud'
Rich tyrian purple, medium single, early to mid season. Delightful flower clusters on long stems. Kurume. 60 × 60cm.   **41**

Azalea 'Purple Glitters'
Violet purple with red stamens, small frilled single, mid season. Grey-green foliage, spreading bushy growth. Kurume. 60 × 60cm.

Azalea 'Purple Splendour'
Light purple, semi double, hose-in-hose, mid season. Hardy, free-flowering. Gable. 120 × 100cm.   **41**

Azalea 'Rain Fire'
Blood red with creamy centre, large wavy single, early to mid season. Compact grower. Harris. 75 × 75cm.

Azalea 'Red Fountain'
Deep orange red with darker throat and spotting, small single, late. Dwarf spreader with occasional erect stems pendulous at the tips. North Tisbury. 30 × 100cm.

Azalea 'Red Poppy'
Intense deep red, large single to semi-double, early to mid season. Deep green foliage turning purplish in winter. Indica. 70 × 90cm.

Azalea 'Red Ruffles'
Deep salmon rose, medium to large, ruffled semi double hose-in-hose, early to mid season. Compact rounded form. Rutherford. 75 × 90cm.

Azalea 'Red Wings'
Bright red, medium double hose-in-hose, early to mid season. Blooms profusely, best in filtered light. Indica. 75 × 75cm.

Azalea 'Redmond'
Pale scarlet red, very large single, late. Handsome foliage. Robin Hill. 75 × 75cm.

Azalea 'Ripples'
Rose pink, frilled double, mid season. Compact growth. Kerrigan. 60 × 60cm.

Azalea 'Rosa Belton'
Pure white, bordered bright mauve with lime throat, large single. Mid season. Open spreading form. Indica. 90 × 100cm.   **24**

Azalea 'Rose Glitters'
Bright carmine red, large single, mid season.

Strong, rounded, upright growth. Kurume. 100 × 100cm.

Azalea 'Rose Queen'
Bright rose pink with spotted throat, medium semi double hose-in-hose, early to mid season. Bushy grower. Rutherford. 75 × 75cm.

Azalea 'Rosebud'
Deep rose pink lightly overlaid mauve, medium triple hose-in-hose, mid season. Compact, upright growth. Gable. 90 × 100cm.

Azalea 'Royal Robe'
Deep mauve, medium semi double hose-in-hose, late. Rounded compact form. Greenwood. 60 × 60cm.

Azalea 'Sadie Kirk'
Delicate shell pink shaded peach with a touch of lime in the throat, large double, mid season. Erect rounded form. Indica. 90 × 90cm.

Azalea 'Saint James'
Brilliant reddish-orange with white throat, medium single, late. Vigorous. Black Acres. 120 × 100cm.

Azalea 'Salmonea'
Bright salmon-rose pink, medium single, early to mid season. Older but still hardy and very prolific, becoming a total mass of bloom. Syn A splendens. Indica. 130 × 130cm.   **41**

Azalea 'Shugetsu'
White, broadly margined lavender, medium to large single, mid season. Spreading compact bush. Satsuki. 75 × 90cm.

Azalea 'Silver Anniversary'
Soft clear pink delicately shaded white at the tips, large frilled semi double hose-in-hose, early to mid season. Erect rounded form. Indica. 90 × 90cm.

Azalea 'Southern Aurora'
Light vermillion marbled white large double, early to mid season. Compact rounded form. Indica. 75 × 90cm.

Azalea 'Star Trek'
Purest white with pale green throat, large ruffled formal double, gardenia-like blooms, mid season. Compact grower. Indica. 75 × 90cm.

Azalea 'Sunburst'
Brilliant orange red, small to medium semi-double, mid season. Small dark green foliage, very compact. Nuccio. 60 × 80cm.

Azalea 'Susannah Hill'
Deep vivid red, small single, late. Glossy foliage, mounding prostrate form. North Tisbury. 40 × 100cm.

Azalea 'Tenino'
Orchid purple, frilled semi double hose-in-hose, late. Low compact growth. Greenwood. 50 × 60cm.

Azalea 'The Teacher'
Pure white delicately margined rose pink, medium double, early to mid season. Compact rounded grower. Indica. 75 × 75cm.   **41**

Azalea 'Tico Tico'
Light lavender, medium to large semi double hose-in-hose, early to mid season. Compact mounding habit. Indica. 75 × 90cm.

Azalea 'Tiny'
Bright rosy pink, small double hose-in-hose, mid season. Compact growth. 50 × 100cm.

Azalea 'Vespers'
Pure white, lightly flared green in the throat, large semi-double, mid season. Light green foliage, upright bushy grower. Glenn Dale. 120 × 140cm.

Azalea 'Violacea Multiflora'
Deep violet purple, medium double, mid season. Vigorous and floriferous. Indica. 75 × 75cm.   **41**

Azalea 'Ward's Ruby'
Brilliant ruby red, small single in profusion, mid season. Compact form. Kurume. 75 × 90cm.   **41**

Azalea 'White Champagne'
White with light red flare in the throat, medium double hose-in-hose, mid season. Compact, bushy grower. Nuccio. 75 × 90cm.

Azalea 'White Rosebud'
Pure white with chartreuse cast in throat, medium double hose-in-hose flowers like miniature rosebuds, mid season. Upright spreading form. Kehr. 90 × 100cm.

Azalea 'Winter Hawk'
Pure white with pale yellowish green throat, medium double hose-in-hose, early to mid season. Low rounded habit. Indica. 50 × 75cm.

Azalea 'Wintergreen'
Orange red, small single, late. Glossy, deep green foliage, low spreading form. North Tisbury. 25 × 100cm.

AZALEA
(DECIDUOUS)

Deciduous Azaleas provide glorious orange, yellow and golden colours as well as delicate pink shades not found in evergreen cultivars. Although worth growing just for impressive spring flowers, they also provide a pleasant bonus of colourful autumn foliage.

Deciduous Azaleas are extremely hardy to cold, but need to be grown in deeply worked, free-draining, organically enriched, moisture-retentive, acid soil. Use peat moss as a soil conditioner and mulch. Aluminium sulphate or flowers of sulphur will achieve desired acidity. While more comfortable in cooler climates, they grow and flower satisfactorily in warm temperate regions where suitable soil conditions exist. Select the coolest location, provide shelter from strong winds, and keep moist during dry spells.

Azalea Anthony Koster Hybrids
Bright golden-yellow shades, trumpet shaped flowers in large trusses carried on long stems. Among the showiest garden shrubs. Cutting-grown cultivars are colour-dependable. If selecting seedling-grown plants, choose desired colour when in flower during October-November.

Azalea Ilam Hybrids
Originally raised by the late Edgar Stead of Christchurch, New Zealand. The strain has won worldwide acclaim for brilliance, form and vigour. Amongst them are orange-reds, bronzy apricots, or flaming red shades, with wide open florets, many with frilled margins. An ever-increasing choice of named cultivars is appearing.

Azalea Knap Hill and Exbury Hybrids
Colourful and hardy Azaleas originally developed from obscure parentage by Anthony Waterer at his Knap Hill nursery. Exbury hybrids have resulted from further development carried out by the late Lionel de Rothschild at Exbury Gardens in the south of England. Both groups are characterized by large trusses of trumpet-shaped florets in a brilliant range of gorgeous colours. **43**

Azalea 'Anthony Koster'
Mollis hybrid. Red buds open to vivid yellow flowers with orange flare, large trusses. Compact bush, free-flowering. Mid season. 1.5m. **42**

Azalea 'Barbecue'
Exbury Solent hybrid. Soft salmon pink flowers with deeper salmon markings. Large trusses. Mid season to late. 1.5m.

Azalea 'Bonbouche'
Exbury Solent hybrid. Tangerine around the margins, blending in the centre to soft golden yellow with gold flare. Large trusses. Mid season to late. 1.5m.

Azalea 'Carmen'
Ilam hybrid. Pale orange, flushed salmon-apricot and coral-pink with golden flare, large single frilled and fragrant florets. One of the first to bloom. Early to mid-season. 1.5m. **42**

Azalea 'Cecile'
Exbury hybrid. Carmine to rose pink with large orange flare. Large single florets. Mid season to late. 1.5m.

Azalea 'Citroen'
Exbury Solent hybrid. Delicate mushroom pink with buff centre and yellow blaze. Large trusses. Mid season to late. 1.5m.

Azalea 'Cockatoo'
Mollis hybrid. Brilliant golden orange flowers, borne profusely on a compact bush, early to mid season. 1.3m.

Azalea 'Crown Supreme'
Exbury Solent hybrid. Golden yellow flowers with deeper gold flare. Large trusses. Mid season to late. 1.5m.

Azalea 'Dawn's Glory'
Exbury Solent hybrid. Deep coral orange flowers with gold blaze. Large trusses. Mid season to late. 1.5m.

Azalea 'Delectable'
Exbury Solent hybrid. Soft peach pink flowers with deeper peach markings and small gold flare. Large trusses. Mid season to late. 1.5m.

Azalea 'Delicatissima'
Occidentale hybrid. The species is native to western North America, a parent of numerous beautiful hybrids. 'Delicatissima' meaning most charming, has fragrant flowers of soft pastel pink, flushed deeper pink with prominent orange flare. Compact, multi-stemmed trusses in great abundance. Mid to late season. 1.5m.

Azalea 'Delicious'
Exbury Solent hybrid. Rich golden yellow with deep peach-pink markings. Large trusses. Mid season to late. 1.5m.

Azalea 'Dorothy Corston'
Knap Hill hybrid. Smaller, deep orange-red or brick-red flowers, mid season, neat compact bushy grower with bronze foliage. 1.3m.

Azalea 'Dreadnought'
Exbury Solent hybrid. Deep salmon-orange flowers with small gold blaze. Large trusses. Mid season to late. 1.5m. **42**

Azalea 'Exquisita'
Occidentale hybrid. Soft pastel-pink, flushed cream with a prominent apricot-yellow flare. Star shaped, very fragrant, mid to late season. 1.5m.

Azalea 'Glow'
Exbury Solent hybrid. Deep yellow flowers with deeper yellow flare. Large trusses. Mid season to late. 1.5m.

Azalea 'Harwell'
Knap Hill hybrid. Deep pink flowers in large trusses, mid season. Considered the best pink Knap Hill hybrid. 1.5m.

Azalea 'Homebush'
Knap Hill hybrid. Small bright vibrant pink, semi-double florets in tight rounded trusses, mid season. Neat upright rounded form. 1.8m.

Azalea 'Impala'
Knap Hill hybrid. Small red flowers on a compact bushy plant, mid season. 1.3m.

Azalea 'Krugerrand'
Exbury Solent hybrid. Deepest golden yellow with tangerine markings and deeper gold blaze. Large trusses. Mid season to late. 1.5m.

Azalea 'Lapwing'
Knap Hill hybrid. Brilliant yellow flowers flushed cream, early season. Among the first to flower. 1.5m.

Azalea 'Lobster Pot'
Exbury Solent hybrid. Salmon pink with deeper salmon markings and gold flare. Large trusses. Mid season to late. 1.5m.

Azalea 'Louis Williams'
Ilam hybrid. Soft pastel-pink, suffused cream with large orange flare, large single waved florets. Slower and smaller growing. Mid season. 1.3m.

Azalea 'Melford Flame'
Ilam hybrid. Bright reddish orange flowers with orange-yellow flare in large, frilled, ball-shaped truss, mid to late season. Strong vigorous grower. 1.5m.

Azalea 'Melford Gold'
Ilam hybrid. Deep golden orange with orange flare, in large trusses, mid season, slightly fragrant. 1.5m.

Azalea 'Mollie'
Ilam hybrid. Deep red flowers on a dense bushy plant, mid season. Considered the best red Ilam hybrid, a mature plant in full bloom most impressive. Named for Mollie Coker of Ilam, Christchurch. 1.5m.

Azalea 'Mountain Mist'
Ilam hybrid. Salmon pink in bud, opening creamy pink to white. Large rounded trusses mid season. Deep bronze spring foliage, vigorous grower. 1.5m.

Azalea 'Paramount'
Knap Hill hybrid. Bright yellow double flowers in tight rounded trusses, late season. One of the latest to flower and to come into new growth. 1.5m.

Azalea 'Pavlova'
Blue Mountain. A group of deciduous Azaleas with double hose-in-hose florets from diverse parentage but with the fragrance and double-flowers of the hardy Ghent hybrids and clean healthy foliage to enhance brilliant autumn colour. The prizewinning cultivar 'Pavlova' has large, pure white, fully double, fragrant blooms. Developed by Blue Mountain Nurseries of Tapanui, New Zealand. 1.5m.

Azalea 'Pink Frills'
Ilam hybrid. Bright pink frilly flowers in large ball trusses, mid season. Considered the best pink Ilam hybrid. 1.5m.

Azalea 'Precious'
Exbury Solent hybrid. Soft golden yellow blending to peach pink in the centre and gold flare. Large trusses. Mid season to late. 1.5m.

Azalea 'Red Gem'
Ilam hybrid. Deep red, flushed scarlet, with orange flare and prominent yellow stamens, large single filled florets. Mid to late season. 1.5m.

Azalea 'Raspberry Ripples'
Ilam Hybrid. Vibrant raspberry pink to red blooms with tangerine flare. Vigorous, highly mildew-resistant and very free-flowering. Late season. 2.5m.

Azalea 'Sunset'
Mollis hybrid. Flame to orange flowers with overall apricot appearance, early to mid season. Compact grower and profuse bloomer. 1.5m.

Azalea 'Sword of State'
Exbury Solent hybrid. Soft pink flowers with prominent gold flare on upper lobe. Large trusses. Mid season to late. 1.5m.

Azalea 'Tender Heart'
Exbury Solent hybrid. Coral pink flowers with golden yellow blaze. Large trusses. Mid season to late. 1.5m.

A genus of ten species of evergreen, South American shrubs and small trees named after J N Azara, 18th century Spanish patron of botany. Grown for attractive form, foliage, and flowers with distinct vanilla fragrance. Locate to avoid the hottest sun and plant in deeply worked, free-draining soil, water frequently during dry spells and trim occasionally to maintain vigour.
   Flacourtiaceae. *All evergreen.*

Azara integrifolia 'Variegata'
Tall shrub from Chile, with smooth, rounded, 2cm leaves with a central zone of deep green, margined bright yellow, deepening to red at the edges and sometimes with lightly toothed margins. Chrome yellow flower clusters appear late winter and spring. Integrifolia — entire or uncut leaf margins. 1.5 × 1m.

Azara lanceolata
Lance-leaf Azara
Graceful arching tree from Chile and Argentina with lush, 5–7cm, lanceolate leaves with serrated margins. Fragrant, mimosa-like, yellow flowers in short clusters, interspersed with the leaves early summer. Under favourable conditions, pale mauve berries appear during autumn. Hardy and easy to grow. 4.5 × 3m.

Azara microphylla
Box Leaf Azara
Dainty shrub from Chile and Argentina with distinctive arching branch pattern, spreading fan-like in two-dimensional effect. Glossy, dark green, 1–2cm, obovate or rounded leaves with entire or obscurely serrated margins. Fragrant, greenish yellow flowers in short clusters late winter. 3 × 2.5m.

Azara microphylla 'Variegata'
Compact, slower growing form with foliage artistically variegated green and creamy gold. 1.5 × 1m

A genus of about 350 species of shrubby plants named for Bacchus, the god of wine, possibly in allusion to the spicy fragrance from the roots. The sole species listed is a dependable little plant for bank or ground cover, especially for its remarkable adaptability to climate and soil, thriving in coastal areas without summer moisture or in almost swampy conditions. Plant in well-drained soil in full sun. In exposed conditions little pruning is required, otherwise remove arching branches and shear to preserve neatness. Valued ground or bank cover with minimum maintenance.
   Compositae.

Baccharis pilularis 'Twin Peaks'
Coyote Brush
Interesting and useful plant from coastal hills and dunes of California. Dense, rather billowy, bright-green mat, densely covered with small, obovate to ovate, serrated, 12mm leaves, like miniature holly leaves without spines. Flowers of little consequence. The cultivar 'Twin Peaks' has smaller, bright green foliage. Pilularis — with little balls, a reference to globular fruits. Evergreen. 20–60cm high, spreading to 2m.

A genus of seven Australian endemic species of trees and shrubs from eastern rainforests named after James Backhouse of York, a 19th century nurseryman. All species are highly ornamental, the foliage charged with aromatic oil, obvious when leaves are crushed. Plant in deeply worked, organically enriched, well-drained soil. Worthy of a place in any garden where frosts are not severe.
   Myrtaceae

Backhousia citriodora
Lemon Scented Myrtle
Attractive medium shrub or small tree from rainforests of north eastern Queensland. Strongly lemon scented leaves, ovate lanceolate, to 12 × 5cm, dark green, margins with small serrations, young shoots reddish bronze. Small, 5–7mm, creamy white flowers crowded in umbels or flat-topped clusters at branch ends through summer and autumn. Citriodora — lemon scented. Evergreen. 4.5 × 3.5m.

BAECKEA

A genus of more than 70 species of prostrate to tall shrubs, mainly Australian, named after Dr Abraham Baeck, 18th century Swedish physician who collected the first recorded species. While distributed in all states, more then fifty are found in south west Western Australia. Coming from different areas, more specific cultural data appears with each of the following species.

Myrtaceae. *All evergreen.*

Baeckea linifolia
Swamp Heath Myrtle

From Queensland, New South Wales and Victoria growing in cool, moist gullies and swamps. Beautiful gracefully pendulous shrub with slender branches clothed with linear, 6–15mm, almost prickly leaves. Drooping young shoots usually reddish bronze. Small, 3–5mm, solitary, white flowers appear in profusion in upper leaf axils almost the year through with massed displays through summer. Adaptable to sun or semi-shade, clay or sandy soils and tolerant of poor drainage. Prune at least annually to keep bushy and encourage new growth and maximum bloom. Linifolia — flax-leaved. 1–2 × 1m.

Baeckea virgata 'La Petite'

The species is widely distributed through Australia's eastern States and Northern Territory, a bushy shrub resembling Thryptomene calycina with dark green, linear-lanceolate, 12–25mm leaves. The cultivar 'La Petite' is a compact, small shrub producing 5–6mm, white flowers in great profusion for several months from mid summer. Suitable for ground cover, rock gardens etc. Hardy, adaptable to most well-drained soils and climates. Plant in full sun. Virgata — twiggy. 30 × 75cm.

BAMBUSA

A genus of about 120 species of clumping bamboos, mostly from tropical and subtropical Asia, named from the Latinized version of the Malaysian vernacular *Bambu*. Besides their use as impenetrable barrier screens, many Bamboo species are excellent landscaping plants for softening architectural lines, providing oriental effects or for creating sheer beauty beside pools or streams. Once established,

Bamboos are tolerant of most climatic conditions encountered in Australasia. They withstand drought and considerable moisture, but dislike boggy conditions. Like any other grass, growth rate is determined by the degree of moisture and feeding.

Gramineae. *All evergreen.*

Bambusa gracilis
Fairy Bamboo

Native to China and Japan. Dense clump bamboo with smooth, slender, 1–2cm, gracefully curving stems well clothed with soft, fresh-green leaves. Has more airy gracefulness than most other cultivated species. Ideal for pool-sides, patios, feature gardens or to soften harsh architectural lines. Gracilis — graceful, slender. 3 × 2m.

Bambusa gracillima
Graceful Bamboo

Chinese native clump bamboo from the Goddess of Mercy Temple, Koom Yam Chuk. Dainty small leafed plant, slow growing and dense. Slender solid stems less than 1cm thick, green when young, becoming orange with age. Stems bend and arch outward in fountain form. Pinnate leaves 1–2cm long held on thin branchlets. Gracillima — most graceful. 2 × 1m.

Bambusa multiplex
Fern Leaf Bamboo

Dense, clump producing bamboo from south China with 3 to 4cm stems, and numerous branchlets coming from the nodes. Small, fern-like, glabrous leaves, deep green with silvery-blue reverse. Multiplex — much-folded. 5 × 2m.

Bambusa multiplex 'Alphonse Karr'

Handsome clump bamboo from Japan. Young stem sheaths striped pink and green, and mature stems about 2cm in diameter have orange-yellow and green stripes of varying widths. Extremely attractive and very popular. 4 × 2m.

Bambusa multiplex 'Wang Tsai'

Chinese native clump bamboo which could be described as a larger form of B gracillima. Gracefully curving, green to orange-brown stems, dark green tufted foliage. 2 × 2m.

Bambusa oldhamii
Oldham Bamboo

Tall, elegant clump forming species from south China and Taiwan. Older plants develop green to yellow stems from 4 to 8cm thick, branching at every node. Broad, 18 × 4cm leaves, dull green above, almost shiny beneath. Useful for tall boundary shelter attaining heights of 15m or more

when established. Heavy frosts may not kill, but cause damage to late-growing succulent shoots and limit height. Grown extensively in warm temperate areas as orchard shelter. Oldhamii — for Richard Oldham, 19th century Kew gardener who collected Chinese plants. 8 × 2m.

Bambusa ventricosa
Buddha's Belly Bamboo

Chinese native clump species with short, swollen internodes suggesting the common name. This is more evident when grown as tub plants or in very dry conditions when stems appear to be turned on a lathe. Grows to a substantial size with 6–7m stems, straight internodes and leaves to 18cm long. Possibly best as a container plant. Ventricosa — having a swelling on one side. 3 × 1.5m.

BANKSIA

The Banksia genus is virtually endemic to Australia with just one of more than 70 species being found in Papua New Guinea. Named after Sir Joseph Banks, president of the Royal Society and famous botanist who travelled with Captain Cook in 1770. About 60 species are found in south Western Australia, in areas of high winter rainfall and dry summer. They include some of the most spectacular and colourful but it must be pointed out that Western Australian species are difficult to grow in areas of high humidity and high rainfall during summer where failure, caused by the root-rot fungus Phytophthora cinnamomi is common. All Banksias attracts hordes of birds.

Eastern species are more amenable to cultivation. Mention is made below of their specific cultural preferences. Generally, Banksias prefer to grow in deep, well-drained friable clay, sandy or gravelly soil in full sun, although some of the western species grow in semi-shade. Once established, they tolerate extended drought and light frost. Banksias with a lignotuber or woody underground root, may if necessary be pruned to ground level for the control of size or shape. Banksias without a lignotuber accept light pruning but not into old wood. A lignotuber acts as food storage and bears latent buds which eventually start to grow if the main stem if damaged or destroyed by fire. Because Banksias grow in soils low in phosphorous, fertilizers with a NPK rating of 10–4–6 may be applied sparingly early autumn and early spring.

Proteaceae. *All evergreen.*

Banksia attenuata
Coast Banksia, Slender Banksia
From Western Australia. Variable form from multistemmed shrub to medium tree with lignotuber and rough, dark grey bark. Leaves usually linear, narrowing towards the base, 8–20 × 1cm, with serrated margins, prominent veins and densely hairy beneath. Showy cylindrical flower heads to 25cm long, bright yellow, fragrant, held above the foliage. Shrubby form more desirable for gardens. Attenuata — narrowing to a point. 3 × 2m.

Banksia baxterii
Bird's Nest Banksia
From south coastal Western Australia. Open spreading to dense medium shrub with lignotuber and reddish, hairy new shoots and horizontal branches. Stiff, dull-green leaves to 15 × 5cm, with slightly prickly, triangular lobes deeply cut to the midrib and hairy beneath. Globular to dome-shaped, yellow-green, terminal flower heads to 10 × 12cm surrounded by leaves and followed by dome shaped cones. Popular cut flower. Named for William Baxter, 19th century botanist. 3 × 2m.

Banksia blechnifolia
Found on sandy heathlands of south Western Australia as a dwarf spreading shrub without a lignotuber, stems often buried with moving sand. Flowers and leaves often look like cut blooms merely stuck into the ground. Young shoots covered with reddish hairs. Leaves to about 45cm, deeply lobed to a prominent midrib and 10cm petiole. Cylindrical flower spikes to 16cm, pink in bud, becoming red or deep salmon pink with yellow stigmas. Vigorous and free-flowering. Ideal for large rock gardens, bank or ground cover. One prolific, flowering specimen is reputed to cover 16 square metres. Blechnifolia — leaves similar to the fern genus Blechnum. 50cm × 2m.

Banksia brownii
Feather-leaved Banksia
From south Western Australia. Upright, open shrub or small tree without lignotuber. Leaves broadly linear to 12 × 1cm and finely lobed almost to the midrib, whitish beneath, appearing featherlike and very soft textured. Cylindrical flower heads to 20 × 10cm bright reddish or golden brown borne amongst the leaves through autumn and winter. Named for Robert Brown, 18–19th century Scottish botanist. 4 × 3m.

Banksia coccinea
Scarlet Banksia, Waratah Banksia
From south Western Australia. Medium to tall shrub with erect, quite hairy branches

and without lignotuber. Leaves somewhat obcordate or obovate, to 10 × 8cm, olive green, leathery, greyish beneath and with toothed margins. Cylindrical flower heads to 12 × 15cm, usually broader than deep, grey and scarlet, borne terminally through winter to early summer. Among the most popular cut flower Banksias. Coccinea — deep red. 3 × 2m.

Banksia ericaefolia
Heath Banksia
From New South Wales, found in wide-ranging conditions from exposed coastal cliffs, in gullies or inland to the Blue Mountains. Compact shrub without lignotuber. Smooth grey branches. Heath-like leaves, linear to 20 × 3mm, deep green, backed silver. Produces great quantities of erect, cylindrical flowers to 30 × 6cm, golden amber to rich orange-brown, studded with hundreds of hooked styles or 'pins' from autumn through spring. Blooms long lasting either on the bush or cut. Ericaefolia — foliage like the genus Erica or heath. 3 × 2m.   **44**

Banksia gardnerii
From south Western Australia. Slow growing, prostrate shrub with a lignotuber or woody root and horizontal branches radiating at ground level to about a metre. Deep green, broadly linear leaves to 40 × 5cm, lobed to about half way to the midrib. Cylindrical flower spikes to 15 × 5cm, light to rusty brown with a hint of pink, carried upright at branch ends during winter and spring. Named for Charles A Gardner, Western Australian botanist. 30cm × 1.5m

Banksia grandis
Great Coned Banksia, Bull Banksia
From the south west corner of Western Australia. Naturally seen either as a stately tree to 10m or large spreading shrub without lignotuber in exposed coastal situations. Large, handsome leaves to 50 × 10cm, lobed almost to the mid-rib into triangular segments, yellowish-green above, silvery beneath. Young shoots may be bright rusty red. Long, cylindrical flower spikes to 40 × 10cm, at first greenish yellow, becoming bright yellow, carried erect at branch ends spring through mid summer. 5 × 4m.

Banksia integrifolia
Coast Banksia
Hardy, evergreen trees, from coastal areas of Queensland, New South Wales and Victoria withstanding strong, salt-laden winds. Open, spreading form with rough, grey, fissured bark. Leaves to 15 × 6, linear or obovate, dark green, silvery beneath, often irregularly toothed despite its name. Pale

yellow cylindrical flower spikes to 12cm, appear early autumn through winter. Integrifolia — with entire leaf margins. 8 × 5m.

Banksia marginata
Silver Banksia
Widely distributed over a range of settings and soil types from coastal scrubs to highland forests in New South Wales, Victoria, Tasmania and South Australia and accordingly variable in size and structure from a compact shrub to tree of 12m, with or without lignotuber. Leaves linear or obovate from 3–10cm × 5–10mm, leathery, deep green, silvery beneath, heavily veined, margins entire, finely toothed or rolled under. Cylindrical, 5–10cm flower spikes, creamy, greenish yellow to bright yellow from late spring through autumn. Dwarf form normally available from nurseries. Marginata — margined. 1 × 1m.

Banksia occidentalis
Red Swamp Banksia
From southern Western Australia growing in swampy, peaty sandy conditions near the coast. Erect, medium shrub or small tree without lignotuber. Bright green, glossy, narrow-linear, 6–12cm leaves, silvery grey beneath with recurved margins. Cylindrical flower heads to 15 × 10cm, creamy yellow with ruby red hooked styles. Occidentalis — western. 4.5 × 3m.

Banksia repens
Creeping Banksia
From southern Western Australia. Prostrate shrub with lignotuber and underground stems which emerge up to 50cm from the centre. Young shoots rusty brown. Amazing leaves to 40 × 15cm, arise from ground level, with entire or finely toothed lobes, appearing ferny or pinnate. Cylindrical flower spikes to 12 × 6cm, yellowish brown to dull red carried erect at branch ends spring through mid summer. Repens — creeping. 50cm × 2m.

Banksia robur
Swamp Banksia
Often seen in large colonies in coastal, sandy or peaty swamps or swamp margins from New South Wales to Cape York Peninsula. Medium shrub with lignotuber, distinguished by large, tough, leathery, obovate, glossy green leaves to 30 × 10cm, with small, irregularly toothed margins and silvery grey beneath. New shoots pink to rusty brown and velvety. Metallic blue-green buds open to cylindrical, yellow-green, flower spikes to 18cm mainly summer through winter and at odd times through the year. Easily grown, preferring conditions which retain moisture. Outstanding as a

specimen and acclaimed for foliage, bud and flower. Robur — Latin for oak-wood or strength. 2 × 1.5m.

Banksia serrata
Saw Banksia, Red Honeysuckle
Frequently seen in scattered colonies as rugged, gnarled, often contorted trees without a lignotuber, growing in poor sandy coastal conditions of Tasmania, Victoria, New South Wales, north to Noosa. Dark grey, furrowed bark with orange blotches, new shoots greyish and softly woolly. Tough and rigid, shiny deep green, obovate leaves to 20 × 3cm, with deeply serrated margins. Cylindrical, 15cm flower spikes, silvery-grey and velvety in bud, open yellow, attractive to honey-eating birds. Curious, large shaggy seed cones represented the 'bad Banksia men' of May Gibb's adventure story books for children. Picturesque specimen tree. Serrata — serrated or toothed leaves. 10 × 5m.

Banksia speciosa
Showy Banksia
From south Western Australia. Forms a rounded, multi-branched, spreading shrub or small tree without lignotuber. Young shoots covered with small, rust-brown hairs. Leaves long, broad-linear to 40cm, glabrous, grey-green, triangular lobed to the midrib and hairy beneath. Erect, terminal, cylindrical flower spikes to 15 × 12cm, rounded at the apex, greyish in bud, open flowers yellow. Amongst the most beautiful banksias. Flowers and cones good for picking. Speciosa — showy. 4 × 4m.

Banksia spinulosa
Hairpin Banksia
Upright growing shrub with lignotuber and smooth, greyish-brown bark, distributed along coastal Queensland and New South Wales usually on hillsides or open forest areas. Leaves narrow linear to 12cm × 7mm, green above, silvery beneath with fine serrations toward the apex and recurved margins. Cylindrical flower spikes to 20 × 8cm, tightly packed with wiry, bright golden yellow styles, usually with contrasting purplish-black styles. Spinulosa — spiny, in reference to toothed leaves. 3 × 2m.

Banksia spinulosa var collina
Hill Banksia
From Queensland, New South Wales and Victoria. Similar to above but with flat and broader leaves, margined with recurved teeth. Conspicuous, 20cm, cylindrical, deep honey coloured flower spikes, enhanced by deep purplish brown protruding styles like hooked pins. Collina — pertaining to the hills. 2.5 × 2m. **44**

Banksia spinulosa var collina
Dwarf Hill Banksia
A low-growing cultivar, selected from coastal stands on the New South Wales coast. Typical, attractive, golden-orange flower spikes borne within branches and foliage when young, becoming more prominent and terminal with maturity. 1 × 1.5m.

Australian endemic genus of three species from moist, sheltered woodland habitats of eastern states, named after 19th century Austrian botanical illustrators Franz and Ferdinand Bauer.

Baueras are most decorative dwarf flowering shrubs of spreading habit, adaptable to varying soil and climatic conditions. They prefer cool, moist slightly acid to neutral soil, deeply worked and conditioned with peat moss and coarse sand, in dappled shade or where they avoid midday heat and protected from hot drying winds. Feed sparingly with slow release fertilizer. Pick flowers for indoors freely and prune back to half way when flowering has finished.
Baueraceae. *All evergreen.*

Bauera rubioides
River Rose
Found in sheltered coastal areas and forests of eastern states and Tasmania. Prostrate, heath-like shrub with slender stems and dainty 12mm leaves arranged in whorls of three. Small, pink, 5–18mm open-petalled flowers appear from leaf axils almost continuously. Rubioides — resembling the genus Rubia. Cultivars include 'Alba' — white, 'Candy Stripe' — pink striped, 'Fairy Pink' — bright pink, 'Plum Duff' — foliage turns plum red in winter. White flowers. 1 × 1.5m.

Bauera 'Ruby Glow'
Hybrid from B rubioides × B sessiliflora resulting in a small, dense rounded shrub with deep, ruby-red flowers. 1 × 1m.

Bauera sessiliflora
Grampians Bauera
Dense, usually upright shrub found along stream banks, gullies and semi-woodland areas of the Victorian Grampians. Dark green, oblong, 25mm leaves in threes. Rosy purple or magenta, 15mm flowers like small briar roses clustered at intervals up each stem provide a delightful display late winter to mid summer. Sessiliflora — with stalkless stems. 1 × 1m.

An interesting genus of about 24 species of xeromorphic, evergreen plants from south USA, Mexico to Guatemala, related to Yucca and Agave. Xeromorphic refers to adaptation for water storage or limitation of loss of moisture.

Plant outdoors in full sun in deeply worked, free-draining soil. Provide adequate protection from sun and cold to plants which have been indoors for prolonged periods until they acclimatize. Slow growth rate allows long term placement in small but high exposure garden areas such as around pools or other outdoor living areas.
Agavaceae.

Beaucarnea recurvata
Ponytail, Bottle Palm
Old, mature specimens are seen with flask-shaped trunks to 8m with swollen, 2m base and few branches and inconspicuous clusters of creamy-white to reddish flowers. Young plants resemble an onion from which arise a rosette or 'mop' of linear, tapering, olive-green leaves to 90 × 2cm, gracefully arching and curving backwards towards the stem. Unusual plant often seen indoors, in large containers on patios, or planted as a garden feature specimen. Recurvata — curved backwards. Evergreen. 1.2 × 1m.

A genus of about 18 Australian endemic species of evergreen shrubs named after Mary Somerset, Duchess of Beaufort, an early 18th century patroness of botany. Most species are from the south west corner of Western Australia, among them many beautiful and colourful dwarf shrubs, somewhat restricted in cultivation.

The Swamp Brush Myrtle has proved to be an excellent garden shrub. Although naturally occurring in swamps, in cultivation it seems to thrive best in light to medium, deeply worked, free draining soil in sun or partial shade. Prune lightly after flowering, and tip prune throughout the growing season. Feed sparingly with slow-release fertilizer early spring and autumn and give infrequent deep watering during dry periods. Closely related to Melaleuca.
Myrtaceae.

Beaufortia sparsa
Swamp Brush Myrtle
Upright to spreading shrub with sparse branches. Small narrow 10 × 5mm leaves clasp each branchlet in two opposite rows. Brilliant scarlet, 5–7cm brush-like flowers appear in mass during summer and autumn. Outstanding flowering shrub. Sparsa — few or far between. Evergreen. 1.5 × 1m.

BEILSCHMIEDIA

A genus of about 100 species of trees and shrubs scattered throughout tropical and subtropical Asia, Africa, Australia, New Zealand, and America, named for German botanist C T Beilschmied. Four Australian endemic species from Queensland rainforests are rarely seen in cultivation. The two New Zealand species grow into large trees, suitable as specimens in public or acreage gardens. Plant them in rich, deeply worked, well drained soil, keep moist until established.
    Lauraceae. *All evergreen.*

Beilschmiedia taraire
New Zealand Taraire
Among New Zealand's most handsome native trees, found in lowland forests and along stream banks mainly in North Auckland. Stately, straight and erect tree with smooth, brown bark. Young shoots covered with rusty brown tomentum, leaves broadly obovate to elliptic, 8–15cm long, heavily veined and glossy. Small flowers without petals in axillary panicles spring and early summer, followed in autumn by purple-bloomed, 3–4cm fruit. 8 × 5m.

Beilschmiedia tawa
New Zealand Tawa
Found in the North Island and northern areas of the South Island, a somewhat erect tree with smooth, almost black bark and graceful, willowy leaves suspended from the branchlets. Leaves lanceolate to narrow elliptic, 5–10cm × 10–25mm, glabrous, light green, glaucous beneath. Small, greenish-yellow flowers in axillary panicles spring and early summer, followed by oval, 2cm, dark purple fruit. 8 × 5m.

BERBERIS

A large genus of about 450 species, found mostly in light woodlands of Northern Asia, Europe and the Americas, named

from *berberys*, Arabic term for the fruit.

Generally easy to grow and versatile, but even though they may thrive under adverse conditions including wet and cold and poor soil, they prefer moderately moist, sandy loam, provide better foliage colour and greater crops of berry in full sun. Thunbergii types respond to light pruning in winter for growth renewal.
    Berberidaceae. *Deciduous except where marked.*

Berberis × stenophylla
Rosemary Barberry
Hybrid of the Chilean species B darwinii × B empetrifolia. Slender, arching, reddish brown stems. Leaves linear-lanceolate to 2cm, dark green and glossy, blue frosted beneath, margins entire. Sweetly fragrant, golden yellow flowers in clusters of six appear in mass during spring, followed by globose, purple-black berries in autumn. Stenophylla — narrow leaved. Evergreen. 1.8 × 1.8m.

Berberis × stenophylla 'Gracilis'
More refined, slower growing and compact form with similar graceful growth habit and leaves. Spring/summer displays of fragrant, golden yellow flowers and crops of fruit in autumn. May be lightly pruned for size control, but be careful to preserve its gracefully weeping manner. Evergreen. 1.3 × 1.3m.

Berberis thunbergii 'Atropurpurea'
Purple Barberry
Striking Japanese shrub valued for deep bronze-purple foliage through spring and summer, turning crimson in autumn. Leaves ovate, 20 × 15mm with entire margins. After a brief deciduous period, vivid new shoots appear. Pale yellow flowers with orange-red sepals in summer, followed by shiny-red berries. Named after 18th century botanist C P Thunberg. 1.3 × 1m.

Berberis thunbergii 'Atrosuperba'
Bolder form with longer arching branches and larger, more rounded leaves coloured rich blackish-red, turning orange-scarlet in autumn. 1.50 × 1.30m.

Berberis thunbergii 'Aurea'
Golden Barberry
Charming, low compact form with slow growth rate. Young shoots pale yellow, becoming brighter yellow during summer, turning gleaming gold in autumn and early winter before falling. Effective amongst darker foliaged shrubs. Plant to avoid midday sunlight and protect from drying winds and spring frost. 60 × 90cm.

Berberis thunbergii 'Golden Ring'
Hardy and colourful shrub, rich wine red leaves with a narrow margin of gold or lime green, becoming intense bright red and orange shades before falling. Clusters of yellow flowers appear during spring. 80cm × 1m.

Berberis thunbergii 'Little Favourite'
Miniature, compact, global form, rounded, purple-red foliage colouring brilliant red in autumn. Ideal rockery plant. 40 × 50cm.

Berberis thunbergii 'Pink Queen'
Vigorous Dutch hybrid with rounded form and dense branchlets. New spring shoots brilliant red, maturing red, intricately variegated in various pink tones. Changes to deep purple red late summer and autumn before falling. Full sun for maximum colour. 1.2 × 1m.

Berberis thunbergii 'Rose Glow'
Dwarf shrub with slender, arching branches. Young shoots bright purple, unfolding leaves intricately mottled silver-pink, cream and bright rose, maturing purple. Most eye-catching foliage shrub and with typical barberry vigour. 1 × 1m.

Berberis thunbergii 'Silver Beauty'
Colourful, variegated bushy shrub with rounded form. New shoots lime green, becoming delicately mottled and splashed silvery cream and green. Colours to brilliant red during autumn. 1 × 1m.

BERZELIA

A genus of about twelve species of South African evergreen shrubs named after Berzelius an early 19th century Swedish chemist. The listed species is an impressive shrub, relatively easy to grow in deeply worked, free-draining, slightly acid to neutral soil, conditioned with peat moss. Enjoys adequate water during dry periods. Locate in full or partial shade where there is good air flow to dry out the foliage. Reasonably hardy.
    Bruniaceae.

Berzelia lanuginosa
Button Bush
Delightful South African shrub resembling an erect conifer in growth habit. Slender upright stems densely covered with feathery, linear-filiform, 6mm rich-green leaves, giving the plant a distinct, soft furry appearance. Each branch is topped with broad panicles of creamy white, rounded,

1cm, 'button' flowers for long periods during spring and early summer. Good for cut blooms. Lanuginosa — woolly. Evergreen. 2 × 1m. **44**

A genus of about 60 species of deciduous trees and shrubs from temperate and arctic regions of the Northern Hemisphere, named from the ancient Latin term for birch. Birch trees have a light and airy gracefulness and ornamental bark adding special beauty and a dimension in landscaping unmatched by other species. The silvery-white trunks of some species create so much garden drama whether planted singly or in groups. Whichever way birches are used, always aim for natural or informal appearance by avoiding precise spacings or regular formation. Choose trees of varying diameter and height and include some with multi-trunks.

Birches are not soil-robbing and their roots don't seem to take off after drains. They grow in average garden conditions, but thorough ground preparation will get them away to a flying start. Frequent deep watering during dry spells for the first year or two is essential for more young birches die of thirst than for any other reason. They thrive on intense winter cold, but pay attention to summer watering.

Desire for instant effects often tempts gardeners to go for advanced specimens, but there's no doubt that younger trees, still in the brown-stem stage are better value and present fewer transplanting problems. And remember, there are others to choose from besides the more familiar Betula pendula or Silver Birch.

Betulaceae. *All deciduous.*

Betula alleghaniensis
Yellow Birch
From eastern North America. Substantial tree with distinctive, curled, yellowish or grey bark which peels in translucent sheets revealing yellow-brown bark beneath. Leaves ovate to ovate-oblong, to 12 × 6cm, coarsely serrated, dull green becoming bright yellow in autumn. Alleghaniensis — from the Allegheny mountains. Syn B lutea. 8 × 5m.

Betula ermanii
Gold Birch, Russian Rock Birch
Tall grower from north east Asia to the Pacific coast of Russia. Peeling bark, white tinged yellow or reddish brown. Young branches orange brown to purple brown. Leaves to 10 × 7cm, deltoid-cordate, with coarse triangular serrations glossy with parallel veins, colouring well in autumn. 8 × 5m.

Betula grossa
Japanese Cherry Birch
Medium size, Japanese species with smooth, greyish black bark becoming grooved as trees mature. Dull-green leaves, ovate-ovoid, to 10 × 6cm with biserrate, incurved margins and silky pubescent beneath. Twigs have a distinctive aroma when bruised. Grossa — very large. 8 × 5m.

Betula maximowicziana
Monarch Birch
Fast growing Japanese species with open crown and thin, peeling bark coloured orange, grey and white. Leaves broadly ovate, to 15 × 10cm, dark green, golden yellow in autumn, often with red veins, double-serrate margins, suspended on 3cm petioles making them highly mobile in the wind. Claimed to have the largest leaves of any Birch. Named for Carl Maximowicz (pronounced maksimovich) 19th century Russian botanist and author. 8 × 4m.

Betula nigra
River Birch, Black Birch
From eastern North America. Grows rapidly in early years eventually becoming a large tree with pyramidal outline. Distinctive peeling bark which flakes and curls, pinkish-brown on young trees, blackish-red on older specimens. Leaves ovate-rhombic, to 9 × 6cm, glossy green above, glaucous beneath, yellow in autumn. Among the best trees for planting in damp areas. Nigra — black. 10 × 5m.

Betula papyrifera
Paper Birch, Canoe Birch
From northern regions of North America. Similar form to Silver Birch, but more open and less weeping. Bark smooth, varying from bright to dull white or grey-brown, peeling in papery layers. Leaves broadly ovate-acute to 9 × 6cm, coarsely serrated, dull dark green, paler beneath. Papyrifera — paper-bearing. 9 × 5m.

Betula papyrifera 'Kenaica'
Alaskan Paper Birch
Similar in most respects to B papyrifera but with tinges of orange on vivid white trunks. 9 × 5m.

Betula pendula
Silver Birch, European White Birch
Notable birch from Europe and Asia Minor, adapted to wide-ranging climatic conditions. Highly valued for prominent white trunks, delicate lacy leaf texture and gracefully pendulous branches. Juvenile bark golden brown, becoming white with black clefts as the tree matures. Broadly ovate, glossy green leaves to 7 × 5cm with tapered point and serrated margins turn yellow in autumn. 8 × 5m.

Betula pendula 'Dalecarlica'
Cut-Leaf Birch
Similar to above, but leaves deeply cut, branches noticeably pendulous and habit delightfully graceful and open. Typical white trunks on mature trees. Less tolerant of prolonged dry spells, foliage often showing stress by late summer. From the province of Dalcarlia in Sweden. 8 × 5m.

Betula pendula 'Purpurea'
Purple Birch
A form of European silver birch with purplish-black twigs. New leaves rich purple-maroon fading to purplish-green in summer, a striking contrast against its white trunk. Best in cool climates. 6 × 4m.

Betula pendula 'Tristis'
Tall graceful tree with erect central leader, slender gracefully pendulous branches forming a narrow, symmetrical head. Vivid white trunk. 8 × 5m.

Betula pendula 'Youngii'
Young's Weeping Birch
More pronounced weeping branches than most pendulous trees. Slender side branches droop straight down to the ground. Stems rich brown, main trunk gradually turns grey. Foliage similar to B pendula. Young plants need the support of a stake and the leading shoot trained upwards until desired height is attained. Forms a dome or mushroom-shaped head with distinct and graceful appearance. Named after Charles and Peter Young, notable nurserymen in Surrey in the early 19th century. 4 × 3m.

Betula platyphylla 'Japonica'
Japanese White Birch
Similar growth habit to B pendula but with larger leaves and distinct pure white bark. Platyphylla — broad-leafed. 8 × 5m.

Betula populifolia
Grey Birch
Native to eastern North America with fairly typical silver birch growth pattern. Trunk distinctly ashen-white and not peeling. Glossy, grass-green, triangular to broadly ovate, coarsely serrated leaves, light yellow in autumn. Hardy tree for all conditions, dry or boggy. Populifolia — leaves like poplar. 8 × 5m.

Betula pubescens
White Birch, Downy Birch
Could easily be confused with silver birch in its young state. Distinguished by dull white to reddish-brown bark which peels in papery strips. Outer shoots semi-erect, smooth without warts and distinctly downy. Leaves broadly ovate to ovate-elliptic, to 6 × 5cm, coarsely serrated, pubescent on both surfaces. Damp tolerant, well suited to planting in marshy conditions. Pubescens — downy. 12 × 7m.

Betula utilis
Himalayan Birch
Attractive medium grower with pink, orange-brown or coppery-brown bark peeling in horizontal papery flakes. Leaves ovate, to 12 × 7cm, coarsely and unevenly serrated, dark green, paler beneath, changing to golden yellow in autumn. Utilis — useful. 8 × 5m.

BORONIA

Australian endemic genus of 95 species, named for Francesco Boroni, 18th century botanist from Milan who died at age 25. Almost half are from Western Australia. The relatively few in cultivation are delightful garden shrubs, mostly with aromatic foliage and fragrant flowers. They need a spot in the garden where their inimitable charm may be appreciated at close range. Some species may be short-lived, but even one season would be good value.

Naturally often found with their roots protected by other plants, boulders or logs. In the garden they benefit from mulching to insulate their roots from heat and retain moisture. Plant in dappled or partial sun in deeply worked, free-draining, slightly acid to neutral soil conditioned with peat moss. They're intolerant of waterlogged conditions, but appreciate moisture during dry periods. Flowers good for picking and the plants benefit from trimming, but as well as this, they need pruning to about half way after flowering for vigorous growth renewal.

A small orange coloured insect may feed on young shoots, either stunting or killing the bush. Their presence can be detected by a sooty fungous which forms on the honey-dew secreted by these insects giving the plant a blackened or dirty appearance. There are sprays for effective control.

Rutaceae. *All evergreen.*

Boronia 'Carousel'
Hybrid Boronia with sturdy, erect, open spreading habit. Delicately fragrant, urn-shaped blooms open soft pink during spring, turning rosy red as the flowers mature. Long flowering period. 1.3 × 1m.

Boronia clavata
Hardy, fast growing, erect, bushy species from Western Australia. Leaves pinnate with up to seven, very narrow, 2cm, strongly aromatic leaflets. Flowers pale greenish-yellow, bell-shaped, 5mm across, delicately fragrant, borne singly in each leaf axil through spring and early summer. One of the easiest Boronias to grow. Clavata — club shaped. 1.5 × 1m.

Boronia crenulata
Graceful Boronia
Small, Western Australian shrub with 15 × 7mm, obovate or spoon shaped, aromatic leaves. Bears masses of pink, 1cm, star-like flowers singly in upper leaf axils late winter through summer. Try it in a dry, semi-shady rock garden or bank. Crenulata — somewhat scalloped. 75 × 50cm.

Boronia denticulata
Toothed Boronia
From Western Australia. Forms a neat, rounded bush with narrow 1–4cm, linear leaves with minutely toothed margins. Lilac-mauve, 1cm, four-petalled flowers in loose clusters from late winter to mid-summer. Easy to grow in average conditions but prefers not to be heavily pruned. Denticulata — slightly toothed. 1 × 1m.

Boronia denticulata 'Pink Falls'
Delightful dwarf grower with weeping habit, producing masses of pink, starry flowers late winter through mid summer. 1 × 1m.

Boronia filifolia
Slender Boronia
From Victoria and South Australia. Ornamental dwarf shrub with numerous branches and narrow linear, 1–2cm, soft-textured leaves often tinged purple. Pink, open-petalled, 1cm flowers, usually in groups of three carried on short stems in each leaf axil through spring and early summer. Filifolia — threadlike leaves. 30 × 50cm.

Boronia fraseri 'Southern Star'
The species fraseri, named after Charles Fraser, Sydney's first Botanic Garden Superintendent, is a small dense shrub with numerous angular branchlets and decorative, pinnate leaves divided into as many as five lanceolate, dark green leaflets often flushed red. Open-petalled, 15mm flowers in terminal clusters appear from early spring.

The cultivar 'Southern Star' bears bright rose-pink, single, starry flowers. 1 × 1m.

Boronia heterophylla
Red Boronia
Vigorous West Australian shrub which quickly forms a dense upright bush with pinnate, bright-green, 3–5cm leaves and long, narrow, dark green leaflets. Fragrant, 10mm, rosy-red flowers like miniature tulips or closed bells borne on slender, axillary stalks in great masses from late winter to early summer. Delightful garden display, good for picking. Heterophylla — diversely leafed. 1.30 × .75m.   **44**

Boronia heterophylla 'Just Margaret'
Excellent cultivar discovered in 1988 in a field of B heterophylla at Tauranga, New Zealand by flower growers Margaret and Jim Pringle.

A healthy, naturally compact, vigorous and floriferous plant with strong constitution and fern-like, bright lettuce green foliage. Commences to bloom two weeks ahead of heterophylla, producing masses of delicate pale pink, bell-shaped flowers with distinctive Boronia fragrance. Lasts well when cut, proved popular as a cut flower and an export success. Named for Mrs Pringle. 100–120 × 60cm.

Boronia heterophylla 'Rose Parfait'
Selected form of the Red Boronia with similar showy bright carmine rose blooms, produced on a bush with striking yellow and green variegated foliage. 1 × .75m.

Boronia megastigma
Brown Boronia
This West Australian has been called 'the most loved and fragrant of Australian flowers'. Upright, compact grower with slender stems, leaves comprising three narrow, 12mm leaflets and great masses of sweetly fragrant, 12mm, goblet flowers deep purple-brown outside, yellow within from winter to early spring. May not always be long lived. Plant several in groups or beneath a window, places where its rich fragrance can be fully appreciated. Megastigma — with large stigma. 1m × 75cm.   **44**

Boronia megastigma 'Chandleri'
Delightfully fragrant flowers, maroon or burgundy-red to very dark brown with greeny-gold interiors. 1m × 75cm.

Boronia megastigma 'Heaven Scent'
Delightful Australian cultivar of dwarf, compact form and dense foliage, completely smothered in spring with great masses of sweetly fragrant, rich-brown flowers with golden interiors. 50 × 30cm.

Above: Azalea 'Princess Maud' **32**

Above: Azalea 'Ward's Ruby' **32**

Above: Azalea 'Violacea Multiflora' **32**
Below: Azalea 'Salmonea' **32**

Above: Azalea 'The Teacher' **32**
Below: Azalea 'Purple Splendour' **32**

42

Above: Azalea deciduous 'Anthony Koster' **33**
Below: Azalea deciduous 'Carmen' **33**

Right: Azalea Knap Hill and Exbury Hybrids **33**
Below: Azalea deciduous 'Dreadnought' **33**

Above: Berzelia lanuginosa **39**

Above: Banksia spinulosa var collina *Hill Banksia* **37**
Below: Banksia ericaefolia **36**

Below: Boronia heterophylla **40**

Above: Boronia megastigma **40**
Below: Boronia megastigma 'Lutea' **49**

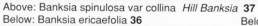

Above: Boronia muelleri 'Sunset Serenade' **49**

Above: Boronia pinnata **49**
Below: Brachychiton acerifolius **49**

Above: Boronia pilosa 'Rose Blossom' **49**

Above: Brachyglottis x greyii 'Otari Cloud' **50**
Below: Brachyglottis repanda 'Purpurea' *Purple Rangiora* **50**

Above: Calliandra tweedii **52**

Above: Brachyscome multifida 'Break o Day' **50**
Below: Callistemon citrinus 'Austraflora Firebrand' **53**   Below: Callistemon citrinus 'Splendens' **53**

Above: Callistemon 'Candy Pink' **53**
Below: Callistemon 'Mauve Mist' **53**

Above: Camellia 'Brushfield's Yellow' **57**
Below: Camellia 'Black Tie' **57**

Above: Camellia 'Anticipation Variegated' **56**

Above: Camellia 'Buttons 'n' Bows' **57**
Below: Camellia 'C M Hovey' **58**

Above: Camellia 'Bob's Tinsie' **57**
Below: Camellia 'Burgundy Boy' **57**

Boronia megastigma 'Lutea'
Yellow Boronia
This cultivar distinguished by lighter green foliage and greenish-yellow flowers. 1m × 75cm. **44**

Boronia muelleri 'Sunset Serenade'
Variable species from Victoria and New South Wales seen as dwarf shrubs to small trees.

The charming cultivar 'Sunset Serenade' has been selected for its dwarf compact form. Light-green, pinnate or fern-like, fragrant leaves with numerous, narrow 12–18mm leaflets. Rich-pink buds open to four-petalled, starry flowers at first creamy white, turning pale pink, then bright cerise-pink, completely covering the bush from early to late spring. Usually blooms profusely the first spring after planting. Named for Sir Ferdinand von Mueller. 1 × 1m. **45**

Boronia pilosa 'Rose Blossom'
Hairy Boronia
South Australia, Tasmania and Victoria is home to the species. The selected cultivar 'Rose Blossom' is a small compact shrub with hairy stems and small, fern-like, pinnate leaves comprising 3–7 crowded, narrow, 6–12mm leaflets. Masses of double, rose-pink, most decorative flowers from mid winter. Prefers a cooler, temperate, non-humid climate. Pilosa — covered with long soft hairs. 60 × 60cm. **45**

Boronia pinnata
From New South Wales. Somewhat erect grower with arching branches and pinnate or fern-like, 5cm leaves with up to nine irregular leaflets to 25mm with a distinct camphor-like fragrance. Scented, four petalled, pale pink, starry flowers, late winter through spring. Pinnata — featherlike leaves. 1.5 × 1m. **45**

Boronia thujona
Bronzy Boronia
Small to medium shrub found growing in shady creek beds of New South Wales. Attractive, pinnate, fern-like leaves with up to fifteen, 3cm, deep green, finely serrated leaflets. Deep pink, 15mm, starry flowers in loose axillary clusters spring and early summer. Thujona — from thujone, an essential oil. 1.3 × 1.3m.

BOUVARDIA

A genus of about 30 soft-wooded herbs and shrubs from Arizona, Texas and Mexico named for Dr Charles Bouvard, 17th century superintendent of the Paris Gardens. Bouvardias are valued for sprays of colourful flowers, some delightfully fragrant. They are relatively easy to grow in deeply worked, well-drained, slightly acid to neutral soil enriched with organic material in a ventilated location, preferably against an east or north facing wall.

Prune to within a few centimetres of the ground each spring and pinch back new shoots as they appear, to develop a compact plant. Cease pinching in February when terminal heads of bloom will appear. Unpruned, they tend to sprawl and become untidy with little resulting bloom. Apply frequent but small applications of well-balanced fertilizer during the growing season.

Rubiaceae. *Semi-evergreen.*

Bouvardia longiflora humboldtii
Scented Bouvardia
Of Mexican origin, this small shrub is a favourite for highly fragrant, narrowly tubular, pure-white, waxy flowers flaring to four lobes 25mm across appearing in terminal clusters during autumn and winter. Woody, flexible stems, leaves ovate or lanceolate, to 5 × 2cm, deep green and glossy. Excellent for picking. Also a variegated leaf form. 1 × 75cm.

Bouvardia ternifolia
Delightful, half-hardy, autumn and winter flowering shrubs of garden origin with slender graceful stems, and ovate to lanceolate leaves prominently veined, glabrous above, pubescent beneath. Flowers borne in terminal clusters autumn and winter. Cultivars include — **'President Cleveland'**, single, rich scarlet. **'President Garfield'**, double flesh-pink. Also a double white flowered form. 75 × 60cm.

BRACHYCHITON

A genus of about thirty species of colourful trees or shrubs mostly endemic to Australia, from the more tropical regions of Queensland and New South Wales, named from the Greek *brachys*, short and *chiton*, a tunic, a reference to the seed coating. The Flame Tree is more widely planted, easily distinguished through spring and summer as a tall stately tree without leaves, entirely covered with spectacular red flowers. Most species shed their leaves as flowers appear, possibly to reduce stress in their dry environment. Regular watering under garden conditions may encourage retention of the foliage.

Large, woody, boat-shaped seed capsules split open when mature, revealing rows of seeds. Handle them carefully as numerous fine hairs surrounding the seeds may cause skin irritation. Although naturally from warm climates with prolonged dry periods, most species can handle a wide range of climatic and soil conditions. Plant in deeply worked, free-draining soil, keep moist during dry periods until well established. Apply slow-release fertilizer spring and autumn. Although taking some years to flower, they merit planting even for the beauty of their leaves.

Sterculiaceae.

Brachychiton acerifolius
Flame Tree
Occurs naturally in coastal bush and rainforest from Cape York Peninsula to Illawarra. Frequently seen in temperate to tropical gardens throughout the world. Could be the best known and most spectacular of Australia's rainforest trees. Narrow, pyramidal or medium spreading form, substantial trunk with greyish, wrinkled bark and glossy, bright green, variably lobed, palmate or maple-like leaves to 25cm across carried on long petioles.

Has the most unusual habit of shedding its leaves during spring to show off a flamboyant display of bloom late spring through summer. Flowers 12mm, vivid scarlet bells produced in great masses in 30cm loosely pendulous, terminal panicles making the tree appear as though on fire. More vivid floral displays often appear after hot dry periods. Leathery, dark brown, 8–10cm, pointed seed capsules. Acerifolius — foliage like the genus Acer or Maple. Deciduous. 10 × 6m. **45**

BRACHYGLOTTIS

A genus of about thirty species of trees, shrubs and vines from New Zealand, Chatham Islands and Tasmania, named from the Greek *brachys*, short and *glottis*, a tongue in reference to the florets. Hardy, evergreen shrubs once classified under Senecio are featured below, among them species for dry or poor soils and coastal exposure.

Generally, they respond to hard pruning. By removing spent flower heads and shortening some of the longer growths, they remain shapely and compact. If the plant becomes rangy, cut almost to ground level and within a few months will be well furnished with new growth. Being surface rooted, take care when weeding or cultivating as root damage can result in rapid deterioration. Mulching lessens the need for any disturbance. Useful for adding a touch of silver or grey.

Compositae. *All evergreen.*

Brachyglottis × greyi
Spreading habit, leaves soft greyish, oblong to oblong-ovate, to 10 × 4.5cm, white felted and prominent midrib beneath, margins entire and slightly wavy. Bright yellow, daisy-like flowers appear in large corymbs through summer. Forms a hardy, spreading, multi branched shrub.

Use in beds or borders, traffic islands, low coastal screens, bank cover or for spot colour contrast. Named after Sir George Grey. 1.2 × 1.2m.

Brachyglottis × greyi 'Leith Gold'
Bushy, rounded shrub, branches and petioles covered with greyish tomentum. Leaves ovate to ovate-oblong, to 16 × 8cm, semi-glossy, mid green above, covered with white tomentum beneath, margins entire and undulating. Soft-yellow, daisy-like flowers borne in erect, multi-branched panicles through spring and again in summer. Name refers to Dunedin's Leith Valley where the plant originated. 1.8 × 1.3m.

Brachyglottis × greyi 'Otari Cloud'
Selected hybrid from B greyii × B laxifolius. Forms a compact, rounded shrub with ovate to broadly elliptic, 6 × 4cm, leaves, white tomentum beneath, on petioles and young shoots giving the plant a bright silvery appearance. Bright yellow, 25mm, semi-double flowers. Plant in full sun for maximum brilliance. 1.2 × 1.2m.   **45**

Brachyglottis × greyi 'Sunshine'
Similar appearance to B greyi, with more spreading habit. Silver-grey downy leaves, white felted beneath, margins not wavy. Yellow, daisy-like flowers through summer. 1.5 × 1.5m.

Brachyglottis monroi
Found in rocky places of more northerly, elevated regions of the South Island. Excellent shrub with neat compact habit, forming a rounded bush with brownish or olive green 12–45mm, narrow oblong foliage, whitish tomentum beneath, margins crisped and wrinkled. Bright yellow flower-heads in terminal racemes through summer. Good for smaller gardens, in dry sunny locations, but tolerant of some shade. 75 × 75cm.

Brachyglottis perdicioides
Raukumara
From the south east coast of New Zealand's North Island. Forms an upright, multi-branched shrub with slender, pubescent branchlets streaked purple. Leaves oblong to elliptic oblong to 5 × 2.5cm, lime green, glossy above, finely tomentose beneath, margins undulating and finely crenate giving a crinkled appearance. Yellow flowers in leafy, terminal corymbs through summer and autumn. Cool spot with good drainage. 1.5 × 1.2m

Brachyglottis repanda 'Purpurea'
Purple Rangiora
The green foliaged form is often seen in coastal or lowland forests or scrubland throughout the North and some parts of the South Islands. The purple form was discovered near Wanganui by a bushman who felled it before noticing the colour of its leaves. A local nurseryman managed to propagate and preserve it.

Large, handsome, broad oblong or ovate-oblong leaves to 20 × 10cm, semi-glossy, deep coppery purple above, silvery white beneath. Leaf colour intensifies during winter Plume-like flower heads with a purplish haze. Quick growing, happy in either sun or shade. Prune lightly early spring. Repanda — with wavy margins. 2.5 × 2m.   **45**

BRACHYSCOME

A genus of about 65 species of annual or perennial herbs or dwarf shrubs from Australia and New Zealand named from the Greek *brachys*, short and *kome*, hair in allusion to a whorl of short delicate bristles in place of the calyx. Few actual species are in cultivation, but numerous cultivars promoted by the nursery industry include many excellent colourful and free-flowering small plants for beds and borders, rock gardens, rock or wall spillers, ground covers, pots, baskets and window boxes.

One of the easiest plants to grow, thriving without pampering. Plant in full sun or dappled shade in deeply worked, free-draining, organically enriched soil. Apply a balanced fertilizer early spring and autumn and water regularly during dry periods. Mulch freely to keep the roots cool and suppress weed growth. Prune back heavily after each crop of bloom for vigorous growth renewal and maximum flower.

Asteraceae. *All evergreen.*

Brachyscome angustifolia
Stiff Daisy, Grassland Daisy
From New South Wales, Victoria, Tasmania and South Australia. Low growing, multi-branched, mat forming plant frequently seen in swampy areas of open forest, spreading by underground stems. Linear, light green leaves to 5cm. Dainty, 2cm, mauve to pink daisy-like flowers for most of the year. Ideal for damp spots at the base of a rockery. Angustifolia — narrow leaved. 30 × 90cm.

Brachyscome ciliaris
Variable Daisy
Low spreading plant found in inland plain and mallee areas of all Australian states. Pinnate leaves to 6cm long divided into linear leaflets with conspicuous white, woolly hairs. Flowers to 3cm across, white or blue with central yellow zone carried on branching stems spring through mid-summer. Full sun, water during dry periods. Ciliaris — fringed with hairs. 10 × 40cm.

Brachyscome multifida
Rock Daisy, Cut Leaf Daisy
Occurs naturally in Victoria, New South Wales and Queensland. Forms a neat, low-spreading wiry plant with finely divided, ferny, bright-green leaves and massed, spring and summer displays of 2cm, multi-petalled, bright-blue daisy flowers with a conspicuous central zone of yellow stamens.

The following cultivars have been selected for colour brilliance and free-flowering qualities over long periods. 'Amethyst' — brilliant blue. 'Break of Day' — brilliant purple-blue. 'Harmony' — deep mauve-blue. 'Valencia' — rosy mauve. 'White Diamond' — clear pure white. Multifida — many times divided, referring to the leaves. 25 × 90cm.   **46**

Brachyscome segmentosa
From Lord Howe Island. A self-layering species found on moist, sheltered ledges and rock faces. Forms an attractive clump with ovate, bright green leaves to 7 × 2cm, deeply and irregularly lobed and divided. White flowers to 35mm across with central yellow disc carried on erect, 15cm stems autumn through mid-summer. Needs protection and moist conditions. Segmentosa — furnished with segments. 20 × 30cm

BRUNFELSIA

A genus of about 40 species of free-flowering evergreen shrubs or small trees from South America and the West Indies, named for Otto Brunfels, 16th century monk, physician and botanical artist. Half-hardy shrubs, they thrive in frost-free, temperate and subtropical regions, smothering themselves in spring and summer with fragrant phlox-like flowers in ever changing colour of deep violet, lavender and white giving rise to the common name. Plant in full sun in deeply worked, organically enriched, well-drained, slightly acid soil. Feed with balanced fertilizer spring and autumn. Prune after flowering to maintain good shape and encourage maximum flower. Solanaceae. *All evergreen.*

Brunfelsia pauciflora 'Eximea'
Yesterday, Today and Tomorrow
Compact, free-branching shrub from Brazil. Dark-green, glossy, oblong to oblong-lanceolate leaves, paler beneath. Becomes a total mass of bloom through spring and summer with sweetly fragrant, phlox-like blooms which seem to lie on top of the bush. They open deep violet, and gradually change over three days from lavender to white. Pauciflora — with few flowers (a misnomer), and eximea — out of the ordinary. 1 × 1m.

Brunfelsia pauciflora 'Floribunda'
Larger form of above with a profusion of fragrant, tubular flowers with 5cm flare, opening deep violet, fading pale violet on the second day and white on the third day, the three colours appearing at the same time with blooms at various stages. 2 × 1.3m.

Brunfelsia latifolia
Yesterday, Today and Tomorrow
Soft-wooded bushy shrub from tropical America with broad, elliptical, greyish-green leaves. Fragrant, phlox-like flowers held in terminal heads open deep-violet, then lavender with white eye, changing later to white, the three colours appearing on the bush at the same time. Containers or sheltered corners outdoors. 1.3 × 1m.

BUDDLEIA

A genus of about 100 species from tropical and subtropical Asia, America and Africa named for Adam Buddle, 17th century English botanist. Buddleias are vigorous growers, tolerant of hard conditions and abuse. They prefer reasonable drainage and enough water to maintain growth, but often will grow in conditions too harsh for other species. Hard pruning each year after flowering prevents them from becoming leggy and untidy. Individual

flowers are beautiful and highly fragrant, attractive to butterflies hence the common name — Butterfly Bush. Plant in full sun.
    Loganiaceae.

Buddleia alternifolia
Fountain Butterfly Bush
Hardy species from China with slender, gracefully arching branches in fountain formation. Lanceolate, dark green leaves to 60 × 15cm arranged alternately, smaller leaves on flowering stems. Fragrant, lilac-purple flower clusters to 45 × 30mm borne profusely along previous year's growth early to mid summer. Prune back flowered growths to the first developing new shoots for next seasons blooms. Alternifolia — leaves on each side of the stem not opposite each other. Deciduous. 3 × 3m.

Buddleia davidii
Butterfly Bush, Summer Lilac
The species is a vigorous, rapid growing shrub from China and Japan with long arching branches densely clothed with dark green, lanceolate, finely serrated leaves to 20 × 7cm, white felted beneath. Through summer and autumn, sweetly fragrant flowers appear in terminal panicles to 30cm long. Davidii — after 18th century missionary and plant collector, Abbe Armand David. Semi-evergreen. 3 × 2.5m.

Numerous garden cultivars of merit, hybrids of B davidii × B davidii nanhoensis and veitchiana, come in a range of colours as follows:

Buddleia 'Black Knight'
Rich deep purple-blue flowers.

Buddleia 'Empire Blue'
Flowers bluish-mauve with orange eye.

Buddleia 'Harlequin'
Leaves variegated creamy-white, flowers reddish purple. Lower growing.

Buddleia 'Nanho Blue'
Multi-branched, compact plant to 1.2m. Slender, cylindrical panicles of light blue flowers.

Buddleia 'Petite Indigo'
Slender, compact grower to 1.3m. Narrow grey-green foliage and short panicles of lavender blue flowers with orange throat..

Buddleia 'Pink Delight'
Large rich pink flower trusses.

Buddleia 'Royal Red'
Intense reddish-purple flowers.

Buddleia 'White Cloud'
Dense panicles of pure white flowers.

Buddleia davidii × fallowiana 'Lochinch'
Medium, bushy, compact shrub of Chinese origin with silvery-grey, pubescent young shoots, foliage becoming grey-green and glabrous above, white tomentose beneath. Dense conical panicles of sweetly fragrant, lilac blue flowers with deep orange eye through late summer and autumn. Evergreen. 2.5 × 2m.

Buddleia globosa
Orange Ball Tree
Impressive South American species. Slender, erect shrub with handsome, dark green, lanceolate leaves to 20 × 5cm, conspicuously veined, wrinkled, glossy and glabrous above, densely woolly beneath. Masses of ball-shaped, orange yellow, sweetly fragrant, pendent flowers appear through summer. Globosa — round, spherical. Evergreen. 3 × 2.5m.

Buddleia lindleyana
Chinese species forming a medium shrub with pale green, ovate or elliptic, 10 × 7cm leaves with entire or crenulate margins. Purple-violet flowers in curved, 20 × 4cm racemes through summer. Evergreen. 3 × 2.5m.

Buddleia salvifolia
South African Sage Wood
South African species, forming a dense, hardy bush with dull-green, narrow lanceolate, matt-surfaced, sage-like leaves to 18 × 5cm, silvery beneath. Terminal sprays of flowers produced spring and summer, pale lilac, orange at the mouth and sweetly fragrant. Responds to regular trimming. Evergreen. 2.5 × 2m.

Buddleia × weyeriana 'Golden Glow'
Hybrid of B davidii and B globosa with globosa characteristics. Sage green, lanceolate leaves, flowers in globose heads light yellow orange suffused lilac. Semi-evergreen. 3 × 2.5m.

BUXUS

A genus of about 70 species of densely branched shrubs or small trees from Eurasia, tropical and South Africa and central America, named from the ancient Latin term for Box. Use of this old world plant goes back to the time of Julius Caesar. Buxus is extremely slow growing but may live for centuries. Box wood timber is yellow in colour, very hard and with dense, uniform grain is popular with wood engravers, in the manufacture of rulers and some musical instruments.

Traditional garden use has been in low formal divisions, edging or topiary. Easily trimmed to almost any form. A long term, dwarf and informal leafy shrub, either planted out or in containers. Very hardy and tolerant of soil and climatic extremes provided they have adequate drainage. Plant to avoid excess midday sunlight. Although long term plants which seem to survive without pampering, a little care with feeding, watering and spraying will result in better colour and more vigour.

Buxaceae. *All evergreen.*

Buxus sempervirens
English Box, Common Box

From southern Europe, western Asia and North Africa. Dwarf, multi-stemmed, stiff, erect grower with deep-green, glossy, ovate, oval-oblong or elliptic leaves to 3cm × 12mm, paler beneath. Slow grower, very hardy, good for formal training whether singly, in groups, in the garden or containers. Sempervirens — ever-green. 1 × .60m.

Buxus sempervirens 'Green Gem'

Canadian hybrid from B sempervirens and B sempervirens koreana. Very dwarf, compact, rounded bush with fresh green colour all year. Requires little training to maintain good form. 80 × 50cm.

Buxus sempervirens 'Marginata'
Variegated Box

Olive green leaves splashed and margined with gold. Slow grower, may be trimmed to any form. 1 × .60m.

Buxus sempervirens 'Suffruticosa'
Edging Box

Low, compact form, glossy, green, ovate to obovate, 2cm leaves. Used extensively in Europe for dwarf edging, garden dividers and fancy topiary. Suffruticosa — somewhat shrubby. 30–75 × 30cm.

A genus of about 200 species of shrubs, small trees and perennial herbs from tropical and subtropical America, India, Madagascar and West Africa, named from the Greek *kalos*, beautiful and *andros*, stamen. The cultivated forms are showy, spreading shrubs with fine, feathery leaves resembling some of the

Acacias. Light-sensitive leaves fold up at night. Flowers like tassels or thistledown comprise many fine stamens earning for some species the name Powder Puff Tree.

Easy to grow in temperate regions, preferring full sun and deeply worked, free-draining soil. Hot, dry conditions encourages more flowers. Light annual pruning will maintain better form and flower production. Ideal under eaves against a sunny wall.

Mimosaceae. *Both evergreen.*

Calliandra portoricensis
Snowflake Acacia

Handsome, feathery, dark-green bipinnate foliage, folding at nightfall. Fluffy, white, fragrant tassel-flowers resembling flakes of snow appear profusely spring through autumn. Open growth habit and interesting branch pattern, at its best against a dark structural background. Portoricensis — of Puerto Rico. 2.5 × 2m.

Calliandra tweedii
Brazilian Flame Bush, Mexican Flamebush

Twiggy, small shrub from Brazil, West Indies and southern USA with fine, feathery, bipinnate, foliage divided into numerous 4–6mm leaflets. Axillary, 5–7cm, tassel-heads of vivid scarlet stamens appear like sheets of flame during spring and summer. Ideal in isolation or blends well with broad-leaf shrubs. Pulcherrima — very beautiful. Syn C pulcherrima. 1.30 × 2m.   **46**

A genus of about 140 species of shrubs and trees from tropical and subtropical America, Asia, Indonesia and Australia named from the Greek *kalli*, beautiful and *karpos*, fruit in reference to their showy clusters of small rounded fruit. The plant tends to be ungainly, but in cooler climates colourful autumn leaves are followed by decorative fruit, admired both in the garden and picked for indoors. Try mass planting Callicarpa, or mingling with gold or white winter-flowering shrubs. Greater crops result from multiple plantings. Plant in rich, deeply worked, free-draining soil in full sun. Prune heavily after berry fall for growth renewal.

Verbenaceae. *All deciduous.*

Callicarpa bodinieri 'Profusion'
Beauty Berry

Chinese shrub with softly pubescent branchlets. Leaves deep green, lanceolate, elliptic

or obovate to 15 × 7cm, with toothed margins and densely pubescent beneath becoming yellow, orange red and purple shades in autumn. Small, lilac pink flowers in summer, followed autumn-winter by clusters of glossy, 2cm, lilac purple fruit. Named for 19th century French missionary and plant collector in China, Emile Bodinieri. 1.5 × 1.3m.

Callicarpa dichotoma
Chinese Beauty Berry

From China and Japan. Small shrub with slender, erect, tawny, pubescent stems and obovate to elliptic, 6 × 2cm leaves. Axillary cymes of small, pink flowers followed by clusters of 2mm, shiny, lilac-purple berries late autumn through winter. 1.5 × 1.30m.

Callicarpa japonica 'Alba Bacca'

Hardy, Japanese species with bushy upright form. Leaves elliptic to ovate-lanceolate, 12 × 6cm, gradually tapering to a fine tip and with finely serrated margins. The species bears metallic-purple fruit. Cultivar *Alba Bacca* produces small, white or pale pink flowers in summer followed by clusters of pure white fruit autumn and winter. Alba — white, Bacca — fruit. 1.5 × 1.2m.

Australian endemic species of about 25 species of shrubs or small trees named from the Greek *kalli*, beautiful and *stemon*, a stamen in reference to their flamboyant flowers. Callistemon, commonly called Bottlebrush is distributed through all states, frequently in areas of high rainfall or besides streams or swamps. Few shrubs so easy to grow can equal the Australian Bottlebrush for spectacular floral displays. Bottlebrush flowers are followed by clusters of quite picturesque, round woody seed capsules, like bands of beads pressed into the bark. Nature planned them as secure fortresses to ensure the viability of their contents for many years until some calamity, usually fire, overtook the plant.

They revel in warm sunny locations in widely varying soil with a preference of slightly acid to neutral. Excess alkalinity may cause chlorosis, yellowing of the leaves and poor performance. Feed sparingly with well-balanced fertilizer in spring and autumn. Although tolerant of sustained drought, they are at their best in moist soils and appreciate infrequent, deep summer watering. New growth emerges from the centre of the flower resulting in the eventual development of seed capsules encircling each stem. Pruning back beyond these capsules as the flowers fade keeps the plant bushy and improves flower production. Callistemon cultivars come in all shapes and sizes for most landscaping purposes.

Myrtaceae. *All evergreen.*

Callistemon 'Candy Pink'
Of northern New South Wales origin. Erect grower with pink, slightly pubescent new shoots. Leaves dark green, lanceolate, sharply pointed to 12 × 1cm. Flowers spikes to 15 × 6cm, pink at first maturing reddish pink. Commences to flower when quite small, producing flushes of bloom throughout the year. Extremely hardy, tolerant of cold and poor drainage. 3 × 2m.   **46**

Callistemon citrinus 'Australflora Firebrand'
A spreading shrub, with arching, weeping branches reaching three metres or more across. Silvery pink new shoots. Leaves lanceolate to 7 × 1cm. Rich bright red, 10 × 6cm flower spikes in profusion through spring and autumn. Good for covering large areas. 75cm × 2.5m.   **46**

Callistemon citrinus 'Splendens'
Vigorous dense growing shrub with silky, pink or red young shoots and lanceolate, rigid, deep-green leaves to 10 × 2.5cm. Flower spikes to 12 × 8cm, brilliant crimson with gold anthers, produced in great profusion spring and early summer and again in autumn. Discovered, named and cultivated extensively in New Zealand. Identical with C citrinus 'Endeavour' as it is known and cultivated in Australia. Citrinus — resembling citron or lemon. Splendens — gleaming. 2 × 2m.   **46**

Callistemon citrinus 'Western Glory'
Erect, medium shrub with pink, very pubescent new shoots. Leathery, lanceolate leaves to 7 × 1cm with pointed tip, glabrous when mature. Deep reddish mauve or deep pink tinged lilac, 12 × 5cm flower spikes, densely arranged in terminal clusters during spring and autumn. 2.5 × 2m.

Callistemon 'King's Park Special'
Vigorous rounded bush with slightly pendulous branches. Lanceolate leaves to 8 × 1cm. Bright red flower spikes to 10 × 6cm carried in terminal clusters during spring and early summer. Discovered in King's Park, Perth. 3 × 3m.

Callistemon 'Little John'
Compact, dwarf grower with narrow-elliptical, dark grey-green, 5cm leaves and masses of short, deep-red, 7cm flower brushes tipped gold mainly through spring and early summer with occasional blooms almost the year round. Often seen mass-planted in public areas, traffic islands etc. Good for rockeries, foregrounds, containers. 75 × 75cm.

Callistemon 'Mauve Mist'
Mauve Bottlebrush
Medium, multi-branched shrub with silvery, silky young growth and stiff, 6 × 1.5cm, lanceolate leaves. A profusion of 10 × 6cm, mauve-pink flower spikes with gold anthers appear throughout summer in dense terminal clusters. 3 × 3m.   **46**

Callistemon pallidus 'Australflora Candle Glow'
Low spreading form. Silvery new growth, grey-green foliage and lemon yellow flowers to 10cm long. Species distributed in three eastern Australian States and Tasmania. 1 × 2.5m.

Callistemon 'Perth Pink'
Large, dense, shapely bush with pink or red new shoots and slender, dark-green, lanceolate leaves. Deep pink flowers borne in terminal clusters spring and autumn. Fast grower, hardy. 3 × 1.5m.

Callistemon pinifolius
Green Bottlebrush
Variable species from New South Wales, seen as either a low spreader or open, erect shrub. Stiff, linear, pine-like leaves to 10cm, grooved on the upper surface and sharply pointed. Compact flower spikes to 8 × 4cm, yellowish-green or apple green through spring and early summer. Pinifolius — pine-like leaves. 1.5 × 1.5m.

Callistemon 'Red Cluster'
Vigorous rounded form, new shoots pink and slightly hairy, lanceolate leaves to 6 × 1cm. Masses of 8 × 4cm, crimson-red flower spikes with gold anthers appear in terminal clusters during spring and autumn. 2.5 × 2m.

Callistemon rigidis 'Superba'
Stiff Bottlebrush
Small to medium rigid shrub native to Queensland and New South Wales, usually growing in damp conditions. Stiff linear-lanceolate leaves to 15 × 6mm, dull green with numerous tiny dots and veins which form ridged margins. Deep red flower spikes to 8 × 3cm with stalkless radiating brushes borne profusely early summer. Extremely hardy, tolerating wind and frost, recommended for sub-zero climates. 3 × 3m.

Callistemon salignus
Willow Bottlebrush, Pink Tips
From Queensland, New South Wales and South Australia usually along stream banks or swamps. Tall shrub to medium tree with graceful weeping form, white papery bark, distinctive, coppery-pink new shoots and narrow-lanceolate, pale green leaves to 10cm × 4mm with prominent veins. Usually takes several years before producing compact, creamy yellow brushes. Suitable for shelter, screens or street planting. Salignus — resembling willow. 5 × 4m.

Callistemon salignus 'Eureka'
Attractive cultivar with upright growth habit, reddish new shoots and attractive willowy foliage. Flower brushes soft pink to lilac borne mainly in spring. Tolerant of most conditions, including coastal areas. 4 × 3m.

Callistemon viminalis
Weeping Bottlebrush
Graceful weeping species from Queensland and New South Wales with arching branches, rough scaly bark and colourful bronzy new shoots. Leaves variable to 7 × 1cm, fresh green and lying closely to the stem. Bright red, terminal flower spikes to 20 × 6cm with open appearance produced spring through early summer. Viminalis — with long slender shoots. 4 × 3m.

Callistemon viminalis 'Captain Cook'
Excellent dwarf shrub with gracefully weeping branches and long, narrow foliage. Masses of dense, bright red flower spikes borne in clusters towards the ends of branches in spring and to a lesser extent in autumn. 1.5 × 1.2m.

Callistemon viminalis 'Hannah Ray'
Small, willowy tree with pendulous branchlets, bright pink new shoots and grey-green foliage. Long, crimson, pendulous flower spikes appear during spring and occasionally autumn. 4 × 3m.

Calluna, a monotypic genus of one species from western North America, Azores and north and western Europe to Siberia, named from the Greek *kalluno*, to sweep, clean or adorn, referring to the use of some species in making brooms. More than 1000 cultivars have arisen from the one species, many useful, free-flowering dwarf shrubs, variable in habit from prostrate forms a few centimetres high to bushes of over a metre.

Callunas, known as Scotch Heather, are closely related to South African ericas or heaths, adapted by nature to exist in some of the most bleak and inclement places, withstanding hot and dry, or damp and cold conditions. Winter foliage colour, a major feature, is more intense in sub-zero temperatures. Plant in full sun in deeply worked, free-draining acid or lime-free soil with peat moss.

Ericaceae. *All evergreen.*

Calluna vulgaris 'Alba Aurea'
Spreading, twiggy growth, dark green foliage, new growths tipped gold. White flowers. 10 × 25cm.

Calluna vulgaris 'Andrew Proudley'
Shrubby plant, foliage yellow becoming tawny, tinted bronze and orange during winter. Heavy clusters of small, purple pink flowers in tiny erect stems. 15 × 20cm.

Calluna vulgaris 'Annabel'
Small compact plant with silvery grey foliage. Double, dark mauve-pink flowers on long spikes. 20 × 30cm.

Calluna vulgaris 'Blaze Away'
Magnificent foliage plant, turning shades of gold, orange, flame and red in winter. Light mauve flowers in summer. 45 × 45cm.

Calluna vulgaris 'Darkness'
Foliage soft bright green, single flowers bright crimson with a hint of purple. Neat and compact growth, with prolific floral displays. Possibly the best in this colour. 30 × 35cm.

Calluna vulgaris 'Elsie Purnell'
Open growth habit, silvery, grey-green foliage. Soft rose-pink, double flowers with white centres carried on long firm spikes. An improvement on 'H E Beale'. 40 × 50cm.

Calluna vulgaris 'Flamingo'
Pale green, upright foliage, soft pink flowers in abundance, excellent for picking. Pinkish new growth in spring. 30 × 30cm.

Calluna vulgaris 'Gold Haze'
Loose, open growth, bright golden foliage on brown stems all year. Good with grey or blue conifers. White flowers in long sprays. 50 × 60cm.

Calluna vulgaris 'Golden Feather'
Soft yellow foliage flushed orange in long feathery plumes, often tinged orange-red during winter. Sparse mauve flowers. 25 × 45cm.

Calluna vulgaris 'Guinea Gold'
Colourful spreader, bright yellow compact foliage. White flowers produced late in the season. 30 × 75cm.

Calluna vulgaris 'Hammondii Aureifolia'
Older leaves dark green with brilliant contrast of golden yellow new growth in spring. White flowers. 40 × 50cm.

Calluna vulgaris 'H E Beale'
Forms a loose mound with dark green leaves. Double silvery-mauve flowers in long spikes during spring. Good for picking. 60 × 60cm.

Calluna vulgaris 'Jimmy Dyce'
Short and somewhat tufted plant with dark green foliage tinged reddish in cold conditions. Bright, pinkish purple flowers, florets rounded on slender spikes. 15 × 25cm.

Calluna vulgaris 'Kinlochruel'
Deep green foliage becoming purplish green during winter months. White, wide open, fully double flowers on short stems. 20 × 25cm.

Calluna vulgaris 'Radnor'
Compact, floriferous plant with dark green foliage. Silvery lilac, double flowers in short, densely packed spikes. Also known as 'Miss Appleby'. 20 × 30cm.

Calluna vulgaris 'Red Favourite'
Dwarf, compact plant with fine, bright green foliage. Rosy-red, double flowers in profusion. 25 × 30cm.

Calluna vulgaris 'Robert Chapman'
Very dense grower with dramatic foliage colour — gold in spring, changing to bronze and finally red and yellow during winter. Flowers soft purple-red. 40 × 50cm.

Calluna vulgaris 'Serlei Aurea'
Erect grower soft, feathery, pale yellow foliage deepening to gold in winter. White flowers in long racemes. 50 × 60cm.

Calluna vulgaris 'Silver Cloud'
Highly regarded for silvery blue foliage, masses of light purple flower. Forms a tight compact mound. 15 × 30cm.

Calluna vulgaris 'Sister Ann'
Charming, dense compact miniature with soft, thick, greyish green foliage, bronze in winter. Abundant pink flowers. 15 × 35cm.

Calluna vulgaris 'Spring Torch'
Spring foliage yellow, shaded apricot, darker towards the tips. Mature leaves greyish green. Pale, lilac rose flowers carried in long spikes. 25 × 30cm.

Calluna vulgaris 'Tib'
Vigorous, upright, compact plant with deep green foliage. Double, rose-red to purple-red flowers in abundance. 30 × 50cm.

Calluna vulgaris 'Wickwar Flame'
Foliage gold and orange, deepening to deep orange and flame in winter. Flowers pale rose in short spikes. Vigorous as a young plant, with outstanding winter colour. 30 × 40cm.

Calluna vulgaris 'Winter Chocolate'
Greenish yellow foliage becoming golden yellow with orange tips, finally dark chocolate brown with reddish tips. Lilac pink flowers, somewhat sparse. Growth close and compact. 25 × 30cm.

A genus of about 70 Australian endemic species of dwarf-growing shrubs to small trees named from the Greek *kalyx*, calyx and *thrix*, a hair, referring to long bristly hairs of the calyx. Often found in light, well drained soil in heathlands, under the protection of rocky outcrops or other plants. The calyx usually reddens, continuing a colourful display long after the flowers have faded. Plant in well-drained, sandy or stony soil in full sun. Apply light applications of slow-release fertilizer early spring. Prune lightly after flowering.

Myrtaceae. *All evergreen.*

Calytrix alpestris
Snow Myrtle
Found in South Australia and Victoria. A shrub with graceful, downy branches, 3–6mm heath-like leaves held perpendicular to the branchlets. Small starry white flowers borne in profusion towards the ends of branches during spring contrast effectively against the darker foliage. 1 × 1m.

Calytrix tetragona
Fringe Myrtle
Found in all states except Northern Territory. Aromatic shrub with slender, erect or spreading branches. Linear, 6mm, heath-like leaves with tiny hairs and fragrant when crushed. Small, 12mm, open-petalled, flowers varying from pure white to shades of pink appear through spring in dense terminal heads followed by persistent reddish calyces. The species now embraces C sullivanii. Tetragona — with four angles. Evergreen. 1 × 1.30m.

CAMELLIA

An amazing genus of around 100 identified species of flowering trees and shrubs, found mainly in tropical and sub-tropical regions of Asia named for George Josef Kamel, a 17th century Jesuit pharmacist and botanist. Camellias have a long and fascinating history, being cultivated in Chinese gardens in the 9th century.

Since their introduction to the western world during the 18th century, thousands of beautiful hybrids have come into being, especially since 1940. Hybridists have concentrated on factors such as desirable growth habit, weather-hardiness of both plant and flower, longer flowering season, self-grooming capabilities as well as flower size and colour. As long as there are gardens, Camellias will be enthusiastically endorsed by both connoisseurs and gardeners throughout the world.

Generally speaking, they're a hardy race, notable for longevity, trouble-free performance, variety of flower-form and colour. Unlike some older varieties, modern Camellia flowers are heavy textured and not easily bruised, lasting well on the bush or picked for indoors. Camellias have a chaste and sculptured beauty possessed by few other flowers.

In addition to their floral charm, handsome foliage and good growth habits, make them ideal landscaping subjects with plants suitable for ground cover or dwarf effects, tall open growers for backgrounds, broad willowy varieties for espaliers and column forms for accent plants. They're excellent in containers or hanging baskets and make beautiful shelter or privacy screens.

Theaceae. *All listed Camellias evergreen.*

Camellia Culture

Camellias generally tolerate full sun, wind and partial shade, but some pale pinks and whites need filtered sunlight and protection. Thoroughly prepare an area for each plant about 60 × 60cm wide by 50cm deep, breaking up the sub-soil without bringing it to the surface and making sure drainage is adequate. Mix in generous equal portions of peat moss, coarse sand and well-rotted animal manure, and at planting time about 85 grams of acid plant food.

A further application of the same fertilizer can be given six weeks after planting. Spray during periods of new growth to control aphids. Thrips can be a problem if Camellias are growing too close to large trees or hedges. Occasionally check the backs of leaves for light brown markings and if present, spray both leaf surfaces.

As Camellias are surface rooted, keep clear of weeds an area equal in diameter to the width of the bush or lawn to facilitate mulching and feeding. Towards the end of the flowering season, and at least once more in the year, apply a mulch of compost, animal manures and peat moss plus acid plant food or blood and bone at the rate of one handful for each year of age of the plant. Grass clippings are not good as mulch as they tend to heat up and may damage young surface roots. During late summer and autumn, larger flowered varieties may be disbudded to one outward facing bud, to encourage extra size, quality and blooms of show standard.

Camellia japonica

The Camellias best known to most of us. There are thousands of named cultivars amongst which will be found all flower forms and colours. They are particularly hardy, their foliage is most handsome, and a careful selection can provide continuous bloom for at least six months of the year. Flower sizes vary from delightful miniatures under 3cm across, up to magnificent semi-doubles, all perfect for garden display or dramatic floral art.

Camellia reticulata

The largest flowered and most spectacular of all Camellias, some blooms attaining a width of 24cm. The ancient Kunming Province in China has records of this magnificent genus dating back over many centuries. 'Captain Rawes' has been in cultivation since the 17th century. The reticulata range is quite extensive and made more exciting by the introduction of numerous hybrids which seem more vigorous and commence their blooming period as early as May.

Camellia sasanqua

Extremely hardy and noted for their free-blooming habits, reliability and early flowering which extends from late summer to early spring. Versatile landscaping plants with more functional uses than many other plants, ideal for specimens, screens, ground or bank cover, espaliers, hanging baskets or containers.

Camellia hybrids

Hybrids, mainly saluenensis, have made a real impact and more and more are being introduced each year. Donation was one of the first and the list now includes many which have become internationally famous. Usually exceptionally strong growers especially when young. Unexcelled for garden display and picking for indoors.

Camellia species

The original species, some of which are parents of past and present varieties, are incredibly hardy, passing on these characteristics to modern day hybrids. Many species are either very graceful in their foliage or growth habit, while others are most floriferous. The wild reticulata is used as a seed parent for amateur and professional hybridists, and has produced many interesting seedlings as well as being an interesting and worthwhile plant in its own right.

Here is a guide to Southern Hemisphere seasons and sizes mentioned in the following descriptions.

Approximate flowering times
Early: April to July
Mid season: July to September
Late: September to November

Approximate flower sizes
Tiny: 1–3cm
Miniature: 3–6.5cm
Small: 6.5–8cm
Medium: 8–10cm
Large: 10–12.5cm
Very large: Over 12.5cm

Dimensions intended only as a rough guide.

CAMELLIA FLOWER FORMS

Single

Semi-double

Formal

Peony

Anemone

Rose form

Camellia 'Adorable'
Hybrid, bright pink, small formal double to rose form, mid season to late. Compact shrubby grower. 1.5 × 1m.

Camellia 'Aino Izumi'
Hybrid, soft pink, small semi-double, late season. Dense, compact grower. 2 × 1.5m.

Camellia 'Alba Plena'
Japonica, white, medium formal double, early to mid season. Average bushy grower, old faithful cultivar. 2.5 × 2m.

Camellia 'Allison Leigh Woodroof'
Japonica, soft pink shading to glowing pink at the margins, small cluster of stamens, medium to small semi-double, mid season. Vigorous upright grower. 1.5 × 1m.

Camellia 'Alpen Glo'
Hybrid, soft pink, tiny, single, mid season to late, seedling from Snowdrop by the same raiser. Clusters of buds open from every leaf axil, leaves lighter coloured and denser than Snowdrop, semi shade preferred, excellent container plant. 1.5 × 1m.

Camellia 'Amanda Lisa'
Reticulata hybrid, bright red, large informal double with neat petal arrangement, mid season to late. 3 × 2m.

Camellia 'Amazing Graces'
Hybrid, white shading to pink at the edges, medium formal double, mid season to late. Dense compact grower. 2.5 × 2m.

Camellia 'Angel Wings'
Hybrid, white shaded orchid pink, medium, semi-double with upright fluted petals, mid season. Upright, bushy growth. 2.5 × 2m.

Camellia 'Annette Carol'
Hybrid, pale pink, small, informal double, mid season. Tall slender growth. 2.5 × 2m.

Camellia 'Anticipation'
Hybrid, deep lavender rose pink, large, full peony to anemone form with full centre, many wavy petaloids and a few stamens, mid season. Erect columnar form. Jury hybrid saluenensis × japonica. 2.5 × 1.5m.

Camellia 'Anticipation Variegated'
Hybrid, rose pink and white, large, informal double, mid season, striking variegated edition. Average upright growth. 2.5 × 2m.   **48**

Camellia 'Applause'
Reticulata hybrid, salmon pink, very large informal double, late season. 3 × 2m.

Camellia 'Apple Blossom'
Sasanqua, white blushed pink, small single, early. Vigorous grower. 2 × 1.5m.

Camellia 'Aquarius'
Japonica, beautiful clear pink, large formal double with neat petal arrangement, mid season. Bushy habit, medium slow grower. 1.2 × 1m.

Camellia 'Ariel Song'
Hybrid, white, tiny, single flowers all along arching branches, early to late. Strong growing. 2.5 × 2m.

Camellia 'Autumn Herald'
Hybrid, white shading to pink at the egdes, miniature single, early to late season. Compact shrubby grower. Similar to the parent species pitardii, but very early flowering. 1.5 × 1m.

Camellia 'Ave Maria'
Japonica, soft, silvery, warm porcelain pink, medium, formal double, early to mid-season, good for picking. 2 × 1.5m.

Camellia 'Aztec'
Reticulata hybrid, salmon pink, very large informal double, late season. 3 × 2m.

Camellia 'Baby Bear'
Hybrid miniature, pink washed white, tiny, semi-double, mid season. Dense and vigorous, unlikely to exceed 1m high. 1 × .75m.

Camellia 'Baby Pearl'
Japonica, white, shading to light pink at edges, small, formal double, mid to late season. Sturdy, compact grower. 1.5 × 1m.

Camellia 'Baby Sis'
Japonica, white striped pink, miniature, single with a mass of central petaloids. Compact grower. 2 × 1.5m.

Camellia 'Baby Willow'
Hybrid, white, tiny, single, mid season to late. Slow, dense spreading and weeping growth habit, good for containers or bonsai. 70 × 90cm.

Camellia 'Ballet Dancer'
Japonica, cream shaded coral pink on petal edges, medium, peony form, early to late. Compact and upright. 2.5 × 2m.

Camellia 'Ballet Queen'
Hybrid, salmon pink, large, peony form, mid to late season. Medium upright growth. 2.5 × 2m.

Camellia 'Ballet Queen Variegata'
Hybrid, salmon pink attractively variegated white, large, full peony form, mid to late season, unique. 2.5 × 2m.

Camellia 'Bambino'
Japonica, coral rose pink, small anemone to formal double, mid season. Strong upright bushy grower. 2 × 1.3m.

Camellia 'Barbara Clark'
Hybrid, bright clear pink, medium to large, semi-double, early to mid-season. Broad pyramidal form, vigorous, free-blooming. 2 × 1.5m.

Camellia 'Barbara Woodroof'
Japonica, light orchid pink outer petals, creamy white petaloids, large, anemone form, mid season, spreading. 2.5 × 2m.

Camellia 'Beatrice Emily'
Sasanqua, white, shading to pink at the edges, large informal double, early season. 2.5 × 2m.

Camellia 'Bellbird'
Hybrid, pink, small, single, medium to late, very free flowering. Strong bushy upright growth, small leaves, ideal in containers. 1.5 × 1m.

Camellia 'Berenice Boddy'
Japonica, light pink, medium semi-double, mid season to late. Slender upright grower, good for picking. 2.5 × 2m.

Camellia 'Bert Jones'
Sasanqua, silvery pink with attractive stamens, small, semi-double, early. 2 × 1.5m.

Camellia 'Bett's Supreme'
Hybrid, soft silver-pink, centre paler at first, gradually intensifying, very large, semi-double, early season. Very floriferous, better colour and texture than its possible parent 'Donation'. 2.5 × 2m.

Camellia 'Betty Patricia'
Sasanqua, persian rose, large, double-rose, early. Vigorous, upright, compact grower. 2.5 × 2m.

Camellia 'Betty Ridley'
Hybrid, soft pink, large, formal double, early to late. Tall, dense, vigorous. 2.5 × 2m.

Camellia 'Betty's Beauty'
Hybrid, white with prominent red border to each petal, large informal double, mid season to late. Sport from Betty Sheffield Supreme, similar but more stable. Average upright grower. 2.5 × 2m.

Camellia 'Betty Sheffield Supreme'
Japonica, palest pink to white with deeper, glowing pink margins, large, semi-double to peony, mid season to late, quite irresistible. 2.5 × 2m.

Camellia 'Billie McFarland'
Japonica, rose pink with attractive yellow stamens, large, semi double, mid season. Vigorous, compact and upright grower. 2.5 × 2m.

Camellia 'Black Lace'
Hybrid, dark velvet red, medium, formal double to rose form with incurved petals, mid to late season. Compact erect grower. 2.5 × 2m.

Camellia 'Black Opal'
Hybrid, very dark red, small semi-double, late season. Like Night Rider, growth slower and more spreading. 2 × 1.5m.

Camellia 'Black Tie'
Japonica, dark red, small, formal double, mid season. Strong dense upright growth. 1.5 × 1m.   **47**

Camellia 'Blondie'
Hybrid, white, miniature anemone form, mid to late season. Compact bushy grower. 2 × 1.5m.

Camellia 'Bob Hope'
Japonica, black red, large, semi-double with irregular petals, mid season. Slow, compact grower. 2 × 1.5m.

Camellia 'Bob's Tinsie'
Japonica, brilliant red, miniature flowers, anemone form, mid season. Upright grower. 2 × 1.5m.   **48**

Camellia 'Bonanza'
Sasanqua, dark crimson, large, full informal double, early. Lax grower when young, can be staked or allowed to spread. 2 × 1.5m.

Camellia 'Bonnie Belle'
Japonica, bright currant red with creamy centre and yellow stamens, small anemone form, mid season to late. Compact pyramid. Good in containers. 1.8 × 1.2m.

Camellia 'Bonsai Baby'
 Sasanqua, deep purplish red, small formal double to rose form, early season. Small foliage, rounded compact grower for ground cover, containers, bonsai. 90 × 100cm.

Camellia 'Botan Yuki'
Hybrid, blush pink, miniature, anemone form with yellow petaloids, mid season. Dwarf and compact. 1.5 × 1m.

Camellia 'Brian'
Hybrid, silvery rose pink, medium semi-double, early to late season. Compact, upright grower. 3 × 2m.

Camellia 'Brigadoon'
Hybrid, rose pink, medium semi-double flowers, outer petals broad and rounded, inner ones curled and flared around the stamens, mid season, like Donation but more floriferous. Compact upright grower. 2.5 × 2m.

Camellia 'Bright Buoy'
Hybrid, bright scarlet red, single, with brilliant golden stamens, early to mid season, heavy flowerer. Vigorous upright grower. 2.5 × 2m.

Camellia 'Brushfield's Yellow'
Hybrid, antique white guard petals with pale primrose to yellow petaloids, medium anemone form, mid season to late. Compact, upright grower. 2.5 × 2m.   **47**

Camellia 'Buddha'
Reticulata, bright tyrian rose, maturing to orchid pink, large, semi-double with irregular, upright, wavy petals and rabbit ears, mid season, vigorous, erect open grower. Magnificent flower. 3 × 2m.

Camellia 'Burgundy Boy'
Japonica, dark red, medium anemone to informal double, mid season to late. Fast, upright open grower. 2.5 × 2m.   **48**

Camellia 'Burgundy Gem'
Japonica, deep burgundy to maroon red, small neat anemone to peony form, mid season. Erect bushy habit. 2.5 × 2m.

Camellia 'Buttons 'n' Bows'
Hybrid, light pink, small formal double with raised and fluted petals, mid season to late. Dense compact grower. 2.5 × 2m.   **48**

Camellia 'Cameron Cooper'
Reticulata, vivid pink, large rose-form double to peony-form, mid season. Vigorous upright grower. 3 × 2m.

Camellia 'Can Can'
Japonica, pale pink with deeper veining and petal edges, medium, full peony form, mid season. 2.5 × 2m.

Camellia 'Captain Rawes'
Reticulata, reddish rose pink, large, semi-double with irregular petals, mid season. Vigorous, hardy, good foliage, open growth habit. 3 × 2m.

Camellia 'Carter's Sunburst'
Japonica, pale pink striped deeper rose pink, very large, semi-double to peony or formal double, early to late. Compact, outstanding award winner. 2.5 × 2m.

Camellia 'Chansonette'
Sasanqua, bright pink, small, formal double to rose form with ruffled petals, early. Upright willowy habit. 2 × 1.5m.

Camellia 'China Doll'
Japonica, palest china pink edged coral, medium to large, loose, high-centred peony form with fluted petals, mid season to late. 2 × 1m.

Camellia 'Choji Guruma'
Sasanqua, bright pink, small anemone form unusual in sasanquas, very early. 2 × 1.5m.

Camellia 'Christmas Daffodil'
Hybrid, white, blush pink at petal tips, small, anemone form with longer central petaloids suggestive of a daffodil, early to mid season. Vigorous, compact grower, unusual. 2 × 1.5m.

Camellia 'Chrysantha'
Species, yellow, small, single to semi-double, mid season to late. Large quilted leaves, not free flowering, fast upright growth. 2.5 × 2m.

Camellia 'Chrysanthemum Petal'
Reticulata, light carmine pink, medium to large, rose form to fully double with fluted or imbricated petals, early to mid season. Slender open grower. 3 × 2m.

Camellia 'Cinderella'
Japonica, white picotee margins shading through pink to red at the centre, unusual wavy petals, informal peony form, mid season. Compact grower, quite spectacular. 1.5 × 1m.

Camellia 'Cinnamon Cindy'
Hybrid, white with pink tinges on petal edges and backs, miniature, semi-double to rose form, fragrant, early to late season. Strong upright grower, lends itself to shaping. 1.5 × 1m.

Camellia 'Clarise Carleton'
Japonica, dark salmon pink to brilliant coral red, very large, irregular semi-double with an outer layer of rounded petals surrounding a loose centre of rabbit ears, petaloids and stamens, early to mid season, compact sturdy grower. Among the largest and best early Camellias. 2 × 1.5m.

Camellia 'C M Hovey'
Japonica, vivid red with prominent veins, large perfect formal double, late season. Strong upright grower. 2.5 × 2m.   **48**

Camellia 'C M Wilson'
Japonica, pale pink, lighter around petals, medium to large anemone form, mid season. Average bushy growth. 2.5 × 2m.

Camellia 'Commander Mulroy'
Hybrid, white shading to pink toward edges, medium formal double, mid season to late. Compact, upright grower. 2.5 × 2m.

Camellia 'Contemplation'
Hybrid, clear pink, medium to large semi-double, mid season to late. Strong upright grower. 2.5 × 2m.

Camellia 'Cornelian'
Reticulata, turkey red to deep rose pink heavily marbled white, very large, semi-double with wavy petals and small petaloids, mid season to late. Medium, bushy, compact grower. 3 × 2m.   **65**

Camellia 'Cornish Snow'
Hybrid, pink flushed buds open to white with occasional pink blush, miniature, single, mid season to late. Dark, narrow leaves, burnished young growth, open erect grower, blooms prolifically, unusual charm and gracefulness. Saluenensis × cuspidata. 2 × 1.5m.

Camellia 'Coronation'
Japonica, purest white, very large, semi-double with beautiful central crown of ruffled and crimped petaloids and golden stamens, mid season. Vigorous, open, spreading grower, large handsome foliage, among the best whites. 2.5 × 2m.

Camellia 'Cotton Candy'
Sasanqua, clear pink, small semi-double with ruffled petals, mid season. Medium upright grower. 2 × 1.5m.

Camellia 'Cover Girl'
Japonica, beautiful pale pink deepening towards the centre, large formal double, mid to late season. Upright bushy grower. 1.8 × 1.3m.

Camellia 'Cranes Feather'
Japonica, pure white with white centre, medium anemone form, mid season. Average upright grower, dependable bloomer. 1.5 × 1m.

Camellia 'Crimson King'
Sasanqua, mahogany red with yellow stamens, small, single, early. Dark green foliage, compact habit. 1.5 × 1m.

Camellia 'Crimson Robe'
Reticulata, bright carmine, very large, semi-double with crepe-textured, wavy, crinkled petals, mid to late. Vigorous, spreading grower, large handsome leaves. 3 × 2m.

Camellia 'Dahlohnega'
Hybrid, creamy white to pale yellow, small to medium formal double, rare Camellia colouring, late to very late. Slow, dense upright grower. 2 × 1.5m.

Camellia 'Daintiness'
Hybrid, medium pink, medium to large, semi-double with bright yellow stamens, mid season. Jury hybrid saluenensis × magnoliaeflora. Free flowering. 2.5 × 2m.

Camellia 'Daitairin'
Japonica, light rose pink, large single with masses of central petaloids, mid season. Vigorous erect grower. 2.5 × 1.5m.

Camellia 'Dave's Weeper'
Hybrid, clear pink, small single, mid season to late. Vigorous grower with numerous long arching branches. Lasts well when cut for indoors. 2 × 1.5m.

Camellia 'Dawn'
Vernalis species, pale pink in bud, white flowers with central cluster of yellow stamens, medium to small semi double, early flowering. Hardy, resembles sasanqua type. 2 × 1.3m.

Camellia 'Dazzler'
Sasanqua, brilliant rose red, large, semi-double, early. Bushy willowy habit. 2 × 1.5m.

Camellia 'Debbie'
Hybrid, hot Thai pink, large, peony form, deep rounded and firm with three rows of petals surrounding a centre of curved rabbit ears, petaloids and stamens, early to late. Strong erect grower with pale green young foliage. Jury hybrid saluenensis × Debutante. 2.5 × 2m.   **65**

Camellia 'Debutante'
Hybrid, clear pink, large informal double, early to mid season. Strong upright grower, reliable. 2.5 × 2m.

Camellia 'Deep Secret'
Japonica, deep cardinal red with conspicuous golden stamens, large semi double, mid season. Upright bushy grower. 2 × 1.5m.

Camellia 'Dellie McCaw'
Japonica, clear pink, medium, formal double, early to late. Attractive addition. 2 × 1.5m.

Camellia 'Demi Tasse'
Japonica, soft peach pink, small to medium, hose-in-hose to 'cup and saucer' form with petaloids, mid season. Vigorous compact upright grower. 2.5 × 2m.

Camellia 'Desire'
Japonica, ivory white, delicately blushed pink on outer edges, large, formal double with incurved petals, mid season. Bushy compact grower. 2.5 × 2m.

Camellia 'Diamond Head'
Hybrid, deep red, large, semi-double with crinkled petals, mid season. Open grower. 2.5 × 2m.

Camellia 'Dixie Knight'
Japonica, rich, deep vibrant red, large, peony form with four or five separate groups of irregular petals and stamens, mid season to late. Vigorous erect grower. 2.5 × 2m.   **65**

Camellia 'Dolly Dyer'
Japonica, bright scarlet, small, tight informal double, mid season to late, prize winning blooms. Compact upright growth. 1.5 × 1m.   **65**

Camellia 'Dona Herzilia de Freitas Magalhaes'
Hybrid, mauve pink at first, deepening to rich deep purple as the plant matures, large informal double, mid season to late. Strong, tall upright grower. 2.5 × 2m.

Camellia 'Donation'
Hybrid, orchid pink with darker veins, large, semi-double, early to late, very floriferous. Vigorous grower. 2.5 × 2m.

Camellia 'Dorothy Culver'
Hybrid, pure white, large anemone form, mid season to late. Strong dense upright grower, good weather resistance for white blooms. 2.5 × 2m.

Camellia 'Drama Girl'
Japonica, deep rose pink to coral salmon, very large, semi-double to peony form, early to late, outstanding and free-flowering. Bold handsome foliage, strong open grower, award winner. 2.5 × 2m.

Camellia 'Dr Burnside'
Japonica, rich red with central petaloid cluster and yellow stamens, peony form, mid season. Free flowering, bushy grower. 1.5 × 1m.

Camellia 'Dr Clifford Parkes'
Reticulata, scarlet with orange cast, very large, semi-double to loose peony form to

full peony form, mid season. Vigorous grower. 3 × 2.5m. **65**

Camellia 'Dream Boat'
Hybrid, bright pink with lavender cast, large, formal double with incurved petals, mid season, vigorous. 2.5 × 2m. **65**

Camellia 'Dream Girl'
Sasanqua × reticulata hybrid, coral salmon, medium to large, semi-double, early to mid season. 2.5 × 1m.

Camellia 'Dr Lilyan Hanchey'
Hybrid, pale blush pink, large formal double, mid season to late. Strong upright grower, weather resistant. 2.5 × 2m.

Camellia 'Dr Tinsley'
Hybrid, pale pink, darker at edges, medium semi-double, mid season to late. Slender upright grower. 2.5 × 2m.

Camellia drupifera
Species, white, small single, buds clustered right along each stem, mid season to late. Slow, dense sturdy grower. Drupifera — bearing fleshy fruits or drupes. 1.5 × 1m.

Camellia 'Early Pearly'
Sasanqua, white with a tinge of pink, small, formal double, early. Average upright growth. 2 × 1.5m.

Camellia 'Easter Morn'
Japonica, soft baby pink, very large, semi-double with irregular petals to full peony form, mid to late season. Upright grower. 2.5 × 2m.

Camellia 'Ecclefield'
Japonica, chalky-white, large, semi-double to peony or anemone form, high built and heavy textured, mid season to late. Outstanding foliage and flower, vigorous, compact grower. 2.5 × 2m.

Camellia 'E G Waterhouse'
Hybrid, pure warm pink, medium, formal double with pointed central bud and notched petals, mid season to late. Distinctive columnar growth, among the best. 2.5 × 1.5m.

Camellia 'El Dorado'
Hybrid, rich warm pink, medium, full peony form, mid season to late. Outstanding, free-flowering, showy, upright, compact grower, does not scorch in full sun. 2.5 × 2m.

Camellia 'Elegans'
Japonica, rose pink, large, anemone form with central petaloids often white, early to mid season. Slow spreading growth. 2 × 2m.

Camellia 'Elegans Champagne'
Japonica, icy white outer petals, creamy petaloids, very large, anemone form, outer petals with serrated margins, early to mid season. Slow spreading growth. 2 × 2m. **66**

Camellia 'Elegans Splendor'
Japonica, soft light pink edged white, very large, anemone form with outer petals serrated, early to mid season. Spreading growth. 2 × 2m. **67**

Camellia 'Elegans Supreme'
Japonica, translucent watermelon pink to deep rose pink, large, semi-double to anemone form, very deep petal serrations, early to mid-season. 2 × 1.5m. **66**

Camellia 'Elegant Beauty'
Hybrid, deep rose to orchid pink, large, loose anemone form, mid season to late. Tall spreading grower, suited to espalier. 2.5 × 2m.

Camellia 'Elfin Rose'
Sasanqua, rose pink, small semi-double, early season. Attractive plant. 2 × 1.5m.

Camellia 'Elsie Jury'
Hybrid, rich clear pink, medium to large, peony form with outer ring of deeply cleft, overlapping petals surrounding central wavy petaloids and stamens, early to late. Strong, upright, compact growth, free flowering. 2.5 × 2m.

Camellia 'Elsie Ruth Marshall'
Hybrid, light pink, large rose form double, mid season. Average upright grower. 2.5 × 2m.

Camellia 'Exquisite'
Sasanqua, pale pink, large single, early to mid season. 2 × 1.5m.

Camellia 'Extravaganza'
Japonica, white, vividly and profusely striped light red, large to very large, anemone form, mid season. Strong upright grower. 2.5 × 2m.

Camellia 'Fairy Wand'
Hybrid, bright rosy red to crimson, miniature, semi-double, mid season to late. Fast bushy grower. 2 × 1.5m.

Camellia 'Fashionata'
Japonica, clear apricot pink, large, semi-double with curled outer petals, occasional clusters of petaloids, mid season. Vigorous open growth. 2.5 × 2m.

Camellia 'Fendig'
Miniature, rich cream, delightful anemone form, 3 to 5cm flowers in profusion, mid season. Compact grower. 2 × 1m.

Camellia 'Fimbriata'
Japonica, pure white, medium, formal double with fimbriated petals, mid season. Rounded bush with semi-pendulous branches. 2 × 2m.

Camellia 'Fire Chief Variegated'
Reticulata hybrid, deep red marbled white, large open semi-double, late. Leaves mottled yellow. Compact bushy grower. 2.5 × 2m.

Camellia 'Fire Falls'
Hybrid, glowing crimson, medium to large full peony form, mid season. Vigorous upright grower. 2.5 × 2m.

Camellia 'Firedance'
Japonica, deep vibrant red with showy stamens, medium, semi-double, mid season, heavy flowering. Vigorous compact upright grower. 2.5 × 2m.

Camellia 'Flower Girl'
Sasanqua × reticulata hybrid, clear pink, large to very large, semi-double to peony form. Vigorous upright growth. 2.5 × 2m.

Camellia 'Fox's Fancy'
Hybrid, deep red, medium full peony form with irregular creped petals, mid season. 2.5 × 2m.

Camellia 'Francie L'
Reticulata hybrid, coral salmon to rose pink, very large, high-centred semi-double, with bold, waxy petals curving and waved towards a mass of golden stamens, mid season to late. Young leaves almost strap-like broadening with age. 2 × 2m.

Camellia 'Fraterna'
Species, white, small, single flowers clustered at each leaf axil, mid season. Fast upright growth with long arching branches. 2.5 × 2m.

Camellia 'Freedom Bell'
Hybrid, bright red, small bell-shaped semi-double, early to late season. Compact upright grower. 2 × 1.5m.

Camellia 'Frivolity'
Sasanqua, white delicately edged pink, large single, early season. 2 × 1.5m.

Camellia 'Fukuzutsumi'
Sasanqua, white broadly edged pink, large single to semi-double, heavily fragrant, early season. 2 × 1.5m.

Camellia 'Gay Baby'
Hybrid, deep orchid rose pink, miniature, semi-double, mid season. Open upright grower. 2 × 1.5m.

Camellia 'Gayborder'
Sasanqua, white with broad rose pink border, large semi-double, early. 2 × 1.5m.

Camellia 'Gayle Walden'
Hybrid, pale pink, shaded deeper pink, medium to large, anemone form, early to late. Exquisite. 2 × 2m.   **66**

Camellia 'Gay Pixie'
Hybrid, light pink with darker pink stripes, medium, informal double, mid season. Compact upright growth. 2.5 × 2m.

Camellia 'Gay Sue'
Sasanqua, white tipped with pink, medium, semi-double, early, highly fragrant. Very popular. 2 × 1.5m.

Camellia 'Ginger'
Japonica, ivory white, miniature peony form, mid to late season. Erect, compact pyramid. 1.5 × 1m.

Camellia 'Glen 40'
Japonica, deep red, large, rose form to formal double, mid season to late, striking flower, excellent for floral art. Handsome foliage and form, slow, compact, erect grower, resistant to cold. 2.5 × 1.5m.

Camellia 'Grace Albritton'
Japonica, white, blushed rose on petal tips and centre, miniature to small, formal double, mid season, Medium upright grower, charming flower. 1.5 × 1m.

Camellia 'Grand Prix'
Japonica, brilliant red with golden stamens, very large, semi double with irregular petals, mid season. Upright grower. 2.5 × 2m.

Camellia 'Grand Slam'
Japonica, brilliant bright red, very large, semi-double to anemone with two or three rows of wavy, recurving petals, mid season. Strong spreading growth, broad, dark green foliage. 2.5 × 2m.   **66**

Camellia 'Guest of Honour'
Japonica, deep salmon rose or carmine, very large, semi-double to peony form with up to 20 petals, mid season, extremely free flowering. Vigorous upright compact grower, disbud for maximum size. 2.5 × 2m.

Camellia 'Guilio Nuccio'
Japonica, deep coral rose to glowing salmon red, very large, semi-double with beautifully wavy and waxy reflexing petals, central zone of petaloids and rabbit ears, and a ring of yellow stamens, mid season. Handsome glossy foliage, vigorous bushy growth, very free flowering, among the most desirable. 2.5 × 2m.   **67**

Camellia 'Gwen Pike'
Sasanqua, soft pink, small, semi-double to rose form, early. Slow dense grower, excellent in containers. 1.5 × 1m.

Camellia 'Gwenyth Morey'
Japonica, rich cream with a touch of yellow, large, anemone form, mid season, the nearest to yellow among Camellias. 2 × 2m.

Camellia 'Hakuhan Kujaku'
Japonica, red and white, remarkable tubular flowers, late season. Arching pendulous branches, long narrow leaves, known as Peacock Camellia. 2.5 × 2m.

Camellia 'Harold L Paige'
Reticulata, bright red, very large full informal double to peony form, late season, outstanding flower. Bushy grower. 2.5 × 2m.

Camellia 'Hawaii'
Japonica, soft pale pink, large, peony form with paler fimbriated margins to the petals resembling a carnation, mid season. Moderate spreading growth. 2.5 × 2m.   **67**

Camellia 'Hiryu'
Sasanqua, bright cerise red, 6cm flowers in abundance, early. Vigorous, hardy, free-flowering. 2.5 × 1.5m.

Camellia 'Holly Bright'
Hybrid, watermelon red, large semi-double, mid to late season. Strong bushy growth. Leaf margins heavily serrated. 2.5 × 2m.

Camellia 'Hopkins Pink'
Miniature, soft pink with occasional streak, spot or petal of red, small 5cm, peony form, mid season to late. Vigorous compact grower, profuse bloomer. 2 × 1m.

Camellia 'Howard Asper'
Reticulata hybrid, coral salmon pink, extra large, high-centred semi-double to peony form with loose erect petaloids and rabbit ears, mid season to late. Vigorous open growth. 3 × 2.5m.

Camellia 'Huia'
Reticulata hybrid, deep rose pink, very large informal double, mid season. Featured in Eden Gardens, Auckland. 3 × 2m.   **67**

Camellia 'Hulyn Smith'
Reticulata, clear pink, very large full informal double with heavy textured petals, late. Sturdy, reliable grower. 3 × 2m.   **66**

Camellia 'Interlude'
Hiemalis hybrid, light pink, large rose form to formal double, early to mid season. 2 × 1.5m.

Camellia 'Isaribi'
Hybrid, clear pink, miniature bell-shaped semi-double, mid season to late. Dense upright grower. Name means 'Fishing Lights' 2.5 × 2m.

Camellia 'Island of Fire'
Japonica, brilliant fiery red, large, peony form, mid season. 2.5 × 1.5m.

Camellia 'Itty Bit'
Hybrid, clear pink, miniature anemone form, mid season to late. Very free-flowering, dwarf compact shrub. Mark Jury hybrid. 1 × 1m.

Camellia 'James Lockington'
Japonica, pure white, medium formal double with symmetrical petal formation, mid season. Medium grower. 2 × 1.5m.

Camellia 'Jamie'
Hybrid, deep glowing red with bright golden stamens, medium, semi-double, mid season. Slow compact upright growth. 2.5 × 2m.   **67**

Camellia 'Jan's Choice'
Hybrid, rich crimson, large anemone form, late to very late. Strong upright grower, good quality late bloomer. 2.5 × 2m.

Camellia 'Jean Clere'
Japonica, red, with petals edged white, medium, full peony form, early to mid season. Bushy growth. 2.5 × 2m.

Camellia 'Jean May'
Sasanqua, soft shell pink, large, semi-double to rose form, early, heavy flowering. 2 × 1.5m.

Camellia 'Jennifer Susan'
Sasanqua, mauve pink, medium, semi-double to peony form, early flowering and distinct. 2 × 1.5m.

Camellia 'Jubilation'
Hybrid, clear rose pink with deeper pink fleck, very large, rose form, mid to late season. Upright grower. 2.5 × 2m.   **68**

Camellia 'Julie Felix'
Japonica, soft pastel pink, large, formal double, mid to late season. Slow growing open habit. 2 × 1.5m.

Camellia 'Jury's Sunglow'
Hybrid, multi-coloured tones of vibrant cyclamen and crimson lake, medium to large, anemone to peony form, mid season. Bushy habit, Les Jury hybrid. 2.5 × 2m.

Camellia 'Jury's Yellow'
Hybrid, ivory white guard petals with a central mass of small, creamy primrose-yellow petaloids, medium anemone form, early to late season. Compact upright grower. 1.8 × 1.5m.

Camellia 'Just Darling'
Japonica, shell-pink, miniature formal double, mid season. Vigorous upright grower. 1.5 × 1m.

Camellia 'Just Sue'
Hybrid, light pink petals bordered red, medium informal double, mid to late season. Strong upright grower. 2.5 × 2m.   **68**

Camellia 'Kelly McKnight'
Sasanqua, rosy red, small formal double, early flowering. Small foliage, bushy grower. 1.5 × 1m.

Camellia 'Kewpie Doll'
Japonica, light chalky pink, miniature, anemone form with high petaloid centre, mid season. Bushy and upright growth. 2.5 × 2m.

Camellia 'Kick Off'
Japonica, pink heavily striped and speckled rosy red, large full peony form, early to late season. Vigorous compact grower. 2.5 × 2m.

Camellia 'Kishu Tsukasa'
Japonica, deep rose pink and white, medium, formal double, mid to late season. Compact upright growth, a real novelty. 2.5 × 2m.

Camellia 'Kitty'
Miniature, creamy white to pale pink, small 4 to 5 cm, formal double, mid season, free flowering. 2 × 1m.

Camellia 'K O Hester'
Reticulata hybrid, orchid pink, very large semi-double, mid season. 3 × 2m.

Camellia 'Kona'
Hybrid, white with green cast, large, very full informal double with serrated margins to each petal, mid season to late. Sport of Hawaii, needing similar weather protection for perfect open blooms. 2.5 × 2m.

Camellia 'Koru Tsubaki'
Hybrid, dark, blackish red, small semi-double, late season. Slow grower. 2 × 1.5m.

Camellia 'Kramer's Fluted Coral'
Hybrid, coral pink, small to medium semi-double, fluted petals, mid season to late. Slow upright grower. 2 × 1.5m.

Camellia 'Kramer's Supreme'
Japonica, glowing turkey red to crimson, large, peony form with mixed petals and petaloids in full rounded form, mid season to late. Rare fragrant Camellia. 2.5 × 2m.

Camellia 'K Sawada'
Japonica, pure white, large, formal double, early to mid season, free flowering, vigorous. 2.5 × 2m.

Camellia 'Lady Clare'
Japonica, deep pink, large, semi-double, mid season. Has been cultivated for over 100 years, vigorous upright grower. 2.5 × 2m.

Camellia 'Lady Loch'
Japonica, light pink with white edged petals, medium informal double, mid season to late. Strong upright grower. 2.5 × 2m.

Camellia 'Lasca Beauty'
Reticulata, soft clear pink and bright golden stamens, very large, semi-double with thick heavy textured petals, mid season. Vigorous open upright grower. 3.5 × 3m.   **68**

Camellia 'Laura Walker'
Japonica, bright red, large, semi-double to anemone form with numerous central petaloids, very late. Most attractive late red, vigorous, upright growth. 2.5 × 1.5m.

Camellia 'Laurie Bray'
Japonica, soft pink, large, semi-double with spaced, ruffled or wavy petals and some petaloids, early to mid season. Upright grower. 2.5 × 2m.

Camellia 'Lemon Drop'
Hybrid, white with lemon centre, miniature anemone form, mid season to late. Average upright grower. 2 × 1.5m.   **68**

Camellia 'Leonard Messel'
Hybrid, bright pink to rose, large, semi-double with heavy textured petals, mid season to late. 2.5 × 2m.

Camellia 'Leonora Novick'
Japonica, white with a touch of cream, large loose anemone form, early to mid season. Highly recommended. 2 × 1.5m.

Camellia 'Les Jury'
Hybrid, deep crimson red, large formal rose to peony form, mid to late season. Upright, vigorous, bushy grower, long flowering season, self grooming. 3.5 × 2m.

Camellia 'Lilemac'
Japonica, pure white, miniature fully double blooms, mid season to late. Medium grower. 1.5 × 1m.

Camellia 'Little Babe'
Japonica, deep red, small, double rose form, early to late, long flowering season. Vigorous compact grower. 1.5 × 1m.

Camellia 'Little Bit'
Hybrid, bright red, small informal double, mid season. Average upright grower. 2 × 1.5m.

Camellia 'Little Bit Variegated'
Hybrid, red marbled white, small informal double, mid season. Average upright grower. 2 × 1.5m.   **77**

Camellia 'Little Lavender'
Hybrid, lavender pink, miniature anemone form, mid season. Compact upright grower. 2 × 1.5m.

Camellia 'Little Michael'
Hybrid, soft pink with creamy white petaloids, miniature anemone form, mid season. Average upright grower. 2 × 1.5m.

Camellia 'Little Pearl'
Sasanqua, rose pink, pearly buds opening pure white, medium informal semi-double, early to mid season. Slow, compact grower. 1.5 × 1m.

Camellia 'Little Red Riding Hood'
Japonica, rich crimson, miniature, formal to peony form, mid to late season. Compact upright grower. 2 × 1.5m.

Camellia 'Little Ruby'
Japonica, rich red, miniature loose peony form to semi double, mid season. Compact grower. 1.5 × 1m.

Camellia 'Little Slam'
Japonica, bright red, small informal double, early to mid season. Average upright grower. 2 × 1.5m.

Camellia 'Lois Shibnault'
Reticulata, medium orchid pink with yellow stamen clusters, very large semi-double with irregular petals ruffled on the edges and erect central petaloids, early to mid season. Medium upright grower. 3 × 2m.

Camellia longicarpa
Species, white, tiny cup-shaped flowers on long stems, mid season to late. Vigorous, spreading, open grower, very narrow leaves. Longicarpa — long fruited. 1.5 × 1.3m.

Camellia 'Look Away'
Japonica, petal edges broadly margined white, merging to deep pink areas and veins, medium large formal double, mid season. Upright grower. 2 × 1.5m.

Camellia 'Lovelight'
Japonica, white, large semi-double with heavy textured petals, mid season. Vigorous upright grower. 2.5 × 2m.

Camellia 'Lovely Lady'
Reticulata, pink, large, formal double, mid season to late. Slender compact upright growth. 3 × 2.5m.

Camellia 'L T Dees'
Hybrid, rich rose red, large to very large formal double, late season. Strong, slender upright grower with handsome appearance. 2.5 × 2m.

Camellia 'Lucinda'
Sasanqua, bright pink, large, peony form, early. Willowy branches excellent for espalier. 2 × 1.5m.

Camellia 'Lulu Belle'
Japonica, pure white, large, semi-double to loose peony form, early season. Upright grower. 2.5 × 2m.

Camellia lutchuensis
Species, white, tiny, single, mid season, profuse bloomer and heavily fragrant. Very small leaves, varying from green to bronze, average slightly open growth. 2.5 × 2m.

Camellia 'Mansize'
Japonica, pure white, miniature, anemone form, mid season. Open upright grower. 2 × 1.5m.

Camellia 'Margaret Bernhardt'
Reticulata hybrid, dark rose pink, large rose form to formal double, mid season. Slow, dense, heavy wooded grower. 3 × 2m.

Camellia 'Margaret Davis'
Japonica, white lightly edged rose, large, peony form, mid season. 2.5 × 2m.   **79**

Camellia 'Margaret Hilford'
Reticulata, dark red, very large, semi-double, mid season, excellent performer. 3 × 2.5m.

Camellia 'Mark Allen'
Japonica, rose to wine red, large, semi-double, early to mid season, free flowering. 2.5 × 2m.   **78**

Camellia 'Maroon and Gold'
Japonica, buds blackish red opening to glowing crimson with bright golden stamens,

medium, peony form with loose petaloids intermingled with stamens, mid season to late, vigorous. 2.5 × 1.5m.   **78**

Camellia 'Mary Alice Cox'
Japonica, pure white, large formal double with a few central yellow stamens, mid season. Upright habit. 2 × 1.5m.

Camellia 'Mary Paige'
Japonica, delicate pale pink, large formal double, mid to early season. Sturdy compact grower. 2 × 1.5m.

Camellia 'Mary Phoebe Taylor'
Hybrid, bright rose pink, large, loose anemone form, early to late. Long stems, good for picking. 2.5 × 2m.

Camellia 'Mary Wheeler'
Japonica, orchid to light pink shaded to white at petal base, large, peony form, mid season. 2 × 1.5m.   **78**

Camellia 'Mathotiana'
Japonica, red with metallic overtones, large, formal double to informal double according to climate, mid to late season, strong bushy growth. 2.5 × 2m.

Camellia 'Mathotiana Supreme'
Japonica, rich crimson, very large, semi-double, irregular petals interspersed with stamens, mid season. 2.5 × 2m.

Camellia 'Maui'
Japonica, pure white, large, anemone form with heavily textured petals, mid season to late. Sturdy dense grower, excellent tub plant. 2 × 1.5m.

Camellia 'Midnight'
Japonica, Black-red buds opening to vivid crimson red, medium to large, semi-double to anemone form with golden stamens, mid season to late, dark foliage. 2 × 1.5m.

Camellia 'Mimosa Jury'
Hybrid, soft lavender pink, medium formal double, mid season to late. Strong upright grower, Felix Jury hybrid. 2.5 × 2m.

Camellia 'Mine no Yuki'
Sasanqua, pure white, small, peony form, early. Popular and very versatile. Syn 'Moonlight'. 2 × 1.5m.

Camellia 'Mini Mint'
Hybrid, white with attractive pink stripe, small formal double, mid season to late. Attractive dwarf shrub. 1.5 × 1m.

Camellia 'Mini Pink'
Hybrid, clear pink, miniature semi-double,

mid season to late. Strong bushy grower. Blooms over a long period. 1.5 × 1m.

Camellia 'Miss Bessie Beville'
Hybrid, pale pink, large formal double, early to mid. Strong bushy grower. 2.5 × 2m.

Camellia 'Miss Charleston'
Japonica, deep red waxy petals, contrasting golden stamens, large, semi-double with high centre, mid to late season. Medium upright growth. 2.5 × 2m.

Camellia 'Miss Tiny Tot Princess'
Hybrid, rose pink, miniature, rose form to formal double, mid season to late. Average upright growth, small foliage. 1.5 × 1m.

Camellia 'Miss Tulare'
Reticulata, bright rosy red, large to very large, informal double, full high centre, mid to late. Vigorous bushy grower. 3 × 2.5m.

Camellia 'Misty Moon'
Sasanqua, light pink, large, semi-double, early. Mature plants produce very large blooms for a sasanqua, dense rounded bushy growth. 2 × 1.5m.

Camellia 'Modern Art'
Hybrid, white boldly striped and spotted pink and red, large anemone form, scented, mid season to late. Strong dense upright grower. 2.5 × 2m.   **78**

Camellia 'Mona Jury'
Hybrid, soft pink shaded apricot pink, large, frilled peony form, early to late season. Upright open growth. 2.5 × 2m.

Camellia 'Moshio'
Japonica, deep flame red, medium, semi-double with open recurving petals, mid season, free flowering. Remarkable colour clarity, upright compact grower. Syn 'Flame'. 2.5 × 2m.

Camellia 'Mouchang'
Reticulata hybrid, salmon pink, very large semi-double, mid season. Strong grower with open branching pattern. 3 × 2m.

Camellia 'Moutancha'
Reticulata, bright pink veined white and striped white on inner petals, large to very large, semi-double to formal double with wavy crimped petals, mid season to late. 3 × 2.5m.

Camellia 'Mrs D W Davis'
Japonica, pale blush pink, very large, single to semi-double with huge boss of stamens and petaloids, mid season to late. Vigorous upright grower. 2.5 × 2m.

Camellia 'Mrs Tingley'
Japonica, salmon silver pink, medium, formal double, mid season to late, prolific bloomer, good stems. 2.5 × 2m.

Camellia 'Myrtifolia'
Japonica, silvery pink, large formal double with incurving petals, late to very late. Strong upright grower. 2,5 × 2m.

Camellia 'Navajo'
Sasanqua, petals white with vivid rosy red margins and golden stamens, medium, single, early. Compact bushy habit. 2 × 1.5m.

Camellia 'Nicky Crisp'
Hybrid, pale lavender pink, small, semi-double, early to late season, high quality flower. Outstanding bush, slow dense bushy growth. 1.5 × 1m.

Camellia 'Night Rider'
Japonica, very dark red, small, semi-double, late season. Dark bronze new growth, very dark green when mature, dense upright growth, very popular. 2.5 × 2m.

Camellia 'Nishiki Kirin'
Hybrid, rose pink with red streaks and occasional red blooms, small, anemone form, early to mid season, free flowering. Dwarf compact and bushy. 1.5 × 1m.

Camellia 'Nokogiri Ba'
Japonica, bright red, small, single, mid season. Long narrow heavily serrated leaves, vigorous bushy grower, known as Sawtooth Leaf Camellia. 2.5 × 2m.

Camellia 'Nonie Haydon'
Hybrid, clear light pink, medium to large informal double, mid season to late. Strong grower, free flowering, bright yellow, long lasting pollen. 2.5 × 2m. **79**

Camellia 'Nuccio's Cameo'
Hybrid, clear pink. large formal double, early to mid season. Strong upright grower. 2.5 × 2m.

Camellia 'Nuccio's Gem'
Japonica, pure white, medium to large, formal double, early to mid season. Compact upright grower. 2.5 × 2m.

Camellia 'Nuccio's Jewel'
Japonica, white, washed and shaded orchid pink, medium, full peony form, mid season. Slow bushy growth. 2 × 1.5m. **79**

Camellia 'Nuccio's Pearl'
Japonica, white, washed and shaded orchid pink, medium, formal double, mid season.

Vigorous compact grower, excellent formal addition. 2.5 × 2m.

Camellia 'Nuccio's Ruby'
Reticulata hybrid, dark red, large semi-double, fluted petals, mid season. 3 × 2m. **79**

Camellia 'Nymph'
Hybrid, blush pink, miniature, semi-double, early to late, scented lutchuensis hybrid, commencing to flower late autumn. Strong bushy growth. 2 × 1.5m.

Camellia 'Odoratissima'
Japonica, rose pink, fragrant, large semi-double to informal double, mid season to late. Average upright grower. 2.5 × 2m.

Camellia 'Ole'
Hybrid, clear pink, small rose form double, late season. Slow bushy grower. 1.5 × 1m.

Camellia oleifera
Species, white tinged pink, small single flowers, mid season. Cultivated in China for the high oil content of the seeds. Variable in form, but the one usually available from nurseries is sasanqua-like. 2.5 × 2m.

Camellia 'Onetia Holland'
Japonica, pure white, very large, peony form with loose petals, mid season to late, excellent white. 2.5 × 1.5m.

Camellia 'Our Betty Variegated'
Hybrid, pink splashed white, large, two hose-in-hose rows of long tubular petals, mid season to late, very free flowering. Fast upright growth. 2.5 × 2m.

Camellia 'Pacific Beauty'
Hybrid, salmon rose pink, large, formal double to occasional peony form, mid to late season. Compact bushy, slow grower. 2 × 1.5m.

Camellia 'Pagoda'
Reticulata, rich bright crimson, large, rose form to formal double, mid season to late, spectacular blooms resemble Begonias or Roses. 3 × 2m. **77**

Camellia 'Parisienne'
Hybrid, vibrant cherry red, occasionally marbled rose pink and white, flared golden yellow stamens, medium to large semi-double, mid season. Compact bushy plant. 2 × 1.5m.

Camellia 'Peach Blossom'
Japonica, light pink, medium semi-double, mid season. Medium compact grower. 2.5 × 2m.

Camellia 'Pink Cameo'
Hybrid, dark pink, large informal double, mid season to late. Compact bushy grower. 2 × 1.5m.

Camellia 'Pink Dahlia'
Hybrid, orchid pink, medium, formal double with separated layers of narrow fluted petals, mid season to late. Long narrow leaves, stiff bushy growth. 2.5 × 2m.

Camellia 'Pink Diddy'
Japonica, warm light salmon pink, medium to large, formal double to rose form, mid season to late. Slightly pendulous growth. 2 × 1.5m.

Camellia 'Pink Gold'
Japonica, clear pink, large semi double with central petaloids interspersed with gold-tipped stamens, early to late long flowering season. Vigorous upright grower. 2 × 1.5m.

Camellia 'Pink Pagoda'
Japonica, rose pink, large, irregular hose-in-hose to formal double, mid season. Exquisitely different, profuse bloomer, vigorous, compact, upright grower. 2.5 × 2m.

Camellia 'Pink Perfection'
Japonica, shell pink to medium pink, small, formal double, mid season to late. Upright, densely foliaged. 2.5 × 2m.

Camellia 'Pink Smoke'
Hybrid, white to very pale pink, miniature with unusual long wispy petals and petaloids, early season. Rapid bushy grower. 2 × 1.5m.

Camellia 'Pirates Gold'
Japonica, dark red with golden stamens, large, semi-double to loose peony form, late season. Spreading bush. 2 × 1.5m.

Camellia pitardii
Species, white flushed pink, small single flowers with bright, long lasting pollen, mid season to late. Slow, twiggy grower. 2 × 1.5.

Camellia 'Plantation Pink'
Sasanqua, mid pink, large, single saucer shaped flowers, early. Vigorous, upright and hardy. 2.5 × 2m.

Camellia 'Pride of California'
Hybrid, pink with faint orange cast, miniature formal double, mid season to late. Strong upright grower. 2 × 1.5m.

Camellia 'Professor Sargent'
Japonica, dark red, medium, full peony, mid season. Vigorous compact upright grower. 2.5 × 2m.

Camellia 'Purple Gown'
Reticulata, dark purple red with pin stripes of white to wine red, large to very large, formal double to peony form with wavy petals. Compact and free flowering. 3 × 2m.   **78**

Camellia 'Queenslander'
Sasanqua, silvery pink, large informal double, early season. Strong grower, light green foliage. 2 × 1.5m.

Camellia 'Quintessence'
Hybrid, pure white with yellow centre, miniature, single, sweet musky fragrance, early to mid season. Slow spreading growth. 1.5 × 1m.

Camellia 'Rainbow'
Sasanqua, white delicately edged red, medium single, early season. 2 × 1.5m.

Camellia 'Raspberry Ice'
Hybrid, white splashed and streaked red and pink, large semi-double with serrated petals, mid season. Strong bushy grower. 2 × 1.5m.

Camellia 'Raspberry Ripple'
Hybrid, white splashed red and pink, large open semi-double, mid season. Strong upright grower. 2.5 × 2m.   **79**

Camellia 'Red Dahlia'
Japonica, scarlet red, medium, loose peony form with wavy petals, mid season. Bushy, upright habit. 2.5 × 2m.

Camellia 'Red Ensign'
Japonica, crimson, large, single to semi double with few petaloids, mid season. Vigorous upright grower. 2.5 × 2m.

Camellia 'Red Red Rose'
Japonica, deep red, small to medium formal double, mid season to late. Slender upright growth. 2.5 × 2m.

Camellia 'Reg Ragland Supreme'
Japonica, rich red, large, anemone to peony form, early to late, extended blooming period. Medium compact growth. 2.5 × 2m.

Camellia 'Reigyoku'
Japonica, orange red, small, single, mid season to late. Green and gold patterned leaves, the yellow portion bright pink when young, slow dense grower. 2 × 1.5m.

Camellia 'Rendezvous'
Hybrid, deep scarlet crimson with large central zone of golden stamens, medium, semi-double, mid season to late. Attractive dark foliage, compact upright growth. 2.5 × 2m.

Camellia 'Richard Nixon'
Hybrid, white shaded and striped pink, large anemone form, mid season. Compact upright grower. 2 × 1.5m.

Camellia 'R L Wheeler'
Japonica, rose pink with occasional white flecks, very large, semi-double to anemone form with heavy outer petals and solid ring of stamens, early to mid season. 2.5 × 2m.

Camellia 'Roger Hall'
Japonica, bright red, small to medium, formal double, early to late season. Handsome foliage, outstanding. 2.5 × 2m.

Camellia 'Rosaeflora'
Species, medium to light pink, small, 2cm single flowers, mid season. Profuse, graceful. 2.5 × 2m.

Camellia 'Rosaeflora Cascade'
Species, very pale pink, small, single, mid season to late. Distinctive, cascading growth habit, top favourite. 2.5 × 2m.

Camellia 'Rose Bouquet'
Hybrid, rose pink, large, double rose form, mid season. Medium spreading growth, very showy. 2.5 × 2m.

Camellia 'Rose Parade'
Hybrid, deep rose pink, medium, formal double to rose form, early to late season. Vigorous compact grower. 2.5 × 2m.

Camellia 'Rosette'
Sasanqua, rose pink, small, semi double to rose form, early. Neat compact form. 2 × 1.5m.

Camellia 'Rudolph'
Hybrid, bright scarlet, large anemone form, early to late season. Average upright grower. 2.5 × 2m.

Camellia salicifolia
Species, white, miniature single blooms late season. Grown mainly for its foliage. Young shoots brick red, mature leaves oblong or elliptic-oblong, to 10 × 2.5cm, dark green and with incurved toothed margins. Rapid twiggy grower, needs regular trimming to maintain good form. Salicifolia — willow-like leaves. 2.5 × 2m.

Camellia 'San Dimas'
Japonica, bright red with golden pollen, large, semi-double, early to late, flowers profusely through the season. Compact bushy grower, among the best in this colour. 2.5 × 2m.

Camellia 'San Marino'
Reticulata hybrid, bright deep red, large semi-double with folded and curled petals, mid season. Strong vigorous grower. 3 × 2.5m.

Camellia 'Sanpei Tsubaki'
Japonica, single pink veined darker pink with petals bordered white, small, single, mid season to late, very free flowering. Strong upright grower. 2.5 × 2m.

Camellia 'Sasanqua Compacta'
Sasanqua, pure white with pink edge, medium single, early season. Forms a dense, dwarf rounded bush. 1 × 1m.

Camellia 'Satans Robe'
Reticulata hybrid, oriental red with golden stamens, large, semi-double, mid season. Vigorous upright habit. 3.5 × 3m.

Camellia 'Sawada's Dream'
Japonica, white to pale cream, outer petals shaded delicate flesh pink, large, formal double, mid season to late. 2.5 × 2m.

Camellia 'Scarlet Ballerina'
Japonica, bright scarlet, small neat hose-in-hose, semi-double, mid season. Vigorous, bushy upright grower. 2.5 × 2m.

Camellia 'Scented Gem'
Hybrid, pink with white central petaloids, miniature, anemone form, exceptionally early to late season, free flowering and fragrant. Vigorous bushy growth, outstanding container plant. 1.5 × 1m.

Camellia 'Scentsation'
Hybrid, clear pink, large informal double, fragrant, mid season to late. Average upright grower. 2.5 × 2m.

Camellia 'Scentuous'
Hybrid, white flushed pink on reverse of petals, small informal double, fragrant, mid season to late. Strong upright grower. Prefers semi-shade. 2 × 1.5m.

Camellia 'Setsugekka'
Sasanqua, pure white, medium semi-double, slight fragrance, early season. Upright rounded form. 2.5 × 2m.

Camellia 'Shirobotan'
Japonica, pure white, medium, semi-double with wavy fluted petals, bright golden stamens, mid season. 2.5 × 2m.

Camellia 'Shishi Gashira'
Sasanqua, light rose red, medium, semi-double to peony form, early. Willowy spreading habit. 2 × 1.5m.

Above: Camellia 'Cornelian' **58**

Above: Camellia 'Dixie Knight' **58**

Above: Camellia 'Dolly Dyer' **58**
Below: Camellia 'Dream Boat' **59**

Above: Camellia 'Debbie' **58**
Below: Camellia 'Dr Clifford Parkes' **58**

66

Above: Camellia 'Elegans Supreme' **59**

Above: Camellia 'Elegans Champagne' **59**
Below: Camellia 'Hulyn Smith' **60**

Above: Camellia 'Grand Slam' **60**
Below: Camellia 'Gayle Walden' **60**

Above: Camellia 'Huia' **60**

Above: Camellia 'Guilio Nuccio' **60**
Below: Camellia 'Hawaii' **60**

Above: Camellia 'Elegans Splendor' **59**
Below: Camellia 'Jamie' **60**

Above: Camellia 'Jubilation' **60**
Below: Camellia 'Lasca Beauty' **61**

Above: Camellia 'Just Sue' **61**
Below: Camellia 'Lemon Drop' **61**

Camellia 'Shocking Pink'
Hybrid, hot bright pink to tyrian rose, medium to large, semi-double to double with ruffled petals and petaloids interspersed with golden stamens, mid season to late, stunning colour. Compact grower. 2.5 × 2m.

Camellia 'Shot Silk'
Reticulata hybrid, spinel pink, large semi-double, mid season. Slender grower. 3 × 2m.

Camellia 'Showa no Sakae'
Sasanqua, soft pastel pink, semi-double to rose form, early to mid season. Slow spreading grower for ground cover, espalier etc. 1.5 × 1.5m.

Camellia 'Showa Supreme'
Sasanqua, rose pink, large, peony form, early, free flowering. Upright spreading habit. 2 × 1.5m.

Camellia 'Show Girl'
Hybrid, clear light pink, very large, semi-double, early to mid season, exceptional bloom, free flowering. 2.5 × 2m.

Camellia 'Silver Anniversary'
Japonica, pure white, very large, semi-double with irregular petals interspersed with gold stamens, mid season, free flowering, exceptional blooms. 2.5 × 2m.

Camellia 'Silver Chalice'
Japonica, waxen white, large, fully double to peony form, mid season, perfect bloom. Large foliage, upright and compact. 2.5 × 2m.

Camellia 'Silver Dollar'
Sasanqua, white, medium, informal double, early, similar flower to Moonlight or Mine no Yuki but on superior dense upright bush. 2 × 1.5m.

Camellia sinensis
Chinese Tea Plant
Species. Shrub or small tree, elliptic leaves to 9 × 3cm, crinkled, glossy, dark green above, lighter green beneath and with incurved, toothed margins. Tiny white single flowers from late summer. Strong bushy grower. 2.5 × 2m.

Camellia 'Snippet'
Hybrid, soft pink, small, semi-double with long, notched, narrow petals, mid season. Dwarf compact bush, good for containers or rock gardens. 1 × 1m.

Camellia 'Snowdrop'
Hybrid, white tinged pink, tiny, single, early to late season with the possibility of flushes of bloom at any time of the year, very free

flowering with clusters of buds at each leaf axil. Vigorous grower with long arching laterals. 1.5 × 1m.

Camellia 'Sparkling Burgundy'
Sasanqua, ruby rose overlaid with a sheen of lavender, medium, peony form with intermingled stamens and petaloids, early. Vigorous willowy habit. 2 × 1.5m.

Camellia 'S P Dunn'
Reticulata hybrid, clear dark red, very large semi-double, mid season to late. Highly recommended. 2.5 × 2m.

Camellia 'Spring Festival'
Hybrid, soft pink, miniature, rose form to semi-double, mid to late season. Small foliage, narrow upright habit, good for containers. 1.5 × 1m.

Camellia 'Spring Mist'
Hybrid, blush pink, miniature, semi-double, very early to late and fragrant. Slow, compact grower. 1.5 × 1m.

Camellia 'Sprite'
Hybrid, light salmon pink, small, informal double, mid season to late. Excellent compact bushy growth. 1.5 × 2m.

Camellia 'Star Above Star'
Sasanqua, white, delicately edged lavender pink, medium semi-double with petals layered in star formation, mid season. Upright bushy grower. 2 × 1.5m.

Camellia 'Strawberry Parfait'
Japonica, rose pink striped crimson, central cluster of pink and white petaloids interspersed with golden stamens, medium to large semi-double to loose peony form, mid season. Bushy upright grower. 2.5 × 2m.

Camellia 'Strawberry Swirl'
Japonica, rose pink margined white, occasionally red striped, medium to large, informal peony, early to late long flowering season. Vigorous upright bushy grower. Jury hybrid. 2.5 × 2m.

Camellia 'Sugar Babe'
Hybrid, clear pink, miniature formal double, mid season to late. Slow upright grower. 1.5 × 1m.

Camellia 'Sugar Dream'
Hybrid, pink with creamy pink centre, medium anemone form, slight fragrance, mid season to late. Open, broadly rounded grower. 2 × 1.5m.

Camellia 'Sundae'
Hybrid, light carmine red guard petals,

central boss of creamy petaloids, small, anemone form, mid season. Vigorous upright habit, Jury hybrid. 2.5 × 2m.

Camellia 'Sunset Oaks'
Japonica, marbled white and pink, some deeper pink, other with more white, yellow stamens, medium semi double, mid season. Upright grower. 2 × 1.5m.

Camellia 'Sunsong'
Japonica, rose pink, large formal double, early to late. Strong bushy grower, reliable bloomer. 2.5 × 2m.

Camellia 'Swan Lake'
Japonica, snow white, medium, semi-double or hose-in-hose form, mid to late. Bushy habit. 2.5 × 2m.

Camellia 'Taishuhai'
Sasanqua, white with a broad band of red around each petal, large, wide open single, early. Fast lacy growth, ideal espalier plant. 2.5 × 2m.

Camellia 'Takanini'
Japonica, glowing dark red, medium, anemone form, very early to late, long flowering season commencing early autumn. Strong bushy grower. 2.5 × 2m.   **79**

Camellia 'Tama no Ura'
Hybrid, red with white border, small single, early to mid. Fast spreading grower. 2 × 2m.

Camellia 'Tammia'
Japonica, white with pink border and centre, miniature to small, formal double with incurved, geometrically arranged petals, mid to late season. Medium, compact, upright grower, exquisite miniature. 1.5 × 1m.

Camellia 'Tanya'
Sasanqua, rose pink, small single, slight fragrance, early to mid season. Slow growing dwarf spreading growth. 1 × 1.2m.

Camellia 'Terrell Weaver'
Reticulata hybrid, flaming scarlet, very large semi-double to peony form, heavy textured petals with waxy sheen, mid season. Upright rounded to spreading growth. 2.5 × 2m.

Camellia 'Thumbellina'
Japonica, rich pink, small to medium formal double, mid season. Upright grower. 1.5 × 1m.

Camellia 'Tiffany'
Japonica, light orchid pink with deeper pink edges, very large, loose peony to anemone form, mid season to late. Hardy, vigorous, great show bloom. 2.5 × 2m.   **78**

Camellia 'Tinker Bell'
Japonica, medium pink often striped white or red, small anemone to double form, mid season. Upright compact grower. 1.5 × 1m.

Camellia 'Tinker Toy'
Japonica, white, lightly speckled and striped rose red, miniature, anemone form, mid season. Medium compact grower, attractive and different. 1.5 × 1m.

Camellia 'Tinsie'
Hybrid, red guard petals, central zone of white petaloids, miniature anemone form, mid season to late. Slender open grower. 2 × 1.5m.   **80**

Camellia 'Tiny Bud'
Japonica, clear pink, miniature semi-double to peony form with erect central petaloids, mid season to late. 1.5 × 1m.

Camellia 'Tiny Princess'
Hybrid, delicate pale pink with white shadings, miniature 2–3cm, semi-double to peony form with loose petals and tiny petaloids, mid season to late. Graceful form, blue-grey foliage. 2 × 1.5m.

Camellia 'Tiny Star'
Hybrid, soft pink, miniature, semi-double, early to mid. Open upright bush. 2 × 1.5m.

Camellia 'Tiptoe'
Hybrid, silvery pink, rose pink margins, medium semi-double, mid to late season. Slender, compact grower. 1.8 × 1m.

Camellia 'Tom Knudsen'
Japonica, dark red with deeper veining, medium to large, formal double to rose or peony form, early to mid season. Compact, upright growth. 2.5 × 2m.

Camellia 'Tom Thumb'
Hybrid, pink petals bordered white, small to medium formal double, medium to late. Strong bushy grower. 2.5 × 2m.   **80**

Camellia 'Tootsie'
Japonica, chalk white, miniature, formal double, mid season. Slow, dense compact growth. 1.5 × 1m.

Camellia transnokoensis
Species, white opening from reddish buds, tiny, single, flowers produced in masses, mid to late season. Dense tiny foliaged bush, ideal for containers. 1.5 × 1m.

Camellia 'Trinket'
Japonica, soft pink, miniature anemone form, mid season. Vigorous upright bushy grower, mid season. 2 × 1.5m.

Camellia 'Tsai'
Species, white, small 2cm, single, fragrant flowers borne in great abundance, mid season. Graceful habit, mahogany new growth. 2.5 × 2m.

Camellia 'Tui Song'
Reticulata, deep rose to red, very large, semi-double with waved petals and prominent stamens, mid season to late, excellent. 3 × 2.5m.

Camellia 'Twilight'
Japonica, light blush pink, medium to large, formal double, mid season. Vigorous, compact, upright growth. 2 × 1.5m.

Camellia 'Twinkle Star'
Japonica, deep glowing crimson overlaid with a glitter effect, medium, formal double to rose form, mid season. Upright bushy habit. 2.5 × 2m.

Camellia 'Un Ryu'
Hybrid, carmine red, small single tubular flowers, mid season. Un Ryu means 'The Corkscrew', so named for its zigzag growth habit, changing direction at each leaf axil. 2 × 1.5m.

Camellia 'Val Parker'
Japonica, deep red, medium semi-double with cup-shaped central petaloids and recurving outer petals, mid season to late. Slower growing to a compact bushy plant. 1.5 × 1m.

Camellia 'Valentine's Day'
Hybrid reticulata, salmon pink, very large, formal double, occasionally semi-double, mid season to late. Strong grower, award winner. 3.5 × 3m.   **80**

Camellia 'Valley Knudsen'
Hybrid, clear orchid pink, large semi-double, mid season to late. Upright pyramidal grower. 2.5 × 2m.

Camellia vietnamensis
Species, white, small, single, fragrant, mid season, from warmer areas of China. 2 × 1.5m.

Camellia 'Ville de Nantes'
Japonica, dark red blotched or marbled white, medium, semi-double with upright, heavily fimbriated petals, early to mid season. Slow, bushy growth. 2 × 1m.

Camellia 'Virginia Franco Rosea'
Japonica, pink with white border, small, formal double, mid season to late. Quick tall slender growth. 2.5 × 2m.   **80**

Camellia 'Volcano'
Hybrid, rich scarlet, large anemone form with long narrow petals and petaloids, mid season to late. Strong upright grower, raised by Camellia Haven, Auckland. 2.5 × 2m.

Camellia 'Waiwhetu Beauty'
Hybrid, light pink, medium informal double, mid season. Slow spreading grower, suited for ground-cover. 60cm × 1.5m

Camellia 'Waterlily'
Hybrid, vivid pink, medium, formal double, mid season to late, charming flower aptly named. Medium upright grower. 2 × 1.5m.   **77**

Camellia 'White Doves Benten'
Sasanqua, white, small informal double, early season. Dwarf grower with small, green and gold variegated leaves. Sport from Mine no Yuki. 1.5 × 1m.

Camellia 'White Hibiscus'
Hybrid, pure white, medium to large semi-double, mid season to late. Average upright grower. 2.5 × 2m.

Camellia 'White Nun'
Japonica, pure white, very large, semi-double with prominent gold stamens. Spreading growth. 2.5 × 2m.

Camellia 'Wilber Foss'
Hybrid, brilliant, pinkish carmine red, large, full peony form, early to late, Vigorous upright growth. 2.5 × 2m.

Camellia 'Wildfire'
Japonica, vibrant sheer scarlet, medium, single to semi-double, mid season, profuse bloomer. Vigorous, upright grower, spectacular colour. 2.5 × 2m.

Camellia 'Wilhelmina'
Miniature, clear soft pink with deeper pink edges and white tipped centres, small 25mm, formal double with incurved petals, early to late. Compact growth, hardy, lasts well as cut flower. 2 × 1.5m.

Camellia 'William Hertrich'
Hybrid reticulata, deep cherry red, very large, semi-double with heavily textured and waved petals and greyish yellow stamens, mid season to late, incredible flower. 3 × 2.5m.

Camellia 'Wirlinga Belle'
Hybrid, soft pink, small single, mid season to late. Strong bushy grower, arching branches. 2.5 × 2m.

Camellia 'Wirlinga Princess'
Hybrid, pale pink fading to white in the centre, miniature single to semi-double, crinkled petals, mid season. 2 × 1.5m.

Camellia 'Woodford Harrison'
Reticulata, deepest rich rose red, large semi-double with heavy texture, mid season to late. Vigorous upright grower. Seedling from 'Crimson Robe'. 2.5 × 2m.

Camellia 'Wyn Rayner'
Hybrid, bright cyclamen pink, medium, semi-double to peony form, early to late, free flowering. Vigorous, hardy. 2.5 × 2m.

Camellia 'Yoimachi'
Sasanqua hybrid, white faintly edged pink, small single, early to late. Strong upright hardy grower blooming over six months. Sasanqua × fraterna. 2.5 × 2m.

Camellia 'Yours Truly'
Japonica, light pink, prominently veined deep pink and bordered white, central cluster of gold-tipped stamens, medium, semi double, mid season. Bushy, slower than normal growth, wavy foliage. 1.5 × 1m.

Camellia 'Yuletide'
Sasanqua, orange red, medium, single with bright yellow stamens, early. Erect compact grower. 2.5 × 2m.

Camellia 'Zambo'
Hybrid, crimson with blue or purple overtones, small formal double, mid season to late. Average upright grower. 2.5 × 2m.

CAMELLIA READY REFERENCE

Red
'Amanda Lisa'
'Black Lace'
'Black Opal'
'Black Tie'
'Bob Hope'
'Bob's Tinsie'
'Bonanza'
'Bonsai Baby'
'Bright Buoy'
'Burgundy Boy'
'Burgundy Gem'
'C M Hovey'
'Captain Rawes'
'Clarise Carleton'
'Crimson King'
'Crimson Robe'
'Dazzler'
'Deep Secret'
'Diamond Head'
'Dixie Knight'
'Dolly Dyer'
'Dr Burnside'
'Dr Clifford Parkes'
'Fairy Wand'
'Fire Falls'
'Firedance'
'Fox's Fancy'
'Freedom Bell'
'Glen 40'
'Grand Prix'
'Grand Slam'
'Guilio Nuccio'
'Harold L Paige'
'Hiryu'
'Holly Bright'
'Island of Fire'
'Jamie'
'Jan's Choice'
'Kelly McKnight'
'Koru Tsubaki'
'Kramer's Supreme'

'L T Dees'
'Laura Walker'
'Les Jury'
'Little Babe'
'Little Bit'
'Little Red Riding Hood'
'Little Ruby'
'Little Slam'
'Margaret Hilford'
'Mark Allen'
'Maroon and Gold'
'Mathotiana Supreme'
'Mathotiana'
'Midnight'
'Miss Charleston'
'Miss Tulare'
'Moshio'
'Night Rider'
'Nokogiri Ba'
'Nuccios Ruby'
'Pagoda'
'Pirates Gold'
'Professor Sargent'
'Red Dahlia'
'Red Ensign'
'Red Red Rose'
'Reg Ragland Supreme'
'Reigyoku'
'Rendezvous'
'Roger Hall'
'Rudolph'
'S P Dunn'
'San Dimas'
'San Marino'
'Satans Robe'
'Scarlet Ballerina'
'Shishi Gashira'
'Takanini'
'Terrell Weaver'
'Tom Knudsen'
'Tui Song'
'Twinkle Star'

'Un Ryu'
'Val Parker'
'Volcano'
'Wilber Foss'
'Wildfire'
'William Hertrich'
'Woodford Harrison'
'Yuletide'

Pink
'Adorable'
'Aino Izumi'
'Allison Leigh Woodroof'
'Alpen Glo'
'Annette Carol'
Anticipation'
'Applause'
'Aquarius'
'Ave Maria'
'Aztec'
'Baby Bear'
'Ballet Queen'
'Bambino'
'Barbara Clark'
'Bellbird'
'Berenice Boddy'
'Bert Jones'
'Bett's Supreme'
'Betty Patricia'
'Betty Ridley'
'Billie McFarland'
'Botan Yuki'
'Brian'
'Brigadoon'
'Buddha'
'Buttons 'n' Bows'
'C M Wilson'
'Cameron Cooper'
'Can Can'
'Chansonette'
'China Doll'
'Choji Guruma'

'Chrysanthemum Petal'
'Contemplation'
'Cornish Snow'
'Cotton Candy'
'Cover Girl'
'Daintiness'
'Daitairin'
'Dave's Weeper'
'Debbie'
'Debutante'
'Dellie McCaw'
'Demi Tasse'
'Donation'
'Dr Lilyan Hanchey'
'Dr Tinsley'
'Drama Girl'
'Dream Girl'
'E G Waterhouse'
'Easter Morn'
'El Dorado'
'Elegans Splendor'
'Elegans Supreme'
'Elegans'
'Elegant Beauty'
'Elfin Rose'
'Elsie Jury'
'Elsie Ruth Marshall'
'Exquisite'
'Fashionata'
'Flower Girl'
'Francie L'
'Fraterna'
'Gay Baby'
'Gay Pixie'
'Gayle Walden'
'Guest of Honour'
'Gwen Pike'
'Hawaii'
'Howard Asper'
'Huia'
'Hulyn Smith'
'Interlude'

'Isaribi'
'Itty Bit'
'Jean May'
'Julie Felix'
'Just Darling'
'K O Hester'
'Kewpie Doll'
'Kramer's Fluted Coral'
'Lady Clare'
'Lasca Beauty'
'Laurie Bray'
'Leonard Messel'
'Little Pearl'
'Lois Shibnault'
'Lovely Lady'
'Lucinda'
'Margaret Bernhardt'
'Mary Paige'
'Mary Phoebe Taylor'
'Mary Wheeler'
'Mini Pink'
'Miss Bessie Beville'
'Miss Tiny Tot Princess'
'Misty Moon'
'Mona Jury'
'Mouchang'
'Mrs D W Davis'
'Mrs Tingley'
'Myrtifolia'
'Nonie Haydon'
'Nuccio's Cameo'
'Nymph'
'Odoratissima'
'Ole'
'Pacific Beauty'
'Peach Blossom'
'Pink Cameo'
'Pink Dahlia'
'Pink Diddy'
'Pink Gold'
'Pink Pagoda'
'Pink Perfection'
'Plantation Pink'
'Pride of California'
'Queenslander'
'Rosaeflora Cascade'
'Rosaeflora'
'Rose Parade'
'Rosette'
'Scentsation'
'Shocking Pink'
'Shot Silk'
'Show Girl'
'Showa no Sakae'
'Showa Supreme'
'Snippet'
'Spring Festival'

'Spring Mist'
'Sprite'
'Sugar Babe'
'Sugar Dream'
'Tanya'
'Thumbellina'
'Tiffany'
'Tiny Bud'
'Tiny Princess'
'Tiny Star'
'Tiptoe'
'Trinket'
'Twilight'
'Valentine's Day'
'Valley Knudsen'
'Virginia Franco Rosea'
'Waiwhetu Beauty'
'Waterlily'
'Wirlinga Belle'
'Wirlinga Princess'
'Wyn Rayner'

White
'Alba Plena'
'Apple Blossom'
'Ariel Song'
'Autumn Herald'
'Baby Pearl'
'Baby Willow'
'Beatrice Emily'
'Blondie'
'Christmas Daffodil'
'Cinnamon Cindy'
'Commander Mulroy'
'Coronation'
'Cranes Feather'
'Dawn'
'Desire'
'Dorothy Culver'
drupifera
'Early Pearly'
'Ecclefield'
'Fimbriata'
'Frivolity'
'Fukuzutsumi'
'Gay Sue'
'Ginger'
'Grace Albritton'
'James Lockington'
'K Sawada'
'Kitty'
'Kona'
'Lemon Drop'
'Lilemac'
longicarpa
'Lovelight'
'Lulu Belle'

lutchuensis
'Mansize'
'Mary Alice Cox'
'Maui'
'Mine no Yuki'
'Nuccio's Gem'
oleifera
'Onetia Holland'
'Pink Smoke'
pitardii
'Quintessence'
salicifolia
'Sasanqua Compacta'
'Setsugekka'
'Shirobotan'
'Silver Anniversary'
'Silver Chalice'
'Silver Dollar'
sinensis
'Snowdrop'
'Star Above Star'
'Swan Lake'
'Tootsie'
transnokoensis
'Tsai'
vietnamensis
'White Doves Benten'
'White Hibiscus'
'White Nun'
'Yoimachi'

Cream and yellow
'Ballet Dancer'
'Brushfield's Yellow'
'Chrysantha'
'Dahlohnega'
'Elegans Champagne'
'Fendig'
'Gwenyth Morey'
'Jury's Yellow'
'Leonora Novick'
'Sawada's Dream'

Mauve
'Dona Herzilia'
'Dream Boat'
'Jennifer Susan'
'Little Lavender'
'Mimosa Jury'
'Nicky Crisp'
'Sparkling Burgundy'
'Zambo'

Multi-colour
'Amazing Graces'
'Angel Wings'
'Anticipation Variegated'

'Baby Sis'
'Ballet Queen Variegata'
'Barbara Woodroof'
'Betty Sheffield Supreme'
'Betty's Beauty'
'Bonnie Belle'
'Carter's Sunburst'
'Cinderella'
'Cornelian'
'Extravaganza'
'Fire Chief Variegated'
'Gayborder'
'Hakuhan Kujaku'
'Hopkins Pink'
'Jubilation'
'Jury's Sunglow'
'Just Sue'
'Kick Off'
'Kishu Tsukasa'
'Lady Loch'
'Little Bit Variegated'
'Little Michael'
'Look Away'
'Margaret Davis'
'Mini Mint'
'Modern Art'
'Moutancha'
'Navajo'
'Nishiki Kirin'
'Nuccio's Jewel'
'Nuccio's Pearl'
'Our Betty Variegated'
'Parisienne'
'Purple Gown'
'R L Wheeler'
'Rainbow'
'Raspberry Ice'
'Raspberry Ripple'
'Richard Nixon'
'Sanpei Tsubaki'
'Scented Gem'
'Scentuous'
'Strawberry Parfait'
'Strawberry Swirl'
'Sundae'
'Sunset Oaks'
'Sunsong'
'Taishuhai'
'Tama no Ura'
'Tammia'
'Tinker Bell'
'Tinker Toy'
'Tinsie'
'Tom Thumb'
'Ville de Nantes'
'Wilhelmina'
'Yours Truly'

CANTUA

A genus of six species of evergreen shrubs and small trees from South America, Cantua being the Quechua vernacular name for C buxifolia. The plants have a loose open, untidy growth habit, but impress with their showy clusters of brilliant tubular flowers. Plant in deeply worked, organically enriched, free-draining soil in full sun. Prune after flowering to maintain good shape, or leave to twine through neighboring shrubs.
Polemoniaceae.

Cantua buxifolia
Sacred Flower of the Incas, Magic Flower
Found at high altitudes in Peru, Bolivia and Chile. Open, woody shrub with twiggy branchlets and variable, elliptic to lanceolate, dull green leaves to 5cm long, mostly much smaller. Striking, 6–8cm tubular flowers, pink or purple with yellow stripes and intense-red flaring lobes to 4cm across, borne gracefully in pendent clusters of 4–8 from all parts of the plant during spring. Buxifolia — box-leafed. Evergreen. 1.5 × 1m. **89**

CAREX

A genus of perhaps 1000 species of grass-like perennial herbs widely distributed throughout the arctic and temperate regions of the world, but mainly China, Japan and Korea, named from the Greek *keiro*, to cut in reference to the sharp leaf margins of some species. Generally, they are found in damp woodlands, alongside lakes or streams, in bogs or alpine locations with high rainfall.

The relatively few in cultivation add a touch of natural alpine ruggedness or tone and texture to rock or feature gardens especially in damp spots. Extremely hardy under almost any garden conditions. Plant in average, deeply worked soil in full sun or partial shade. Feed occasionally with a balanced fertilizer, and water deeply during dry spells. When plants become untidy, cut off top growth to within 5cm of the ground. They recover rapidly with renewed vigour.
Cyperaceae. *All evergreen.*

Carex buchananii
Attractive, New Zealand native grass forming a densely tufted, tussock-like plant with dark bronze purple leaves to 75cm × 1–2mm. Upright, graceful form for special effects. Hardy to wind and cold and grows in any soil. 80 × 50cm.

Carex comans
New Zealand native, densely tufted, tussock grass with blue-green foliage to 40cm × 1–2mm, bleached and curled at the ends. Good for mass planting. Comans — hairy. 30 × 50cm.

Carex dissita
New Zealand native, tall densely tufted sedge with flat, smooth, dark green, deeply grooved, grass-like leaves to 75cm × 6mm. Flower spikes with pale brown, nodding spikelets appear spring to mid summer. Dissita — lying apart or well spaced. 90 × 75cm.

Carex flagellifera
New Zealand native dwarf grass or tussock-like plant with slender leaves to 30cm × 1mm tapering to a point, coloured light brown to bronze purple, pinkish when young, curving to the ground. Flagellifera — bearing long, thin or supple shoots. 40 × 50cm.

Carex flagellifera 'Frosted Curls'
Attractive variation, forming a dwarf tussock-like plant with light silver leaves. Graceful, hardy and valuable for special landscaping effects. 40 × 50cm.

Carex lucida
At first glance not obviously distinctive from C flagellifera, but with richer brown colouring, a little taller and more elegant. At its best in groups. Lucida — bright, shining or clear. 50 × 50cm.

Carex morrowii 'Evergold'
Japanese sedge with tapering leaves to 60cm × 8mm, richly variegated green with bright creamy yellow band, gracefully arching and spreading out from ground level. Forms a neat compact and colourful clump. Best in shaded feature gardens or container plant. Refurbishes well after hard pruning. Syn C morrowii variegata. 30 × 30cm.

Carex testacea
New Zealand native, loosely tufted, clump forming tussock grass with distinctive green and brick-orange foliage. Hardy to cold and wind and grows in most soils. Testacea — brick coloured. 60 × 50cm.

Carex trifida
New Zealand native, robust, tall weeping grass with smooth, rigid leaves to 1.5m × 12mm and fine rough margins, green at first later becoming quite blue. Nodding flower spikes with attractive large brown seed heads in summer. Trifida — cleft into three parts. 1.5 × 1m.

CARMICHAELIA

Apart from one found on Lord Howe Island, the genus of some 40 species is confined to New Zealand and named after 18th–19th century Scottish army officer, botanist and plant collector Captain Dugald Carmichael. An unusual and remarkable group varying from small depressed shrubs of a few centimetres to small trees. When mature, most species are leafless, the grooved, flattened or rounded branchlets which have stomata and contain chlorophyll function as leaves. They bear pea-like flowers.

New Zealand Broom as it is commonly known is worth growing for attractive growth patterns, unusual stem texture and floral beauty. Mostly very hardy, tolerant of coastal exposure and varying soil conditions, either poorly drained or dry soils. They have a preference for good garden conditions with adequate moisture.
Leguminosae. *All evergreen.*

Carmichaelia aligera
Erect shrub with finely grooved branchlets. Compound juvenile leaves with up to seven obcordate to obovate-cuneate, 15 × 12mm leaflets. Green, wide-flattened, weeping mature stems smothered in summer with racemes of small white, yellow and purple pea-shaped flowers followed by obliquely oblong, 10 × 5mm fruit with orange seeds. 3 × 2m.

Carmichaelia odorata
Compact, multi-branched shrub with spreading branches and drooping, grooved and flanged branchlets about 2mm wide. Sweetly fragrant, white flowers veined and mottled purple, 3–4mm long, borne through summer in racemes of up to ten, followed by straw coloured pods. Discovered between Wairoa and Waikaremoana in 1843 by William Colenso who named it odorata for its strong fragrance. 2 × 1.5m.

Carmichaelia williamsii
Occurs in coastal and semi-coastal areas from Poor Knights Island to East Cape, Bay of Plenty. An erect, multi-branched shrub with thin, glabrous, 8–12mm close-grooved branchlets. Juvenile leaves trifoliate with narrow, obovate or obcordate leaflets. Large,

25mm, pale yellow flowers veined and blotched purple maroon appear in racemes of up to six, spring and early summer, followed by dark brown or black 30 × 7mm seed capsules. Prefers good drainage. Named for Bishop Williams of Waiapu who found the species at Hicks Bay. 2.5 × 1.5m.

CARPENTARIA

A genus of one species of solitary palms, endemic to northern Australia, named for a former Governor General of the Dutch East Indies, P de Carpentier. Although from the tropical north, this stately palm has been grown as far south as Sydney. However, in temperate to subtropical gardens, this palm requires shelter from strong winds and frost, deeply worked, organically enriched, well drained soil, deep mulching and adequate moisture at all times.
Palmae.

Carpentaria acuminata
Carpentaria Palm
Found along the margins of lowland rainforests and banks of streams in Northern Territory near Darwin, a stately palm with slender, smooth, grey, ringed trunk terminating in a smooth green crownshaft from which faded leaves fall naturally. Arching, pinnately divided fronds to 3m long with about 88 pairs of deep green leaflets. During late winter and spring, large clusters of creamy white flowers appear below the crownshaft, followed by bunches of bright crimson, 15mm, fruit with yellow calyx, ripe early summer. Majestic, graceful palm for avenue planting, parks and home landscaping in suitable climatic zones. Acuminata — tapering to a sharp, narrow point. Evergreen. 15 × 5m.

CARPINUS

A genus of around 35 species of hardy deciduous trees belonging to the beech family found over the temperate regions of the Europe, East Asia, North and Central America. Meaning of Carpinus is obscure, but Hornbeam is said to arise from the use of the bone-hard wood in making ox-yokes. Hornbeams are very beautiful trees, bearing curious yellow catkins in spring, pendulous clusters of winged fruit and brilliant leaves in autumn, plus handsome bark and

picturesque branch pattern during winter. Carpinus grows in almost any reasonable soil.
Carpinaceae.

Carpinus betulus
European Hornbeam
From Europe, Asia Minor. Grows moderately in dense pyramidal form, maturing to a broad outline, grey bark, networked with metallic-blue striations and drooping outer branches. Young shoots covered with light grey downy hairs. Leaves ovate to ovate-oblong, green, deeply ribbed, to 12 × 6cm with small irregular margins, turning yellow, dark red or rich brown in autumn and remaining on the tree almost through winter.

Male flowers in the form of 7cm, pendent catkins comprised of three-lobed bracts. Female catkins appear at the end of each twig. Male catkins fall after shedding pollen followed in autumn by the development on female flowers, of small 5mm ovate one-seeded nuts in pairs attached to three-lobed wings enjoyed by birds and other wildlife. Remaining seeds are carried away by the wind, borne aloft by three-pointed wings to germinate on the forest floor some eighteen months later. Betulus — resembling birch. Deciduous. 15 × 10m.

CARPODETUS

A genus of about ten species of shrubs and small trees from Papua New Guinea and one from New Zealand named from the Greek *karpos*, fruit and *detos*, bound, in reference to the fruit being contracted in the centre. Original specimens were collected in Queen Charlotte Sound by botanists Banks and Solander accompanying Captain Cook on his first voyage in 1769. A worthwhile tree to grow as an isolated specimen or small canopy to lightly shade or shelter plants beneath it. Hardy, grows moderately fast. Best in a semi-shady location in deeply-dug, good garden soil which tends to remain moist.
Escalloniaceae.

Carpodetus serratus
Putaputaweta
From coastal, lowland and mountain forests and along the banks of streams throughout the North, South and Stewart Islands. Forms a small flat-topped, shapely small tree distinguished by pale greyish-white bark. Juvenile leaves to 3cm, broadly elliptic, almost rounded. Adult leaves to 6cm, ovate-elliptic, leathery, dark green with attractive lighter marbling, and with waved and

toothed margins. Small, 5mm, white flowers carried in 5cm panicles early summer to mid autumn, followed by small, pea-sized, black capsules. Serratus — saw-toothed. Evergreen. 5 × 3m.

CARYA

A genus of about 25 species of large, deciduous trees from eastern USA, central and south east China, named from the Greek *karya*, a nut bearing tree. The genus includes Pecan and Hickory trees. Apart from their nut-bearing qualities, Carya species grow into magnificent specimen or shade trees with stately boles and impressive crowns of pinnate leaves which colour brilliantly in autumn.

Plant in deeply worked, organically enriched, free-draining soil which tends to retain moisture. Mulch freely and water generously until the tree is well established. Stake securely and remove lower branches early to allow adequate headroom.
Juglandaceae.

Carya ovata
Shagbark Hickory
Grows to a sizeable tree with shaggy, greyish bark. Palmate leaves to about 30cm, pubescent beneath at first, five leaflets obovate to elliptic to 15cm, becoming rich yellow in autumn. Attractive spring catkin display, followed in autumn by ellipsoid, angled, thin-shelled, white nuts. Numerous selected cultivars for superior nut production are listed in the Northern Hemisphere. Ovata — ovate or egg-shaped. Deciduous. 8 × 6m.

CARYOPTERIS

A genus of about six species of herbs or shrubs from east Asia, named from the Greek *karyon*, nut and *pteron*, wing in reference to winged seeds. Hardy, easily grown plants valued for aromatic leaves and clusters of blue flowers through summer and autumn. Excellent amongst herbaceous plants, annuals or shrubs in beds or borders to take advantage of its colour. Grow in full sun in deeply worked, organically enriched, free-draining soil. Prune hard late winter for growth renewal and maximum flower production. Pruning after each wave of flower encourages near-constant blooms.
Verbenaceae.

Caryopteris × clandonensis
Blue Spiraea, Bluebeard
An English hybrid shrub valued for its contribution of blue to the garden during summer and autumn. Leaves elliptic to ovate lanceolate to 10cm, grey-green above, greyish white beneath with slightly toothed margins. Terminal and axillary clusters of bright blue flowers from early summer to late autumn. A tidy grower, bringing a contribution of true blue to any garden. Deciduous. 1 × 1m.

CASSIA

A genus of more than 500 species of annuals, shrubs and small trees mostly from warm temperate or tropical regions of both hemispheres named from the Greek *kasia*. Some species yield the senna leaves and pods of pharmacy. The New RHS Dictionary of Gardening now includes most Cassia species in the genus Senna. The cultivar 'John Ball' has for years been amongst the most popular shrubs for its brilliant displays of golden yellow flowers at a time of the year when garden colour is scarce. Plant in deeply worked, free-draining soil in sunny, open conditions without excessive wind. Flowers on current season's shoots and benefits from annual pruning to keep compact and encourage maximum bloom.
    Leguminosae.

Cassia corymbosa 'John Ball'
Buttercup Tree
From southern USA, Uruguay and Argentina. Forms a shapely rounded bush with dark green, pinnate leaves divided into three or four pairs of oblanceolate, 5cm leaflets which fold at night. Becomes a total mass of bloom as shining rich yellow, cup-shaped flowers with prominent golden stamens, like big buttercups appear from mid autumn, well into winter. Hardy in all but the coldest districts. Corymbosa — provided with corymbs. Evergreen. 2 × 2m.   **89**

CASSINIA

A genus of twenty species of evergreen shrubs from Australia, New Zealand and South Africa named for Count Henri de Cassini, early 19th century French botanist specializing in Compositae. Hardy, easily grown shrubs with heathlike leaves and white, cotton-like flowers,

valued for the ability to grow in almost any soil type in dry, exposed places and for the protection they afford more tender species. Annual pruning after flowering will keep them neat and compact.
    Compositae. *All evergreen.*

Cassinia fulvida
Golden Taihinu, Golden Cottonwood
Abounds in riverbeds or sandy coastal areas on eastern coastal areas of New Zealand's North Island. Erect shrub with slender, tomentose and sticky, gold coloured, stems and foliage. Crowded, linear leaves to 8 × 2mm with slightly recurved margins, greenish above, yellow beneath. Creamy, 5mm flowerheads in dense corymbs. Fulvida — tawny yellow. 1m × 80cm.

Cassinia retorta
Hardy New Zealand species with tomentose branches and crowded, linear- obovate, 5 × 2mm, leathery, glabrous, blue-grey to silvery green leaves with recurved margins, white tomentose beneath. White flowers clustered above the foliage in small corymbs. Retorta — twisted back. Evergreen. 1 × 80cm.

Cassinia vauvilliersii
Mountain Cottonwood
From drier areas of subalpine scrubland or grassland south of Auckland, New Zealand. Forms an erect, multi-branched, bushy shrub, its stout, furrowed branches covered with yellowish tomentum, and leathery, dark green, linear-obovate leaves to 12 × 3mm, quite viscid above, covered with tawny yellow tomentum beneath. White flowers clustered in rounded corymbs. A form known as C vauvilliersii albida is similar but with white tomentose branches. 1.5 × 1m.

CASTANEA

A genus of about twelve species of deciduous trees from eastern North America, southern Europe, China and Japan, named from the Latin, *castanea*. The Sweet Chestnut has been cultivated for more than 3000 years and become naturalized in many parts of the world. The Romans introduced it to Britain during their long spell of occupation between AD 42 and AD 410 as a food source for their troops, but although the trees flourished, the English climate seemed unsuitable for bountiful harvests.
    Castaneas are attractive, drought tolerant, trees, hardy in all climates, perfect for wide open spaces which in time

will develop into a large spreading tree up to 30m high with a trunk 4m or more. Imposing specimen for schools, parks, reserves, farms or motor camps where it quickly provides shade and becomes more and more majestic over generations. They have a preference for deeply worked, free-draining, slightly acid, loamy soil. Water deeply during dry periods for the first two years until obviously established.
    Fagaceae.

Castanea sativa
Sweet Chestnut
Forms a tall, stately tree with furrowed, dark grey to black bark. Winter twigs stout, angular and marked by ridges and large, plump pinkish brown buds. Oblong-lanceolate, glossy, green leaves to 25 × 10cm with prominent veins and sharply toothed margins. Slender catkins which open mid-summer usually carry both male and female flowers. Fruit is in the form of a prickly burr enclosing up to three large brown nuts, pleasant to eat when roasted. Sativa — cultivated rather than spontaneous. Deciduous. 15 × 9m.

CASUARINA

A genus of about 40 species of trees and shrubs from Australia and the Pacific, named from the fancied resemblance of long drooping branches to the feathers of the Cassowary. The term Sheoke or She Oak arises from a similarity of the wood to Quercus or Oak trees. Some thirty species are endemic in Australia, distinctive trees, with unique character and pleasing appearance. Re-classified in 1982, a number of Australian species now appear under Allocasuarina including C torulosa. However, it is retained here for simplicity.
    Casuarinas grow rapidly and without fuss, adapt to extremes of soil and climate and perform where other species struggle. Some revel in poor, dry, sandy conditions exposed to salt-laden coastal winds. Adequate soil preparation and watering during the establishment will get them away to a flying start. Use Casuarinas for softening architectural lines, rapid screening, protection from wind and sun or erosion control.
    Casuarinaceae. *All evergreen.*

Casuarina cunninghamiana
River She Oak
The tallest of Australia's Casuarinas, majestic trees found along the banks of rivers

and streams of Queensland, New South Wales and Northern Territory. Graceful, branch and stem structure, densely covered with drooping, very fine, almost hair-like, deep green branchlets. Small reddish-brown flowers and rectangular, 8cm cones. Suitable as a wind or noise barrier, screen or shade tree in public or private gardens. Valuable for erosion control near streams or dams. Named for A Cunningham. 8 × 5m.

Casuarina glauca
Swamp She Oak
Medium growing, somewhat upright tree with attractive clusters of fine, rich grey-green, pendulous branchlets. Found naturally in saline marshes in Queensland, New South Wales and Victoria. Thrives in harsh conditions such as damp, brackish swamps, salty or poor dry soil. Spreading by underground suckers, it has proved excellent as a sand or soil binder. Versatile tree for garden, park, stock shelter or erosion control. Glauca — having grey or whitish powdery coating. 8 × 4m.

Casuarina torulosa
Forest Oak
One of many Australian Casuarinas now listed as Allocasuarina. Found frequently on gravelly or sandy soils in open forests of Queensland and New South Wales. A small tree with rough, corky bark, shaped like a pyramid or cone with colourful, drooping, finely textured branchlets, distinctly reddish purple in colour. When in flower, the tree appears quite rusty or dark brown. Effective from the moment of planting. Excellent suburban tree. Torulosa — thickened at intervals. 6 × 4m.

CATALPA

A genus of eleven species of deciduous, large-leaved trees from North America, Cuba, south west China and Tibet, Catalpa being the North American Indian name.

Distinctly beautiful, lawn and avenue trees with tropical appearance, particularly showy when in flower during spring. Adaptable to extremes of heat and cold and grows in cool, moist, loamy, fertile soil in full sun. Choose a site with maximum protection from wind to minimize damage to large leaves. Train when young to develop a clean stem with enough clearance beneath lower branches.

Bignoniaceae. *All deciduous.*

Catalpa bignonioides
Tree Bignonia
North American native tree with rounded crown and clean, straight, shapely trunk and light brown bark. Large, green, 10–20cm, cordate to ovate, heart-shaped leaves resembling Pawlonia usually carried in pairs, with unpleasant odour when crushed. Spectacular in spring and summer with magnificent creamy-white, 5cm flowers, striped purple and spotted yellow. Flowers trumpet-shaped like bignonia, carried in large, erect, pyramidal clusters displayed over a carpet of lush foliage. Bean-shaped capsules to 35cm long. Bignonioides — resembling Bignonia. 8 × 6m.

Catalpa bignonioides 'Aurea'
Attractive cultivar, retaining its handsome, butter-yellow, velvety foliage spring through autumn. As above, but somewhat smaller. 5 × 4m.

Catalpa speciosa
Western Catalpa
Native to central United States, naturally a large, pyramidal tree to 30m with 3m trunk. Large, green, glabrous leaves to 30x20cm, cordate or heart-shaped, pubescent beneath and without odour when crushed. Bell-shaped flowers with a 5cm flare, white spotted purple and with yellow stripes in the throat produced about two weeks ahead of C bignonioides. Flowers larger, but less in each cluster. Bean-like capsules to 55cm long. Speciosa — showy. 9 × 7m.

CAVENDISHIA

A genus of about 100 species of evergreen shrubs or small trees from tropical South America, named for the 18th–19th century Duke of Devonshire, William Spencer Cavendish of Chatsworth House in Derbyshire.

Closely related to Agapetes, Leucothoe and Pieris, enjoying similar conditions — deeply worked, organically enriched, slightly acid, free-draining soil in partial shade. Mulch deeply to keep the roots cool and retain moisture. Water freely during dry periods. Prune lightly after flowering.

Ericaceae.

Cavendishia acuminata
Colombian Heath
Handsome shrub from the Andes Mountains of Colombia and Ecuador. Gracefully pendulous branches, new shoots pink to coral red. Firm, leathery, 5–8cm, ovate to lanceolate, dark green leaves with lighter reverse. Showy, bright crimson, 2cm flowers with pale green tips, enclosed in coral red bracts, borne in short racemes late spring through autumn. Acuminata — tapering to a long narrow point. Evergreen. 1.8 × 1.3m.

CEANOTHUS

North America and in particular California is home to some 55 species of hardy evergreen Ceanothus named from the Greek *keanothos*, a spiny plant, although few species are prickly to the touch. They abound throughout the mountains and foothills of California in forms ranging from carpets to trees. Commonly known as Californian Lilac, they've become one of the most cultivated blue-flowered shrubs in many parts of the world.

They have a preference for hot, dry, free-draining soil in full sun. Yearly pruning to half way prevents legginess and preserves vigour. Taller growers need staking in exposed locations as excessive movement causes root damage and the ultimate collapse of the plant. There are types for ground, rock or bank cover, backgrounds, foregrounds and single specimens.

Rhamnaceae. *All evergreen.*

Ceanothus 'Blue Carpet'
Low-growing plant with small, glossy green foliage and masses of rich blue, 'candy floss' flowers during spring. Forms a dense carpet, ideal for rockeries, ground cover or spilling over walls. 60 × 1.5m.

Ceanothus 'Blue Cushion'
Fast growing spreading shrub or ground cover. Small, rich green foliage and an abundance of rich blue flowers. New Zealand registered cultivar, possibly of C gloriosus. .75 × 1.5m.

Ceanothus gloriosus 'Emily Brown'
Fast growing ground cover spreading by rooting branches. Thick, dark green, glossy, holly-like, 25mm leaves. Masses of dark violet-blue flowers in short, 25mm clusters. Will fill large areas. 60cm–1m × 2.5–4m.

Ceanothus griseus horizontalis 'Yankee Point'
Carmel Creeper
Excellent, refined ground cover with dense, dark-green, glossy, 35mm leaves and profuse clusters of bright blue flowers. 60cm–1m × 2.5m.

Above: Camellia 'Pagoda' **63**
Below: Camellia 'Waterlily' **70**

Below: Camellia 'Little Bit Variegated' **61**

78

Above: Camellia 'Mark Allen' **62**

Above: Camellia 'Tiffany' **69**

Above: Camellia 'Purple Gown' **64**
Below: Camellia 'Modern Art' **62**

Above: Camellia 'Maroon and Gold' **62**
Below: Camellia 'Mary Wheeler' **62**

Above: Camellia 'Nonie Haydon' **63**

Above: Camellia 'Nuccio's Jewel' **63**

Above: Camellia 'Margaret Davis' **62**
Below: Camellia 'Takanini' **69**

Above: Camellia 'Nuccios Ruby' **63**
Below: Camellia 'Raspberry Ripple' **64**

Above: Camellia 'Tinsie' **70**
Below: Camellia 'Tom Thumb' **70**

Above: Camellia 'Valentine's Day' **70**
Below: Camellia 'Virginia Franco Rosea' **70**

Ceanothus impressus
Santa Barbara Ceanothus
Distinguished by dense, flexuous branches and small, wrinkled, furrowed, dark green, 6–12mm leaves. Branches covered in spring with rich, deep-blue flowers. Impressus — sunken or impressed. 1.30 × 1.30m.

Ceanothus 'Joyce Coulter'
Very vigorous, extremely wide-spreading plant, leaves and flowers resembling C roweanus. Good bank or ground cover. 1 × 4m.

Ceanothus 'Julia Phelps'
Deep indigo-blue flowers in 25mm clusters. Small, 12mm, dark green leaves. Wide-growing shrub splendid for screens or specimen. Similar to C impressus. 2 × 3m.

Ceanothus 'Marie Simon'
Excellent pink-flowered variety with small leaves and distinctive reddish-brown stems. Blooms throughout summer. Requires less pruning. Semi-deciduous. 1.30 × 1m.

Ceanothus papillosus 'Roweanus'
Wart Leaf Ceanothus
Brilliant deep-blue heads of bloom almost cover the whole plant. Dark-green, linear to oblong, 10mm leaves with small raised spots. Neat compact habit. Excellent choice as a blue-flowered shrub. Papillosus — having surface protuberances. 2 × 1.5m.　　　　**89**

C E D R E L A

A genus of about twenty species of trees from tropical America, China, India, Malaysia and Australia named from the Greek *kedros* a cedar. The heartwood of some species has a resemblance to that of the cedar in colour and fragrance, but the two genus are not remotely related. Chinese Toon is widely planted in temperate gardens for spectacular pink new growth. Plant in deeply worked, organically enriched, free-draining soil in full sun, protected from wind. Winter pruning will encourage better foliage displays and more compact growth.
　　Meliaceae.

Cedrela sinensis 'Flamingo'
Chinese Toon
Strikingly handsome Chinese tree with slender, erect branches. Pinnate leaves to 60cm, divided into 10–20, oblong-lanceolate, 8–12cm leaflets, pubescent beneath, margins entire or finely serrated. Special

beauty is the rich warm pink colouring of each leaflet, enhanced with bright red midrib and petiole in early spring. As they unfold and develop to full size, foliage becomes creamy pink before maturing green. Small white inconspicuous flowers. Sinensis — Chinese. Deciduous. 4 × 3m.　　**89**

C E D R U S

A genus of just two species of evergreen coniferous trees named from the Greek *kedros*, cedar. Their tall stately dignity, elegant pyramidal form, graceful branch structure, rich colouring and long life have earned the respect of tree lovers everywhere. Everything about cedars is good — the way they hold their branches, colour and texture of their needle leaves, even the way they hold their cones adds up to a most picturesque tree.
　　Plant in deeply worked soil with peat moss and sand. Stake for support and to protect the central leader. Side branches may be pruned to reduce width. Use as lawn specimens, street trees, in parks or reserves, farms, caravan parks, school grounds where they'll not be overcrowded and fully display their individuality.
　　Pinaceae. *All evergreen.*

Cedrus atlantica
Atlas Cedar
Native to Algeria. Distinctly pyramidal in youth with open angular habit. Gently curved branches ascend slightly at the tips. With advancing years, limbs become more horizontal and the tree broadly pyramidal. Branches and twigs densely covered with tufts of short, green needle foliage. 12 × 6m.

Cedrus atlantica 'Aurea'
Golden Atlas Cedar
Choice and rare with outer leaves overlaid with gold. Formation and appearance as above though a little smaller. 6 × 4m.　　**89**

Cedrus atlantica 'Glauca'
Blue Atlas Cedar
Handsome blue form surpassing the larger blue conifers for performance and beauty. Gently curving and ascending branches from ground level clothed with rich, glaucous-blue needles distinctly frosted. Suitable for average gardens if future overcrowding can be avoided. 6 × 4m.

Cedrus atlantica 'Glauca Pendula'
Weeping Blue Cedar
Imposing weeping form with curtains of silvery grey foliage cascading from an

umbrella or dome shaped crown. Staking when young essential. 4 × 3m.

Cedrus deodara
Indian Cedar, Deodar Cedar
From the Himalayas, a beautiful majestic tree, distinctly upright from the start with pyramidal form and evenly spaced branches gracefully pendulous at the tips. Blue-grey needle foliage generously frosted. Adds a special touch of grandeur and dignity to any landscape. 8 × 5m.

Cedrus deodara 'Aurea'
Golden Deodar
Smaller edition of Indian Cedar, similar in form and structure but with foliage overlaid bright gold. 6 × 4m.

Cedrus libani 'Sargentii'
Cedar of Lebanon
The ancient Lebanon Cedar has innumerable Biblical and historical associations. The cultivar Sargentii is a slow-growing, procumbent plant with dense, weeping branches clothed with characteristic, blue-green needle foliage. Superb plant for rock or feature gardens. Libani — of Mount Lebanon. 1 × 2m.

C E L T I S

Genus of over 70 species of deciduous and evergreen trees or shrubs from temperate regions of south east Europe and North America related to elms and embracing Hackberries and Nettle trees. Being deep rooted, they can be planted in confined places or near paved areas without surface roots causing damage. While young, they need staking for stability but once established, Celtis is tolerant of wind, heat, considerable drought and alkaline soils. Best in deep fertile soils, but will grow in a wide range of conditions with high summer temperatures.
　　Ulmaceae.

Celtis occidentalis
Common Hackberry
Native to the eastern USA. Forms a substantial tree with rounded crown, spreading branches, sometimes with pendulous tips and grey, rough, furrowed, warted, corky bark. Leaves to 12cm, ovate to broadly lanceolate, margins sharply but finely serrated, glossy green above, slightly pubescent beneath. Abundant globose fruit to 1cm, at first yellow or red, deep purple when mature in autumn. Occidentalis — western. Deciduous. 8 × 5m.

CERATOPETALUM

A genus of five species of glabrous trees and shrubs from Australia and New Guinea named from the Greek *keras*, a horn and *petalon*, a petal, referring to the lobed petals of one species resembling a stag's horn. They are handsome trees found in moist forests or rainforests, well known for impressive displays of colourful calyces. Seems reasonably hardy, known to survive temperatures of less than 6°C. Plant in deeply worked, organically enriched, free-draining soil. Mulch freely and provide ample deep watering over dry spells.

Cunoniaceae. *All evergreen.*

Ceratopetalum gummiferum
Sydney Christmas Bush
Exceptionally beautiful small tree from New South Wales forests. Forms a tall shrub or small tree. Trifoliate leaves with narrowly oblong leaflets to 7 × 1.5cm, margins shallowly serrated, dark green above, paler beneath. Inconspicuous terminal bracts of 6mm, creamy white flowers. After pollination the sepals enlarge, become deep red causing the entire tree to become a blaze of colour during spring and early summer. Last well when cut for indoors. Gummiferum — gum producing. 4 × 2.5m.

Ceratopetalum gummiferum 'Emerald N'Lace'
A selection made from a spectacular example near Auckland, New Zealand. Forms a smaller and more compact, upright growing tree, very free-flowering and exceptional display of red sepals. 3 × 2.5.

Ceratopetalum gummiferum 'Rubies & Lace'
Selected for its rich coppery red new foliage. Attractive summer display of small white feathery flowers, followed by bright red sepals. 3 × 2.5m.

Ceratopetalum gummiferum 'Wildfire'
From Australia, chosen for bright-red spring growth, earlier flowering, vivid red sepal display and upright compact habit. 3 × 2.5m.

CERATOSTIGMA

A genus of about eight species of small shrubs or woody perennials from Himalayas, central China, south east Asia and tropical Africa named from the Greek *keras*, a horn and *stigma*, referring to horn-like excrescences on the stigma. Valued for brilliant blue flower clusters through summer and autumn and colourful autumn leaves. Plant in full sun in loose, free-draining soil. Flowering on current season's growth, they can be pruned to at least half way in spring for growth renewal and maximum bloom. Slightly frost-tender, but rapid recovery.

Plumbaginaceae

Ceratostigma plumbagioides
Dwarf Plumbago
Dwarf shrub or perennial ground cover from western China. In loose soil, the plant spreads by underground runners, sending up numerous slender wiry stems. Thin-textured, bright green, obovate leaves to 8cm turn reddish brown in cold areas. The plant becomes a mass of 2cm, open, five-petalled, intense blue flowers through summer and autumn. Plumbagioides — like Plumbago. Evergreen. 30 × 90cm.

Ceratostigma willmottianum
Chinese Plumbago
Native to western China, a charming dwarf, semi-deciduous shrub producing from the base numerous thin, wiry, angled stems with narrow lanceolate, dull green leaves about 3cm long, bristly on both sides. Foliage yellow or orange-red prior to falling in late autumn. Throughout summer, the bush is covered with 25mm, bright gentian blue, phlox-like flowers in rounded clusters 5–6cm across. Named for Miss E A Willmott (1860–1934) celebrated English amateur gardener. Semi-deciduous. 60cm × 1m.

CERCIDIPHYLLUM

A genus of just one species, a deciduous tree from China and Japan named from *Cercis* and the Greek *phyllon* in reference to the similarity of its leaves to Cercis. Unusual tree with colourful foliage when the new shoots appear in spring and again with autumn colours. Prefers deeply worked, humus-rich, slightly acid soil which retains moisture during summer. Mulch freely, protect from hot sun and drying winds and water regularly during the growth season.

Cercidiphyllaceae.

Cercidiphyllum japonicum
Katsura Tree
Beautiful tree with varying growth habits, some with single trunks, more often with multiple stems angled upward and outwards. Leaves orbicular to ovate, 10–15cm, purplish pink as they first appear, maturing dark blue-green above, greyish beneath, neatly arranged in pairs along gracefully arching branches.

During autumn, foliage becomes scarlet and yellow and emits a strong spicy fragrance suggestive of caramel or burnt sugar. Small flowers appear before the leaves in spring. Deciduous. 7 × 5m.

CERCIS

A genus of about six species of deciduous trees and shrubs from southern Europe, North America and eastern Asia, often found along banks of streams or in moist, sandy or loamy soils in forests, named from the Greek *kerkis*, a weaver's shuttle, thought to describe the woody, flattened seed capsules. A tree with year-round interest. A profusion of small pea-shaped flowers on bare twigs and branches during spring, summer foliage, autumn leaf colour as well as picturesque, bare branches and seed pods in winter.

Plant in deeply worked, organically enriched, free-draining, moisture retentive soil in full sun, preferably sheltered from cold, drying winds. Mulch freely and water regularly during dry periods. Avoid advanced specimens as younger trees transplant with greater success. Prune only to remove deadwood or crossing branches. Old tired plants may be cut back to within 30cm of the ground, but will not flower until the second year. Stake and train young Cercis to a single main stem.

Caesalpiniaceae. *All deciduous.*

Cercis canadensis
Eastern Redbud, North American Redbud
From eastern North America, this small tree forms a broad rounded head with tiered branches as it ages. Distinguished from the Judas Tree by thinner, suborbicular-cordate, bright green leaves to 12cm long with pointed tips. In early spring, brownish branches are clothed in small, 12mm, pea-shaped, rosy pink, crimson or lilac flowers. Canadensis — of Canada, usually embracing north eastern United States. 5 × 4m.

Cercis canadensis 'Alba'
Forms a small tree with broad, rounded head. Clusters of pure white, pea-shaped flowers late spring, early summer. 5 × 4m.

Cercis canadensis 'Forest Pansy'
Selected cultivar forming a small round-headed tree. Young stems and leaves deep wine red to dark purple. Foliage matures bronzy-green through summer, red in autumn. Becomes a total mass of pale, rose-pink, pea-shaped flowers in spring. 3 × 3m.

Cercis canadensis 'Ruby Atkinson'
Round headed, medium tree with tiered, horizontal branch pattern and fresh green, cordate or heart-shaped leaves. Shell pink or pastel mauve pink, pea-shaped flowers borne profusely along every branch from early spring. 5 × 4m.

Cercis chinensis
Chinese Redbud
Native of southern China, seen mostly as a densely branching, open small tree with 5–12cm, rounded-cordate, rather glossy, bright green leaves. Clusters of 15–20mm, pea-shaped, deep rose, almost rosy purple flowers in profusion during spring. Vigorous, hardy species flowering three or four weeks earlier than Judas tree. 3.5 × 2.5m.

Cercis chinensis 'Avondale'
Choice dwarf-growing form discovered in New Zealand in the Auckland suburb of Avondale. Produces from an early age, a profusion of deep cerise-pink flowers on bare branches in spring. Heart-shaped, rich green leaves turn yellow in autumn. Prefers a sunny, warm sheltered location. 2.5 × 2m.

Cercis siliquastrum
Judas Tree European Redbud
Judas Tree is indigenous to Mediterranean regions and western Asia and reputed to be the tree upon which Judas hanged himself after the betrayal of Jesus. Rather more open and irregularly branched than the preceding species. Leaves to 10 × 12cm, reniform to broadly and bluntly obcordate, glabrous, coppery at first, maturing matt green. Spectacular in spring when the whole tree is clothed with pea-shaped, bright purplish-rose flowers. Siliquastrum — ancient Latin for a pod-bearing tree. 6 × 5m. **89**

CHAENOMELES

A genus of three species of deciduous shrubs or small trees from east Asia, named from the Greek *chaino*, to gape and *melon*, an apple, from an erroneous belief that the fruit is split. Among the first spring shrubs to bloom, each bare branch becoming a riot of colour from mid winter. They usually have thorns and bear fruit like small quinces, suggesting the name Flowering Quince.

Tolerant of a range of soil types and climatic extremes. Plant in moderately fertile, well-drained soil in full sun. To preserve shape and vigour pruning can be carried out at virtually any time, perhaps best when flowering stems can be picked and taken indoors. Excellent espalier plant or included in a shrub border. At one time classified as Cydonia and often referred to as 'Japonica'. Most cultivars are hybrids of Chinese C speciosa × Japanese C japonica.
Rosaceae. *All deciduous.*

Chaenomeles 'Alba'
Snow white single flowers with green centre. Vigorous upright grower.1.8 × 1.5m.

Chaenomeles 'Cameo'
Delicately shaded, soft apricot blushed pink double blooms borne freely on a compact bushy shrub. 1.2 × 1m.

Chaenomeles 'Cardinal'
Large, brilliant deep red single blossoms, long, profuse flowering period, strong vigorous grower. 1.8 × 1.5m.

Chaenomeles 'Chochuragaki'
Large, double, deep salmon-orange flowers with light apricot outer petals. Beautiful and strong growing. 1.5 × 1m.

Chaenomeles 'Crimson & Gold'
Intense crimson flowers with contrasting golden stamens. 1 × 1m.

Chaenomeles 'Dr Burton'
Large, deep orange-red flowers. Hardy, winter flowering and non-suckering. 1.5 × 1m.

Chaenomeles 'Green Ice'
Chartreuse buds open to semi-double, white flowers tinged green. Hardy and very showy. 1.8 × 1.5m.

Chaenomeles 'Riccartonii'
Large, very bright orange-red flowers, hardy, semi-deciduous. 1.8 × 1.5m.

Chaenomeles 'Rowallane'
Large, blood-crimson flowers in great profusion. 1.8 × 1.5m.

Chaenomeles 'Sunset Gold'
Single, rose pink flowers completely cover every branch. Bears fruit heavily. 1.8 × 1.5m.

CHAMAECYPARIS

A genus of about six species from eastern Asia and North America, named from the Greek *khamai*, on the ground and *kuparissos*, cypress. Close relatives of Cupressus or cypress, they are probably the most important group of landscaping conifers, differing mainly in flattened, frond-like or 'bookleaf' branchlets. Large numbers of excellent hybrids are cultivated in virtually any size, shape, colour or texture. There are carpets, buns, cushions, spires, globes, pyramids and columns in blue-green, yellow-green, grey-green, dark-greens, silver, gold or variegated.

Gardens featuring conifers exclusively have a well-groomed appearance at all times with minimum maintenance. Most dislike heavy soil and exposure to drying winds. Deeply dug, free-draining soil with peat moss, plus a mulch of peat moss or bark and occasional deep watering will keep the roots cool through hot periods. Natural branch formation is preferable to a trimmed appearance. Pruning unnecessary apart from obvious shaping or the removal of dead wood.
Cupressaceae. *All evergreen.*

Chamaecyparis lawsoniana 'Aurea Densa'
Compact conical form with upright sprays of bright golden yellow foliage. Always neat and tidy. Lawsoniana — named for Charles Lawson, 19th century botanical author and nurseryman. 1 × .75m.

Chamaecyparis lawsoniana 'Azurea'
Upright, compact, columnar to pyramidal form with ruffled frost-blue foliage. One of the best blue conifers. 4 × 2m.

Chamaecyparis lawsoniana 'B D Edginton'
Stately pyramidal form, rich golden yellow foliage. Old but reliable. 5 × 2m.

Chamaecyparis lawsoniana 'Blue Mountain'
Neat conical form with vivid blue-grey foliage all year. Originated as a sport of the once well-known, blue-foliaged C 'Ellwoodii'. Superior to its parent and to most other Chamaecyparis in this form and colouring. 1.5m × .60m.

Chamaecyparis lawsoniana 'Blue Weeper'
Informal grower, no central leader, wide spreading habit, blue-green weeping foliage. Very attractive. 3 × 1.5m.

Chamaecyparis lawsoniana 'Dutch Gold'
Upright, pyramidal, neat and tidy habit, bright golden yellow foliage. Excellent addition. 4 × 2.5m.

Chamaecyparis lawsoniana 'Ellwood's Gold'
Forms a neat conical spire with the tips of its mid-green foliage touched light gold. Relatively slow grower. 1 × .50m.

Chamaecyparis lawsoniana 'Erecta Viridis'
Bushy, upright, flame-shape with deep green foliage on long erect branches. Creates an imposing profile alongside driveways and boundaries or as accent specimen. Erecta — erect or upright. Viridis — green. 2.5 × .60m.

Chamaecyparis lawsoniana 'Forsteckensis'
Forms a neat, dense, rounded bush of light green foliage. Good for rock gardens and can be kept to size by removing protruding tip growths. 30 × 50cm.

Chamaecyparis lawsoniana 'Grayswood Feather'
Upright, compact, columnar habit with feathery, deep green foliage, soft textured and attractive. 3.5 × 1m.

Chamaecyparis lawsoniana 'Grayswood Pillar'
Extremely narrow columnar form, tightly packed ascending branches and striking bluish green foliage. Possibly the slenderest member of the Lawsoniana family and valuable in areas where other erect-growing conifers tend to loose their strict form. 3 × .45m.

Chamaecyparis lawsoniana 'Green Globe'
Perfect miniature globe shape with rich green foliage, very slow grower. 60 × 60cm.

Chamaecyparis lawsoniana 'Imbricata Pendula'
Graceful weeping habit, whip-cord foliage falls in long streamers to 1m long like a cascading waterfall. A unique conifer of great beauty. Imbricata — overlapping like tiles or scales. 2.5 × 1m.

Chamaecyparis lawsoniana 'Jonesii'
Broad conical form, bright yellow foliage sprays, retains good colour in sun or semi-shade. 2 × 1m.

Chamaecyparis lawsoniana 'Minima Aurea'
Dense conical dwarf with tightly packed, golden yellow foliage, slow growing. Minima — smallest. 50 × 35cm.

Chamaecyparis lawsoniana 'Moerheimi'
Somewhat open pyramidal form with golden yellow, semi-pendulous tips and picturesque branches when young. Vigorous grower, older but reliable. 5 × 2m.

Chamaecyparis lawsoniana 'Pembury Blue'
Erect, broad columnar outline with open or informal foliage in the brightest of blue-green. Better in cooler climates. 3 × 1m.

Chamaecyparis lawsoniana 'Pygmaea Argentea'
Compact, globular but open dwarf, whorls of deep green foliage beneath silvery-white tips which intensify during spring giving a frosted appearance. Argentea — silvery. 45 × 45cm.

Chamaecyparis lawsoniana 'Silver Queen'
Upright, pyramidal form, clothed to the ground with soft, silvery-grey foliage. Conspicuous in spring with creamy white pendulous new growth. 3 × 1.5m.

Chamaecyparis lawsoniana 'Southern Gold'
Somewhat open pyramidal to weeping form with lemon coloured foliage. Slow grower with graceful habit. Best in semi-shade. Dislikes salt wind. 2 × 1.5m.

Chamaecyparis lawsoniana 'Stewartii'
Medium sized, conical shaped shrub with bookleaf sprays of golden yellow, truly elegant. 3.5 × 1.5m.

Chamaecyparis lawsoniana 'Wallis Gold'
Dense, upright habit, with bookleaf sprays of rich, golden yellow foliage. 3 × 1.5m.

Chamaecyparis lawsoniana 'Yellow Transparent'
Broad pyramidal outline and fascinating bookleaf sprays of rich yellow foliage seen best with light shining through it. Brightest effects with each burst of fresh growth, turning brownish in winter. 1.8 × .80m.

Chamaecyparis obtusa 'Albovariegata'
Slow growing form of Hinoki Cypress, semi-open habit and dark green foliage irregularly splashed creamy white. Obtusa — blunt. 1 × .50m.

Chamaecyparis obtusa 'Caespitosa'
One of the smallest miniature conifers, forming a flattened irregular cushion of rich green foliage held in tiny compressed fans. A real midget which needs protection from climatic extremes. Caespitosa — growing in dense clumps. 10 × 7cm.

Chamaecyparis obtusa 'Confucius'
Vigorous, informal, compact pyramidal habit, bright golden fan-like foliage sprays. 1 × 1m.

Chamaecyparis obtusa 'Contorta'
Unusual dwarf with green twisted and contorted twiglets. Contorta — twisted, bent irregularly. 25 × 25cm.

Chamaecyparis obtusa 'Crippsii'
Golden Hinoki Cypress
Broad, pyramidal shape with golden yellow frond-like sprays drooping at the tips. Graceful appearance, makes a first class lawn specimen, one of the most beautiful of conifers. 3.5 × 2.5m.

Chamaecyparis obtusa 'Ericoides'
Fresh glaucous green, heath-like juvenile foliage with the odd terminal shoot of adult, rich green foliage protruding irregularly. Upright bush with billowy habit. 1.5 × 1m.

Chamaecyparis obtusa 'Fernspray Gold'
Informal, arching, pagoda-like habit. Attractive fern-like sprays bright yellow in summer, deepening to burnished gold in winter. 2 × 1m.

Chamaecyparis obtusa 'Flabelliformis'
Very slow growing, pointed squat pyramidal form with deep green foliage in attractive whorled fans. Flabelliformis — fan-shaped. 25 × 25cm.

Chamaecyparis obtusa 'Hage'
Miniature dwarf globe with tiered layers of lustrous deep green foliage. 25 × 30cm.

Chamaecyparis obtusa 'Juniperoides'
Very dwarf, globose or low mound form with rich dark green foliage in fan-shaped decurving sprays. Juniperoides — resembling Juniper. 20 × 20cm.

Chamaecyparis obtusa 'Kosteri'
Most elegant, informal grower with large fans of lush green foliage sprays curiously twisted, creating a fascinating, tiered oriental-looking plant. May tend to sprawl, but can be sculptured as desired. 80 × 80cm.

Chamaecyparis obtusa 'Lycopodioides Aurea'
Colour variation of Lycopodioides with those parts of the bush exposed to light being lemon-yellow. Similar informal habit but slower growing. Lycopodioides — resembling Lycopodium or club-moss. 1 × 1m.

Chamaecyparis obtusa 'Mariesii'
Slow grower gradually building a small pyramid with variegated foliage, brilliant creamy-white in summer, mellowing to yellowish green for the winter. 30 × 30cm.

Chamaecyparis obtusa 'Minima'
Maybe the world's most compact conifer, a mere ball of tightly packed green foliage looking rather like a pincushion. Minima — smallest. In ten years would grow only 6 × 10cm.

Chamaecyparis obtusa 'Nana'
Miniature dome shape, with tiered layers of tufty branchlets in deep lustrous green. Fits the smallest garden. 60 × 50cm.

Chamaecyparis obtusa 'Nana Aurea'
Dwarf Golden Hinoki
Compact, conical dwarf with nuggety sprays of golden yellow foliage. Looks mature even when young. 50 × 30cm.

Chamaecyparis obtusa 'Nana Gracilis'
Excellent dwarf informal habit with lustrous, dark-green foliage sprays arranged in loosely held fans. 1 × .40m.

Chamaecyparis obtusa 'Nana Lutea'
Extremely slow growing, very dwarf compact mound gradually building height. Fine foliage in delicate shade of creamy gold over emerald green. 60 × 60cm.

Chamaecyparis obtusa 'Nana Verdonii'
Upright compact habit, slow-growing, otherwise similar to Nana Aurea but with deeper winter colour. 75 × 30cm.

Chamaecyparis obtusa 'Pygmaea'
Bushy, spreading dwarf with rounded fan-like habit and flat loosely arranged branchlets which take on a reddish tinge in summer deepening to bronze in winter. .60 × 1m.

Chamaecyparis obtusa 'Rigid Dwarf'
Forms an erect but informal vase shape with fan-like, dark, almost black-green foliage sprays. Slow grower. 75 × 30cm.

Chamaecyparis obtusa 'Tempelhof'
Dwarf, compact rounded shrub with broad, overlapping whorls of deep green foliage, burnished with bronze in winter. 1 × 1m.

Chamaecyparis obtusa 'Tetragona Aurea'
Bushy upright habit, unusually angular branches with rich, golden-yellow, moss-like sprays assuming a bronzy sheen in winter. Distinctly oriental appearance. Tetragona — four-angled. 2 × 1.25m.

Chamaecyparis obtusa 'Tonia'
Compact, globular dwarf, dense tufts of dark green foliage with occasional curious flecks of creamy white. 75 × 75cm.

Chamaecyparis obtusa 'Youngii'
Very similar to Nana Aurea but more open and with faster rate of growth. Rich golden foliage. 60 × 30cm.

Chamaecyparis pisifera 'Boulevard'
Dense pyramidal shrub with intense silvery-blue foliage very soft to the touch. Outstanding colour and form. Pisifera — pea bearing. 1.5 × 1m.

Chamaecyparis pisifera 'Compacta Variegata'
Compact, bun shaped bush, tightly packed, dark-green foliage with bold contrasting flecks of yellow. 60 × 70cm.

Chamaecyparis pisifera 'Filifera Aurea'
Broadly conical habit with cascading fountain of long, brilliant yellow, pendulous threads. Very graceful. Filifera — thread bearing. 1.25 × 1.25m.

Chamaecyparis pisifera 'Gold Spangle'
Attractive, low rounded bush, bright, golden yellow foliage with both thread-like and larger open leaves. Responds to regular pruning to maintain compact form. .50 × 1m.

Chamaecyparis pisifera 'Nana Aureovariegata'
Grows very slowly, around 3cm each year to form a ground hugging, bun. Dense, rich green foliage highlighted with a golden sheen, particularly attractive in spring and summer. 15 × 30cm.

Chamaecyparis pisifera 'Plumosa Aurea'
Bushy upright habit, feathery branchlets rich golden, deepening to bronze in winter. 2 × 1.5m.

Chamaecyparis pisifera 'Plumosa Compressa'
Rounded bun-shaped dwarf, extremely dense, moss-like foliage with vivid white tips during spring and summer. 45 × 50cm.

Chamaecyparis pisifera 'Plumosa Rogersii'
Dwarf conical shape, densely congested foliage which colours up like a butter ball during summer and golden toning in winter. 60 × 50cm.

Chamaecyparis pisifera 'Tsukoma'
Very dwarf and compact yet develops rapidly. Rich green foliage. 25 × 25cm.

Chamaecyparis thyoides 'Andelyensis Nana'
Attractive slow grower with variable form and blue-green foliage clusters turning rich purple in winter. Thyoides — resembling Thuja. 1 × .30m.

Chamaecyparis thyoides 'Ericoides'
Colourful, upright to conical grower with attractive plum-purple mossy foliage during late winter. New spring and summer growth sea-green with a trace of bronze. Similar appearance to Thuja 'Ericoides' but firmer to the touch. Ericoides — resembling Erica or heath. 1.5 × 1m.

Chamaecyparis thyoides 'Ericoides Red Star'
Dwarf, columnar cone of soft, purple-green summer foliage, becoming plum-purple in winter. Showy, colourful and different. Needs ample moisture. 1.4 × .60m.

Chamaecyparis thyoides 'Juvenalis Stricta'
Slender conical dwarf, broadening with age. Soft plumy, blue-grey foliage. 1.25 × .75m.

CHAMAEROPS

A genus of one species, a shrubby palm from western Mediterranean regions of Algeria, Morocco and southern Spain, thought to be the only palm native to Europe and named from the Greek *chamai*, dwarf and *rhops*, a bush. Leaf fibres yield vegetable 'horsehair' used in upholstery.

Has adapted well in most climates, flourishing in hot sun or shade in warm coastal conditions to sub-zero temperatures and is quite wind and drought tolerant once established. Naturally found in nutritionally poor, rocky or sandy conditions. Grows under almost any garden conditions. Versatile landscaping palm either as a specimen in groves or containers.
Palmae.

Chamaerops humilis
Mediterranean Fan Palm
Extremely hardy, clustering fan palm, varying from a solitary, 6m trunk to an attractive cluster of short, ground-hugging stems to 2m. Stiff, grey-green to blue-green, fan-shaped leaves to 90cm with spiny petioles. Produces panicles of small yellow flowers hidden among the leaves followed by brown or yellow, 2cm fruits. Humilis — low or small. Evergreen. 2 × 2.5m.

CHAMELAUCIUM

Australian endemic genus of about 20 species of shrubs restricted to south west Western Australia. Derivation and meaning of the name is obscure. Beautiful shrubs with an airy grace, particularly C uncinatum, cherished for long lasting cut blooms. Large plantations for flower production are established in Australia and other parts of the world. Foliage of most species is pleasantly fragrant when crushed.

Plant in deeply worked, free-draining, light to heavy-textured, loose, sandy or gravelly, neutral to slightly acid soil, in full sun or light shade. Withstands long periods of drought, and hardy to light frost. Be sparing with fertilizer. Cut freely for indoors plus heavy pruning when flowering has finished. Excellent selected cultivars have been introduced into cultivation.

Myrtaceae.

Chamelaucium uncinatum
Geraldton Wax Flower
Medium to tall shrub with numerous slender branches and open to dense habit. Bright green, 3–4cm, linear, almost cylindrical, lemon scented leaves, hooked at the ends. Showy sprays of waxy, five-petalled, wide open, 12–25mm flowers in white, pink, mauve, purple or dull red, through spring and mid-summer. Uncinatum — hooked at the end. The following named cultivars are all evergreen and grow approximately 2 × 2m.

Chamelaucium uncinatum 'Album'
Exquisite white flowers in profusion.

Chamelaucium uncinatum 'Burgundy Blush'
Selected for vigour, erect growth and deep mauve-purple flowers.

Chamelaucium 'Lady Stephanie'
Vigorous hybrid producing masses of pale pink flowers through spring becoming deeper pink as they mature.

Chamelaucium uncinatum 'Newmarracarra'
Flowers pale pink turning reddish purple with maturity.

Chamelaucium uncinatum 'Purple Pride'
Dense terminal clusters of reddish purple flowers with a fine white central ring.

CHIMONANTHUS

A genus of about six species of deciduous or evergreen shrubs from China, named from the Greek *cheimon*, winter and *anthos*, a flower. The only cultivated species, valued for sweet fragrance and waxy flowers during winter was introduced to England in 1766.

Grows easily and hardy anywhere. Plant in deeply worked, free-draining soil in full sun, sheltered from strong wind. Pick flowering stems freely for indoors, otherwise, as flowers appear on second year wood, prune only to remove dead or misplaced branches. Best in climates with cold winters and dry summers. Locate where the sweet fragrance can be enjoyed.

Calycanthaceae. *All deciduous.*

Chimonanthus praecox
Allspice, Winter Sweet
A bushy, twiggy shrub with grey-green new shoots, brown when mature. Leaves ovate-lanceolate to 20 × 7cm, upper surface rough and lustrous green, becoming rich golden colour before falling in areas with a cold, dry autumn. Delightfully violet scented, 25mm flowers, outer petals sulphur yellow, inner petals purple or brown, produced in pairs along every bare branch in mid-winter. Praecox — early. 2.5 × 2m.

Chimonanthus praecox 'Luteus'
Selected form with larger, more conspicuous, waxy, sulphur yellow flowers with the same sweet fragrance. Blooms a few weeks later than C praecox and grows more upright. 3 × 2m.

CHINOCHLOA

A genus of about twenty species of coarse, perennial tussock grasses from New Zealand, one from Australia, named from the Greek *chion*, snow and *chloe*, grass in allusion to the appearance of the foliage. Although tussock grasses have long been associated with wild alpine and subalpine grasslands, strong form and elegant flower has earned them recognition in urban landscaping especially in adverse conditions or where minimal maintenance is called for.

Although hardy to extreme temperatures, under garden conditions they perform best when sheltered from persist-ent cold, drying winds and planted in loose, sandy, free-draining, moisture retentive, fertile soil in full sun. Old shabby plants may be cut to within a few centimetres of the ground for rapid growth renewal. Excellent among rocks, on banks or in borders.

Gramineae. *All evergreen.*

Chinochloa conspicua
Snow Tussock, Plumed Tussock
Large tussock found throughout New Zealand, usually alongside streams in lowland and subalpine forests or clearings. Leaves 45cm–1.2m × 6–8mm with prominent nerves and softly hairy margins. Handsome, 45cm, creamy flower panicles on long stems appear late spring through mid-summer. 1.2 × 1m.

Chinochloa flavescens
Broad-leaved Snow Tussock
From alpine regions of both islands. Forms bold tussocks of greenish-yellow leaves and drooping panicles of feathery, creamy yellow flowers held above the leaves on long arching stems. Resembles a miniature Toetoe. 75cm × 1m.

Chinochloa rubra
Red Tussock
Found from sea level to 1800m south of East Cape and Mt Egmont in New Zealand but more frequently in alpine regions of the South Island. Forms large, bronzy-red tussocks with long, slender rolled leaves. Foliage colour persists all year. 1 × 1m.

CHIONANTHUS

A genus of three or four species of deciduous, essentially dioecious trees and shrubs from east Asia, Korea, Japan and eastern USA, named from the Greek *chion*, snow and *anthos*, a flower. Following summer floral displays, if both sexes are present, although some flowers may be bisexual, female trees produce damson-like fruit. Plant in deeply worked, organically enriched, free-draining, moisture retentive, neutral to slightly acid soil in full sun for maximum flower.

Oleaceae.

Chionanthus virginicus
Fringe Tree, Old Man's Beard
Native to eastern USA, a slow-growing airy shrub or small tree with obovate leaves to 20cm, glossy and dark green above, downy and prominently veined beneath. Bright

yellow autumn foliage colour. Flowers pure white, slightly fragrant with four extremely slender petals hanging loosely like threads borne early summer in drooping, 20cm, pointed panicles resembling a beard. Pollinated female flowers produce dark blue, damson-like fruits. Deciduous. 5 × 4m.

CHOISYA

A genus of nine species of aromatic shrubs from southern USA and Mexico named after 19th century Swiss botanist Jacques D Choisy.

Grown for rich, glossy green foliage and persistent floral displays spring through autumn. Simple to grow, preferring slightly acid, deeply worked, free-draining soil in sun or partial shade. Good for multiple planting, backgrounds, blank areas or low screens. Remove straggling shoots or spent flower heads to encourage further bloom and prune to maintain neat compact form.

Rutaceae. *All evergreen.*

Choisya ternata
Mexican Orange Blossom
Handsome shrub from Mexico, quickly forming a neat, rounded bush. Palmate leaves divided into three oblong to obovate leaflets, the terminal one to 8cm, lateral leaflets shorter, rich deep green, lustrous, leathery. Bruised leaves have a strong but not unpleasant odour. Pure white, five-petalled flowers to 24mm, produced in terminal clusters have the appearance and fragrance of orange blossom and cover the entire bush from late winter through spring, and intermittently during summer. Ternata — in clusters of three. 1.5 × 1.5m. **90**

Choisya ternata 'Sundance'
Slower growing, smaller cultivar with lime-green to golden yellow foliage. White flowers as above. Protect from strong wind and hottest midday sun. 1 × 1.2m.

CHORDOSPARTIUM

A genus of two New Zealand endemic species or shrubs or small trees discovered by a Mr George Stevenson earlier this century near the mouth of the Clarence River on the seaward side of the Kaikoura mountains of New Zealand's South Island. The name arises from the

Greek *chorde*, string and *spartium*, a genus of broom. Very hardy, tolerant of poor dry soils, but responds to better conditions. Prefers locations with hot summers and dry autumns. Tends to be by-passed as it is somewhat unattractive when young, but merits extensive use as a modern landscaping feature specimen. Give space to display its unique individuality.

Leguminosae.

Chordospartium stevensonii
Weeping Broom
A handsome, rare, broom-like shrub or small tree with long, graceful, leafless branches drooping almost to the ground, resembling a miniature weeping willow. These slender cordlike, brownish-green streamers 60–90cm long burst forth with a profusion of pea-shaped, wisteria-blue to rosy-purple flowers late spring through mid-summer. Grows 6–7m in nature but smaller dimensions can be expected under garden conditions. Evergreen. 3 × 2.5m.

CHORISIA

A genus of 5 species of deciduous small to medium trees from tropical America named after botanical artist Ludwig Choris, who accompanied Russian navigator Kotzebue on a scientific expedition to the Pacific in the 19th century. A tree for mild climates to −7°C. Plant in full sun in deeply worked, free-draining, soil. Water deeply during dry periods.

Bombacaceae.

Chorisia speciosa
Floss Silk Tree
From Brazil and Argentina. Unusual tree with heavy, tapering trunk, studded with stout, rose-like spines, grass-green when young, grey with age. Fast growing and slender when young, later slowing to form a broad crown. Palmate leaves divided fanwise into five to seven, 12 × 3cm, lanceolate leaflets with finely serrated margins.

Flowers to 15cm across, somewhat like Hibiscus with five narrow petals in orchid pink, purplish rose or burgundy. Petal bases ivory or white, spotted or striped brown. Variation in flower shape and colour normal. Pear-shaped fruits contain silky, floss covered seeds. Flowers freely in autumn and early winter after dropping the bulk of its leaves. Speciosa — showy. Semi-evergreen. 7.5 × 4.5m.

CHRYSOCOMA

A genus of about 20 species of annual and perennial herbs and shrubs from South Africa. The Greek *chryso*, gold and *kome*, hair, are descriptive of the woolly golden flowers. Plant in deeply worked, gravelly or sandy, free-draining soil in full sun. Water sparingly during dry periods and feed every four weeks through the growing season with liquid fertilizer. After flowering, shear the bush back to at least half way for growth renewal and maximum flower. Blooms freely during the first year from seed and may be treated as an annual in frost free areas. Excellent for rock gardens, edgings etc.

Compositae.

Chrysocoma coma-aurea
Golden Hair, Goldilocks
Charming South African dwarf shrub. Forms a compact mound with many erect stems and lobed, linear, heather-like leaves. Round, golden yellow flowers with bell-shaped involucre or calyx, like woolly buttons or knobs atop each slender stem making a brilliant display through autumn. Coma-aurea — golden hair. Evergreen. .60 × 1m.

CINNAMOMUM

A genus of over 250 species of evergreen trees from south east Asia and Australia, named from the classical Greek term for cinnamon. The species C zeylanicum yields cinnamon but is seldom grown ornamentally. C camphora is the species more generally grown and valued for its yields of camphor. Good shade tree for larger areas in warmer climates but has an unfortunate competitive root system. Grows freely in almost any soil, withstands drought but needs deep watering during dry spells until established.

Lauraceae.

Cinnamomum camphora
Camphor Tree
Slow-growing, eventually 12–15m in height and almost as wide with picturesque structure. Spring growth pink, red or bronze tinted. Glossy, light-green, ovate-lanceolate leaves to 10cm. Tiny, yellow, fragrant flowers in late autumn, followed by small blackish fruit. Every part of the tree is charged with the aromatic compound which produces camphor when distilled. Evergreen. 9 × 7m.

CISTUS

A genus of about 20 species of small to medium evergreen or semi-evergreen flowering plants from southern Europe and north Africa named from the ancient Greek name *kistos*. Valued for continual displays of colourful, crepe-like flowers resembling old-fashioned single roses and the aromatic leaves of some species. They're at home in dry, sunny gardens, one of the first choices for banks, rock gardens or coastal planting, their hardiness matched by beauty as dense masses of brilliant bloom appear through warmer months.

Once established, they resist drought, prefer poor lean soil, tolerate hot sunshine and desert conditions and flourish in reach of salt spray and ocean winds. Maintain vigour by removing from the base only a portion of the older stems. Tip-pinching early growth encourages bushiness and maximum flower. They resent hard pruning, root disturbance or over-feeding. Use for dry bank cover, mass bedding, shrub borders, hot rockery pockets or coastal gardens.

Cistaceae. *All evergreen.*

Cistus 'Bennett's White'
Larger growing cultivar forming an impressive bushy shrub. Leaves elliptic to 8 × 4cm, deep green, covered with fine hairs. Showy, pure white flowers to 10cm across with five crepe-like petals and prominent central cluster of yellow stamens. 1.8 × 2m.   **90**

Cistus incanus
Rock Rose
Dwarf with erect or divaricate branches and shaggily hairy young shoots. Leaves ovate to elliptic to 7 × 3cm, green or silvery pubescent, margins often undulate. Pink-purple, crepe-like flowers to 6cm across with yellow central zone. Syn C villosus. Incanus — hoary, quite grey. 1 × 1m.

Cistus incanus 'Pink Cloud'
Excellent cultivar, selected for medium-size, lilac-pink flowers with prominent golden-yellow centre, borne freely through spring and summer. 1.5 × 1.5m.

Cistus ladanifer
Gum Cistus
Native to south west Europe and North Africa. Rather clammy, glutinous shoots and foliage. Leaves linear-lanceolate to 10 × 2.5cm, green and glabrous, grey pubescent beneath, exuding a resinous substance giving the plant an attractive leaden appearance, especially in cooler weather. Solitary flowers 7–10cm across, pure white with prominent crimson blotch at the base of each crinkled petal. Ladanifer — refers to ladanum, fragrant, resinous juice used in medicine, the myrrh mentioned in the Bible. 1 × 1m.

Cistus laurifolius
Rock Rose
Erect grower with young stems covered with an aromatic, sticky substance. Leaves ovate to ovate-lanceolate to 9 × 3cm, margins undulate, dark green and glabrous with white pubescence, clammy beneath. Flowers white with yellow basal spot, to 5–6cm, borne in clusters on long stems. Laurifolius — Bay-leaved. 1.5 × 1m.

Cistus × lusitanicus
Rock Rose
Compact dwarf hybrid of C ladanifer and C hirsutus. Shoots resinous and clammy, leaves to 65mm, oblong-lanceolate, dull grey-green above, thinly pubescent beneath. Flowers to 7cm across with five broadly ovate sepals, white with crimson basal spot, held in terminal clusters of three to five. Lusitanicus — of Lusitania, Portugal. 75 × 75cm.

Cistus × lusitanicus 'Decumbens'
Low, spreading grower, becoming a mass of white flowers with crimson basal blotch during summer. Decumbens — trailing with upright tips. 60cm × 1m.

Cistus × pulverulentus 'Sunset'
Rock Rose
Forms a multi-branched, dense compact shrub with 3–5cm, oblong, grey, hairy leaves and an abundance of rose-pink, 50mm flowers appearing at frequent intervals throughout the year. Pulverulentus — powdered as with dust. 70 × 90cm.

Cistus × purpureus 'Brilliancy'
Orchid Rock Rose
Forms a rounded bush, young shoots pubescent and sticky. Leaves to 5cm, oblong-lanceolate, dark green above, grey-hairy beneath. Crepe-like flowers to 7cm across, deep rosy pink with a maroon or brown spot at the base of each petal and a central bunch of yellow stamens. Hybrid from C ladanifer × C incanus ssp. creticus. 1.30 × 1.50m.   **90**

Cistus salviifolius
Sageleaf Rockrose
Wide spreading form with pubescent young shoots. Leaves ovate-oblong, light grey-green, to 4cm long, crinkled, crisp, felted beneath. Flowers 4cm across, white with yellow spots at the base of each petal, produced freely late spring. Salviifolius — salvia-like leaves. .60 × 2m.

Cistus salviifolius 'Snowmound'
Forms a rounded mound becoming a total mass of 25–30mm, pure white, crepe-like flowers from early spring, about three weeks earlier than White Gem. Selection from Auckland Regional Botanic Gardens. 1 × 1m.   **90**

Cistus salviifolius 'White Gem'
A spreading plant well clothed with foliage to ground level, growing attractively over rocks or spilling over walls. Produces masses of 30mm pure white flowers during spring. Selection from Auckland Regional Botanic Gardens. .40 × 1m.

Cistus 'Silver Pink'
Rock Rose
Low, spreading, bushy plant with downy stems. Dull sage-green, ovate-lanceolate, downy, fragrant leaves to 7cm, pale grey beneath. Clear silvery-pink flowers to 7cm across, with central cluster of gold stamens carried in clusters of three to five. Garden hybrid. 80 × 90cm.

Cistus × skanbergii
Rock Rose
Forms a dense, wide-spreading bush with white pubescent stems. Fine, grey-green, oblong-lanceolate leaves to 5 × 1cm, prominently veined, downy beneath. Beautiful, clear pink, 25mm, silky, crepe-like flowers borne profusely in cymes up to six through spring and summer. From Greece. 45cm × 1m.

CLADRASTIS

A genus of five species of hardy deciduous trees from east Asia and eastern North America, named from the Greek *klados*, a branch and *thraustos*, fragile, from the brittle nature of the twigs. Although flowers may be scarce for the first decade, the tree is worth planting for good form, handsome autumn foliage and the promise of spectacular flowers in due time.

Most handsome, slow-growing and useful tree for lawn, terrace or patio, whether or not in bloom. Plant in full sun in deeply worked, organically enriched, free-draining, alkaline to neutral soil. Carefully plan the location to avoid subsequent moving. Shorten side branches when young, removing them entirely when the tree reaches desired height.

Leguminosae.

Above: Cantua buxifolia
Sacred Flower of the Incas **73**

Above: Cassia corymbosa 'John Ball' **75**
Below: Ceanothus papillosus 'Roweanus' **81**

Above and inset: Cercis siliquastrum *Judas Tree* **83**
Below: Cedrus atlantica 'Aurea' *Golden Atlas Cedar* **81**

Below: Cedrela sinensis 'Flamingo' **81**

Above: Choisya ternata *Mexican Orange Blossom* **87**

Above: Cistus x purpureus 'Brilliancy' *Orchid Rock Rose* **88**

Above: Cistus salviifolius 'Snowmound' **88**
Below: Convolvulus cneorum **94**

Above: Clerodendrum ugandense *Blue Butterfly Bush* **93**
Below: Cistus 'Bennett's White' **88**

Above: Coleonema album *Breath of Heaven* **94**

Above: Clianthus puniceus 'Red Cardinal' *Red Kaka Beak* **94**
Below: Coleonema pulchrum *Pink Diosma Confetti Bush* **94**

Above and below: Coleonema pulchrum 'Sunset Gold' **94**

Above: Coprosma 'Beatson's Gold' **95**

Above: Coprosma 'Greensleeves' **95**

Above: Coprosma 'Kiwi Silver' **96**

Above: Coprosma repens 'Goldsplash' **96**
Below: Coprosma repens 'Pink Splendour' **96**

Below: Coprosma repens 'Variegata' **96**

Above: Coprosma repens 'Marble Queen' **96**
Below: Coprosma 'Yvonne' **97**

Cladrastis lutea
Kentucky Yellow Wood

Native to Kentucky, Tennessee and North Carolina. Rather slow grower, forming a broad, rounded head. Leaves pinnate, to 30cm long, divided into 7–11 ovate, 10–12cm leaflets with prominent veins, bright green during summer, turning brilliant yellow in autumn, somewhat resembling the English walnut. During early summer, 15–25cm clusters of white, highly fragrant wisteria-like flowers appear in spectacular masses, followed by 8–10cm, long flat seedpods. May take ten years before blooming and occasionally skips a season. Lutea — yellow, from yellow dye found in the heartwood. Deciduous. 8 × 5m.

CLERODENDRUM

A genus of about 300–400 species of trees, shrubs and woody climbers from tropical and subtropical regions of Asia and Africa named from the Greek *kleros*, chance and *dendron*, tree, possible reference to its variable medicinal qualities. Within the genus are many beautiful and spectacular plants for subtropical to tropical climates, often grown indoors in temperate regions. The listed species thrive in most temperate areas with few special demands. Plant in full sun in deeply worked, free-draining soil.

Verbenaceae.

Clerodendrum trichotomum 'Fargesii'
Harlequin Glorybower

Shrub from western China attractive at all seasons. Large ovate leaves to 20 × 10cm, purplish when young, maturing bright green, slightly hairy on both surfaces, margins entire or finely serrated. Through late summer, large terminal clusters of sweetly fragrant, 25mm, white starry flowers appear, set in a green calyx. Calyx persists to late autumn, becomes bright red and encloses attractive porcelain-blue fruit. Been around for decades and deserves more attention. Fargesii — for 19th century French missionary and naturalist Paul Farges. Deciduous. 2.5 × 1.5m.

Clerodendrum ugandense
Blue Butterfly Bush

Rapid-growing shrub from tropical Africa. Narrowly obovate to elliptic, 5–10cm leaves, mid green, glabrous and coarsely toothed. Orchid-like, two-toned, light and deep blue flowers resembling small butterflies appear in terminal panicles through summer and autumn. Will stand considerable frost in fairly dry conditions. Prune heavily each spring even to ground level for growth renewal. Tip prune early through the growing season to maintain a compact bush and maximum flower. Ugandense — of Uganda. Evergreen 1.5 × 1m. **90**

CLETHRA

A genus of about 30 species of evergreen and deciduous trees and shrubs from Asia, eastern North America and Madiera Islands, named from *klethra*, Greek term for alder, given for the similarity of its foliage. Grown mainly for beautiful floral racemes with spicy fragrance. Clethra is quite hardy, growing naturally on wooded mountainsides with roots in the shade.

Conditions suited to Rhododendrons are ideal, full sun in cool areas, light shade in warmer regions, deeply worked, organically enriched, free-draining, lime-free, acid soil. Mulch freely and water deeply during dry spells. Not really a tree for hot locations, but worth growing wherever Rhododendrons and Azaleas thrive. Spray for thrips usually evidenced by a silvery-grey appearance on the leaves.

Clethraceae.

Clethra alnifolia
Sweet Pepper Bush

Native to eastern United States. Strong, slender, erect, growth pattern, tending to form a bushy clump from underground shoots. Obovate to oblong, wedge-shaped leaves, dark green, to 10cm long, margins serrate, bright yellow in autumn. Small, 1cm, cup-shaped, gleaming white flowers with spicy fragrance appear in densely packed, cylindrical, 15cm, terminal racemes through late summer and autumn. Alnifolia — with alder-like leaves. Deciduous. 2 × 1m.

Clethra arborea
Lily of the Valley Tree

Native to the Madeira Islands off the coast of Morocco. Forms a neat, erect-growing shrub or small tree. Young pubescent shoots shaded rusty copper provide an attractive feature with each burst of new growth. Tree densely clothed with smooth, rich-green, elliptic to oblanceolate leaves to 15 × 5cm long, margins finely serrated, slightly felted beneath. Pure white, cup-shaped, 8mm flowers appear through summer and autumn in slender racemes resembling lily of the valley blossom, even to the fragrance. Arborea — growing treelike. Evergreen. 6 × 4m.

Clethra arborea 'Flore Pleno'

Rare, unusual and floriferous cultivar with wide-open, fully double, 2cm, fragrant white sterile flowers borne in pendent panicles through autumn. Typical C arborea vigour and foliage, but without untidy seed pods. Evergreen. 3 × 2.5m.

CLEYERA

A genus of about 17 species of evergreen or deciduous trees and shrubs from Japan to Himalayas and Mexico to Panama, named for Dr Andreas Cleyer, 17th century German doctor and botanist. A close relationship to Camellia is evident in the leathery, glossy foliage. In Japan, leafy branches are used in Shinto rituals. This magnificent foliage shrub is for semi-shady locations in deeply worked, organically enriched, free-draining soil, deeply mulched and kept moist during dry periods. Protect from strong wind and frost.

Theaceae.

Cleyera japonica 'Tricolor'

Beautiful glabrous shrub with gracefully arching, wide-spread branches. Young shoots tinged coppery red. Leaves narrowly elliptic or linear-lanceolate to 8 × 3cm, bright green, with stripes of grey and golden-yellow with a touch of rose-pink towards the margins. On mature plants, small, pale yellow flowers appear in autumn followed by small, dark red puffy berries. Attractive, slow-growing shrub for foliage effects. Syn C japonica 'Fortunei'. Evergreen. 1.5 × 1.3.

CLIANTHUS

New Zealand and Australia each have one of the two species belonging to this genus named from the Greek *kleos*, glory and *anthos*, a flower. Sturt's Desert Pea, C formosus is one of Australia's most admired wildflowers, while C puniceus, Kaka Beak or 'kowhai-ngutu-kaka' is among New Zealand's better known natives. Native to northern parts of New Zealand, Kaka Beak is virtually extinct in its natural state.

Locate in sun or partial shade protected from strong wind and heavy frost. Plant in deeply worked, free-draining soil, mulch heavily and keep moist during dry periods or while in bloom. Grow Clianthus as a shrub, espalier or climber.

Regular tip pruning early in the growth period will encourage more flower. Prune after flowering to preserve shape and vigour.

Leguminosae. *All semi-evergreen.*

Clianthus puniceus
Kaka Beak, Parrot Beak, Lobster Claw
Fast-growing plant with wide-spread, long-arching branches. Dark green, fern-like, 7–15cm pinnate leaves with up to 25, narrow-oblong, 2–3cm leaflets. Flowers to 7–8cm, pea-shaped with standard and keel, the lower keel resembling a parrot's beak, suspended in drooping racemes of up to 15 through early summer. Rich in nectar and attractive to birds. Puniceus — reddish purple. 2 × 2m.

Clianthus puniceus 'Flamingo'
Pink Kaka Beak
Deep rose-pink parrot-beak flowers. Syn C puniceus 'Roseus'.

Clianthus puniceus 'Red Cardinal'
Red Kaka Beak
Brilliant scarlet red parrot-beak flowers. Syn C puniceus.   **91**

Clianthus puniceus 'White Heron'
Cool, ivory white parrot-beak flowers. Syn C puniceus 'Albus'.

CLIVIA

The genus of four species of perennial, evergreen herbs from warm dry forests areas of Natal, is named for Lady Charlotte Cliver, 19th century Duchess of Northumberland. Ideal plants for dry shady areas beneath larger trees where colonies may be left undisturbed for years. Choose a frost-free location with deeply worked, free-draining soil with peat or sand, keeping in mind their preference for dry atmospheres and absence of direct sunlight. Plant with the top of the tuber just showing above the soil.

Although Clivia will bloom even if neglected, regular watering during the growing period and weekly liquid feeding as buds appear results in superior flower size and colour. After flowering, remove faded blooms at the base and cease watering. They dislike root disturbance and flower more profusely when left to themselves. Excellent container plants grown in some shady spot and brought into view at flowering time.

Amaryllidaceae.

Clivia miniata
Kaffir Lily
Herbaceous plants with fleshy, tuberous roots, forming robust colonies of bright-green, ligulate, strap-like leaves to 60 × 7cm. Spectacular flower heads resembling agapanthus on 45–75cm stems containing 12–20 brilliant orange or flame red, funnel-shaped flowers with yellow throat appearing late winter through early summer. Miniata — vermillion or scarlet with a mixture of yellow. Evergreen.

COLEONEMA

A genus of about eight species of multi-branched, erect shrubs from South Africa named from the Greek koleos, a sheath and *nema*, a thread referring to the way stamens are enfolded in channels. Attractive, filmy, refined, fast-growing shrubs with slender stems, fine-textured, heath-like foliage and masses of tiny flowers from late winter through early summer.

Plant in full sun in deeply worked, loose, free-draining soil. Reasonably hardy, standing considerable drought and heat. Shear lightly after the main flower crop has finished to maintain compact form and thin out some of the interior stems if overcrowding seems apparent. Plant alongside paths or patios where it can be admired at close range. Use as a single specimen, in shrub or herbaceous borders, or mass planted on banks.

Rutaceae. *All evergreen.*

Coleonema album
Breath of Heaven
South African native, forming a closely twigged bushy shrub furnished with small, heathlike, linear-oblanceolate, 13 × 1mm leaves, highly aromatic when crushed. In early spring the tips of each branchlet become crowded with small, 6mm, starry, white flowers. Locate where the pleasant fragrance of bruised foliage may often be enjoyed. Syn Diosma ericoides. Album — white. 1 × 1.3m.   **91**

Coleonema pulchrum
Pink Diosma, Confetti Bush
Neat, South African shrub with erect, bushy habit, and slender, wispy branches which sway in the breeze. Linear, pale green, 15mm, heath-like leaves. Myriads of small, 10mm, starry rose-pink flowers crowd toward the end of every branch with the first touch of warm spring weather, continuing well into summer. Odd flowers are likely to appear throughout the year. Sprigs of bloom

good for picking. Pulchrum — beautiful. 1.5 × 1.5m.   **91**

Coleonema pulchrum 'Compactum'
Green-foliaged form of Coleonema 'Sunset Gold' with similar growth habit and pale pink flowers early summer. 30–70cm × 1.2m.

Coleonema pulchrum 'Rubrum'
Deep rose pink form developed in Western Australia. More intensely coloured than pulchrum but somewhat less vigorous. 1.5 × 1.5m.

Coleonema pulchrum 'Sunset Gold'
Delightful low-spreading shrub also from Western Australia, valued for its dense, bright golden, aromatic foliage throughout the year but more intense through summer and autumn. A small number of starry, pale pink flowers appears early summer. Prostrate form and brilliant foliage makes this one of the finest ground-cover shrubs. Mass plant in sunny beds, banks, traffic islands etc. For maximum brilliance, plant in full sun, don't over-water or over-feed. Can be clipped to desired shape or size if necessary. Excellent in containers. 30–70cm × 1.2m.   **91**

Coleonema pulchrum 'Winter Charm'
Differs significantly from C pulchrum, flowering at least two months earlier and with compact growth habit more like C album. Beautiful flowering shrub, studded with pink starry flowers during winter. 1.2 × 1.5m

CONVOLVULUS
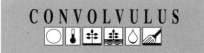

A genus of about 250 species of annual or perennial, shrubby, climbing or scrambling herbs and shrubs widely distributed throughout the earth's subtropical and tropical regions, named from the Latin *convolvo*, to entwine. C cneorum is a charming dwarf shrub, excellent on hot, dry banks or rock gardens, very effective when massed. Plant in open, sunny situations in light, deeply worked, free-draining soil. Prefers not to be watered in dry periods. Easy to grow, quite hardy, prune lightly from time to time to maintain good form.

Convolvulaceae.

Convolvulus cneorum
Excellent small shrub native to Mediterranean regions. Grows rapidly to form a compact, rounded bush with attractive, 4–6cm, silvery-grey, oblanceolate to linear

leaves, covered with fine hair, giving a silky-smooth texture. Great masses of white, open-trumpet, 3–4cm flowers, with bluish tinge, shaded yellow in the throat and with fine hair on the reverse appear early summer through autumn. Attractive combination of foliage and flower. Cneorum — from the Greek *kneoron*, a shrub resembling an olive. Evergreen. .60 × 1m.   **90**

C O P R O S M A

A genus of 90 species of evergreen shrubs and small trees of which about half are found in New Zealand, the remainder throughout the Pacific, Java, Borneo, Hawaii and Tasmania. Genus named from the Greek *kopros*, dung and *osme*, smell, a reference to the foetid smell from crushed leaves of one common, scrubby species. Many New Zealand native species and cultivars are acclaimed worldwide for landscaping adaptability, ornamental value and easy culture.

Coprosmas are versatile and an ever-increasing range of forms, textures and colours includes plants for use as wall-spillers, bank covers, screens, divisions, foregrounds, ground covers and specimen shrubs. They are drought tolerant, grow in almost any soil, revel in sun or shade, withstand ocean spray and respond to shaping or pruning once or twice a year. The term Mirror Plant refers to reflecting qualities of the highly polished leaves of some species.
Rubiaceae. *All evergreen.*

Coprosma acerosa
Sand Dune Coprosma
Unique and picturesque dwarf shrub or ground cover. Forms a cushiony mound of slender, irregularly curving, springy, intertwining, light tan branchlets. Leaves 12 × 1.5mm, deep-green. Tiny flowers if fertilized, produce translucent, pale-blue, 7mm, egg-shaped fruit, ripening autumn. Quite at home in poor, dry, sandy conditions. Acerosa — needle-like. 45cm × 1.5m.

Coprosma acerosa 'Hawera'
Flat-growing, groundcover, spreading prostrate almost like a lawn, gradually mounding with age. Leaves olive-green, very small and narrow. Discovered on coastal cliffs west of Hawera. Tolerant of wind and cold. 30cm × 2m.

Coprosma acerosa 'Taiko'
Spreading, mounding form, building an attractive mound of dark green foliage,

creating cascade effects with branchlets weeping to ground level. Vigorous and hardy. 40cm × 1m.

Coprosma australis
Kanono
Tall growing, large-leaved, fruiting species widely distributed from Three Kings Islands to North Canterbury. Forms a large shrub or small tree with glabrous branches. Leaves broadly elliptic to obovate, to 20 × 10cm, bright green and very glossy in shade, thicker and yellowish- green in the open. Flowers occur late autumn and winter, usually with the previous season's drupes which may take a year to mature. Bright orange to reddish orange, glossy, oval, 9mm drupes borne in large ornamental clusters. Excellent under-storey shrub. Can be trained with a single trunk or multi-stems. Australis — southern. 3 × 2.5m.

Coprosma 'Beatson's Brown'
Desirable small shrub, slender arching branches, narrow, oval brown leaves. Perfect against a large boulder or rock wall. A mutant sport from Beatson's Gold, named for Mr Beatson of Glenfield, retired engineer and native plant enthusiast. 1 × 1m.

Coprosma 'Beatson's Gold'
Rounded shrub, slender angular branches, twiggy branchlets. Leaves broadly ovate, 10–20 × 6–15mm, deep green to olive green, variegated yellow in the centre and along the margins. Best colour in full sun. 1.2 × 1m.   **92**

Coprosma brunnea
Stem and leaf structure not unlike acerosa, growth habit sprawling with interlacing branchlets forming rather open, flattened mats. Small 3mm flowers early spring which if fertilized develop attractive, translucent, blue, 6mm fruits, ripening autumn. Colourful fruit the main attraction. Needs sun and good drainage. 15cm × 1.5m.

Coprosma 'Chocolate Soldier'
Stiffly ascending branches, erect narrow form. Small bronzy-green leaves become rich chocolate-bronze in winter. 2.5 × 1.2m.

Coprosma 'Coppershine'
Handsome, compact shrub with neat and tidy appearance all year. Leaves ovate to elliptic, slightly waved, 20–40 × 10–20mm, dark green, overlaid rich copper, highly polished. Excellent low screen and colour contrast. 1.5 × 1.3m.

Coprosma × cunninghamii 'Purpurea'
Interesting hybrid with 40 × 10mm leaves, dark green in summer, but as the weather

become cooler, foliage turns rich bronzy purple, most attractive when glistening in the sunlight. Better in southern gardens and full exposure. Needs pruning to preserve size and form. 1.5 × 1.5m

Coprosma 'Cutie'
Compact grower with striking, small rounded, 15mm, deep bronze leaves which turn glossy bronze-black in winter. Almost conical form. Good rock garden plant. Withstands dry. 60 × 50cm.

Coprosma 'Glistener'
Upright main stems with lax, pendulous branches. Attractive, glossy, olive-green leaves at times shaded purplish-brown, deepening in winter. Profusion of orange berries during summer and autumn. 2.5 × 1.5m.

Coprosma 'Greensleeves'
Erect, compact form, leaves ovate to ovate-oblong, to 50 × 25mm, deep-green, glossy and curiously rolled to appear saddle-shaped. Reasonable leafy 'filler' shrub. 2 × 1.5m.   **92**

Coprosma × kirkii
Closely branched plant rapidly forming a dense mat of shining, deep olive-green, linear oblong to linear lanceolate leaves to 35 × 15mm, providing one of the best ground covers. Seldom exceeds 30cm in height, one plant spreading to 1.5m. Great wall-spiller, bank cover, sturdy enough for traffic islands. Effectively covers steep or difficult areas. Lends itself to hard trimming or shearing. 30cm × 1.5m.

Coprosma × kirkii 'Goldstream'
Distinctive cultivar collected from Mt Maunganui, selected for its orange-golden stems, which with typical olive-green leaves give the plant an entirely different overall appearance. Somewhat flatter growing and in many respects superior to C kirkii. 30cm × 1.5m.

Coprosma × kirkii 'Variegata'
Excellent variegated form with similar growth patterns but sage-green leaves edged creamy white. Useful plant for almost any situation where a hardy, rapid-growing, easily maintained ground cover or wall-spiller is called for. 30cm × 1.5m.

Coprosma 'Kiwi Gold'
Low growing spreader with small, polished, golden yellow and lime-green variegated, 25 × 8mm leaves on clear yellow branchlets. Handsome foliage effects all year round. Appears to be a variegated form of C prostrata. Remove any green reverting

shoots as soon as they appear. Excellent rock garden or ground cover plant. 50cm × 2m.

Coprosma 'Kiwi Silver'
Excellent spreading plant with 25 × 8mm leaves richly variegated green and silvery white with a hint of pink. Useful for rock garden, ground cover or mass planting. Could also be of C prostrata parentage. 20 × 90cm.   **92**

Coprosma lucida
Shining Karamu
Strong growing shrub or small tree widely distributed through New Zealand in forest undergrowth, often as a epiphyte on fallen trees. Branches robust, glabrous, reddish brown. Leaves obovate to broad-elliptic, to 15 × 5cm, glossy, dark green, paler beneath. Creamy flowers during spring followed in winter by attractive, 10mm, orange-red drupes. Lucida — bright, shining. 3 × 2.5m.

Coprosma 'Middlemore'
Hardy, versatile compact bushy shrub with 30 × 15mm, rich green, glossy, rounded leaves. Resembles C repens, but hardier to frost. 1 × 1m.

Coprosma parviflora 'Tuffet'
Densely interlacing, twiggy shrub with tiny, coppery-bronze leaves forming a low cushion. Parviflora — with small flowers. 90 × 90cm.

Coprosma 'Pride'
Eye catching variegated Coprosma derived from Coppershine with similar leaf size and shape but splashed with yellow, turning quite bright during growth periods. Hints of orange also present intensifying in autumn and becoming quite vivid. Hardy, colourful, compact, easy to care for and likes full exposure. 80 × 80cm.

Coprosma propinqua
Shrub or small tree, divaricate branches, twiggy, tangling branchlets, brown or dark grey bark. Leaves linear-oblong to linear obovate, to 15 × 3mm. Globose, 8mm, translucent-blue to dark blue fruit. Survives in constantly wet ground or in windy locations. Propinqua — related. 3 × 2.5m.

Coprosma prostrata
Forms a perfect mat only a few centimetres high, and grows so densely that rarely can weeds appear through it. Elliptic to elliptic-oblong, rich green, highly polished, leaves, usually no more than 25mm long densely cover the plant. Not a rampant grower, bit steadily fills the required area, gently spilling over rocks and walls. Tolerant of drought and heat and most climatic extremes. Rarely

needs trimming, but remove any vertical shoots which sometimes appear. 15cm × 1.5m.

Coprosma repens 'Goldsplash'
Selected for superior golden-yellow variegation, less tendency to revert and more erect growth habit than C repens 'Variegata'. A chance seedling discovered by Graeme Platt at his Albany nursery. Syn C 'Taupata Gold'. Repens — creeping. 2 × 1.5m.   **92**

Coprosma repens 'Marble Queen'
Typical rounded leaves of the repens group, basically creamy white with deep-green central zone and slight 'overspraying' of green on the margins. 1.3 × 1m.   **92**

Coprosma repens 'Picturata'
Highly polished, rounded leaves with rich green margins and irregular central blotch of creamy yellow and yellow-green. Rather more upright than other repens types. 1.3 × 1m.

Coprosma repens 'Pink Splendour'
Striking cultivar with 40 × 20mm, wavy leaves, variegated as in C repens 'Variegata' but with a distinctive pink wash over the foliage, deepening with cooler autumn and winter temperatures, providing an attractive colourful shrub for months. Easily grown, wind and salt tolerant. Prune or train to any desired shape. 1.5 × 1.5m.   **92**

Coprosma repens 'Poor Knights'
Very prostrate-growing form, rounded, glossy deep-green leaves. Discovered on Poor Knights Islands, east of Whangarei. May be frost tender. 70cm × 2m.

Coprosma repens 'Silver Queen'
More compact with less reach and gracefully arching branches but in many respects like repens variegata. Rounded, rich green foliage with silvery, creamy-white margins. 45cm × 1.5m.

Coprosma repens 'Variegata'
Leaves broad-oblong to broadly ovate-oblong, to 5 × 4cm, highly polished, rich green central zone, broadly and irregularly margined bright yellow. May be trained to almost any form. Easily grown, hardy and colourful foliage shrub. 45cm–1.5m × 1–3m.   **92**

Coprosma rhamnoides
Unique small spreading Coprosma with interlacing branches and short almost thornlike branchlets sparsely covered with deep green, rounded leaves. Small, usually solitary flowers occur during spring succeeded early summer by small 3–4mm

berries, ripe and red the following winter, later turning dark crimson or black. Extremely hardy, withstanding constant exposure to strong winds. Rhamnoides — resembling the genus Rhamnus. 80 × 80cm.

Coprosma robusta
Karamu
A common free-growing species found through New Zealand's main and outer islands. Leaves to 12 × 4cm, dark green and glossy above, paler beneath. Female bush bears bright orange-red fruits in abundance. Naturally somewhat rangy, but can be trained to a compact bush with good form. Robusta — strong in growth. 2 × 1.5m.

Coprosma robusta 'Gordon's Gold'
Resembles C robusta in foliage and form. Leaves clear bright golden yellow where exposed to sun, attractive lime-green in shade. Locate to avoid hottest midday sun and protect from hard frost. Named for Ron Gordon of Taihape who found the plant near Gisborne. 1 × 1m.

Coprosma robusta 'Williamsii Variegata'
Rather graceful with slender, flexible stems providing an open, semi-pendulous effect. Foliage soft and uncrinkled, 8 × 2cm, basically creamy white with marbled central zone of light green and irregular dark green blotches. Prefers semi-shade. 1.5 × 1m.

Coprosma 'Roys Red'
Rather bushy grower with tiny, 10mm, bronze red leaves, becoming more intense during autumn and winter. Easily trained to compact form. 80 × 80cm.

Coprosma rugosa
Variable species with rigid, divaricating, tangling branchlets with dark, reddish brown bark. Leathery leaves, linear to narrowly cuneate, to 12 × 2mm. Typical species forms an erect bush, but the clone described here, collected at high elevation on East Dome in the Air Mountain in Southland, is a flat ground-cover, forming a ground-hugging thicket. Leaves deep bronze-green especially through winter. Branchlets quite golden during summer. Female form bears translucent, pale-blue fruit. Very hardy. Rugosa — wrinkled. 10cm × 1.5m.

Coprosma rugosa 'Clearwater Gold'
Erect growing, male form, more typical of the species, with distinct bronzy gold hue in young shoots. Extremely hardy and excellent for hedges or screens in difficult, exposed locations. 2 × 1.3m.

Coprosma 'Stumpy'

Forms an upright, compact pyramid. Glossy leaves green, suffused wine-red, deep purple in winter. Good in containers. 1m × 60cm.

Coprosma 'The Shiner'

Densely foliaged shrub with leaves 25–60 × 12–35mm, broadly oval, highly polished, slightly curled and bright green. Open erect habit, excellent for screens or backgrounds. 2.5 × 1.5m.

Coprosma 'Thompsons Hybrid'

Excellent groundcover plant with golden stems and very small, 10 × 2mm, bronzy green foliage. Hardy and easily grown. Possible C acerosa parentage. Covers 1m, mounding to 30cm with age.

Coprosma 'Walter Brockie'

Compact grower with glossy, slightly undulating leaves retaining distinctive brown colouring throughout the year, more intensely over winter. Similar to Coppershine but with better colour. 1.2 × 1m.

Coprosma 'Yvonne'

Very dark, glossy, bronzy green, wavy foliage, deepening in winter to almost black. Ideal for contrast or group planting. Better than C Purple Hybrid which it seems to have superseded. Very hardy. Trim to maintain form. 1.5 × 1m.   **92**

CORDYLINE

A genus of fifteen species of woody plants or palm-like trees or shrubs from south east Asia, Polynesia, Hawaii, New Zealand and Australia, named from the Greek *kordyle*, a club, in allusion to large carrot-like, fleshy roots of some species. Cordyline adds a tropical or exotic dimension in landscape design. Easily accommodated, not soil-robbing and quite indifferent to soil or climatic conditions. Spray for caterpillars at the first sign of infestation. Otherwise, an occasional feed and grooming is their only need for care. Agavaceae. *All evergreen.*

Cordyline australis
Cabbage Tree

Commonly found in association with other trees or in colonies in open places of both North and South Islands of New Zealand and in many public and private gardens. Tapering central stem with rough fissured bark. Arching, deep green, sword-like, lanceolate to linear leaves to 90 × 6cm, attached directly to the trunk, clothe the plant to ground level as a juvenile. Having reached 2–3m in height three or four branches develop, each with a rosette of leaves, forming a broad head and clean trunk after the style of a tropical palm.

Impressive drooping spikes to 90cm long comprising myriads of 8mm, sweetly fragrant, creamy-white flowers appear early summer. Compact effects easily created by cutting the main stem at any height, even to ground level. Multiple trunks soon develop. Versatile landscaping plants, either singly, in groups or in containers. Australis — southern. The term Cabbage Tree arose from early settlers who used tender heart-shoots as a vegetable. 6 × 2m.   **109**

Cordyline australis 'Albertii'

Magnificent variegated form, dull-green leaves heavily banded rich creamy-yellow shading to red at the base. New growth tinted salmon rose. Formal upright habit. Among the most handsome of foliage plants, perfect as a dramatic container specimen. 4 × 1.5m.   **109**

Cordyline australis 'Purpurea'

Closely resembles C australis but with rich, bronzy-purple leaves. Somewhat slower growth rate and less ultimate height. Mostly grown from seed, so expect minor variation. 5 × 2m.

Cordyline banksii
Forest Cabbage Tree

Found naturally in forests from North Cape to Westland at altitudes to 1000m. Distinguished from C australis by shorter, slender stems, longer and fewer leaves, and drooping panicles of white flowers. Clumping, bushy, compact habit. Slender, linear-lanceolate, drooping leaves to 1.5m × 8cm, usually with central vein in red, yellow or darker green. Beautiful, drooping, 75cm panicles of white, highly fragrant flowers appear early summer. Most garden situations, but at its best in cool, moist conditions. Banksii — for Sir Joseph Banks, botanist on Cook's New Zealand voyage in 1769. 2.5 × 1.5m.

Cordyline banksii 'Purple Tower'

Hybrid cultivar from C banksii with vigorous upright habit and striking heads of broad, arching, deep reddish-purple foliage with faint glaucous bloom. Large panicles of fragrant, creamy-white flowers, followed by small blue fruit. Handsome, exotic-looking plant. 4 × 2m.

Cordyline baueri
Cabbage Palm

Handsome species from Norfolk Island. Neat, slender, clump-forming plant, each slender stem crowned with a dense cluster of arching, linear-lanceolate, rich-green leaves to 60 × 6cm, narrowed at the base and with a broad midrib. Leaves differ from C australis being shorter, broader and uniformly veined. White fragrant flowers borne above the foliage early summer. Has distinctly fresh or lush appearance especially as a juvenile. Baueri — for Franz and Ferdinand Bauer, 18–19th century botanical artists. 2.5 × 1.5m.

Cordyline baueri (purple form)
Bronze Cabbage Palm

Bronze-leaved version with broader leaves and smaller growth pattern. Fragrant white flowers through summer. Tropical appearance. 2.5 × 1m.

Cordyline 'Green Goddess'

Interesting hybrid cultivar from C kaspar which forms multiple branches close to the ground, densely clothed with short, broad, fresh green, sword-like foliage. Tends to remain as a compact clump rather than forming a terminal head. Small, creamy-white flowers in panicles to 75cm appear amongst the foliage early summer, followed by small, deep-blue fruit. 2.5 × 1.5m.

Cordyline indivisa
Toi, Mountain Cabbage Tree

Most handsome species from cool mountain regions of the lower half of the North Island and parts of the South Island in high rainfall areas, frequently shrouded in mist. A somewhat massive tree, usually with single trunk. Immense, leathery, sword-shaped, narrowly lanceolate leaves to 1.8m × 12cm, green or purplish-green above, glaucous beneath, often with reddish or orange midrib. White flowers tinted mauve in densely branched, pendulous clusters to 1.5m long, appear early summer, followed by deep purplish blue, 7mm fruit.

This magnificent, tropical-looking specimen is not the easiest to manage, preferring cool, moist, mountain conditions which few gardens possess. If inclined to try, plant in rich, deeply dug soil in full or semi-shade, water generously during dry periods and mulch with peat moss, bark or leaves. Indivisa — undivided, referring to the single stem with which it is usually found. 3 × 1m.

Cordyline pumilio

Distinctive small Cordyline, stem to 1.5m, often arching. Grasslike, narrowly linear leaves to 100 × 2cm. Well-spaced white or bluish-white flowers in loosely branched panicles to 60 cm long, followed by 5mm, rounded, bluish-white fruit. Found north of Raglan and Bay of Plenty. Pumilio — dwarf. 1 × 1m.

CORNUS

A genus of about 45 species of shrubs or small trees and semi-woody herbs distributed throughout cooler regions of Siberia, China, Japan, Himalayas, northern and eastern United States, called by the Latin name *cornus*.

The Cornus or Dogwood family provides garden interest all year with either beautiful flowers, foliage, handsome stems or one with strawberry fruit. Generally they prefer low winter temperature and hot dry autumn. The cultivar 'Eddie's White Wonder' is known to bloom well in more temperate climates.

Plant in deeply worked, organically enriched, free-draining, neutral to acid soil conditioned with peat moss. Avoid hot windswept locations and keep the roots cool and moist. Frequent watering and mulching with bark or peat moss will help achieve this. The term 'Dogwood' is said to have originated from the use of a mixture made from the bark of one species for bathing mangy dogs.

Cornaceae. *Mostly deciduous.*

Cornus alba 'Elegantissima'

Rampant, hardy shrub from Siberia, northern China and Korea forming a thicket of erect, glabrous, blood-red stems. Variable, ovate-elliptic, 4–8cm, grey-green leaves with wide, irregular white margins, brilliant autumn colour. Cream, 3–5cm flowers in narrow cymes early summer. Fruit white flushed light blue. Easy to grow, very hardy to cold. Elegantissima — very elegant. 2 × 1.5m.

Cornus capitata
Himalayan Strawberry Tree

Larger growing evergreen species from Himalayas and China. Forms a medium, round-headed tree with horizontal branches and grey, downy young shoots. Leaves ovate to lanceolate, to 12cm long, dull grey-green, tinted reddish bronze in winter, leathery, distinctly curled.

Inconspicuous, creamy white, four petalled flowers through mid-summer, which may take up to ten years before appearing. Blossom followed by 5cm, orange scarlet, strawberry-like, edible fruit in autumn. Allow adequate space and avoid locating the tree where fallen fruit may become an annoyance. Some leaves show autumn and winter colour and in cooler areas a proportion may fall. Capitata — growing in a head. Evergreen. 8 × 7m.

Cornus controversa
Giant Dogwood

Native to Japan, China and Himalayas. Magnificent, tree-like species with picturesque, horizontal, sweeping branches in tiers, brown shoots thickly frosted with white bloom. Luxuriant, alternate leaves, ovate to broadly elliptic, to 15cm long, glossy, dark green above, glaucous beneath, glowing, rich purple-red in autumn, persisting well into winter. Creamy-white, 13mm flowers in broad, flat, fluffy, 10–18cm cymes during spring, followed in autumn by rounded, 6mm, blue-black fruit, relished by birds. Individual flowers unspectacular, but the great masses on every branch provide an impressive display. Enjoys full sun and moist soil. Controversa — doubtful, controversial. 10 × 8m.

Cornus 'Eddies White Wonder'

Hybrid from C florida × C nuttalii raised by Eddie's Nurseries, Vancouver, Canada, highly regarded for good form and magnificent floral display. Superb, hardy tree with erect, pyramidal form, branches loosely pendulous. Broadly rounded, deep green leaves become yellow, orange and scarlet in autumn. Large, pure white flowers to 12cm produced in bracts of up to six during spring. Flowers tinted pink late in the season. Clusters of small red fruit ripen in autumn. Unlike many Dogwoods, this hybrid is known to flower satisfactorily in milder regions of New Zealand's North Island. 4 × 3m.

Cornus florida
North American Dogwood

The North American species and its cultivars are popular amongst both American and European gardeners. Interesting plant for all seasons. Slender erect trunk, branches in horizontal tiered pattern, terminating with upright, greyish twigs. Broadly oval to ovate, 7–15cm, dull-green leaves, white downy beneath, vivid orange, red or violet in autumn. Myriads of pure white, 4cm, upward facing, four-petalled, obovate bracts enclosing 12mm, dome-shaped clusters of tiny greenish petals, arranged in layers on twiggy branches. Small clusters of ovoid, 1cm, reddish fruit in autumn, remain until eaten by birds. Florida — flowering. 4 × 3m.   **109**

Cornus florida 'Cherokee Chief'

Choice American hybrid from Tennessee claimed to be the deepest red flowering Cornus. Four-petalled, deep rose flower bracts paler at the base. New spring growth bright bronzy red, deep green and glossy through summer, yellow, scarlet and wine-red in autumn. 4 × 3m.

Cornus florida 'Cherokee Daybreak'

Excellent selected hybrid cultivar. Leaves fresh green with broad, creamy white outer zone and waved margins, turning salmon pink to rosy purple in autumn. Large snow white flower bracts. 3 × 2m.

Cornus florida 'Cherokee Princess'

Superior hybrid cultivar. Vigorous grower with wide-spreading branches. Leaves light green and glossy, turning a fiery blend of orange apricot and red in autumn. Medium sized, creamy white flower bracts with curiously twisted petals borne in great profusion. 4 × 3m.

Cornus florida 'Cherokee Sunset'

Vigorous, improved selection, young shoots tipped pinkish-red, mature leaves dark green, broadly margined lemon yellow, turning shades of rose pink, red and purple in autumn. Impressive, large purplish-red flower bracts. Disease resistant. 3 × 2.5m.

Cornus florida 'Cloud Nine'

American selection noted for impressive displays of pure white, extra large, rounded bracts and central green flower clusters at an early age, followed by red fruit in autumn. Strong grower, rounded spreading growth habit, leaves elliptic, bright green in summer, yellow, scarlet, orange and purple in autumn. Performs best in cooler climates but reasonably tolerant of heat and lack of winter chill. 4 × 3m.

Cornus florida 'Pendula'
Weeping Dogwood

Attractive, slow-growing cultivar with distinctive, stiffly drooping branches. Deep green summer foliage becoming deep purple, suffused scarlet in autumn. Pure white flower bracts. Impressive lawn specimen. 3–4 × 2.5m.

Cornus florida 'Rainbow'

Excellent, pyramidal small tree with horizontal branch structure. New shoots lime green at first becoming deep green, splashed golden yellow around the leaf margins. Autumn foliage brilliant rainbow colours from pink to carmine red, lavender-blue to purple-red. Small white flower bracts in spring followed by small reddish fruit in autumn. 4 × 3m.

Cornus florida 'Spring Song'

Excellent small round headed tree with slender trunk and spreading branches. New spring shoots green suffused red, fresh green through summer, changing in autumn to orange, red, wine-purple intensifying to deep purple. Soft rosy pink flower bracts, small red fruit in autumn. 4 × 3m.

Cornus florida 'Stokes Pink'

Strong grower, forming an elegant, round-headed tree with ascending branch structure. Clear rich pink flower bracts in abundance in spring. Autumn foliage a blend of red and purple persisting well into winter. Known to flower satisfactorily in milder regions of New Zealand's North Island. 4 × 3m.

Cornus kousa
Kousa Dogwood, Japanese Dogwood

Native to Japan and Korea. Forms a large multi-stemmed shrub, or can be trained to a small, single-stem tree with spreading, dense, horizontal habit of growth and delicate branch structure. Lustrous, medium green, ovate, 5–9cm, leaves with serrated margins and conspicuous tufts of rust-brown hairs on the undersides of the leaf axils. Autumn foliage colours vivid yellow and scarlet. Blooms early summer, later than other Dogwoods, creamy white, pointed four-petalled bracts, 7cm across, becoming pink along the edges, poised on slender erect stems above the foliage. Red, 2cm, strawberry-like fruit suspended below the branches in autumn. Very hardy but requires good soil conditions. 4 × 3m.

Cornus kousa 'Southern Cross'

Specially selected for creamy-white flower bracts produced in abundance early summer and effective, vivid red autumn foliage colours. 3–4 × 2.5m.

Cornus mas
Cornelian Cherry

Found naturally in southern Europe and the Orient. Usually an airy, twiggy shrub but trainable as a small, spreading, densely branched tree. Young branches covered with greyish-green pubescence. Leaves ovate to 10cm long, glossy, green, turning yellow, red or purple in autumn. One of the earliest Dogwoods to bloom, producing an abundance of 2cm, bright yellow bracts in clusters of three or four on naked twigs late winter-early spring, followed in autumn by clusters of bright scarlet, 2cm, edible fruit used in making preserves and relished by birds. Withstands sub-zero temperatures and alkaline soil. Mas — from masculine, used by early writers in a metaphorical sense to distinguish robust species from the more delicate. 5 × 3m.

Cornus stolonifera 'Kelseyi'
Red Osier Dogwood

Vigorous shrub from eastern North America with procumbent branches suckering freely. Distinctive, glabrous, dark purple-red young shoots. Leaves ovate to oval-lanceolate, to 10cm long, dark green above, glaucous blue-green beneath with fine, adpressed hairs on both surfaces, turning red in autumn. Dull-white flowers in 4cm cymes followed in autumn by 6–8mm, white, globose fruit. The cultivar C Kelseyi, forms a compact mounded bush with bright red stems. Suitable for ground cover and wet sites. Stolonifera — having stolons, root runners. Syn C stolonifera 'Nana'. 60cm × 1m.

COROKIA

A genus of about six species of evergreen shrubs from New Zealand and Australia named from an adaptation of the Maori name *korokio*. Corokias are extremely hardy and useful plants, characterized by twiggy branch patterns, myriads of fragrant, starry, yellow flowers and colourful drupes. They thrive in practically any soil with good drainage, are tolerant of coastal extremes, open situations in full sun or beneath larger trees, can be severely trimmed or shaped and are one of the easiest plants to establish. Birds enjoy the prolific crops of ornamental berries.
Cornaceae. *All evergreen.*

Corokia buddleoides
Korokio

Found in the North Island from Mangonui to Rotorua and East Cape growing in or along margins of coastal or lowland forests. Slender, multi-branched shrub with yellowish to dark green, lanceolate, 12 × 2cm leaves, silvery-grey beneath. Starry, bright yellow, 12mm flowers, followed by dark red to black 7mm berries. Excellent border shrub. Buddleoides — resembling Buddleia. 2 × 1.5m.

Corokia cotoneaster
Wire Netting Bush

Found in the drier river flats or rocky places of the North and South Islands and Three Kings Islands. Forms a sparsely foliaged roundish shrub with slender, angular, twiggy, rigid branches, tortuous and very interlaced suggestive of its common name. Sparse, orbicular, 12–20mm leaves, dark green to dark maroon above, white felted beneath. Bright yellow, 12mm, starry flowers carried in small clusters towards the twig ends spring through early summer, followed late summer and autumn by small, round, deep orange or red berries. 2.5 × 1m.

Corokia cotoneaster 'Little Prince'

Small, slender, erect, twiggy shrub with zig-zagging branches and black bark. Leaves orbicular, to 4 × 4mm on a broad, or winged, 6mm petiole, green with silvery reverse. Masses of small, starry, yellow flowers, followed by red berries. 1.2 × .90m.

Corokia macrocarpa
Whakatata

From the forests of Chatham Islands. Seen either as an erect or somewhat spreading shrub or small tree with robust branches and dark, rough bark. Leaves lanceolate, to 8 × 3cm, glossy, grey-green to sage-green, silvery beneath. Starry, bright yellow, 15mm flowers with a central orange zone, carried in axillary racemes through spring, followed by red or orange drupes in autumn and winter. Withstands dry areas and grows beneath large trees. Macrocarpa — large fruited. 3 × 2m.

Corokia × virgata 'Bronze King'

Resembles C 'Cheesemanii'. Leaves glossy, dark green, suffused bronze around margins and base, silver beneath. Heavy crops of deep red fruit. 2 × 1.2m.

Corokia × virgata 'Bronze Lady'

Generally resembles C 'Cheesemanii', but perhaps taller and with very dense branches. Leaves bronze, covered with fine hairs, oblong-lanceolate or elliptic-oblong, margins sinuate or wavy. Bright red fruit in moderate quantities. 2.4 × 1.5m.

Corokia × virgata 'Cheesemanii'

Natural hybrid from C cotoneaster × C buddleoides occurring in various localities of New Zealand's North Island. The clone selected for cultivation forms a slender, erect, multi-branched shrub with dense, twiggy, zig-zagging branches, somewhat less interlaced than C cotoneaster. Leaves oblanceolate-elliptic to 45 × 10mm, dark green and glossy, silvery beneath. Literally smothers itself with bright canary-yellow, 12mm flowers in axillary and terminal panicles during spring followed by 5–7mm, oblong-ovate, reddish berries. Good specimen or screen especially for dry, windy locations. 2 × 1.2m. **109**

Corokia × virgata 'Frosted Chocolate'

Resembles C 'Cheesemanii', but with distinctive, dusky, pinkish-brown or chocolate-brown leaves, intensifying during cooler months. 2 × 1.2m.

Corokia × virgata 'Geenty's Green'

Resembles C 'Cheesemanii', selected for bright green foliage with silvery reverse. 2 × 1.2m.

Corokia × virgata 'Red Wonder'

Upright, slender shrub, narrow bronzy green leaves to 45mm with white undersides, in most respects resembling C 'Cheesemanii'. Starry yellow flowers followed by heavy crops of polished, bright-red berries. One of the best Corokias for fruit display. 2 × 1.2m.

Corokia × virgata 'Sunsplash'

Attractive cultivar with 30 x 10mm, creamy-yellow leaves splashed green and a touch of pink, silvery felted beneath. Mature stems almost black. Open, sunny location for best colour. 2 × 1.2m.   **109**

Corokia × virgata 'Yellow Wonder'

Upright shrub, more densely branched and vigorous than Red Wonder, leaves 12–50 × 7–16mm, elliptic to oblanceolate, green and glossy. Starry yellow flowers followed by abundant crops of glossy, golden yellow berries. Somewhat resembles C buddleoides. Distinctive and beautiful. 2 × 1.2m.

CORONILLA

The genus comprises about 20 species of shrubs and herbs from central or southern Europe, Orient and North Africa The Latin *corona*, a crown, refers to golden, radiating umbels. The listed species is a charming, easily grown little shrub. Plant in deeply worked, free-draining soil in a warm, sunny location. Pinch back often, provide support if necessary or allow to scramble over rocks or walls.

Leguminosae.

Coronilla valentina ssp glauca 'Variegata'
Daffodil Bush

Charming glabrous shrub from southern Spain and Portugal. Attractive, pinnate, clover-like leaves, with three to six pairs of broadly ovate, leaflets to 20 × 10mm, sea green, heavily splashed and bordered rich creamy-white. Pea-shaped, golden-yellow, 7–12mm flowers, strongly fragrant during the day, produced in umbels of up to twelve on 75mm stems through spring summer and into autumn. Valentina — from Valentia, Spain. Evergreen. 1 × 1.2m.

CORREA

A genus of about 11 species of Australian shrubs, mainly from south eastern regions, named for Jose Francesco Correa de Serra, 18th century Portugese botanist. Flowers suggestive of the common name Australian Fuchsia, but there the similar-

ity ends. Beautiful, compact shrubs providing year-round bloom, rich in nectar and attractive to birds.

Correas flower best in full sun in fast draining, loamy, rocky or sandy soil, even if inclined to be slightly alkaline. Overwatering and overfeeding is a sure killer, although during the growth season they respond to light dressings of slow-release fertilizer. Most species respond to heavy pruning, even by a third at planting time, and then each year for vigorous growth and maximum bloom. Useful as ground cover, in shrub borders, on banks or slopes, as container plants or wherever they can be enjoyed at close range.

Rutaceae. *All evergreen.*

Correa alba
White Correa

Compact, spreading shrub with light brown, woolly branchlets, ovate to orbicular leaves to 4cm covered with fine grey or brown tomentum and white tomentum beneath. White, waxy, four-petalled, open bell-shaped, 25mm flowers with reflexed lobes, carried singly, in pairs or threes through autumn to early spring and spasmodically through the year. C alba var pannosa has smaller leaves and grows only 50cm high with a spread of two metres. 1.2 × 1.2m.

Correa backhousiana

Small, dense, spreading shrub with rusty-hairy stems and branches. Leaves ovate to elliptic, to 3cm, green, smooth, leathery, hairy beneath. Tubular, pendulous flowers to 25mm, creamy-yellow to pale green, early winter through late spring. Will bloom freely in semi-shade. Named for Jas Backhouse, English missionary and botanist. 1.5 × 2m.

Correa 'Dusky Bells'

Low growing hybrid with spreading, reddish brown branchlets. Leaves to 35 × 20mm, cordate, pale to medium green, hairy on both surfaces at first, glabrous when mature. Tubular, carmine-pink, 4cm flowers autumn through spring. Reliable shrub for temperate, non humid areas. Excellent, long lived ground cover. 50cm × 2m.

Correa 'Mannii'

Hybrid cultivar, probably from C pulchella × C reflexa. Leaves cordate, to 30 × 20mm, glossy, dark green, lighter below. Beautiful, 4cm tubular flowers with reflexed tips, red outside, pink within, autumn through spring and sporadically through the year. Prefers partial shade. 1 × 2m.

Correa 'Marian's Marvel'

Wide-spreading form with masses of 30mm, pendulous, pale pink, bell-shaped flowers,

suffused lime-green near the tip, autumn through early spring. Hybrid from C backhousiana × C reflexa. 1.5 × 2m.

Correa pulchella

Attractive, South Australian shrub. Smooth, green, 12–20mm, oval to elliptic leaves. Tubular flowers in pink and salmon, borne in mass autumn through spring and sporadically through the year. Partial sun or shade. Pulchella — pretty. 20–100cm × 1.5m

Correa reflexa 'Fat Fred'

The species is widely distributed in all States except Northern Territory. Leaves to 50 × 30mm, broadly lanceolate, often cordate and usually smooth. The cultivar 'Fat Fred' has large, 30 × 12mm, tubular flowers with flared mouth, red with greenish yellow tips. Reflexa — turned sharply back, referring to the foliage. 1 × 2m.

CORTADERIA

The genus comprises about 24 species of large perennial grasses from tropical and temperate South America, New Zealand and New Guinea, named from *cordadera*, Argentinian name for Pampas grass. Although boasting plume-like inflorescences and graceful tussock-forming habit, both the mauve-plumed South American species, C jubata and white-plumed C selloana have reached almost plague proportions in many areas, invading and smothering young forest trees or creating fire hazards.

Under strictly controlled conditions, Pampas Grass or Toe Toe can provide an impervious and rapid windbreak. The more ornamental cultivars are valuable landscaping plants in difficult situations. Periodic grooming is necessary to dispose of dead leaves and spent flower stems, a task practically impossible by hand on account of razor-sharp leaf margins. Setting fire to the tussock late winter or early spring is most effective and new growth will quickly appear. New Zealand native species are less aggressive.

Graminae. *All evergreen.*

Cortaderia fulvida
Mountain Toetoe, Kakaho

New Zealand species from grassland or forest margins, and alongside streams from sea-level to sub-alpine regions of the North Island. Arching, grass-like foliage and tawny, creamy-buff flower plumes on 2m stems resembling Toe Toe. Hardy to wind and frost. Fulvida — buff. 2 × 1.5m.

Cortaderia richardii
South Island Toetoe, Plumed Tussock
Familiar along New Zealand's South Island rivers. Plumes to 60cm on long petioles, white, tinged yellow or silver. Narrow leaves to 120cm, leathery and tough, growing more or less erect then drooping at the tips. 2.5 × 2m.

Cortaderia selloana
Silver Pampas Grass
From temperate South America. Aggressive grower with deep green, narrow, arching, leaves to 2.5m, margins finely saw-toothed. Silvery-white or pink, 30–60cm flower plumes on long stems, arise above the leaves. Grows anywhere, withstanding hot, dry, arid wasteland, gale force winds and salt spray. Forms a natural windbreak, the razor sharp leaves making it impervious to man and beast. Windborne seeds germinate freely. Grub them out or spray as soon as they appear. Named for Friederich Sellow, 19th century German traveller and naturalist. 3 × 2m.

Cortaderia selloana 'Gold Band'
General appearance and hardiness as for selloana but less aggressive. Leaves attractively margined golden yellow. Rapid dense screen in suitable areas and an attractive landscaping plant. Syn C selloana 'Aureo-Lineata'. 2 × 2m. **109**

CORYLOPSIS

A genus of about thirty species of deciduous, spreading shrubs or small trees from Bhutan to Japan, named from the Greek *korylos*, hazel and *opsis*, like or similar, from the resemblance to corylus. Hardy, oriental shrubs, related to Hamamelis or Witch Hazel. At their best in association with other shrubs such as Azaleas, Rhododendrons, Camellias, Pieris etc, in borders or woodland setting. Plant in a sheltered location, in sun or partial shade, with cool, moist acid soil conditions and water frequently in dry periods.
Hamamelidaceae.

Corylopsis spicata
Winter Hazel
Hardy Japanese shrub with rather open structure, attractive delicate branching pattern and woolly young shoots. Leaves to 11cm, greyish-green, ovate to obovate with cordate base, margins toothed, conspicuously veined, downy beneath. Masses of very fragrant, yellow, bell-shaped flowers in 6–8cm racemes resembling flowering currant blossoms, appear very early spring on bare branches, bursting forth from greenish-yellow bracts. Spicata — bearing spikes. Deciduous. 1.8 × 2m.

CORYLUS

A genus of about 15 species of hardy, deciduous shrubs or small trees from north temperate Asia, Europe and America, Corylus being the classical Latin name. Grown for distinctive branching habits, handsome foliage, conspicuous spring catkins and nut-bearing qualities. Extremely hardy in the bleakest places and grow freely in any reasonable soil. Occasional deep watering and mulching minimizes leaf burn, an unsightly problem under dry summer conditions.
Corylaceae. *All deciduous.*

Corylus avellana
Hazelnut
European species forming a dense, suckering thicket of stems with greyish-brown bark peeling in thin, curling strips. Leaves orbicular or roundish to 10 × 10cm, deep green, turning yellow in autumn. Brownish-yellow, 5–10cm male flower catkins appear early spring before the leaves. Ovoid, 5mm, female catkins when pollinated produce rounded nuts of good flavour, usually enclosed by two irregularly lobed bracts. Good hardy screen or filler with year-round interest. Avellana — old generic name of the hazel. Named cultivars selected for high quality nuts include 'Alexandra', 'Appleby', 'Barcelona', 'Ennis', 'Merville de Bolwiller', 'Nottingham', 'Whispit', 'White Filbert', 'White Heart'. 4 × 3m.

Corylus avellana 'Contorta'
Harry Lauder's Walking Stick
Upright shrub with twisted, waved and curled, corkscrew-like stems. Leaves resemble C avellana but somewhat smaller. Ornamental, greenish-yellow catkins late winter to early spring. Locate where its curiosity value may be appreciated. Cut branches valuable for floral art. Common name refers to the cane of a Scottish comedian from a bygone era. Contorta — irregularly bent, twisted. 3 × 2.5m.

Corylus maxima 'Atropurpurea'
Purple Leafed Filbert
Distinctive branching pattern and handsome, dark purple, almost black leaves in spring and summer, rivalling many other foliage trees for colour intensity. The colour changes to dull purplish-green in summer. Rounded leaves, margins serrated, slightly lobed and prominently veined, resembling copper beech. Creates exciting contrasts with golden or paler leaved trees. Locate to avoid the hottest midday sun and keep moist through dry periods. Maxima — largest. Atropurpurea — dark purple. 2.5 × 2.5m.

CORYNOCARPUS

A genus of four species of evergreen trees from New Zealand, New Caledonia and Vanuatu named from the Greek *koryne*, a club and karpos, fruit, from the shape of the fruit. Earlier Maoris valued the fruit, ate the flesh raw, but thoroughly prepared the kernels which untreated were most unpalatable and highly poisonous, causing convulsions, paralysis and even death.

Young shoots may suffer frost damage. Select a warm location where fallen fruit will not create a mess. Plant in rich, deeply worked soil with adequate drainage and keep moist during dry periods until well established. Matures slowly, retaining its handsome form without attention for years. Specimens, backgrounds, screens or containers.
Corynocarpaceae.

Corynocarpus laevigatus
Karaka, New Zealand Laurel
Extremely handsome, upright tree seen frequently in eastern and western coastal or lowland forests of New Zealand's North and South Islands as far south as Banks Peninsula and Greymouth. Leaves to 18 × 9cm, elliptic-oblong to obovate-oblong, laurel-like, dark green, leathery and glossy. Insignificant panicles of greenish, 5mm flowers, followed during summer and autumn by heavy crops of 25–40mmm, elliptic to narrowly-ovoid, smooth, orange coloured fruit resembling a fleshy plum. Laevigatus — smooth and polished. Evergreen. 8 × 5m.

COTINUS

A genus of three species of woody, deciduous shrubs or small trees from North America, Europe, Himalayas and China, named from the Greek *kotinus*, wild-olive — application uncertain. Highly valued for leaf colour and curious flower effects. Closely allied to the Rhus family, they are easy to grow in any open

situation and cool, free-draining, soil. Over-rich soil may encourage coarse, rank growth and poor leaf colour. Prune heavily after leaf fall for growth renewal, a neater growing bush and better foliage display.

More intense colour can be expected in areas with cold winters and dry summers. However, they're worth planting in milder climates. Perfect for adding colour to shrub borders, backgrounds or lawn specimens.

Anacardiaceae. *All deciduous.*

Cotinus coggygria
European Smoke Bush, *Venetian Sumach*
From southern Europe to central China. Bushy, spreading shrub developing into a broad, urn-shaped mass. Leaves to 75mm, bright green, smooth, broadly elliptic to oblong-ovate, yellow to orange-red in autumn. A profusion of multi-branched, 20cm panicles of fawny-purple, misty flowers in fuzzy looking plumes early summer, become smoky-grey by late summer and suggest the common name. Coggygria — from the Greek *kokkugia*, a smoke bush. 3 × 3m.

Cotinus coggygria 'Foliis Purpureis'
Purple Smoke Bush
Rich, wine-purple foliage through spring and early summer, turning purplish-green through summer and light red shades in autumn. During summer plumes of tiny, reddish-purple flowers give a hazy, smoky appearance. 2.5 × 2.5m.

Cotinus coggygria 'Royal Purple'
Richly coloured form with deepest wine-purple, paddle shaped leaves covered with a distinct waxy or satiny bloom, quite translucent in the sun's rays. Purple colour retained throughout summer, becoming bright orange and scarlet in autumn. Greyish, pinky-mauve flowers in immense terminal panicles create a smoky haze over the bush mid-summer. 2.5 × 2m.

Cotinus obovatus
American Smokewood
Choice, larger growing species from south-eastern United States. Leaves broad elliptic to obovate, to 12cm, blue-grey with slender, red petioles, fresh green through summer, becoming a riot of scarlet, orange, yellow and purple in autumn, persisting well into winter in sheltered locations. Flowers few and without smoky effects, but worth planting for outstanding autumn colour alone. Obovatus — egg-shaped with the broadest end uppermost. Syn C americanus. 5 × 3m.

COTONEASTER

A widespread genus of more than 70 species from Europe, North Africa and east Asia, Siberia and Himalayas, named from the Latin *cotoneum*, quince and *aster*, incomplete resemblance. Highly valued for autumn and winter berries, graceful branch pattern and a bonus of spring blossom. Among the numerous species and cultivars are ground covers, dwarf and medium shrubs and trees.

They like full sun, grow in most soils and climates, and thrive with little care and attention. Cotoneasters look best with naturally arching branch pattern. Restrict pruning to removing old or dead branches rather than shortening back those which carry the next crop of flower and berry. Avoid cramping for space to allow free branch development.

Rosaceae. *All semi-evergreen.*

Cotoneaster adpressus
Creeping Cotoneaster
Prostrate, ground hugging species from western China, slow growing but eventually wide-spreading with rigid branches, smooth, broad-ovate or obovate, 6–15mm, dull-green leaves which turn reddish in autumn before falling. Tiny red and white flowers, followed by a brilliant display of 8mm, somewhat globose, bright red fruit. Excellent bank or ground cover. Follows ground and rock contours and drapes over walls. Adpressus — a reference to the way certain leaves are pressed against a stem. 30cm × 2m.

Cotoneaster congestus
Native to the Himalayas. Scandent or prostrate shrub, slowly forming a dense, rounded bush with branches curving downwards. Leaves to 11cm, obovate-elliptic, spirally arranged, dull bluish-green, whitish beneath. Flowers white shaded pink and carmine red, 9mm fruit. Follows rock contours well, foregrounds or containers. Congestus — arranged very closely together. 1 × 1m.

Cotoneaster conspicuus 'Decorus'
Necklace Rockspray
Almost prostrate grower from south eastern Tibet. Short, rigid branches from main stems form a low dense mat. Leaves to 20mm, oblong or lanceolate, deep green, densely cover each branch. White, 10mm flowers followed by shiny, scarlet, 9mm, somewhat globose fruit. Ground or bank cover, rock gardens or containers. Name — conspicuous and decorative. 15cm × 2m.

Cotoneaster dammeri
Chinese species forming an excellent, ground-hugging carpet flowing over and around rocks and cascading over walls. Vigorous, long, prostrate rooting branches covered with elliptic to obovate leaves to 30 × 14mm, dark green and glossy above, whitish beneath. White spring flowers to 13mm and showy, bright red, somewhat globose, 5mm berries in autumn and winter. 15cm × 3m.

Cotoneaster dammeri 'Royal Beauty'
Vigorous ground-hugging form with small 10cm leaves and long-trailing stems covering an area 3–4 square metres in 5–10 years. Heavy crops of orange-red fruit in autumn, attractive to birds. Ideal for ground cover or sunny banks. 15cm × 3m.

Cotoneaster dammeri 'Skogholm'
Smaller foliage than above, but with similar gracefully curving branches and prostrate, wide-spreading habit. Bright orange fruit, borne earlier and more prolifically. 30cm × 2.5m.

Cotoneaster harrovianus
Chinese species. Graceful, arching branches, leaves elliptic-oblong to 45mm, dark green and glossy above, buff pubescence beneath. White flowers in 4cm corymbs followed autumn and winter with pendulous clusters of waxy, 8mm, nearly globose, red fruit. Fine berry shrub in the top of its class. 2.5 × 2m.

Cotoneaster horizontalis
From western China. Low growing, wide spreading habit with stiffly angled stems and fan or herring-bone branchlets laying flat on the ground. Leaves, broadly elliptic to 13mm, bright green and glossy, paler beneath, turning vivid orange and red in autumn. Red and white flowers followed by masses of shiny, bright red, 5mm fruit. Bank or ground cover, large rockeries, low traffic barriers or espalier. Avoid planting alongside paths or driveways where branches would have to be cut back. Allow room to spread and develop naturally. 30cm × 3m.

Cotoneaster horizontalis 'Superba'
Similar to above, but with larger and more widespread foliage fans. Larger leaves and berries. Tends to display its fascinating branch pattern better, but otherwise of equal size and merit. 30cm × 3m.

Cotoneaster horizontalis 'Variegatus'
Delightful cultivar with smaller, 6mm leaves artistically variegated cream and white, suffused red. Excellent, small-scale, decorative foliage plant. Produces berries but not profusely. 30cm × 1m.

Cotoneaster microphyllus
Rockspray Cotoneaster
Native of Himalayas and south west China. Useful, versatile, compact dwarf shrub, main branches usually trailing and root-forming, with secondary branches more erect. Leaves to 8mm, ovate to obovate, glossy, dark green, grey beneath. Masses of 8mm white flowers followed by 7mm, carmine red fruits. Remove upright branches for lower form. Microphyllus — small leafed. 1 × 2m.

Cotoneaster microphyllus 'Cochleatus'
From western China and south east Tibet. More prostrate and compact than above. Flower, fruit and foliage similar, but leaves brighter, broader and with edges that tend to curl. Moulds to ground or rock contours and probably the best ground cover in the microphyllus group. Cochleatus — leaves spiralling like a snail shell. 60cm × 2m.

Cotoneaster microphyllus 'Thymifolius'
More compact than the species but with stiff, upright branches. Leaves narrower, flowers similar, fruit smaller and in clusters. Tends to become woody. Pruning to thin out and shorten branches may be necessary. Thymifolius — thyme-like leaves. 1 × 2m.

Cotoneaster microphyllus 'Thymifolius Variegatus'
Resembles above in form and foliage, but leaves attractively variegated creamy-yellow, green with a hint of red. 1 × 2m.

Cotoneaster prostratus
Vigorous, Himalayan, semi-prostrate species with elongated, arching branches, at first sparsely hairy, becoming glabrous with greyish-brown bark forming a dense, rounded bush. Leaves broad obovate-elliptic to 13 × 6mm, glossy, dark green, ash-grey beneath. Solitary, white flowers to 10mm followed by 10mm, globose, crimson fruit. Prostratus — flat or prostrate. 1 × 1.5m.

Cotoneaster 'Red Fan'
Forms a large rounded shrub with masses of bright red fruit borne fanwise on flat herringbone-type branches. Showy fruit persists well into winter and valued for floral art. Extremely hardy. 3–4 × 3m.

Cotoneaster salicifolius 'Autumn Fire'
Willowleaf Cotoneaster
The Chinese species C salicifolius is a vigorous upright grower with arching branches to 4–5m, narrow willow-like leaves and invasive roots. 'Autumn Fire' is a delightful prostrate form with lax, procumbent to pendulous branches. Leaves elliptic, to 80 × 25mm, glossy, dark green and slightly wrinkled above, sea-green beneath with fine, purplish veins. White, 5mm flowers in clusters of up to 12, followed in autumn by heavy crops of orange-red fruit. Excellent hardy bank or groundcover or wall-spiller. Lends itself to training on a single stem with weeping crown. Syn. C s 'Herbstfeuer'. Salicifolius — willow-leaved. 25cm × 2m.

Cotoneaster salicifolius 'Scarlet Leader'
Similar in many respects to C dammeri 'Skogholm' but with dark red to scarlet stems, dark green foliage and coral red fruit. Graceful spreading habit ideal for grafting on a standard. 30cm × 2.5m.

Cotoneaster × watereri 'Cornubia'
Large, vigorous shrub, branches rise diagonally then arch in somewhat open formation. Leaves oblong-lanceolate to 10 × 4cm, dark green above, wrinkled with irregular veins beneath. White flowers followed by large, bright red, globose, almost pendent fruit, considered the largest and heaviest crop among Cotoneasters. 4 × 3m.

CRATAEGUS

A genus of between 100 and 200 species of deciduous shrubs or small trees mostly from temperate regions of the northern hemisphere, named from the Greek *kratos*, strength, referring to the strength and hardness of the wood. A hardy group of small, dense and thorny trees, thriving almost anywhere but seen at their best in areas of distinct seasons and cold winters. Free-flowering members of the Rose family, with profuse spring blossom after the leaves have formed and showy fruits like tiny apples or pears through summer and autumn. Birds and bees love these trees. Commonly known as Hawthorn, most species have thorny branches.

Grow them in full or partial sun in deeply worked, free-draining, moisture retentive, but not over-rich soil. Avoid over-feeding to discourage excessive, succulent growth. After flowering, prune for shape and thin excess twiggy growth. Despite such negative factors as aggressive thorns, possible fireblight disease and attacks from pests like aphids, pear slug or slug worm, true garden lovers cannot help but admire these trees and have an irresistible desire to possess at least one.

Rosaceae. *All deciduous.*

Crataegus ellwangeriana
Hardy, eastern North American species. Small tree with ascending branches, sparse, 3–5cm thorns. Leaves ovate to oval to 8cm, margins with shallow lobes, green and quite pubescent above, shaggy beneath especially young leaves. White, 2cm flowers with pink anthers in large clusters up to ten, followed by impressive displays of 15mm, bright crimson-red, oblong fruit. Syn C cordata. 5 × 4m.

Crataegus laevigata 'Chapel'
Hardy erect grower literally smothered with clusters of rich pink, fully double flowers mid spring. Resembles 'Paul's Scarlet' except for colour. Originated in Taihape, New Zealand. Laevigata — smooth, referring to the foliage. 5 × 3m.

Crataegus laevigata 'Paul's Scarlet'
Crimson Hawthorn
Delightful cultivar from European, North African and Indian species. Forms a shapely, round-headed small tree with 25mm thorns. Leaves to 6cm across, obovate in outline, 3–5 shallow rounded lobes with serrated margins, dark green, glabrous above, paler beneath. Impressive, bright crimson, fully double, 25mm flowers appearing with lush foliage, literally smother each branch late spring. Not one for fruit, but hard to equal for sheer floral beauty. Syn C oxycantha. Syn C 'Coccinea Plena'. 5 × 3m. **110**

Crataegus laevigata 'Plena'
White Hawthorn
Resembles Paul's Scarlet, but with white, fully double flowers maturing pale pink. 4.5 × 3m.

Crataegus laevigata 'Roseo-Plena'
Double Pink Hawthorn
Resembles Paul's Scarlet but with masses of highly fragrant, double, pink blossoms. 4.5 × 3m.

Crataegus pedicellata
Scarlet Haw
From north east North America. Forms a small tree with widespread crown, slender branches, straight or slightly curved thorns to 5mm. Leaves broad-ovate to 10cm with 4–5 pairs of shallow lobes, margins serrated, dark green and wrinkled above, glabrous beneath, rich autumn colours. White, 15–20mm flowers with reddish anthers in crowded corymbs followed by clusters of pear-shaped, bright red, 10mm fruit. Pedicellata — relating to stalk of flower or fruit. 5 × 5m.

Crataegus phaenopyrum
Washington Thorn
From south east USA. Graceful tree with open branch structure and rounded crown, occasionally branched. Maple-like leaves to

7 × 3cm, triangular to broadly ovate, 3–5 lobed and sharply serrated, bright green, glossy, turning orange-red in autumn. White, 10mm flowers with pink anthers in 7cm corymbs, followed in autumn by 5cm, almost globose, bright orange-red fruit which hang on through winter. Seems to resist fireblight. Syn C cordata. 8 × 7m.

Crataegus pubescens
Mexican Hawthorn
Vigorous Mexican species reputed to be hardy regardless of its origin. Leaves elliptic to obovate, scalloped and sharply toothed margins, glossy, green above, felted beneath. White, 20mm flowers in 6–15cm, densely woolly corymbs followed by orange-yellow, globular to pear-shaped, edible fruit. Pubescens — downy. Syn C stipulacea. Semi-evergreen. 5 × 3m.

CRINODENDRON

A genus of two species of shrubs or small trees from Argentina and Chile named from the Greek *krinon*, lily and *dendron*, tree in reference to the flowers of C patagua. Handsome evergreen, highly regarded for foliage, flower, fragrance and form. Crinodendron is hardy to −10°C, performing best in cool summer areas. Choose a location sheltered from cold wind and plant in deeply worked, free-draining, fertile, organically enriched, moisture retentive, acid soil. Mulch freely and keep moist during dry spells.

Crinodendron may be grown as a large shrubby bush, but if you want a tree with clean bole and rounded crown, commence training and staking early, selecting a strong leader and removing lower branches for adequate head height. Excellent lawn specimen. Keep clear of walkways as fallen seed capsules can be messy.

Elaeocarpaceae. *All evergreen.*

Crinodendron hookerianum
Chilean Lantern Tree
A multi-stemmed shrub or small tree with stiff, erect branches clothed with narrowly oblong-lanceolate, sharply toothed, glossy, dark green, 5–7cm leaves with a few bristly hairs and prominent veins, downy beneath. Opening from buds resembling cherries, lantern-like or urn-shaped, scarlet to carmine, 2cm, fleshy flowers hang below the branches on red-tinted, 5cm, downy pedicels late spring through summer. 3 × 3m.

Crinodendron patagua
Lily of the Valley Tree
Chilean native. Will form a multi-stemmed, upright shrub or trained to a small round headed tree, appearing like an evergreen oak but with flowers. Deep green, glossy, elliptic to oblong-ovate leaves, 5–7cm long, with irregularly toothed margins, resembling oak. Impressive displays of white, 25mm flowers like bells or fringed cups, hang beneath the branches on 3cm, green pedicels, late spring through summer, followed by decorative cream and red seed capsules. 4 × 3m.

CROTALARIA

The genus comprises 500–600 species of annual and perennial herbs and shrubs from the world's warmer regions, in particular east and south Tropical Africa, named from the Greek *krotalon*, a castanet or clapper, referring to the seeds which rattle inside inflated pods. Those in cultivation are fascinating flowering shrubs for mild areas, growing rapidly and bearing impressive clusters of bird-like flowers.

Plant in full sun, protected from wind and heavy frost in deeply worked, free-draining, sandy soil. In milder areas, almost continual floral displays may be encouraged by pruning two or three times a year which also keeps the bush compact. Thin out criss-cross branches and shorten brittle stems to lighten the foliage and flower load.

Leguminosae. *All evergreen.*

Crotalaria agatiflora
Canary Bird Flower
Rapid growing native of East Africa. Trifoliate leaves consist of three elliptic-ovate, grey-green leaflets to 60 × 35mm. Spectacular, pure yellow to olive green, 6cm flowers resembling birds hanging by their beaks, produced in terminal racemes to 40cm long. Good for picking, or garden colour. Mix with other flowering shrubs or use as colour contrast against darker walls or backgrounds. Agatiflora — flowers resembling Agati, synonym for Sesbania. 2 × 1.5m.

Crotalaria spectabilis
Indian Rattlebox
From India and Malaysia. Erect, woody herb or shrub with simple leaves to 14 × 8cm, oblanceolate to obovate, softly downy on both surfaces and heavily ribbed. Rich golden yellow, 25mm, pea-shaped flowers lined purple-red, appear through spring and summer in terminal or axillary racemes up

to 50cm long, followed by inflated, puffy seed capsules which rattle in the wind. Syn C semperflorens. Spectabilis — spectacular or showy. 2 × 1m.

CROWEA

Australian endemic genus of three species, one from south Western Australia and two from New South Wales and Victoria, named for Dr James Crow, 18th century British botanist. Croweas are delightful dwarf flowering shrubs closely related to boronia and eriostemon, preferring loose, free-draining, acid soil with peat moss, sand or scoria, full sun to partial shade in an open situation, without excessive fertilizer or summer moisture. Trim lightly after flowering. One of those charming plants to have at close range where its beauty can be fully appreciated.

Rutaceae. *All evergreen.*

Crowea 'exalata'
Small Crowea
From New South Wales and Victoria. Forms a neat, dwarf but open plant with linear 20–50 × 2–5mm, glabrous leaves with spicy, aniseed fragrance when crushed. Elegant sprays of five-petalled, pink to mauve, starry, waxy, 2cm, solitary flowers in leaf axils or branch terminals mainly spring through mid winter and at other times during the year. Good for picking. Exalata — without wings. 50–90 × 50–90cm.

Crowea 'exalata 'Bindelong Compact'
Charming, very compact form with aromatic foliage and clear pink, five-petalled, star-shaped flowers covering the plant late spring through autumn. 50 × 50cm.

Crowea 'exalata 'White Star'
Small rounded shrub with neat sage-green linear leaves and masses of small, pure white, star shaped flowers in abundance during spring and summer. 50 × 50cm.

Crowea 'Festival'
Small, dense shrub, leaves narrow-elliptic to 40 × 5mm, deep-green, margins entire, highly aromatic. Deep cyclamen-pink, 2cm starry flowers with delicate paler shading towards the centre, borne freely in leaf axils early summer through autumn and sporadically through the year. Excellent cut flower. Hybrid from C exalata × C saligna. 1 × 1m.

Crowea 'Poorinda Ecstasy'
Handsome rounded shrub with glossy, aromatic leaves. Masses of pink, waxy, star-

shaped flowers during spring and summer and periodically through the year. Hybrid from C exalata × C saligna. 1 × 1m.

Crowea saligna
Red Wax Flower
Rounded, bushy shrub with angular branches and narrow, elliptic to lanceolate, 5cm leaves. Deep-pink, 3–5cm, star-like, waxy flowers with petals slightly curled at the tips borne profusely summer and autumn. Saligna — resembling willow. 1 × 1m.

CRYPTOMERIA

A genus of one species from Japan and China named from the Greek *kryptos*, to hide and *meris*, a part, referring to concealed floral parts. Many highly ornamental forms have been selected, some hardly recognizable as cultivars of C japonica. Amongst the hardiest of conifers, easy to transplant and grow under a wide range of soil and climatic conditions. They range from real dwarfs to large trees.

Japanese Cedar is planted extensively for permanent boundary shelter or divisions in orchards and farms. Set at 2m centres it can attain 12m in three years or 18m after 12 years. Has proved canker-free and lends itself to high trimming at little more than 1m wide. Suitable as Christmas trees in containers. As a specimen has tall pyramidal outline. Resents prolonged drought during establishment but otherwise easy to grow in almost any fertile soil with good drainage.

Cupressaceae. *All evergreen.*

Cryptomeria japonica
Japanese Cedar
Grows quickly as a juvenile, new growth bronze later turning deep green. Forms a tall, stately pyramidal structure with straight columnar trunk, reddish brown bark and slightly pendulous, spreading branches clothed with short, curved, needle foliage. 11 × 6m.

Cryptomeria japonica 'Araucarioides'
Curious cultivar of the Japanese Cedar, starting out in life as a single stem clothed with needle foliage after the style of Araucaria or Norfolk Pine, hence the name. After a few years, branches form with clusters of foliage at each branch tip. Odd but attractive. 1.5 × 1m.

Cryptomeria japonica 'Bandai-Sugi'
Forms a strong leader with congested miniature and half-size foliage in tightly packed clusters in no particular sequence. Unusual oddity prized for miniature stature and charming irregularities. 1 × 1m.

Cryptomeria japonica 'Compressa'
Very slow growing dwarf bush forming a compact, somewhat flat-topped globe. Densely crowded foliage turns reddish purple in winter. Great rock garden plant. 75 × 75cm.

Cryptomeria japonica 'Elegans'
Plume Cedar
Distinct, graceful conifer with soft textured, feathery or plumy foliage, at first green, changing to rich copper, red or purple during autumn and winter. Matures slowly to broad, pyramidal form clothed to the ground. Removing alternate branches provides a tiered, oriental effect and opens up the tree for better air circulation, preventing bare patches caused by naturally overcrowded branches. 6 × 3m.

Cryptomeria japonica 'Elegans Aurea'
Similar in many respects to the Plume Cedar but with yellowish-green foliage intensifying to gold in winter. 5 × 3m.

Cryptomeria japonica 'Elegans Compacta'
Compact form of the Plume Cedar with less inclination to form a central leader. Needles longer, winter colour bronze with inner foliage remaining green. Pyramidal outline. Compact but not dwarf. 2 × 1.5m.

Cryptomeria japonica 'Elegans Nana'
Sport of Plume Cedar sometimes referred to as C elegans compacta, somewhat slower in growth. Softer, more plumy foliage with distinct billowy appearance. Rich purple winter toning. 2 × 1m.

Cryptomeria japonica 'Jindai-Sugi'
Small, dense, slow grower, compact conical form with open irregular branches. Foliage and form almost appears as a miniature version of C japonica. Retains green colour throughout the year. 1 × .75m.

Cryptomeria japonica 'Monstrosa Nana'
Compact form, normal needle-type foliage from which arises thickened stems of heavy growth with bunches of monstrous congested foliage, green for most of the year, bronze in winter. 1 × 1m.

Cryptomeria japonica 'Spiralis'
Named for the way many of the leaves are twisted around the branchlets after the manner of a cork-screw. Forms a compact bush with open habit and light green to pale yellow new growths. 50 × 50cm.

Cryptomeria japonica 'Vilmoriniana'
Very slow growing dwarf conifer with small crowded branchlets and leaves forming a dense, congested and rigid globe. Foliage deep green through summer, turning reddish-purple in colder regions. Ideal rock garden conifer. 50 × 50cm.

CUNONIA

A genus of about 15 species of trees and shrubs from New Caledonia and South Africa, named for John Christian Cuno of Amsterdam, 18th century garden enthusiast and poet. The South African species in cultivation is a handsome small tree or large shrub with good form, handsome foliage, fascinating buds and flowers. Plant in full sun in deeply worked, organically enriched, free-draining soil. Seems tolerant of dry or cold conditions. Good shrub to be seen at close range. Locate in patios, entryways, alongside paths or in containers.

Cunoniaceae.

Cunonia capensis
Butter Knife Bush
Fast growing South African tree found at altitudes to 1000m in forests especially near streams of the Cape and southern coastal regions. A multi-stemmed shrub with smooth, wine-red twigs and branches. Young shoots rich bronzy-red, lustrous, dark green, pinnate leaves with 5–7 narrow, 10 × 3cm, oblong to lanceolate leaflets, margins serrulate or slightly toothed.

Seldom without flattish buds in pairs, shaped like butter knives held on long stalks, remaining unchanged for months. Inflorescence resembles a pair of erect, woolly candles in vee formation as 15cm racemes comprising hundreds of tiny white, fragrant flowers with protruding stamens open late summer. May be trained to a single trunk. Capensis — from the Cape of Good Hope. Evergreen. 4 × 3m.

CUPHEA

A genus of some 250 species of herbs and shrubs from south east USA, Mexico, Guatemala, Bolivia and Brazil, named from *kyphos*, curved, referring to curved seed capsules. Delightful little plant which seem constantly in bloom, performing without fuss under average garden conditions in a diversity of temperate to subtropical climates.

Plant in full sun, in average, deeply worked, free-draining, not over-rich soil and water regularly during dry periods. Pinch back tips for compact growth and prune old plants to just above ground level in early spring for growth renewal. As they seed and germinate freely, old rangy plants may be discarded. Cupheas are petite plants for bedding, borders, massed or individually. May be grown in pots for spot colour.

Lythraceae. *All evergreen.*

Cuphea hyssopifolia
False Heather, Elfin Herb
Delightful, compact, shrublets from Mexico and Guatemala with dense, flexible, leafy branchlets. Leaves glossy, dark green, linear-lanceolate to 20mm long. Small, 1cm, lilac, lavender, pink or white flowers from each leaf axil smother the whole bush for long periods, mainly through summer and autumn. Seedlings often appear beneath the plant. Hyssopifolia — with leaves like hyssop. Named cultivars include — **'Golden Ruby'**, green and gold leaves, lilac flowers. **'Pink Blush'**, bright pink flowers. **'Robs Mauve'**, pinkish mauve flowers. **'Ruby'**, reddish purple flowers. **'White Whisper'**, pure white flowers. 40 × 40cm.

Cuphea ignea
Cigarette Plant, Firecracker Plant
Pretty, leafy shrub from Mexico and Jamaica with dark green, elliptic, 3–4cm leaves. Tubular, 25mm, bright red flowers with a white slightly flared tip and protruding black stamens, hence the common name. Flowers mass produced mainly through summer and autumn. Colourful, little plant that seems to fit in anywhere. 60 × 60cm.

Cuphea ignea 'Gold Flash'
Variegated Cigarette Plant
Attractive yellow and green variegated leaves together with tubular, bright red flowers. Colourful small shrub. 60 × 60cm.

CUPRESSOCYPARIS

Interesting hybrid conifer combining the vigour and drought tolerance of Cupressus macrocarpa from Monterey, California and the resilience to cold of Chamaecyparis nootkatensis from north west America, Canada and Alaska. General appearance closely resembles Chamaecyparis although cones and seeds take after Cupressus. C leylandii has dense, columnar habit with ascending branches, deep green foliage in flattened, irregular or slightly drooping sprays.

Amongst the fastest growing conifers, tolerant of coastal exposure, a variety of soils and climates and strong wind. Growth of a metre annually can be expected. Grows 4–5m in three years or ultimately to 20m. Mostly used as screens, tall hedges or specimens. May be pruned hard or regularly trimmed.

Cupressaceae. *All evergreen.*

Cupressocyparis leylandii
Leyland Cypress
Forms a columnar to conic or pyramidal crown densely covered with flat sprays of dark green foliage tinged grey. 5 × 3m.

Cupressocyparis leylandii 'Castlewellan Gold'
Popular, slower growing form, foliage tinted golden yellow. 4 × 2.5m.

Cupressocyparis leylandii 'Leighton Green'
Narrow, columnar form with apparent central leader, irregular branches and dense, distinctly flattened, green to olive green foliage. 5 × 3m.

Cupressocyparis leylandii 'Naylor's Blue'
Narrow columnar form, greyish-green foliage noticeably glaucous during winter, darker beneath. Like Leighton's Green but with more open branches. 5 × 3m.

Cupressocyparis leylandii 'Robinson's Gold'
More compact and conical habit, leaves larger than Castlewellan Gold, bronze in spring, becoming lemon-green and finally gold. Vigorous and fast growing. Syn C leylandii 'Mellow Yellow'. 5 × 3m.

CUPRESSUS

A genus of 15–20 species of evergreen coniferous trees or shrubs, mostly from mountainous areas of China, Himalayas, northern and central America and the Mediterranean, named from the Greek *kuparissos*, cypress tree. Closely related to Chamaecyparis, differing in the foliage which in Chamaecyparis is in flattened sprays. Many Cupressus species are larger growing with bold symmetrical outlines and seem more tolerant of cultural and climatic extremes. Plant in any reasonable, deeply worked soil. Used as screens, backgrounds or specimens.

Cupressaceae. *All evergreen.*

Cupressus glabra 'Arctic'
Smooth Arizona Cypress
Native to Arizona, northern Mexico and particularly drought resistant. Strong-growing form, developing strong ascending branches. Soft green foliage develops a creamy frosting through winter. This cultivar and the following valued for fast-growing screens, backgrounds or specimens. Glabra — without hairs, refers to smooth, cherry red bark from which the species gets its common name. Often incorrectly listed as C arizonica. 7 × 4m.

Cupressus glabra 'Blue Ice'
Ascending branches and upright pyramidal form combined with compact, tidy habit. Foliage attractively frosted blue. 5 × 3.5m.

Cupressus glabra 'Golden Pyramid'
Similar to Blue Pyramid, but with golden tinted foliage. 6 × 4m.

Cupressus lusitanica 'Benthamii'
Bentham Cypress
Once grown extensively as a hardy, rapid growing shelter tree. Similar appearance to C macrocarpa but with glaucous foliage, softer to the touch. Grows under a wide range of conditions, withstands heavy trimming and more resistant to cypress canker. Lusitanica — of Portugal, even though a native of Mexico. 3–8 × 2–5m

Cupressus macrocarpa
Monterey Cypress
Grows naturally on the Californian coast and tolerant of seaside conditions. Once a prominent shelter tree, but a tendency to develop bare patches after trimming and skin-irritating foliage led to its replacement by Bentham Cypress. Eventually grows to a large spreading, somewhat untidy tree with little ornamental value.

Cupressus macrocarpa 'Aurea Saligna'
Golden Weeping Cypress
Perfect, symmetrical, erect, pyramidal form, long pendulous, threadlike branchlets and rich, golden yellow foliage. Excellent weeping lawn specimen. Support the main stem for two or three years and remove any reverting non-weeping growths. 4 × 3m.

Cupressus macrocarpa 'Brunniana Aurea'
Stately pillar or conical form with rich gold colour and soft foliage. Rapid growth, responds well to trimming and has proved an excellent garden variety. 4 × 1.2m.

Cupressus macrocarpa 'Golden Pillar'
Selected, compact, conical pillar-like form with dense, yellow shoots and foliage. Good for accenting large conifer gardens, or lawn specimen. 2.5 × 1m.

Cupressus macrocarpa 'Finegold'
Vigorous grower, compact, sturdy, pyramidal form, rich golden foliage closely addressed to slender, twiggy branchlets. 4 × 3m.

Cupressus macrocarpa 'Greenstead Magnificent'
Dwarf, spreading and mounding form with intense, blue glaucous foliage all year. Good ground cover or feature plant, but allow space for development. 50cm × 2m.

Cupressus macrocarpa 'Lambertiana Aurea'
Symmetrical, pyramidal, upright form, horizontal to slightly ascending branches and bright golden-yellow foliage where exposed to light, contrasting with the green inner leaves. Hardy, indifferent to soil and climate. Allow space for development. 6 × 4m.

Cupressus sempervirens 'Gold Rocket'
Resembles Swane's Golden, in fact it is difficult to see any real difference in colour or form. Sempervirens — evergreen. 2 × .45m.

Cupressus sempervirens 'Gracillis'
Superior New Zealand raised form of Upright Cypress with more refined, threadlike foliage, fresh green colour, and perfect column form tapering to a point. Retains good form without the bad habit of branch 'fall-out'. Propagated from cuttings ensuring each plant identical. Deeply worked soil, sun or partial shade, open situation. Gracillis — graceful and slender. 3m × 35cm.

Cupressus sempervirens 'Stricta'
Upright Cypress
Ancient classical trees from the Mediterranean forming a narrow column of strictly ascending branches and branchlets with dense, dark-green foliage. Grows to a sizeable specimen if left unpruned but occasional trimming preserves better shape and keeps the plant healthier. Useful for architectural and formal landscaping but can be too dominant if overdone. Sempervirens — ever-green, stricta — erect or upright. 4m × 60cm.

Cupressus sempervirens 'Swanes Golden'
Golden Upright Cypress
True golden foliage, compact, slow-growing, slender and narrowly erect,

retaining perfect form without trimming or tying. Well-worked, free-draining soil, full sun and open situation. Raised by Swanes of Sydney. Good colour and form have made this one of the most widely planted conifers. 3m × 35cm. **110**

Cupressus sempervirens 'Totem'
Slender form, erect, threadlike, dark green foliage. Provides a neat vertical line. 2m × 35cm.

Cupressus torulosa
Bhutan Cypress, Himalayan Cypress
Native to the western Himalayas, where it is seen as a tall, handsome, pyramidal tree up to 50m. In cultivation, more of a slender, symmetrical, tall-conical shrub with dense, green foliage. Prefers cooler, wetter conditions. 5 × 2m.

An incredible genus of some 600 species of Tree Ferns widely distributed through tropical and sub-tropical regions, named from the Greek *kyatheion*, a small cup, in reference to the formation of spore cases. Both Australia and New Zealand have a good share of these magnificent plants. They revel in cool sylvan glades besides streams or on shady hillsides, their fronds casting cool shade upon stems and roots. It is important to remember this when attempting to transplant.

Tree Ferns often have all fronds removed and roots balled up when offered for sale. Trunks less than 90cm have a greater chance of success.

Choose a shady or semi-shady location with deeply worked soil conditioned with peat moss, leaf-mould or compost. Soak the roots thoroughly and plant with 5cm of soil on top of the root ball. Sprinkle a handful of blood and bone or well-balanced, slow-release fertilizer around the plant and mulch with peat moss or bark, watering regularly during dry periods. Although somewhat unsightly, a sack tied around the stem and kept moist until fronds begin to form will help the plant until it can provide its own shade.

Tree Ferns are better planted in groups both aesthetically and for the support they afford each other. Useful for softening architectural lines particularly on the cooler side of buildings. Exploit the filtered sunlight they create by underplanting shade-loving plants such as azaleas, rhododendrons, kalmias,

Pieris etc. Once established and growing strongly Tree Ferns demand little attention apart from occasional grooming. See also Dicksonia.
Cyatheaceae. *All evergreen.*

Cyathea australis
Rough Tree Fern, Hard Tree Fern
Adaptable species from Australia's eastern states forming a massive trunk, the bottom portion fibrous and with rough, rasp-like marks left by fallen fronds and conspicuous, shiny brown scales around the upper half. Fronds to 4m, finely divided, dark green. Grows in a wide range of conditions including moist or dry soils and exposure to sun. Australis — southern. 5 × 4m.

Cyathea cooperi
Cicatrice Tree Fern
Hardy, fast-growing tree fern from New South Wales and Queensland with handsome and unusual appearance. The upper portion of the trunk and new unfolding fronds have long, soft, white, silky hair-like scales. As mature fronds fall, the trunk where they were attached is permanently marked by large oval cicatrices or scars reminiscent of the skin of a giant reptile. Graceful ferny fronds to 3m long on natural specimens which may have trunks to 12m. Adaptable to most situations except unreasonable extremes of heat and cold. Named for Thomas Cooper, 19th century English gardener and plant collector. 4 × 3m.

Cyathea dealbata
Silver Fern
The inspiration for New Zealand's national emblem. Often seen in lowland and mountain forests throughout the North and South Islands, Chatham Islands and Lord Howe Island. Young plants have fresh green leaves, the undersides taking several years to receive their silver coating. Rather smaller growing than the more common C medullaris, fronds stiffer and not as soft to the touch. Although hardy, tends to become ragged and untidy if exposed. Dealbata — covered with white powder. 4 × 3m.

Cyathea medullaris
Black Ponga, Black Punga
The most common and distinctive of New Zealand's Tree Ferns seen throughout the three main islands except parts of the eastern side of the South Island, also in Tasmania, Victoria and some of the Pacific Islands. Slender, black trunk and large crown of gracefully arching fronds add a gracious touch to any garden. The pith from the trunk and starchy contents of the frond bases were at one time baked and eaten by Maoris. Medullaris — pithy. 5 × 3m. **110**

Cyathea smithii
New Zealand Whe

Found naturally in damp lowlands and mountain forests of New Zealand's main islands where specimens grow 8m high with 22cm trunks. A magnificent tree fern, distinguished by soft, horizontally spreading fronds with prominent yellowish midrib and slender trunk often covered with thickly matted fibrous, aerial rootlets. Although quite hardy to low temperatures, it is wise to locate this fern in sheltered areas to prevent damage to soft fronds by strong winds. Possibly seen at its best beneath large trees. 4 × 3m.

CYCAS

A remarkable genus of about forty species of palm-like plants distributed through Asia, Malaysia, Philippines, Indonesia, New Guinea, tropical Australia, Africa, Madagascar and a few Western Pacific islands. The name is derived from the Greek *koikas* for a type of palm. Cycas is neither fern nor palm. It belongs to a family which embraces the most primitive of plants, survivors of what was once an important part of the earth's vegetation. Although a form of sago can be made from the pithy material present in the trunks, commercial enterprises in Florida and Australia ceased to operate in the 1920s. Cycads are becoming increasingly popular landscaping plants, used extensively around public buildings and suburban gardens.

Handsome foliage, elegant structure, longevity and low maintenance set them in a class of their own. Their growth rate and dimensions are quite predictable, a valuable factor in garden planning. Cycads adapt to a wide range of soil types, although the more fertile the soil, the better the performance. Deeply worked, free-draining, organically enriched, slightly acid to neutral sandy loam is recommended.

Incorporate a light application of slow-release fertilizer into the planting hole, plant with the top of the root ball no more than a centimetre below the soil surface and water thoroughly. Deep mulching will retain moisture, suppress weed growth and insulate the roots from excessive heat. Apply light dressings of balanced fertilizer annually when the soil is moist, once spring growth has commenced. Grooming dead or damaged leaves is about the only pruning necessary.

Cycadaceae.

Cycas revoluta
Sago Palm

In its youth, cycas has an airy, lacy, ferny appearance, but as it ages, it has the appearance of a palm. They are renowned for highly decorative, glossy, deep-green leaves held in rosettes on a central trunk. Each leaf comprises something like a hundred or more leaflets with rolled margins, 10–20cm long, making a hard, stiff, 75cm frond like a giant feather. A long term plant, beautiful from the time of its first leaf, becoming increasingly handsome and distinctive as it grows and develops over centuries. Revoluta — rolled backwards, referring to the foliage. Evergreen. 1 × 1m.   **110**

CYPERUS

A genus of more than 600 species of grasslike, rhizomatous, annual and perennial herbs from numerous temperate to tropical regions, named from the ancient Greek word for these plants. C papyrus is probably the best known species. The reed or flower stem is the source of parchment upon which many manuscripts of sacred and classic literature were written. As far back as 2750 BC, the Egyptians cut pith-like tissue into strips and after laying them out with overlapping edges, united them under pressure. Also thought to be the bulrushes in which the child Moses was hidden.

Although mostly bog plants by nature, they grow just as well under normal garden conditions as they do at the edge of ponds or streams with roots submerged. Cyprus has few demands once established apart from occasional grooming. When clumps become too large, divide and replant vigorous outside divisions, discarding overgrown centres during spring when they'll rapidly re-establish themselves. Locate in full sun, in rich soil and keep moist.

Cyperaceae.

Cyperus papyrus
Egyptian Papyrus

Graceful plants, native to north Africa, building a colony of underground rhizomes from which arise slender, smooth, leafless green reeds or stems topped with umbel-shaped heads of 100–200, drooping, thread-like rays. The unusual, exotic appearance of this plant has led to its extensive use in contemporary landscaping, alongside authentic or simulated ponds or streams, outdoor living areas or feature gardens. Evergreen. 2 × 1m.

CYTISUS

A genus of about 30 species of shrubs mostly from Mediterranean regions and the Canary Islands, named from the Greek *kytisos*, a term used for various woody members of the pea family. They share the common name of flowering Brooms with Genista and Spartium. Cytisus have a reputation for being one of the hardiest and easiest shrubs to grow, some species becoming established as wild flowers. Given a reasonable start, they will from an early age provide a colourful display of pea-shaped flowers over many weeks in spring and summer.

Plant in full sun in any reasonable, deeply worked, free-draining soil that is not over-rich. Usually, they'll bloom within a few weeks of planting. Cut back to at least half way for strong growth renewal. Left unpruned, brooms become lanky and woody, so hard cutting back after flowering each year is advisable. Beautiful shrubs which merit inclusion wherever spring and early summer colour is desired, and they are good for picking.

Leguminosae. *All evergreen.*

Cytisus × dallimorei 'Lena'

Hybrid from C multiflorus × C scoparius. Lena is a spectacular dwarf cultivar, flowers lemon yellow and cream with ruby-red wings. 1.5 × 1m.

Cytisus × dallimorei 'Lilac Time'

Australian hybrid, small, light lilac-pink flowers. Graceful, arching dwarf grower. 1.5 × 1m.

Cytisus multiflorus 'Albus'
White Spanish Broom

Native to Spain, Portugal and north west Africa. Erect, multibranched shrub, each slender, greyish-green stem covered with 9mm, pure-white, fragrant, pea-shaped flowers during spring. Provides good garden display and plenty of flowers for indoors. Multiflorus — many flowered. Albus — white. 2 × 1.5m.

Cytisus × praecox
Warminster Broom

Hybrid from C multiflorus × C purgens. Delightful, dense grower with a tumbling mass of slender, ash-green branches and silky new shoots. Fragrant, rich cream or sulphur-yellow flowers massed on slender weeping branches during spring. Praecox — very early. 1 × 1m.

Above: Cordyline australis 'Albertii' **97**

Above: Cordyline australis **97**
Below: Corokia x virgata 'Cheesemanii' **99**

Above: Cornus florida *North American Dogwood* **98**
Below: Corokia x virgata 'Sunsplash' **100**

Below: Cortaderia selloana 'Gold Band' **101**

Above: Crataegus laevigata 'Paul's Scarlet' **103**

Above: Cupressus sempervirens 'Swanes Golden' **107**
Below: Cyathea medullaris *Black Ponga* **107**

Above: Cycas revoluta *Sago Palm* **108**
Below: Daphne odora 'Rubra' **114**

Above: Deutzia x hybrida 'Pink Pompon' **116**

Above: Dombeya 'Pink Cloud' **117**
Below: Deutzia x kalmiiflora **116**

Above: Elaeocarpus dentatus *Hinau* **119**
Below: Deutzia purpurascens **116**

Above: Embothrium coccineum 'Inca Flame' **119**
Below: Erica canaliculata *Purple Heath* **125**

Above: Embothrium coccineum 'Longifolium' *Chilean Fire Bush* **119**
Below: Erica conica 'Compact' **125**

Cytisus × praecox 'All Gold'
Outstanding shrub with slender weeping branches and long lasting sprays of golden yellow flowers. 1 × 1m.

Cytisus scoparius
Scotch Broom
The species is native to western Europe and Britain. Many ornamental Brooms under cultivation are hybrids from this species, C multiflorus and C × dallimorei. Forms an erect, vigorous bush with numerous erect, slender green stems which in spring become a mass of highly coloured, pea-shaped flowers. Scoparius — broomlike. 2 × 1m.

Cytisus scoparius 'Andreanus'
Deep crimson and bronzy-gold flowers. 2 × 1m.

Cytisus scoparius 'Burkwoodii'
Deep red shaded rose, keel tipped yellow. 2 × 1m.

Cytisus scoparius 'Crimson King'
Intense crimson flowers. Strong grower, very floriferous. 2 × 1m.

Cytisus scoparius 'Geoffrey Skipworth'
Smaller flowers in purplish rose and cerise shades. Among the first to flower. Graceful arching sprays. 2 × 1m.

Cytisus scoparius 'Lord Lambourne'
Pale cream flushed lilac, wings carmine edged gold. Strong, upright, compact grower. 2 × 1m.

Cytisus scoparius 'Ruby'
Deep mahogany red. Vigorous compact grower. 2 × 1m.

DABOECIA

A genus of two species of low shrubs from western Europe to the Azores, named for Irish Saint Daboec. Closely allied to and resemble heaths or ericas. They are long-lived hardy plants, and form low growing, spreading shrubs with dark green, short, needle-like leaves. Require similar conditions to Ericas, but often thrive where ericas may be difficult to establish. Plant in full sun in deeply worked, free-draining acid soil conditioned with peat moss.
Ericaceae. *All evergreen.*

Daboecia cantabrica 'Alba'
St Daboec's Heath, Irish Heath
The species D cantabrica is from south west Ireland and northern Spain. Somewhat straggling branches, small, dark green leaves with fine white hair on the under-surface, giving a silvery appearance when branches are lifted. Pendent flowers to 12mm, distinctly urn-shaped, the wild species usually pale rose. Cultivar 'Alba' is a vigorous grower with light green, glossy foliage and large, pure white bell or urn-shaped flowers in long spikes late spring through early autumn. Cantabrica — from Cantabrian mountains of Spain. 40 × 45cm.

Daboecia cantabrica 'Praegerae'
Dark green foliage with distinctive purplish sheen, silvery beneath. Urn-shaped, clear salmon pink flowers in erect spikes late spring through early summer. Spreading growth habit. Regarded as one of the finest cultivars. 25 × 40cm.

Daboecia cantabrica 'William Buchanan'
Dark green, shiny foliage, low compact growth. Bright rose-purple, bell-shaped flowers in erect spikes almost cover the bush from late spring through early autumn. Quite spectacular. 20 × 30cm.

DACRYCARPUS

A genus of about nine species of coniferous trees from Malaysia, Philippines, New Caledonia, Fiji and New Zealand, named from *Dacrydium* and *Podocarpus* from the relationship to these genera. Listed species reputed to be New Zealand's tallest native tree, one specimen in Westland measured at over 60m. Naturally a tree for moist valleys or swampy forests. Under cultivation prefers moist situations, alongside streams, lakes or ponds and will even grow with its feet in water. Slow grower as a garden specimen, attaining about 9–10m in 20 years. Plant in deeply worked, not over rich soil, keep damp and shaded when young. Excellent as a specimen or in groups for motor camps, farms, school grounds or parks, especially in swampy conditions.
Podocarpaceae

Dacrycarpus dacrydioides
Kahikatea, White Pine
Described as the tallest and noblest New Zealand native tree with clean unbranched trunk for almost 25m. Occurs through the three main islands, mostly in swampy areas. Timber very light in colour, one of New Zealands most useful soft-woods. Juvenile leaves linear, 6mm long, green tinged gold or red in winter, arranged spirally in two opposite rows. Mature leaves green, scale-like, 2–3mm long, resembling some of the cypress. Male and female flowers appear on separate trees. After pollination, a rounded crimson swollen peduncle or flower stalk, 6mm across forms, with a shiny blue-black nut embedded in its tip. Syn Podocarpus dacrydioides. Dacrydioides — resembling Dacrydium or Rimu. Evergreen. 7 × 4m.

DACRYDIUM

A genus of about thirty species of coniferous trees from Malaysia, Chile, Tasmania, New Caledonia and New Zealand named from the Greek *dakrydion*, a small tear, referring to the resin drops which they commonly exude. Some of New Zealand's finest trees are found in this group, in particular the Rimu with highly ornamental timber. Outclasses other conifers of similar dimensions for sheer beauty.
Consider their natural habitat, dense shade, and cool, moist root conditions when growing young forest trees. Young nursery-grown trees are easier to transplant and preferable to seedlings gathered from the bush. Plant in partial shade, or provide temporary shade until well established. Deeply worked soil with peat moss, ground-bark or leaf mould encourages healthy root action. Mulching after planting insulates the roots and helps retain moisture. See also Halocarpus.
Podocarpaceae.

Dacrydium cupressinum
Rimu
Found in lowland and alpine forests of New Zealand's North, South and Stewart Islands. A slow grower and one of the most handsome specimen trees as a juvenile, quite comfortable in suburban gardens for at least three or four decades. Perfectly straight, slender, tapering stem and long, drooping, flexible branches with bright green, tiny, cypress-like foliage, bronzing over various seasons. A most graceful tree, preferring cool, moist conditions, protected from the hottest sun and strongest winds until well established. Cupressinum — cypress-like. Evergreen. 6 × 3m.

DAMPIERA

Australian endemic genus of about 65 species of herbaceous perennial plants and small erect or procumbent shrubs.

The genus and a Western Australian town is named after William Dampier, English navigator and explorer who in 1688 landed on the WA coast. Many species found in WA, growing under all kinds of conditions from sea level to higher altitudes. Plant in full sun or partial shade in moist, loose clay or sandy, well drained soils and keep watered during dry periods. Useful as ground cover, spilling over rocks, logs or walls or in a hanging basket.
Goodeniaceae.

Dampiera diversifolia

A delightful and widely grown WA species in the form of a dwarf, suckering and ground hugging plant with slender angular stems. Small, 10 × 5mm, oblanceolate, deep green leaves with toothed margins. Masses of brilliant, purple blue, 15mm flowers with yellow central zone smother the plant through spring and summer. Diversifolia — leaves variable. Evergreen. 15cm × 1.5m.

A genus of about 50 species of deciduous and evergreen shrubs from Europe, North Africa, temperate and subtropical Asia, named from the Greek term for Laurus nobilis, later applied to these plants. Daphnes are small shrubs with charming, intensely fragrant flower clusters adored by gardeners throughout the world's temperate climates.

They generally prefer semi-shade, and cool, friable, deeply worked, free-draining, organically enriched, moisture retentive, lime-free soil. Leaves turning yellow can usually be traced to poor drainage or chlorosis, a symptom of iron deficiency. If drainage is not to blame, the condition can be remedied by applying iron chelates, aluminium sulphate or flowers of sulphur.

Prune during or immediately after flowering. Regulate the desired shape by pruning to inside buds for upright growth or outside buds for a spreading bush. Troublesome virus infection of Daphne odora cultivars over many years has largely been overcome by the cultivation of virus-free plants identified with the letters FKV — 'Free of Known Virus'.
Thymelaeaceae.

Daphne bholua
Himalayan Daphne
A sturdy, somewhat variable grower from the Himalayas, forming either an erect or spreading, compact or loosely branched shrub. Dull deep green leaves to 10cm long, elliptic or oblanceolate, leathery, prominently veined and with undulating margins. Pale purple to rose-pink, sweetly fragrant flowers with white centres in terminal or axillary clusters to fifteen, produced for long periods from late winter, followed by black, 7mm ovoid fruit. Train early for desired form. Bholua — from the Himalayan native name Bholu Swa. Evergreen to semi-deciduous. 2.5 × 2m.

Daphne burkwoodii
Burkwood Daphne
Beautiful hybrid from D cneorum × D caucasica, forming a neat, rounded bush with erect stems covered with closely set, linear-oblanceolate, bright green leaves to 40 × 12mm. Highly fragrant, soft lilac-pink, starry flowers in rounded, terminal clusters up to sixteen, almost cover the bush for long periods from late spring, and again late summer. Excellent for garden display and picking. Semi-deciduous. 1.2 × 1.2m.

Daphne burkwoodii 'Somerset'
More vigorous form with larger foliage, flowers with purple-pink tube and light pink lobes to 13mm. Semi-deciduous. 1.5 × 1.3m.

Daphne burkwoodii 'Variegata'
Rounded compact shrub with handsome variegated leaves, deep-green finely margined cream. Pale pink, highly fragrant flowers in terminal clusters. Semi-deciduous. 1 × 1m.

Daphne cneorum
Garland Flower
Native to central and southern Europe. Possibly the most popular hardy species. Forms a low shrub with trailing branches covered with dull-green, oblanceolate, 10–25mm leaves crowded toward branch tips. Sweetly scented, rosy-pink, starry flowers in dense, rounded, terminal clusters almost cover the plant for long periods from spring through early summer. May bloom again late summer. Ideal for rock gardens, along the top of walls etc.

Full sun in cooler climates, partial shade in warmer areas. Mulch with peat moss to insulate roots and encourage rooting of trailing stems. Cneorum — from the Greek name for a shrub resembling an olive. Evergreen. 30cm × 1m.

Daphne cneorum 'Variegata'
Compact grower, variegated leaves dark green with yellow margins. Abundance of soft pink, fragrant flower clusters in spring. Evergreen. 30cm × 1m.

Daphne genkwa
Chinese Daphne
Chinese native species, forming a slender, erect, sparsely branched shrub with greyish green stems. Dull-green, lanceolate to ovate leaves, lighter beneath, to 60 × 25mm, silky textured when young. Masses of amethyst or lilac-blue flowers with 10mm tubes appear in axillary clusters of up to seven early spring before the foliage. Sheer beauty and quantity of bloom offsets lack of fragrance. Genkwa — from the Chinese name *Genk'wa*. Deciduous. 90 × 60cm.

Daphne mezereum
Winter Daphne
Hardy, European native with limited, upright, greyish brown branches. Soft grey-green, oblanceolate, somewhat spiralling leaves to 8cm. Highly fragrant, reddish purple flowers appear in small, close clusters on wood of the previous year during winter, continuing to early spring, followed by bright red, bead-like, globose fruit borne on bare stems beneath the foliage. Prefers neutral to slightly alkaline soil. Better left unpruned. Mezereum — from the Latin *mezereon*. Deciduous. 1.2 × 1m.

Daphne odora 'Leucanthe'
Upright Daphne
Resembles the well-known 'Pink Daphne' but branches more erect forming a neat, rounded compact bush. Leaves larger, firmer and deeper green. Flowers deep pink shaded white, sweetly fragrant in larger clusters massed on short stems close to the branches. Leucanthe — white flowered. A white form is seldom available. Evergreen. 1 × 1m

Daphne odora 'Rubra'
Pink Daphne
Native to China and Japan, introduced from the orient in 1771. Somewhat spreading or informal grower with lanceolate-elliptic, glossy, deep green, leathery leaves to 8 × 3cm. Sweetly fragrant, reddish pink flowers, white within, held on long stalks in tight nosegay clusters from mid-winter through spring. Grow this old-fashioned Daphne near a frequently used path or entrance to fully appreciate its sweet fragrance. Odora — fragrant. Evergreen. 60cm × 1m.   **110**

Daphne odora 'Rubra Variegata'
Distinctive variegated leaves, deep green with creamy-yellow margins. Growth habit and fragrant flowers resemble D odora 'Rubra'. Evergreen. 60cm × 1m.

Daphne tangutica
Native to north west China. Attractive shrub with either erect and open, or rounded

densely branched habit. Leathery, oblanceolate, deep green, glossy leaves to 6 × 2cm. Fragrant, rosy-purple flowers with white suffused purple interiors borne in crowded terminal clusters to 7cm across through spring and early summer, followed by fleshy red fruit. Tangutica — of Kansu. Evergreen. 1.5 × 1m.

DAUBENTONIA

The genus Daubentonia, named for Louis Jean Marie Daubenton, an 18th century French naturalist is invariably associated with the genus Sesbania. Consequently, the species D tripetii is often listed by the synonym Sesbania tripetii.

By any name it's a beautiful, rapid growing, though short-lived shrub for temperate, frost-free, sunny locations. Plant in deeply worked, free-draining soil in full sun. Water freely during dry periods. Prune hard early spring for growth renewal and maximum flower. Can be trained as a broad-topped, standard tree and is good in containers. Fabaceae.

Daubentonia tripetii
Scarlet Wisteria Tree
Native to Brazil and northern Argentina. Forms a slender, erect-growing shrub, deep green, pinnate leaves resembling virgilia with up to 20 pairs of narrow, oval, 25mm leaflets. Bright orange-red and yellow, 25mm, pea-shaped flowers in showy, drooping 15–20cm racemes from each leaf axil, open from the centre from spring through summer. Cut off seed pods as they form to prolong flowering. Evergreen. 3 × 2m.

DAVIDIA

A genus of one species, a deciduous tree from south west China, named for Abbe Armand David, 19th century French missionary and plant collector who discovered the tree in China in 1869. Reasonably fast- growing specimen tree for spacious gardens, with well-groomed appearance whether in leaf or bare, best seen against a background of dark foliage to highlight the curious flowers which resemble white doves.

May take a decade to commence blooming but then, the floral display improves with each succeeding year.

Allow ample space to avoid competition with other flowering trees or shrubs. Locate in sun or partial shade, sheltered from strong wind. Plant in deeply worked, free-draining, moisture retentive soil, mulch freely, stake and protect young trees until well established. Nyssaceae.

Davidia involucrata 'Vilminiana'
Dove Tree
Forms a stately tree with rounded crown, robust branches and flaking, greyish-brown bark, glabrous shoots and buds with glossy red scales. Broadly ovate to cordate, 15 × 12cm leaves, aromatic when young, quite glossy, rich green above, covered with white tomentum beneath, margins sharply serrated.

Flowers comprise 2cm clusters of red anthers carried between two large unequal white bracts, one about 15cm long, the other 10cm, appearing to rest among the leaves like white doves or small white handkerchiefs hung out to dry, late spring and early summer. Ovoid, 3cm fruit at first green then brown-purple follow autumn and winter. Cultivar 'Vilminiana', a superior form, is the one usually seen in cultivation. Involucrata — with an involucre, with reference to the showy bracts. Deciduous. 8 × 5m.

DESFONTAINEA

Monotypic genus from the Andes of Peru and Chile named for Rene Louiche Desfontaines, 18th–19th century French botanist. A slow-growing shrub from a cool, moist environment, valued for glossy, holly-like leaves and spectacular trumpet-shaped flowers.

Plant in deeply worked, organically enriched, free-draining, moisture retentive, acid soil. Although tolerant of sub-zero temperatures, in cooler climates, plant against a warm wall sheltered from cold winds. In warmer regions, locate in semi-shade or where it will avoid the midday sun. Loganiaceae.

Desfontainea spinosa
An attractive and hardy, narrowly upright, evergreen shrub with tough, leathery, glossy, dark green, 35–60mm, oval-ovate, holly-like leaves with spiny to dentate margins. Very showy, solitary, 7cm, crimson to orange-scarlet, tubular or trumpet flowers with five yellow lobes and green calyx, scattered freely throughout the bush summer and autumn. Cherry-like berries follow. Rather

slow grower, but commences to bloom early. Spinosa — spiny leafed. Evergreen. 2 × 1.2m.

DEUTZIA

A genus of about 60 species of flowering shrubs from temperate Asia, including Japan, Philippines and Himalayas, and the mountains of central America, named for Johann van der Deutz, friend of the 18th century Swedish botanist Thunberg who founded the genus. A beautiful, free-flowering, extremely hardy, easily grown group of plants, excellent amongst colourful spring-flowering annuals, bulbs or perennials.

Deutzia grows in any fertile soil, preferring deeply worked, free-draining, moisture retentive, organically enriched loam, located to avoid the hottest midday sun in an open situation and not overshadowed by other trees or shrubs. Remove at ground level flowered shoots that are at least two years old to encourage new growths and better flower production.

Saxifragaceae. *All deciduous.*

Deutzia 'Dorothy Hamilton'
Compact growing garden hybrid originating at Hamilton Gardens, Lake Hayes, Central Otago. Foliage bright green at first, maturing to bronze through summer and intensifying in autumn before falling. The plant smothers itself with small, soft pink flowers in spring. Useful, hardy small shrub. 75 × 75cm.

Deutzia compacta 'Lavender Time'
Native to China. Forms a compact bush with densely hairy young shoots, later becoming glabrous. Leaves ovate-lanceolate, to 70 × 25mm, dark green above, greyish green beneath, with scattered rayed hairs on both surfaces and finely toothed margins. Flowers lilac to pale lavender borne in numerous flat compact panicles through early summer. 1.5 × 1m.

Deutzia crenata 'Nikko'
Delightful low spreading form of the graceful Japanese species.

First Deutzia to flower, producing masses of tiny, snowy white, nearly tubular blossoms from mid winter, covering every branch and twig. Dwarf compact habit, useful as a background for colourful borders of annuals, perennials, bulbs or ground cover. Syn D gracilis 'Nikko'. Crenata — cut in rounded scallops referring to leaf margins. 60 × 90cm.

Deutzia × elegantissima 'Rosealind'
A beautiful clone arising from D purpurascens × D sieboldiana, reputed to be the
deepest and best pink flowered Deutzia.
Handsome erect form and rounded clusters
of deep carmine pink flowers prominently
displayed from mid spring. 1.5 × 1m.

Deutzia gracilis
Wedding Bells
From Japan, a low growing shrub with
arching branches. Bright green, thin-
textured, lanceolate to ovate leaves to
60 × 40mm, margins with small forward
pointing teeth. Pure white, strongly fragrant
flowers, 15–20mm across, borne in 40–
60cm racemes through early summer.
Gracilis — graceful, slender. 1 × 1m.

Deutzia × hybrida 'Joconde'
Hybrids of garden origin considered to be
from Chinese species D longifolia × D
discolor. Strong-growing shrub, large pale
lilac-white flowers, streaked and shaded
rose-purple on the outside. 1.5 × 1.2m.

Deutzia × hybrida 'Magician'
Forms an erect and slender shrub, leaves
lanceolate to 10cm. Large, bold, lilac-pink
flowers, each petal edged white and with a
purple streak on the reverse borne profusely
through spring. 1.5 × 1.2m.

Deutzia × hybrida 'Mont Rose'
Attractive hybrid, forming a graceful,
rounded to upright bush, wide-open, soft
pink to pale mauve-pink flowers with
prominent yellow anthers borne prolifically
in large elegant panicles. One of the best
coloured hybrids. 1.5 × 1m.

Deutzia × hybrida 'Pink Pompon'
Attractive and quite distinct hybrid forming
a rounded to upright bush with gracefully
curving branches, massed with rose-pink,
double, tightly packed flowers in spring.
2 × 1.2m.   **111**

Deutzia × kalmiiflora
An attractive hybrid from D purpurascens ×
D parviflora with long, arching branches
crowded through late spring and early
summer with dainty, starry, 18mm, white or
pale pink flowers, red on the outside,
suggestive of Kalmia, borne in loose trusses
of up to twelve. 1.5 × 1m.   **111**

Deutzia magnifica
Vigorous, strong upright grower with sturdy
branches. Leaves deep green, ovate-oblong
to 6cm long, margins with fine, sharp teeth.
Fully double, pure white flowers in short
dense panicles in early summer. Magnifica
— splendid, magnificent. 2 × 1.5m.

Deutzia purpurascens
Slender, arching Yunnanense species with
sweetly fragrant, 18mm, white flowers,
tinted rich purplish-crimson on the outside
borne in 5cm clusters spring through to
early summer. Leaves ovate-lanceolate to
70 × 30mm, deep green, margins with
forward pointing teeth. Purpurascens —
tending to purple. 1.5 × 1m.   **111**

Deutzia × rosea 'Carminea'
Pink Wedding Bells
Hybrid of garden origin with dainty arching
branches. Leaves elliptic to lanceolate, dark
green, margined with forward pointing teeth.
Bell-shaped, soft-pink flowers flushed
carmine, in dense panicles spring — early
summer. Avoid overcrowding. 1 × 1.5m.

Deutzia scabra
Fuzzy Deutzia
Erect-growing, vigorous Japanese species.
Leaves broadly ovate to 8 × 4cm, dark green,
rough hairy surface and coarse forward
pointing toothed margins. Pure white,
honey-scented flowers in loose, pyramidal
panicles early summer. Very floriferous.
Scabra — rough. 2.5 × 1.5m.

Deutzia scabra 'Candidissima'
Similar to above with larges panicles of
tightly packed, almost spherical, fully
double, pure white flowers late spring and
early summer. Candidissima — very white.
2 × 1.5m.

Deutzia scabra 'Pink Minor'
Dwarf cultivar with arching, spreading
growth habit. Bears masses of pink and
white shaded flowers through spring.
70 × 90cm.

Deutzia scabra 'Pride of Rochester'
White, fully double, frilled flowers, flushed
rose-purple on the outside in large panicles.
2 × 1.5m.

DICKSONIA

A genus of about 20 species of tree ferns
from America, south east Asia, Australasia and Polynesia, named for James
Dickson, 18th century botanist. Dicksonia
tree ferns are less bulky than Cyathea,
and are ideal for working in amongst
shade loving plants in borders, woodland
gardens, in groups or in containers. Refer
Cyathea for cultural requirements.
Dicksoniaceae. *All evergreen.*

Dicksonia antarctica
Tasmanian Tree Fern, Soft Tree Fern
Beautiful species from the fern gullies of
south eastern Australia where aged specimens can be seen with massive, 6m trunks,
their buttressed base covered with a jacket
of reddish, ginger-brown, soft fibrous
rootlets. The trunk is crowned with numerous arching, 2–3m, dark-green fronds, soft
to the touch and with smooth stems.
Antarctica — used in botany for regions
south of 45°. 2 × 1.5m.

Dicksonia fibrosa
Wheki-ponga
New Zealand species, found in lowland and
lower mountain forests of the North and
South Island. Closely related to D antarctica
but of lesser dimensions. Thick trunk
covered with densely matted fibrous roots.
Fronds to 2.4m, at first almost erect before
gradually spreading and merging into a wide
canopy. Slow growing, but performs well
under average garden conditions. 2 × 1.5m.

Dicksonia squarrosa
Wheki
Found in lowland and hilly forests throughout New Zealand and one of the most
abundant native tree ferns. Distinguished by
slender trunk, clothed with the hardened
remains of frond stalks and a dense skirt of
dead fronds beneath its crown. Rhizomatous
rooting system travels underground for some
distance before sending up new plants. By
this means the species often appears
profusely after bush fires. Relatively small
dimensions and hardiness makes it an
excellent garden variety for almost any
conditions. Squarrosa — spreading or
recurved at the ends. 2 × 1.5m.

DODONAEA

A mostly Australian genus of about 50
species ranging from woody, prostrate
shrubs to small trees, mostly with male
and female flowers on separate trees.
Named for Rembert Dodoens, 16th century Flemish royal physician and herbalist. Sometimes referred to as Hop Bush
as some species were used in brewing by
early settlers as a substitute for hops.
Dodonaea is valued for its ability to grow
in adverse conditions, colourful foliage
and ornamental inflated seed capsules.
    Dodonaea viscosa is probably the
hardiest species, surviving almost zero
temperatures, drought, salt laden winds
and polluted atmospheres, foliage protected by a dried coating of sticky exudate.

Provides an ornamental screen or specimen, serves well in erosion control or reclamation. Light trimming to size will encourage colourful new growth. They resent being pruned back to old wood. Plant in any reasonable, free-draining soil, feed sparingly with balanced fertilizer, water regularly until established.

Sapindaceae.

Dodonaea viscosa 'Purpurea'
Purple Ake Ake, *Hop Bush*
Dodonaea viscosa is distributed throughout all Australian States, New Zealand, South Africa and Mexico. The purple-leaved form, discovered late last century on the banks of the Wairau River in Marlborough, New Zealand, is widely acclaimed as a handsome foliage shrub. Forms a neat, slender, erect, densely foliaged shrub.

Leaves oblanceolate to narrow-elliptic, to 10 × 3cm, tapering at the stalk end, slightly waved margins, purple-bronze to purple-violet according to conditions and seasons. Purplish-red, 3–winged seed capsules appear in great quantities. Plants grown in poorer conditions colour better than if overfed and pampered. Viscosa — sticky. Ake Ake — Maori forever, refers to the durable wood, used for clubs and other weapons in bygone days. Evergreen. 3 × 1m.

DOMBEYA

A genus of about 200 species of deciduous or evergreen shrubs or small trees from Africa, Madagascar and Mascarene Islands named for the 18th century French botanist Joseph Dombey. Grown for lush, tropical-looking foliage and beautiful, rounded, drooping clusters of fragrant flowers. Locate in a warm, sheltered spot in full sun or partial shade, preferably protected from the hottest midday sun. Plant in deeply worked, organically enriched, fibrous, free-draining loam. Mulch freely, water during the growth period. Remove faded flowers and prune previous season's growth to half way after flowering.

Sterculiaceae.

Dombeya spectabilis 'Pink Cloud'
Native to Madagascar. Classified as a small tree but mostly regarded as a shrub. Leaves ovate to suborbicular to 18 × 13cm, deep green, semi-glossy, margins almost entire. Clusters of woolly buds open to clear pink. open flowers, borne in terminal racemes spring through autumn. Spectabilis — spectacular. Semi-evergreen. 2.5 × 2m. **111**

DRACAENA

A genus of about 40 species of herbaceous or woody shrubs or trees, many from west Africa and the Canary Islands, named from the Greek *drakaina*, a female dragon, or as has been suggested, after Sir Francis Drake. Draceanas are best known as decorative house plants, especially the numerous attractive cultivars of D fragrans. The listed species is a fascinating plant for warm temperate climates, worth growing for curiosity value alone. Dragon trees are unique creations of the flora of the Canary Islands.

They grow on rocky precipices along the coast of Tenerife, forming massive trees to 20m high with monstrous trunks to 5m diameter. Many are centuries old. Gnarled old trunks divide into several ascending branches, then into sub-branches, all grotesquely contorted. Each branchlet is crowned with a rosette of strap-like, pointed leaves, not unlike an old New Zealand cordyline. When the trunk is cut, a red gum oozes out. Legend has it that this resin became dragon's blood with curious properties. In their natural environment they revel in heat and humidity. Plant in free-draining, stony or sandy soil in a warm, frost-free location and water sparingly.

Agavaceae.

Dracaena draco
Dragon Tree
Dracaena draco has different character as a juvenile. Young plants have smooth, thick, glaucous-green, linear-lanceolate, sword-shaped leaves to 60cm long with translucent edges, outlined in red if grown in sunshine, attached directly to a straight, erect stem, forming a terminal rosette from which large panicles of very small, greenish white flowers appear. Orange-red, spherical, 15mm fruit borne on mature trees. In temperate climates, a plant may take years before attempting to branch or bloom. At whatever stage in its development, it is a showy plant with dramatic silhouette, ideal for creating tropical or exotic effects. Draco — dragon. Evergreen. 2 × 1m.

DRYANDRA

A genus of about 60 species endemic to Western Australia, named for Jonas Dryander, 18th century Swedish botanist.

Dryandra flowers are hard and stiff, appearing to be finely sculptured from precious metals. The blooms are long lasting and perfect for floral art. Although so very beautiful, Dryandras are not easy to establish beyond their home State.

They resent pampering, preferring dry, poor, natural stony or sandy soils rather than the rich fertile soil of cultivated gardens. Root disease Phytophthora cinnamomi is a prevalent cause of failure. Tests have shown that a layer of limestone chips below the plant may be a possible solution to this problem.

Plant in light to medium, free-draining soil conditioned with coarse sand or gravel, in a situation where soil moisture is constant. Withstands some frost and coastal winds, in fact, a well-ventilated position if preferable. Don't hesitate to cut blooms for indoors and prune hard when flowering has finished.

Proteaceae. *All evergreen.*

Dryandra formosa
Showy Dryandra
Found mainly on the Stirling Range in the south west growing in peaty or gravelly soil. A medium to large open grower with soft-textured, broadly linear leaves to 20cm, deep green above, greyish beneath, deeply toothed to the midrib into triangular sections. Handsome, 10cm flower heads, comprising numerous curved, orange-yellow styles forming a perfect cone topped with fine creamy hairs, surrounded with floral leaves, carried at the terminal of each branch and lateral branchlets spring and early summer. Grown extensively for cut blooms. Formosa — beautiful. 2.5 × 1.5m.

Dryandra ferruginea
Low growing shrub with dense habit, often with underground stems. Leaves to 45cm × 35mm, blue-green and smooth above, with rusty hairs beneath, margins with well-spaced, narrow, triangular, 10mm teeth extending more than half way to the midrib. Flowerheads to 9cm across, comprising central yellow styles surrounded by orange-brown bracts, borne on short stems spring and early summer. Blooms resemble South African Proteas. Ferruginea — rust coloured. 40 × 90cm.

Dryandra nivea
Couch Honeypot
Dwarf, prostrate shrub with erect, spreading or underground branches. Linear leaves to 40cm × 8mm, glabrous, dark green above, pale green or white beneath, margins cut deeply to the midrib into narrow triangular sections giving the foliage a fern-like appearance. Terminal, brownish yellow,

40mm flower heads with hairy bracts and hollow centre suggestive of the common name. Blooms appear winter through spring. Excellent rockery plant. Nivea — snow white, growing near snow. 40 × 90cm.

DURANTA

A genus of about 30 species of trees or shrubs from tropical America, named for Castore Durante, 16th century physician and botanist in Rome. Sky Flower is grown for attractive blue flowers and clusters of yellow fruit. It grows rapidly, is indifferent to soil conditions and thrives in hot summer areas but prefers constant moisture. Tends to form numerous stems and needs regular thinning and pruning to preserve shape.
     Verbenaceae

Duranta erecta
Sky Flower
From Brazil, Mexico, West Indies and southern Florida. A dense, twiggy, bushy shrub, stems sometimes spiny. Leaves obovate to ovate-elliptic, to 75 × 35mm, mid green, shaded purplish-blue in winter. An abundance of tubular, violet-blue flowers in terminal or axillary racemes through summer, attractive to butterflies, followed by 15cm clusters of yellow, 12mm fruit. Syn D repens, D plumieri. Erecta — erect or upright. Evergreen. 2.5 × 2m.

ECHIUM

A genus of about 40 species of annual or perennial herbs or shrubs from Europe, Canary Islands, Africa and western Asia named from the Greek *echion*, a fancied cure or protection against snake bites.

     Many Echium species with impressive flowering spires are good focal plants in large herbaceous or shrub borders. They like full sun, good drainage, thrive in almost any reasonable soil, survive temperatures almost to zero and are ideal for coastal gardens. Lightly prune to preserve bushiness and remove flowers as they fade. Good for colour accent against walls, amongst shrubs or other plants.
     Boraginaceae

Echium candicans
Pride of Madeira
Large, picturesque shrubby perennial from Madeira Island. Forms a multi-branched plant with silvery pubescent, grey-green, lanceolate leaves arranged in irregular rounded mounds at the end of each stem. Bold and dramatic, 30cm, terminal, cylindrical spikes or clusters of purplish-blue, 12mm flowers are held well above the foliage through spring and summer. Syn E fastuosum. Candicans — shining or woolly white. Evergreen. 2 × 1m.

EDGEWORTHIA

A small genus of three deciduous or semi-evergreen shrubs native to Himalayas and China, named for M P Edgeworth, 19th century botanist with the East India Company. Interesting and beautiful Chinese native shrubs, long cultivated in Japan for the long, snow-white fibres used in the manufacture of thin but very strong paper. An excellent garden subject with good form and exquisite, fragrant flowers. Plant in deeply worked, organically enriched, moisture retentive, slightly acid soil. Mulch with peat moss or granulated bark and water deeply during dry periods. Light pruning only, keeping in mind that flowers are borne on previous year's wood.
     Thymelaeaceae. *All deciduous.*

Edgeworthia papyrifera
Yellow Daphne, Paper Bush
An open bush with stout, ascending, greyish-brown, clean branching stems and twigs, so tough they can be tied into knots without breaking. Leaves lanceolate to oblong, to 10cm, dull-green with grey-green undersides. In late winter, clusters of flaring, tubular, lemon, cream and yellow flowers, covered on the outside with tiny hairs, appear on naked branches. Flower resembles a yellow daphne. Beautiful shrub in full bloom, giving a long lasting display prior to new leaves. Papyrifera — paper bearing. 1.5 × 1m.

Edgeworthia papyrifera 'Grandiflora'
Closely resembles above, but more compact and with significantly larger flower heads. 1 × 1m.

ELAEAGNUS

A genus of about 45 species of shrubs or trees from Asia, southern Europe and North America, named from the Greek *elaia*, the olive tree and *agnos*, a name applied by Theophrastus to a species of willow, probably in reference to the oily, edible fruit and narrow, willow-like leaves of E angustifolia. E *pungens* with extreme hardiness and rapid growth was at one time extensively planted for shelter. It soon became out of control in a tangled mass of long thorny shoots if not regularly trimmed, so the species is no longer grown.

     The highly ornamental cultivars of E pungens and E × ebbingei are useful shrubs, especially in cooler regions, tolerating heat, cold, wind, coastal conditions and long periods of drought once established. Plant in full sun in any reasonable, free-draining soil. Prune or shear to shape. Remove immediately any green-reverting shoots. Elaeagnaceae. *All evergreen.*

Elaeagnus × ebbingei 'Gilt Edge'
Silverberry
Excellent hybrid with erect, thornless branches, at first brown, becoming grey and scaly, new shoots silvery. Leaves elliptic, to 11cm long, glossy, dark green with striking gold margins and silvery reverse. Small, waxy, creamy-white, intensely fragrant flowers during autumn followed by orange-red, silver speckled, oval fruit, excellent in preserves. Named after J W Ebbinge of Boskoop, Holland. 2 × 1m.

Elaeagnus × ebbingei 'Limelight'
Resembles above but with greyish-green leaves delicately splashed pale yellow and lime-green, silvery beneath. 2 × 1m.

Elaeagnus pungens 'Maculata'
Gold-Leaf Silverberry
Broadly spreading or angular growth habit. Ornamental, oval to oblong leaves to 8cm, lustrous olive-green with prominent central splash of gold, margins wavy, silvery and cinnamon beneath. Hardy, useful foliage shrub for garden highlighting and floral art. Maculata — blotched, referring to the leaves. 1.5 × 1.5m.

ELAEOCARPUS

A genus of about 60 species of trees and shrubs mostly from India and Malaysia with a few extending through the Pacific Islands, Australia and New Zealand, named from the Greek *elaia*, olive and *karpos*, fruit, from the olive-like fruit. Grown for beauty of foliage, small fringed and fragrant flowers and decorative fruit. The listed species may take many years

to commence flowering, but is an attractive foliage tree in the meantime. Grows in sun or partial shade in deeply worked, organically enriched, free-draining, moisture retentive soil. Mulch freely and keep moist during dry periods.
Eleaocarpaceae.

Elaeocarpus dentatus
Hinau
Among the most beautiful flowering New Zealand natives, from lowland forests throughout the North and South Islands. Handsome, obovate- oblong, 5–10cm leaves, leathery, dark green and glossy, paler and downy beneath, margins entire or very finely serrated. Creamy-white flowers resembling lily-of-the-valley but with dainty silky fringes, appear in 10cm terminal racemes spring through summer, followed in autumn by purple-blue, 15mm, oval fruit, attractive to birds and one of the vegetable foods of the Maori. In moist climates eventually reaches 12m, but in average garden conditions seldom grows more than shrub proportions. Dentatus — toothed. Evergreen. 3 × 2m.	**111**

ELINGAMITA

A monotypic genus endemic to Three Kings Islands, about 48 kilometres north west of New Zealand's northernmost tip, named after the steamer Elingamite, wrecked off the west island in 1902 not far from where this plant was discovered in 1950 by plant enthusiast Major M E Johnson. These wild, rugged and almost inaccessible islands are exposed to the fury of gales and high seas which sweep in from the Tasman Sea. Elingamita trees were found growing in full sun, protected from prevailing westerlies by a ridge. Although obviously exposed to salt-laden spray they appeared to be thriving in this harsh environment.

Apart from historical interest, the tree has handsome foliage and ornamental fruit and a worthwhile addition to any garden. Plant in a sunny, open position in deeply worked, free-draining, moisture-retentive soil.
Myrsinaceae

Elingamita johnsonii
Forms a large shrub or small tree. Leaves elliptic to obovate to 17 × 7cm, glossy deep green, tough and leathery, margins entire. Light cream flowers with a tinge of pink freely produced through summer, followed by bright red, 2cm fruit set against a

background of foliage in terminal clusters of 20 or more. They may take 12 months to fully ripen but persist on the tree for long periods. A rare and handsome tree for the discerning gardener. Evergreen. 4 × 2.5.

EMBOTHRIUM

A genus of eight species of evergreen shrubs or trees from the Andes, South America, named from the Greek, *en*, in and *bothrion*, a little pit, referring to the anthers. The Fire Bush is aptly named, a dense canopy of brilliant red through spring and early summer. Coming from cool, shaded valleys high in the Andes mountains, exposed to heavy rainfall with rapid run-off, it's not surprising that some difficulty may be experienced in getting them established.

Plant in full sun in deeply worked, free-draining, moisture-retentive, lime-free, acid soil with peat moss but without organic material or animal manure. Once planted, they resent any disturbance. Mulch freely and keep moist during dry periods.
Proteaceae. *Both evergreen.*

Embothrium coccineum 'Inca Flame'
Selected form of 'Longifolium' with erect growth habit, and a profuse display of brilliant orange-scarlet flowers like catherine wheels during spring and early summer. 6 × 3m.	**112**

Embothrium coccineum 'Longifolium'
Chilean Fire Bush
A distinct geographical species, considered superior to the original, more robust, with better poise and more easily grown. Graceful growth habit with numerous side branches drooping to within 1m of the ground with the weight of blossom. Leaves deep green, oblong-lanceolate to 11cm long. Characteristic spring and early summer displays of vivid flame-red flowers for which the Chilean Fire Bush is famous, borne along each branch rather than at the tips. 5 × 3m.	**112**

ENKIANTHUS

A genus of about 10 species of shrubs belonging to the Heath family from China, Japan and Himalayas, named from the Greek *enkyos*, pregnant and *anthos*, a flower, referring to the flower

of one species which seems to carry another inside it. Delightful shrubs which revel in unpolluted, clear mountain conditions, often at sub-zero temperatures. Valued in cool-climate gardens for pendent clusters of bell-shaped flowers. Plant in deeply worked, organically enriched, moisture retentive, lime-free, acid soil in sun or partial shade. They enjoy similar soil and growing conditions to Rhododendrons and Azaleas and make good companion plants.
Ericaceae. *All deciduous.*

Enkianthus campanulatus
Red Vein Bell Flower
Desirable Japanese species with smooth, reddish young shoots. Leaves obovate-elliptic, to 65 × 35mm, dull green, gold and scarlet in autumn. In spring, arching outer branches produce short, pendulous racemes of dainty, 8–12mm bell-flowers resembling lily-of-the-valley, pale cream with a touch of green and reddish veins. Campanulatus — bell-shaped. 1.5 × 1m.

Enkianthus campanulatus 'Palibini'
Resembles above, but with broadly ovate leaves with rusty-downy midrib, becoming fiery red during autumn. Pendent racemes of rich red, smaller, bell-shaped flowers in spring. 2 × 1m.

Enkianthus campanulatus 'Rubrum'
Small to medium growth with outward spreading branches and brilliant fiery red leaves in autumn. Intense red, bell-shaped flowers in pendent racemes during spring. 1.5 × 1m.

ENSETE

A genus of seven species of giant, perennial, Musa-like herbs from central and east Africa growing in moist conditions at altitudes to 2300m. Ensete is from the Amharic vernacular *anset*. Imposing banana-like plants for bold, dramatic, tropical effects in patios or feature gardens where sheltered, frost-free conditions prevail. Plant in full sun, in loose, free-draining soil. Removing flower heads as they appear may encourage longer life.
Musaceae. Both evergreen.

Ensete ventricosum
Ethiopian Banana
Lush, gigantic plants with stout, erect, polished stem, swollen at the base. Immense, 3–4m × 50cm, bright-green leaves with red

petiole and midrib clustered at the top of the stem. After producing dark red bracts, insignificant white flowers, and fertile seeds, the plant dies. New plants are easily raised from seed. Ventricosum — having a swelling on one side. 5 × 4m.

Ensete ventricosum maurelii
Red Ethiopian Banana
Attractive juvenile leaves, almost completely blackish red. As the plant develops, the thick shiny trunk, foliage on both surfaces, petiole and midrib become distinctly wine red. Mature leaves to 2.5m × 50cm, deep-green, generously suffused wine red. 3 × 2m.

ENTELEA

A monotypic genus named from the Greek *enteles*, complete or perfect, referring to all fertile stamens. Interesting and handsome, New Zealand native tree, quite rare in its indigenous state but growing happily under cultivation. Entelea is frost tender, but grows rapidly in warm, sunny or partly shady locations in reasonably good loamy soil. Good leafy filler for backgrounds or screens. The wood is extremely light, about half the weight of cork and was used by the Maoris for floats and small rafts.

Tiliaceae.

Entelea arborescens
Whau
Handsome tree, easily identified by large leaves and bristly seed capsules. Leaves cordate, to 25 × 20cm, bright-green, glossy, paler beneath, margins double-toothed with small triangular lobes, soft and prominently veined, carried on 20cm petioles. Foliage inspires the common name of N Z Mulberry. White, 25mm, single flowers with prominent yellow stamens appear in erect terminal or axillary cymes, spring through early summer, followed by spine-covered, 2cm capsules, resembling a chestnut burr, containing inedible, orange seeds. Arborescens — tree-like. Evergreen. 3 × 2m.

EPACRIS

A genus of about 35 species of heath-like evergreen shrubs from south east Australia, New Zealand and New Caledonia, named from the Greek *epi*, upon and *akris*, a summit, referring to the lofty environment of some species. These beautiful shrubs are grown for exuberant displays of exquisite flowers in crowded spikes borne on slender stems. The various species are found from sea level to reasonably high altitudes, some with roots in moist sandy or peaty conditions, others amongst drier gravel or rocks on hillsides.

Under garden conditions, they require deeply worked, organically enriched, free-draining, moisture retentive, neutral to acid soil with little or no fertilizer. Best in dappled shade with roots protected from direct sun. Mulch freely and keep moist through prolonged dry periods. Pruning after flowering preserves good form and encourages strong growth.

Epacridaceae.

Epacris impressa
Common Heath
Most attractive shrub from coastal heathlands and forests of New South Wales. Victoria, Tasmania and South Australia. The floral emblem of Victoria. A dwarf to medium grower usually with erect, twiggy branches which unpruned tend to become spindly. Leaves to 15 × 5mm, linear-lanceolate to narrow ovate, narrowing to a sharp point, deep green and glabrous. Tubular, bright rosy red, pendent flowers to 25 × 5mm with five flaring lobes carried in erect terminal racemes. Flowers appear through the year, especially early autumn to late spring, especially through winter. Impressa — sunken or impressed. Evergreen. 75 × 90cm.

ERICA

A genus of over 700 species of shrubs and small trees, 90% of which belong to South Africa, the rest to Europe and North Africa, named from the Greek *ereike*, classical name for E arborea. All heaths have one thing in common, leaves of one narrow, needle style. Flowers come in three main shapes, bells, tubes or urns, and almost every conceivable shade is represented. Very few are fragrant.

South African species are generally more demanding in cultural requirements, being sensitive to soil and climate. European ericas are climatically hardy and more tolerant of garden soils. They differ widely in size, habit and adaptability with low growers for rock gardens, ground or bank cover, foregrounds or massed bedding, or taller ones for shrub borders or feature specimens. A portion of the garden given entirely to ericas can be most rewarding, special requirements being satisfied and a selection of varieties providing almost year-round colour.

Grow ericas in full sun, in deeply worked, free-draining, moisture-retentive, slightly acid soil with the addition of peat moss, sand or fine gravel. Sharp drainage essential as roots must never be soggy. Never fertilize heavily, but feed sparingly with acid manure, and avoid lime in any form. During prolonged dry spells, water deeply but infrequently, mulch with peat moss or granulated bark to conserve moisture, suppress weed growth and minimize cultivation which could damage roots. Shear low growing ericas after flowering. Cut taller growers back below spent blooms, but never into bare wood. Pruning preserves shape and stimulates new growth.

Ericaceae. *All evergreen.*

Erica arborea
Tree Heath
European. Large, erect-growing, hardy shrub, young shoots hairy, dark green leaves in whorls of three or four. Small, 4mm. bell-shaped flowers, pink in bud, white with a touch or grey when open, borne in lax, 40cm racemes during winter. Arborea — growing in tree-like form. 1.5 × 1m.

Erica 'Aurora'
Hybrid Cape Heath
South African. Outstanding hybrid with soft, 6mm, conifer-like, deep green leaves. Rich, bright coral-red or rosy scarlet, 18–25mm tubular flowers densely clustered on erect stems throughout winter and spring. 80 × 50cm. **122**

Erica australis
Spanish Heath
Larger upright form from Spain and Portugal, described as one of the showiest Tree Heaths. Branches soft-hairy when young, linear, 6mm leaves in whorls of four. Rosy purple, tubular to bell-shaped flowers in small clusters late spring and summer. Australis — southern. 95 × 30cm.

Erica australis 'Mr Robert'
European. Excellent, selected cultivar with upright habit, pale fresh-green leaves, large, pure-white flowers with golden anthers. 95 × 30cm.

Erica australis 'Riverslea'
European. Beautiful cultivar with good form, foliage somewhat glaucous, fuchsia-purple flowers, deeper colour than E australis. Good for picking. 95 × 30cm.

Above: Erica x darleyensis 'Arthur Johnson' **126**

Above: Erica perspicua 'Pink Tubes' **127**
Below: Erica cerinthoides 'Pink Ice' **125**

Above: Erica colorans 'White Delight' **125**
Below: Erica nana **126**

Above: Erica perspicua 'Ivory Tubes'
Prince of Wales Heath **127**

Above: Below: Erica cerinthoides *Red Hairy Heath* **125**
Below: Erica cyathiiformis **125**   Below: Erica conica *Knobby Heath* **125**

Above: Erica peziza *Velvet Heath* **127**
Below: Erica 'Aurora' *Hybrid Cape Heath* **120**

Above: Erica regia 'Variegata' *Royal Heath* **127**
Below: Erica ventricosa 'Rosea' **127**

Above: Erica sessiliflora **127**
Below: Erica ventricosa 'Globosa' *Wax Heath* **127**

Above: Eucalyptus ficifolia *Red Gum* **129**

Above: Erythrina sykesii *Indian Coral Bean* **128**
Below: Euonymus fortunei 'Emerald'n Gold' **131**

Above: Eriostemon myoporoides 'Profusion' **128**
Below: Euonymus japonica 'Aureo-marginatus' **131**

Erica baccans
Berry Flower Heath
South African. Masses of 6mm, rosy pink, globular, firm, papery bells, on erect stems late winter to spring. Make a faint sibilance when shaken. Narrow, 5–7mm, stem clasping leaves in fours. Strong grower, naturalized in parts of NZ, Victoria, Tasmania. Tolerates heavier soils and more exposure than most South African species. Valued as cut blooms. Baccans — berry-like. 1 × 1m.

Erica bauera 'Pink Maiden'
Bridal Heath
South African. The species is noted for being almost continuously in bloom. This excellent cultivar has large, slightly inflated, 18mm clear pink, waxy tubes hanging in masses around erect, wiry stems. 75 × 75cm.

Erica caffra
Kaffir Heath
South African. Tall shrub with narrowly urn-shaped 6mm flowers, cream to pale greenish yellow with honey fragrance appearing in the upper leaf axils. Narrow, 9–12mm leaves. Unusual, but lacks lustre. 1 × .75m.

Erica canaliculata
Purple Heath
South African. Amongst the most popular flowering shrubs becoming a total mass of rose-purple, 5mm bells with black anthers, completely covering the foliage during autumn and early winter. Leaves dark green, 6mm long in threes, with a tiny, narrow channel on the upper surface, hence the specific name. The bush carries a strong fragrance. Syn E melanthera. Canaliculata — channelled or grooved. 1.5 × 1m.   **112**

Erica carnea 'Cecilia M Beale Pink'
European. Low globose grower with erect branchlets and mid-green foliage. Masses of pink flowers winter through early spring. Sport from 'Cecilia M Beale'. 15 × 30cm

Erica carnea 'Eileen Porter'
European. Neat rounded plant, deep green foliage, rich carmine-rose bell flowers massed on stiff stems through autumn, winter and spring. 15 × 20cm.

Erica carnea 'Myretoun Ruby'
European. Excellent form, low spreading growth, very dark green foliage, large flowers reddish-brown in bud, opening pink, intensifying to bright ruby red with black anthers in late winter and spring. 25 × 50cm.

Erica carnea 'Springwood Pink'
Mountain Heath
European. Low spreading habit, new growth brownish-pink, leaves mid green in summer, bronzy green in autumn. Profusion of pink, urn-shaped, 1cm flowers late winter to spring. Forms a spreading mound, good as a filler for weed control. Hardy, one of the few lime-tolerant heaths. 15 × 50cm.

Erica carnea 'Springwood White'
European. Vigorous, fast growing, neat heath, forming a spreading mound of bright green foliage. Large flowers greenish in bud, opening pure white with prominent brown anthers, massed in long spikes late winter through spring. 15 × 60cm.

Erica cerinthoides
Red Hairy Heath
South African. Narrow, 12–15mm, hairy foliage. Bright scarlet, hairy, inflated tubular, 3cm flowers in pendent, 7cm clusters spring and early summer. Many weeks of gorgeous bloom. Cerinthoides — resembling the genus cerinth. 100 × 75cm.   **122**

Erica cerinthoides Pink Form
Pink Hairy Heath
South African. Resembles above. A compact shrub with masses of slender stems carrying terminal clusters of bright pink flowers late spring through early summer. 100 × 75cm.

Erica cerinthoides 'Pink Ice'
South African. Attractive salmon pink and white, inflated tubular flowers clustered at the tips of each stem during late winter and spring. 90 × 60cm.   **121**

Erica cinerea 'Golden Hue'
Bell Heath
European. Erica cinerea is the common, hardy 'bell-heather' which covers vast highland areas of the British Isles where it endures intense cold. Forms mats of wiry stems and produces masses of 6mm urn-shaped, rosy purple bells in long racemes from early summer through to autumn. 'Golden Hue' forms a neat cushion of pale yellow foliage, often becoming red in winter. Pale purple flowers rather sparse. Trim regularly to main good form. 25 × 30cm.

Erica cinerea 'Pink Spangles'
European. Hardy, low-spreading growth, deep green foliage, bicolour flowers in pale lilac pink and rose-pink. 20 × 45cm.

Erica cinerea 'Golden Drop'
European. Mat-like habit, burnished gold or copper foliage in summer, bright rusty red in winter. Mauve pink flowers. 15 × 25cm.

Erica cinerea 'Purple Beauty'
European. Dark green foliage, vigorous, semi prostrate form with masses of large purple flowers. 20 × 35cm.

Erica colorans 'White Delight'
South African. Upright grower, tiny, crowded, deep green foliage. Narrow, tubular 15mm flowers, pale pink in bud, opening white tinged pink, in long, crowded, spike-like clusters autumn through spring. 1 × 1m.   **121**

Erica conica
Knobby Heath
South African. Excellent, compact growing heath with small, short, open-mouthed, deep pink flowers densely clustered in knobby heads at the tops of each branch winter and spring. Quite rigid, 6mm leaves with minute points and rolled margins. Conica — cone-shaped. 1 × 1m.   **122**

Erica conica 'Compact'
South African. Delightful shrub with compact rounded form, becoming a mass of rich rose-pink to purple-pink, bell-shaped flowers through spring. 75 × 75cm.   **112**

Erica cruenta
Blood-Red Heath
South African. Strong grower, somewhat loose habit, sparse, 6mm, deep green, rough-edged leaves and very showy, 25mm curved tubular flower in vivid scarlet-red. Mainly autumn flowering, but flowers appear in short bottlebrush clusters throughout the year. Cruenta — blood coloured. 90 × 90cm.

Erica cyathiiformis
South African. Slender small shrub with lax branches densely covered with tiny, deep green leaves. Smothered through late winter with small, cup-shaped, deep-pink flowers. Prefers moisture-retentive, free-draining soil. Prune after flowering. Raised in New Zealand. Cyathiiformis — in the form of a little cup. 75 × 75cm.   **122**

Erica × darleyensis
Darley Heath, Winter Heather
European. Extremely hardy hybrid, inheriting favourable traits of two worthy parents, E carnea — bright colours and long flowering tendencies and E erigena — rapid growth and floriferous nature. Leaves needle-like, 6–12mm with rolled edges. Pale lilac-rose, 10mm, urn-shaped flowers in leafy spikes to 15cm long. Very hardy, thrives in virtually any soil and flowers throughout winter and well into spring. Annual light trimming will maintain neat rounded specimens. Darleyensis — of Darley Dale, Derbyshire. 45 × 60cm.

Erica × darleyensis 'Ada S Collings'
European. Low compact grower, deep green foliage, white flowers through winter and early spring. 30 × 50cm.

Erica × darleyensis 'Arthur Johnson'
European. Light green foliage, bright mauve-pink flowers in very long spikes, excellent for garden display and for picking. Raised by the late A T Johnson. 45 × 60cm.   **121**

Erica × darleyensis 'Darley Dale'
European. Vigorous, bushy grower, medium to dark green foliage, pale lilac-rose flowers becoming deeper in colour towards the end of the season. Excellent ground cover. Thought to be the original hybrid and synonymous with E × darleyensis. 45 × 60cm

Erica × darleyensis 'Furzey'
European. Foliage dark green, becoming even darker in winter. Flowers bright deep pink produced freely in strong spikes. Good ground cover. 30 × 45cm.

Erica × darleyensis 'Jack H Brummage'
European. New growth light yellow, retained through spring and summer turning golden green or clear gold in winter depending on amount of sunlight. In cooler areas red tints are evident. Deep pink flowers in massed short spikes. 30 × 40cm.

Erica × darleyensis 'J W Porter'
European. New growth red and cream maturing to very dark green. Bright purple pink flowers in good spikes once the plant is established. Neatly rounded habit. 25 × 45cm.

Erica × darleyensis 'Silver Beads'
European. Neatly rounded plant with deep green glossy foliage. Rounded bell-flowers, silver white with brown anthers, are borne profusely from early autumn through late spring. Syn E Silberschmelze. 30 × 45cm.

Erica erigena 'Alba'
Irish Heath
European. Charming heath, dense, compact habit, dark- green, 9mm, needle leaves with margins half rolled under. Masses of 6mm, white, urn-shaped flowers with prominent dark anthers appear in dense clusters during winter. Fine shrub, blooms profusely, easy to grow and lime tolerant. Erigena — from Erin or Ireland where many cultivated forms had their origin. 60 × 30cm.

Erica erigena 'Golden Lady'
Forms a compact bushy mound of bright, golden-yellow foliage accented with small white flowers. Ideal ground cover or contrast plant. Sport from Erica 'W T Radcliff', originating at Bloom's Nursery, England. 40 × 50cm.

Erica erigena 'Irish Salmon'
European. Light grey foliage with reddish tinge to new stems. Flowers clear pink with no trace of purple. Named from its rich dark salmon buds, as much a feature of the plant as the paler flowers. Quite distinct. 50 × 25cm.

Erica erigena 'Nana'
European. Neat, low-growing spreading form, foliage grey-green in summer, becoming rich bronze with cooler weather. Masses of shell pink flowers late winter. Ideal for rock gardens or front borders. 30 × 75cm.

Erica erigena 'Rosslare'
European. Upright, fairly dense growth habit with dull, dark green foliage. Light purple-pink flowers in abundance. Raised in New Zealand. 50 × 25cm.

Erica erigena 'W T Rackliff'
European. Neat rounded form, foliage rich green, lighter new shoots. Large, white bell-flowers with prominent brown anthers, borne in short crowded spikes in such quantities that the bush is completely covered through spring and often in autumn. 30 × 35cm.

Erica formosa
South African. Compact, tidy grower, white, globular, fluted, slightly sticky, 4mm flowers borne in profusion winter through early summer. Excellent winter flowering erica, useful for picking. Formosa — handsome or beautiful. 75 × 75cm.

Erica hirtiflora
Hairy-Flowered Heath
South African. Unusual small shrub with tiny, 4mm, deep purple-pink, ovoid, bell-shaped flowers carried in nodding clusters at the ends of short side branches through spring and summer. Small, 6mm, narrow, bluish green foliage. Leaves, shoots and flowers covered with minute hairs. Hirtiflora — hairy flowered. 60 × 60cm.

Erica hybrida
South African. Neat, upright, rapid growing hybrid heath of unknown origin with soft-green, cylindrical leaves densely packed on each branch resembling a conifer. Tubular, bright salmon scarlet flowers in 4cm, lupin-like clusters during spring. Spectacular dwarf shrub. 1 × .60m.

Erica mammosa 'Gilva'
South African. Larger-growing, erect, strongly branched shrub, producing through mid-summer attractive lime-green to yellowish white, 15–20mm, pendent tubu-lar flowers in long pseudospikes. Excellent for picking. Mammosa — being furnished with nipples. Gilva — dull yellow. 1.5 × 1m.

Erica mauritanica 'Spring Charm'
South African. Forms an upright, compact shrub with numerous fine-hairy branches, densely covered with small, erect leaves in whorls of four. Mauve-pink, 2–3mm cup-shaped flowers set in a green or red calyx, mass-produced on long stems, excellent for picking. Prune after flowering. Raised in New Zealand from South African seed. 1m × 75cm.

Erica multiflora 'Daviesii'
Pearl Heath
European hybrid. Excellent New Zealand raised cultivar forming an erect, pyramidal bush becoming a total mass of tiny, delicate lavender-pink bells during spring, completely hiding its small narrow foliage. The bush has distinct silvery appearance in full bloom. 1 × .60m.

Erica nana
South African. Low, compact, somewhat spreading, glabrous shrub. Leaves 4–8mm in erect or spreading whorls of four. Yellow, waxy, tubular, 22mm flowers with small spreading lobes borne through spring in pendent whorls of three, massed at the end of every branch. Nana — dwarf. 15 × 25cm.   **121**

Erica onosmaeflora
South African. Forms an erect shrub with stiff branches, producing clusters of scarlet-red, tubular flowers almost all year. Quite hardy and adaptable to most free-draining soils. Prune lightly. Onosmaeflora — from the Greek *onos*, an ass, *osme*, smell, *flora*, a flower. 75 × 75cm.

Erica 'Parkeri'
South African. Waxy, satin-pink, 3–4cm, tubular flowers in large clusters mainly through spring and summer, although bush is rarely without some bloom. Open, semi-erect growth habit. Easy to grow. 1 × .75m.

Erica persoluta
Pink Garland Heath
South African. Very narrow, smooth, bright green leaves less than 6mm long carried in threes on slender, soft-hairy stems. Tiny, 4mm, deep pink bells massed on spreading lateral shoots, crowded on erect main stems during spring. Although the plant will withstand cold conditions, protect from strong winds. 75 × 50cm.

Erica perspicua 'Ivory Tubes'
Prince of Wales Heath
South African. Multi-branched upright grower, erect to spreading, 3–4mm leaves in whorls of 3 or 4. Ivory-white, waxy, tubular, 16–24mm flowers with small spreading lobes in spike-like clusters on each erect stem almost the year through. Good for picking. Perspicua — transparent. 1 × .80m.   **122**

Erica perspicua 'John Bone'
South African. Forms a bushy shrub with magnificent, densely packed spikes to 30cm long of rosy purple, tubular, 25mm flowers during summer and autumn. Narrow hairy leaves less than 6mm, arranged in fours on hairy stems. Named for its raiser in Oamaru, New Zealand. 1 × .80m.

Erica perspicua 'Pink Tubes'
South African. Resembles 'White Tubes' in its growth habit. Buds pink with white tips, tubular flowers deep pink, paler at the tips, carried on erect stems in dense spikes from late winter. Good for picking. 1 × .80m.   **121**

Erica peziza
Velvet Heath
South African. Small, dainty and remarkable heath with a profusion of honey-scented flowers in threes appearing somewhat like tiny, 3mm white woolly bells, crowded on every branchlet from spring. Narrow, glossy, 3–4mm leaves carried in threes on downy, reddish stems. 75 × 75cm.   **122**

Erica regia 'Variegata'
Royal Heath
South African. Delightful, 25mm, tubular flowers, white with scarlet tip, appear as if made of white wax, carefully dipped in red ink. Open, erect habit, inclined to be short-lived but worth trying. 1 × .60m.   **123**

Erica rubens
Red Heath
South African. Small, 6mm, rich rosy red, Chinese-globe shaped flowers borne profusely during spring and intermittently throughout the year. Dense, compact grower with 6mm deep-green cylindrical leaves. Rubens — red. 75 × 60cm.

Erica sessiliflora
South African. Erect, multi-branched habit, rich green, slightly curved, conifer-like, 5–10mm leaves. Exquisite, pale lime-green, 20–30mm, tubular flowers in crowded terminal clusters winter and early spring. Sessiliflora — stalkless flowers. 1 × .75m.   **123**

Erica sparsa 'Lavender Mist'
South African. Strong grower, upright habit, long stems crowded with small, smoky lavender-pink bell flowers from late winter. Soft and fine dark green foliage. Sparsa — few, far between. 1 × .75m.

Erica subdivaricata 'Autumn Snow'
South African. Masses of tiny, white, bell-shaped, sweetly fragrant flowers envelope the plant from late summer. Very popular for floral decorations. Erect, compact grower, numerous thin, finely-hairy branches. Subdivaricata — somewhat spreading. 75 × 75cm.

Erica tetralix 'Alba Mollis'
Cross-Leaved Heath
European. Excellent compact dwarf heath with numerous ascending stems. Lanceolate, 6mm, frosted, light silvery-grey leaves in whorls of four. Flowers ovoid or oval pitcher-shaped, pure white, produced on current season's growth in terminal clusters atop each upright stem from early summer through autumn. Tetralix — with leaves in fours. 20 × 30cm.

Erica vagans 'Alba'
Cornish Heath
Species found in Cornwall, south-west France, northern Spain and Ireland, often thriving in heavier, moderately alkaline soil. Vigorous, low growing heath with decumbent or horizontal branches ascending at the tips and vivid green foliage. Pure white, bell-shaped flowers individually tiny, but arranged in closely packed spikes through summer and autumn. All vagans cultivars are neat, free-flowering plants, excellent for rapid ground cover. Vagans — widely distributed or wandering. 30 × 50cm.

Erica vagans 'Fiddlestone'
European. Fresh green foliage and cerise to dark red flowers, closely resembling, if not somewhat inferior to Mrs D F Maxwell. 25 × 35cm.

Erica vagans 'Mrs D F Maxwell'
European. Deep green, glossy foliage and cerise to dark red flowers in dense racemes summer through autumn. Neat bushy grower, among the most popular summer flowering Ericas. Found by Mr & Mrs Maxwell while on honeymoon in Cornwall. 25 × 35cm.

Erica vagans 'St Keverne'
European. Compact, bushy heath, fresh, light green foliage. Bright-pink, bell-shaped flowers in abundance summer through autumn. 25 × 35cm.

Erica ventricosa 'Globosa'
Wax Heath
South African. Pretty, free-flowering heath found naturally at altitudes of 2000m. Exquisite, swollen, highly polished, pale-pink, waxy, flask-shaped flowers with deeper flared lip and red interior, carried in generous clusters late spring through summer. Soft, narrow leaves to 12mm, fringed with tiny hairs. Prefers cooler conditions with protection from frost. Ventricosa — having a swelling on one side. 50 × 75cm.   **123**

Erica ventricosa 'Rosea'
More compact grower suitable for rock gardens or containers. Flask-shaped, bright rose-pink flowers with paler flared lip, literally smothering the whole bush from late spring. 30 × 35cm.   **123**

Erica verticillata
South Africa. Forms a medium shrub with neat, erect habit, freely producing purple-pink, finely-hairy, 20mm tubular flowers in whorls or spikes near the top of each erect stem, mostly through summer and autumn, occasionally through the year. Grows easily, long lived, average garden conditions. Verticillata — in whorls. 1.3 × 1m.

Erica walkerii
South African. One of the most attractive Ericas. Forms a low-growing bush, producing an abundance of pyramidal spikes of china-pink, delightfully fragrant, starry flowers mid spring. Excellent for picking, but flowering season somewhat short. Hardy and reasonably frost-tolerant. 39 × 50cm.

Erica × watsonii 'Dawn'
European. One of many hybrids from E ciliaris × E tetralix, developed by D F Maxwell, heather enthusiast of England. 'Dawn' has compact bushy bun-form, new growth tipped yellow and tangerine, becoming deep green through summer. The whole plant covered in early summer through early autumn with clusters of arge, rounded, deep rose-pink bell-shaped flowers. 15 × 30cm.

Erica wilmorei
South African. The wilmorei heaths are of unrecorded hybrid origin. Extremely beautiful, erect, compact, bushy plants with tapering stems. Tubular flowers, pink tipped white, borne in clusters, interspersed with the foliage winter and early spring. Requires the best of erica conditions and protection from the hottest sun. E wilmorei 'Plena' has soft pink flowers with a distinct, fully double, starry mouth tipped white. 90 × 75cm.

Erica 'Wittunga Satin'

Excellent hybrid Erica selected for excellence of flower and growth habit. Forms a small to medium shrub bearing masses of lustrous, mauve-pink, bell-shaped flowers in long arching sprays. Good garden display and long-lasting in floral arrangements. Hybrid from E mauritanica × E quadrangularis, from Wittunga Botanical Gardens, Adelaide. 1m × 75cm.

ERIOSTEMON

Australian endemic genus comprising over thirty species of small to medium shrubs, named from the Greek *erion*, wool and *stemon*, a stamen, in reference to their woolly stamens. Genus distributed over all States excluding Northern Territory. Commonly known as Wax Flower because of smooth, heavy petals. Popular garden shrub with starry flowers appearing in massed displays for long periods. The crushed leaves give off a sweet aroma.

Plant in full sun or partial shade in deeply worked, free-draining, slightly acid to neutral soil with coarse sand or fine gravel. Once established they withstand extensive drought and seem hardy to zero temperatures. Don't hesitate to pick flowers for indoors or prune lightly to preserve shape and vigour.

Rutaceae. *All evergreen.*

Eriostemon myoporoides
Wax Flower

Found in eastern Sates from Queensland to Victoria. A floriferous and adaptable shrub with broadly ovate leaves to 8cm, greyish green, covered with pellucid dots or oil glands visible if the leaf is held to the light. Crushed leaves emit a strong fresh fragrance. From the leaf axils, clusters of up to 8 pink buds open to starry, five-petalled, 15–20cm, waxy white flowers with orange anthers, appearing in great masses autumn through mid summer. Myoporoides — resembling the genus Myoporum. 1.3 × 1.5m.

Eriostemon myoporoides 'Profusion'

Profusion has shorter, thicker leaves, more compact habit, and even greater masses of superior flowers. One of the finest dwarf shrubs. 1.3 × 1.5m. **124**

Eriostemon myoporoides 'Stardust'

Hybrid from E myoporoides × E verrucosus. Stems inclined to be warty, leaves more rounded. Large, waxy-white flowers in great profusion. 1.5 × 1.5m.

ERYTHRINA

A genus of more than 100 species of trees or shrubs from North and South America, tropical Africa, Asia and Australia, named from *erythros*, red, referring to the predominant flower colour. Noted for spectacular racemes of papilionaceous flowers, resembling Clianthus, usually in vivid blood red colours. Adaptable to wide-ranging climatic conditions and grow in virtually any free-draining soil in an open, sunny situation.

Fabaceae. *Both deciduous.*

Erythrina crista-galli
Brazilian Coral Tree

Unusual species from the rainy areas of Brazil. Climatic variations influence its growth pattern. In warmer, relatively frost-free areas it becomes a multi-branched, rough barked tree to 6m high and almost as wide. Dies down in cooler regions to almost ground level each winter from which it makes tremendous growth in spring to form a bushy plant of two or three metres with tapering unbranched stems studded with stout spines. Leaflets to 15 × 8cm long, oblong lanceolate, leathery, slightly glaucous, usually found in threes on a long spiny stalk.

Impressive summer floral displays of brilliant, crimson-scarlet, 7cm, pea-shaped flowers arranged amongst the foliage in stiff terminal racemes to 50cm long, followed by long green seed pods. As many as three crops of bloom may occur annually according to climatic conditions. Remove old flower stems and deadened branch ends after each burst of bloom. Crista-galli — cock's comb descriptive of a flower cluster. 3 × 2m.

Erythrina sykesii
Indian Coral Bean

Spectacular Australian hybrid of Asian parentage providing brilliant winter colour throughout temperate regions. Quickly forms an open branched, spreading specimen with brilliant scarlet, spikey flower trusses all over the tree during late winter and early spring before the leaves appear. Forms a dense canopy through summer of broadly ovate or heart-shaped leaves. Does not produce seed capsules but easily propagated from cuttings, or large pieces planted as 'instant trees' which take root quickly but need firmly staking against wind. Often incorrectly called E variegata, E indica or E pulcherrima. 6 × 5m. **124**

ESCALLONIA

A genus of about 60 species of shrubs or small trees from South America, mostly native to Chile, named for Senor Escallon, Spanish traveller in South America in the 18th century. Useful border shrubs or screens with handsome foliage and almost everblooming habit. Flowers comprise five spoon-shaped petals in tubular or chalice form, borne in large panicles through spring and summer.

Hardy, easy to grow, quite indifferent to soil conditions, salt- tolerant, sun or partial shade. Although withstanding some drought, they respond to occasional deep watering in summer. Rejuvenate old plants by pruning almost to ground level. Tip-pinching will keep growing plants compact. Trimming back flowered shoots as they fade may encourage a second flush of bloom. Regular shearing to size or form may inhibit flower production.

Escalloniaceae. *All evergreen.*

Escallonia 'Alice'

First class hybrid with large leaves and clusters of rosy red flowers. 1.5 × 1m.

Escallonia 'Field's Scarlet'

Masses of small, bright scarlet flowers. Small foliage. 1.5 × 1m.

Escallonia × langleyensis 'Apple Blossom'

Hybrid E rubra and E virgata. Attractive, slow grower, arching branches, glossy, deep green leaves, masses of pinkish white flowers open from pink buds late spring through autumn. 1.5 × 1m.

Escallonia × langleyensis 'Donard Seedling'

Medium sized shrub with arching branches, small leaves and large, apple-blossom pink flowers borne in large panicles through spring and summer. Extremely hardy. Resembles E 'Slieve Donard'. 1.5 × 1m.

Escallonia 'Red Elf'

Dwarf compact grower with deep, reddish-pink flowers in abundance through summer. Excellent hybrid cultivar — E rosea × E langleyensis. 1.5 × 1m.

Escallonia rubra var macrantha
Common Escallonia

Hardy, rapid-grower, glossy, deep-green, 3–7cm leaves. Bright, rose pink, 18mm, chalice-shaped flowers in large clusters spring through summer. Ideal for backgrounds, screens or shelter. Train or trim to any size or shape. Rubra — red. Macrantha — large flowered. 2 × 1m.

EUCALYPTUS

A genus of at least 600 species ranging from small, bushy shrubs to immense timber trees, all but eight endemic in Australia, six occurring in Australia and New Guinea and two not found at all in Australia. Genus named from the Greek *eu*, well and *kalypto*, to cover as with a lid, referring to the calyx which covers the stamens in bud. Eucalyptus have adapted to many countries of the world. Almost all have distinct fragrance, although some leaves need to be crushed before this is evident. Some are grown for artistic trunks or handsome form, others for beautiful flowers, foliage or capsules. Attraction to many forms of wildlife is sufficient reason to plant at least one.

Eucalyptus are easy to grow, provided the right one is chosen for a particular area. Generally they require free-draining soil and a sunny aspect. A sprinkling of fertilizer at planting time is about all they ever need and once established, watering is unnecessary. Stake until the plant can support itself. Pruning and training amounts to either stopping the central leader, removing competitive branches, cutting out or shortening misshapen or low side branches.

Myrtaceae. *All evergreen.*

Eucalyptus cinerea
Silver Dollar Gum, Mealy Stringybark
As a juvenile, leaves resembling 5–6cm silver discs in pairs on slender stems are grey- green, lightly dusted with whitish bloom. Some trees retain this disc foliage as the tree matures, but more often adult leaves are longer and pointed. Very adaptable and grows under most garden conditions. Small white flowers followed by conical seed capsules. Excellent for rapid privacy or protection screens. Locate clear of drains or pavement and allow adequate space. Cinerea — ash or grey coloured. 8 × 5m.

Eucalyptus cladocalyx 'Nana'
Bushy Sugar Gum
Small, open to moderately dense tree from Kangaroo Island and Eyre Peninsula. Smooth, grey to bluish grey bark, sheds large patches in autumn to reveal yellow or light brown beneath. Young leaves elliptic, to 6 × 9cm, dark green with reddish margins.

Adult leaves lanceolate, to 15 × 2.5cm, dark green, glossy. Creamy-white, 15mm flowers in large clusters, followed by 15 × 10mm barrel-shaped capsules with prominent ribs. Widely planted for shelter. 8 × 5m.

Eucalyptus cordata
Heart-leaved Silver Gum
Tasmanian species forming a small to medium, dense-growing tree with smooth white bark with green or purplish patches. Adult foliage silver-grey, heart-shaped, 6–10cm long, sessile or without stalks. Unattractive, white, spring flowers, followed by 12mm roundish and flattened capsules. Handsome tree for larger areas, particularly in cold, moist climates. Cordata — heart-shaped. 10 × 5m.

Eucalyptus delegatensis
Alpine Ash
Grows naturally at altitudes to 1500m forming gigantic specimens over 60m with almost 2m bole. Forms a thickset specimen with long, straight trunk covered with brown, fibrous bark. Branches smooth, creamy white or blue-grey. Juvenile foliage ovate and silvery grey. Adult leaves curled, elliptic to ovate, blue-green, to 35cm long. Insignificant white flowers late summer, capsules woody and pear-shaped. A fast growing tree of bold dimensions, hardy, cold resistant, suitable for outlines, shade, shelter or seclusion in public areas or farms. Delegatensis — for the town Delegate, NSW. 18 × 10m.

Eucalyptus ficifolia
Red Flowered Gum
Possibly the best known flowering Eucalyptus. Handsome form, usually a single-trunked, round-headed tree with compact crown, or may be trained as a multi-stemmed bush. Stringy, browny red to grey fibrous bark. Leaves broad-lanceolate, to 14 × 5cm, deep green, glossy with reddish rib, varying little from juvenile to adult. Spectacular flowers, mostly deep red, although orange, pink or white may occur in seedling trees, displayed well above the foliage in large clusters during summer. Seed capsules 25mm wide, shaped like miniature goblets. Ideal tree for avenues, specimens, shade, colour effects, singly or in groups, in home gardens or public areas. Grows naturally in high rainfall areas, so prefers adequate moisture, but shelter from frost, especially when young. Ficifolia — leaves like ficus. 7 × 5m.   **124**

Eucalyptus fraxinioides
White Mountain Ash
Tree of variable size with moderately dense canopy, found at altitudes frequently

shrouded in mist in the coastal ranges of southern New South Wales and Victoria. Rough, dark grey to almost black bark near the base, grey or pale brown for the top two thirds, shedding in autumn to reveal white or yellow bark beneath. Young leaves elliptic or broadly lanceolate, to 20 × 6cm, blue-green or reddish. Adult leaves green, lanceolate or sickle-shaped, to 16 × 2.5cm. Flowers creamy-white, to 15mm across, borne profusely, followed by 11 × 11mm urn-shaped capsules. Mainly used in forestry or as a shade tree in parks, farms or acreage properties. Fraxinioides — resembling Fraxinus. 15 × 12m.

Eucalyptus globulus ssp bicostata
Southern Blue Gum
Vigorous tree, popular as a juvenile for the delightful colourings of its growing shoots. Ovate to broadly lanceolate leaves in opposite pairs, greyish green, edged and overlaid with a distinct purple sheen, held on almost square, four-sided branchlets. Mature leaves to 25cm long, sickle-shaped and deep green. Older trees develop rough green or brown bark at the base which becomes rather shaggy. Upper trunk and limbs smooth and blue-grey. Flowers white. Allow adequate space for development. Fast-growing shelter or timber tree. Globulus — round, spherical, bicostata — refers to two ridges on the calyx of each bud. 10 × 5m.

Eucalyptus nicholii
Willow Peppermint
Graceful weeping tree with ascending main stem, soft brown bark and spreading branches. Young shoots distinctly plum coloured, leaves light green, narrow lanceolate, to 12cm, with peppermint fragrance when crushed. Inconspicuous, small white autumn flowers and seed capsules. A beautiful tree for fine-textured foliage and willowy form. Ideal as a street tree, lawn specimen, for shade or screen. Makes rapid progress, hardy to frost and drought and grows in average conditions. Nicholii — for R Nichol, formerly at Royal Botanic Gardens, Sydney. 10 × 6m.

Eucalyptus nutans
Nodding Gum
Ornamental, rather bushy and spreading shrub, commencing to bloom when about 2m high, possibly three years after planting. Lanceolate leaves to 12cm, rich green with a hint of red around the edges, carried on reddish twigs. From late spring, clusters of acorn-shaped buds open into rich crimson flowers with white-tipped anthers, followed by cone-shaped seed capsules. Buds and fruit held in clusters of up to seven on one short

130   *Palmer's Manual*

stem, often drooping and expressed in the name nutans which means nodding. Grows in sandy, stony or dry free-draining soil and tolerates drought. Excellent, showy small tree for avenues backgrounds slopes or lawns. 4 × 3m.

Eucalyptus pauciflora
Snow Gum, Weeping Gum
Snow Gums are highly photogenic with their picturesque, contorted trunks in beautiful patterns and colours. Found in various habitats from coastal plains to altitudes of 1500m south of the Queensland border to Tasmania and South Australia. Forms a small tree either with single trunk or contorted branches near the base, bark smooth, grey, white or pale brown, shedding in patches in autumn to reveal whitish new bark. Adult leaves broad-lanceolate, to 15 × 5cm, blue-green to glaucous. Creamy-white, 15mm flowers in axillary clusters followed by 11 × 11mm cup-shaped capsules. Pauciflora — few-flowered. 8 × 6m.

Eucalyptus pulchella
White Peppermint
Tasmanian species with handsome form, trunk and foliage. A small tree with reasonably dense canopy. Smooth bark artistically patterned in white, cream, grey or brown, shedding small patches during autumn.

Bluish-green juvenile leaves lanceolate to linear, to 7 × 1cm. Adult leaves linear-lanceolate to 10cm × 6mm, green to grey-green, aromatic when crushed. Axillary clusters of 15mm creamy flowers followed by small cup-shaped capsules. Pulchella — beautiful. 8 × 6m.

Eucalyptus scoparia
Wallangarra White Gum
Attractive, fast growing gum from the Wallangarra district on the Queensland-New South Wales border. Forms slender, straight or contorted trunk with spreading crown of pendulous foliage. Ornamental bark smooth, white, reddish brown mottled grey and quite powdery. Young leaves oblong to lanceolate, to 6cm × 6mm, dark green and glossy. Adult leaves linear-lanceolate, green, glossy on both surfaces and gracefully pendulous. White, 15mm flowers followed by small ovoid capsules. Scoparia — broom-like. 8 × 6cm.

Eucalyptus sideroxylon 'Rosea'
Pink Ironbark
One of the hardiest gums, occurring naturally in areas where annual rainfall is little more than 65cm, where summer temperatures often exceed 40°C or where twenty frosts could be experienced in one winter. Thriving under such conditions on poor,

shallow soil is evidence of extreme vigour. Pink Ironbark is rather variable in growth, the trend in young plants a guide to ultimate development, open or dense, slender or wide, pendulous or erect. Non-shedding bark, deeply furrowed, almost black and very hard. Darker leaves could indicate deeper flower shadings. Leaves narrow lanceolate to 12cm long, blue-green with a bronzy hue in winter. Light pink fluffy flowers in pendulous clusters mostly from autumn to late spring, followed by 1cm goblet-shaped seed capsules. Sideroxylon — from the Greek *sideros*, iron and *xylon*, wood, from the hardness of its heart timber. 10 × 6m.

A genus of about six species of trees and shrubs from Chile and south east Australia, named from *eu*, well and *kryphios*, covered, referring to the sepals which form a cap. Relatively unknown in cultivation in the Southern Hemisphere, but grown in England for many decades where a number of excellent hybrids have arisen from Chilean and Australian species. Highly ornamental trees and shrubs, all with masses of wide-open, nectar-rich, strongly fragrant flowers with prominent stamens.

Eucryphia is easy to grow, frost hardy, grows in shade or dappled sun, full sun in cold climates. Plant in deeply worked, organically enriched, free-draining, neutral to slightly acid soil. Mulch freely to keep the roots cool and water frequently during dry periods. They enjoy being amongst other trees or shrubs which shade their roots but where they can reach the light, ideal in moist woodland situations.

Euchryphiaceae. *All evergreen.*

Eucryphia cordifolia
Chilean. Broad, columnar tree with tomentose young shoots. Heart-shaped or oblong leaves, cordate to rounded at the base, to 7 × 4cm, margins crenate or serrate, glabrous above, grey downy beneath. Flowers white, 5cm across. Beautiful large shrub. Cordifolia — with heart-shaped leaves. 3 × 2m.

Eucryphia lucida
Leatherwood
Small to medium tree from high-rainfall forests of Tasmania. Pale green, sticky young shoots. Leaves elliptic or narrow lanceolate to 45 × 20mm, leathery, dark green, glossy, glaucous beneath. Beautiful white, fragrant, 4cm flowers with four wide-open petals and

numerous stamens, resembling a single rose, borne prolifically late spring through summer. Lucida — bright, shining. 3 × 2m.

Eucryphia lucida 'Ballerina'
Resembles above, but with soft pink flowers, deeper pink margins and conspicuous crimson-pink central eye. Unusual colouring for the genus. 3 × 2m.

Eucryphia lucida 'Gilt Edge'
Distinctive, trifoliate, deep green leaves margined golden yellow. Otherwise resembles the species. 3 × 2m.

Eucryphia lucida 'Leatherwood Cream'
Impressive cultivar with beautiful variegated leaves, deep green with creamy margins. Quite distinct from 'Gilt Edge'. 3 × 2m.

Eucryphia × nymansensis 'Nymansay'
Excellent hybrid from E cordifolia × E glutinosa from Chile, described as the ultimate selection. Leaves either simple or compound, elliptic-lanceolate to 6cm long, margins sharply serrated. Compound leaves usually in threes, the central one to 8 × 4cm. Exquisite, large, fragrant white flowers to 75mm resembling Rose of Sharon appear in great profusion late summer and autumn. Named for Nymans, Sussex. 3 × 2m.

A genus of over 170 species trees or shrubs distributed throughout Asia, Europe, North and Central America, Madagascar and Australia named from the Latin *euonymus*, of good name, an ironic reference to its toxicity to animals. Euonymus are highly valued for foliage, form and year-round colour, among the few golden foliaged shrubs undamaged by sun or drought. Deciduous species are noted for autumn foliage colour and brilliant autumn fruits. Some species provide for ground cover or rock gardens and there are narrow erect forms for sentinels or screens.

They're easy to grow in most localities or soils with reasonable drainage, prefer full sun, but accept partial shade. In areas of high summer humidity, E japonica cultivars are notorious for mildew. Locate in full sun with good air circulation and spray to control mildew, scale and other insect pests. Remove immediately any green reverting shoots which may appear on variegated plants.

Celastraceae. *Evergreen except where marked.*

Euonymus europaeus
Spindle Tree
Deciduous shrub from Europe to western Asia. Green, angular branches with corky stripes. Leaves ovate-elliptic to oblong, to 8cm long assuming rich tints of orange and red in autumn. Inconspicuous, greenish-yellow, 10mm flowers with yellow anthers appear in cymes of five or more in spring followed in autumn by curious, four-lobed, 2cm, scarlet-crimson fruit. They burst open to display shiny, bright orange seeds which persist in great quantities through winter. Hardy anywhere, preferring alkaline soil. Common name from the fact that its hard wood was once used in making spindles. Deciduous. 3 × 2m.

Euonymus europaeus 'Red Cascade'
Selected form of Spindle Tree with arching branches, often pendulous under the burden of tremendous crops of rich, rosy red berries in autumn and winter. Brilliant red autumn foliage colour. Deciduous. 3 × 2m.

Euonymus fortunei 'Emerald'n Gold'
Extremely hardy, trailing shrub supporting itself by aerial rootlets, providing either ground or wall cover. Ovate-elliptic, leaves to 6cm, finely serrated margins, beautifully variegated, central zone of emerald green, irregularly margined with gold and a touch of pink. Excellent ground or rock cover or dwarf shrub. Fortunei — after Robert Fortune, 19th century Scottish horticulturist. 60 × 90cm. **124**

Euonymus japonica 'Albo-marginatus'
Silver Japanese Laurel
Compact form with erect, bushy growth, oval or elliptic leaves with an irregular central green zone narrowly margined creamy white. Japonica — of Japan, Albo-marginatus — white margined. 1 × 1m.

Euonymus japonica 'Aureo-marginatus'
Golden Japanese Laurel
Narrow, erect and compact growth, easily clipped to any desired shape, always gleaming, bright and clean. Glossy, 7cm, lightly serrated, ovate to elliptic leaves, dark green with an irregular margin of gold. Ideal specimen, container plant, avenue plant or screen. Amongst the finest golden variegated evergreen shrubs in cultivation. Aureo-marginatus — yellow margined. Easily trained from 1 to 3m high. As a screen, plant at 75cm centres. **124**

Euonymus japonica 'Aureo-picta'
More compact than 'Aureo-marginatus' with shorter, twiggy growth. Young stems gold, glossy foliage intense bright yellow, margined deep green, with many leaves entirely yellow. Choice attractive shrub. Aureo-picta — painted or brightly coloured gold. 2 × 1.5m.

Euonymus japonica 'Ovatus Aureus'
Dwarf Golden Japanese Laurel
Low-growing compact form, ovate to elliptic, 5–6cm leaves, distinctly curled, brilliant yellow with green markings. During spring and autumn foliage seems almost entirely yellow making the bush literally glow. Ovatus — egg-shaped. 1 × 1m.

Euonymus japonica 'Silver King'
Bushy upright form, large narrow leaves, deep green with silvery white margin. Easy to grow and hardy to –6°C. 2 × 1.5m.

EUPHORBIA

Extensive genus in excess of 1500 species of trees, shrubs and herbs with milky-white latex, mainly from Africa, Madagascar, south and south-east Asia, named for Euphorbus, physician to King Juba of Mauritania. To most gardeners, the genus is best represented by the familiar Poinsettia, a vigorous flamboyant plant for frost-free, sunny conditions with free-draining soil, sheltered from strong wind. Hard pruning each year after flowering will maintain compact form and encourage new flowering shoots.
Euphorbiaceae.

Euphorbia characias ssp wulfenii
A novel and hardy species from the Balkans. Compact, rounded bush with numerous unbranched stems densely clothed with linear to obovate, 12 × 1cm, greyish green leaves. Decorative in winter and early spring with showy, pyramidal heads of cup-shaped, chartreuse or bright greenish yellow bracts. Withstands neglect, but prune after flowering. Named for von Wulfen, 18th century Austrian botanist. Evergreen. 1 × 1m.

Euphorbia milii
Crown of Thorns
Native to Madagascar. Succulent, scrambling shrub, with almost leafless, irregular angular stems, armed with long, sharp spines. Sparse, obovate, light-green leaves to 35 × 15mm, usually near branch ends. Bright scarlet bracts in clustered pairs appear amongst the foliage almost the year through. Left to itself, forms a low twiggy mound about 1 × 1m. to 60cm high. May be trained on a small frame or trellis against a sheltered wall. Full sun or partial shade. Drought tolerant, but responds to infrequent deep watering through dry periods. Syn E splendens. Evergreen. 60cm × 1m.

Euphorbia pulcherrima
Poinsettia
Mexican. Strong grower, producing long slender stems clothed with large, medium green, lanceolate to ovate-elliptic leaves to 15cm or more, usually deeply lobed. Clusters of small yellow flowers surrounded by flamboyant, intense scarlet bracts through winter and early spring. Few other plants rival poinsettia for winter brightness. Pulcherrima — very beautiful. An improved form is known as 'Barbara Ecke Supreme'. Deciduous. 2 × 1.5m. **133**

Euphorbia pulcherrima 'Alba'
Flower bracts white. Improved form — 'Ecke's White'.Deciduous. 2 × 1.5m.

Euphorbia pulcherrima 'Crema'
Flower bracts of pale yellow. Deciduous. 2 × 1.5m. **133**

Euphorbia pulcherrima 'New Reich'
Superior selected cultivar for frost-free outdoor locations. Forms a branched shrub with bright red bracts with a background of blackish foliage. 1.5 × 1.5m.

Euphorbia pulcherrima 'Plenissima'
Magnificent form with wide-spreading, rich scarlet outer bracts and a heavy central cluster of smaller bract 'petals'. Improved clone — 'Henrietta Ecke'. Deciduous. 2 × 1.5m. **133**

Euphorbia pulcherrima 'Rosea'
Flower bracts in bright pink, leaves pale green. Improved form — 'New Pink'. Deciduous. 2 × 1.5m.

EURYA

A genus of about 70 species of mostly evergreen trees and shrubs from south and east Asia and the Pacific Islands named from the Greek euru, broad. Grown for its beautiful foliage and attractive branching pattern. Belongs to the same family as Camellia and grows under similar conditions. Grow in organically enriched, free-draining, moisture retentive soil in sun or partial shade.
Theaceae.

Eurya japonica 'Variegata'
From Japan and Korea. Slow-growing, bush with slender, willowy, spreading branches,

laterals arranged in neat herringbone formation. Young shoots tinged pink, leaves oval to obovate, to 8 × 3cm, leathery, smooth and pliable, beautifully variegated dark green, milky green, irregularly marked creamy-white around the margins. Inconspicuous, 5–6mm, off-white flowers with unpleasant odour appear on older plants followed by small glossy berries. Evergreen. 1.5 × 1.3m.

EURYOPS

A genus of about 100 species of shrubs or perennial herbs mainly from South Africa, named from the Greek *euryops*, with large eyes referring to the immense flowers of some species.

Euryops are valuable easy-grown shrubs, providing massed displays of yellow daisy-flowers for long periods, surviving temperatures to almost zero and thriving near the coast. Plant in full sun, in deeply worked, free-draining soil. Once established, they can do with little water. During their long flowering season, pick off old blooms and cut the plant back by half when flowering is over.

Compositae. *All evergreen.*

Euryops pectinatus
Grey Haired Euryops
Desirable South African dwarf shrub with ferny, woolly-grey, pinnate leaves to 10 × 5cm, deeply cut into 8–20 narrow linear lobes. Rich yellow, 4cm daisy flowers on 15cm stalks displayed above the foliage, appear late spring through summer. Pectinatus — comb-like. 1 × .75m.   **133**

Euryops tenuissimus
Paris Daisy
Neat South African shrub with finely divided, soft, ferny, deep-green foliage and rounded, bushy form. Great quantities of bright yellow, daisy-like, 5cm flowers carried on slender stems about 10cm above the bush through winter and spring. Tenuissimus — very slender. 1 × 1m.

Euryops virgineus 'Glitters'
Compact, multi-branched shrub from South Africa. Leaves obovate to oblanceolate to 12 × 5mm, with 3–7 small lanceolate lobes, deep green leathery, crowded and overlapping on twiggy branchlets. Small, 15mm bright yellow flowers in great masses, appearing as myriads of golden stars almost completely cover the bush through winter and spring. 1 × 1m.   **133**

EUTAXIA

Australian endemic genus of eight species of pea-flowered dwarf shrubs, all but one, E microphylla, from south west Western Australia, named from the Greek *eu*, well, and *taxis*, arranged, possibly referring to a well ordered leaf arrangement. Delightful dwarf shrubs, growing without fuss. becoming a total mass of bloom for long periods during spring. Prefers light, well drained soil, but tolerant of varying conditions, either in full sun or the dappled shade of larger trees. Prune heavily after flowering.

Fabaceae.

Eutaxia obovata
From Western Australia. One of the easiest and most colourful shrubs to grow. Forms a bushy, closely twigged plant, fully clothed with linear to obovate-oblong, 2cm leaves, neatly arranged in four rows along each stem. Covered through spring and early summer with masses of 12mm, pea-shaped, bright yellow, red and orange flowers, set in clusters of four between each set of leaves. Obovatus — egg-shaped with the broadest end uppermost. Evergreen. 1 × 1m.

EVOLVULUS

A genus of about 100 species of annual or perennial herbs or subshrubs, many from Central and South America, others from tropical and subtropical regions including Australia, named from the Latin *evolvo*, to unravel or disentangle, a reference to the non-climbing tendency of the genus. Found naturally in dry, open, sunny situations, scrambling over rocks.

In the garden, Evolvulus makes an excellent wall spiller, ground cover or rock garden plant for sunny, frost-free locations. Ideal for hanging baskets or tumbling over containers. Grows readily in almost any loose, free-draining soil in a warm, frost-free location in full sun. Cut back to almost ground level for growth renewal, or grow new plants from divisions.

Convolvulaceae.

Evolvulus pilosus Blue Sapphire'
Desirable little plant from southern states of the USA. Forms a bushy, compact mound of numerous slender stems. Leaves elliptic-ovate to 25 × 10cm, dull sage green above,

paler beneath, margins entire. Buds, branchlets, leaf undersides and stems covered with fine silky hairs. Bright blue flowers to 25mm across, with small pure white central star and white anthers, borne terminally on branchlets or leaf axils almost continuously, spring through autumn. Pilosus — covered with long soft hairs. Evergreen. 50 × 90cm.   **134**

FAGUS

A genus of some ten species of deciduous trees from temperate Asia and Europe, called by the Greek and Latin name for Beech. Richness of foliage and picturesque framework have earned, especially for Fagus sylvatica cultivars, the respect of garden connoisseurs everywhere. Although slow growers and somewhat thin and unshapely when young, they develop a broad, pyramidal or conical outline, with lower branches sweeping to ground level. The tree needs space to look its best and should never be overcrowded.

Although from cooler climates, Fagus perform in warmer areas where strong prevailing wind or salt spray can be avoided. They grow in any good garden soil, in full sun or partial shade, but require adequate drainage. Mulch young trees to keep the roots cool and moist during dry periods. Ideal as specimens, backgrounds, silhouettes, in containers or bonsai. Good focal point for home gardens where space is not cramped. Consider carefully where you plant. They are long-term trees growing more and more beautiful over many decades, and to relocate or chop one down would simply be unthinkable.

Fagaceae. *All deciduous.*

Fagus sylvatica
Common European Beech
Forms a tall pyramidal tree with irregular outline and lower branches sweeping to the ground. Smooth, grey bark and soft, dark green, glossy, 10 × 6cm, elliptic-ovate leaves with prominent veins, reddish brown in autumn, persisting well into winter. After leaf fall, pointed winter buds and intricate twigs make picturesque patterns. New leaves in spring have a silky sheen.

Although Common Beech is offered by some nurseries, the ornamental cultivars are more generally planted. Native to Europe. Sylvatica — of a wood or forest in the natural sense, rather than cultivated. 10 × 6m.

Above: Euphorbia pulcherrima *Poinsettia* **131**

Above: Euphorbia pulcherrima 'Plenissima' **131**
Below: Euryops pectinatus *Grey Haired Euryops* **132**

Above: Euphorbia pulcherrima 'Crema' **131**
Below: Euryops virgineus 'Glitters' **132**

Above: Evolvulus 'Blue Saphire' **132**

Above: Gardenia augusta 'Radicans' *Dwarf Gardenia* **140**
Below: Fagus sylvatica 'Riversii' *River's Copper Beech* **137**

Above: Gordonia axillaris *Fried Egg Tree* **142**

Above: Gardenia augusta 'Mystery' **140**
Below: Gardenia augusta 'Veitchii' **140**

Above: Grevillea x gaudichaudi **143**

Above: Grevillea 'Poorinda Royal Mantle' **144**

Above: Garrya elliptica 'James Roof' **141**
Below: Gleditsia triacanthos 'Sunburst' *Sunbust Honey Locust* **142**

Above: Grevillea 'Robyn Gordon' **145**
Below: Grevillea 'Superb' **145**

Above: Grevillea brachystylis 'Bushfire' **143**

Above: Grevillea 'Bonnie Prince Charlie' **143**

Above: Grevillea rosmarinifolia 'Scarlet Sprite' **145**

Above: Grevillea 'Tickled Pink' **145**
Below: Grevillea prostrata 'Aurea' **144**

Above: Grevillea alpina 'Dallachiana' **143**
Below: Grevillea 'Poorinda Peter' **144**

Above: Grevillea lanigera 'Mt Tamboritha' **144**
Below: Ginkgo biloba **141**

Fagus sylvatica 'Atropunicea'

Beautiful form of F purpurea, selected for spectacular deep reddish-purple spring foliage, bronze through summer. Atropunicea — dark reddish purple. 10 × 6m.

Fagus sylvatica 'Heterophylla'
Cut-Leaf Beech

One of the most effective large ornamental trees. Attractive leaves, deeply cut almost to the midrib into finger-like lobes. Variations of this form include asplinifolia, incisa and laciniata. Heterophylla — diversely leafed. 7 × 4m.

Fagus sylvatica 'Purpurea'
Purple Beech

Handsome leaves, elliptic-ovate, pointed, toothed and prominently veined, often reddish at first, lightly covered with fine hairs. Mature leaves deep purple, almost black. Rather gaunt when young, they gradually form a dense, ornately branched pyramid. 10 × 6m.

Fagus sylvatica 'Purpurea Pendula'
Weeping Purple Beech

Rare, gracefully pendulous and perhaps the most beautiful of all weeping trees. Grafted on a tall stem, slender branches reach for the ground, clothed in spring with rich purple foliage.

Grows with little or no training. In the early stages of development, more height and less width can be achieved if a strong leading branch is staked to grow erect. From this weeping side branches will develop. A tree for discerning gardeners. 3 × 3m.

Fagus sylvatica 'Riversii'
River's Copper Beech

Selected form, foliage larger than 'Purpurea', and rich deep purple-black. Holds its colour more or less constant until autumn when the leaves drop cleanly rather than retaining an untidy portion through winter. Large dome-shaped tree. 10 × 6m.   **134**

Fagus sylvatica 'Rohanii'
Purple Fern-Leaf Beech

Foliage deeply lobed with rounded serrations, deep reddish purple in spring, more muted by late summer. Raised on the property of Prince Camille de Rohan and named in his honour. 7 × 4m.

Fagus sylvatica 'Tricolor'

Interesting variation in which the young spring growths are purplish, edged and blotched with rose and pinkish white. The foliage is decorative for several months eventually losing brilliance and turning dull purplish green before falling. 7 × 4m.

Fagus sylvatica 'Zlatia'
Golden Beech

Unusual form with beautiful golden yellow leaves in spring, aging to greenish yellow through summer and autumn. Slower growing and smaller tree. Zlatia — from the Serbian *zlatos*. 6 × 4m.

FATSHEDERA

A bigeneric hybrid from Fatsia japonica 'Moseri', French seedling Japanese aralia and Irish ivy, Hedera hibernica. An interesting evergreen shrub-vine with characteristics of both parents. Less demanding of space than Japanese Aralia, its vertical lines most effective against walls. Guide and tie branches before they become too brittle. Tips may be pinched at any time to induce branching.

As a climber, provide strong support, encouraging new basal shoots to cover older stems which may become bare in the lower regions. It can be used indoors but is more vigorous and effective in outdoor situations. Full sun or partial shade, tolerant of light frost, any reasonable, free-draining soil. Mulch freely and keep moist in dry periods. Watch for aphids, scale insects, mealy bug, slugs and snails. If the plant becomes ungainly, cut to ground level and it quickly re-grows.

Araliaceae.

Fatshedera lizei

Highly polished, leathery, 15–20cm, prominently veined, palmate leaves with three to five pointed lobes resembling a small aralia leaf, deep green in shady locations, lighter green in full sun, often with a reddish tinge. The plant sends up long, trailing or climbing stems, strong enough to be self-supporting if away from wind. Young stems carry foliage from tip to base, but tend to loose lower leaves with age. Also a creamy white variegated form. Evergreen. Height and width variable according to training.

FATSIA

A genus of three species of thick stemmed shrubs or small trees from Japan, Taiwan and Bonin Island called by an adaptation of *Fatsi*, the Japanese name for Fatsia japonica. Widely used in landscaping for its large leaves, tropical appearance, frost-resistance and tolerance of salt-laden winds and pollution. Often used indoors but prefers the freedom of growing outside, performing without fuss, appearing handsome and healthy all year round. Good in containers, singly or in groups of various sizes.

Grows in full sun, partial or full shade, leaf colour varying from light to deep green according to exposure. Grows in almost any deeply worked, free-draining soil. Mulch freely, feed with balanced fertilizer spring and autumn and keep moist through dry periods. Rejuvenate tired plants by hard pruning in early spring. Hose down occasionally to remove dust and discourage insects. Light spraying with a weak summer oil solution gives a high gloss finish to the foliage and controls many insect pests.

Araliaceae.

Fatsia japonica
Japanese Aralia

Sparingly branched and densely foliaged plant, although lower leaves may eventually fall. Leaves deeply lobed palmate, to 30cm, dark green, glossy, held on strong, clean petioles. Rounded clusters of small white flowers during autumn and winter succeeded by small black berries. Also F japonica 'Variegata' with leaves edged golden yellow to creamy white. Evergreen. 2 × 1.5m.

FEIJOA

Genus of two species of shrubs from Brazil named for Don de Silva Feijoa, 19th century Brazilian botanist. The popular fruiting Feijoa selloviana is also a valuable landscaping plant. Used extensively for screens or hedges, can be worked into shrub borders or used as a specimen shrub. Hardy to almost zero temperatures, tolerant of drought and coastal exposure once established. Plant in any reasonable, deeply worked, free-draining soil. Mulch freely, apply nitrogen-rich fertilizer spring and autumn and water through dry periods for fruit production. Seedling-grown trees unpredictable as to fruit quality. Selected vegetatively propagated clones are preferable. Crops dependant on good cross-pollination, always better in group planting.

Myrtaceae.

Feijoa selloviana
Pineapple Guava

Forms a dense, bushy tree with branches and foliage to ground level. Leaves elliptic-oblong to 75mm, deep green and glossy above, white-woolly beneath. Handsome flowers to 35mm across with four fleshy, cupped petals, white tomentose outside, purplish within, with a conspicuous tuft of dark red stamens. Fleshy petals are said to be edible. Luscious oval or oblong fruit, 5–10cm long, dull green with whitish bloom. Flavour suggestive of pineapple and strawberry, when fully ripe. Selloviana — for Friedrich Sellow, 18th–19th century German naturalist. Evergreen. 3 × 2m.

FELICIA

A genus of about 80 species of annual or perennial herbs from tropical and South Africa and Arabia named for Felix, early 19th century German official at Regensburg. Felicias are pretty little shrubs, usually with blue daisy flowers. Grow them in full sun, in deeply worked, free-draining soil. Water frequently during dry spells. Pick plenty of flowers and prune hard late summer for growth renewal. Semi-prostrate habit, suited to spilling over banks and walls, filling large rockery pockets or massed bedding.
Compositae. *All evergreen.*

Felicia amelloides
Blue Marguerite
Low-growing, spreading and tidy subshrub from South Africa. Handsome leaves ovate to obovate to 3cm long, deep green, glossy, margins almost entire. Clear light blue flowers to 4cm across with conspicuous central yellow eye borne on 18cm stems, mainly through spring and summer but always seems to be in bloom. Note also the following cultivars — 'Felicity' white daisy flowers, 'Pink Star' pink daisy flowers. 'Sapphire' variegated cream and green foliage, kingfisher-blue flowers. 30 × 90cm.

Felicia fruticosa
Kingfisher Daisy
More shrubby South African form with linear, 12mm, angular densely arranged leaves, margins entire. Masses of 3cm, amethyst-violet daisy flowers borne on 10cm stems, covering the bush through spring and summer. Fruticosa — shrubby or bushy. 90 × 90cm.

FESTUCA

A genus of some 300 species of perennial grasses, from cooler temperate regions named from the Latin *festuca*, a stalk straw or stem. A few have become popular landscaping subjects, particularly F ovina 'Glauca' with good colour, neat appearance and rapid development. Useful for edging, ground cover, geometric garden designs, rock or feature gardens etc. Grow readily in most locations but resent soggy, poorly drained conditions. Clip to within 2–3cm of the ground after flowering or whenever the plants become untidy. A dressing of balanced fertilizer after clipping is advised. Fresh growth soon appears. Overgrown plants may be pulled apart and small divisions replanted.
Graminae. *All evergreen.*

Festuca coxii
Chatham Island Fescue
Native to the Chatham Islands. Excellent little grass with slender blue glaucous leaves. Often confused with F ovina 'Glauca' which it resembles, but without the browning effect of older leaves. Considered a better all-round plant but will not survive hot and dry conditions. 25 × 25cm.

Festuca ovina 'Glauca'
Blue Fescue
European, densely clumping grass with flimsy, finely filiform, blue-grey blades growing in dense tussocks from ground level. Ovina — relating to fodder for sheep. 25 × 25cm.

FICUS

A genus of about 800 species of trees, shrubs or woody vines found throughout the world's tropics and subtropics called by *ficus* the Latin name for fig. Amazing diversity of form and function is evident even in the relatively few species under cultivation. Besides tree forms, there are small leafed clinging vines, the common fruiting fig, and handsome large leafed species frequently used as house plants. Moreton Bay Fig grows almost anywhere if sheltered from frosts, but rapidly outgrows average suburban situations. Splendid container and landscaping tree in juvenile form.
Moraceae.

Ficus macrophylla
Moreton Bay Fig
Native to northern regions of Australia, eventually forming a massive, thick trunk with buttressed roots, attaining great proportions of height and width. Leathery, oblong to elliptic, glossy leaves to 25 × 12cm. Rose coloured leaf-sheaths appear like candles at branch ends. Macrophylla — large leaf. Evergreen. 10 × 6m.

FORSYTHIA

A genus of six species of free flowering, hardy shrubs from central Asia and central Europe, named for William Forsyth, 18th century superintendent of the Royal Gardens, Kensington. Mostly fountain shaped shrubs, in spring providing gleaming displays of yellow flowers on bare branches. They blend well with other spring flowering shrubs such as blue ceanothus, red chaenomeles, pink weigela or white philadelphus, underplanted with annuals or spring flowering bulbs. Long flowering stems ideal for picking.
Extremely hardy, rarely needing attention apart from annual pruning. Performs best in colder regions. Almost any deeply worked, free-draining soil in full sun. While tolerating neglect, occasional feeding and summer watering encourages better floral displays. Established plants may be pruned by cutting to ground level a third of the branches that have flowered plus any dead wood.
Oleaceae. *All deciduous.*

Forsythia × intermedia 'Beatrix Farrand'
Hybrid cultivar from the Chinese species F suspensa × F viridissima. Erect and spreading, greenish-gold branches. Leaves ovate-lanceolate, mid-green, margins serrated. Yellow flowers in clusters of three borne prolifically through spring. 'Beatrix Farrand' is an erect grower with thick-set branches wreathed in spring with 5–6cm, deep canary yellow flowers marked orange in the throat. Intermedia — intermediate in colour, form or habit. 2.5 × 1.5m.

Forsythia × intermedia 'Fiesta'
Compact, bushy grower, attractive variegated leaves green, with central zones of bright cream and gold. Golden yellow spring flowers. Sport of 'Minigold'. 1 × 1m.

Forsythia × intermedia 'Karl Sax'
Large, deep golden-yellow, bell-shaped flowers in spring before the leaves appear. Lower growing, neater and more graceful than Beatrix Farrand but equally floriferous. Upright and bushy. 1.8 × 1m.

Forsythia × intermedia 'Lynwood Gold'
Erect central stems, semi-pendulous side branches. Becomes a total mass of large,

golden yellow flowers through spring. 1.8 × 1.5m.

Forsythia × intermedia 'Minigold'
Erect, compact, rounded bushy shrub of semi-dwarf habit. Handsome deep green foliage. Masses of yellow blooms cover bare branches early spring. 1 × 1m.

Forsythia × intermedia 'Spectabilis'
Upright growth. Masses of dark yellow flowers with twisted lobes densely packed on erect stems through spring. 2 × 1.3m.

FRANKLINIA

A genus of 70 species of trees and shrubs from south east USA and south east Asia, named for Benjamin Franklin, 18th century American printer, scientist, philosopher and statesman. The listed species discovered in Georgia in 1764, was apparently exterminated in the wild by 1803 through indiscriminate collecting by nurserymen for propagation. Highly valued for the long succession of fragrant flowers and the fiery scarlet autumn colours. Plant in deeply worked, organically enriched, free-draining, moisture-retentive, neutral to slightly acid soil in sun or partial shade. Mulch freely and keep moist through dry spells. Related to Camellias and grows in similar conditions to Rhododendrons.
Theaceae.

Franklinia alatamaha
Grows moderately with slender form, reddish brown bark with faint striping. Large, bright-green, lustrous, obovate-oblong, somewhat spoon-shaped, 10–15cm leaves which turn bright scarlet in autumn. Opening from round, white buds held on long erect stalks, deliciously fragrant, 7cm, cup-shaped, single creamy white flowers with central cluster of yellow stamens appear, sometimes coinciding with autumn leaf display. A gorgeous autumn flowering shrub revelling in hot continental summers when its ripened growths withstand zero winters. Alatamaha — of the Alatamaha River, Georgia, USA. Deciduous. 5 × 3m.

FRAXINUS

A genus of about 65 species scattered over the cooler temperate regions of the northern hemisphere named from the

Latin *fraxinus*, an ash tree. Rapid growing trees including some of the hardiest and adaptable species for shade, seclusion and sheer beauty. Leaves beautiful from spring through autumn. Winter bare branch structure is most picturesque.

They grow in almost any deeply worked, fertile soil, tolerate poor drainage and are not unduly troubled by pests or diseases. However, deep soil preparation, staking and ample deep watering during establishment assists rapid development. Use as lawn specimens, shade trees, screens, backgrounds, avenue or street trees. Fraxinus are one of the last trees to come into leaf in spring.
Oleaceae. *All deciduous.*

Fraxinus americana
White Ash
Native to eastern USA, quickly forming a noble shade tree with straight trunk and oval-pointed crown. Pinnate leaves to 35cm long with up to nine oblong-lanceolate, 15 × 9cm, dark green leaflets, whitish grey and downy beneath, rich purple in autumn. Avoid excessive exposure to strong winds to prevent foliage burn. 15 × 6m.

Fraxinus excelsior
Common European Ash
Forms a large tree with wide, rounded head providing ideal shade or shelter in larger areas, especially in heavy soils or moist conditions. Smooth stems studded with characteristic black buds. Pinnate leaves to 25cm with as many as eleven obovate, 10cm leaflets, dark green above, paler beneath. No autumn colour. Ideal stock shelter. Excelsior — very tall. 15 × 10m.

Fraxinus excelsior 'Aurea'
Golden Ash
This European hybrid is one of the most desirable trees for year round beauty. Smooth, golden yellow, gracefully curving branches and twigs, studded with big black buds provide unique and beautiful bare branch patterns through winter. Pinnate leaves to 30cm long with up to eleven obovate, 8cm, lime yellow leaflets, yellow through summer, brilliant golden yellow in autumn. Foliage persists into winter before laying a carpet of gold. Responds to pruning and training to shape or size. To encourage top growth and form a shapely head, rub off lower buds as they develop. Good for shade, screening, backgrounds in average gardens. Lawn grows beneath it. 6 × 5m.

Fraxinus excelsior 'Aurea Pendula'
Weeping Golden Ash
Grafted on a 2.5m standard, the plant when mature makes an impressive specimen.

Branch, bud and foliage colour similar to Golden Ash, but with a greater proportion of pendulous branches weeping gracefully to the ground. 3 × 2m.

Fraxinus ornus
Flowering Ash, Manna Ash
From southern Europe and Asia Minor. Rapid grower with broad rounded crown, greyish-brown dormant buds. Handsome pinnate foliage to 20cm with up to seven, obovate, 7cm, dark green leaflets, paler beneath, margins toothed. Autumn colours soft lavender-bronze and yellow. White to greenish white, fragrant, fluffy flowers in 10cm terminal clusters provide an unusual display in spring, followed by decorative samaras or seed clusters which appear as the leaves take on their autumn hues and persist through winter. A sugary substance referred to as manna exudes from this tree. Ornus — mountain ash. 10 × 5m.

Fraxinus oxycarpa 'Raywoodii'
Claret Ash
Most beautiful and popular deciduous tree with elegant framework and neat pyramidal habit. Handsome pinnate leaves to 30cm long, with up to thirteen, 7cm, oblong-lanceolate bright green leaflets gradually becoming rich purple-claret-red in autumn, holding well into winter before falling. Well-mannered and fits in to limited spaces. Australian hybrid. 8 × 5m.

FUCHSIA

A genus of about 100 species, mostly shrubs or small trees native to central and South America, Tahiti and New Zealand, named for Leonhart Fuchs, 16th century botanist and artist. Extensive breeding has provided endless, beautiful varieties in an infinite range of colour combinations and forms. Fuchsias prefer cool summer temperatures, good winter drainage and adequate moisture. Plant in deeply worked, organically enriched, free-draining, moisture retentive soil in a location sheltered from strong wind which avoids the hottest summer sun.

Fuchsias have an insatiable thirst during summer. Mulching and frequent overhead watering provides moisture, cleanses the foliage and increases humidity. Regular feeding, watering and pinching encourages healthy growth and an abundance of bloom. Remove spent flowers to avoid the formation of berries which weaken the plant. Healthy plants more resistant to pests and diseases but spraying for thrips, aphids and cater-pillars may be required. Use Fuchsias in hanging baskets, as standards, in containers, raised beds, along walls or in cool woodland areas. No attempt is made in this book to list the multitudes of named cultivars continually being introduced.

Onagraceae. *All evergreen.*

Fuchsia arborescens
Tree Fuchsia
Easily grown Mexican species. Forms a bushy tree with narrow, elliptic to oblanceoate, dark green, glossy leaves to 20 × 8cm, paler beneath. Slender, tubular, pinkish-purple flowers in large terminal clusters in abundance through spring and summer. Needs winter protection when young, ideal against a sunny wall. Arborescens — growing in tree-like form. 2.5 × 1.5m.

Fuchsia magellanica 'Tricolor'
Hardy species from southern Chile that will prove to be a valuable, free-flowering shrub with long arching branches and an abundance of bloom throughout the growing season. Pendent, nodding, 40mm flowers produced by the hundreds in pairs or fours at every leaf axil have a bright scarlet calyx enclosing a bluish or purple skirt and long protruding stamens and stigma. Flowers though small are very dainty. 'Tricolor' has attractive, variegated leaves, green margined creamy yellow and flushed pink. Magellanica — from the Straits of Megellan. 2 × 1m.

Fuchsia procumbens
Creeping Fuchsia
Found along coastal regions of north eastern New Zealand, growing in sandy or gravelly soil or among rocks, often within reach of extra high tides. Prostrate or trailing plant with slender, glabrous brownish stems. Leaves ovate to orbicular, to 12mm, bright green, paler beneath with prominent veins and midrib. Flowers to 20mm long, calyx orange-yellow on the outside, green within and reflexing, sepals dark purplish, filaments bright red, borne erect from leaf axils spring through early summer, followed mid-summer through autumn by bright red or magenta, 2cm fruit. Rare and endangered. For rock gardens, trailing over walls, hanging baskets. Procumbens — prostrate. 15 × 90cm.

Fuchsia triphylla 'Gartenmeister Bronstedt'
Vigorous upright grower with numerous slender stems, densely covered with large, elliptic or oblanceolate, 7–8cm, downy leaves, dark bronze above, purple-red beneath. Slender, 5–6cm, tubular, bright salmon-red flowers in large terminal clusters or racemes, mass produced through summer and autumn. Selected form from West Indies. 1 × 1m.

GARDENIA

A genus of about 250 species of evergreen shrubs or small trees natives of Asia, China, Africa and Australia, named for Dr Alexander Garden, 18th century physician in South Carolina and correspondent of Linnaeus. Gardenia is one of the most treasured plants for fragrant, exotic blooms. A healthy plant produces hundreds of flowers over many weeks depending on warmth, moisture, humidity and feeding. Locate in full sun or partial shade sheltered from frost and chilling winds.

Plant in deeply worked, organically enriched, free-draining, moisture retentive, slightly acid soil with generous amounts of peat moss, granulated bark and sand. Mulch freely after planting to insulate the roots and conserve moisture. Water frequently during dry periods and syringe or lightly hose plants in hot weather to raise humidity. Feed periodically with balanced slow-release fertilizer. Don't hesitate to pick blooms for indoors. Prune lightly after flowering. Spray for aphids or scale. Yellowing of the foliage, a symptom of chlorosis, may be corrected with iron chelates or sulphate of iron. Rangy plants may be cut almost to ground level for growth renewal.

Rubiaceae. *All evergreen.*

Gardenia augusta 'Mystery'
The species is native to China, Taiwan and Japan and along with its cultivars never fails to charm with exotic and fragrant blooms. 'Mystery' forms a bushy, compact plant with large, deep green, glossy leaves and produces 8–10cm, creamy white, fragrant, semi-double to double blooms spring through early summer. Syn G jasminoides. Augusta — majestic, notable. 1.2 × 1m.   **134**

Gardenia augusta 'Professor Pucci'
Strong grower with large foliage, and fully double flowers to 8cm across. Somewhat hardier and more vigorous. 1 × 1m.

Gardenia augusta 'Radicans'
Dwarf Gardenia
Spreading dwarf forming multi-branched, densely foliaged plant, becoming a total mass of white, semi-double, sweetly fragrant flowers to 55mm across late spring and early summer. Appears to be covered with snow. Leaves oblanceolate to elliptic, to 50 × 15mm, deep green, glossy, lighter beneath with prominent midrib. Suitable for ground cover, rockeries, wall spillers, hanging baskets or containers. Radicans — with rooting stems. 20 × 75cm.   **134**

Gardenia augusta 'Veitchii'
Compact, semi-erect grower, leaves oblanceolate to elliptic, to 11 × 5cm, glossy deep green above, lighter beneath, margins entire. Flowers pure white, highly fragrant, fully double to 5cm diameter, produced in abundance through spring and early summer. 90 × 90cm.   **134**

Gardenia thunbergia
White Gardenia
Native to South Africa. A shrub with rigid, erect branches and smooth grey bark. Leaves in whorls of three, elliptic, to 14 × 6cm, glossy, very dark green. Long tubular, terminal buds open into white or pale cream, 5–6cm, single flowers with lobes reflexed in such a manner that each bloom resembles a small umbrella. Deliciously fragrant at night. Blooms appear winter through spring, followed by ovoid, 7 × 4cm greyish-green fruit. Thunbergia — for Carl Peter Thunberg, (1743–1828) plant collector and student of Linnaeus. 2 × 3m.

GARRYA

A genus of about fifteen species of trees and shrubs from western USA, Mexico and West Indies named for Nicholas Garry, 19th century secretary of the Hudson Bay Company who assisted in the exploration of North America. Garrya elliptica and cultivars are commonly grown, valued for handsome foliage and attractive catkins during winter.

Easy to grow in sun or partial shade, thrives near the coast or inland and tolerates drought. Plant in loose, free-draining, not over-fertile soil. Dramatic shrub as lawn specimen, in shrub borders or sunny banks. Locate where the beauty of the winter floral display may be fully appreciated.

Garryaceae. *All evergreen.*

Garrya elliptica
Catkin Bush, Silk Tassel
Hardy, winter-blooming shrub from the coastal ranges of California and Oregon, with most unusual, tassel-like flowers hanging from the tips of each branch. Forms a bushy shrub with oblong-elliptic, 8cm

leaves, dark-green above, grey woolly beneath and wavy margins. Pendent clusters of greyish-green flowers in 15cm catkins produced on male plants during winter. Female plants rarely available, but if cross-pollinated bear clusters of purplish fruit covered with grey tomentum. Elliptica — elliptical. 2.5 × 2m.

Garrya elliptica 'James Roof'
From a selection made at the Regional Botanic Garden, Berkeley, California and named after the director. The best male form with very dark green foliage and 20cm, silvery, grey-green catkins in dense clusters. 2.5 × 2m. **135**

GAULTHERIA

A genus of about 170 low growing evergreen shrubs (which includes Pernettya) from America, West Indies, Japan to Australasia, named for Jean Francois Gaultier, 18th century French physician and botanist.

Valued for handsome foliage, fragrant flowers and fleshy fruits. Mostly found naturally as understorey plants. Best in shade or semi-shade in moisture-retentive, deeply worked, free-draining, lime-free acid soil. Mulch freely and keep moist during dry periods. Prune regularly to preserve shape and vigour. Use as a wide-spreading filler or in containers.

Ericaceae. *All evergreen.*

Gaultheria mucronata 'Bell's Seedling'
Attractive Chilean species spreading by underground suckers to form dense thickets of erect, wiry stems. Young shoots tinged red. Dense deep-green leathery, oval or oblong-elliptic leaves to 18 × 6mm, terminating abruptly with a hard sharp point (the meaning of mucronata). Some leaves become bronze or red in winter.

Myriads of small urn-shaped white heath-like flowers late autumn, followed by dense clusters of lustrous, marble-like, 12mm crimson fruit. Berries toxic, untouched by birds and remain on the bush all winter. True Bell's Seedling plants have both male and female flowers on the one plant. Syn Pernettya mucronata 'Bell's Seedling'. 60cm × 1m.

Gaultheria mucronata 'Alba'
Resembles above, but with crops of glistening white fruit faintly tinged pink. 60cm × 1m.

GENISTA

A genus of about 90 shrubs or small trees found in Europe, north Africa and western Asia named from the Latin genista — the plant broom. Genistas are free-flowering relatives of cytisus and spartium generally quite hardy and bear great masses of colourful pea-shaped flowers. Plant in full sun in light, free-draining soil. Withstands wind, coastal exposure and dry conditions. Good subjects for dry banks, rock gardens or sunny borders. Less aggressive than other Brooms. Pruning hardly necessary except for shaping.

Fabaceae. *All evergreen.*

Genista lydia
Balkan's Golden Broom
From the Balkans and Syria. An outstanding dwarf grower forming a rounded bush with slender, sparsely foliaged, ascending and curving stems. Leaves linear-elliptic to 8 × 3mm, deep green, carried in clusters. A profusion of bright yellow, pea-shaped flowers borne in short racemes literally cover the plant late spring, early summer. Excellent for rock gardens or prominent border positions. Quite hardy. Named from Lydia in Asia Minor. 60cm × 1m.

Genista monosperma
Bridal Veil Broom
Fine textured shrub with light, airy gracefulness, from western Mediterranean regions. A well grown specimen produces myriads of tiny, white, fragrant, pea-shaped flowers with purple calyx in spring, showered over long, fine, pendulous branches weeping almost to the ground. Narrow, 12mm, silky leaves few and far between. Syn Retama monosperma. 2.5 × 2m.

Genista 'Yellow Imp'
Compact bushy form producing a profusion of bright golden yellow blooms for prolonged periods from late spring. Trim after flowering to encourage further blooms in autumn. 1 × 1m.

GINKGO

The Chinese native Ginkgo is a most interesting and magnificent monotypic genus, reputed to be the last of a race which ages before the time of man, occupied a prominent position in the flora of the world. The name arises from the Japanese *ginkyo*, silver apricot.

Ginkgo is a hardy tree of great beauty. Somewhat gawky in youth, it develops a well proportioned head with picturesque branch structure. Female trees when pollinated, produce fleshy and rather messy fruits with unpleasant odour. Superior grafted male trees are the only ones worth growing. Plant in deeply worked, free-draining soil. Mulch freely and keep moist during dry periods until established. Stake young trees to develop a straight trunk. Magnificent lawn specimens. Allow space to show their distinct individuality.

Ginkgoaceae. *All deciduous.*

Ginkgo biloba
Maidenhair Tree
Forms a pyramidal tree with whorled symmetrical branches and grey, furrowed, corky bark. Broad, fan-like, leathery, light green leaves to 12cm across, resembling sections of a maidenhair fern. Leaves spirally arranged on long shoots and in whorls of five on shorter shoots. A spectacular sight in autumn as foliage turns brilliant gold lighting up the whole tree over long periods before the leaves fall to lay a carpet of gold. 7 × 4m. **136**

Ginkgo biloba 'Autumn Gold'
Selected male clone, growing slowly to a medium to large tree with symmetrical rounded crown and brilliant golden-yellow foliage early autumn. 7 × 4m.

Ginkgo biloba 'Fairmount'
Selected male clone, strong central leader, erect, conical habit. Summer foliage deep green, bright golden-yellow in autumn. 7 × 4m.

Ginkgo biloba 'Saratoga'
Selected male clone. Erect pyramidal outline when young, becoming rounded with maturity. Distinctive deep-green, elongated, deeply notched leaves suspended in a pendulous manner giving the tree a graceful weeping appearance. Brilliant golden autumn colours. 7 × 4m.

GLEDITSIA

A genus of about 14 hardy deciduous trees, many armed with single or branched thorns, named for Johann Gleditsch, 18th century director of the Berlin Botanical Gardens. The species triacanthos, (armed with sharp thorns), is native to North America and called Honey Locust for the sweetish pulp which lines seed pods. The species is seldom planted as an ornamental because of its thorns. A thorn-free form, G triacanthos 'Inermis', (unarmed), has given rise to a number of excellent cultivars. They are virtually thornless, have no pods to clean up, grow more slowly and fit comfortably into suburban gardens.

Honey Locusts are tolerant of acid or alkaline soil, heat or cold, and considerable drought. Avoid excessive exposure to wind to avoid breakage and leaf-burn. Give enough space to allow the trees to display their individuality. Their fine ferny leaves don't unfold until late spring, provide a light shade canopy during summer, colour early autumn before falling and soon disappear into surrounding lawn. Ornamental Honey Locusts are becoming more and more utilized in home landscaping.

Caesalpinioidaceae. *All deciduous.*

Gleditsia triacanthos 'Inermis'
Honey Locust
A tree with erect trunk and spreading arching branches. Ornamental, 20cm, bipinnate leaves with up to sixteen pairs of pinnae, each with as many as 32, small oblong-lanceolate leaflets. Numerous excellent colourful cultivars have arisen from this form. 4 × 3m.

Gleditsia triacanthos 'Emerald Kascade'
Weeping Honey Locust
Graceful, naturally pendulous branches, weeping almost to the ground, clothed with delicate, finely divided, rich dark emerald-green foliage, turning bright yellow in autumn. Excellent graceful feathery weeping tree, suitable for smaller areas. Thrive in warm temperate climates. Discovered and developed in New Plymouth, New Zealand. Ultimate dimensions dependent on training. 4 × 3m.

Gleditsia triacanthos 'Ruby Lace'
Forms a graceful, round headed small tree with finely divided frond-like foliage, ruby-red in spring, bronzy red through summer, becoming more intense prior to falling. 'Ruby Lace' aptly describes this beautiful cultivar. 5 × 4m.

Gleditsia triacanthos 'Skyline'
Upright in form, with straight trunk and compact branching structure in pyramidal form. Dense, deep green, finely divided foliage. Excellent shade or specimen tree, especially where space is limited. 6 × 4m.

Gleditsia triacanthos 'Sunburst'
Sunburst Honey Locust
Forms a neatly rounded tree with picturesque branching pattern. Casts light, dappled shade, sufficient to provide pleasant conditions for people, and open enough to allow lawn to grow beneath it. Lacy, double pinnate foliage, lime-yellow in spring, deepening to fresh green through summer, bronze-yellow in autumn. Successive new growth through summer contrasts against older leaves. Magnificent shade tree for lawn, patio, or garden feature. 6 × 5m.   **135**

GLYPTOSTROBUS

Genus of one species, a coniferous, deciduous tree from south east China and north Vietnam, named from the Greek *glypto*, to carve and *strobilus*, a cone, in reference to pitted cone scales. Naturally, a small tree found in saturated conditions, somewhat resembling the Swamp Cypress but without pneumataphores or 'cypress knees'. Used extensively around paddy fields and along river banks for erosion control. Essentially a tree for hot, humid summers, in wet, swampy conditions, even standing in water.

Cupressaceae.

Glyptostrobus pensilis
Chinese Swamp Cypress
Although a small to medium tree in the wild, it is more a large shrub in cultivation with brownish grey, weakly furrowed bark. Soft, flat, scale-like, overlapping leaves to 15 × 1mm arranged spirally, resembling Dawn Redwood. Foliage bright grass-green, glaucous green to yellow-green through spring and summer, rich orange-brown in autumn. Valued for autumn colour and ability to grow with its roots under water. Syn G lineatus. Pensilis — hanging or pendent. Deciduous. 4 × 2.5m.

GORDONIA

Genus of about thirty species of evergreen and deciduous shrubs and trees, from USA and east and south east Asia, named for James Gordon, 18th century English nurseryman. Closely related to Camellia which it closely resembles both in appearance and quantity of flower and the growing conditions it prefers. Plant in sun or semi-shade in deeply worked, organically enriched, free-draining, moisture retentive, slightly acid soil. Performs well under average garden conditions and tolerates a wide range of temperatures.

Theaceae.

Gordonia axillaris
Fried Egg Tree, Crepe Camellia
Hardy, versatile large shrub or small tree from Taiwan to Vietnam. Forms a multi-stemmed bush with elliptic-oblong to oblanceolate leaves to 15 × 4cm, thick, glossy, dark green, remotely toothed and with a blunt apex. A profusion of creamy white, 8–10cm flowers with six, broad, crepe-like, wide-open petals and a prominent central cluster of yellow stamens appears late autumn through spring. Axillaris — borne in leaf axil, referring to the flowers. Evergreen. 3 × 2m.   **134**

GREVILLEA

Most of the 250 or more species of Grevillea are endemic to Australia and have potential as cultivated ornamentals. The genus is named for Charles F Greville, a founder of the London Horticultural Society in the 18th century.

Grevilleas are a versatile and adaptable group of species and hybrid cultivars with types for practically every garden situation — ground covers, wall-spillers, dwarf shrubs, medium shrubs and tall trees and for wide-ranging cultural and climatic differences. Would be possible to choose a range of Grevilleas for year-round floral and foliage effects. Part of the garden devoted entirely to them would always be full of interest.

A few demand special conditions, but generally they thrive in poor, dry, or not so dry, light or heavy soils with good drainage. They revel in sunshine and withstand strong winds. Grevilleas prefer not to be overfed, thrive on neglect and grow rapidly, producing myriads of colourful and curious snail or spider flowers throughout the year.

Most Grevilleas are tolerant of drought, and rarely need artificial watering. Light applications of slow-release fertilizer low in phosphorus may be applied in spring. Most respond to pruning for growth renewal and maximum flower. Some of the small shrubby cultivars may be tip pruned through the growing season.

Proteaceae. *All evergreen.*

Grevillea acanthifolia 'Summerleas'
Hardy species from the Blue Mountains, New South Wales. Variable form from almost prostrate to upright spreading, bronzy new shoots and deep green leaves to 75 × 35mm, pinnately divided almost to the midrib into as many as fifteen, spreading, curved, sharply pointed segments. Toothbrush-like, pink to purplish pink, 3–9cm, terminal or axillary flowers, appear in profusion late spring through autumn. Acanthifolia — leaves resembling Acanthus. 30cm-2.5m × 3m.

Grevillea alpina 'Dallachiana'
Low-growing shrub with soft, slightly hairy, 20 × 3mm, narrow-lanceolate leaves with grooved midrib and tiny point. Red and creamy-yellow flowers in pendent, terminal clusters mainly winter through early summer. Alpina — of the mountains. Syn G alpestris. Possibly a hybrid from G rosmarinifolia × G alpina. Victoria. 75 × 75cm. **136**

Grevillea alpina 'Gold Rush'
Bold, beautiful, neat and tidy shrub with rich green foliage, compact growth habit and bright, golden-yellow curled spider flowers with distinctive red streak in the stigma. Long flowering period commencing early winter. 1.5 × 1.5m.

Grevillea aquifolium 'Carpenter Rocks'
Prickly Grevillea
Variable species from western Victoria and South Australia. Varies from a prostrate ground hugger to low arching shrub. New shoots pink to red and quite velvety. Leaves ovate to oblong, to 10 × 5cm, greyish-green, margins toothed with sharp points and wavy. Flowers soft greenish-pink in toothbrush racemes early spring through mid summer. Excellent ground cover. Aquifolium — holly-leaved. 30cm × 2.5m.

Grevillea 'Austraflora Canterbury Gold'
Vigorous grower, semi-prostrate growth, arching branches reaching to 60cm with a spread of 3–4m and lanceolate leaves to 60 × 8mm, light green and smooth above, silky hairy beneath. Clusters of large yellow 'snail' flowers with greenish tip borne prolifically winter through summer. Bank or ground cover or massed planting. 60cm × 3m.

Grevillea 'Austraflora McDonald Park'
Free-flowering, bushy, spreading, compact grower, bronze young shoots, leaves linear-lanceolate to 25 × 4mm, green and with few hairs. Distinctive, orange-red flowers tipped bright yellow, borne profusely winter through mid summer. Rock gardens, containers, borders. Listed in New Zealand as G 'Highland Laddie'. 20cm × 1.5m.

Grevillea 'Bonnie Prince Charlie'
Similar parentage to G Austraflora McDonald Park. Dwarf bushy grower, dark green, oblong, 40 × 5mm slightly hairy leaves. Orange-red and yellow 'snail' flowers in profuse terminal clusters, winter through mid summer. 20 × 60cm. **136**

Grevillea brachystylis 'Bushfire'
Most ornamental species from south west Western Australia. Forms an open, slender, low-growing bush, with hairy stems, leaves and flowers. Leaves linear or narrow-elliptical to 14 × 1cm, deep green with recurved or curled margins. Bright orange-red to deep red, somewhat woolly flowers with black-tipped style, borne in terminal or axillary, few-flowered racemes mid winter through early summer. Brachystylis — short styles. 1m × 50cm. **136**

Grevillea 'Bronze Rambler'
Dense, sprawling shrub valued for foliage, flower and adaptability. Bronzy red new shoots, attractive, blemish-free, much-divided leaves to 10cm long, lobes sharply pointed. Red toothbrush flowers in 80mm racemes early spring through autumn. Vigorous groundcover for banks, median strips or verges. Under 30cm with a spread of 3m.

Grevillea 'Canberra Gem'
Dense, rounded shrub, crowded, linear leaves to 30 × 1mm, sharply pointed. Waxy, deep rose pink flowers in large racemes, prolific winter through mid summer. Good all purpose shrub. Vigorous hybrid from G rosmarinifolia × G juniperina. 1.5 × 1.5m.

Grevillea 'Clearview David'
Hardy, strong-growing, erect, bushy shrub. Young shoots often reddish, leaves narrow-linear, to 30 × 2mm, deep green, tapering point. A profusion of deep reddish-crimson 'spider' flowers with cream curls winter through spring. Hybrid from G rosmarinifolia × G lavendulacea from Maffra, Victoria. 2 × 2m.

Grevillea diminuta
Very hardy, spreading shrub with neat, elliptic, 2cm leaves, glossy, dark green above, silky-hairy beneath and sharply pointed. Rusty red and pink flowers covered with hairs, in dense pendulous clusters mid-summer through autumn. Found in higher altitudes in A.C.T. and New South Wales. Diminuta — made small. 50cm × 1.5m.

Grevillea 'Evelyn's Coronet'
Adaptable, hybrid cultivar. Small to medium shrub with erect to somewhat spreading branches. Leaves narrow-linear to 25 × 3mm, green, glabrous, rough, paler and hairy beneath. Apex pointed, sometimes hooked. Unusual flowers, cream at first, then pink and finally grey with erect red styles, borne in dense, rounded, terminal racemes of up to thirty, spring through autumn. 1.5 × 1.5m.

Grevillea fasciculata
Beautiful, low, cascading shrub, ideal for rock gardens or ground cover. Produces masses of orange-scarlet flowers almost the year round particularly winter through spring. Dull green, lanceolate leaves to 3cm long with recurved margins. Hot, dry locations. Often short lived in humid climates. Fasciculata — clustered or grouped in bundles in reference to the flowers. Western Australia. 20cm × 1m.

Grevillea × gaudichaudi
Ground hugging form with attractive reddish new shoots, narrow-ovate, deep green leaves deeply divided almost to the midrib into sharply pointed segments. Dark red toothbrush flowers spring through early winter. Excellent ground cover or wall spiller for well-drained sunny locations and resistant to salt spray. From the Blue Mountains, New South Wales. Natural hybrid from G laurifolia × G acanthifolia. Named for Gaudichaud-Beaupre, 19th century French botanist. 15cm × 2m. **135**

Grevillea glabrata
Smooth Grevillea
Distinct, 4cm, light-green, broad-cuneate, trident foliage on willowy branches, gracefully pendent like weeping maple. Throughout spring and early summer the whole bush becomes a mass of small white spidery flowers. Most effective shrub, hardy, fast growing, responds to pruning and effective for floral decoration. Glabrata — smooth, a likely reference to the whole plant which is hairless. Western Australia. 2 × 1.5m.

Grevillea 'Glen Sandra'
Vigorous cultivar, possibly from G juniperina × G rosmarinifolia. Bushy shrub with erect to spreading branches, young shoots densely covered with silky hairs. Needle-like, linear, 40 × 1mm leaves. Flowers cerise pink, red and cream with red styles, borne in profuse racemes. 2.5 × 2.5m.

Grevillea 'Ivanhoe'
Hardy shrub with dense, spreading branches, young shoots bronze or reddish. Attractive, pinnate leaves to 16 × 3cm, deeply lobed to the midrib into numerous deep green, glossy

segments. Light red toothbrush flowers in abundance winter through spring and again mid-summer, attractive to birds. Named for the Melbourne suburb of Ivanhoe. 2.5 × 3m.

Grevillea juniperina 'Sulphurea'
Forms a dense shrub with arching branches and fine, needle-like, dark green linear, sharp-pointed leaves in crowded clusters. Sulphur yellow flowers in terminal clusters produced winter through spring and at other times through the year. Hardy and easy to grow. Juniperina — juniper-like 2 × 2m.

Grevillea 'King's Glow'
Compact with attractive green and cream variegated foliage. Clusters of red flowers with white lip, mass produced through winter. Prune after flowering. 1.5 × 1.3m.

Grevillea lanigera
Woolly Grevillea
Erect, compact form, grey or rust coloured, densely hairy new shoots. Branches and branchlets hairy. Attractive leaves linear to narrow-oblong, to 30 × 4mm, greyish green, somewhat roughly textured and hairy. Flowers reddish pink with a touch of lime-green and cream, styles reddish pink, borne profusely in conspicuous, umbel-like racemes, autumn through summer. Lanigera — woolly. Victoria, New South Wales. 1 × 1m.

Grevillea lanigera 'Mt Tamboritha'
Prostrate, dense bushy growth habit and small, rounded, grey-green foliage with turned down margins, tending to point upwards. Distinctive, creamy white and red spidery flowers produced in great masses during winter and spring. Excellent rockery plant, for beds, borders or containers. Named for Mt Tamboritha, south eastern Victoria. 50cm × 1m.   **136**

Grevillea lavendulaceus 'Victor Harbor'
Lavender Grevillea
Erect, semi-spreading form, young growth covered with silky hairs. Leaves narrow-linear to elliptic, to 35 × 7cm, and dark green. Conspicuous, bright red flowers in terminal, pendent, umbel-like racemes appear winter through spring and mid-summer through autumn. From the Fleurieu Peninsula, South Australia and Victoria.

Grevillea 'Masons Hybrid'
Hybrid cultivar with the same parents as the popular G 'Robyn Gordon'. Very similar in foliage, form and flower but blooms paler red, especially when they first open. Long flowering season and hardy. Syn G 'Ned Kelly'. 1.5 × 1.5m.

Grevillea 'Olympic Flame'
Dense rounded bush, sharp, needle-like, 12–18mm leaves and rather large, slightly pendulous clusters of red and cream flowers borne prolifically during winter and spring. Named from the 1956 Olympic Games in Melbourne. Very hardy. 1 × 1m.

Grevillea 'Pink Star'
Seedling cultivar from the Australian National Botanic Garden, Canberra. Upright open grower at first, more spreading with age. Reddish, hairy new shoots, light green, lanceolate leaves to 22 × 3mm, hairy at first, becoming shiny, margins waved and re-curved. Flowers pink and cream with green and deep pink styles, borne in semi-pendent, terminal racemes spring through early summer. 1.5 × 1.3m.

Grevillea 'Poorinda Elegance'
Small to medium grower, hairy young shoots, branches upright to spreading, leaves elliptic, to 40 × 6mm, bright green, shiny, densely covered with silky hairs beneath. Flowers apricot, reddish and apricot-yellow with pinkish-red styles, borne in pendent, terminal racemes mainly winter through early summer. Parentage — G juniperina × G alpina × G obtusifolia. Possibly lacking vigour, but heavy on colour and charm. 1.5 × 2m.

Grevillea 'Poorinda Peter'
Very vigorous grower rapidly reaching full dimensions as an open and spreading bush. Young shoots burgundy red and silky hairy, branchlets deep reddish brown and hairy. Leaves shiny dark green, 15 × 4cm, deeply lobed into 12 sparsely toothed segments, hairy beneath. Rosy-pink to purple-red, 6cm toothbrush flowers appear early spring through summer. Tolerates reasonable moisture, excellent cut flower, very attractive to birds for nectar and nesting. 2.5 × 3.5m.   **136**

Grevillea 'Poorinda Rondeau'
Compact bush, young shoots reddish and hairy, branches upright to spreading. Leaves elliptic to ovate, to 15 × 5mm, shiny dark green, pale green beneath, crowded on reddish, densely hairy branchlets. Flowers bright reddish pink and white with red, hairy styles, borne in conspicuous terminal racemes winter through spring. 1.3 × 1.3m.

Grevillea 'Poorinda Royal Mantle'
Vigorous ground-hugging stems with coppery red new shoots and handsome, 15 × 5cm, broad-lanceolate to elliptic leaves either lobed or entire with waved and recurved margins. Deep burgundy-red, 8cm toothbrush flowers in great masses winter

through mid summer and sporadically over the year. Rapid and reliable ground cover. May be grafted on to G robusta as a standard weeping plant. As ground cover grows less than 15cm high with a spread of 2m.   **135**

Grevillea 'Poorinda Tranquility'
A more subdued and pretty Grevillea in the form of a small, bushy shrub with soft-green, oblanceolate to oblong, 35 × 6mm, deep greyish-green, sharply pointed leaves. Pale pastel-pink flowers tipped cream, with pinkish styles in few-flowered racemes winter through spring. Hardy almost anywhere in full sun. 1.5 × 1.5m.

Grevillea prostrata 'Aurea'
Low, spreading habit, bright green foliage, and masses of sulphur yellow flowers in erect clusters during spring and summer. Ground cover, wall spiller, rock gardens. Prostrata — lying flat on the ground. 30cm × 1m.   **136**

Grevillea 'Red Cloud'
Lavendulacea hybrid. Forms a low mound of slender, graceful branchlets densely covered with silvery grey foliage. For long periods from mid winter the whole bush is covered with short spikes of deep red flowers. 1 × 2m.

Grevillea 'Red Cluster'
Small semi-spreading shrub with soft, glossy, bright green foliage which becomes bronzy red in winter. Clusters of deep-red flowers almost cover the whole bush in mid-winter. Parentage unknown. 1 × 1m.

Grevillea 'Red Dragon'
Attractive form of the popular G 'Clearview David' with creamy white and light green variegated, 20 × 5mm foliage and showy rich red spidery flowers during spring and early summer. Hardy, bushy plant of rugged constitution in light soils. 1 × 1.5m.

Grevillea 'Robin Hood'
Scarlet Toothbrush Grevillea
Possibly a form of G aspleniifolia with similar herringbone foliage. Easily grown, attractive garden shrub displaying scarlet flower spikes at branch tips spring through summer. Grows rapidly, withstands cold and dry, but needs staking against strong wind. 3 × 2m.

Grevillea robusta
Silky Oak
Tree-form Grevillea growing rapidly with neat pyramidal form when young, becoming broad and open with age. Handsome fern-like, pinnate leaves to 30cm long, with as many as 24 narrow, tapered lobes, deep

green above, grey-green beneath. Cone-like, 15cm, rich, golden-orange flower clusters are crowded along the top of every branch, the whole tree becoming a mass of bloom from early spring. May be pruned to size or shape. Advisable to stake until self supporting. Queensland, New South Wales. Robusta — stout, strong in growth. 8 × 5m.

Grevillea 'Robyn Gordon'
Forms a broad, spreading bush with branches gracefully arching to the ground, densely clothed with handsome, 10–18cm, deeply divided, pinnate leaves, dark green with silvery undersides. Bright red, spidery flowers in large 15cm cylindrical racemes or brushes at the end of arching branchlets continue opening towards the tips to provide a magnificent floral display over most of the year. Birds enjoy the constant nectar supply. Hybrid from G bipinnatifidum × G banksii raised in Queensland and regarded as one of the finest cultivars amongst Grevilleas. 1 × 1.5m.　**135**

Grevillea rosmarinifolia 'Pink Pixie'
Dwarf compact grower, dense, needle-like, lanceolate, 22 × 3mm, light green foliage and clusters of bright, candy-pink and white flowers in 5cm heads winter through spring. Syn G rosmarinifolia 'Nana'. 60 × 60cm.

Grevillea rosmarinifolia 'Scarlet Sprite'
Low spreading shrub with dense, arching habit and narrow, linear, dark green, sharply pointed, 3cm leaves. Bright red and cream flowers borne in spidery clusters winter through spring. One of the brightest flowered Grevilleas. 1.3 × 1.3.　**136**

Grevillea 'Superb'
A hybrid cultivar with the same parentage as 'Robyn Gordon' and 'Mason's Hybrid', with similar qualities, perhaps intermediate between the two as to foliage and form. Flowers pinkish-yellow, maturing deep pink with brighter pink styles. 1 × 1.5m.　**135**

Grevillea thelemanniana
Spider Net Grevillea
Dwarf to medium, spreading growth, leaves trilobed to pinnate, soft, finely divided. Red flowers tipped creamy yellow in loose, toothbrush-like, pendent racemes borne mainly on short branchlets winter through spring. Western Australia. 1 × 1.5m.

Grevillea thelemanniana 'Obtusifolia'
Prostrate, spreading shrub. Leaves dark green, linear to oblong, to 35 × 3mm, margins recurved, blunt apex, sometimes with a small point. Small numbers of pale red and green flowers autumn through spring. Ground cover and wall spiller in hot,

dry conditions. Obtusifolia — leaves blunt, rounded at the ends. Western Australia. 15cm × 1m.

Grevillea 'Tickled Pink'
Superior, pink-flowered cultivar with spreading growth habit, erect branches and light green, needle-like, non-prickly leaves. Attractive, two-toned pink 'snail' flowers borne in large clusters autumn through spring.　**136**

Grevillea victoriae
Royal Grevillea
Dwarf to medium grower, new shoots rust coloured and hairy. Leaves lanceolate to ovate, to 14 × 5cm, greyish green to green, silvery and hairy beneath. Rust-red or orange red flowers in pendent, terminal racemes, often very showy, summer to early winter, through spring and sporadically through the year. Queensland, New South Wales, Victoria. Named for 19th century Queen Victoria of England. 2 × 2m.

Grevillea 'White Wings'
Vigorous, dense, spreading grower. Leaves light green, to 4 × 4cm, irregularly lobed and sharply pointed segments. White and yellow, sweetly fragrant flowers in loose, terminal or axillary, 25mm racemes terminally and in the leaf axils throughout the year. 2 × 3m.

Grevillea 'Winpara Gem'
Vigorous, hardy shrub, dark green leaves to 65 × 4mm, deeply lobed into 3–5 narrow, segments. Pink buds open to scarlet, spidery flowers turning orange with maturity, produced in compact, 7 × 5cm, axillary racemes almost all year but mostly winter through summer. 1.5 × 1.5m.

GREWIA

A genus of about 150 species of shrubs, trees or climbers from south and east Asia, Africa and Australia, named for Nehemiah Grew, 17th century physician, pioneer microscopist and botanical author. The following species could never be described as spectacular, but quiet unassuming plants with subtle charm. Sprawling, flattened branching pattern makes an ideal shrub for growing against a wall or fence, especially as espalier.

Grows rapidly, and easily trained to cover walls or trellis, as a single stemmed specimen, or, by removing upright growths, encouraged to function as ground or bank cover. Overgrown or woody plants may be cut hard back to a

couple of basal stems for complete growth renewal. Plant in full sun, in deeply worked, free-draining soil. Water freely during dry periods and feed with slow release balanced fertilizer spring and autumn.

Tiliaceae.

Grewia occidentalis 'Mauve Star'
Lavender Star Flower
Charming South African native with slender stems and branchlets. Mid green, lanceolate to ovate or diamond-shaped leaves to 10cm long with finely toothed margins. Starlike, 3cm, lavender-pink flowers with yellow centres, scattered over the bush in axillary clusters up to six late spring through autumn. Occidentalis — western. Evergreen. 2 × 2m.　**153**

GRISELINIA

A genus of eight species of trees and shrubs confined to New Zealand, Brazil and Chile named for 18th century Venetian naturalist Francesco Griselini. Two species endemic to New Zealand, six to Chile and Brazil, an example of the close association between the plants of these two countries. The New Zealand species and cultivars are handsome foliage plants. Kapuka especially is tolerant of rough coastal conditions and heavy frosts.

They grow reasonably fast without over-crowding in almost any reasonable, free-draining soil. Occasional feeding and trimming is about all the care they need. Use for backgrounds, screens, shelter, lawn specimens, streets or containers. Excellent, hardy, evergreen trees worthy of extensive planting.

Cornaceae. *All evergreen.*

Griselinia littoralis
Kapuka, Native Broadleaf
Handsome and hardy shrub or small tree found almost from one end of New Zealand to the other. First observed near the shores of Akaroa in 1840 and given the name littoralis meaning of the seashore. Forms a tidy, well-groomed, densely branched shrub with smooth twigs and branchlets. Leaves broadly ovate or egg-shaped, to 10 × 6cm, smooth, polished and leathery, rich deep green with slightly waved edges. Male and female flowers borne on different trees through spring. When pollinated, insignificant, blackish purple, 6mm fruits appear late autumn. Grown for beauty of form, clean-cut foliage, elegant good looks and hardiness. 3 × 2m.

Griselinia littoralis 'Dixon's Cream'

Leaves splashed and blotched creamy yellow in the centre, surrounded by a yellowish green zone, and narrow, irregular, deep green area around the margins. Better in partial shade. 2 × 1m.

Griselinia littoralis 'Green Jewel'

Forms an upright, rounded shrub with narrower leaves, deep green with irregular creamy-yellow marginal variegation and faint grey-green markings within the central zone. Maintains best colour in full sun. 2.5 × 1.5m.

Griselinia littoralis 'Variegata'

Valuable, hardy variegated shrub with leaves similar in shape and size to Kapuka but irregularly blotched and margined pale gold. Excellent in containers. 2 × 1m.

Griselinia lucida
Puka, Akapuka

Found naturally from North Cape to Foveaux Strait, often perched high in the forks of forest trees from where it sends down aerial roots to ground level for further support and nourishment. Found also on the sea coast as a terrestrial plant growing in pockets of soil sheltered by rocks and varying in size according to the available nourishment. An impressive plant with broad-ovate or egg-shaped, thick, leathery, glossy, rich deep-green leaves 7–18cm long, characterized by unequal sided blades.

Inconspicuous female flowers without petals and small yellowish male flowers produced in panicles from leaf axils. Although naturally an epiphyte, it will develop into a small spreading, hardy and easily grown tree, thriving in either sun or shade and provide luxuriant foliage effects. The name Puka is also applied to other New Zealand plants including Meryta sinclairii. Lucida — shining, a reference to its polished leaves. 2 × 1m.

GUNNERA

A genus of more than thirty species of rhizomatous plants from South Africa, South America, Pacific region, and Australia named for Ernst Gunnerus, 18th century Norwegian bishop and botanist. Listed species a magnificent giant plant, focal point at the edge of ponds or streams, semi-woodland areas or dominating a bed of low, fine-textured ground cover plants. Prefers semi-shade, soil rich in organic material, and continual moisture for ultimate development,

although it will grow under normal garden conditions.

Gunneraceae.

Gunnera tinctoria

Awesome Chilean native with enormous foliage. Leaves deep-green, 60–150cm across, somewhat kidney-shaped, palmately lobed, roughly puckered, conspicuously veined, supported on thick, light-brown stalks, studded with small, reddish and prickly hairs. Habit and general appearance suggestive of mammoth rhubarb.

Greenish flowers and fruit clusters resembling reddish corn cobs are formed near the base of the plant. Remove as soon as they appear to aid production of larger leaves. A magnificent plant and quite a conversation piece, given enough space and in the right setting. Tinctoria — applied to plants used at some time in dyeing. Evergreen. 2 × 2m.   153

GYMNOCLADUS

A genus of five species of pod-bearing trees from North America and China named from *gymnos*, naked and *klados*, a branch, referring to bare winter branches. The seeds of Kentucky Coffee Tree were used as a coffee substitute, and its fruit as soap. A handsome, slow-growing tree, resistant to pollution, with picturesque winter outline, handsome leaves and ornamental fruit. This fascinating tree is worthy of a place in larger gardens. Grow in deeply worked, moisture retentive, free-draining soil. Once established will tolerate drought and extremes of heat and cold.

Leguminosae.

Gymnocladus dioica
Kentucky Coffee Tree

Native to eastern United States, growing quickly in narrow form as a juvenile, slowing down and becoming broader with heavy contorted branches with maturity. One of the most handsome of all hardy trees, picturesque when bare with light grey, almost white, stout young twigs, artistically arranged over the bold outline of the tree. Large pinnate leaves, 30–80cm long, with four or five pairs of 25–75mm leaflets, pink tinted or violet as they unfold, deep-green in summer, clear yellow prior to falling. Inconspicuous, dull greenish-white flowers in 10cm racemes, followed by 15 × 4cm, flat, reddish brown pods containing hard black seeds. Dioica — furnished with two berries or nuts. Deciduous. 7 × 5m. ·

HAKEA

A genus of some 150 species of shrubs or small trees, all endemic to Australia, named for Baron Christian Ludwig von Hake, 18th century German patron of botany. Hakeas are well represented in the south western regions of Western Australia and central Australia, also in eastern states to a lesser degree. Admired for varied leaf designs, conspicuous flowers and curiously formed seed capsules.

Many of the more desirable western species have proved difficult to grow in eastern Australian or New Zealand gardens and possibly for this reason, relatively few are found in these areas. The listed species grow without fuss in coastal or inland gardens in light, acid, well-drained soil and full sun. Stake securely and prune to shape and size. Withstands dry conditions and best with little or no fertilizer.

Proteaceae. *All evergreen.*

Hakea laurina
Pincushion Flower

This West Australian shrub has a profusion of rosy red flowers in globose heads to 6cm across, resembling pin cushions covered with creamy stamens or pins during autumn and winter. When the bud-covers first lift, little colour is evident, but this gradually deepens, and the pins unfold to display the full beauty of flowers which are excellent for picking. Oblong-lanceolate, bluish-green leaves, to 15 × 3cm, prominently veined, resemble eucalyptus foliage. Forms a shapely, erect bush, grows rapidly. Laurina — resembling Laurus or laurel. 3 × 2m.

Hakea salicifolia 'Gold Medal'
Willow-leaved Hakea

The species from New South Wales and Queensland is used extensively as a hardy and vigorous screen tree. The cultivar 'Gold Medal' is valued for foliage colour. Forms a medium shrub densely clothed with elliptic to narrowly ovate leaves to 10 × 2cm, variegated yellow and green. During winter the colour intensifies in hues of mahogany and pink. Syn H saligna. Salicifolia — willow-leaved. 3 × 2m.

HALIMIUM

A genus of about 12 species of shrubs allied to Cistus and Helianthemum from

the Mediterranean, south west Europe, North Africa and Asia Minor, named from the Greek *halimos*, maritime. They are sun-loving plants with grey leaves and masses of bloom, closely resembling Cistus or Rock Rose and growing under similar conditions.
Cistaceae

Halimium lasianthum
Spreading shrub with erect, grey-pubescent stems. Ovate, 15–30mm, grey-pubescent leaves with rounded apex. Bright yellow, 4cm flowers with reddish-brown basal spot on each petal in loose clusters spring through mid summer. Syn Cistus formosus. Lasianthum — woolly-flowered. Evergreen. 90 × 90cm. **153**

HALOCARPUS

A genus of three species of coniferous trees, endemic to New Zealand named from the Greek *halos*, halo and *karpos*, fruit, in reference to a white collar at the base of the carpel. New Zealand Mountain Pine is closely related to Dacrydium or Rimu and at one time was included in the genus. Prefers to grow in deeply worked, moisture retentive, free-draining soil with adequate moisture until established.
Podocarpaceae.

Halocarpus biformis
Found mainly in mountain or sub-alpine forests of New Zealand's three main islands, south of National Park. Characterized by the unusual effect of distinct adult and juvenile foliage on the one branch. Rather slow-growing, remaining a dwarf for many years, eventually a handsome, small tree with lower branches reaching to the ground. Syn Dacrydium biforme. Biformis — having leaves of two distinct forms. Evergreen. 3 × 1.5m.

HAMAMELIS

A genus of five species of hardy, deciduous shrubs from North America, Europe and East Asia, called by the Greek name for a plant with pear-shaped fruit. Quaint shrubs, popular for distinctly oriental branching patterns, handsome autumn foliage and curious, spider-like winter blooms. Angular twigs and branches quite downy when young, picturesque when loaded with knobbly buds. The term

Witch Hazel was allegedly given to these plants by early American settlers who noticed a close resemblance in the leaves of a native species to the common English hazel extensively used in water divining.

Hamamelis is remarkably hardy in all districts, tolerant of sub-zero temperatures. Plant in deeply worked, organically enriched, free-draining, moisture retentive, slightly acid soil, in full sun or partial shade, protected from persistent, cold, drying winds. Mulch freely and water frequently during dry periods. Avoid overcrowding with other shrubs to best display the open, zigzag branches and winter floral display. Flowering stems perfect for dramatic floral arrangements.
Hamamelidaceae. *All deciduous.*

Hamamelis × intermedia
The result of hybridizing H japonica and H mollis. The following clones have arisen in cultivation and include very interesting and delightful forms.

Hamamelis × intermedia 'Arnold Promise'
Small growing, neat, upright, vase-shaped grower. Abundant, deep sulphur-yellow, fragrant flowers in dense clusters late winter through early spring. 1.5 × 1.3m.

Hamamelis × intermedia 'Carmine Red'
Large flowers with wavy petals, pale bronze, suffused copper and carmine tips. Vigorous spreading growth. Ovate or rounded , 12cm leaves, yellow autumn colour. 3 × 2m.

Hamamelis × intermedia 'Dianne'
Neat rounded form, large carmine-red, densely clustered flowers with straight petals. Claimed as the best red-flowered Witch Hazel. Rich orange-red autumn foliage. 1.8 × 1.3m.

Hamamelis × intermedia 'Jelena'
Vigorous spreading habit, large ovate leaves to 17 × 15cm, broad and softly hairy, scarlet, bronze, orange and red in autumn. Flowers in dense clusters with twisted petals yellow, suffused deep coppery red, and burgundy. 2.5 × 2m.

Hamamelis × intermedia 'Primavera'
Upright, spreading grower. Dense primrose-yellow flower clusters with broad, sickle-shaped petals winter through early spring. 2 × 1.3m.

Hamamelis × intermedia 'Ruby Glow'
Medium grower with erect branches, rounded or ovate, 16 × 12cm leaves, scarlet, orange and bronze in autumn. Flowers deep coppery red. 2 × 1.3m.

Hamamelis × intermedia 'Westerstede'
Vigorous erect growth habit with ascending branches forming a large rounded shrub. Large primrose-yellow flowers with long straight petals in clusters, late winter. Autumn foliage yellow. 3 × 2m.

Hamamelis mollis
Chinese Witch Hazel
Every bare branch is wreathed from mid winter through spring with sweetly fragrant, 4cm, golden-yellow, spidery flowers ahead of the leaves. Round to broad ovate, 16 × 11cm leaves, dark green and rough above, grey-felted beneath, turning rich, clear yellow in autumn. Mollis — soft with fine hairs. 3 × 2m.

Hamamelis mollis 'Goldcrest'
Vigorous, upright, later-flowering form with large, exceptionally fragrant, rich golden-yellow flowers, burgundy at the base of the petals. Yellow autumn foliage. 3 × 2m.

Hamamelis mollis 'Pallida'
Neat spreading grower. Large sulphur-yellow flowers with strong, sweet, delicate fragrance in dense clusters along naked stems. Autumn colour yellow. 2.5 × 2m.

Hamamelis virginiana
Virginian Witch Hazel
Native of eastern North America and the commercial source of Witch Hazel. Rather open, spreading growth habit with characteristic roundish leaves without grey felting beneath, yellow to orange in autumn. Golden-yellow, 2cm blooms appear during early winter, somewhat hidden by the leaves. Hardy and vigorous, often used as under-stock for more glamorous cultivars. 4 × 3m.

HARPEPHYLLUM

A monotypic genus named from the Greek *harpe*, sickle and *phyllon*, leaf in reference to the shape of the leaves. An attractive tree for virtually frost-free climates with good form, foliage and fruit. Rapidly forms a handsome, round-headed, spreading tree with straight, smooth bole, making a perfect lawn or shade tree with a well-groomed, tropical appearance. Can also be trained as a multi-stemmed specimen, developing into a quaint and picturesque tree with age. Select a warm aspect in full sun, protected from frost when young and plant in fertile, deeply worked, free-draining, moisture retentive soil.
Anacardiaceae.

Harpephyllum caffrum
Kaffir Plum

Magnificent South African tree with attractive compound, leathery leaves, with 5–17, narrow lanceolate or ovate leaflets to 10 × 3cm, coppery red as they unfold, later turning dark green. Small, cream to yellowish-green spring flowers followed on female trees by edible, dark red, 25mm fruits resembling large olives, slightly acid to the taste. Caffrum — of South Africa. Evergreen. 7 × 5m.

A genus of 75–100 species of shrubs and small trees named for the Greek goddess of youth. About eighty species are confined to New Zealand but the genus also extends to south east Australia, Tasmania, South America, Falkland Islands and New Guinea's highlands. Many valuable landscaping plants are amongst them, either for beauty of flower, form or foliage. Flowering varieties are easy to grow, thriving in any reasonable soil, withstanding exposure to wind, salt, sun and light frost, in fact they can be rated as the least troublesome of dwarf flowering shrubs. Periodic pruning and feeding after each burst of flower encourages lush growth and maximum floral display.

Whipcord varieties generally, have scale-like leaves not unlike cypress and are grown more for texture and foliage colour. Excellent for rock or scree gardens, blending with conifers and other plants to create natural alpine effects. Plant in open, airy situations in sun or partial shade in free-draining, stony or crumbly soil. Little pruning is required with most whipcords. They dislike summer heat and humidity. A strategically placed rock may offer protection.

Scrophulariaceae. *All evergreen with one exception.*

Hebe albicans

Found in rocky places and sub-alpine scrub in mountain regions of the Nelson Province at altitudes from 1000 to 1375 metres. Low growing, multi-branched, spreading shrub, ovate leaves, to 3cm long, glaucous on both surfaces. Flowers pink in bud, opening white with purple anthers, densely packed on short spikes mid-summer through autumn. Hardy, handsome and floriferous. 60 × 75cm.

Hebe 'Andersonii Variegata'

Strong growing, large foliaged shrub, with rounded outline, ovate-lanceolate leaves to 10cm long, variegated mid to dark green and grey green with irregular cream band around the margins. Light violet flowers in close 10cm spikes through summer and sporadically autumn through spring. Beautiful flowers and foliage Remove any reverting growths. 1.2 × 1.2m.

Hebe 'Anomala'

Hardy, erect and floriferous multi-branched shrub with greenish-yellow branchlets tipped purple. Leaves linear-oblong to elliptic lanceolate to 22 × 2mm, dark green, glossy, leathery, paler beneath. White flowers with purple anthers in short, crowded, terminal panicles through summer. Thought to be a cultivar of H odora. Anomala — deviating from normal, referring to the calyx having three or four lobes. 75 × 75cm.

Hebe 'Autumn Glory'

Attractive small shrub, erect, sparsely branched with dark purplish stems, 35mm obovate leaves, dark to grey green, paler beneath. Beautiful violet flowers, in short 45mm spikes crowded at the ends of each branch late summer through autumn. Good for mass planting. 50 × 75cm.

Hebe × 'Bishopiana'

Natural hybrid of H obtusata × H stricta, found straggling over rocky outcrops around Huia on the Manukau Harbour, west of Auckland. Purple stems and dark green, narrow elliptic leaves to 75mm. Lavender flower spikes up to 10cm long in late summer. Semi prostrate. Evergreen. 30 × 60cm.

Hebe brachysiphon

Compact, rounded, slow-growing shrub with semi-erect stems. Leaves elliptic to lanceolate, to 25 × 6mm, mid green, paler beneath. From mauve-tinted buds, white flowers in short terminal racemes through summer. Brachysiphon — short tube, referring to the corolla. 1.3 × 1.2m.

Hebe buchananii

Attractive small species found in the Southern Alps at 900–2100 metres. Multi-branched, low-grower, spreading in clumps to 90cm across with sturdy branches, almost black, closely scarred and tortuous. Broadly ovate, dull and dark green leaves to 7mm, paler beneath. Flowers white in short crowded spikes, rather hidden amongst the foliage through summer. Hardy, sun or shade, but more glaucous in sun. Good texture plant for rock gardens, mass planting. 10–30 × 90cm.

Hebe 'Carnea Variegata'

Garden hybrid which arose during the 19th century, probably related to H speciosa. A multi-branched spreading shrub with slender branchlets densely covered with glabrous 4–8cm, oblong, variegated leaves coloured grey-green, with a broad margin of cream, heavily suffused rose pink during autumn and winter. Rosy purple flower spikes to 90 × 25mm produced near the ends of the branchlets in summer often again in winter. Slightly frost tender, excellent for milder areas. 1 × 1m.

Hebe chathamica

Small scrambling shrub found on the Chatham Islands, 800km east of Christchurch, growing on rocks and cliffs close to the sea. Prostrate, wide-spreading grower with slender branchlets, rooting at the nodes. Leaves spreading, inclined to one plane, to 30 × 12mm, elliptic-oblong, thick and fleshy, dull-green above, paler beneath. Flowers predominantly white in squat, dense, 4cm racemes from early summer through autumn. For coastal gardens, ground or bank cover and wall spiller. 20cm × 1m.

Hebe 'County Park'

Spreading, ground cover plant with branchlets ascending at the tips. Leaves ovate to 125 × 6mm, grey green edged red, suffused pinkish-mauve in winter. Violet, 25mm flowers in short terminal spikes through winter. Raised and named by County Park Nursery, Essex. 45 × 75cm.

Hebe cupressoides

Distinct Hebe of the whipcord group, forming a symmetrically rounded shrub with numerous thin, crowded, erect, vivid bright green branchlets. Small scale-like leaves give the plant a conifer-like appearance. Reluctant to bloom when young but when it starts, the plant appears shrouded in pale blue mist as myriads of tiny flowers appear on each branch tip. Found on river flats, terraces and sub-alpine regions of the South Island. Cupressoides — like cypress. 1 × 1m.

Hebe decumbens

Small spreading shrub with slender, shiny, dark purple or purplish brown branchlets. Leaves elliptic to 20 × 8mm wide, yellow-green to dark-green with distinct reddish margins. White, almost sessile flowers in 25mm spikes borne toward the branch ends through summer. Decumbens — trailing with upright tips. 45 × 90cm.

Hebe diosmifolia

Delightful shrub found in the North Island from Kaipara to North Cape. Forms a low, multi-branched, spreading bush with close-set, obovate to lanceolate, 25 × 6mm leaves, dark green above and paler beneath. Flowers pale lavender, fading to white, freely produced in flattened heads early spring through mid-summer. Diosmifolia — diosma-like leaves. 75 × 75cm. **153**

Hebe diosmifolia 'Garden Beauty'
Loosely erect shrub with pale reddish brown branchlets. Typical diosmifolia, deep green leaves. Flowers lavender at first, gradually turning white, borne in large racemes spring and early summer. 1 × 1m.

Hebe diosmifolia 'Lavender Lass'
Forms a tidy bush somewhat larger than the species but with typical diosmifolia leaves. Bears a profusion of lilac coloured flowers in clusters like its parent, early spring through mid-summer. 1 × 1m.

Hebe diosmifolia 'Otari Delight'
Rather more vigorous than H diosmifolia, growing strongly into a uniformly low rounded bush. Pale-lilac flower spikes completely cover the plant in spring. Originated at Otari Native Plant Reserve. 70cm × 1m.

Hebe diosmifolia 'Wairua Beauty'
Originally found near Wairua Falls, near Whangarei. Bears larger corymbs of heliotrope flowers, more spectacular in bloom for about four weeks spring and early summer. Leaves pale or yellowish green to 25mm long. 1 × 1m.

Hebe elliptica
Hardy species from the western shoreline of both islands, south from Cape Egmont, growing to within a few metres of highwater mark, withstanding gales and salt spray. In cultivation, forms a spreading bush with elliptic, 2–4cm, somewhat fleshy leaves, dark green and shining. White to pale violet flowers larger than most Hebes early summer through autumn. Commences blooming when quite young. 1.2 × 1m.

Hebe elliptica var crassifolia
Larger grower with sturdy branchlets. Leaves oblong to broadly ovate to 30 × 15mm, somewhat fleshy, pale green. Large 2cm, white flowers in terminal or lateral racemes. From coastal foothills of Mt Taranaki and Kapiti Island, New Zealand. 1.2 × 1m.

Hebe 'Emerald Green'
Multi-branched, semi-whipcord Hebe with ascending branchlets forming a cushion-like shrub. Tiny, 3 × 1.5mm, dull, yellowish-green leaves with entire margins, closely spaced in four ranks at an angle of 45°. Crenated margins on juvenile foliage evidence of whipcord parentage. Small white flowers in summer. Syn H 'Emerald Gem' 30 × 60cm.

Hebe 'Eveline'
Showy, compact, rounded, multi-branched shrub with green stems. Leaves lanceolate or oblanceolate to 7 × 2mm, deep green, glossy, paler beneath. Deep purple-pink flowers in 15cm terminal spikes early to mid spring. From Guernsey, Channel Islands. Syn H 'Rainer's Beauty' 1.3 × 1m.

Hebe evenosa
From the Tararua Range, North Island. Sturdy, spreading main branches and branchlets. Leaves obovate-oblong, to 20 × 6mm, mat green, paler beneath. White flowers in short 25–30mm spikes during summer. 1 × 1m.

Hebe franciscana 'Blue Gem'
Handsome, multi-branched, spreading shrub with broad obovate, 65 × 25mm, dark green glossy leaves. Lavender-mauve flowers in dense 65mm spikes through summer and autumn. Hybrid from H speciosa × Falkland Island form of H elliptica, originating in England mid 19th century, introduced to New Zealand as Veronica lobellioides. 1 × 1m.

Hebe franciscana 'Variegata'
Resembles 'Blue Gem' but leaves broadly margined and overlaid with creamy yellow. Magnificent low-growing foliage shrub, maintaining leaf colour throughout the year. Violet-blue flowers in large spikes during summer. Syn H franciscana 'Waireka'. 90 × 90cm.

Hebe glaucophylla
Found on banks and gullies in tussock areas of Marlborough and Canterbury in the South Island. Slender brown branches maturing grey, forming an erect bush with rounded outline. Leaves lanceolate, to 20 × 4mm, grey-green and glabrous. Lilac flowers in short 35mm racemes borne in leaf axils near the ends of branchlets in summer. Glaucophylla — blue-grey foliage. 1 × 1m.

Hebe 'Hartii'
Hybrid cultivar of unknown parentage, forming a slender, prostrate, spreading shrub with small, 12mm, lanceolate leaves, glossy, green to slightly purplish. Flowers mauve fading to white, in loose 5cm spikes through summer. Full sun or partial shade. Rock gardens or wall-spiller. 10 × 75cm. **154**

Hebe hulkeana
New Zealand Lilac
Found along banks and rocky bluffs from sea level to 900 metres in Marlborough and North Canterbury. Erect, rather loosely branched spreading shrub with slender purplish red, finely pubescent branches. Leaves oblong-elliptic, 4 × 2cm, dark green above, paler beneath, margins finely toothed and reddish. Masses of lavender to white flowers carried in broad, terminal panicles to 25cm long, spring through early summer. Small individual flowers produced in great masses over long periods makes this an excellent garden shrub, regarded as the most spectacular of New Zealand's Hebes. Dry areas with low humidity. Subject to downy mildew in warm moist climates. 90 × 90cm.

Hebe 'Inspiration'
New Zealand hybrid between H speciosa and H diosmifolia. Forms a neat, compact, rather spreading shrub with oblanceolate, 25 × 10mm, dark green shining leaves. Purple flowers in 4cm terminal racemes smother the bush during summer and sporadically winter through spring. Beautiful dwarf flowering shrub. 75 × 75cm. **154**

Hebe 'Karo Golden Esk'
Slowly forms a rounded spreading bush with main stems arching outward from the centre. Typical whipcord, thick, softly flexible juvenile yellow-green leaves closely adpressed to the stem, turning rich gold in winter. Tiny mature foliage more spreading and open. Sparse, small white flowers in spring. Natural hybrid from upper Esk Valley, Southern Alps. Highly rated. 60 × 75cm.

Hebe 'La Seduisante'
Erect, multi-branched shrub with purple-brown, finely pubescent stems. Leaves broadly elliptic, 70 × 45mm, dark green, glossy, paler beneath, midrib purple-brown. Violet purple flowers in dense, 10 × 2cm spikes through summer. 'La Seduisante' — French for attractive. 1.3 × 1m.

Hebe 'Lavender Lace'
Attractive, free-flowering hybrid of unknown origin, forming a low growing shrub, with narrow leaves to 40 × 5mm. Flowers lavender, fading to white borne in branched racemes to 8cm long spring and summer. 75cm × 1m.

Hebe 'Lavender Spray'
Excellent vigorous spreading plant, rich green, ovate to elliptic leaves in formal ranks on reddish stems and masses of clear lavender-mauve flowers in crowded racemes through spring and early summer. Ideal for bedding, ground cover or wall-spiller. 60cm × 1.3m. **153**

Hebe 'Lewisii'
Forms an erect but branching shrub with stout, brown branchlets. Leaves elliptic-oblong, to 65 × 25mm, bright glossy green,

slightly wavy. Flowers violet and white, borne in crowded tapering 65mm spikes through summer, occasionally in autumn and winter. Blooms more profusely when grown hard. Excellent hardy winter-flowering shrub. Hybrid from H elliptica × H salicifolia. 1.2 × 1m.

Hebe 'MacEwanii'

Somewhat compact shrub with erect growth, dark purple stems. Leaves oblong-lanceolate, 15 × 5mm, glaucous on both surfaces. Lavender blue to pale violet flowers in 65mm racemes in early summer. British hybrid, H pimelioides as one parent. 45 × 45cm.

Hebe macrocarpa 'Latisepala'

Hardy handsome shrub from Great and Little Barrier Islands, Coromandel Peninsula and Whangarei Heads. Erect, stiffly branched shrub with narrow-oblong, 8–10cm leaves, dark green with a dull gloss and slightly fleshy. Rich, deep-purple flowers produced winter through early summer in dense 10cm racemes. Deepest colour among known Hebes. Macrocarpa — large fruited. Latisepala — wide sepals. 1 × 1m.

Hebe 'Mary Antoinette'

Attractive spreading plant with slightly pendulous outer branches. Leaves oblanceolate, to 35 × 7mm, deep green, new shoots with distinctive dusky magenta-pink reverse. Small dainty flowers, deep crimson in bud, opening cerise, shading through pink to white, borne in tapering, 5cm, terminal racemes spring through late autumn. From a batch of H speciosa seedlings discovered and developed by Annton Nursery, Cambridge, New Zealand. 50 × 75cm.

Hebe 'McKeanii'

Compact rounded or irregular dwarf shrub with tiny, scale-like 5 × 2mm, fresh green leaves along slender branchlets. Maintains year-round colour, could easily be mistaken for a conifer. Seems to be the only whipcord type Hebe which performs in areas of high humidity. Discovered in the Ruahine Ranges, New Zealand by Angus McKean. Deciduous. 60 × 60cm.

Hebe obtusata

Semi-prostrate or spreading species occurring on Auckland's west coast between Manukau Heads and Muriwai. Reddish to purple stems, obovate to oblong leaves to 55 × 25mm, yellowish green, somewhat fleshy and quite glabrous. Pale lavender mauve flowers in 10cm racemes prominently displayed summer through autumn. Good ground or bank cover, spilling over walls or banks. 45 × 75cm.

Hebe ochracea 'James Stirling'

Confined to alpine regions of western Nelson in the South Island growing in damp snow-tussock country at altitudes of 1200–1700 metres. Distinctive whipcord Hebe with dense spreading growth habit. Four-sided, yellowish green, glossy branchlets, covered with tiny overlapping leaves pressed closely to the stem. Colour intensifies during winter. Small white flowers in short spikes at branch ends in summer. Effective form, foliage and flower. Selected and brought into cultivation by James Stirling of the Government Gardens in Wellington. 45 × 90cm.

Hebe odora

An inhabitant of mountain regions of the North, South, Stewart and Auckland Islands, usually in wet areas on river flats to 1400 metres. Forms a neat symmetrical, ball-shaped bush with yellowish-green young stems. Leaves elliptic ovate, to 20 × 8mm, dark-green, glossy, resembling buxus. White flowers in loose terminal racemes spring through autumn. Odora — fragrant. 1 × 1m.

Hebe 'Oratia Beauty'

Hybrid of unknown origin from the Auckland area with possibly H albicans as one parent. Compact growing shrub with closely placed, deep green leaves to 6 × 2cm. Flowers pink in bud fading to white as they mature, in compact racemes during summer. Named by Hugh B Redgrove of Auckland in 1982. 75 × 75cm.

Hebe parviflora

Found in forest margins and alongside streams in both islands. An almost dome-shaped bush with slender branches, linear-lanceolate, fresh light-green leaves to 70 × 6mm. Pale lilac to white flowers in 65mm racemes produced freely near branch tips through summer. Parviflora — small-flowered. 1 × 1m.

Hebe pimelioides

From the drier mountain regions in the South Island, southwards from Marlborough. Charming species with slender dark purplish stems. Leaves narrow lanceolate to ovate, to 8 × 2mm, glaucous with yellowish or reddish margins. Bluish purple flowers in long racemes through summer. Pimelioides — like pimelia. 30 × 75cm.

Hebe pimelioides 'Quicksilver'

Multi-branched spreading shrub with purplish-brown stems. Leaves elliptic to orbicular, to 4 × 2mm, light grey and glaucous, held at right angles to the stem. Racemes of bluish purple flowers through summer. Full sun for brightest leaf colour. 30 × 75cm.

Hebe pinguifolia

Small prostrate shrublet found in sub-alpine scrub and rocky places in the drier eastern areas of the South Island. Sturdy branches with prominent old leaf scars. Leaves broadly ovate, to 10 × 5mm, thick and glabrous, glaucous on both sides often with reddish margins. White flowers in densely packed spikes during summer. Rock gardens, informal edging, traffic islands etc. Pinguifolia — fat leaves. 25 × 75cm.

Hebe pinguifolia 'Pageii'

Quite distinct from the species. Forms a low, wide-spreading plant with dark purplish, glaucous branchlets. Leaves broad ovate to 14 × 10mm, very glaucous, margined reddish or purple. Ideal for ground-cover, best in full sun. 30 × 90cm.

Hebe pinguifolia 'Sutherlandii'

Cultivar of unknown origin, decumbent and spreading with ascending branchlets. Ovate to rounded leaves to 8 × 6mm, grey-green with pale yellow margins. White flowers as above. Ground or bank cover with at least 1m spread. 30cm × 1m.

Hebe propinqua

Whipcord Hebe from peaty and grasslands areas in subalpine regions from 760–1500m, South Canterbury to Southland. Multi-branched variable shrub with short, spreading or erect, tortuous branchlets. Tiny, 2mm, scale-like, light yellow-green leaves pressed closely to the stems. Spikes of white flowers appear towards branch ends in summer. Propinqua — near related. 75 × 75cm.

Hebe raoulii

Small, variable, multi-branched, somewhat straggling to compact plant with purplish, pubescent branchlets. Leaves oblong or spatula-shaped to 25 × 8mm, mid green, leathery with reddish margins, toothed near the apex. Lavender or pinkish flowers in terminal panicles late spring. Named for Edouard F Raoul, 19th century Medical Office on the ship *L'Aube*. 25 × 75cm.

Hebe recurva

From rocky places along rivers and streams in north west Nelson. Low compact grower with sparsely hairy, light brown to red branchlets. Leaves narrow-lanceolate, to 50 × 6mm, glaucous blue-green, turned abruptly downwards. White flowers in 7cm spikes at branch ends through summer. Grow in full sun as for all glaucous-leaved plants. Recurva — curved backwards. 60 × 60cm.

Hebe salicifolia

Attractive, multi-branched, erect to spreading shrub. Leaves willow-like, narrow-lanceolate to 125 × 12mm, glossy, mid green, paler beneath. White flowers in attractive racemes through summer. South Island from sea-level to 1000m, also Chile. Salicifolia — willow-leaved. 1.5 × 1.3m.

Hebe 'Snowdrift'
Neat, multi-branched shrub with light green 3–4cm leaves. White flowers in 75mm racemes borne profusely late spring and early and again in autumn. Most likely a hybrid of H parviflora. 1 × 1m.

Hebe speciosa
Very beautiful species, originally found at the southern head of Hokianga Harbour and as far south as Pelorous Sound, although natural specimens are now rare. Forms a rounded, bushy shrub with sturdy, smooth green branchlets. Leaves broad elliptic or obovate, to 10 × 5cm, rather fleshy, dark-green, glossy, paler beneath. Reddish purple or beetroot-purple flowers appear in large, closely packed racemes for long periods through summer and autumn. Long flowering season, depth of colour and handsome foliage places this Hebe in a class of its own. Various colour forms such as magenta red, pink and violet offered by some nurserymen. Speciosa — showy. 1 × 1m.

Hebe speciosa 'Variegata'
Similar to above but with foliage attractively variegated grey-green and pale grey-green, broadly and irregularly margined and overlaid cream. During colder months, young leaves heavily suffused rosy pink. More tender than H speciosa. Syn H speciosa 'Tricolor'. 75 × 75cm.

Hebe stricta
Found in hilly and lowland country north of Manawatu. Free-branching spreading shrub with lanceolate to linear lanceolate leaves to 12 × 2cm, deep green, dull gloss, paler beneath. White flowers, occasionally bluish tinted appear in erect 7–15cm spikes during summer. Stricta — erect. 1.5 × 1m.

Hebe subalpina
Grows in high rainfall areas on western mountain-sides in Westland, Fiordland and Canterbury at 750–1370m. Multi-branched shrub with rounded form, sturdy green to purple branchlets. Leaves lanceolate to narrow-elliptic, 25 × 6mm, apple green, glossy upper surface. White flowers in crowded 3–4cm spikes freely produced towards the tips of branches through summer. Handsome and floriferous. 1 × 1m.

Hebe topiaria
Shapely ball-shaped shrub with clipped appearance. Leaves broadly elliptic to obovate, to 12 × 6mm, somewhat fleshy, mid green, glaucous, and slightly glossy. Flowers white, appearing between the leaves during summer. Immaculate outline needs contrasting against other foliage. Topiaria — as if shaped by trimming. 90 × 75cm.   **154**

Hebe townsonii
Found in the regions of Mt Messenger in Taranaki and on rocky hills near Westport. Erect, bushy shrub with yellowy green branchlets. Leaves linear-lanceolate, to 40 × 6mm, bright green, paler beneath. White flowers with a hint of mauve in 5cm, loosely arranged racemes spring through early summer. 1 × 1m.

Hebe venustula
Inhabits sub-alpine growth at 750–1500m in North Island mountains. Forms a rounded, compact bush, branchlets yellow green. Leaves elliptic oblong to 12 × 6mm, bright green and glossy, paler beneath. White or pale violet flowers appear from early summer. Venustula — graceful. 1.3 × 1.3m.

Hebe vernicosa
Naturally grows on Beech forest floors from sea level to timberline in Marlborough, eastern Nelson Province and western Amuri area. Attractive semi-erect shrub with globular form and greeny-brown branchlets. Leaves elliptic to obovate, to 10 × 5mm, lustrous, dark green. Flowers white or lavender fading to white in short spikes crowded towards the tips of the branches spring through early summer. Vernicosa — varnished referring to the leaves. 75 × 75cm.

Hebe 'Waikiki'
Upright growing bush, branchlets green with brown nodes. Leaves ovate-elliptic, to 40 × 12mm, mid green, semi-glossy, paler beneath, young shoots coppery red. Bluish-mauve flowers in 7cm spikes early to mid-summer. Named after Waikiki Beach, Honolulu. 1.2 × 1m.

Hebe 'Wiri Charm'
The 'Wiri' series of Hebes have been bred, selected and named by Jack Hobbs of Auckland Regional Botanic Gardens in Auckland, New Zealand. 'Wiri Charm' is a compact spreading shrub, ideal for mass planting or general garden use. Deep rose-purple flowers appear in summer and sporadically through winter. 60 × 80cm.

Hebe 'Wiri Cloud'
Compact shrub with small rounded foliage, suitable for rock gardens. Small, soft pink flowers through summer. 35 × 30cm.

Hebe 'Wiri Dawn'
Spreading shrub with narrow, fresh green foliage. Soft pink flowers in summer and sporadically early winter. Good ground cover and wall spiller. 40 × 70cm.

Hebe 'Wiri Gem'
Neat compact upright grower, medium green foliage. An abundance of rose-purple flower spikes late winter and late summer. 80 × 80cm.

Hebe 'Wiri Image'
Dense, vigorous grower with glossy green foliage. Soft, methyl-violet flowers in long racemes through summer. 1.2 × 1.2m.

Hebe 'Wiri Mist'
Compact spreading shrub with green fleshy foliage. Becomes a mass of white flowers late spring. Ideal for mass planting or perennial or shrub borders. Very disease resistant. 50 × 80cm.   **154**

Hebe 'Wiri Prince'
Tall vigorous shrub with large dark green foliage. Intense deep purple flowers in long racemes through winter and again in summer. 1.5 × 1m.

Hebe 'Wiri Splash'
Compact shrub with attractive, narrow, golden-green foliage. Covered through early summer in a profusion of lavender-lilac flowers. Disease resistant. Suited to massed bedding. 40 × 60cm.

Hebe 'Wiri Vision'
Vigorous cultivar with handsome undulating foliage. Reddish purple flowers in attractive racemes for long periods through autumn and winter and again in summer. 90cm × 1.2m.

Hebe 'Youngii'
Low-growing form with decumbent, purple-brown stems. Leaves broad obovate, to 12 × 5mm, mid-green, paler beneath. Violet flowers in 4cm loose racemes appear at branch ends through summer. Distinct cultivar, useful in rock gardens and for edging beds and borders. Hybrid from H elliptica × H pimelioides named for James Young, once curator of Christchurch Botanic Gardens. 25 × 50cm.

HEDYCARYA

A genus of about twelve species of trees and shrubs from Australia, New Zealand and the South Pacific named from the

Greek *hedys*, sweet and *karyon*, a nut. A handsome specimen for public gardens, farms or acreage in warm areas. Plant in full sun in deeply worked, organically enriched, free-draining, moisture retentive soil, sheltered from strong wind and frosts, especially when young.
Monimiaceae

Hedycarya arborea
Pigeonwood
The sole New Zealand species, found in lowland to mountain forests of the North, South and Three Kings Islands from sea level to 750m. An erect-growing medium tree with ascending branches and dark brown bark. Leaves linear oblong to obovate, to 12 × 5cm, leathery, pliable, shining, dark green, coarsely toothed margins. Flowers from trees of both sexes needed to obtain fruit, which are orange to bright red drupes, relished by native birds. Arborea — growing in tree-like form. Evergreen. 5 × 4m.

A genus of about 500 species of annual and perennial herbs, shrubs and sub-shrubs, mainly from South Africa and Australia, named from the Greek *helios*, the sun and *chrysos*, golden. Highly regarded for free-flowering qualities, their papery flowers excellent for brilliant garden displays and for cutting and drying. Plant in deeply worked, free-draining, loose open soil in full or filtered sun. Mulch freely, water occasionally in dry periods and apply light dressings of a balanced fertilizer early spring and autumn. Prune fairly hard after flowering and tip prune during early growth.
Compositae. *All evergreen.*

Helichrysum argenteum
Low growing upright plant with decorative glistening white flowers with golden centres. The flowers may be picked and used either fresh or dried. Best in dry sandy soil. Argenteum — silvery. 50 × 50cm.

Helichrysum argyrophyllum
Trailing, prostrate, mat-forming plant with silvery-white appearance. Leaves obovate to obovate-spathulate, to 3cm long, nearly glabrous and quite silvery. Papery flowers lemon yellow with golden brown outer bracts, borne in lax corymbs to 20cm across. Excellent ground or bank cover and wall spiller. Very salt-wind tolerant. Argyrophyllum — silver-leaved. 1 × 2m.

Helichrysum bracteatum
Golden Everlasting, Strawflower
Annual or perennial herb, usually found as a spreading, plant with erect stems, widely distributed in most Australian States. Leaves oblong-lanceolate to linear-lanceolate, to 12cm long, green to grey-green, quite hairy, margins entire. Flowerheads to 8cm across borne singly on erect stems through spring and summer. Colours vary, white to cream, yellow to golden yellow. Several excellent cultivars available. Bracteatum — with bracts. 20–90 × 30–90cm.

Helichrysum bracteatum 'Apricot'
Large apricot flowers with glossy, papery bracts. 50 × 75cm.

Helichrysum bracteatum 'Cream'
Large cream flowers with glossy papery bracts. 50 × 75cm.   **155**

Helichrysum bracteatum 'Diamond Head'
Bright yellow 3cm flowers with orange centre borne on long stems well above the foliage. Excellent low-growing form, ideal for rockery planting or containers. 20 × 50cm.   **155**

Helichrysum bracteatum 'Pink Surprise'
Large pink flowers with glossy, papery bracts. 50 × 75cm.

Helichrysum bracteatum 'Princess of Wales'
Excellent, very free-flowering, bushy cultivar, producing a profusion of 6cm rich golden-yellow flowerheads for long periods through spring and summer. 60 × 90cm.   **155**

Helichrysum bracteatum 'White'
Large white flowers to 8cm across with prominent yellow centre borne profusely on long stems through spring and summer. 50 × 75cm.   **155**

A genus of about 60 species of perennial grasses from temperate regions of the Northern Hemisphere and South Africa named from the Greek *heliktos*, twisted and *trichos*, spine in reference to the shape of the awn or bristle-like appendage on the glume. These vigorous tussock-forming grasses are grown for attractive form and arching infloresence. Plant in deeply worked, free-draining soil in full sun. Combine with other grasses or sword-leaved plants with rocks or boulders. Hardy to –15°C. Groom as necessary by pulling out any dead leaves.
Graminae.

Helictotrichon sempervirens
Blue Oat Grass
From south west Europe where it occurs in rocky and stony pasture on calcereous soils where they build up rounded hummocks or fountains of bright bluish grey, narrow leaves resembling giant editions of the familiar Blue Fescue. Tightly rolled or flat, rigid or gracefully curved, glaucous leaf blades to 22cm × 3mm. Straw-coloured flowers with purple markings borne in loose open panicles on 18cm stems. Evergreen. 1.2m × 75cm.

A genus of about 100 species of annual or perennial herbs or shrubs from Australia and South Africa, named from the Greek *helios*, sun and *pteron*, wing or feather, in reference to feathery pappus hairs, distinguishing them from the related Helichrysum which has barbed pappus hairs. Helipterum is valued for long-lasting papery flower heads used in fresh or dried floral arrangements. They're low-growing bushy plants, excellent for garden bedding.

Helipterum grows freely from seed and commences flowering within 2–3 months of sowing. Plant in deeply worked, free-draining, organically enriched, friable soil in full or partial sun. Tip-prune young plants to encourage bushiness and remove faded flowers to extend the flowering season and the plant's lifespan.
Compositae

Helipterum anthemioides 'Paper Baby'
Chamomile Sunray
Found in all eastern Australian States. Dwarf-growing shrubby herb sending up numerous erect or branching stems from a carrot-like root. Leaves narrow-oblanceolate to linear, to 18 × 2mm, greyish green, glabrous to minutely hairy, margins entire, with chamomile fragrance when crushed. Solitary, terminal flower-heads to 3cm diameter, with central cluster of golden-yellow disc florets, surrounded by pure white, papery ray florets, borne on long pedicels winter through mid-summer. Evergreen. 25 × 90cm.   **154**

Above: Gunnera tinctoria **146**

Above: Hebe diosmifolia **148**

Above: Grewia occidentalis 'Mauve Star' **145**
Below: Halimium lasianthum **147**

Above and below: Hebe 'Lavender Spray' **149**

Above: Hebe topiaria **151**

Above and below: Hebe 'Inspiration' **149**

Above: Hebe 'Wiri Mist' **151**
Below: Hebe 'Hartii' **149**

Below: Helipterum anthemioides 'Paper Baby' *Chamomile Sunray* **152**

Above: Helichrysum bracteatum 'Cream' **152**

Above: Helichrysum bracteatum 'Princess of Wales' **152**
Below: Hibbertia empetrifolia **161**

Above: Helichrysum bracteatum 'Diamond Head' **152**
Below: Helichrysum bracteatum 'White' **152**

Above: Hibiscus 'Ben James' **162**
Below: Hibiscus 'Golden Belle' **163**

Below: Hibiscus 'Surfrider' **164**

Above: Hibiscus 'Lemon Chiffon' **163**

Above: Hibiscus 'Marjorie Coral' **163**

Above: Hibiscus 'Anvil Sparks' **162**
Below: Hibiscus 'Mollie Cummings' **163**

Above: Hibiscus 'Mary Wallace' **163**
Below: Hibiscus syriacus 'Blue Bird' **164**

Above: Hypericum leschenaultii **168**

Above: Koelreuteria paniculata *Golden Rain Tree* **175**

Above: Hypocalymma cordifolium 'Golden Veil' **169**
Below: Juniperas conferta *Shore Juniper* **172**

Above: Jacaranda mimosifolia *Jacaranda* **171**
Below: Justicia carnea *Brazilian Plume Flower* **174**

Above: Kalmia latifolia **174**

Above: Laburnum x watereri **176**
Below: Idesia polycarpa *Wonder Tree* **169**

Above: Lagerstroemia indica 'Petite Orchid' **176**
Below: Knightia excelsa *Rewarewa* **175**

Above: Lantana 'Pink Frolic' **181**

Above: Lantana montevidensis *Trailing Lantana* **181**
Below: Lantana 'Source d'Or' **181**

Above: Lantana 'Sunset' **181**
Below: Lantana 'Cream Carpet' **181**

HETEROCENTRON

The genus comprises about 25 species of herbs and low shrubs from Central and South America, named from the Greek *heteros*, different and *kentron*, a spur or sharp point, referring to bristle-like appendages. The listed species is admired for the intense colour it provides as bank or ground cover, draping over walls, creeping through rocks or over old stumps and in hanging baskets.

Although a mere creeping herb, it has many useful landscaping functions. Plant in sun or partial shade in deeply worked, free-draining average garden soil. Needs protection from frost and adequate moisture through dry periods.

Melastomataceae.

Heterocentron elegans
Spanish Shawl
Native of Mexico, Guatemala and Honduras. Forms a dense carpet or mat of threadlike stems which root at each node. Leaves ovate to oblong-ovate, 10–25mm long, veins well-defined, deep green, slightly hairy, margins entire. During cooler months, both leaves and stems become reddish, especially in full sun. The whole plant becomes a solid mass of 25mm, wide open, cyclamen-pink or magenta to mauve flowers, providing a spectacular summer display. Plant three or four to a square metre for rapid coverage. Syn Schizocentron. Elegans — elegant. Evergreen.

HIBBERTIA

Most of the one hundred species of Hibbertia are found in Australia as small, desirable, shrubby plants with yellow or orange flowers, seen at their best in rock gardens. The genus is named for George Hibbert, 18th–19th century, distinguished patron of botany. Not the easiest to grow, often falling victim to the root disease Phytophthera cinnamomi. Provide sandy or stony soil, perfect drainage, in a built-up bed or rockery in full sun.

Dilleniaceae. *All evergreen.*

Hibbertia empetrifolia
Found in South Australia, Victoria, Tasmania and New South Wales. Woody spreading shrub with small, dark green leaves and masses of deep golden-yellow flowers through spring and early summer. A reliable Hibbertia, good for bank or ground cover. Try in hanging baskets. Empetrifolia — foliage resembles Empetrium or Crowberry. 30–60cm × 1.5m. **155**

Hibbertia obtusifolia
Grey Guinea Flower
Distributed through the eastern States, a tiny ground-hugging plant with 3–5cm, hoary, greyish leaves, broad-tipped and quite blunt. Bears 2cm, canary-yellow, primrose-like flowers spring through mid-summer. Dry, stony soil. 20cm × 1m.

Hibbertia procumbens
Spreading Guinea Flower
From Victoria and Tasmania. Neat little prostrate trailing plant with narrow, 12–25mm, hairless leaves and well-displayed, bright yellow, 2–3cm flowers during spring. Good for rockeries in cooler areas. 20 × 60cm.

Hibbertia stellaris
Orange Stars
Claimed as the most floriferous and beautiful Hibbertia. Straggly, wiry dwarf shrub with fine, narrow, 12–25mm leaves on slender trailing stems and charming, golden-orange, 12mm, five-petalled flowers for most of the year. 20 × 75cm.

HIBISCUS
(TROPICAL)

A genus of over 300 species of shrubs, trees, annual or perennial herbs distributed throughout tropical and subtropical regions of the world, named from *hibiskos*, Greek for marshmallow, Althea officinalis. It is usually the flamboyant Hawaiian hibiscus that spring to mind when the genus is mentioned. In 1923 Hibiscus became the floral emblem of Hawaii by joint resolution of the legislature.

Many of the magnificent hybrid cultivars we know today have arisen from some of the Hawaiian native species crossed with the Chinese species H rosa sinensis. Now thousands of beautiful hybrids delight gardeners throughout the tropical and subtropical world, either from Hawaii or local breeding programmes.

In Australia and New Zealand there could be six hundred or more cultivars or varieties grown. The Australian Hibiscus Society features over 350 of which a third were bred in Australia.

Modern hibiscus hybrids willingly provide year round displays of magnificent colourful blooms on compact and shapely bushes, placing them amongst the most favoured shrubs for tropical, subtropical or warm-temperate gardens.

Some grow more vigorously and bloom better than others. A flower of exquisite form or colour may be tempting, but not always the best performer. Extensive breeding has deprived some varieties of the ability to develop vigorous root systems, making it necessary to graft on hardy rootstock. The stronger roots assimilate more water and nutrients for better growth and flower, are more tolerant of soil and weather conditions and have greater resistance to disease. Choosing grafted plants whenever possible is recommended.

In selecting Hibiscus, a little research will avoid disappointing results. Keep an eye on private or public gardens for robust, free-flowering plants. Visit reputable Hibiscus nurseries. This will put you on the right track to obtaining good plants for your particular situation.
All tropical Hibiscus evergreen.

Hibiscus Culture
Position: Hibiscus are at their best in maximum sunlight. They'll grow in shade, but need full sun for optimum flower production. Avoid placing them with other plants which compete for available root space and nutrients. A north facing bed devoted entirely to Hibiscus is ideal.

Soil: Deeply worked, free-draining, moisture-retentive soil with a pH level of 6.2 to 6.5, enriched with animal manure or compost is ideal. Probably more Hibiscus fail through wet feet than frost damage, so drainage is very important.

Planting: Assuming the plant is well rooted and hardened, water freely in the container and allow to stand for an hour or so. Remove the plant from its container without disturbing the roots and place in the prepared hole with the top of the root ball no more than 1cm below garden soil level. Firm the soil to ensure there is contact on all sides of the roots. Secure the plant to a stake if strong winds are expected.

Watering: Hibiscus thrive on a steady water supply but cannot stand wet feet. If the soil is free-draining it's doubtful if overwatering will occur. After planting give a thorough soaking and repeat every second or third day if it doesn't rain. This is a vital time for growth and flower development. During winter, and after pruning in spring, the need for moisture may not be as great, but at all seasons, if dry weather persists, regular deep watering is essential, preferably during the day to allow foliage to dry before sunset.

Mulching: Mulching occurs naturally in the wild and is a vital function under garden conditions. It helps retain moisture, creates a suitable environment for surface feeding roots essential for healthy growth, protects the soil from packing down and any erosion during heavy downpours. It constantly adds organic matter to the soil, controls weed growth and improves the appearance of garden beds. Mulch immediately after planting.

Feeding: Hibiscus use up considerable energy and feed heavily to maintain an almost continual production of bloom especially in warmer areas where flowering persists through winter. As well as the nutritive value of mulching, a regular feeding programme on the basis of 'little and often' encourages healthy growth and consistent floral displays. Feed new plants three weeks after planting and then at three-week intervals. Start feeding mature plants about a month after pruning, mid to late October, continuing at three-week intervals, even through winter in warmer areas. Scatter fertilizer within the drip line of the plant and water before and after application.

Australian Hibiscus Society suggests either a complete granular fertilizer — Nitrophoska Blue with a NPK rating of 12–5–14, or water- soluble plant foods such as Phostrogen or Maxicrop. As a guide, application rates for granular fertilizers are — a teaspoon for new or young plants under 60cm, a dessertspoon for plants to a metre and double this for plants to 1.5 metres. Larger specimens may be given one or two handfuls according to size. Continue this feeding programme at 3–4 weekly intervals. Checking for soil acidity in mid summer is recommended. Dressings of lime or dolomite may be required to bring the pH to 6.2 to 6.5. For fertilizer to be effective, correct pH is essential.

Pruning: Annual pruning is a vital part of successful Hibiscus culture, encouraging healthy growth, good flower production and neat, compact plants. When the weather begins to warm up in spring, remove about one third of the previous season's growth, using sharp secatuers to make a slanting cut above an outward pointing bud. Completely remove any crossed or wayward branches or any which overcrowd the centre of the bush. Cut off branches within 30cm of the ground, to create clearance for mulching,

fertilizing etc. Your bushes may look somewhat denuded after pruning but soon rebound into vigorous new life.

Pest Control: Thriving, robust plants seem to handle pests and diseases far better than weak unhealthy ones but even so, some control may be necessary particularly during summer months. Pests commonly found on Hibiscus are Caterpillars, Aphids, Mites and Grasshoppers. Check with your local stockist for the appropriate spray.

Bloom size
Miniature: Under 10cm
Medium: 10–15cm
Large: 15–20cm
Extra large: 20–25cm

Bush height
Low: Under 1m
Average: 1–2m
Tall: 2–3m
Very tall: Over 3m

Hibiscus 'Agnes Gault'
Bright satin pink to purplish rose, large overlapped single flower. Vigorous, tall upright grower.

Hibiscus 'Ali Uii'
Reddish orange or tomato red flowers speckled lemon yellow. Medium, overlapped single, trumpet shape. Tall, prolific grower.

Hibiscus 'All Gold'
Bright golden yellow, medium double flowers, slightly ruffled petals. Average grower.

Hibiscus 'Ann Miller'
Pink with white markings, medium single blooms, regular and reliable. Average bush, slow grower, inclined to be woody.

Hibiscus 'Anvil Sparks'
Vivid orange shaded red, large single bloom. Average grower. Outstanding. **157**

Hibiscus 'Apricot Beauty'
Clear apricot with red eye, medium single with overlapping petals. Low bushy grower, prolific flowerer.

Hibiscus 'Apricot Parade'
Apricot-orange with a red eye and lavender-pink overtone. Medium cup and saucer double. Tall, well-branched, vigorous, reasonably prolific.

Hibiscus 'Augie Miller'
Bronze to burnt orange with yellow shadings and a prominent maroon central zone. Medium overlapped single and ruffled

flower. Low to medium grower. Grafted plant essential.

Hibiscus 'Ben James'
Deep rose pink to tomato red flowers, medium single with crinkly petals. Average grower. **156**

Hibiscus 'Black Beauty'
Rich purplish red, white veins on outer petals, medium single flowers somewhat bell-shaped with overlapping slightly tufted petals. Average upright grower. Handsome and prolific.

Hibiscus 'Brucei'
Bright yellow with white eye, medium single bloom. Average grower, hardy and prolific.

Hibiscus 'Butterfly Wings'
Ivory with central flush of pink giving mother of pearl effect. Medium to large fully double. Average erect grower.

Hibiscus 'Cameo Queen'
Pale primrose yellow shading to soft-pink in centre. Large single cartwheel flower, overlapping ruffled petals. Average bushy grower, free flowering. Syn Ruffled Giant.

Hibiscus 'Canary Girl'
Bright golden yellow with white zone and pink flush in the centre, medium single blooms. Average to tall bushy grower.

Hibiscus 'Capitola'
Soft apricot with red centre, miniature semi-double, fringed and ruffled petals, pendulous flowers. Average grower, prolific bloomer.

Hibiscus 'Celia'
Pale apricot orange with pink eye, medium single blooms in abundance. Average bushy grower.

Hibiscus 'Celia Double'
Pastel apricot flowers with pink centre, medium double. Tall grower, prolific flowerer.

Hibiscus 'Claret Rose'
Deep wine-red, medium to large double flowers. Average grower.

Hibiscus 'Conqueror'
Buff apricot with crimson throat, medium single flower, free blooming. Tall bushy grower.

Hibiscus 'Covakanic'
Yellow on the outer edges, with orange-red, fawn and pink blending toward the centre and red eye. Medium, single, overlapping petals, prolific bloomer. Average grower. Syn 'Hawaiian Girl'.

Hibiscus 'Cromwell'
White flushed pale pink, nearest to white in tropical Hibiscus, large single flower. Lower bushy grower.

Hibiscus 'Crown of Bohemia'
Golden yellow flushed orange with red eye, becoming deeper in winter. Large double bloom. Free flowering, medium bushy grower.

Hibiscus 'Crown of Warringah'
Soft fawny apricot with pink halo, white centre, medium cup and saucer semi-double. Prolific flowerer. Average grower.

Hibiscus 'D J O'Brien'
Bright orange tangerine with carmine throat. Medium semi-double flowers with ruffled petals. Average, upright grower, vigorous and free flowering.

Hibiscus 'Dr Kutsuki'
Yellow merging with orange at the centre, large single flowers prominently frilled and ruffled. Low bushy grower.

Hibiscus 'El Capitolio'
Bright red flowers with petals edged white. Miniature semi-double, ruffled blooms with elongated stems. Prolific, average grower.

Hibiscus 'Eldorado'
Rich golden yellow with reddish throat, small to medium double flower with ruffled central petals. Low compact grower.

Hibiscus 'Fiji Flame'
Tangerine scarlet with primrose spotted throat, medium single blooms. Tall vigorous grower. Almost everblooming.

Hibiscus 'Fijian Pink'
Clear soft pink with prominent dark red central splash. Miniature open single flower. Free flowering, average to tall grower, lush glossy foliage.

Hibiscus 'Fire Engine'
Bright orange scarlet, large, single over-lapped blooms. Prolific, low to average grower. Grafted plants preferable.

Hibiscus 'Full Moon'
Clear, bright golden yellow blooms with white eye. Medium, cup and saucer double blooms. Prolific, average to tall grower. Syn 'Mrs James Henderson'.

Hibiscus 'Garden Glory'
Clear light pink, large single blooms. Average bushy grower, free-flowering.

Hibiscus 'Gay Rose'
Rich flamingo-pink with creamy white centre, medium, ruffled and tufted single bloom. Flowers well. Average grower.

Hibiscus 'Gold Dust'
Apricot gold with irregular creamy lemon flecks and yellow reverse, medium single blooms with overlapping, ruffled and tufted petals. Low to medium, slow grower, free-blooming. Grafting recommended.

Hibiscus 'Gold Sovereign'
Rich orange-yellow with red centre, medium fully double blooms. Average to tall grower, free flowering.

Hibiscus 'Golden Belle'
Pure rich bright golden yellow, large to extra large, overlapped, ruffled and tufted, single flower. Prolific bloomer, low to medium grower. Must be grafted. **156**

Hibiscus 'Golden Oriel'
Apricot to golden yellow, bright crimson eye and pink halo, medium single flowers. Average to tall bushy grower.

Hibiscus 'Harmony'
Brilliant intense red, medium to large single flower. Average grower.

Hibiscus 'Hawaiian Sunset'
Cerise pink shading to lemon yellow at the edges. Large, overlapped, frilled and ruffled single bloom. Prolific, bushy, average grower.

Hibiscus 'Hiawatha'
Deep red, miniature double, pendulous blooms with long stalks. Average grower.

Hibiscus 'Honey Gold'
Golden yellow with white centre, medium double blooms. Average bushy grower. Free flowering, quite outstanding.

Hibiscus 'Hubba Hubba'
Rich cyclamen pink shading to gold, large single blooms. Strong average grower.

Hibiscus 'Island Empress'
Deep cerise pink with red centre. Medium semi-double flowers. Blooms freely, average grower. Very hardy.

Hibiscus 'Isobel Baird'
Dark lavender with red eye, medium semi-double, 2–day flower. Average upright grower.

Hibiscus 'Jacks'
Dark orange blending to pink towards the centre, medium double flowers. Low grower.

Hibiscus 'Jerry Smith'
Rich golden yellow shading to apricot yellow. Large fully double, 2–day flower. Medium bushy grower.

Hibiscus 'Johnsonii'
Apricot gold to orange with pinkish red centre, medium single blooms with over-lapping petals. Low to average bushy grower.

Hibiscus 'Kitty Beebe'
Deep smoky lavender mauve with red eye. Large, overlapped, ruffled and tufted, single, two day flowers. Low bushy grower.

Hibiscus 'Kuimala'
Burnt orange with red centre, medium to large single flower, overlapping petals. Low bushy grower, free-flowering.

Hibiscus 'Lemon Chiffon'
Pale cream with wide lemon yellow edges, flushed pink in the throat. Large, crepe-textured, single, beautiful flowers. Prolific, hardy, average grower. **157**

Hibiscus 'Light Fantastic'
Rich deep pink, large double blooms. Average bushy grower.

Hibiscus 'Madonna'
White with a hint of palest pink, red eye and central veining, large single flower with overlapping, ruffled and tufted petals. Average grower and very beautiful. Grafting recommended.

Hibiscus 'Marjorie Coral'
Intense pink with red eye, large single with overlapping, ruffled and tufted petals. Average bushy grower. Outstanding example. **157**

Hibiscus 'Mary Forbes'
Rich vibrant orange with light red eye. Large, overlapped, tufted, single blooms. Prolific, average grower.

Hibiscus 'Mary Wallace'
Vivid, deep orange red edged light yellow. Large, fully overlapped, single blooms with light texture. Prolific, medium, bushy grower. **157**

Hibiscus 'Mollie Cummings'
Rich dark velvet red with glowing sheen. Large, fully overlapped, single flower. Prolific, average, upright grower. **157**

Hibiscus 'Mystic Charm'
Brightest cerise red with irregular white border which broadens as the season progresses. Medium to large single flower

with overlapping, slightly ruffled petals. Prolific bloomer. Low to medium grower.

Hibiscus 'Nagao 20'
Rich deep velvet red. Large, fully overlapped, two-day single blooms. Very prolific, average, somewhat untidy grower with glossy foliage. Must be grafted.

Hibiscus 'Nathan Charles'
Rich carmine crimson, shaded lighter towards outer petals. Large, cartwheel, overlapped, single, two-day flower with heavily crimped and ruffled petals. Low to medium, bushy grower. Grafting recommended.

Hibiscus 'Old Gold'
Rich glowing golden yellow to apricot, large single with ruffled overlapping petals. Glows like molten brass. Low to average grower.

Hibiscus 'Peach Blow'
Rich peach pink with carmine centre. Medium, fully double flowers. Average, bushy grower, very free flowering.

Hibiscus 'Pink Satin'
Rich pink, large single flowers, average growing bush.

Hibiscus 'Pride of Lockley'
Light rosy red, medium, fully double blooms. Average grower, vigorous and free flowering.

Hibiscus 'Rosa Sinensis'
Rose of China, Shoe Black Plant
Vigorous branching shrub, thought to have originated in China, certainly from tropical Asia. Leaves ovate to broadly lanceolate, to 12 × 10cm, glossy deep green, paler beneath, margins deeply serrated or lobed. Flowers intense bright red with maroon throat, medium single, borne singly in upper leaf axils. Forms a relatively hardy, strong-growing bush. The original species from which countless hybrids have been developed. An attractive shrub in its own right.

Hibiscus 'Ross Estey'
Soft rose pink, suffused and edged apricot. Large, full overlapped, single flowers. Prolific, average bushy grower.

Hibiscus 'Royal Highness'
Margins pale apricot, shaded red towards the centre with a deeper red eye, large single. Average grower.

Hibiscus 'Ruby'
Rosy red, medium single flowers with reflexed petals. Vigorous average to tall grower, free flowering.

Hibiscus 'Saffron'
Broad margin of soft yellow shading to large pale pink central zone, large single with ruffled overlapping petals. Average grower.

Hibiscus 'Sandy Chun'
Bright golden orange with large red central zone and veining. Changes to golden yellow on second day. Large, overlapped, ruffled and tufted, single blooms. Low bushy grower. Must be grafted.

Hibiscus 'Simmonds Red'
Bright tomato red with pink eye, large single flower. Strong vigorous average to tall grower.

Hibiscus 'Smokey Blue'
Lavender edged pink, fading to apricot and with red eye, medium semi-double, 3-day flower. Average grower.

Hibiscus 'Sunshine'
Vivid burnt orange, medium semi-double with overlapping petals. Average grower.

Hibiscus 'Surfrider'
Rich apricot to orange with prominent red eye. Large to extra large, overlapped, ruffled and tufted, single blooms with heavy texture. Very prolific, low, spreading grower.   **156**

Hibiscus 'Suva Queen'
Combination of bright cerise and deep rose pink, medium to large fully double flowers. Vigorous tall grower and very free flowering.

Hibiscus 'Tahiti Orange'
Bright orange-yellow with pink overtone and gold eye, large single flowers. Average grower.

Hibiscus 'Tango'
Bright tangerine red with carmine eye and greyish pink halo. Takes on coppery hues during winter. Large, overlapped, tufted single blooms. Prolific bloomer, average open grower.

Hibiscus 'Vivid'
Clear vibrant orange, large single ruffled flowers. Average grower.

Hibiscus 'Warriewood Gem'
Rich glowing scarlet, medium single blooms with overlapping petals. Average bushy grower, dark green leaves.

Hibiscus 'Warrior'
Rich deep red, medium single blooms. Average bushy grower.

HIBISCUS
(TEMPERATE)

When Linnaeus conferred the epithet *syriacus* to this deciduous species, he obviously thought it was indigenous to the Middle East. Rose of Sharon is actually native to temperate and warm temperate regions of eastern Asia. Although lacking the flamboyance of tropical Hibiscus they are valuable garden shrubs, hardy to −15°C, but show great versatility by flowering freely in subtropical conditions.

Vigorous upright growers with numerous slender stems, leaves often tri-lobed to 7cm long, deep green and coarsely toothed. Flowers somewhat resembling hollyhock, appear through summer and autumn when other shrubs in flower are scarce. Plant in deeply worked, free-draining, moisture-retentive soil in full sun. Benefit from annual pruning to about half way after flowering to preserve shape and encourage more and better flowers.

Malvaceae. *All deciduous.*

Hibiscus syriacus 'Blue Bird'
Rose of Sharon, Syrian Rose
Violet blue with darker eye, single, very free flowering. 2 × 1.30m.   **157**

Hibiscus syriacus 'Flying Flag'
White with showy red throat. Single blooms. 2 × 1.30m.

Hibiscus syriacus 'Heidi'
Light violet blue, double blooms. Dwarf grower. 1.2 × 1m.

Hibiscus syriacus 'Violacea Plena'
Deep violet purple, fully double flowers. 2 × 1.30m.

HOHERIA

A genus of five species or evergreen shrubs and trees, confined to New Zealand, called by a Latinized form of the Maori name *Houhere*. Lacebark, the common name, alludes to the artistic lace-like character of the netted, fibrous layer found beneath the outer bark, once used for numerous ornamental purposes such as trimming hats, basketwork etc.

Lacebark presents few cultural problems, growing rapidly under average garden conditions. Specimens becoming ragged may be hard pruned, soon re-growing with heathy vigour. Being soil-robbing plants, other species are best kept at a distance. Spray for caterpillars, and at the same time use a fungicide for the prevention of a gall disease, recognized by a lumpy growth appearing on twigs which distort some of the foliage. Cut off and burn affected parts, give a fungicidal spray and feed the plant with a balanced fertilizer.

Malvaceae. *All evergreen.*

Hoheria populnea
Lacebark

Found in coastal and lowland forests of the North Island from North Cape to Waikato. Extremely graceful evergreen with slender branches and broadly-ovate to ovate-lanceolate leaves to 14 × 6cm, fresh light green, semi-glossy, prominently veined, margins sharply toothed. Great masses of beautiful, starry, snow white, 2cm flowers provide a magnificent floral display late summer and autumn almost obscuring the leaves. Appears hardy in most districts. Excellent for rapid screening, backgrounds, boundaries, groves etc. Populnea — poplar-like. 5 × 3m.

Hoheria populnea 'Alba Variegata'
White Variegated Lacebark

Excellent cultivar with attractive variegated leaves, dark green, heavily and irregularly margined creamy white with young growths often tinged pink. Impressive in its own right or in association with other foliage shrubs. 3 × 2m.

Hoheria populnea 'Purple Wave'
Purple Lacebark

Selected form with leaves purple-blue on the undersides, most effective when the foliage rustles in the breeze. Masses of starry white flowers also with blue stamens. Syn H populnea 'Purpurea'. 3 × 2m.

Hoheria populnea 'Variegata'
Yellow Variegated Lacebark

Showy form with larger leaves, dark green with irregular central blotch of greenish yellow, also marked or blotched yellow-green, giving the appearance of yellowish leaves margined green. Not as handsome as 'Alba Variegata' and a little tender when exposed to frost. 3 × 2m.

Hoheria sexstylosa
Graceful Lacebark

From the lowland and lower mountain forests of both islands of New Zealand. Resembles H populnea but distinguished by graceful weeping growth habit, narrower and more serrated foliage. Slightly smaller flowers borne profusely in large clusters mid summer through autumn not only filling the air with sweet fragrance but compelling closer inspection. A very beautiful tree, in many respects preferable. Sexstylosa — with six styles. 5 × 3m.

A genus of 40 species of clump-forming herbaceous plants from Japan, China and Korea, named for Nicholaus Thomas Host (1761–1834) physician to the Austrian Emperor. Hostas are long-lived, robust plants, grown mainly for handsome luxuriant leaves in varying textures, sizes and shapes and flowers of considerable beauty. More than a thousand registered cultivars are in existence throughout the world.

Generally, Hostas are shade-lovers, seen at their best in light woodland settings, amongst shrubs or trees or in shaded parts of a herbaceous border. Their natural habitat is an environment of semi-permanent mist and high humidity, either in moist grasslands, besides rocky streams in the dappled shade of larger trees or on bleak shaded hillsides. Similar conditions may not always prevail in garden situations, but even so, few gardeners fail to grow Hostas satisfactorily. Basic requirements are shade or partial shade for development of luxuriant foliage and sunlight for flower production.

They thrive in deeply worked, organically enriched, free-draining, moisture retentive, slightly acid to neutral soil. Mulch freely and water regularly during dry periods. Avoid overhead watering which may cause scorch or splash marks on delicate leaf surfaces. Mulch early spring with well-rotted stable or chicken manure. Through spring and summer, monthly applications of high nitrogen liquid foliar fertilizer will produce outstanding results.

Hosta clumps resent disturbance and may be left to themselves for years. Delay any division for at least three years after planting. Slugs and snails relish their succulent leaves. Control with slug pellets or by sprinkling plants and surrounding soil with liquid aluminium sulphate.

Liliaceae.

Hosta 'August Moon'

Corrugated, pale golden yellow, faintly glaucous leaves. Pale mauve, almost white flowers. Vigorous grower. 60cm.

Hosta 'Big Daddy'

Large, 45cm, rounded, heavily puckered, deep blue glaucous leaves. Near-white flowers in short spikes early summer. 90cm.

Hosta 'Blue Skies'

Small neat grower, clear blue foliage. White flowers in hyacinth-like spikes during summer. 30cm.

Hosta 'Celebration'

Neat leaves, bright gold edged green fading to cream in the centre. Lavender flowers in dense spikes. First to emerge after winter. 30cm.

Hosta 'Emerald Skies'

Dwarf with shiny dark-green, thick-textured leaves. White to mauve flowers in hyacinth-like clusters. Ideal rockery plant. 10cm.

Hosta 'Francee'

Deep forest green leaves with prominent brilliant white margins. Lavender blooms in dense spikes. 45cm.

Hosta 'Fringe Benefit'

Base colour light greyish green with wide white margin. Early spikes of pale lavender flowers. Strong growing. 70cm.

Hosta 'Gold Edger'

Small heart shaped, pale gold leaves. Light mauve, midsummer flowers. Increases rapidly, making ground cover or edging. 25cm.

Hosta 'Gold Standard'

Heart-shaped leaves, chartreuse green to light yellow, intensifying to butter gold with narrow and irregular dark green margin. Lavender flowers mid season. 45cm.

Hosta 'Golden Tiara'

Green heart-shaped leaves margined brilliant gold. A profusion of lavender flowers in tall racemes. Rapidly forms a neat clump. 30cm.

Hosta 'Ground Master'

Lanceolate-ovate leaves to 25cm, matt dark green with broad, irregular white, wavy margin. Deep lavender flowers in tall spikes. 30cm.

Hosta 'Hadspan Blue'

Compact grower, smooth cordate leaves to 15cm, closely veined, deep blue and glaucous. Pale lavender or lilac flowers on short spikes. 40cm.

Hosta 'Kabitan'

Narrow, lance-shaped, very ruffled leaves, chartreuse yellow with fine dark green margin. Deep violet purple flowers in tall spikes. 30cm.

Hosta 'Little Aurora'

Small, gold leaves, somewhat cupped, puckered by irregular lines and veins. Flowers near-white in large racemes. 20cm.

Hosta 'Ruffles'

Mid-green ruffled leaves with impressed veins. Bell-shaped lilac flowers in tall racemes. 55cm.

Hosta 'Samurai'

Huge, spectacular, blue-green leaves, boldly margined creamy yellow. Off-white flowers in dense compact spike. 80cm.

Hosta 'Shade Fanfare'

Heartshaped, pale green to gold leaves with creamy-yellow margin. Masses of lavender flowers mid summer. 40cm.

Hosta 'Shade Master'

Vigorous grower, forms a dense mound of mid gold leaves. 60cm.

Hosta 'Sum and Substance'

Huge, smooth, very heavy textured, chartreuse yellow leaves to 45cm. Pale lavender flowers in tall spikes late summer. Strong grower. 90cm.

Hosta 'Sun Power'

Pointed, pale chartreuse to bright gold leaves, twisted and with wavy margins. Flowers pale lavender late summer. 60cm.

Hosta 'Treasure Trove'

Light green foliage irregularly margined creamy yellow, fading to white through summer. Lavender flowers. Robust. 45cm.

Hosta 'Vera Verde'

Narrow lance-shaped, somewhat rugose, rich green leaves, finely margined white. Small grower suitable for edging. Lavender flowers. 20cm.

Hosta 'Wide Brim'

Heavily puckered, dark bluish-green leaves with wide, irregular cream and gold margins. Lavender flowers in dense spires through summer. 45cm.

Hosta 'Zounds'

Glossy, heavily puckered leaves, gold with metallic sheen. Pale lavender flowers. Strong grower. 60cm.

HOWEA

A small genus of two species, slender, solitary, unarmed palms endemic in Lord Howe Island, from which the genus is named. An understory plant, found on steep slopes in moist forest areas, the magnificent Kentia Palm, introduced into Europe in the Victorian era and now highly valued throughout the world for indoor and outdoor decoration. As an indoor plant, Kentia Palm is sturdy, elegant and tolerant of considerable abuse.

At its best in maximum light away from prolonged direct sun. Feed early spring and autumn with a balanced fertilizer, keep adequately watered and take outdoors periodically for either rain or hose to cleanse dust off the foliage. Sponge or spray diluted Summer Oil to control scale and polish the leaves. In frost free conditions, Kentia Palm can be grown successfully outdoors in deeply worked, free draining, organically enriched soil, preferably in partial shade, at least when the plant is small. Water frequently and feed early spring and autumn.

Palmae.

Howea forsteriana
Kentia Palm, Thatch Palm

Abounds in sandy, lowland forests of Lord Howe Island. Forms a slender, dark green trunk with prominent rings, crowned with a magnificent head of graceful pinnate fronds with deep green, leathery leaflets. From a mass of brown fibres below the lowest leaves, multiple flower stalks appear followed by oblong, 3–4cm, orange to reddish brown fruit. Forsteriana — for William Forster, former NSW Senator. Evergreen. 6 × 3m.

HYDRANGEA

A genus of about 100 species of shrubs, trees or climbers from North and South America, China, Japan, Himalayas, Philippines and Indonesia named from the Greek *hydor*, water and *aggos*, a vessel, referring to cup-shaped seed heads. Hydrangeas are grown principally for flower although some species have ornamental leaves. Cultivars of H macrophylla with large 'Mophead' flowers of pink red and blue are a familiar sight in summer. Those with 'Lacecap' flowers are becoming more popular. Flower colour largely dependent on availability of aluminium, determined by soil pH and the response of various plants.

In general terms, deep blue colours occur in plants growing in soil with a pH of 4.5–5.5. This can be achieved and maintained with aluminium sulphate applied at seven to fourteen day intervals during the growth season at the rate of 85 grams dissolved in 14 litres of water. Pink or red colours are evident in alkaline soils, resulting from generous applications of lime or superphosphate. The treatment needs to be well in advance of flowering. In some gardens, obvious change may take several seasons, or where pH is extreme either way, soil chemistry may be better left as it is.

Hydrangeas exist with little attention, usually forming large plants with masses of smaller blooms. Some gardeners may accept this, but more compact plants with greatly enlarged flowerheads can be achieved with pruning and feeding. Blooms are usually formed on the terminals of previous season's wood so take care not to remove buds which are going to flower. Pruning consists of removing old flowered stems, cutting back to a pair of swollen buds near the base. Also remove any weak or congested growth. Old tired plants may be cut down to almost ground level. Thin out new shoots, leaving the strongest to form flower buds.

Fortnightly liquid feeding during the growth period and after flowers have formed helps to develop enormous heads. Plant in deeply worked, organically enriched, free-draining soil. Mulch freely and water generously through dry spell. Ideal for mass bedding, low screens, summer border colour and dramatic container plants for Christmas flowers.

All deciduous.

Hydrangea aspera
Star Hydrangea

Native to Himalayas, China, Taiwan and Indonesia. A spreading shrub with lanceolate to narrowly ovate leaves to 25 × 10cm, mid green and sparsely hairy above, densely covered with soft down beneath, margins with forward facing teeth. Inflorescence in 25cm flattened corymbs comprising a central zone of small, pale porcelain-blue fertile flowers surrounded by sterile, white or lilac-pink ray florets during summer. Extremely hardy, valued for foliage and flower. Syn H villosa. Aspera — rough. 3 × 3m.

Hydrangea macrophylla

Possibly the most familiar species, seen throughout temperate gardens as a rounded bush covered entirely with red, blue or white flowers. Over 500 cultivars recorded in two distinct flower forms — Mophead and Lacecap. As mentioned above, soil chemistry has a major influence on flower colour.

Approximate heights
Dwarf: 60cm
Medium: 60–90cm
Tall: Over 1m

Hydrangea macrophylla 'Blue Wave'
Lacecap. Corymbs of small blue fertile flowers open from green buds, surrounded by blue to pink single ray florets. Tall.

Hydrangea macrophylla 'Carton Baucle Kunhert'
Mophead. Pale blue heads of flower. Dwarf.

Hydrangea macrophylla 'Geoffrey Chadbund'
Improved European 'lacecap' type, responding well to chemical treatment for either blue or pink flowers. Medium to dwarf.

Hydrangea macrophylla 'Glory of Brussels'
Mophead. Larger than average flower heads, seen at its best in mid to rich pink with lime treatment. Medium to dwarf.

Hydrangea macrophylla 'Hadfield Rose'
Typical mophead, rich pink flowers. Tall.

Hydrangea macrophylla 'Heine Seidel'
Mophead. Large heads, carmine rose flowers. Tall.

Hydrangea macrophylla 'Holstein'
Mophead. Clear sky blue, large heads. Tall.

Hydrangea macrophylla 'Juliana'
Old-fashioned white, often edged blue. Largest mophead flowers of any white flowered cultivar to date. Vigorous and reliable. Tall.

Hydrangea macrophylla 'Lanarth White'
Lacecap. Small fertile flowers pink or blue, ray florets white. Medium.

Hydrangea macrophylla 'Le Cyge'
The Swan
Mophead. Charming white flowers, large rounded heads. Medium.

Hydrangea macrophylla 'Lemon Wave'
Lacecap. New shoots broadly banded white. Leaves mid green, marbled grey-green, margined creamy white, irregularly highlighted lemon-yellow. Small fertile gentian blue flowers encircled by soft creamy blue ray florets. Prefers semi-shade. Tall.

Hydrangea macrophylla 'Maculata'
Lacecap. Attractive grey-green variegated leaves broadly margined creamy white. Blue fertile flowers in flattened corymbs encircled by white ray florets. Tall.

Hydrangea macrophylla 'Matilda Geutges'
Mophead. Outstanding cultivar from Europe, responding easily and quickly to treatment making it possibly the best and most free flowering blue Hydrangea. Medium to dwarf.

Hydrangea macrophylla 'Mein Leibling'
Mophead, medium-size, light pink flowers. Tall.

Hydrangea macrophylla 'Pia'
Mophead. True genetic dwarf with normal sized pink to red irregular blooms, at its best when treated with lime. Perfectly hardy, excellent for rock gardens or tub culture. Grows less than 40cm in three years. Syn 'Winning Edge'. Syn 'Piamina'. Very dwarf.

Hydrangea macrophylla 'President Doumier'
Mophead. Dark crimson red flowers, large heads. Dwarf grower.

Hydrangea macrophylla 'President K Touchard'
Mophead. Large heads, clear pinkish red. Medium.

Hydrangea macrophylla 'Preziosa'
Mophead. Garden hybrid from H macrophylla × H serrata, forming a handsome shrub with purplish red stems and purple tinged leaves when young. Attractive globular heads of large rose-pink florets deepening to reddish purple in autumn. Tall.

Hydrangea macrophylla 'Red Emperor'
Mophead. Heads of the deepest crimson flowers. Dwarf.

Hydrangea macrophylla 'Red Star'
Mophead. Cherry red, large heads. Medium.

Hydrangea macrophylla 'Rose Supreme'
Mophead. Deep rose pink, large heads. Medium.

Hydrangea macrophylla 'Schandendorf Perle'
Mophead. Large heads of rich pink flowers. Dwarf.

Hydrangea macrophylla 'Sensation'
Mophead. Claimed as the first true bi-coloured Hydrangea. Florets rose pink margined white, borne in large heads. Prefers filtered sunlight and cool root conditions. 1 × 1m.

Hydrangea macrophylla 'Todi'
Mophead. Rosy red flowers, very large heads. Medium.

Hydrangea macrophylla 'Tosca'
Mophead. Double blooms in light pink. Dwarf.

Hydrangea macrophylla 'Tricolor'
Lacecap. Variegated leaves mottled pale and dark green, cream and yellow. Flattened corymbs of pale blue fertile flowers encircled by white ray florets. Tall.

Hydrangea macrophylla 'Triumph'
Mophead flowers with pointed, slightly curled petals, coloured clear pink in alkaline soils. Tall.

Hydrangea macrophylla 'Voster Fruhot'
Mophead. Smaller heads and florets, but regularly treated with lime will produce the most vivid red flowers. Very dwarf.

Hydrangea macrophylla 'White Wave'
Lacecap. Small fertile flowers pink or blue, encircled by pearly white ray florets. Tall.

Hydrangea paniculata 'Grandiflora'
Pee Gee Hydrangea
Beautiful Chinese and Japanese native amongst the showiest of flowering shrubs. Forms a multi-stemmed shrub densely clothed with dark green, ovate leaves to 15 × 8cm, turning bronze in autumn. Spectacular, erect, pyramidal heads of bloom to 30cm long, densely packed with 25mm creamy white florets, gradually deepening to pink or purplish rose as they mature. Flowers, which cover the entire bush during spring, last for months and are excellent for picking. Enormous flower heads can be developed by thinning out flowering shoots. Prune to any desired height or train as a single-trunk specimen. Paniculata — flowers in panicles. 2.5 × 2.5m.

Hydrangea quercifolia
Oak Leaf Hydrangea
Magnificent foliage shrub native to south eastern USA. Forms a broad, rounded bush with woolly shoots and handsome, broadly ovate-rounded, deeply lobed and prominently veined, oak-like, rich-green leaves to 20 × 17cm, white-downy beneath, turning orange, red and wine-purple in autumn, persisting well into winter. Flowers creamy white in open pyramidal clusters gradually turning delicate pink or violet. May be pruned to the ground early each spring to form a dense, compact shrub to 1m. Interesting container plant. Tolerant of drier conditions than other species. Quercifolia — leaves resembling quercus or oak. 2 × 1.5m.

Hydrangea robusta
Chinese native, forming a loose, spreading shrub, young shoots downy at first becoming

glabrous. Leaves rounded-ovate to 18 × 10cm, mid green, thick textured, margins sharply toothed, stiff-hairy above, dense bristly beneath. Inflorescence in large flattened corymbs to 30cm across with small blue fertile flowers and twenty or more 3–4cm white sterile ray florets summer through autumn. Extremely hardy. Robusta — strong in growth. 2.5 × 2.5m.

Hydrangea serrata 'Grayswood'
Species native to Japan and Korea. Attractive spreading shrub, young shoots finely pubescent at first, later glabrous. Leaves lanceolate to 15 × 7cm, glabrous above, prominently veined and short-hairy beneath, mid green through spring and summer, yellow-green and reddish brown in autumn. Inflorescence in flattened corymbs to 10cm across with blue fertile flowers encircled by 15mm sterile ray florets at first white, gradually turning rose and finally deep carmine red. 1.5 × 1m.

HYMENOSPORUM

Australian endemic genus of one species, found in Queensland and New South Wales, related to Pittosporum and one of Australia's outstanding flowering trees named from the Greek *hymen*, a membrane and *spora*, a seed, referring to seeds having a membranous wing.

Grown extensively for picturesque, open branch structure, handsome foliage and masses of creamy, fragrant flowers. Develops rapidly and adapts to varying climates and soils. Best in deeply worked, organically enriched, free-draining, moisture retentive soil. Mulch freely and water frequently during prolonged dry periods. Flowering seems more profuse in open sites, but shelter from prevailing winds is preferred. Thin out weedy limbs and strengthen branches by frequent pinching. Excellent lawn or patio specimen, against walls fences or backgrounds.

Pittosporaceae.

Hymenosporum flavum
Australian Frangipani
A small tree with graceful, erect, slender open form, handsome foliage and beautiful flowers. Branches often horizontal, bark brownish grey and fairly smooth. Leaves lanceolate, thin textured, glossy, dark green, paler beneath, clustered towards branch ends. Tubular, 3–4cm, flowers with five spreading lobes, at first pale cream, maturing orange-yellow, distinctly orange-blossom or honey scented, carried in terminal 20cm, umbel-shaped corymbs for long periods spring through summer. Blooms somewhat resemble tropical frangipani but no relationship exists between the two species. Flavum — pure yellow. Evergreen. 6 × 3m.

HYPERICUM

A large genus of over 400 species of herbs, shrubs and sub-shrubs found in temperate regions of the Northern Hemisphere named from the Greek *hyper*, above and *eikon*, picture or image from the fancied resemblance to a figure of the upper parts of the flower. It is interesting that the common name spelt 'wort' is a plant or herb. Apparently flowers of some species were thought to restrain evil at some ancient midsummer festival which later became the feast of St John.

Highly ornamental shrubs, characterized by open, cup-shaped, golden flowers with shapely ovary and stigma encircled with a central ring of stamens. They are easy to grow, make rapid progress, and few pests seem to bother them. Plant in sun or semi-shade, in deeply worked, free-draining soil and prune late winter to preserve shape. Taller growers add colour to shrub borders. Lower ones are good for rock gardens, ground or bank cover or wall spillers.

Hypericaceae. *All evergreen.*

Hypericum calycinum
Aaron's Beard, Creeping St John's Wort
Hardy evergreen shrub from southern Europe which spreads by vigorous, creeping underground branches. Erect, unbranched stems, leaves elliptic to narrowly ovate, to 10 × 4cm, leathery, medium-green in sun, yellowish in shade. Star-shaped, bright-yellow, 7cm flowers produced freely through summer.

Provides tough, dense ground cover in sun or shade, thriving under trees or in poor soil. Helps contain erosion on banks or hillsides. Clip or mow almost to ground level every two or three years. Calycinum — calyx-like. 30cm × 1m.

Hypericum cerastioides
Prostrate Goldflower
From southern Europe. A perennial herb with stems creeping at ground level, rooting at nodes, erect at the tips. Leaves elliptic to ovate, to 30 × 13mm, grey-green, thick papery texture and downy, paler beneath. From soft downy buds, an abundance of bright-yellow, star-shaped flowers to 45mm across covers the plant late spring through summer. Ground cover or front border plant for sunny, well-drained sites. Cerastioides — resembling Cerastium or chickweed. 10 × 90cm.

Hypericum 'Hidcote'
Excellent hybrid of uncertain origin regarded as one of the most popular of all flowering shrubs. Compact grower with arching or spreading branches. Leaves triangular-lanceolate to 6cm long, thick papery texture, conspicuously veined, paler beneath. Saucer-shaped, golden yellow flowers to 65mm across, produced in great quantities for long periods spring through autumn. Syn H 'Hidcote Gold'. 2 × 2m.

Hypericum leschenaultii
Vigorous and impressive shrub from the mountains of Java with erect slender stems. Leaves triangular-lanceolate to ovate, to 80 × 35mm, smooth, rich green, paler and glaucous beneath. Rich yellow, waxy, saucer-shaped, 7cm flowers with well rounded overlapping petals, and central ring of stamens produced in abundance in clusters of two or three through summer. Good shrub for colour highlights. Named for Louis T Leschenault de la Tour, French botanist. 2 × 1.5m.   **158**

Hypericum moserianum 'Tricolor'
Beautiful prostrate grower of hybrid origin with the most colourful leaves, marbled green, creamy white and pink held on reddish, slender arching stems which form a low mound. Yellow flowers to 5cm across, not freely produced. Stands on the merits of coloured foliage and graceful form. Use in rock gardens, ground cover, wall spiller etc. Named for Moser a French nurseryman. 5cm × 1m.

Hypericum olympicum 'Citrinum'
Charming dwarf shrub from southern Europe with erect, arched or spreading stems. Leaves oblong to elliptic to 36 × 12mm, grey-green and somewhat leathery. Masses of soft lemon-yellow flowers through summer. Olympicum — of Mount Olympus, high mountains of the Balkan Peninsula, Asia Minor etc. Citrinum — lemon coloured. 20 × 30cm.

Hypericum patulum 'Sungold'
Excellent dwarf shrub, forming a neat, spreading bush with arching branches. Large, 5–7cm, golden yellow flowers produced abundantly late summer. Excellent for massing, or highlighting foregrounds, perennial or shrub borders. Patulum — spreading. 60cm × 1m.

HYPOCALYMMA

A genus of 13 species all endemic to Western Australia, named from the Greek *hypo*, under and *kalymma*, a veil or covering, referring to the cap of the calyx. All species are most ornamental, usually small woody shrubs with slender wiry stems, good form, foliage and flower. Plant in partial shade or dappled shade in deeply worked, free-draining, moisture retentive, slightly acid to neutral sandy loam. Mulch freely and water regularly through dry periods. Apply slow-release, low phosphorus fertilizer sparingly spring and autumn. Hypocalymma responds to pruning to maintain good form and encourage strong growth.
   Myrtaceae. *All evergreen.*

Hypocalymma cordifolium 'Golden Veil'
Compact rounded shrub found in swampy ground in jarrah forests. Square stems and orbicular-cordate or heart-shaped 1cm leaves in opposite pairs, placed alternately along each erect branchlet. Cultivar 'Golden Veil' has red young twigs maturing light brown and olive-green leaves heavily margined cream. Small, unimpressive white flowers in the leaf axils during spring. Grown for its colourful young shoots and foliage. Cordifolium — heart-shaped leaves. 75 × 75cm.   **158**

Hypocalymma robustum
Swan River Myrtle
Beautiful small erect shrub from Western Australia thriving in sandy woodlands and jarrah forests. Shining, stiff, narrow linear to linear-lanceolate, 25mm leaves green with bronzy tone. Mauve-pink, 1cm flowers with prominent gold-tipped anthers and pleasant spicy fragrance, produced in crowded clusters from each leaf axil, appearing like miniature sprays of cherry or peach blossom. Outstanding species harvested commercially for cut blooms. Robustum — strong in growth. 90 × 90cm.

IDESIA

A genus of one species, a deciduous tree from southern Japan, Taiwan, China and Korea named for Eberhard Ides, 17th century Dutch explorer in China. Idesia is grown for incredible crops of shiny red berries. Being dioecious, both male and female trees need to be present for cross-pollination and berry production. For this reason, grafted pairs are preferable to seedling-grown trees. Plant in deeply worked, free-draining, moisture retentive, neutral to slightly acid soil in sun or light shade. Mulch freely and water frequently during the establishment period. Hardy to –15°, best when sheltered from strong wind, but otherwise not at all difficult to grow. Excellent lawn specimen.
   Flacourtiaceae.

Idesia polycarpa
Wonder Tree
A most handsome tree, native to China and Japan, with tiered, horizontal branch structure and broad crown. Thick cordate-ovate leaves to 20 × 20cm on red 20cm petioles, medium green with reddish veins, yellow in autumn. Small, yellowish green, fragrant but inconspicuous flowers borne in 30cm, terminal or axillary, drooping racemes appear in summer. On female trees they develop into showy crowded clusters of 10mm berries, at first green, then brown, and finally, waxy, bright red resembling loose bunches of small grapes, seen at their best after leaf fall. Berries untouched by birds and often retain their brilliance until new leaves appear in spring. Polycarpa — many fruited. Deciduous. 7 × 5m.   **159**

ILEX

A genus of over 400 species of evergreen and deciduous shrubs and trees from the temperate and tropical regions of the world named from the Latin term for *Quercus ilex*, evergreen oak. In the northern hemisphere, holly berries are an essential part of a white Christmas. Holly is adaptable to wide-ranging climatic and cultural conditions, thriving in temperate or cool regions, sun or shade, wet soil or dry.
   The preference is for deeply worked, free-draining, moisture retentive, slightly acid soil. Mulch freely with peat moss or granulated bark to keep roots cool, conserve moisture and eliminate weeding which may upset surface roots. Water frequently during dry periods until well established. Spray for Mealy bug or scale as required.
   Aquifoliaceae. *All evergreen.*

Ilex × altaclarensis 'Golden King'
Large almost spineless leaves to 10 × 6cm, rich green in the centre with broad bright golden-yellow margins. Excellent golden-variegated holly. Altaclarensis — of High-clere (Alta Clera) where it is thought to have originated. 3 × 2m.

Ilex × altaclarensis 'Lawsoniana'
Outstanding shrub, green stems streaked yellow, spineless leaves to 11 × 7cm, dark green with irregular central splashes of gold and lighter green. Female, but not very productive. 2 × 1.3m

Ilex aquifolium
Common Holly, English Holly
Extremely hardy, familiar evergreen forming a well-branched, densely foliaged, pyramidal specimen with glossy, deep green, elliptic or ovate, wavy-edged leaves to 9 × 6cm, margins sharply spined when young, probably as a protection from browsing stock. Leaf-spines practically absent on mature trees. Female trees bear liberal crops of red berries. Although capable of reaching 12m or more, as a garden specimen, its height would possibly be no more than 5m after 15–20 years. Aquifolium — Latin name for holly. 4 × 2m.

Ilex aquifolium 'Bacciflava'
Yellow-fruited Holly
Spectacular shrub though autumn and winter with heavy crops of bright yellow fruit. Syn I 'Fructu Luteo'. Bacciflava — pure yellow berries. Female. 3 × 2m.

Ilex aquifolium 'Crispa Aureopicta'
Thick leathery, twisted and curled leaves with a sharp spine at the tip, dark green with a central splash of yellow and pale green. Male. Crispa — finely waved or closely curled. 3 × 2m.

Ilex aquifolium 'Flavescens'
Moonlight Holly
Stems purplish red, leaves to 8 × 4cm, suffused canary yellow overlaid old gold which persists in full sun. Older leaves and those in shade mature green. New growth most attractive. Female, red fruited. Best in full sun. Flavescens — yellowish. 3 × 2m.

Ilex aquifolium 'Handsworth New Silver'
Attractive purple stems, spiny leaves oblong-elliptic to 9 × 3cm, deep green, mottled grey, broadly margined creamy white. Heavy crops of bright red berries. Female. 3 × 2m.

Ilex aquifolium 'J C Van Tol'
Excellent hybrid with smooth, dark purplish stems and black-green, shining, almost spineless elliptic leaves to 75 × 40mm. A self-fertile form, producing large clusters of shining red berries which remain throughout winter. 3 × 2m.

Ilex aquifolium 'Madame Briot'

Attractive purple stems, leaves broadly ovate to 10 × 5cm, strongly spiny, deep green mottled and margined bright yellow. Scarlet berries. Female. 3 × 2m.

Ilex aquifolium 'Silver Milkboy'

Attractive cultivar with spiny leaves, dark green with broad central creamy white blotch. Remove any green reverting leaves. Male. 3 × 2m.

Ilex aquifolium 'Silver Queen'

Dense, low growing bush with blackish purple stems and a tinge of pink in young shoots. Leaves elliptic to 6 × 4cm, spiny, dark green, marbled grey with creamy white central blotch. Male. 2 × 1.3m.

Ilex cornuta 'Burfordii'
Chinese Holly

Dense rounded compact bush with unusual rectangular leaves to 7 × 4cm, glossy, green, leathery, margins entire except for a short terminal spine. Bears large crops of red berries. Female. Cornuta — horned or horn-shaped. 2 × 2m.

Ilex crenata 'Convexa'
Box-leaved Holly, Japanese Holly

Neat dwarf holly from Japan and Korea with purple stems. Leaves ovate or elliptic to 30 × 15mm, surface blistered or puckered, glossy black-green and few spines. Good crops of black fruit. Suitable for topiary training. Female. Crenata — cut in rounded scallops. 75 × 75cm.

Ilex crenata 'Golden Gem'
Dwarf Golden Holly

Dwarf, compact form, bright golden foliage throughout the year. Female, but rarely flowers. Ideal for rock gardens or front border in full sun. 30 × 75cm.

Ilex crenata 'Mariesii'
Dwarf Japanese Holly

Dwarf, very slow-growing cultivar with tiny, crowded, orbicular or rounded, deep green leaves. Black berries. Hardly resembles a holly. Good for rock gardens, bonsai, etc. Female. 30 × 30cm.

INDIGOFERA

A genus of more than 700 shrubs and perennial herbs distributed throughout the warmer parts of the world with about 30 in Australia, named for the indigo dye obtained from some species. Grown for attractive foliage and masses of bloom summer through autumn. The listed species, distributed through all states is hardy and grows in almost any deeply worked, free-draining, slightly acid to neutral soil. Prefers semi-shade or dappled shade. Relatively hardy to zero temperatures. Flowers on current season's wood. Pinch tips through the growing season and prune hard after flowering. Old jaded plants may be cut almost to ground level.

Papilionaceae. *All evergreen.*

Indigofera australis
Austral Indigo

An attractive, rapid growing flowering shrub found in all States. Branches reddish brown, erect at first usually becoming pendulous or arching. Dainty, pinnate, bluish green leaves to 10 × 5cm, black hairy at first, with up to 21 ovate to oblong leaflets to 25 × 9mm, dark green to bluish green, paler beneath. Pea-shaped, mauve-pink flowers in loose axillary racemes somewhat resembling Hardenbergia, borne freely late winter through spring. Australis — southern. 1.5 × 1m.

Indigofera decora
Chinese Indigo

Native to Japan and China. Dwarf deciduous shrub with delicate, smooth, cylindrical, rusty brown to red stems. Pinnate leaves to 20cm long with up to 13 narrow-oblong, dark green glabrous leaflets to 40 × 15mm, pale green beneath. Clematis pink flowers in crowded 20cm racemes through spring and summer. Decora — decorative, becoming, lovely. 60 × 60cm.

IOCHROMA

A genus of about 20 species of shrubs or small trees from tropical America named from the Greek *ion*, violet and *chroma* from the flower colour of some species. Fast growing, soft-wooded shrubs of the potato family, related to many popular plants such as Cestrum, Datura, Petunia, Solanum and Streptosolen.

Iochromas are attractive flowering shrubs for frost-free gardens in areas with low rainfall and maximum sunshine. Plant in deeply worked, free-draining, moisture-retentive soil in full sun and sheltered from frost and strong wind. Suitable as espalier or free-standing shrub, but prune hard after flowering, and tip prune during the growth season.

Solanaceae.

Iochroma cyaneum

Fast-growing, soft-wooded, pubescent shrub from South America. Leaves lanceolate to 15 × 8cm, dull dark-green, greyish pubescence on both surfaces, margins entire and lightly waved. Purplish blue, 5cm, tubular or trumpet-shaped flowers borne in pendulous umbels up to 20 through summer and autumn. Cyaneum — blue. Evergreen. 2.5 × 1.5m.

ISOPOGON

Australian endemic genus of about 35 species mainly from Western Australia, with a few from temperate regions of eastern states, named from the Greek *isos*, equal and *pogon*, a beard referring to a beard-like fringe on the fruits. Isopogon is valued for exquisite cone-shaped flowerheads, ornamental leaves and decorative fruiting cones. Because of their long-lasting qualities, they're grown commercially for the cut-flower market. In suitable areas, they rank highly as ornamental flowering shrubs.

They prefer deeply worked, free-draining, acidic, sandy or loamy soil which is not over-rich and resent water-logging. Locate in plenty of sunshine or in dappled shade for part of the day. Most species withstand temperatures to −5°C. High summer humidity may be detrimental to development and can cause sudden collapse from root fungal attacks.

Feeding rarely necessary, but if you can't resist, give meagre dressings of slow-release fertilizer with little or no phosphorus. After establishment, watering seldom necessary and certainly not during hot summer conditions. Cut freely for indoors and prune after flowering. Tip pruning during the growth period will keep the bush compact and encourage strong flower production.

Proteaceae. *All evergreen.*

Isopogon anemonifolius
Broad-leaf Drumsticks

Attractive species from heathland and dry forests along the coast and Tablelands of New South Wales. Dwarf grower with hairy, often reddish young shoots, branches and branchlets. Leaves light green or minutely hairy, to 10 × 8cm, bipinnate, divided into three linear segments which are in turn divided into linear lobes, sometimes with prickly points. Yellow and cream flowers in conspicuous, globular, 4cm terminal heads borne profusely through spring and early summer followed by globular 2cm cones. Anemonifolius — leaves resembling Anemone. 1.3 × 1m.

Isopogon buxifolius

Low grower from south west Western Australia. Young shoots, ascending branches and branchlets somewhat hairy and reddish. Leaves ovate, to 35 × 15mm, thick, leathery, dull to greyish green, glabrous with a turned down point at the apex. Silky hairy, pale to deep mauve-pink flowers tipped purple carried in terminal, 3cm heads through winter and spring followed by 1cm cones. Buxifolia — leaves resembling Buxus. 1.3 × 1m.

ITEA

A genus of about 10 species of trees and shrubs from north east Asia and eastern North America, named from the Greek *itea*, a willow, referring to the catkins. Not a flamboyant shrub but admired for its graceful habit and long pendulous catkins. Useful as espalier against a dark wall or as a feature plant near ponds or water gardens. Plant in deeply worked, free-draining, moisture-retentive, slightly acid soil in sun or partial shade.
Grossulariaceae.

Itea illicifolia
Hollyleaf Sweetspire
Shrub or small holly-like tree from western China with graceful, lax, arching, open growth. Leaves elliptic to 12 × 7cm, glossy dark green above, paler and slightly scurfy beneath, margins spiny toothed. Small, fragrant greenish white flowers in closely packed, pendent racemes to 35cm long through late summer and autumn. Flowers more profusely in cooler climates. Illicifolia — holly-leaved. Evergreen. 3 × 2m.

JACARANDA

A genus of about 45 species of medium to large trees from tropical America, called by the Latinized Brazilian name. The familiar Brazilian Jacaranda mimosifolia appears to be the only generally cultivated species. Throughout the warm-temperate and subtropical world it never fails to totally envelope itself through spring and summer with spectacular blue flowers.
Jacaranda is a tree for warm sunny locations in climates where temperatures

don't fall below –4°C. Plant in deeply worked, free-draining, moisture-retentive soil. Stake securely when young and prune to encourage a sturdy single trunk. Excellent lawn or patio tree, picturesque when branching over a wall or driveway and pleasing when viewed from above a deck or upstairs window. Flowers may not appear for five years, but a handsome tree from the moment of planting. Although a tropical evergreen, leaves may fall in cooler climates.
Bignoniaceae.

Jacaranda mimosifolia
Jacaranda
Amongst the world's most beautiful and greatly admired trees. Handsome form with open, irregular head, usually with single trunk. Soft, ferny bipinnate leaves to 45cm long, finely divided into myriads of tiny, oval leaflets. Mauve-blue, tubular, bignonia-like, 5cm flowers with flaring trumpets, borne in 30cm terminal racemes spring through summer, followed by roundish, flat, disc-shaped seed capsules, useful in floral arrangements. Mimosifolia — mimosa-like leaves. Semi-evergreen. 7 × 5m.   **158**

JUNIPERUS

A genus of about 55 hardy evergreen trees and shrubs widely distributed through cold and warmer regions of the northern hemisphere named from the Latin *iuniperus*, the juniper tree. (*i* replaces *j*). Either in their own right or grouped with chamaecyparis or other conifers, Junipers are fine subjects for modern gardens. Extensive hybridizing has provided a wide range of types, colours and textures.
Prostrate forms excellent for ground covers, permanent low foundation plants or planter boxes. Medium growers come as wide-spreaders, columns or pyramids while formal or informal outlines can be found in tall Junipers. Rugged growth and vigorous rooting system enables Junipers to withstand strong winds, considerable variation in climatic and soil conditions. They rank highly in low-maintenance gardens, providing year-round impact under extreme cultural conditions.
Cupressaceae. *All listed Junipers evergreen.*

Juniperus chinensis
Chinese Juniper
Important ornamental species and parent of numerous excellent cultivars. Found natur-

ally over a wide area of the Himalayas, China and Japan. Dense pyramidal compact tree with semi-informal structure. Deep-green, awl-shaped juvenile leaves and scale-like adult leaves appear at the same time. Hardy, tolerant of extremes, quick growing. May be sheared to almost any shape. Chinensis — of China. 3 × 2.5m.

Juniperus chinensis 'Aurea'
Young's Golden Juniper
Tall, slender, columnar habit with lacy, bright yellow foliage. Retains colour well through winter. Both adult and juvenile foliage on the same plant. Tends to burn in full sun. 1.5m × 75cm.

Juniperus chinensis 'Blue Alp'
Similar shape to African Juniper, a little more open and faster growing but with very blue foliage. 1.5 × 1.25m.

Juniperus chinensis 'Blue Point'
Dense pyramidal form with blue-grey foliage. Formal outline resembles a large teardrop. 2.5 × 1.5m.

Juniperus chinensis 'Columnaris Glauca'
Dense columnar habit, slightly wider at the base, gradually tapering to a point. Foliage awl-shaped, sharply pointed and attractive glaucous blue. 2.5 × 1m.

Juniperus chinensis 'Kaizuka'
Hollywood Juniper
Fascinating oriental appearance. Long gracefully curving branches held at all angles, growing in a distinctly spiralling, upward direction. Scale-like, bright green foliage in dense clusters. Perfect isolated focal point or architectural feature plant. 2 × 1m.

Juniperus chinensis 'Kaizuka Variegata'
Interesting sport of Hollywood Juniper. Without spiralling branches but slowly develops a narrow columnar outline. Foliage smooth to the touch, highlighted with bold patches of bright creamy yellow. 1.8m × 30cm.

Juniperus chinensis 'Kuriwao Gold'
Spreading or wide fountain form with gracefully pendulous tips. Fresh golden-yellow foliage throughout the year, most intense during winter. Relatively slow grower, tolerant of wind and salt air. 1 × 1m.

Juniperus chinensis 'Pyramidalis'
Dense, slow grower with neat, formal, compact, pyramidal outline. Foliage almost entirely juvenile and prickly, blue green with silvery sheen. Most attractive. 1.5 × 1.25m.

Juniperus chinensis 'Robusta Green'
Majestic and outstanding cultivar. Dense, tufted, brilliant blue-green foliage. Rugged, upright, irregular pyramidal habit. 2 × 1m.

Juniperus chinensis 'San Jose'
Excellent low-growing form with sage green, whipcord and juvenile foliage. Slow grower, at its best when exposed to the elements. Ground or bank cover to 30cm high with a spread of 2m.

Juniperus chinensis 'Spartan'
Quickly forms a dense, compact pyramid. Rich dark green foliage. Excellent, hardy and ornamental. 3 × 1.5m.

Juniperus chinensis 'Variegata'
Cream Fleck Juniper
Fascinating, irregular, semi-pyramidal growth pattern, building gradually to dramatic informal oriental outline. Glaucous green foliage interspersed with creamy white sprigs. 2.5 × 1m.

Juniperus communis
Common Juniper
Widely distributed through North America, eastward through Europe, Asia to Korea and Japan. Valuable species usually seen as an erect bush with awl-shaped, silver-backed, prickly leaves. Berries rounded, 6mm across, black, covered with glaucous bloom and take two or three years to ripen. Rarely used ornamentally, but some of the finest conifers are found amongst its cultivars. Communis — common or growing in company. 3.5 × 2m.

Juniperus communis 'Compressa'
Dwarf Column Juniper
Slender, spire-like dwarf with short, erect branchlets, crowded grey-green, awl-shaped prickly leaves. Forms a petite upright column ideal for miniature gardens or containers. 75 × 30cm.

Juniperus communis 'Depressa Aurea'
Delightful ground hugging, prostrate shrub with closely woven foliage, bright buttery yellow in spring turning rich golden bronze in winter. Striking contrast beneath taller green conifers and excellent wall spiller. Depressa — flattened, pressed down. 20cm × 1.5m.

Juniperus communis 'Depressed Star'
Dense low-spreading bun-shaped conifer with glistening lime-green foliage ascending at the tips. Attractive form, year round colour especially in full spring growth. Ground cover, spot colour or contrast. 75cm × 1.25m.

Juniperus communis 'Gold Cone'
Upright conical compact habit, tightly packed glaucous foliage tipped canary yellow. Yellow toning prominent during spring and summer. 1.2m × 75cm.

Juniperus communis 'Repanda'
Prostrate ground-hugging carpet-forming juniper with dark green, densely packed leaves. Excellent ground cover, artistic over rocks. Repanda — with slightly waved margins. 15cm × 1.5m.

Juniperus communis 'Suecica Nana'
Not unlike J c 'Compressa' in its general appearance, with narrow erect outline and dense compact glaucous foliage appearing to be regularly shorn. Remove any obviously reverting shoots. Good hardy accent conifer. Suecica — from Sweden. 2m × 60cm.

Juniperus conferta
Shore Juniper
Native to Japan and Sakhalin where it grows on sandy sea shores. Dense, prostrate species with supple stems and short ascending branchlets forming dense, prickly carpets of bright apple-green foliage. Globose 1cm fruit, purplish black and covered with bloom. Vigorous rich-textured wall spiller and ground cover. Conferta — crowded. 20cm × 2m.   **158**

Juniperus conferta 'Blue Pacific'
Reasonably fast and clean-growing ground cover with prominent soft non-prickly, bluish green foliage. Good for filling between shrubs or trees, cascading over rocks or spilling over banks or walls. 25cm × 3m.

Juniperus conferta 'Emerald Ruffles'
Selected clone of Shore Juniper with attractive bright green foliage, spreading ground-cover form and upright lateral shoots with ruffled leaves giving a soft billowy appearance. 30cm × 3m.

Juniperus davurica 'Expansa'
Robust wide-spreader with ground-hugging appearance but which has rigid horizontal branches supported a few centimetres above the ground, making it easier to weed and cultivate beneath it. Obvious mixture of juvenile and adult, rich green foliage. 60cm × 1.5m.

Juniperus davurica 'Expansa Aureospicata'
General appearance as for Expansa Variegata, but with mainly juvenile foliage, less vigorous growth habit and butter-yellow variegations. 50cm × 1.3m.

Juniperus horizontalis
Creeping Juniper
North America native species found inhabiting sea cliffs, gravelly slopes and swamps. Dwarf prostrate grower with long branches eventually forming carpets several metres across, glaucous green, grey green, blue, often with plum or purple shades in winter. 10cm × 2m.

Juniperus horizontalis 'Bar Harbor'
Vigorous, prostrate ground cover with long branches spreading in all directions. Foliage soft-grey blue in summer, deep mauve with silvery bloom in winter. Beautiful and functional. 10cm × 1.5m.

Juniperus horizontalis 'Blue Chip'
Lays its branches flat on the ground in overlapping layers to completely cover the ground with a beautiful carpet of silvery blue foliage intensifying rich blue in winter. Moderate growth rate. 10cm × 2m.

Juniperus horizontalis 'Glauca'
Completely prostrate habit, with dense whipcord steel-blue foliage intensifying during winter. New growth superimposed on old, gradually building up a thick, spongy living carpet. Ideal ground or rock cover and wall spiller. 15cm × 2m.

Juniperus horizontalis 'Hughes'
Neat, vigorous ground cover, with distinctive silvery blue foliage. 10cm × 2m.

Juniperus horizontalis 'Plumosa'
Andorra Juniper
Dense compact form with graceful branches gradually ascending at 45°, clothed with feathery, grey-green, awl-shaped leaves turning rich purplish plum in winter. Soft plumy appearance. 75cm × 1.25m.

Juniperus horizontalis 'Turquoise Spreader'
Bright-blue variation of these low carpet forming Junipers. Moderate growth rate. 10cm × 2m.

Juniperus × media
The term × media refers to cultivars of J chinensis × J sabina in which the characteristics of both parents are evident. Some are thought to be natural hybrids from north east Asia and include some of the most beautiful forms and colourings. Media — intermediate between parents.

Juniperus × media 'Blaauw'
Compact erect vase shape with gracefully ascending branches turning outwards at the tips. Dense scale-like, heavy textured, deep greyish blue leaves in feathery sprays.

Colour persists throughout the year. Slow grower with great charm. 1.25m × 75cm.

Juniperus × media 'Gold Coast'
Juniper of great merit with low spreading graceful fountain-like habit and fine golden foliage. Bright lime-yellow new growth, striking in spring. Compact moderate grower. 60cm × 1.5m.

Juniperus × media 'Milky Way'
Handsome low but wide spreader with bold arching branches and gracefully pendulous tips. Foliage rich green prominently flecked or stippled creamy white. 75cm × 2m.

Juniperus × media 'Mint Julep'
Low shrub with graceful fountain form and rich mint green foliage. Young leaves lime green, a bright feature in spring. Neat habit, good contrast, very hardy. 1 × 1m.

Juniperus × media 'Pfitzeriana Aurea'
Golden Pfitzer
Handsome wide-spreading shrub with bold arching branches. Gracefully pendulous golden yellow tips in summer, yellowish green in winter. Excellent feature, filler, ground or bank cover. 75cm × 2m.

Juniperus × media 'Pfitzeriana Glauca'
Blue Pfitzer
Graceful spreading or wide fountain form with branches rising at 45° with pendulous tips. Somewhat denser than other Pfitzers and foliage rich glaucous blue overlaid silvery grey. Plant in bold groups for high visual impact. 75cm × 1.5m.

Juniperus × media 'Plumosa Aurea'
Gold Dust Juniper
Broad spreading shrub with ascending, arching branches, gracefully curving at the tips, densely clothed with plumose sprays of scale-like, deep golden yellow foliage, intensifying to bronze-gold in winter. Slow growing. High decorative value. 75cm × 1.25m.

Juniperus × media 'Sulphur Spray'
Gracefully ascending to prostrate branch pattern. Foliage soft light green with unusual sulphur tips. Handsome blending of colour and form. 75 × 75cm.

Juniperus procumbens
Creeping Juniper
Naturally inhabits coastal areas of Japan. Dwarf wide-spreading plant with long stiff branches. Growing tips raised upwards, branches crowded with awl-shaped, glaucous green, sharply pointed leaves. Vigorous ground cover for open sunny locations. Procumbens — prostrate. 20cm × 2m.

Juniperus procumbens 'Nana'
More petite in all respects to above, ideally suited to rock garden pockets or limited spaces. Builds compact cushions of glaucous, apple-green foliage, maturing bluish green. 20cm × 1.2m.

Juniperus recurva 'Coxii'
Coffin Juniper
Unusual juniper from upper Burma. Forms a small pyramidal tree with long slender pendulous branches and glaucous or silvery green foliage. Common name is said to refer to long lasting properties of the timber, highly esteemed by the Chinese for coffins. Recurva — curved backwards. 3 × 2m.

Juniperus sabina 'Blue Danube'
Species widely distributed from mountains of southern and central Europe to the Caucasus. Extremely variable procumbent, wide spreading shrub with slender plumose branches. 'Blue Danube' is a delightful low spreading form with prostrate branches curving upwards at the tips and with crowded branchlets. Leaves mostly scale-like, soft greyish green with blue overtones. Dense ground cover and vigorous grower. 75cm × 2m.

Juniperus sabina 'Tamariscifolia'
Low spreading shrub with horizontal overlapping branches, densely clothed with attractive blue-green foliage. Perfect ground cover. 25cm × 2m.

Juniperus scopulorum 'Blue Heaven'
Rocky Mountain Juniper
Species native to British Columbia, Arizona and Texas, a small cypress-like tree with conical form. 'Blue Heaven' has neat compact pyramidal outline and exceptionally blue foliage all year round. Scopulorum — of cliffs, crags and projecting rocks. 2 × 1m.

Juniperus scopulorum 'Grey Gleam'
Trim narrow columnar spire with attractive silvery grey foliage. A plant of great symmetry durability and permanence, handsome throughout the year especially in winter when its silvery colour is more accentuated. Slow grower and maintains precise form with trimming. 1m × 25cm.

Juniperus scopulorum 'Moonglow'
One of the best silver upright Junipers. Excellent formal pyramid of intense silver-blue. Neat and eye-catching. 2m × 60cm.

Juniperus scopulorum 'Pathfinder'
Distinctive upright and erect grower with neat pyramidal form and soft fine silvery blue-grey foliage. 3 × 1m.

Juniperus squamata 'Blue Star'
Excellent blue dwarf Juniper with low compact cushion or bun form and bright steel-blue foliage in glaucous, star-like clusters in the style of the well known Meyer Juniper. Squamata — with small scale-like leaves. 50cm × 1m.

Juniperus squamata 'Meyeri'
Meyer Juniper
Variable species widely distributed throughout Asia from Afghanistan eastwards to China. 'Meyeri' has gracefully informal branching pattern with semi-erect and angular branches packed with glaucous blue foliage with distinct silvery sheen. 1.5 × 1m.

Juniperus squamata 'Pygmaea'
A smaller member of the squamata family forming a low compact mound or dwarf cushion with fine glaucous green to bronzy green foliage. Ideal rockery subject. 1 × 1m.

Juniperus squamata 'Wilsoni'
Refined edition of Meyer Juniper with graceful informal branches, semi-erect form and typical nodding tips. Finer bright green foliage with two bluish white bands on the inner side giving the bush a distinct silvery effect in certain lights. 1.3 × 1.3m.

Juniperus taxifolia 'Lutchuensis'
Ground hugging carpet-juniper with soft, closely knit, pastel green foliage. One of the few conifers to lay flat over the face of a wall, ideal as ground cover or spilling over rocks. Taxifolia — with leaves like Taxus or Yew. 10cm × 1.5m.

Juniperus virginiana 'Silver Spreader'
North American species. One of the few low-growers in the virginiana group. Informal layers of horizontal branches grow in all directions, densely covered with silvery grey-green foliage. First class low accent shrub. Virginiana — Virginian. 50cm × 2m.

Juniperus virginiana 'Skyrocket'
Pencil Juniper
A natural seedling, perhaps the slenderest of all columnar conifers. Strong, reasonably rapid grower with dense strictly erect branches, tapering to a terminal point and well covered with blue-grey foliage. Good accent plant wherever a strong vertical line is needed. 2.5 × 50cm.

A genus of some 40 species of perennial herbs or shrubs from tropical America,

named for James Justice, celebrated 18th century Scottish gardener. Beautiful soft-wooded plants which need to be grown in deeply worked, free-draining, organically enriched soil in sun or semi-shade, protected from frost and strong wind. Ideal along sunny walls, sheltered from cold and excessive moisture by overhanging eaves. Prune after flowering.

Acanthaceae. *All evergreen.*

Justicia carnea
Brazilian Plume Flower, Flamingo Plant
Charming, soft-wooded plant often seen thriving in dry, sheltered positions against walls or fences. Erect, purplish stems, leaves ovate, to 25cm long, dark-green with soft fine hairs above, purplish beneath, margins entire. Deep pink, curved-tubular hooded flowers in dense, compact terminal plumes appear for long periods through summer and autumn. Decorative on the bush or picked for indoors. Syn Jacobinia carnea. Carnea — flesh-coloured. 1.5 × 1m.   **158**

Justicia rissinii
Paradise Plant
Neat, dwarf-growing, floriferous Brazilian shrub. Forms a small rounded, multi-branched plant, leaves oblong-elliptic to obovate, 2cm long, mid green, margins entire. Masses of 25mm, pendent, tubular, bright red flowers tipped bright yellow, borne singly in leaf axils throughout the whole plant, spring through summer and into winter. Syn Jacobinia pauciflora. 75 × 75cm.

A genus of seven species of shrubs from North America and Cuba named for Peter Kalm, 18th century Swedish botanist and student of Linnaeus who travelled widely in USA. Kalmias are simply adored for their exquisite flowers produced through spring and summer. Mountain Laurel grows at high altitudes in rocky conditions as an understorey plant in forests of eastern USA, in a cool moist atmosphere subject to persistent rainfall and good drainage, mulched freely from fallen leaves of large deciduous trees and with just the right amount of sunlight.

Related to Azaleas and Rhododendrons, they grow under similar conditions, surviving temperatures as low as −18°C, preferring frosty winters to mild areas with high summer humidity. Locate in a cool semi-shady position beneath large deciduous trees, in shade

houses or on the cool side of a wall.

Plant in deeply worked, organically enriched, free-draining, moisture-retentive, sandy loam with a pH 4.5 to 5.5. Mulch freely with peat moss or similar material to insulate the roots and eliminate weeding and cultivation which may disturb surface roots. Feed sparingly with acid fertilizer. During dry spells, water deeply and spray the foliage. Apart from removing spent flowers or crossed branches, pruning is unnecessary. A delightful shrub worth every effort to grow at least one.

Ericaceae. *All evergreen.*

Kalmia latifolia
Calico Bush, Mountain Laurel
Native to eastern USA, the State Flower of Pennsylvania. Forms an open, rounded bush with glossy, elliptic-lanceolate, laurel-like leaves to 12 × 3cm, deep green above, paler beneath. Colourful buds resemble starry drops of icing ready to decorate a birthday cake. Exquisite rose pink, 25mm flowers shaped like saucers, lampshades or open parachutes, borne in terminal 15cm corymbs. Unopened buds and flowers appear together over long periods through spring. Irresistibly beautiful. Latifolia — broad-leaved. 2 × 1.5m.   **159**

Kalmia latifolia 'Bullseye'
Reddish white buds, flowers with conspicuous reddish purple central zone and white margins. Leaves tinged red. 1.5 × 1m.

Kalmia latifolia 'Carousel'
Buds reddish white. Flowers banded and rayed deep red with white central zone and distinctive white border. Strong grower, rich green foliage. 1.5 × 1m.

Kalmia latifolia 'Elf'
Small compact grower, buds light pink, flowers palest pink almost white. 1.2 × 1m.

Kalmia latifolia 'Freckles'
Light pink buds, flowers palest pink to white with an inner band of small purple or maroon spots. 1.5 × 1m.

Kalmia latifolia 'Nipmuck'
Intense red buds open to soft pink flowers. 1.5 × 1m.

Kalmia latifolia 'Ostbo Red'
Buds deep red, opening clear pink, becoming deep pink. 1.2 × 1m.

Kalmia latifolia 'Pink Charm'
Sturdy vigorous cultivar. Warm salmon pink buds, rich pink flowers. Attractive foliage and form. 1.2 × 1m.

Kalmia latifolia 'Yankee Doodle'
Buds red, opening to white flowers flushed pink with prominent inner band of maroon near margin. Tidy, robust grower. 1.2 × 1m.

A genus of one species, a shrub from China and Japan, named for William Kerr, 18th century Kew gardener and plant collector. Admired for its green stems, rich green foliage and intense yellow flowers. Enjoys full sun, preferably shaded from midday heat. Plant in deeply worked, free-draining, moisture retentive soil. Mulch freely and water during dry periods. Blooms borne on growth from the previous season, so prune only to remove flowered or overcrowding stems. Old tired bushes may be rejuvenated by pruning hard to the base late winter. Hardy to −20°C.

Rosaceae. *All deciduous.*

Kerria japonica
Japanese Rose, Jew's Mallow
Builds a colony of green, glabrous, rod-like stems from underground suckers. Leaves ovate to 70 × 35mm, clear deep-green, coarsely serrated and prominently veined, yellow in autumn. Masses of single, bright golden yellow, 5cm flowers scattered along arching branches throughout the entire bush through spring. Effective in shrub borders, against walls or fences. Japonica — of Japan. 1.5 × 1.2m.

Kerria japonica 'Pleniflora'
Batchelor's Button
Vigorous form with sturdier more stiffly erect stems and stronger suckering habit. Masses of fully double, bright golden yellow flowers wreath every arching stem through spring. Excellent for cutting. Pleniflora — with double flowers. 1.5 × 1.2m.

Kerria japonica 'Variegata'
Variegated Japanese Rose
Smaller grower with variegated leaves deeply and irregularly margined white. Bright yellow single flowers in spring. Prefers semi or dappled shade. 1.2 × 1m.

A genus of three species of trees and shrubs from New Caledonia and New Zealand named for Thomas Andrew

Knight (1759–1838) pomologist and past president of the London Horticultural Society. One of the few New Zealand members of the Protea family. An outstanding, poplar-like tree, first discovered during Cook's initial voyage. Finely grained timber referred to as New Zealand oak, prized for fine woodwork. Enjoys association with other trees when young, maturing into a stately specimen. Branches and roots keep within bounds with minimal pruning. Average well-worked soils and summer moisture until established.

Proteaceae.

Knightia excelsa
Rewarewa
Widely distributed from North Cape to Marlborough Sounds. Forms a slender erect tapering tree with poplar-like form, handsome foliage and ornamental flowers. New shoots and undersides of young leaves covered with fine brown tomentum. Leaves linear lanceolate, to 15 × 4cm, leathery, deep-green, glossy, prominent midrib, margins coarsely and bluntly toothed. Curious reddish brown flowers with protruding white tipped anthers appear in dense 7cm racemes spring through early summer, attracting native birds which enjoy nectar secreted from four small glands at the base of each flower. Curious 5cm seed vessels split in two when ripe, each shaped like a miniature canoe. Excelsa — tall. Evergreen. 7 × 2m. **159**

KOELREUTERIA

A small genus of about three species of shrubs or trees from China and Taiwan named for Joseph G Koelreuter, 18th century German professor of botany and national history. Golden Rain Tree has many talents — summer flowers, colourful autumn fruit, handsome leaves and good form.

Tolerant of cold, heat, drought, a reasonable amount of wind and alkaline soil, but at its best in temperate or subtropical areas with hot summers, dry autumns and cold winters. Serves well as a lawn or garden shade tree or street tree. Quite indifferent to soil conditions in full sun or partial shade. Plant in deeply worked, free-draining soil, water regularly when young and prune to shape. Drops myriads of seeds which germinate freely. Pull out unwanted seedlings as they appear.

Sapindaceae.

Koelreuteria paniculata
Golden Rain Tree, Varnish Tree
Interesting small tree from northern China with picturesque, open spreading form. Pinnate leaves to 40cm long with 7–15 narrowly ovate, toothed or lobed, 3–8cm, deep green leaflets. Foliage turns brilliant yellow in autumn in cooler areas. During summer, 12mm, yellow, four-petalled flowers appear in erect, 30cm, loose pyramidal clusters. The whole tree is spectacular for long periods in autumn as curious inflated papery capsules resembling clusters of small Chinese lanterns appear, turning from pale green through pink or light red and finally brown, containing dark brown pea-sized seeds. Paniculata — with flowers in panicles. Deciduous. 6 × 3m. **158**

KOLKWITZIA

A monotypic genus named for Richard Kolkwitz, professor of botany in Berlin early 20th century. Native of central China where the species is found among rocky areas in excess of 3000m. Admired for great masses of beautiful flowers and easy culture.

Performs better in cold climates, hardy to –20°C although late frosts may burn new growth. Plant in fertile, free-draining soil in full sun. Mulch freely and water during dry periods. To enjoy fruit display, lightly thin out wood which has flowered the previous year. Avoid heavy trimming which takes away next year's flowering wood. However, old tired plants may be cut to ground level for growth renewal. Excellent for colour amongst shrubs, herbaceous perennials or annuals.

Caprifoliaceae.

Kolkwitzia amabilis 'Pink Cloud'
Beauty Bush
This selected cultivar forms a dense, multi-branched shrub, uppermost stems gracefully arching. Broad-ovate leaves to 75 × 50mm, dull green, slightly hairy, margins finely serrated. Bright rosy pink buds burst into masses of 15mm, bell-shaped, five-lobed flowers, pink outside, orange throat and dots within, late spring and early summer followed by conspicuous pinky brown, bristly, egg-shaped fruits which prolong the display of colour. Blooms better as the bush ages and when grown under harsh conditions. Brown flaky bark gradually peels from the stems during winter. Amabilis — lovely. Deciduous. 2 × 2m.

KUNZEA

Australian endemic genus of about 25 species of shrubs or small trees named for Gustav Kunze, 19th century professor of botany at Leipzig.

Kunzea has attractive fluffy flowers largely comprised of anthers. Good drainage and full sun and light stony or sandy soil are the main cultural requirements. Prune to shape after flowering and avoid overfeeding or overwatering.

Myrtaceae. *All evergreen.*

Kunzea baxteri
Open, spreading shrub with narrow, fresh green, linear-oblong leaves about 2cm long, radiating in all directions. Spectacular bottlebrush flowers, 7cm long and as wide, comprise rich red or crimson stamens with contrasting yellow anthers freely produced through spring and summer. May take two or three years before blooming seriously. From Western Australia. Named for William Baxter. 19th century English gardener and plant collector. 2 × 2m.

Kunzea ericifolia
Slightly pendulous shrub with open growth habit, heath-like leaves and globular heads of yellow flowers during spring. Inclined to be short-lived in cultivation. From Western Australia. Ericifolia — with heath-like leaves. Syn K vestita. 1.5 × 1m.

Kunzea parvifolia
Open twiggy shrub from Victoria and New South Wales, with small, heath-like, soft downy leaves less than 5mm long. Attractive during summer when every twig produces terminal clusters of fluffy, rounded, deep mauve flowers. Very hardy. Parvifolia — small leafed. 1.5 × 1.5m.

LABURNOCYTISUS

Laburnocytisus adamii
A graft hybrid between the yellow-flowered Laburnum anagyroides and lilac-flushed-crimson flowered Chamaecytisus purpureus. The process of graft-hybridization results in a plant constructed of tissues of differing genetic composition, a process known as chimaera. In this case, the resulting tree somewhat resembles L anagyroides but with smaller leaflets to 65mm and, if the tree remains true to type, the inflorescence will be 18cm racemes of attractive smaller,

yellow flowers tinged purple appearing coppery pink.

Frequently the chimaera breaks down leading to the fascinating oddity of flowers and leaves of both parents appearing together with blooms halfway between the two. So in L adamii, expect racemes of golden yellow and purple as well as coppery pink on the same tree. Flowers appear in spring. Culture as for Laburnum. Leguminosae. Deciduous. 3.5 × 2.5m

LABURNUM

A genus of only three species of trees or shrubs from southern Europe and western Asia, called by the classical Latin name. Sometimes referred to as Golden Chain, descriptive of their drooping racemes of yellow pea-shaped flowers. All parts of the plants are poisonous, particularly the seeds. Remove and burn them as they form. This also helps preserve the plant's vitality. Plant in deeply worked, fertile, free-draining, moisture-retentive soil in full sun. Mulch freely and water during dry periods. Use as a lawn specimen or blend with other shrubs for colour accent. Stake and train from an early age for good form.

Fabaceae. *All deciduous.*

Laburnum alpinum
Scotch Laburnum, Alpine Golden Chain
More compact form than Common Laburnum. Trifoliate, shining deep green leaves with 8cm, elliptic leaflets, paler and slightly hairy beneath. Fragrant, golden yellow flowers in drooping 35cm+ racemes in spring, followed by flattened glabrous shining pods. From central and southern Europe. Alpinum — from high mountains. 3.5 × 2.5m.

Laburnum anagyroides
Common Laburnum, Golden Chain
A spectacular sight early summer when covered with pendulous 20cm racemes of beautiful golden flowers like glittering chains. Characteristic tri-lobed leaves with greyish, elliptic-obovate, 8cm leaflets, silky hairy beneath when young. European. Anagyroides — resembling anagris, a genus of shrubs. 4 × 2m.

Laburnum × watereri
Selected hybrid from L anagyroides and L alpinum. Delightful small tree with glossy trifoliate leaves with elliptic, 7cm leaflets. Rich golden yellow fragrant flowers in 50cm slender pendent racemes.

Resembles L Vossii, but blooms a little later in spring. 3 × 2m.   **159**

Laburnum × watereri 'Vossii'
Forms a small tree with compact rounded head and ascending branches. A magnificent sight late spring when festooned with deep golden yellow floral chains to 60cm long. Both hybrids set very few or no seed pods. 3 × 2m.

LAGERSTROEMIA

The genus which includes more than 50 evergreen and deciduous species from south east Asia, New Guinea and Australia is named for Magnus von Lagerstroem of Gottenburg, an 18th century merchant, and friend of renowned botanist Linnaeus. Crepe Myrtles are elegant flowering shrubs which smother themselves with attractive, crepe paper-like flowers all summer through. The picturesque branch pattern and smooth grey or light brown bark are also attractive features.

Plant Crepe Myrtles in full sun, in average, deeply worked, free-draining, slightly acid soil with no lime. Feed moderately and provide occasional deep watering in dry periods. Remove spent flower heads and untidy twigs on dwarf-growing plants. Larger growers may be pruned more heavily to the desired size and shape. Single trunks with dense rounded head, or a multi-stemmed bush can be encouraged with early training. Crepe Myrtles revel in heat and show this with vivid garden colour all summer through.

Lythraceae. *All deciduous.*

Lagerstroemia indica
Crepe Myrtle
Native to China and Korea, a beautiful large shrub with attractively mottled stems. Leaves to 8cm long, light green with bronzy toning at first, maturing deep green, turning to shades of yellow, orange and red over a dry winter. Magnificent cone-shaped panicles of bloom from 15–30cm high and almost as wide, packed with 4cm, crinkled, crepe-like, six petalled flowers, borne in terminal panicles almost obscuring the foliage through summer.

Numerous magnificent cultivars are available, in white, lavender, pink or crimson. Indica — Indian, an epithet casually applied by early explorers to numerous plants discovered anywhere in the east. 3 × 2m.

Lagerstroemia indica 'Bergerac'
Masses of crimped magenta blossoms borne in large terminal panicles mid summer through autumn. Upright bushy specimen, selected for its long flowering season. 3.5 × 2.5m.

Lagerstroemia indica 'Kimono'
Pure white crepe flowers enhanced by golden stamens. Compact bushy grower. 2.5 × 2m.

Lagerstroemia indica 'La Mousson'
Showy, vivid pink crepe blossoms freely produced mid summer through autumn. Possibly the earliest to flower. Excellent bush, effective when trained as a standard specimen. 3 × 2m.

Lagerstroemia indica 'Petite Embers'
Compact bushy grower, with rich rosy red crepe flowers in profusion on young growths through summer. Vigorous upright habit, attractive bronzy young shoots. 1.5 × 1m

Lagerstroemia indica 'Petite Orchid'
Cerise-purple, crepe flowers held in dense terminal panicles through summer. 1.5 × 1m.   **159**

Lagerstroemia indica 'Petite Pinkie'
Outstanding displays of rich pink crepe flowers in terminal panicles through summer. 1.5 × 1m.

Lagerstroemia indica 'Souvinir D'Hubert Puard'
Vigorous, bushy upright grower with mauve-lilac, crepe-like blooms mass produced mid-summer through autumn. French hybrid. 3.5 × 2.5m.

Lagerstroemia indica 'Saint Emilion'
Large, bright reddish crimson flowers borne prolifically. Vigorous, erect grower. 3.5 × 2.5m.

Lagerstroemia indica 'Soir D'Ete'
Delicate, soft almond-pink flowers. Very free flowering, graceful spreading habit. 2.5 × 2m.

Lagerstroemia indica 'Terre Chinoise'
Claret crepe flowers in great profusion on long robust branches. 3.5 × 2.5m.

Lagerstroemia indica 'Yang Tse'
Vigorous, erect grower with long arching branches. Crimson red buds open to rich pink, frilly flowers through summer and autumn. Glossy foliage. French hybrid. 3.5 × 2.5m.

Above: Lavendula dentata **182**

Above: Leptospermum scoparium 'Burgundy Queen' **184**
Below: Leptospermum flavescens 'Pink Cascade' **184**

Above: Leptospermum scoparium 'Fascination' **184**
Below: Leptospermum scoparium 'Jubilee' **184**

178

Above: Leptospermum scoparium
'Kotuku' **185**

Above: Leptospermum scoparium 'Martinii' **185**
Below: Leptospermum scoparium 'Wiri Susan' **185**

Above: Leucadendron argenteum *Silver tree* **186**
Below: Leptospermum scoparium 'Spectrocolor' **185**

Below: Leptospermum scoparium 'Rose Glory' **185**

Above: Leucadendron 'Bell's Sunrise' **186**

Above: Leucadendron floridum 'Pisa' **186**

Above: Leucadendron laureolum 'Rewa Gold' **186**
Below: Leucadendron 'Safari Sunset' **187**

Above: Leucadendron 'Red Gem' **186**
Below: Leucadendron salignum 'Early Yellow' **187**

Above: Leucospermum cordifolium **187**
Below: Leucospermum reflexum **188**

Below: Leucospermum cuneiforme **187**

LAGUNARIA

A monotypic genus first discovered in Norfolk Island and subsequently in Lord Howe Island and Queensland, named for Andrea Laguna, 16th century Spanish botanist. With maritime heritage, it is an ideal tree for coastal planting, quite tolerant of exposure to coastal wind and salt spray where it seems to flower more prolifically. Plant in full sun in well-worked soil, paying attention to feeding and watering until the tree is established. It then survives extensive drought. Excellent single specimen, screen, shelter, street or avenue tree.

Malvaceae. *All evergreen.*

Lagunaria patersonii
Norfolk Island Hibiscus
One of the most handsome evergreen trees with erect, stately, narrow-pyramidal outline. Densely foliaged with 5–10cm, thick textured, ovate to broadly lanceolate, olive green leaves with grey undersides. Light to deep pink, 6cm open flowers with five recurved petals, appear amongst the foliage mainly through summer and autumn. Flowers somewhat resemble small single-flowered Hibiscus to which the tree is related. Obovoid, pubescent seed capsules, at first green then turning brown, contain numerous fine spicules or splinters which tend to penetrate the skin, causing slight irritation if handled carelessly. 8 × 4m.

Lagunaria patersonii 'Princess Rose'
Selected for shapely pyramidal form and limited size. Leaves ovate to broadly lanceolate, grey-green to 10cm long. Deep rose-pink silky, five-petalled flowers. 4.5 × 3m.

Lagunaria patersonii 'Royal Purple'
Selected for deep rosy purple flowers, erect branching pattern, free-flowering from an early age. Narrow pyramidal outline. 4.5 × 3m.

LANTANA

A genus of more than 150 species of evergreen shrubs and perennial herbs mostly from tropical and sub-tropical America and Africa. Lantana is an old Latin term for Viburnum. The familiar ornamental Lantanas are developed from the Jamaican or Central American species L camara, or, are hybrids from L camara × L montevidensis. Camara is a West Indian word for a plant. Usually in bloom when planted, they make tremendous growth and continue flowering through a greater part of the year. While some species grow rampantly, and declared noxious weeds in many parts of the tropical world, cultivated hybrids are well behaved and valued as useful landscaping plants.

Dwarf or trailing forms provide excellent ground or bank cover, spilling gracefully over walls. Shrubby forms good for bedding, spot color and containers. Plant in full sun and deeply worked soil with good drainage. Tolerate coastal winds and salt spray, thriving a few metres from ocean blasts. Excessive shade, water or overcast conditions causes mildew on the foliage. Bloom more profuse when underwatered and underfed. Frequent pinching encourages good form and maximum flower. Plants which becomes untidy or overgrown may be pruned to ground level.

Verbenaceae. *All evergreen.*

Lantana 'Chelsea Gem'
Showy, compact shrub with brilliant crimson flowers shaded orange-red. Blooms constantly, always outstanding. 75 × 75cm.

Lantana 'Christine'
Large grower, with masses of cerise-pink flowers. Prune to desired size and form. 2 × 1.5m.

Lantana 'Cream Carpet'
Medium spreader, flowers cream with bright yellow throat. 60cm × 2m. **160**

Lantana 'Eden Garden'
Originated in Eden Gardens, Auckland. Outstanding, large growing bush producing great quantities of flowers in rounded heads, shaded from brilliant cerise to orange and golden yellow. Large deep green foliage overlaid purple. 2 × 1.5m.

Lantana 'Golconda'
Delightful little dwarf grower, smothering itself throughout summer and autumn with bright, coppery orange flowers shaded red. 60 × 60cm.

Lantana montevidensis
Trailing Lantana
South American species providing rapid coverage of rocks, banks, beds, old tree stumps, or bare areas. Massed displays of lavender pink or mauve flowers through spring, summer and autumn. May be trimmed as a low divider or twined through old sparse bushes. Versatile, easy grown and floriferous plant for sunny locations. 35cm–1m × 2–3m. **160**

Lantana 'Pink Frolic'
Medium spreader, with showy flowers in pink and yellow. 60cm × 2m. **160**

Lantana 'Snowflake'
Compact, spreading shrub with almost continual masses of pure white flowers. 1 × 1m.

Lantana 'Source d'Or'
Compact grower with masses of yellow flowers, paler with age. 1 × 1m. **160**

Lantana 'Spreading Sunshine'
Low, spreading plants with compact growth, rich, dark green leaves and an abundance of bright, sunshine-yellow flowers creating a blanket of garden colour. 60cm × 2m.

Lantana 'Sunset'
Low spreading form, with masses of red, orange and yellow flowers during summer. 1 × 1m. **160**

LARIX

A genus of about 12 species of deciduous, rapid-growing conifers widely distributed through the northern hemisphere, notable for utility, beauty and hardiness. Not a tree for warm climates, usually seen in cool temperate maritime climates in areas of high rainfall with adequate run-off. Although more often seen in plantations, the beauty of spring and autumn foliage may be enjoyed in garden situations where there is enough space for natural development.

Pinaceae. *All deciduous.*

Larix decidua
European Larch
Forms a slender pyramid with horizontal branches and pendulous branchlets. Needle-like, 12–40mm leaves soft to the touch, and woody, roundish, 20–40cm cones spread along the branches. Young shoots yellowish green becoming soft fresh-green through summer, brilliant yellow and orange before falling. Naked winter branches enhanced by cones create picturesque patterns. 8 × 5m.

Larix kaempferi
Japanese Larch
Vigorous tree of great forest dimensions. Distinctive reddish twigs create a purplish haze in late winter. Summer foliage soft

bluish green, turning whitish buff prior to falling. Responds to systematic and creative pruning and shaping for seasonal beauty to be enjoyed in home garden situations. Makes an excellent tub plant. From the island of Hondo. Syn L leptolepis. 3 × 1.5m.

LAURELIA

A genus of two species of trees from New Zealand, Chile and Peru called by its Latin name. The New Zealand Pukatea is found in lowland, swampy forest areas, along banks of streams and shady gullies of both North and South Islands. Shelter from winds, otherwise hardy to –5°C. Plant in deeply worked, moisture-retentive, fertile soil including alkaline soil, in sun or partial shade.
Monimaceae

Laurelia novae-zelandiae
Pukatea
Tall handsome tree with whitish bark and deeply buttressed trunk. Leaves elliptic oblong to obovate, 3–7cm long, thick, leathery, deep-green, lighter beneath, margins entire or saw-toothed. Branches and twigs shiny black, flowers and fruit of little consequence. Although a forest giant, slow growth rate enables it to be used as a fresh leafy tree in average gardens, particularly in wet or shady locations, or in a spot at the edge of lakes or streams. Evergreen. 6 × 4m.

LAURUS

A genus of two species of trees or shrubs from southern Europe, Canary Islands and Azores, called by the Latin name. Laurus nobilis, widely distributed around the Mediterranean, usually grows in moist rocky valleys. It provided laurel crowns for ancient Greek heroes of games and wars and was valued for the medicinal properties of its fruits and leaves. Plant in deeply worked, free-draining, moisture retentive, fertile soil in sun or semi-shade in hot summer areas. Hardy to –5°C and thrives near the coast. Clip to almost any shape, excellent for formal specimens, containers, screens or backgrounds.
Lauraceae

Laurus nobilis
Bay Laurel, Sweet Bay
Forms a hardy, compact, broad-based pyramidal shrub or tree. Leaves lanceolate-

elliptic, to 10 × 4cm, leathery, dark green and highly aromatic. The traditional culinary bay leaves. Small yellow flowers in clusters followed by 25–40mm, oval, black or dark-purple berries yielding oil used in perfumery. Nobilis — excellent, notable, famous or renowned. Evergreen. 4 × 3m.

LAVANDULA

A genus of 28 species of hardy shrubs and perennials from Mediterranean regions, North Africa, western Asia, Arabia and India named from the Latin *lavo*, to wash or bathe, from the use of lavender oil in various toiletries. Many cultivated species are grown for beauty as well as fragrant properties. To use in sachets, cut flower clusters as soon as colour shows and dry in a cool shady place. Fragrance is retained for long periods.

Generally found in exposed, often parched and hot conditions on rocky hillsides, usually in calcareous soils. However, they thrive in almost any deeply worked, free-draining soil in full sun and prefer a minimum of fertilizer or moisture. Pruning or clipping after flowering keeps them neat and compact. Good in coastal gardens. Ideal as low dividing hedges, flanking a pathway or amongst herbaceous perennials especially those which like it hot and dry.
Labiatae. *All evergreen.*

Lavandula angustifolia
English Lavender
Cultivated in England since the mid-16th century, the classic perfume lavender, perhaps the most highly prized of aromatic shrubs. Forms a dense, compact bush with square, greyish stems and lanceolate to linear, smooth, pale silvery grey, aromatic leaves to 6cm long. Numerous closely packed spikes of tiny greyish blue fragrant flowers carried on thin stems 30–45cm long. Syn L spica, L officinalis, L vera. Angustifolia — with narrow leaves. 75 × 75cm.

Lavandula angustifolia 'Alba'
Taller, robust grower, narrow grey-green leaves and white flowers on 90cm to 1.2m stems mid-summer. 1m × 75cm.

Lavandula angustifolia 'Arabian Nights'
Selected for rich purple flowers and intense fragrance. Hardy, easily grown. 40 × 75cm.

Lavandula angustifolia 'Avon View'
Vigorous short-stemmed variety with spikes of deep lavender flowers 60 × 90cm.

Lavandula angustifolia 'Blue Mountain'
Deep violet-blue flowers produced on a compact bush through summer. Suitable for drying. Originated at Tapanui, New Zealand. 50 × 75cm.

Lavandula angustifolia 'Byjong'
Large heads of lavender-blue flowers held well above the foliage through summer. Good for cut flowers and production of lavender oil. 90 × 90cm.

Lavandula angustifolia 'Dilly Dilly'
Small compact grower, richly fragrant, blue flower spikes spring through summer. 50 × 75cm.

Lavandula angustifolia 'Grey Lady'
Very compact form with frosty-grey leaves and deep violet-purple flowers in dense spikes. 30 × 30cm.

Lavandula angustifolia 'Hidcote'
Compact form, grey lanceolate leaves and stems. Lilac flowers with deep lilac calyx in dense spikes early summer. Slow grower. 30 × 30cm.

Lavandula angustifolia 'Munstead'
Earlier flowering compact shrub with small leaves and large blue-lilac flowers in loose spikes with purple calyx. 30 × 45cm.

Lavandula angustifolia 'Rosea'
Compact form with narrow green leaves and lavender-pink flowers on 60–75cm stems mid-summer. Oil used in Eau de Cologne. 50 × 75cm.

Lavandula angustifolia 'Wilson's Giant'
Vigorous plant with large heads of lavender-blue flowers carried on long stems through summer. High yields of lavender oil, excellent cut flowers, good for drying and very ornamental. 75 × 75cm.

Lavandula dentata
Toothed Lavender
From Spain and North Africa. Vigorous grower with grey-green, linear or lanceolate leaves to 35mm long with square-toothed margins. Lilac-purple flowers in short, spike-like clusters, topped with petal-like bracts autumn through early summer. Lacks fragrance but blooms almost continually in mild areas. Dentata — furnished with teeth. 1 × 1m.   177

Lavandula latifolia
Spike Lavender
Dwarf grower from southern France resembling English Lavender. Stems and foliage grey tomentose, leaves elliptic to spatula-shaped, 60 × 12mm, more tomentose be-

neath. Fragrant flowers purple to dark-purple in branched spikes through summer. Latifolia — broad leaved. 80 × 60cm.

Lavandula stoechas
French Lavender
Found along the Mediterranean from Spain to Greece. Dwarf intensely aromatic shrublet with 10–40mm, grey-green, linear to oblong-lanceolate leaves. Dark purple flower heads borne in 5cm spikes, topped with prominent lilac-pink, petal-like bracts during summer. Shoots and leaves have distinct pine-like fragrance when crushed. Stoechas — of the Stoechades off the coast of France near Toulon (now the Isles d'Hyéres.) 50 × 50cm.

Lavandula stoechas 'Helmsdale'
Compact growing form, large, deep wine red flowers through spring and summer. 60 × 60cm.

Lavandula stoechas 'Marshwood'
Compact, upright plant with long flower spikes. Purple-pink bracts with a hint of green in long spikes spring through autumn. 80 × 80cm.

Lavandula stoechas 'Pedunculata'
Resembles L stoechas but the foliage is light-green and softly textured. Reddish-brown flowers with prominent reddish-purple, petal-like bracts on 10–25cm peduncles or stems spring and early summer. Pedunculata — with a stalk or peduncle. 75 × 60cm.

LECHENAULTIA

A genus of about twenty species of shrubs and herbs, mainly from Western Australia named for Louis Theodore Leschenault de la Tour, 18–19th century French botanist. Other species found in New Guinea, Indonesia and Malaysia. Name variation may be attributed to Robert Brown who omitted the 's' when first describing the plant. Admired for long-lasting displays of brilliant flowers unsurpassed by few others. May be difficult to get established and could be short-lived.

Plant in sun or semi-shade in deeply worked, free-draining, moisture retentive, sandy or friable-clay soil. Lechenaultia is moderately frost resistant but brittle stems need protection from strong wind. They like summer moisture, but cannot tolerate high humidity. Ideal in elevated rockery pockets with a little dappled

shade. **Although short-lived, they strike readily from cuttings. Propagate extra plants as replacements.**
Goodeniaceae. *All evergreen.*

Lechenaultia biloba
Blue Lechenaultia
Rather straggling habit with soft needle-like, linear 10 × 1mm leaves on slender stems. Flowers of purest blue, around 20mm across with five wedge-shaped petals mass-produced during spring. Spills nicely over rocks. Biloba — two-lobed. 25 × 75cm.

Lechenaultia biloba 'Blue Mountain'
Compact, upright form with narrow, soft green leaves. Masses of gentian-blue flowers late spring and early summer. 60 × 60cm.

Lechenaultia × biloba 'Fantail Ultra Violet'
Hybrid from L biloba × L formosa. Forms a small erect plant with masses of fan-shaped violet-blue flowers with mauve centre late autumn through spring. Good for pot culture. 35 × 50cm.

Lechenaultia × biloba 'Fantail Starburst'
Hybrid from L biloba × L formosa. Small prostrate grower. Red fan-shaped flowers with orange-yellow centre borne in great masses late autumn through spring. Ideal in containers. 10 × 50cm.

Lechenaultia formosa
Red Lechenaultia
Beautiful small multi-branched, spreading or suckering plant with fine, soft, light-green to grey-green, linear leaves to 12mm. Large showy brick-red flowers in abundance late winter through autumn. Formosa — handsome, beautiful. 50cm × 1m.

Lechenaultia formosa 'Flamingo'
Compact spreading shrublet with bright flamingo-pink, fan-shaped flowers autumn through early summer. One of the easiest of this genus to grow, withstanding cold and apparently unaffected by over-moist soil. 20 × 40cm.

Lechenaultia formosa 'Pink Princess'
Spreading shrub with fine soft foliage and masses of beautiful pink flowers late winter through spring. 30 × 30cm.

Lechenaultia formosa 'Sunrise'
Compact, suckering, spreading dwarf shrub with greyish leaves and masses of brilliant red flowers with orange-yellow centres borne mid-winter through autumn. 30 × 60cm.

LEONOTIS

A genus of 30 species of sub-shrubs, annual or perennial herbs from South Africa and India named from the Greek *leon*, **a lion and** *ous*, **an ear from a fancied resemblance of the hairy corolla lip to a lion's ear. The shrubby species L leonurus is a popular, easily grown species with masses of flowers for long periods late spring through autumn.**

Reasonably hardy, drought resistant, grows in deeply worked, free-draining, fertile soil in full sun. Don't overwater or overfeed. Pick flowers for indoors and prune after flowering. Use as lawn specimen or in shrub borders amongst other heat lovers.
Labiatae. *All evergreen.*

Leonotis leonurus
Lions Tail, Lion's Ear
South African soft-wooded, easily grown shrub. Sage-like, lanceolate to oblanceolate leaves to 12cm long, downy, dull-green, slightly toothed at the edges. Brilliant orange-red, tubular, two-lipped flowers to 6cm long, covered with furry hairs, carried in dense clusters or whorls at intervals on erect stems to 2m providing spectacular displays through summer and autumn. Blooms suggestive of a lion's tail. Leonurus — from the Greek *leon*, a lion and *ouros*, a tail. 2 × 1.5m.

Leonotis leonurus 'Albiflora'
White Lion's Tail
Closely resembles above in growth habit but with furry, tubular, creamy-white flowers in dense whorls interspersed with leaves on erect stems. Syn L leonurus 'Alba'. 2 × 1.5m.

LEPIDOTHAMNUS

A genus of three species of shrubs or trees from southern Chile and New Zealand named from the Greek *lepis*, **scale and** *thamnos*, **shrub. The listed species along with the Chilean L fonkii, said to be the world's smallest conifers are found at high altitudes under almost continuous rain or dampness. Two forms of L laxifolius have been identified, the one listed, the other with green summer foliage which turns plum red in winter. An attractive trailing shrub for rockery pockets or spilling over walls. Grows in sun or partial shade in**

loose, free, damp soil. Mulch freely and water regularly during dry periods.
   Podocarpaceae.

Lepidothamnus laxifolius 'Blue Pygmy'
Pygmy Pine, Mountain Rimu
First discovered in 1839 near Mt Ngauruhoe in the central North Island and later in the South Island and Stewart Islands usually in boggy ground in alpine and subalpine scrub. Most attractive, small usually prostrate shrub forming mats of slender wiry branches to 90cm long and erect branchlets to 15cm. Juvenile leaves subulate or awl-shaped to 12mm, adult leaves linear-oblong to 3mm, sharply pointed and overlapping, glaucous blue in summer, changing to green or brown in winter. Both leaf forms appear on the same branch. Flowers appear in spring followed late summer and autumn by a swollen, succulent, 5–7cm, crimson capsule with protruding black pointed seed. Syn Dacrydium laxifolius. Laxifolius — loose-leaved. Evergreen. 15 × 90cm.

LEPTOSPERMUM

A genus of about 75 species of trees and shrubs mostly Australian, a few from New Zealand, New Caledonia and Malaysia, named from the Greek *leptos*, slender and *sperma*, seed, a reference to narrow seeds. Commonly known as Tea Tree, Leptospermum is grown for floral beauty, a wealth of bloom which seems to cover the entire bush. They're found on mountains or cliffs dwarfed by wind, on the seashore, in swamps or dry areas, low bushes a few centimetres high to trees of several metres. Generally quite hardy and adaptable to wide changes of environment.
   Plant in any deeply worked, free-draining soil in full sun. Water frequently during dry periods until established. Annual trimming and occasional pinching keeps the plants neat and compact. Sooty mould, a black soot-like residue forming on stems and branches, caused by a scale pest may need control. Delightful shrubs to work in just about anywhere, individually or in massed groups.
   Myrtaceae. *All evergreen.*

Leptospermum flavescens 'Pacific Beauty'
Native to New South Wales and Queensland, semi-prostrate form, pendulous branches, oblong, 2cm leaves and a profusion of 15mm white flowers from pink buds late spring and summer. Reliable and floriferous. Flavescens — yellowish. 1.5 × 2m.

Leptospermum flavescens 'Pink Cascade'
Semi-prostrate cascading branching pattern, new shoots red, foliage dark green when mature. Masses of single, two-toned pink flowers through spring and again in autumn. 50cm × 1.5m.   **177**

Leptospermum macrocarpum 'Copper Sheen'
Shiny Tea Tree
Variable species found on exposed and often dry rocky places on the central coast and tablelands of New South Wales. The cultivar 'Copper Sheen' has reddish young stems, narrow elliptical, deep bronze-purple glossy leaves and 12–25mm, single flowers, with reddish petals, greenish sepals, prominent green centre and white stamens. Hardy and tolerant of moist conditions. 1.5 × 1m.

Leptospermum macrocarpum 'Green Eye'
Forms an attractive bushy shrub with rich bronzy red foliage and white flowers with conspicuous green centre through spring. 1 × 1m.

Leptospermum scoparium
Tea Tree, Manuka
Distributed through New Zealand, New South Wales, Victoria and Tasmania but the species is seldom seen under cultivation. L scoparium cultivars have mostly originated in New Zealand, often occurring as chance seedling in various nurseries. All have narrow-lanceolate to ovate, sharply pointed leaves to 20 × 6mm. Single flowered varieties have five rounded petals arranged around a hard central cone which after petal fall form 6mm goblet-shaped seed capsules. Both single and double forms commence blooming at an early age, literally smothering every branch with colourful blooms over many months from late autumn, through winter and into spring. Early voyagers and settlers once used dried leaves in place of tea. Scoparium — broom-like, in reference to twiggy branches which in earlier days served as brooms.

Leptospermum scoparium 'Black Robin'
Neat rounded bush with dark purplish foliage. Light pink single flowers deepening towards the centre entirely cover the bush for long periods late spring through summer. 75 × 75cm.

Leptospermum scoparium 'Blossom'
Large double coral pink flowers in great abundance winter and spring, sometimes through summer. Bushy grower, green foliage. 2 × 1.5m.

Leptospermum scoparium 'Burgundy Queen'
Exquisite double flowers of deep burgundy-red late winter and spring. Dark reddish bronze foliage. 2 × 1.5m.   **177**

Leptospermum scoparium 'Charmer'
Large single flowers, pastel pink and white toned rose pink with a dark eye. Vigorous, upright bushy grower, small olive green foliage. 2 × 1.5m.

Leptospermum scoparium 'Cherry Brandy'
Large deep pink single flowers in spring. Compact semi-dwarf habit, deep bronze-purple new growth. 75 × 50cm.

Leptospermum scoparium 'Coral Candy'
Vigorous free-flowering bush with masses of fully double flowers striped red and candy-pink. Striking through spring and autumn. 1.5 × 1m.

Leptospermum scoparium 'Crimson Glory'
Double crimson flowers freely produced in spring. Compact bushy grower, reddish bronze foliage. 1 × 1m.

Leptospermum scoparium 'Elizabeth Jane'
Deep pink single flowers in great profusion. Neat growth habit, deep purple-red foliage. 45 × 45cm.

Leptospermum scoparium 'Fascination'
Frilly double blooms of light and deep candy-pink late spring and summer. Bushy habit, green foliage. 1.5 × 1m.   **177**

Leptospermum scoparium 'Gaiety Girl'
Double flowers in unusual tones of pink tinted lilac during spring. Reddish foliage and bushy growth habit. 1.5 × 1m.

Leptospermum scoparium 'Huia'
One of the delightful dwarf nanum group named after New Zealand native birds. Huia produces single 15mm deep pink to red flowers in masses for long periods during spring. 30 × 45cm.

Leptospermum scoparium 'Jubilee'
Double pink flowers deepening to bright red from autumn to spring. Reddish foliage and open growth habit. 2 × 1.5m.   **177**

Leptospermum scoparium 'Karekare'
Discovered at Karekare on Auckland's West Coast and introduced into cultivation by nurseryman Graeme Platt. Considered one of the finest foliage shrubs in the Lepto-

spermum collection at Auckland Botanic Gardens. Slower and sturdier growth than most larger growers with broad, distinctive and attractive foliage. Good quality pure white single flowers produced abundantly through spring. 2 × 1.5m

Leptospermum scoparium 'Kea'
Compact densely branched dwarf shrub with single pale pink flowers in autumn and early winter. Small olive-bronze foliage. Blooms early but not profusely, tending to hide its flowers amongst the foliage. 30 × 45cm.

Leptospermum scoparium 'Keatleyi'
Single soft pink flowers with wavy petals, usually as large as a 20 cent coin, borne in profusion during winter and spring. Light green habit, open growth habit. 2 × 1.5m.

Leptospermum scoparium 'Kiwi'
Single light red flowers en masse spring and early summer. One of the dwarf nanum group, amongst the showiest miniature shrubs. 30 × 45cm.

Leptospermum scoparium 'Kotuku'
Single soft rose-pink flowers with deeper blush during early spring. Dwarf compact grower, bronze foliage. One of the nanum group. 45 × 45cm. **178**

Leptospermum scoparium 'Martinii'
Large single rich deep pink to red flowers in great masses from late winter to early summer. Outstanding shrub, magnificent in full bloom. Compact growth habit. 2 × 1.5m. **178**

Leptospermum scoparium 'Pink Champagne'
Medium grower, light green foliage, masses of pale pink single flowers through summer. 1 × 1m.

Leptospermum scoparium 'Pink Lady'
Very compact. Small light red leaves, masses of pale pink single flowers. 50 × 50cm.

Leptospermum scoparium 'Red Damask'
Compact, upright grower with bronze foliage. Crimson to cherry red double flowers in great profusion late winter through mid summer. Amongst the most outstanding Leptospermums. 2 × 1.5m.

Leptospermum scoparium 'Red Ensign'
Bright glowing crimson single flowers produced in great profusion. Upright, bushy habit. 2 × 1.5m.

Leptospermum scoparium 'Red Falls'
Semi prostrate grower with some stems at ground level, others to a metre high with long trailing branches. Rich red single flowers from late winter. Good for multiple planting and effective as a standard weeping tree. 1.5 × 1m.

Leptospermum scoparium 'Rose Glory'
Rose-pink to red double flowers during winter and spring. Reddish foliage and upright habit. 2 × 1.5m. **178**

Leptospermum scoparium 'Rose Queen'
Tall grower with bright rose-pink full double flowers for long periods through winter and spring. 1.5 × 1.3m.

Leptospermum scoparium 'Rosy Morn'
Fascinating variation of colours from light pink to cerise from autumn through spring. Reddish foliage, compact grower. 1.5 × 1m.

Leptospermum scoparium 'Ruru'
Single deep pink flowers completely cover the plant during late spring and early summer. One of the nanum group. Excellent dwarf flowering shrub. 30 × 45cm.

Leptospermum scoparium 'Sherryl Lee'
Vigorous tall grower with silvery sheen to new growth and attractive foliage. Large salmon pink single flowers resembling L Keatleyi winter through spring. Introduced by nurseryman Graeme Platt and named after his daughter. 2 × 1.5m.

Leptospermum scoparium 'Snow Flurry'
Erect grower with pale green silky hairy young shoots and deep green leaves. White, fully double flowers to 17mm, odd petals with a touch of crimson late spring to mid summer. 1.5 × 1m.

Leptospermum scoparium 'Spectrocolor'
Erect grower with silky new shoots and stiff dark-green leaves. Fully double flowers in various shades ranging from almost white with green eye to light pink and red with dark eye. Free-flowering. 1.5 × 1m. **178**

Leptospermum scoparium 'Sunraysia'
Vigorous bush with mid-green foliage. Fully double flowers open deep pink, fading to pale pink. 2.5 × 1.5m.

Leptospermum scoparium 'Tui'
Single white flushed pale pink flowers with a dark eye during spring. One of the nanum group with more erect growth habit, very free flowering. 45 × 45cm.

Leptospermum scoparium 'Wairere'
Superior vigorous prostrate form with lighter green foliage and masses of rich pink single flowers during summer. Cascades over walls or rocks or can be trained as a weeping standard. 60 × 90cm.

Leptospermum scoparium 'Winter Cheer'
Large double bright red flowers produced freely through winter and in the early spring. Reddish foliage and bushy habit. 1.5 × 1m.

Leptospermum scoparium 'Wiri Amy'
Forms a semi-dwarf conical shrub with deep red single flowers resembling L Martini but with rosy red central zone and white edges, borne freely through winter and late spring. The 'Wiri' series are a result of a breeding programme supervised by Jack Hobbs, Curator of Auckland Botanic Gardens, selected as distinct from existing cultivars. 1 × 1m.

Leptospermum scoparium 'Wiri Donna'
Vigorous grower with bronze foliage. Medium to large deep-red single flowers with gold stamens through spring. 1.5 × 1.5m.

Leptospermum scoparium 'Wiri Joan'
Attractive green foliage and distinctive small, bright red double flowers which remain tightly in bud throughout winter. Flowers have no stamens and form very few seed capsules. 2 × 1.5m.

Leptospermum scoparium 'Wiri Kerry'
Compact grower with small bronze foliage. Rose-red fully double flowers autumn through spring. First compact Leptospermum with double flowers. 80 × 60cm

Leptospermum scoparium 'Wiri Linda'
Vigorous grower with fresh green foliage. White fully double flowers with ruffled petals, early autumn and spring. 1.7 × 1.5m.

Leptospermum scoparium 'Wiri Sandra'
Medium grower with green foliage. The bush is smothered in spring with rich pink perfectly formed flowers. 1.3 × 1m.

Leptospermum scoparium 'Wiri Shelly'
Tall erect grower with green foliage. Distinctive rose-red smallish single flowers through spring. Vibrant colour. 1.7 × 1m.

Leptospermum scoparium 'Wiri Susan'
Medium grower with green foliage. Becomes a mass of large, perfectly formed glistening white single flowers through spring. 1.2 × 1m. **178**

LEUCADENDRON

A genus of about 80 species of South African shrubs and trees, named from the Greek *leucos*, white and *dendron*, a tree, alluding to the leaves of L argenteum. Leucadendrons are dioecious, male and female flowers borne on separate plants. Tiny female flowers appear on a seed bearing cone, while the male flowers take the form of small fluffy pompons. Most species have highly coloured yellow orange or red terminal leaves surrounding the flowers often changing colour with seasons. Most species found in the south western Cape region.

Leucadendrons should be grown in deeply worked, free-draining, moisture retentive acid soil with a pH of about 5.5, conditioned with sand or peat moss. As they thrive in impoverished soil conditions in their native habitat, fertilizing cultivated plants is rarely necessary. Naturally they're found on mountain slopes within sight of the ocean, enjoying constant sea-breezes. Many are hardy to −5°C, will stand summer heat but are likely to fail in conditions of high humidity. Locate for maximum air circulation. Leucadendrons are amongst the most spectacular flowering shrubs, widely grown for cut blooms.

Proteaceae. *All evergreen*

Leucadendron argenteum
Silver Tree
In suitable conditions this magnificent species grows to a sizeable tree with handsome lanceolate leaves, to 15 × 2cm, greyish and covered on both sides with shining silvery down. Foliage covers the branches entirely, giving the tree the appearance of a shining silver pyramid. Terminal heads of 4cm flowers during summer followed by black or brown seed cones of little significance. Few trees have the same dominating personality as Silver Tree. Argenteum — silvery. 5 × 3m. **178**

Leucadendron 'Bell's Sunrise'
From the same parentage as 'Safari Sunset' and 'Red Gem', but perhaps a little less vigorous. Forms a dense, multi-branched bush. Lime-gold bracts become delicately tinged orange-red at the tips as they mature. Prominent rounded green and gold central cone. Easily grown and becoming popular for cut blooms. Male hybrid of L salignum × L laureolum, developed by and named for Ian Bell of Wanganui, New Zealand. 1.5 × 1.5m. **179**

Leucadendron 'Brook's Red'
Forms a large dense bulky shrub. Leaves linear to 80 × 3mm, medium green, bronze-tinted much of the year, with pointed red tips intensifying towards the bracts. Bronzy red bracts commence to form in autumn increasing in size and colour through winter, opening to 10cm wide in spring at which stage they're suffused light yellow and display a central female cone. Flowerheads borne on long stems in great profusion, excellent for picking. Natural hybrid from L salignum. 2.5 × 3m.

Leucadendron 'Cherry Glow'
Selected male hybrid from L procerum. Forms a low-growing bushy shrub with elliptic, medium green leaves to 40 × 5mm. Flowerheads comprise yellow bracts to 4cm across surrounding a deep wine-red cone which with pollen production becomes yellow, borne on 15–20cm stems mid spring, often with multi-heads. Excellent for garden display and floral art. 50 × 50cm.

Leucadendron 'Cloudbank Ginny'
Vigorous hybrid from L discolor × L gandogeri. Forms a dense, compact bush, leaves elliptic to 70 × 20mm, surface and margins covered with silvery-white pubescence at first, maturing more glabrous and with a prominent red tip. Creamy flower bracts to 12cm across with an attractive rich-orange central male cone, borne profusely on long stems from early spring to early summer. Bred and named at Cloudbank Nursery, Maui, by Colin and Ginny Lennox. 1.3 × 1.3m.

Leucadendron 'Firecracker'
New Zealand raised selection of L discolor. Forms a slender erect plant with long stems of silvery foliage and terminal light yellow bracts enclosing attractive silvery grey cones. Intolerant of heavy frost. 2 × 1m.

Leucadendron floridum 'Pisa'
Distinctly upright habit, producing 1m stems clothed with silky, grey-green leaves, topped with bright yellow bracts surrounding a silvery cone, which as it matures enlarges to become a highly decorative feature. Excellent plant for fine silver foliage, useful for cutting either for leaves bracts or cones. Floridum — rich in flowers. 1.5 × 1m. **179**

Leucadendron 'Inca Gold'
Hybrid cultivar from L laureolum × L salignum. An upright grower, producing long reddish stems of butter-yellow, tulip-like bracts, finely tipped crimson during winter. Excellent plant for cut flower and landscape use. 2 × 1.5m.

Leucadendron 'Julie'
Possibly a hybrid from L salignum. Attractive medium erect shrub with small glaucous-green foliage. Produces an abundance of yellow flushed red, multi-headed, medium sized, goblet-shaped bracts autumn through mid winter intensifying with maturity. Popular cut flower. 1.5 × 1m.

Leucadendron lanigerum
Slow-growing, dense, bushy shrub. Leaves narrow-elliptic to 25 × 6mm, tending to clasp the stems, red tipped at the apex, becoming margined and flushed red nearer the flower bracts. Yellow flushed red, daisy-like, bracts to 50mm across with central yellow cone, borne singly or in multiple heads late winter and early spring. Colourful garden shrub and excellent for cutting. 1.3 × 1.3m.

Leucadendron laureolum
Forms a broad medium shrub with numerous ascending branches and oblong leaves to 95mm, green tinged red. In the male plant, broad tapering terminal brilliant golden yellow bracts surrounded by yellow leaves make the whole bush gleam during spring. Female plants have smaller less showy bracts. 2 × 1.5m.

Leucadendron laureolum 'Rewa Gold'
Excellent selection with long straight stems of large yellow bracts which develop reddish bronze edges. Very desirable cut flower. 2 × 1.5m. **179**

Leucadendron 'Maui Sunset'
Of hybrid origin from Hawaii. Low growing spreading habit, producing through late winter and spring, whitish-cream bracts delicately flushed pink intensifying with age. Hardy and suitable for picking. 1 × 1.5m.

Leucadendron 'Mrs Stanley'
Female form with soft pinkish-red bracts in autumn, deepening to rich burgundy in winter. Low bushy spreading habit, bright and spectacular. 1 × 1m.

Leucadendron 'Red Gem'
Closely related to L 'Safari Sunset' and L 'Bell's Sunrise', raised from the same parent plants. Bushy low-branching habit, with outer stems somewhat curving. Leaves narrowly elliptic to 85 × 15mm, medium green flushed bronze through some seasons, rounded tips deep red with fine silvery hairs. Flowerheads comprise cup-shaped bracts to 10cm across, at first deep bronzed-red, changing through cream and orange-bronze in spring. Excellent cut flower. 1.5 × 2m. **179**

Leucadendron 'Safari Sunset'

Particularly vigorous hybrid from L salignum × L laureolum developed in New Zealand. Strong erect growth habit, bushy and densely branched. Deep green leaves to 90 × 15mm flushed red nearer each terminal. Female bracts on long stems light red in autumn, intensifying to rich wine red in winter, paling to golden yellow in the centre near the end of the season. Excellent garden display, grown extensively for cut flower production. 2.5 × 2m. **179**

Leucadendron 'Safari Sunshine'

Variegated leaf selection of L Safari Sunset. This striking bush has leaves with showy salmon pink and cream margins and outstanding floral bracts edged bright pink with deeper red central zone. Not as vigorous as Safari Sunset, but blooms freely on strong stems, excellent as a cut flower. Syn L 'Jester' 2 × 1.5m.

Leucadendron salignum

Widely distributed species from which numerous cultivars have been developed. Usually seen as an erect, dense bush with linear, deep green to lighter green leaves to 50 × 5mm, often with a prominent red tip at the apex. Uppermost leaves and terminal bracts fill with colour, providing vivid garden displays and cut blooms for indoors. Syn L adscendens. Salignum — willow-like.

Leucadendron salignum 'Durban Gold'

Dense tidy grower with narrow leaves. Rich butter-yellow female bracts tinged red borne freely late winter. 1.3 × 1m.

Leucadendron salignum 'Early Yellow'

Clear golden yellow bracts to 20mm across by 80mm in depth, borne in long stems from late autumn and through winter. 1.3 × 1m. **179**

Leucadendron salignum 'Yellow Devil'

Bright yellow bracts in winter borne on 40–50cm stems. 1.3 × 1m.

Leucadendron 'Super Star'

New Zealand hybrid from L lanigerum × L salignum. Forms a low, slender, multi-branched spreading bush. Numerous small leaves closely pressed to the stem. Terminal reddish bracts blending to creamy yellow in the centre surround bright-yellow male flower clusters, borne on long stems mid winter through spring. 80 × 60cm.

Leucadendron thymifolium

Forms an erect bushy shrub. Small, elliptic, stem-clasping leaves to 16 × 4mm, soft grey-green and slightly pubescent. Female bushes cultivated for flowerheads which develop into fascinating 15mm cones becoming pink or mauve late summer, persisting on the bush for many months. Excellent garden shrub and Superb for floral arrangements. 3 × 2m.

LEUCOSPERMUM

A genus of about 45 species of shrubs or small trees from South Africa and Zimbabwe named from the Greek *leucos*, white and *sperma*, seed, referring to smooth whitish seeds. Mostly from the south western Cape regions, they're among the world's most magnificent shrubs. A bush carrying hundreds of blooms in brilliant orange or yellow shades is a breathtaking sight from early spring well into summer. When not in bloom, Leucospermums may be distinguished from other Proteaceae family members by small toothed indentations on the tips of the leaves with raised edges usually outlined in red.

They prefer an open situation with adequate air movement to disperse excessive moisture from the foliage. Plant in deeply worked, free draining, volcanic, sandy or friable clay, acid soil without artificial or animal manures. A minimum of fertilizer is essential for success. Avoid coddling or overwatering during dry spells, but protection from frost is recommended, especially when plants are young. Pick blooms freely but little pruning is needed, apart from shaping. Few shrubs provide such a wealth of bloom in such glorious colours over such long periods.

Proteaceae. *All evergreen.*

Leucospermum cordifolium

Beautiful low shrubs with gracefully curving branches and greyish green, downy, lanceolate, 10cm leaves. In spring, every branch carries exquisite dome-shaped rich orange blossoms formed by numerous prominent styles or pins which spring from the centre, curving outwards and upwards to form perfect symmetrical pin cushion flowers, entirely covering the bush through spring and summer. Perfect garden feature and excellent for picking. Numerous colour forms and hybrids are constantly being introduced. Cordifolium — with heart shaped leaves. Syn L nutans, Syn L bolusii. 1.5 × 2m. **180**

Leucospermum cordifolium 'Aurora'

Compact grower. Abundant, waratah-like flowerheads in apricot and soft orange tones, late spring through summer. 1.5 × 1.5m.

Leucospermum cordifolium 'Harry Chittick'

Specially selected cultivar producing spectacular orange-red flowers on long stems, particularly attractive for cutflowers. 2 × 1.5m.

Leucospermum cuneiforme

Forms a well-rounded bush with luxuriant, grey-green, leathery, 5 × 2cm leaves, deeply notched across blunt tips. Gorgeous blooms basically buttercup yellow with numerous erect, deeper yellow, 6cm styles or pins, freely produced spring through summer. Syn L attenuatum. Cuneiforme — wedge-shaped leaves. 1.5 × 1.5m. **180**

Leucospermum cuneiforme 'Goldie'

Of South African origin. Erect, slender-stemmed plant producing attractive pin-cushion heads of yellow flowers late spring through mid summer. Prune after flowering to encourage compact growth. 1–2 × 1m.

Leucospermum cuneiforme 'Honey Glow'

Clear golden-yellow flowers with soft orange tints to inner flowers, produced from early summer. Erect growing bush. 2 × 1.5m.

Leucospermum hybrid 'Caroline'

Hawaiian hybrid from L tottum × L cordifolium. Excellent introduction with attractive rounded growth habit. Large rounded pin-cushion flower heads, orange tinted salmon, borne on long stems through spring and early summer. Such hybrids may eventually replace older species and cultivars due to greater disease resistance. 1–2 × 1.5m.

Leucospermum hybrid 'Firefly'

Choice hybrid from L tottum × L vestitum. Neat, compact grower with elliptic· grey-green leaves to 55 × 15mm, with three conspicuous red-tipped notches at the apex. Compact, rounded rich-red, pin-cushion flowers to 10cm across, becoming more intense with maturity, borne profusely on 30cm stems mid spring through midsummer. 1 × 1.5m. **189**

Leucospermum hybrid 'Scarlet Ribbons'

Excellent cultivar with outstanding, deep salmon pink, broad cone shaped flowers with scarlet perianth ribbons on 35–50cm stems. Unopened florets lightly covered with blue-grey down which combined with orange styles creates unusual pastel effects. Vigorous plant with upright growth. Blooms earlier than L cordifolium cultivars. 1.5 × 1.5m. **189**

Leucospermum hybrid 'Sunrise'
South African hybrid from L cordifolium × L patersonii hybrid. Vigorous grower with somewhat open and straggly growth habit. This is compensated by freely produced, large, deep orange-red flowers appearing late winter through spring. Hard pruning after flowering encourage better form. 1.5 × 1.5m.

Leucospermum hybrid 'Veldfire'
South African hybrid, vigorous, upright, rounded tidy growth habit, producing conspicuous soft yellow blooms with recurved perianth straps deepening through gold and orange shades, glowing brightly with maturity. Foliage well covered with soft grey hairs. 2 × 1.5m.   **189**

Leucospermum lineare 'Flame'
The species lineare differs from most Leucospermums with narrow, almost needle-like leaves to 70 × 3mm, deep olive-green with prominent red tip. Vivid clear orange-red flowers to 12cm wide becoming deep red with maturity borne on 30–40cm stems early spring through mid summer. Forms a neat compact upright bush, spectacular for garden display and excellent for picking. Natural mountain dweller, hardier to frost than most species. Lineare — narrow, with sides nearly parallel. 2 × 1.5m.

Leucospermum lineare 'Red Sunset'
Hawaiian hybrid from L lineare × L cordifolium. Vigorous, compact, erect, rounded bush with attractive leaves typical of the species. Flowers creamy lemon at first with apricot styles tipped red, maturing deep orange-red, borne on slender stems often in clusters of 2–3. 1.5 × 1.5m.

Leucospermum prostratum 'Ground Fire'
Prostrate grower with long trailing branches, narrow-oval, soft grey-green, slightly pubescent leaves to 40 × 6mm. Small, 2–3cm, pompon flowers in great masses appear spring through autumn, or almost the year through in suitable conditions. Flowers light yellow at first, developing through soft orange, maturing dark orange-red, which appearing in all stages at the same time provide a unique multi-coloured effect. Exceptional ground and bank cover in sandy or loose free, acid soil conditions. Protect from heavy frost. 30cm × 1.5m.

Leucospermum reflexum
Larger grower, forming a rounded shrub with erect branches densely covered with dark silvery grey foliage. Produces hundreds of bright orange-red flower heads. Lower bracts reflex to form a skirt around the base of each flower which are carried on long stems well above the foliage in a fancied resemblance to sky-rockets in full flight. A good focal point in any landscape setting. Blooms excellent for floral arrangements. Reflexum — bent sharply backwards. 3 × 2m.   **180**

Leucospermum reflexum 'Luteum'
This attractive form bears masses of bright clear yellow reflexed flowers through spring and summer. Exceptional garden display and a magnificent cut flower. Syn L 'Cape Gold'. 3 × 2m.

Leucospermum tottum
Forms a neatly rounded bush with deep green oblong leaves to 40 × 10mm, tinged reddish, almost without notches and loosely arranged on sturdy stems. Flowers pale salmon at first, becoming deep pink to scarlet and expanding to 10cm across, well covering the plant. Flowers have soft or lacy appearance and open a little later than the cordifolium types. Naturally from altitudes exceeding 1500m, L tottum is quite resistant to cold. 1 × 1m.

Leucospermum tottum 'Champagne'
Attractive, low-growing shrub with bushy habit. Flower heads more flattened than usual in rich salmon pink, borne freely on long slender stems through spring. Excellent landscaping shrub and good for picking. Prune lightly after flowering. 1 × 1.5m.

Leucospermum tottum 'Fantasy'
Rather sprawling habit when young, more upright with maturity. Gorgeous salmon-buff flowers tipped vermillion, inner central zone pastel pink, deepening with age. 1.5 × 1.5m.

A genus of about 44 species of evergreen shrubs and trees named for Leucothoe of Greek mythology, beloved of Apollo and daughter of Orchamus king of Babylon. Shade tolerant shrubs grown for handsome foliage and beautiful white flowers.

Plant in partial or dappled shade in deeply worked, free-draining, organically enriched, moisture-retentive, slightly acid soil. Mulch freely and water regularly through dry periods. Prune by removing old flower stems. If growth becomes rank and untidy, cut all stems to just above ground level to give it a fresh start. Effective when massed beneath other acid lovers such as rhododendron, azalea, kalmia etc.
    Ericaceae. *All evergreen.*

Leucothoe fontanesiana
Lily of the Valley Shrub
A graceful shrub related to Pieris, native to the south eastern USA, sometimes incorrectly referred to as L catesbaei. Long arching branches drooping gently to the ground, clothed with leathery, oblong-lanceolate, 6–15cm, dark green and lustrous leaves which turn bronzy purple in autumn and winter. Creamy white, almost cylindric, lily of the valley-like flowers in 6cm axillary pendulous racemes early spring. Fontanesiana — for Rene Louiche Desfontaines, 18th century botanical author. 1 × 1m.

Leucothoe fontanesiana 'Rainbow'
Forms a small rounded shrub with graceful arching stems and characteristic sprays of small white lily of the valley flowers. Young shoots crimson. Leaves attractively variegated pink and cream, maturing white and green. Syn L 'Girard's Rainbow'. 1 × 1m.

A genus of about 20 species of fibrous rooted herbs distributed through Australia, New Zealand and South America. The genus was named for Marie A Libert, 19th century Belgian writer on botanical subjects. Grown for its small strap-like leaves, dainty flowers like miniature Iris and colourful seed capsules. Naturally found in damp places among sand dunes or in mossy places. Very hardy, enjoys full or partial sun, deeply worked, loose moisture-retentive soil. This is an extremely useful plant for rock or feature gardens, at its best when growing through a bed of stones, pebbles etc.
    Iridaceae. *All evergreen.*

Libertia grandiflora
Mikoikoi
Larger-flowered species found in damp situations in New Zealand forests. Brownish green linear leaves to 90 × 1.5cm, tapering to a point. Attractive white 3–5cm flowers with olive or bronze keel are carried on 90cm lightly branched stems in early summer, followed in autumn by decorative golden-brown seed capsules. 90 × 75cm.

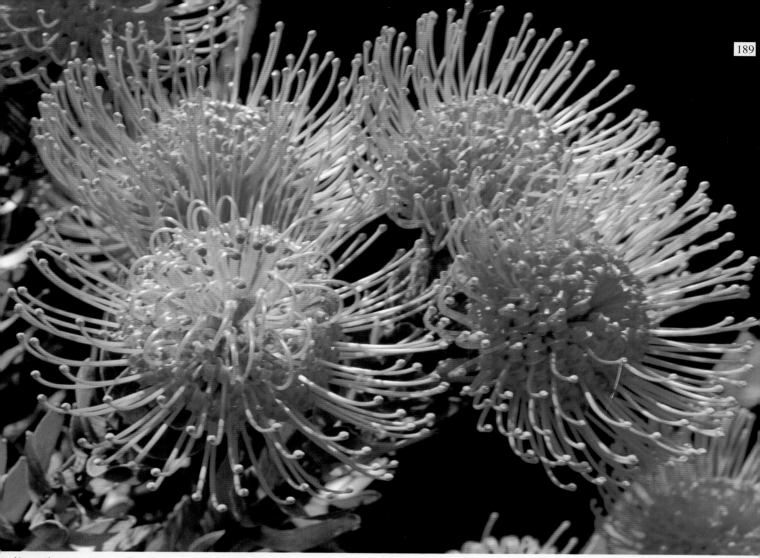

Above: Leucospermum 'Fire Fly' **187**
Below: Leucospermum hybrid 'Scarlet Ribbons' **187**

Below: Leucospermum hybrid 'Veldfire' **188**

Above: Macropiper excelsum 'Psittacorum' **197**

Above: Magnolia campbellii 'Charles Raffill' **197**
Below: Magnolia stellata **200**

Above: Liquidambar styraciflua *American Sweet Gum* **194**
Below: Liriodendron tulipifera *Tulip Tree Yellow Poplar* **194**

Above: Lophostemon conferta 'Variegatus' **195**

Above: Luculia gratissima **196**
Below: Liriodendron tulipifera 'Aureo-Marginatum' **194**

Below: Libertia peregrinans *New Zealand Iris* **193**

Above: Lophostemon conferta **195**
Below: Lithodora diffusa **195**

Above: Magnolia x soulangeana 'Lennei Alba' **200**
Below: Magnolia x soulangeana *Tulip Magnolia* **200**

Below: Magnolia x soulangeana 'Lennei' **200**

Libertia ixioides
New Zealand Iris, Tukauki
Found in coastal and inland areas throughout New Zealand. Forms a colony of rigid linear dark green leaves with brownish midrib, to 40cm × 6mm, tapering to a fine point. Pure white, three-petalled, 25–40mm flowers tinted brown or green, carried in broad panicles on 30–60cm stems early summer, followed by conical to oblong 10mm capsules in autumn, at first yellow, maturing brown. Ixioides — resembling Ixia. 60 × 50cm.

Libertia peregrinans
New Zealand Iris
Simple but interesting plant often found in damp hollows among sand dunes, resembling miniature flax. Sword-like leaves to 25 × 2cm, brownish green or khaki with well defined orange-yellow midriff, tapering to a sharp point, arranged in fans. The plant is sustained by underground rhizomes from which new fans of leaves appear up to 30cm away from the parent. They form a small colony but are seldom invasive or a nuisance. Small white three-petalled flowers on short stems in spring, followed by bronzy yellow capsules. Peregrinans — roaming or travelling. 25cm × +−1m.   **191**

LIBOCEDRUS

A genus of about five species of trees found in New Caledonia and New Zealand named from the Greek *libos* a tear or drop and *cedrus*, cedar, an apparent reference to gummy, tear-like exudations. The two New Zealand endemic species are amongst the most beautiful conifers and L plumosa in particular is worthy of extensive planting. Although large in natural forests, slow growth-rate allows free use in average gardens. As with most larger New Zealand trees, they are suitable for areas of high rainfall. Hardy to cold, but prefers semi-shade when young. Deeply worked soil conditioned and mulched with peat moss. Water deeply through dry spells.
    Cupressaceae. *All evergreen.*

Libocedrus bidwillii
Kaikawaka, Southern Cedar
A fastigiate or slender erect tree which tapers rapidly, forming a perfect cone-shaped head with short branches and rich green, fine ferny foliage. Differs from Kawaka, having smaller leaves and cones and four-sided branchlets. More prevalent in southern New Zealand, reaching its northernmost

limit on Te Aroha Mountain. Extremely hardy to cold. Named for J C Bidwell, 19th century Director of Botanic Gardens in Sydney and collector of New Zealand plants. 3 × 1.

Libocedrus plumosa
Kawaka, Plume Incense Cedar
Handsome symmetrical pyramidal tree with clean straight stems to 24m high, easily distinguished by old bark falling away in long thin ribbons. Found mainly in Northland with limited distribution in Hawkes Bay and Nelson.
    Forms a slender erect specimen with bright green scale-like leaves arranged on flattened fern-like branchlets. Very rare, highly aromatic timber, suggestive of the common name. Delightful in juvenile form, even in small gardens. Ideal accent and container plant. Plumosa — feathery. 2.5 × 1m.

LIGUSTRUM

A genus of about 50 hardy trees and shrubs distributed through east and south east Asia, Europe, North Africa and Australia, called by the Latin term for Privet. Variegated forms have handsome foliage, but also valued for tolerance of abuse and climatic extremes. Indifferent to soil conditions, heat or cold, wet or dry and polluted air. Few pests or diseases bother them. Ideal for boundary screens, specimens, backgrounds or fillers. Trim to encourage colourful new growth. Well fed and watered plants respond with healthier appearance and better foliage displays. Keep invasive rooting habits in mind when locating Privet.
    Oleaceae. *All evergreen.*

Ligustrum ovalifolium 'Allgold'
Selected and named for clear yellow foliage without green variegation. More spreading than 'Aureum'. Best in semi-shade and lightly pruned or clipped to maintain good shape and fresh bursts of new growth. 1.5 × 1.5m.

Ligustrum ovalifolium 'Aureum'
Golden Privet
Brilliant gold and green variegated foliage with each burst of new growth. Leaves elliptic-ovate to 7cm long, deep green heavily margined with gold, some completely gold. Tends to drop a portion of its leaves in winter but only for brief periods. Trim regularly for growth renewal, compactness and shaping. 2 × 1.5m.

LINUM

A genus of about 200 species of annual or perennial herbs or shrubs widely distributed through temperate and subtropical regions of both hemispheres, called by the Latin term *linum* for flax or linen. Linum species are noted for a long succession of perfectly formed satiny flowers. The listed species is endemic in New Zealand found mainly on rocky cliffs or dunes in coastal areas from the far North to Stewart Island. Grows in any deeply worked, free-draining soil in full sun or partial shade. After flowering, prune to within 15cm from the base. May be short-lived, but fallen seeds germinate readily beneath the bush if capsules are left to ripen.
    Linaceae.

Linum monogynum
Rauhuia
Most ornamental, soft-wooded shrub with erect or spreading branches. Linear to lanceolate leaves to 25 × 4mm, smooth and leathery, pale green to almost glaucous. White five-petalled 25mm flowers with perfect form born profusely in terminal corymbs spring through summer, followed in autumn by light-brown, 4–10mm seed capsules. Showy plant for rock gardens, borders or massed bedding. Monogynum — with one pistil. Evergreen. 40 × 50cm.

LIQUIDAMBAR

The genus comprises four species of deciduous trees belonging to Asia Minor, China and North America, named from the Latin *liquidus*, liquid and *ambar*, amber, referring to the fragrant resin or sweet gum known as liquid storax, an ingredient of various cosmetic, medical and technical processes. Main source of storax is from the soft inner bark of L orientalis, but is also present in L styraciflua. American Sweet Gum is one of the finest deciduous trees for autumn colour with moderate growth rate, good form, picturesque branch pattern and corky bark. Maple-like, artistically lobed leaves with intense autumn colour either in warm or cooler regions.
    Plant in fertile, deeply worked, moisture retentive, neutral or slightly acid soil. Stake securely, mulch freely and water deeply during the establishment period

or regularly through dry periods. Feed early spring with well-balanced fertilizer. In the early stages prune only to shape, leaving lower branches intact if possible unless future headroom is desired. Locate for unhindered development, although wide-spreading branches may be shortened back in winter if tending to overcrowd.

Hamamelidaceae. *All deciduous.*

Liquidambar orientalis
Oriental Sweetgum
Native to Asia Minor. Small slow growing tree with spreading or rounded head. Deep green palmate leaves to 7cm across usually with five deeply cut and coarsely margined lobes, autumn colour from deep gold to bright red in cooler areas, dull brownish-purple in warmer climates. Small greenish flowers appear with new spring leaves. Grows larger in warm dry climates. Orientalis — eastern. 5 × 3m.

Liquidambar styraciflua
American Sweet Gum
Native to eastern United States. Forms a stately pyramidal tree with picturesque framework, well spaced branches and rugged corky bark. Handsome shining dark green, maple-like leaves to 15cm across with five or seven triangular lobes, changing in autumn to shades of red, orange, yellow and purple making the whole tree a riot of colour. Hardy in all climates but equally colourful in warm or cooler areas. Ultimately grows to a sizeable tree but easily accommodated in average gardens for many years. Styraciflua — flowing with storax. 7 × 5m.   **190**

Liquidambar styraciflua 'Aurora'
Selected for compact, pyramidal, slow growing form, large maple leaves and brilliant autumn displays in shades of yellow, orange, red and purple. Ideal for smaller gardens. 4 × 3m.

Liquidambar styraciflua 'Burgundy'
Selected clone with distinguished narrow pyramidal form, larger leaves which appear early spring and rich deep burgundy red autumn colours often persisting through winter. 5 × 3m.

Liquidambar styraciflua 'Golden Treasure'
An Australian introduction and amongst the most colourful foliage trees. Shapely pyramidal outline and green and gold variegated leaves providing good colour spring through summer. In autumn the gold changes to cream then white and inner green to vivid shades of burgundy, orange and pink. 5 × 3m.

Liquidambar styraciflua 'Kia'
Outstanding selection, erect pyramidal spreading form and large deeply lobed maple-leaves. Bright autumn tones of orange, crimson deepening to purple before falling. 6 × 4m.

Liquidambar styraciflua 'Palo Alto'
Narrow upright pyramidal form, rich green summer foliage, bright red in autumn intensifying to fiery scarlet before falling. 7 × 5m.

Liquidambar styraciflua 'Richard'
Upright pyramidal form with outer branches gracefully drooping. Finely cut and lobed leaves with autumn shades of orange and apricot then becoming purple. Resembles L 'Worplesdon' but with better autumn colour. 8 × 5m.

Liquidambar styraciflua 'Richmond'
Beautiful form of American Sweet Gum selected for an excellent mix of orange, gold, scarlet and crimson-black leaves in autumn. 5 × 5m.

Liquidambar styraciflua 'Rotundiloba'
Fruitless Sweetgum
Instead of typical pointed lobes to its leaves, this cultivar is distinguished by rounded lobes. Foliage green through summer becoming dark burgundy red in autumn. Does not produce fruit. 6 × 4m.

Liquidambar styraciflua 'Worplesdon'
Upright, pyramidal form, outer branches gracefully drooping, finely cut and lobed leaves taking on autumn shades of pale orange and apricot then becoming purple. 8 × 5m.

A genus of two species of trees from China, Indochina and North America named from the Greek *leirion*, a lily and *dendron*, a tree. Of ancient lineage, fossil records from Alaska, Greenland and Europe suggest extensive distribution in pre-glacial times. The American native L tulipifera was at one time thought to be the sole species until 19th century discovery of L chinense. Related to Magnolia, they are grown for beauty of form, unusual foliage and tulip-like flowers.

Not the easiest trees to transplant so select either container grown or small field grown plants. Plant in deeply worked, slightly acid, free-draining, moisture retentive soil in full sun, shel-tered from prevailing wind. Mulch freely for root insulation and water deeply through summer. Excellent tree for larger gardens, public areas or farms.

Magnoliaceae. *All deciduous.*

Liriodendron chinense
Chinese Tulip Tree
Discovered in the Lushan Mountains of central China in 1875. Resembles L tulipifera but smaller, to 15m in its natural habitat. Leaves somewhat larger, lobes more deeply cut, more glaucous beneath and tinted purple when young. Tulip-shaped flowers smaller, green outside and yellowish within. 6 × 4m.

Liriodendron tulipifera
Tulip Tree, Yellow Poplar
Native to eastern North America. Fast growing tree to 60m in its natural state, with arrow-straight trunk, thick, greyish, ridged bark and spreading ascending branches forming a tall pyramidal crown. Curious lyre-shaped leaves to 12cm with about six angular lobes, cut more or less squarely at the apex instead of a point, smooth textured, bright green spring and summer, rich butter-yellow in autumn.

Tulip or cup-shaped, 5cm, fragrant, lime-green flowers banded orange at the base of each reflexed petal and with conspicuous cluster of stamens. Blooms which appear after the leaves in early summer are beautiful at close range, but too high and hidden amongst the leaves to be showy on the tree. Cone-shaped fruit comprises numerous winged seeds. May take up to ten years to commence blooming. Tulipifera — tulip-bearing. 10 × 6m.   **190**

Liriodendron tulipifera 'Arnold'
Narrow upright columnar form, more useful in confined spaces. Similar foliage and flower but may commence to bloom as early as three years from planting. 8 × 5m.

Liriodendron tulipifera 'Aureo-Marginatum'
Amongst the finest colour-foliage trees. Unique lyre-shaped leaves variegated with various shades of green, broadly and irregularly margined yellow. Bright in spring, tends to lose colour intensity in summer but returns in autumn. Fragrant orange green and yellow flowers late spring. 6 × 4m.   **191**

Liriodendron tulipifera 'Fastigiatum'
Similar foliage and flower to the Tulip Tree, but with narrow erect form, excellent for confined spaces or dramatic avenue planting in larger areas. Fastigiatum — with erect branches close together to form a column. 8 × 4m.

LITHODORA

A genus of about seven species of perennial herbs and sub-shrubs from south west Europe to Asia Minor, named from the Greek *lithos*, a stone and *doron*, a gift. Cultivars of L diffusa valued for intense blue flowers. Plant in full sun in deeply worked, free-draining, moisture-retentive, lime-free soil. Mulch freely and water during dry periods, but avoid waterlogging at all times. Under these conditions the plant is hardy to –15°C. Trim or shear after flowering. Excellent for rock gardens, wall spillers, banks, front border etc.

Boraginaceae. *All evergreen.*

Lithodora diffusa
Prostrate to slightly mounded shrublet from southern Europe. Stems slightly hairy. Leaves elliptic to linear, to 35 × 8mm, deep green, somewhat bristly. Plant studded during summer with 20mm, bright gentian blue or purple starry flowers with a dense ring of white hairs within. Syn Lithospermum diffusum. Diffusa — spreading. 40 × 90cm. **191**

Lithodora diffusa 'Alba'
Prostrate grower with masses of white flowers often faintly tinted blue through summer. Good ground cover. 25 × 90cm.

Lithodora diffusa 'Grace Ward'
Exquisite bright azure blue flowers during spring and early summer. Narrow dark green foliage, low trailing habit. Perfect rockery or ground cover plant. 15 × 90cm.

Lithodora diffusa 'Irish Crystal'
Low prostrate grower, foliage deep green. Flowers sparkling white delicately tinted misty blue. 10 × 90cm.

LOMATIA

A genus of about 12 species, mostly from eastern Australia, three from Chile, named from the Greek *loma*, a border or edge in reference to the papery wings around the seeds. Ornamental evergreen trees with handsome foliage and attractive flowers. The listed species is hardy to about –10°C but prefers shelter from cold drying winds. Plant in deeply worked, organically enriched, moisture-retentive, peaty soil with pH of 5–6 in a sunny location. Mulch freely and water during dry periods. Excellent feature plant.

Proteaceae.

Lomatia ferruginea
From Chile, magnificent foliage shrub or small tree with stems and young growth coated with rusty velvety down. Narrowly triangular, bipinnate, fern-like leaves to 20 × 10cm with up to 17 leathery, olive green leaflets, resembling silky oak but somewhat smaller stiffer and more refined. Magnificent golden yellow and deep rose, 12mm flowers with a touch of green, borne during summer in axillary racemes to 7cm long. Develops slowly, at first a single erect stem with handsome leaves directly attached, branching later to form a neat compact small tree. Ferruginea — rust coloured. Evergreen. 3 × 2m.

LONICERA

A genus of about 180 species of shrubs and climbers spread throughout the northern hemisphere, named for Adam Lonitzer, 16th century German botanist. A diverse genus with numerous applications, many with attractive flowers. All species readily transplanted, grow rapidly and perform in any reasonable soil or climate in full or partial sun. The Climbing Plant section of this book features ornamental climbing Honeysuckles.

Caprifoliaceae. *All evergreen.*

Lonicera nitida
Box Honeysuckle
Densely branched small-foliaged shrub from China with short twiggy stems, densely covered with ovate to rounded, 12mm, dark green, highly polished leaves. Small creamy white fragrant 10mm flowers in early summer followed by translucent, purple-blue 6mm fruit. Usually seen as a low hedge or screen from 50–125cm high and 30cm wide although flowers and fruit are non-existent when plants are clipped. Plant 40cm apart and nip to half way at planting time. Nitidis — shining.

Lonicera nitida 'Aurea'
Similar to above in general appearance but slower in growth and leaves coloured lime-yellow, intensifying to deep yellow in full sun and soil which is not over-rich.

Lonicera nitida 'Fertilis'
Rather stiff shrub with erect leading shoots. Leaves in four ranks, broadly ovate or elliptic to 15mm long. Lateral shoots long and arching with smaller leaves. Prolific flowers and fruit. Fertilis — fruitful.

LOPHOSTEMON

A genus of six species of trees or large shrubs from Australia and New Guinea named from the Greek *lophos*, a crest and *stemon*, a stamen. The two listed are found in rainforests of eastern Queensland and New South Wales, magnificent noble specimens with reddish trunk and soaring branches to 35–40m. Readily trained to more manageable proportions. Has become a popular and desirable tree for parks, school grounds, motor camps, farms, streets or avenues.

Although a little frost tender when young, withstands light frosts and considerable drought once established. Plant in full sun in deeply worked, free-draining average fertile soil. Mulch freely, provide shelter and moisture when young. Train early either for a clean single stem, or pinch to develop low-branching.

Myrtaceae. *All evergreen.*

Lophostemon conferta
Queensland Box, Brisbane Box
Neat erect symmetrical tree, somewhat upright at first, later developing a broad rounded crown. Trunk and limbs with reddish bark which peels back to reveal a layer of smooth, lighter coloured bark beneath. Leaves lanceolate to 15 × 5cm, leathery, bright green and glossy, clustered at the ends of branchlets. Creamy white, 12mm flowers resembling eucalyptus blossom, in clusters of 3–7 during summer, followed by woody capsules like gumnuts. Syn Tristania conferta. Conferta — crowded. 7 × 5m. **191**

Lophostemon conferta 'Variegata'
Resembles above but smaller growing. Most attractive variegated leaves, light green margins and irregular central brilliant yellow blotch with reddish midrib and petioles at first, maturing dark green and creamy yellow. Extremely ornamental tree. 6 × 4m. **191**

LOROPETALUM

A genus of two species of evergreen shrubs from Himalayas, China and Japan closely related to hamamelis, named from the Greek, *loron* a strap or thong and *petalon*, petal referring to long narrow petals. **L chinense**, naturally a sizeable tree, is more of a shrub in cultivation, valued for its distinct oriental appearance and abundance of flower. Easy to grow in slightly acid, deeply worked, free draining, moisture-retentive soil conditioned with peat moss and sand. Enjoys summer moisture, occasional feeding, but little pruning. Full sun or semi-shade. Excellent for rock or feature gardens. **Hamamelidaceae.**

Loropetalum chinense
Fringe Flower
A shrub with subtle beauty and unique charm. Slowly forms a compact shrub with tiered, graceful, arching, somewhat spreading, semi-pendulous branches. Leaves ovate to elliptic, 4–5cm long, dull dark green and prominently veined. Flowers white or greenish white, each with four narrow twisted 2cm strap-like petals resembling witch hazel, mass-produced in clusters of up to eight at the end of each twig for long periods late winter through spring. Picturesque and beautiful all year, quite irresistible in full bloom. Evergreen. 1.5 × 1m.

A genus of 5 species of shrubs and small trees from temperate east Asia, named from *lukuli swa*, Nepalese for Luculia gratissima. The species listed are two of the most beautiful flowering shrubs admired also for handsome foliage. Locate in full sun in areas free of all but light frost. Plant in rich deeply worked, free-draining, moisture retentive soil with sand and peat moss. Mulch freely and water deeply but infrequently during dry periods. They are reasonably drought tolerant but resent wet feet. Pruning to half way after flowering preserves shape, encourages vigorous growth and maximum flower. Although classified as evergreen, both species tend to drop a portion of their leaves during colder months. **Rubiaceae.** *All semi-evergreen.*

Luculia grandifolia
White Luculia, Bhutan Luculia
Exquisite flowering and foliage shrub from Bhutan, discovered at 2500m. Distinctive appearance with sturdy erect stems. Handsome ovate to elliptic leaves to 35 × 25cm, prominently veined and coarsely textured, deep dull-green, turning rich red or reddish purple in autumn. Worth growing just for the beauty of its foliage. Pure white, fragrant,

trumpet shaped flowers to 7cm long, borne in erect cymes to 20cm across through late spring, summer and autumn. Excellent for floral arrangements. Hardier than L gratissima, but requires a sunny warm location away from heavy frost. 1.5 × 1.5m.

Luculia gratissima
Pink Luculia Himalayan Luculia
The pink-flowered Himalayan luculia in full bloom is a winter attraction in warmer areas. Forms an open bush with soft, olive green, deeply ribbed, ovate to elliptic leaves to 20 × 10cm. Foliage becomes bronzy red in autumn and winter, a proportion falling except under very warm conditions. Sweetly fragrant, light to deep pink, slender tube-shaped flowers with flaring lobes in terminal rounded clusters to 24cm across through autumn and winter. A bush in full bloom is one of the garden's greatest assets. Perfect for picking. Enjoys the support of other shrubs for protection from wind or frost, but needs plenty of sun. Seedling plants variable in colour. Selected cutting-grown or named cultivars more reliable. Gratissima — very agreeable or pleasant. 2 × 1.5m.   **191**

Luculia gratissima 'Early Dawn'
Selected for high quality deep pink fragrant flowers. Syn L 'Egmont Pink'. 2 × 1.5m.

Luculia pinceana 'Fragrant Cloud'
Native from Nepal to Yunnan. Strong grower with pubescent stems. Leaves lanceolate or ovate to elliptic to 15 × 5cm, deep-green, leathery, sparsely pubescent beneath. Almond-pink, tubular flowers to 5cm long with 5cm flaring lobes borne through winter in 20cm corymbs, followed by obovoid ribbed 15 × 10mm fruit. Named for Robert T Pince, 19th century Exeter nurseryman. 2.5 × 2m.

LYONOTHAMNUS

A genus of one species, a slender evergreen tree, native to Santa Catalina Islands off California, named for W S Lyon (1851–1916), US plant collector, and from Greek *thamnos*, a shrub. Admired for slender graceful form, attractive leaves, peeling bark and pretty flower clusters, more particularly the Fernleaf Catalina Ironwood. Grows best in warm maritime conditions in sun or semi-shade in deeply worked, free-draining, rich fertile soil. Mulch freely, water during dry periods until established, but then is tolerant of considerable drought. Prune in winter to maintain good

form and cut off faded flower clusters. **Rosaceae.** *All evergreen.*

Lyonothamnus floribundus
Catalina Ironwood
Slender tree with narrow crown and reddish brown bark which peels in long thin strips. Leaves simple to pinnate, lanceolate-oblong to 16cm long, glossy, deep green, pubescent beneath, margins lobed or scallop-toothed. White flowers in terminal compound panicles to 20cm across through spring and summer. 9 × 6m.

Lyonothamnus f ssp asplenifolius
Fernleaf, Catalina Ironwood
Slender, graceful tree, admired for handsome ferny foliage. Bipinnate leaves to 16cm long, divided into 3–7 deeply notched or lobed leaflets, deep green and glossy above, grey and pubescent beneath. Small white flowers in corymbs to 30cm across held above the foliage spring through summer. Young shoots often reddish. Reddish brown bark peeling in long thin strips an attractive feature. Asplenifolius — leaves feathery, fernlike. 9 × 6m.

LYSIMACHIA

A genus of about 150 species of annual and perennial herbs widely distributed throughout subtropical and temperate regions, named for King Lysimachos of Thrace (360–281 BC) who is reputed to have calmed a wild bull with a piece of this plant. The king's name is from the Greek *lysimachos*, ending strife. One of the species is commonly called Loosestrife. The listed species is used mainly as ground cover, in rockeries or hanging baskets. Plant in deeply worked, free-draining, organically enriched, loose, fertile soil in partial shade and keep moist during dry periods. Apply small dressings of balanced fertilizer spring and autumn. Runners may be trimmed as required and plants periodically divided. Plant at 30–45cm centres for ground cover. **Primulaceae.**

Lysimachia nummalaria 'Gold Clusters'
Creeping Jenny
Glabrous creeping prostrate perennial from Central Europe with long runners which take root at each node. Stems reddish brown, covered with silky hairs. Leaves ovate to orbicular in pairs, olive green with lighter reverse, to 45mm long. Clusters of waxy bright golden yellow flowers with deeper

throat, bell-shaped with five flaring petals and prominent central stamen, borne profusely spring through early summer. Nummalaria — with coin-shaped leaves. Evergreen. 10 × 75cm.

MACROPIPER

A genus of nine species of shrubs and small trees from Polynesia, New Guinea and New Zealand named from the Greek *makros*, large and *peperi*, piper or pepper. Belongs to the Pepper family which includes interesting species such as *Piper nigrum* from southern India and Sri Lanka, source of black and white pepper and the South Pacific *Piper methysticum* from which kava drink is made. Aromatic fruit and leaves of Macropiper excelsum are said to be stimulating. Roots were chewed by early Maoris with toothache.

Handsome New Zealand native shrub for sun or shade in warmer coastal regions. Grown in shade, the leaves are soft and dark green. In the open they tend to be somewhat yellow and thick-textured. Plant in deeply worked, organically enriched, free-draining fertile soil, sheltered from strong wind and frost. Responds to periodic feeding. Mulch freely, but once established, grows in either moist or dry conditions. Watch and spray for chewing insects.

Piperaceae. *All evergreen.*

Macropiper excelsum
Kawa-kawa, Pepper Tree
Found in coastal forests and scrublands through the North Island, north eastern South Island and Chatham Islands. Glabrous aromatic shrub or small tree with dark, flexuous, meandering, somewhat erect branches with distended joints and nodes. Aromatic leaves broadly ovate to sub-orbicular, to 10 × 11cm, dark green to yellow-green and glossy above, paler beneath. Minute flowers closely set in erect spikes succeeded by closely set yellow to bright orange fruits on 25–75mm spikes. Excelsum — tall. 4 × 2.5m.

Macropiper excelsum 'Psittacorum'
From offshore islands around the northern coastline of New Zealand. Extremely handsome form with larger leaves to 15 × 20cm, prominently veined, generally yellow-green and very glossy. Orange flower and fruiting spikes to 15cm long contrast admirably against the foliage. Syn M excelsum 'Majus'. Psittacorum — of parrots. 4 × 2.5m. **190**

MAGNOLIA

A genus of about 120 species of evergreen and deciduous trees and shrubs, natives of northern and central America, east Asia and the Himalayas named for Pierre Magnol, director of the Montpelier Botanic Gardens over two centuries ago. Magnolias are true aristocrats among flowering shrubs and trees, each with a distinctive personality, good poise, elegant stems and leaves, shapely buds and beautiful flowers. The range is extensive and includes many species of horticultural merit including star-flowered stellata, dozens of tulip-flowered types and magnificent evergreen laurel Magnolias.

Choose planting sites carefully to avoid moving once established, especially deciduous forms. Some grow quite large and need space to display their individuality. Don't overcrowd or damage fleshy roots through deep digging or cultivation. Give them full sun, cool roots and shelter from strong winds. Plant in organically enriched, deeply worked, free-draining, moisture-retentive, neutral to slightly acid soil. Plant at original soil level, stake tall or larger specimens securely and avoid treading too firmly. Mulch freely after planting to insulate roots from the sun and conserve moisture. Water deeply and frequently during establishment, but avoid drowning the roots.

Topdress with acid fertilizer after planting and at least once a year to maintain healthy growth. Never apply lime. Pests and diseases seldom bother magnolias. Poor growth or unhealthy appearance usually caused by unsuitable soil conditions or soil deficiencies. As lawn specimens, provide large areas free of grass for mulching, feeding and watering. Limited cutting to shape may be necessary with young plants. Otherwise, pruning is restricted to removing damaged limbs, watershoots or grooming, immediately after flowering. Overgrown specimens may be hard pruned for size control.

Magnoliaceae. *All deciduous except M grandiflora.*

Magnolia acuminata 'Golden Glow'
Cucumber Tree
Native to eastern USA. Conical when young becoming widespread and pyramidal with ranks of tiered branches, trunk brown suffused grey, bark coarse and grooved. Bold leathery leaves, ovate to elliptic to 24cm long, fresh dark green above, grey-downy beneath, falling in autumn without colouring. Erect cup-shaped, golden yellow flowers to 9 × 3cm in spring followed by green oblong-cylindric cucumber-like cones becoming reddish brown. Needs plenty of space for unhindered development. Acuminata — tapering to a long narrow point. 8 × 5m.

Magnolia × brooklynensis 'Woodsman'
Interesting hybrid from two remote species, M acuminata × M liliflora featuring unusual greenish yellow to purple or chocolate flowers with soft pink centres fading to white. Moderately vigorous upright grower. Popular for floral arrangements. 4 × 3m.

Magnolia campbellii
Pink Tulip Tree
Magnificent tree from Himalayas producing spectacular giant blooms. Forms a lightly branched tree with spreading crown. Leaves elliptic-ovate to 25 × 12cm, dark green above, paler beneath. Opening from big greyish brown woolly buds, flowers at first goblet-shaped later wide-spreading to 25cm, pinkish white within, deep rose on the outside, deliciously fragrant, appearing freely on naked branches early to mid spring. An established specimen carrying hundreds of flowers an unforgettable sight, justifying the decade it may take to commence blooming. Named for Dr Archibald Campbell of Sikkim. 7 × 5m.

Magnolia campbellii 'Alba'
Beautiful creamy white fragrant form of M campbellii with large open cup or tulip-shaped blooms late winter through early spring. Maybe a decade before commencing to flower but worth waiting for. 7 × 5m.

Magnolia campbellii 'Charles Raffill'
Forms a broad domed crown with gracefully ascending branches. Immense clear soft rose-pink bowl-shaped blooms with white interiors held elegantly on naked branches early spring, somewhat later than other campbelli cultivars. May flower within 7 years of planting. Raised by Charles Raffill at Kew Gardens around 1946. 7 × 5m. **190**

Magnolia campbellii 'Lanarth'
An erect tree with ascending branches in narrow pyramidal form. Large cup-shaped deep reddish purple flowers with prominent central stamen cluster late winter to early spring. May commence blooming within 7 years of planting. Named for the great Cornish garden of Lanarth where the first specimen introduced from north western China was planted. 7 × 5m.

Magnolia campbellii 'Mollicomata'
From Tibet Yunan and east Himalayas. Sturdy erect open-domed tree with ascending branches, thick bronze-downy twigs and handsome 20–30cm smooth heavily veined dull-grey leaves, downy beneath. Flowers cup and saucer-shaped, 15–18cm across, rich-pink lightly tinged rose with lavender shadings, appearing before the leaves early spring, followed by bright red fruits. Commences to bloom at an earlier age, but not as clear coloured as M campbellii. Mollicomata — soft-haired. 5 × 4m.

Magnolia denudata
Yulan Magnolia
Handsome Chinese native with broadly pyramidal form. Leaves obovate to ovate, to 15cm long abruptly pointed and downy beneath. During winter large conspicuous buds covered with a grey shaggy hair. Goblet-shaped, 15cm, citrus-scented, pure white flowers with broad fleshy petals appear on naked branches early spring. Distinct oriental appearance, amongst the most beautiful white-flowered deciduous magnolias. Denudata — bare or naked. 5 × 4m.

Magnolia denudata 'Forrest's Pink'
Exquisite cultivar with nicely textured tulip or bell-shaped, soft raspberry pink flowers and light fruity fragrance early spring. Vigorous grower, tree-like form and commences to bloom at an early age. An outstanding Magnolia. 4 × 2.5m.

Magnolia grandiflora
Laurel Magnolia
Among the grandest and most beautiful evergreen flowering trees. Native to south eastern USA where impressive aged specimens to 30x15m flourish in rich swamplands. Large handsome elliptic to ovate, deep green glossy leaves to 20 × 9cm rusty-brown felted beneath. Large 25cm powerfully fragrant waxy white flowers turning buff with age produced through summer and autumn.

Somewhat variable in form, but easily trained to a single trunk. With lower branches removed it makes an ideal shade tree. May be shaped into virtually any form without resenting heavy pruning for size reduction if necessary. Ideal street lawn or patio tree and good in containers. Evergreen. 7 × 5m.

Magnolia grandiflora 'Ferruginea'
Sturdy selected form distinguished by rust-coloured felt beneath large glossy foliage. Forms an elegant round-headed specimen tree bearing immense fragrant creamy white flowers. Ferruginea — rust coloured. Evergreen. 7 × 5m.

Magnolia grandiflora 'Goliath'
Upright round-headed bushy tree producing at an early age very large creamy white globular flowers. Handsome short broad blistered glossy foliage, glabrous beneath. Evergreen. 4.5 × 4m.

Magnolia grandiflora 'Little Gem'
American selection, forming a small compact, narrowly columnar tree. Dense foliage, glossy deep green, heavily fluted beneath. Characteristic creamy white, wide open flowers somewhat smaller in proportion to the tree, produced freely from an early age. Evergreen. 5–8 × 4m.

Magnolia grandiflora 'Maryland'
Upright densely branched round-crowned tree bearing for long periods in spring large creamy white blooms with intense lemon fragrance. Excellent hybrid, handsome foliage. Evergreen. 6 × 4.5m.

Magnolia grandiflora 'Russet'
Compact narrow upright pyramidal habit, narrow pointed dark green foliage rusty suede-like beneath. Large 25cm fragrant cream flowers produced early. Evergreen. 5 × 4m.

Magnolia grandiflora 'Saint Mary'
Smaller compact grower, bright glistening leaves to 30cm long, dark rusty tomentose beneath. Very large cup-shaped fragrant white flowers from an early age. Evergreen. 5 × 4m.

Magnolia grandiflora 'Samuel Sommer'
Distinctive neat glossy dark green leaves, prominently ribbed, bright russet brown felt or suede beneath. Very fragrant large 30–40cm creamy flowers in spring. Evergreen. 6 × 4.5m.

Magnolia Gresham Hybrids
A range of impressive hybrids developed by Mr Drury Todd Gresham of Santa Cruz, California. Generally they grow into reasonably sized bushes, commence blooming at an early age and produce magnificent flowers regularly and prolifically. Listed alphabetically with other hybrids, identified as **Gresham hybrid.**

Magnolia hybrid 'Apollo'
Jury hybrid. Forms a neat small tree with open spreading habit. Deep rose-pink buds open to 23cm bowl-shaped rosy-red flowers with rich fruity fragrance, shaded light purple at the base of each petal, similar but lighter inside. Rounded overlapping petals with heavy-texture. Flowering may commence on 2 year-old trees, mid to late season. M liliflora 'Nigra' × M c 'Lanarth'. 6 × 4m.

Magnolia hybrid 'Athene'
Jury Hybrid. Erect vase-shaped form when young, becoming rounded with maturity. From an early age, a profusion of large 20–25cm, richly fragrant, cup and saucer-shaped flowers with rounded silky-textured petals, white at the rim shading to rosy purple with ivory white interiors appear from mid spring. M s 'Lennei Alba' × M 'Mark Jury'. 6 × 4m.

Magnolia hybrid 'Atlas'
Jury hybrid. Claimed as the world's largest Magnolia flower. Forms an erect open round-headed small tree. Immense 35cm, heavy-textured, cup-shaped, lilac-pink flowers with creamy-white interiors produced from an early age. Protect from frost and wind for unblemished blooms. M s 'Lennei' × M 'Mark Jury'. 6 × 4m.

Magnolia hybrid 'Betty'
Kosar hybrid. Multi-branched compact grower. Large upright tulip-shaped blooms, soft rose-pink tinged purple, interiors flushed white. Blooms heavily in spring. M liliflora × M stellata. 2.5 × 2m.

Magnolia hybrid 'Caerhay's Belle'
Magnificent large clear pink blooms like M campbellii unfold like crushed satin into immense bowl-shaped flowers. Attractive upright spreading grower. Takes several years to commence blooming. Absolutely exquisite. M sprengeri 'Diva' × M sargentiana 'Robusta'. 5 × 4m.

Magnolia hybrid 'Galaxy'
Kosar hybrid. Large reddish purple, distinctly fragrant blooms late spring. Formal upright pyramidal habit. Flowers freely from a young age. M liliflora 'Nigra' × M sprengeri 'Diva'. 5 × 3m.

Magnolia hybrid 'Heaven Scent'
Gresham hybrid. Upright rounded form with erect pastel lavender pink blooms toned more softly towards the tips and with white interiors. Unique colour amongst Magnolias and strongly fragrant. M liliflora 'Nigra' × M veitchii. 4 × 2.5m.

Magnolia hybrid 'Iolanthe'
Jury hybrid. Beautiful cultivar forming a neat round-headed tree with open airy branch structure. Rich deep pink buds open to large 25cm cup-shaped delicate pastel rose-pink flowers deepening towards the base of each petal and with creamy pink interiors. Commences to bloom from year two. Flowering persists over a five week period. M s 'Lennei' × M 'Mark Jury'. 6 × 4m.

Magnolia hybrid 'Manchu Fan'
Gresham hybrid. Vigorous grower with erect pyramidal form. Medium sized, delicately fragrant, goblet-shaped creamy white flowers flushed light purple at the base freely produced in spring. M lennei 'Alba' × M veitchii. 4 × 3m.

Magnolia hybrid 'Mark Jury'
Jury hybrid. Forms a narrow tree with steeply ascending branches covered in spring with a profusion of large cup-shaped, pure light pink flowers flushed rose-pink, margins tinged soft lavender. May take seven years to commence blooming. M c 'Lanarth' × M sargentiana 'Robusta'. 7 × 5m.

Magnolia hybrid 'Milky Way'
Jury hybrid. Erect neatly rounded tree. Cup-shaped, medium-sized heavy-textured, fragrant flowers, icy-white delicately shaded rose-pink towards the base and pure white inside, borne prolifically on bare branches early to mid spring. Commences to flower when young. M s 'Lennei Alba' × M 'Mark Jury'. 5 × 3.5m.

Magnolia hybrid 'Peppermint Stick'
Gresham hybrid. Vigorous erect rounded form. Cup and saucer-like flowers with erect central petals, basically white stained lavender pink at the base with a fine violet stripe extending up each petal. M liliflora 'Nigra' × M veitchii. 4 × 3m.

Magnolia hybrid 'Ricki'
Kosar hybrid. Forms a multi-stemmed bush with upright habit. Long slender erect buds open to cup-shaped rosy purple flowers, deepening towards the base and with white flushed purple interiors. massed on bare branches early spring. M liliflora × M stellata. 2.5 × 2m.

Magnolia hybrid 'Royal Crown'
Gresham hybrid. Forms a shapely rounded small tree with a reliable display of magnificent flowers from mid spring. Immense cup and saucer-shaped flowers to 30cm across with slender elongated reddish violet cup, creamy white within. M liliflora 'Nigra' × M veitchii. 4 × 3m.

Magnolia hybrid 'Ruby'
Impressive goblet-shaped delicately fragrant rich ruby-red flowers with fine white picotee edge to the petals and white interior. Heavy textured petals. Hybrid from M soulangeana 'Picture'. 4 × 3m.

Magnolia hybrid 'Sayonara'
Gresham hybrid. Magnificent small tree with bushy upright habit. Large ivory-white globe-shaped flowers faintly flushed lavender-pink on the exterior late spring. M veitchii × M soulangeana 'Lennei Alba'. 4 × 3m.

Magnolia hybrid 'Serene'
Jury hybrid. Strong growing, erect sparsely branched tree when young becoming more spreading and rounded. Massive rounded bowl-shaped 25cm, slightly fragrant blooms, deepest rosy pink shaded purplish carmine toward the base, inside ivory-white tinged purple toward the margin. Flowers from an early age, blooms mid-spring for long periods. M liliflora × M 'Mark Jury'. 5 × 4m.

Magnolia hybrid 'Spectrum'
Kosar hybrid. Sturdy upright to pyramidal tree. Remarkable very large dark rosy purple cup-shaped blooms, white interior, profuse in late spring. Flowers from an early age. M liliflora 'Nigra' × M sprengeri diva. 5 × 4m.

Magnolia hybrid 'Star Wars'
Neat erect rounded medium growth habit. Immense bright rosy-pink flushed white blooms with satiny texture produced freely on bare branches late winter through early spring. Raised by Mr O Blumhardt of Whangarei from M liliflora × M campbellii. Flowers strongly resemble M campbelli but the tree commences to bloom during the third year from grafting. 5 × 4m.

Magnolia hybrid 'Sundance'
Elegant tulip-shaped deep yellow fragrant flowers to 20cm across in mid spring. Tidy conical form, attractive deep-green foliage. M acuminata × M denudata. 5 × 4m.

Magnolia hybrid 'Susan'
Kosar hybrid. Forms an upright, multi-branched shrub. Erect long-tapered, deep claret-purple buds open to slightly fragrant glowing reddish violet blooms with white tinged violet interiors borne in great abundance late spring. M liliflora × M stellata. 2.5 × 2m.

Magnolia hybrid 'Vulcan'
Jury hybrid. Erect open-branched habit at first becoming narrowly rounded at maturity. Massive 25–30cm brilliant ruby-red flowers with rich fruity fragrance opening from wine-purple buds from late winter. Flowers comprise twelve heavy-textured fleshy petals forming a rounded bloom of great substance, appearing from an early age. Possibly the most impressive Jury hybrid yet to appear. 6 × 4.5m.

Magnolia Jury Hybrids
Many superb large flowered prolific blooming hybrids commencing to flower at an early age, developed by Felix M Jury and his son Mark C Jury of Taranaki, New Zealand are listed alphabetically with other hybrids, identified as **Jury hybrid**.

Magnolia kobus 'Borealis'
Hardy sturdy Japanese variety with smooth branches, downy winter buds and broad ovate leaves to 18 × 10cm. Starry 10cm blooms resembling M stellata, creamy white, faintly stained purple at the base. Kobus — Japanese name for the species. Borealis — northern. 7 × 5m.

Magnolia Kosar hybrids
A hybridizing programme carried out at the US National Arboretum in the late 1950s using mainly M liliflora and M stellata as parents has resulted in an excellent range of shrubby, small-growing, multi-stemmed cultivars. They are hardy, prolific and commence blooming early, often during the first year. Bright green ornamental leaves. Listed alphabetically with other hybrids, identified as **Kosar hybrid**.

Magnolia liliflora
Lily Magnolia
Delightful smaller growing Chinese variety forming a low many branched shrub, slowly increasing its width at the base by forming new erect-growing basal shoots. Long erect buds like slender tulips, rich purple outside, almost white within gradually opening to lily-form flowers from early spring, some flowers persisting through summer. Good for picking if taken before the buds are fully open. Liliflora — lily-flowered. 2.5 × 2m.

Magnolia liliflora 'Nigra'
Slightly more compact and slender cultivar from Japan, tending to produce less basal shoots. Slender curved pansy-black buds open dark maroon-purple with creamy white interiors stained purplish pink, flowering profusely from an early age over two months through spring and summer. The deepest-coloured Magnolia. 2 × 1.5m.

Magnolia loebneri 'Leonard Messel'
A magnificent open branched small tree bearing a profusion of fragrant, narrow petalled, star-shaped, soft lavender-pink, 13cm blooms with white interiors, opening from deeper buds. Beautiful hybrid possibly M kobus × M stellata 'Rosea' originating at Nymans, Sussex, a grand garden made by the late Colonel Messel. 4 × 3m.

Magnolia loebneri 'Merrill'
Forms a large shrub with picturesque, multi-branched structure and flowers resembling Star Magnolia, larger but with fewer

petals. Blooms fragrant, pure white, quite waxy, freely produced before the leaves in spring. Hybrid M kobus × M stellata. 4 × 2.5m.

Magnolia macrophylla
Large-Leaved Cucumber Tree
Native to south eastern USA where specimens to 20m with widespread branches and 45cm trunk may be found although relatively rare in cultivation. Has larger foliage and flowers than most deciduous trees. Leaves elliptic to oblong-ovate, to 75 × 30cm, pale green, glabrous, thin-textured, glaucous and downy beneath. Fragrant 30cm ivory or cream flowers spotted or tinged purple towards the base appearing early summer, followed by 9cm ovoid or globose rose-pink cones.

The foliage is easily damaged so the tree requires a position in full sun protected from strong winds. Macrophylla — large leaved. 6 × 5m.

Magnolia sargentiana 'Robusta'
Tall vase-shaped tree from western China, forming a broad multi-branched tree with glossy deep-green, oblanceolate leaves to 20 × 9cm, grey-downy on the undersides. Quite breathtaking 30cm fragrant blooms with 12–16 petals, purplish crimson in bud, opening mauve pink with paler interiors, at first erect, later horizontal or facing downwards on naked branches. May take 6–8 years to commence flowering. Spectacular tree for cooler areas. Named for Professor Charles Sargent, 1841–1927, founder of Arnold Arboretum, Mass, USA. Robusta — strong and stout. 10 × 8m.

Magnolia sieboldii
Oyama Magnolia
Wide spreading Japanese shrub with slender downy branches and oblong to ovate-elliptic, prominently veined leaves to 12 × 10cm, dark green above, glaucous and downy beneath. Buds resembling Japanese lanterns open to creamy white, cup-shaped, fragrant, 7–10cm flowers with central bunch of crimson stamens, followed by spectacular crimson fruit clusters. Blooming commences spring, continuing intermittently for up to three months.

As blooms are pendulous or horizontal, plant up a slope or above a wall so it can be viewed from beneath. Named for Philip von Siebold, 18th–19th century Dutch botanist and plant collector in Japan. 3 × 2.5m.

Magnolia × soulangeana
Tulip Magnolia, Saucer Magnolia
Magnificent French-raised hybrid from M denudata × M liliflora. Broadly elliptic leaves to 16 × 12cm, shiny dark green above, often with minute soft hairs beneath. Bears masses of open globe-shaped, creamy white flowers flushed pink and purple at the base and with white interiors, held erect on naked stems. Commences early, quite often in bloom when first planted. Named for the raiser, Etienne Soulange-Bodin, 18th–19th century horticulturist at Fromont, near Paris. 5 × 4m.   **192**

Magnolia × soulangeana 'Alexandrina'
Vigorous erect and free flowering plant, producing early spring pear-shaped soft rosy purple flowers with creamy white interior. 3 × 2m.

Magnolia × soulangeana 'Lennei'
Vigorous compact upright tree producing immense globe-shaped rosy purple flowers with white interiors and pleasantly fragrant. Beautifully moulded flowers, each petal incurving at the tips. 4 × 3m.   **192**

Magnolia × soulangeana 'Lennei Alba'
Neat round-headed small tree, often multi-stemmed with outstanding large goblet-shaped pure ivory white, globular blooms with recurved petal tips somewhat resembling M denudata. 4 × 3m.   **192**

Magnolia × soulangeana 'Rustica Rubra'
Hardy vigorous grower, more tree-like in habit and splendid for larger areas. Large chalice or pear-shaped, soft rosy purple flowers with milky white interiors borne mid season, often followed by 15cm dark rose seed pods. Sport from M Lennei. Rustica — of wild places. 7 × 6m.

Magnolia × soulangeana 'San Jose'
This is a delightful Californian hybrid. Large fragrant cup or chalice-shaped creamy white flowers are delicately shaded pastel rose-pink, deeper at the base with milky white interiors. Blooms early spring providing an impressive display of bloom on bare branches. 6 × 4.5m.

Magnolia × soulangeana 'Verbanica'
Rounded pear-shaped blooms of soft light rose-pink flushed purple with white interiors. Blooms mid to late spring, flowers often appearing with the foliage when most other Magnolias are falling. 5 × 4m.

Magnolia sprengeri 'Diva'
Goddess Magnolia
Spectacular Magnolia from western China. Forms a large broad tree with smooth yellowish green young shoots. Leaves obovate to lanceolate-elliptic, to 14 × 7cm, glabrous dark green above, paler and downy beneath. Beautiful, sweet-musky fragrant flowers to 20cm, rich rosy carmine outside, white interiors lined and suffused pink. Blooms cup and saucer-shaped held erect on bare branches for long periods early to mid spring. Commences to flower within five to seven years.

This cultivar was named for German Carl Sprenger, a nurseryman at Vomero near Naples. Diva — Latin term for a god or goddess. 5 × 4m.

Magnolia stellata
Star Magnolia
Charming Japanese shrubby Magnolia, among the first to bloom. Forms a compact rounded multi-branched twiggy bush with narrow-oblong to obovate, dark green leaves to 13 × 6cm, often golden in autumn. In early winter each twiggy branch is covered with grey hairy buds. Starry pure white fragrant flowers to 70mm across with 13–33, laxly spreading straplike petals appear in great masses for long periods from mid winter, continuing until the leaves appear in spring. Commences to flower at an early age, often in bloom at planting time. Stellata — star-like. 2 × 2m.   **190**

Magnolia stellata 'King Rose'
Smaller slower growing form of the delightful Star Magnolia with rounded bushy habit. Masses of soft rose-pink buds in spring open to white flowers with a touch of pale pink at the base of each petal. Superior to M stellata 'Rosea'. 2 × 2m.

Magnolia stellata 'Rosea'
Pink Star Magnolia
Resembles M stellata but with pink buds and fragrant pink flushed flowers gradually fading to white. Blooms regular in form and with more petals. Vigorous erect and shapely bush. 2.5 × 2m.

Magnolia stellata 'Royal Star'
Vigorous cultivar from USA forming a compact, densely branched spreading bush with larger flowers than M stellata and produced with even greater enthusiasm. Pink buds, petals flushed pale pink as flowers open, eventually pure white. Flowers about two weeks later. Hardy to −35°C. 2.5 × 2m.

Magnolia stellata 'Waterlily'
Vigorous USA cultivar. Medium sized compact densely branched shrub rather more erect and twiggy than other Star Magnolias. Large semi-double flowers with many petals, opening from palest pink buds to starry white with pink blush on the outside. 2 × 2m.

Above: Mahonia lomariifolia *Chinese Holly Grape* **205**

Above: Malus floribunda *Japanese Crab* **205**
Below: Melaleuca bracteata 'Revolution Gold' **207**

Above: Malus coronaria 'Charlottae' **205**
Below: Malus ioensis 'Plena' *Bechtel Crab, Prairie Crab* **206**

Above: Metrosideros excelsa 'Aurea' *Yellow Pohutukawa* **209**

Above: Metrosideros excelsa 'Springfire' **209**
Below: Metrosideros thomasii *Ohia-Lehua* **210**

Above: Metrosideros excelsa *New Zealand Christmas Tree* **209**
Below: Metrosideros kermadecensis 'Variegata' **210**

Above: Myrtus bullata 'Matai Bay' **213**

Above: Michelia doltsopa 'Silver Cloud' **210**
Below: Monstera deliciosa **211**

Above: Myrtus x ralphii 'Barry's Multicolor' **213**
Below: Myrtus x ralphii 'Kathryn' **213**

Above: Nandina domestica 'Richmond' **214**
Below: Meryta sinclairii 'Moonlight' **208**

Above: Nandina domestica 'Pygmy' *Dwarf Heavenly Bamboo* **214**
Below: Meryta sinclairii *New Zealand Puka* **208**

MAHONIA

A genus of about 70 species of hardy evergreen shrubs and small trees from north western USA and the Orient named for Bernard McMahon, early nineteenth century American horticulturist. They are beautiful shrubs related to Berberis but with dramatic pinnate foliage, colourful flower sprays, grape-like berries, picturesque stems and artistic outline. Perfect against backgrounds of stone, glass, brick or stained timbers. Useful in a wide range of landscaping situations easy to grow and attractive all year through.

Plant in semi-shade, protected from strong winds, in deeply worked, organically enriched, free-draining, moisture-retentive, slightly acid to neutral soil. Mulch freely and water regularly during dry spells. Pruning necessary only when plants become lanky or aged. Cut almost to ground level and new clean vigorous growth will soon appear. Few pests seem interested but watch for caterpillars. In some areas leaf spotting may require control with a fungicidal spray.

Berberidaceae. *All evergreen.*

Mahonia bealei
Leatherleaf Mahonia
Unusual species from China forming a dramatic shrub with erect stems. Impressive pinnate leaves to 50cm long, with 7–9 pairs of thick leathery leaflets, dull grey or metallic green above, olive green beneath, margined with up to six spiny teeth, the terminal leaflet often larger than the others. Small bright yellow flowers in erect 10–15cm terminal racemes followed by clusters of ovoid powdery greyish blue fruit. Named for T C Beale, 19th century Portuguese consul in Shanghai. 2 × 1.5m.

Mahonia japonica
From China and Taiwan, closely related to M bealei. Erect stems topped with pinnate leaves to 45cm long with up to 19 oblong-ovate tough rigid glossy grey-green leaflets usually red-tinted in winter, margins serrated with six spiny teeth on each side. Yellow, highly fragrant flowers in loose pendent 25cm racemes late winter through early spring followed by clusters of 9mm ovoid mauve glaucous fruit. 2 × 1.5m.

Mahonia lomariifolia
Chinese Holly Grape
Handsome plant from western China and Burma said to possess the most beautiful leaf design of any ornamental shrub. Large pinnate leathery leaves to 50cm long, with as many as twenty pairs of oblong-ovate glabrous deep green 7–10cm leaflets with up to seven sharply pointed spines on each side. Leaflets set in regularly spaced pairs along the midrib, attached directly in horizontal plane, clustered near the top of each erect stem.

Yellow flowers in crowded erect clusters to 15cm long appear at the tip of each stem winter or early spring, followed by ovoid blue-black powdery fruit relished by birds. Young plants usually with one single unbranched stem. Further stems grow from basal shoots to form a colony of erect branches of varying heights. Height and width variable according to age and training. Lomariifolia — with ferny leaves like lomaria. 2 × 1.5m. **201**

MALUS

A genus of about 35 species of flowering and fruiting deciduous trees or shrubs including forerunners of the common apple tree, from Europe, Asia and north America, called *malus*, Latin for apple tree. Crab as applied to these trees has nothing to do with crustaceans but with the sharp taste of the fruit. Malus provides delightful combinations of flower, fruit, foliage and ornamental stems unequalled in other genus. Edible fruit is a bonus. Excellent lawn specimens, street or avenue trees. Spring flowering annuals, perennials or bulbs growing beneath flowering Malus provide spring colour beyond compare.

Locate in full sun sheltered from strong wind and plant in deeply worked, free-draining, moisture-retentive, mildly acid to slightly alkaline soil which is not over-rich. Mulch with well-rotted animal manure or feed occasionallly with well-balanced fertilizer to encourage flower and fruit formation. Early training will build a good framework. During the first spring allow the tree to blossom and cut flowering stems for indoors.

Prune remaining branches by two thirds when flowers have faded to encourage strong root action and desirable shape. After flowering the following spring, wood made during the previous season may be reduced by half. Subsequently no further pruning is needed apart from obvious shaping. Old unshapely trees may be hard pruned for growth renewal. Watch and spray fruiting Crabs for insects and other pests.

Rosaceae. *All deciduous.*

Malus × arnoldiana
Small round-headed tree with widely arching drooping branches. Leaves elliptic to ovate to 8cm long tapering to a point, margins roughly serrated. Carmine-red buds open to pale pink single flowers fading to white followed by 15mm globose yellow-green fruit flushed red. Garden hybrid — M baccata × M floribunda. Arnoldiana — originating at Arnold Arboretum, near Boston, USA. 4 × 2.5m

Malus coronaria 'Charlottae'
Excellent cultivar from north eastern USA. Forms a small spreading tree with numerous short-thorned laterals. Leaves ovate-oblong to 10cm roughly serrated and lobed, scarlet stained orange in autumn. Beautiful 5cm shell pink double flowers resembling Japanese cherry with delightful violet fragrance early summer. Coronaria — resembling a crown. Charlottae — after Mrs Charlotte de Wolf who discovered it in 1902. 2.5 × 2m. **201**

Malus floribunda
Japanese Crab
Long gracefully arching branches crowded along the whole length with myriads of bright pink buds opening to 25–30mm white to pale pink flowers followed by small yellow fruits flushed red. Maybe the most flowers to be seen on any spring blossom trees and possibly the earliest Malus to bloom. Floribunda — flowering freely. 3 × 2.5m. **201**

Malus × gloriosa 'Echtermeyer'
Weeping Crab Apple
Usually grafted on 2m standards forming a graceful widespreading specimen with maroon-black stems weeping elegantly to the ground. Leaves tinted red at first changing to purple as they open maturing bronze green. Rosy carmine 3–4cm single flowers, deeper in bud, appear along the full length of each cascading branch in spring, followed by 25mm reddish purple fruit in autumn. One of the finest weeping trees. Remove any branches which tend to grow stiffly erect. Hybrid of garden origin — M pumila × M schiedeckeri. 2.5 × 2m.

Malus hybrid 'Crimson Rod'
Stronger growing form of Malus Gorgeous producing an abundance of crimson red fruit which weigh down the branches through autumn and winter. Similar parentage to M Gorgeous — M sieboldii × M halliana. 4 × 3m.

Malus hybrid 'Gorgeous'
Forms a rounded bush with white or pale pink single flowers resembling a fruiting

apple tree followed by spectacular crops of 25mm glossy bright crimson red fruit, orange red beneath. This impressive crop of fruit hangs like cherries on long thin stalks weighing down outer branches. It persists until late autumn or early winter, usually brought to an end by birds devouring fully ripe fruit. Excellent culinary variety. New Zealand hybrid — M sieboldii × M halliana raised by early 20th century nurseryman Haywood Wright of Auckland. Grown on regular or dwarfing stock. As a dwarf it makes a bush of less than 2m, ideal for beds borders or single specimen. Regular 3 × 2m. Dwarf 2 × 1.5m.

Malus hybrid 'Jack Humm'
Exceptional fruiting crab. Strong growing rounded tree with masses of white single flowers. Large oval 25–30mm bright crimson glossy fruit flushed yellow and orange beneath provide a magnificent winter display which persists after leaf fall. Fruit good for jelly. For some reason fruit is untouched by birds unless there's nothing else about. New Zealand hybrid of M Gorgeous and the English cultivar John Downie. Grown on regular or dwarfing stock. As a dwarf it makes a bush of less than 2m, ideal for beds borders or single specimen. Regular 3 × 2m. Dwarf 2 × 1.5m.

Malus hybrid 'Kaitoke'
Red Weeping Crab Apple
Forms a large shrub with purplish red young growths becoming green. Every branched clothed with masses of crimson buds which burst open to carmine-red blossom through spring. Originated in Kaitoke, New Zealand. 2.5 × 2m.

Malus hybrid 'Sovereign'
Forms a rounded small tree. White single flowers from pink buds, then attractive golden yellow 25mm fruit flushed red which persist through winter. Green summer foliage, yellow in autumn. Usually grown on dwarfing stock. New Zealand hybrid M 'Jack Humm' × M schiedeckeri. 2 × 2m.

Malus hybrid 'Van Eseltine'
Small columnar or vase-like tree with stiffly erect branches. Large, 35–50mm semi-double flowers, rose-scarlet in bud opening deep rose-pink followed by 20mm fruit either pure yellow or yellow flushed red. Spectacular in flower and fruit. Ideal for small gardens. USA hybrid — M arnoldiana × M spectabilis. 3 × 1.5m.

Malus hybrid 'Wandin Glory'
Weeping Fruiting Apple
Develops into an excellent weeping tree with umbrella head and dense green foliage.

Masses of spring blossoms followed in summer by good crops of full-sized, highly coloured, sweetly flavoured apples. Originated in Wandin, Victoria, Australia. 2 × 2m.

Malus hybrid 'Wright's Scarlet'
Said to have been bred by Hayward Wright, early 20th century nurseryman in New Zealand who crossed Malus 'Gorgeous' with fruiting apple 'Delicious'. From a number of seedlings, 'Wright's Scarlet' was selected for large clusters of 50mm flattish deep crimson fruits, highly ornamental and excellent for jelly. 3 × 3m.

Malus ioensis 'Plena'
Bechtel Crab, Prairie Crab
Forms a small vase-shaped bush with well-spaced angular branches. Leaves oblong-ovate to 10cm, dark green and glabrous above, yellow-green and felted beneath, margins deeply serrated, deep red or yellow in autumn. Very large, soft-pink fully double flowers resembling rambling roses with violet-like fragrance produced freely during spring, followed by sparse greenish yellow 3cm fruit. Beautiful flowering crab. Ioensis — of Iowa, USA. Plena — double flowered. 2 × 2m.   **201**

Malus × moerlandsii 'Profusion'
Amongst the most free flowering, a first class hybrid producing masses of 4cm purplish wine-red slightly fragrant single flowers borne in clusters up to seven. Small 10cm ox-blood red fruit. Young shoots bright coppery crimson, bronze later. Vigorous grower, commences flowering when very young, usually a mass of bloom in nursery rows. Excellent garden display, lasts well when picked. Dutch hybrid of garden origin M 'Lemoinei' × M sieboldii. 3 × 2.5m.

Malus × robusta
Erect conical shrub or small tree with spreading branches somewhat pendulous at the tips. Leaves elliptic to 11cm long, bright green with scalloped margins. White or occasionally pink single 3–4cm flowers in corymbs of up to 8, followed by rounded red or yellow 1–3cm fruit suspended on long stalks resembling cherries which persist on the tree into winter. M baccata × M prunifolia. 4 × 3m.

Malus × schiedeckeri 'Ballerina'
Vigorous grower, forming a shapely small tree. Early each spring, clusters of rosy red buds along every branch burst open to a profusion of large, pink, frilly, fully double flowers which pale prior to falling, followed in autumn by attractive large salmon-apricot crab apples. Outstanding cultivar raised in Wanganui, New Zealand. 3 × 2.5m.

Malus × schiedeckeri 'Barbara Ann'
Shrubby rounded form with erect stems. Leaves ovate bright green to bronze-green, paler and downy beneath, margins coarsely serrated, red tinted in autumn. Large wine-red double flowers fading to pink followed in autumn by 12mm purplish red fruits. Distinctive cultivar of garden origin from USA — M floribunda × M prunifolia. 3 × 2.5m.

Malus × schiedeckeri 'Red Jade'
Dramatic semi-weeping flowering and fruiting crab with gracefully cascading branches almost to the ground. A delight in spring when masses of pink buds open to blush white single flowers. Loaded in autumn with ovate 15mm brilliant red fruit. Glossy rich green leaves, yellow in autumn. Picturesque bare branch pattern in winter. Originated Brooklyn Botanical Gardens, New York — M floribunda × M prunifolia. 3 × 2m.

Malus sieboldii 'Snowbright'
Somewhat dwarf compact semi-weeping bush with ovate-elliptic, long tapered dark-green leaves to 6cm long, paler beneath, both surfaces downy, margins lobed and deeply toothed, red and yellow in autumn. Dainty snow-white single flowers in massed clusters opening from salmon-pink buds in spring followed by polished bright-red marble-size fruit in autumn through winter. 3 × 2m.

Malus trilobata
Rare and distinct species from western Asia with erect pyramidal form. Maple-like leaves with three distinct lobes, margins also lobed and sharply toothed, glossy green, intense red orange or scarlet in autumn. White 35mm flowers in clusters of 6–8 followed by yellow flushed red pear-shaped 2cm fruit. Flowers white, fruit yellowish but shy bearing. Worthy of extensive planting in public gardens or where space permits. Trilobata — three-lobed. 5 × 3m.

Malus tschonoskii
Japanese species, pyramidal when young more spreading with maturity. Leaves ovate-elliptic to 12cm long, at first white felted and silvery green, bright green and glabrous through summer, white felted beneath, margins roughly serrated to lobed, yellow orange scarlet and purple in autumn. White tinged pink single 35mm flowers in clusters of 2–5, followed by 20mm globose or ellipsoid, lime-green fruit flushed reddish purple. Somewhat unspectacular flower and fruit, but excellent for autumn colour. Merits extensive planting in public areas or larger gardens. Named for Tschonoski, Japanese plant collector. 8 × 4m.

Malus × zumi 'Golden Hornet'
Upright pyramidal habit, pink buds white single flowers in spring followed by spectacular 25–30mm glossy golden-yellow fruit in great profusion suspended on long stalks, persisting into winter. Highly ornamental and good for jelly. Foliage green through summer, yellow in autumn. Top garden variety. Cultivar from England originating from M baccata × M sieboldii. 3 × 2.5m.

MAYTENUS

A genus of over 200 species of trees and shrubs from tropical and sub-tropical regions, named from *maiten* the Chilean term for these trees. Maytenus boaria is grown for gracefully weeping branches and handsome evergreen foliage. Provides the charm and gracefulness of Weeping Willow without the problem of invasive roots. Choice lawn or patio specimen growing moderately to 6m in ten years, thereafter slowly doubling its size.

Plant in reasonable, deeply worked soil with good drainage. Prefers full sun, quite hardy and suitable for cooler districts to −10°C. Has a tendency to send up multiple stems and laterals. Stake securely and remove side growths unless some are required for multiple trunk effects.

Listed species is quite drought tolerant once established, but keeps greener and healthier with periodic deep watering which also prevents surface roots invading garden beds. Sometimes after cold periods or blooming the tree may shed a portion of its leaves, but recovery is rapid. Locate to effectively display its full branch pattern.

Celastraceae.

Maytenus boaria
Mayten Tree
A graceful small evergreen tree from Chile with long slender pendulous branchlets which hang down from the branch framework, giving it daintiness and grace. Leaves lanceolate to narrowly elliptic to 5 × 2cm, glossy deep green above, paler beneath, margins closely and finely serrated. Small white tinged green inconspicuous flowers followed by leathery yellow capsules. Habit and foliage somewhat resembles a small-scale weeping willow but obviously much tidier and more easily controlled. Boaria — of cattle which forage the leaves. Evergreen. 6 × 4.5m.

MELALEUCA

A genus of over 200 species of trees and shrubs, mostly Australian, named from the Greek *melas*, black and *leukos*, white in reference to light coloured trunks and darker leaves or branches of some species. Closely allied to Callistemon, many species have similar bottlebrush flowers but with longer stamens united into bundles in multiples of five. Clusters of woody seed capsules persist in odd decorative formations around twigs and branches for many years. Some have interesting contorted branches, others thick paper-like bark which peels in layers.

Melaleucas are decorative fast growing shrubs, hardy and tolerant of heat, wind, poor soil, drought, wet feet and salt air. Their extreme vigour can be controlled by cutting or shortening branches rather than shearing. Plant in deeply worked acid soil. Mulch freely and keep moist during dry periods.

Myrtaceae. *All evergreen.*

Melaleuca bracteata 'Revolution Gold'
The species occurs in all mainland Australian states except Victoria, shrubby in arid regions or tree-like near streams. Leaves linear-lanceolate to 15mm long, flowers white or cream in 5cm leafy cylindrical spikes through spring and early summer. The cultivar 'Revolution Gold' is a tall erect shrub with golden leaves and reddish stems, prominent in new growth. Excellent for background planting or screens. Benefits from occasional pruning for size and shape and growth renewal. Bracteata — having bracts. 2.5 × 2m. **201**

Melaleuca 'Mountain Fire'
Forms a tidy erect bush with narrow green leaves. Admired for brilliant fiery purple-red new foliage throughout the year, intensifying in cooler weather. Small white bottlebrush flowers autumn and summer. Frost tolerant, thrives in most soils and situations and adapts well to damp conditions. 2.5 × 1m.

MELASTOMA

A genus of about seventy species of shrubs and small trees from south east Asia, India, China, Malaysia, Pacific Islands and Australia named from the Greek *melas*, black and *stoma*, mouth in reference to the edible berries of some species which if eaten may stain the mouth or tongue black or dark blue. Belonging to the same family and has similar features to the better known Tibouchina or Lasiandra. Naturally found in swamp forest or rainforest or in moist sandy areas nearby.

Suitable for frost-free locations in sun or partial shade in deeply worked, organically enriched, moisture-retentive soil, deeply mulched and frequently watered during dry periods. Heavy pruning after flowering and occasional tip pinching during the growth period maintains good form and a profusion of bloom.

Melastomataceae.

Melastoma malabathricum
Indian Rhododendron
Spreading shrub, branches almost four-angled, densely covered with adpressed scales. Leaves ovate to broadly lanceolate to 10cm long covered with sharp stiff adpressed hairs with somewhat sandpapery surface. Flowers 4–5cm across resembling Tibouchina, at first pale pink, becoming lavender-pink and finally deep pink, borne profusely in corymbs of 1–5 for 6–8 weeks from mid summer, followed by 8mm fruit with reddish pulp used medicinally by native peoples. Malabathricum — *malabar*, from the Malabar Coast, southern India; *thricum*, from *trix*, hair. Evergreen. 1.5 × 1m.

MELIA

A genus of five species of deciduous trees or shrubs from India, China, East Indies and Australia named from the Greek term for Ash which has similar foliage. Melia azedarach is a rapid-growing tree, valued for open branch framework, handsome foliage, pretty flowers, decorative fruit and attraction to birdlife. Grows in almost any deeply worked, free-draining soil, prefers full sun and withstands considerable exposure to wind and drought. Protect from frost when young but moderately hardy once established. Start training early for single stem with adequate head-height beneath lower branches. Ideal lawn or patio tree, excellent for street or avenue planting.

Meliaceae.

Melia azedarach
Indian Lilac, Bead Tree, Chinaberry
Native to India and China, widely cultivated in temperate regions of many countries.

Strong growing as a juvenile with a straight erect 2–3m stem before branching to form a broad topped specimen with open branch structure. Stems and branches smooth and greyish black. Handsome double pinnate leaves to 60cm long, ovate to elliptic, 5cm leaflets, deep green glossy, margins shallow toothed, yellow in autumn, persisting often to mid winter.

Lilac, 2cm, chocolate or caramel scented flowers in loose terminal panicles produced freely on current season's growth along with the leaves in spring, followed in autumn by clusters of smooth shiny round-ovate 12mm fruit, at first green, ripening bright yellow. Fruit clusters hang on the tree for months, long after leaf fall, ornamental through winter months and relished by birds which visit daily and gorge themselves for hours. Fruit, which is toxic to humans, contains a five-sided yellowish brown stone used in Italy for rosaries. Azedarach — a contraction of the Persian vernacular *azaddhirakt* or noble tree. Deciduous. 7 × 5m.

MELICOPE

A genus of about 50 species of trees and shrubs from India, Malaysia, Australia, Pacific Islands and New Zealand, named from the Greek *meli*, honey and *kope*, division, in reference to four honey glands at the base of the ovary.

Grown for its bright shining leaves, aromatic when crushed and elegant form. Needs protection from heavy frost and strong wind. Grows in sun or semi-shade and in coastal situations. Plant in deeply worked, organically enriched, free-draining soil. Mulch freely keep moist during dry periods. Useful wherever a fresh looking evergreen is called for.

Rutaceae.

Melicope ternata
Wharangi
Endemic in New Zealand found in coastal and lowland forests of the North Island and northern regions of the South Island. Slender yellowish green branchlets. Trifoliate leaves with obovate-oblong to elliptic leaflets to 10 × 4cm, bright glossy fresh green above, paler beneath, margins entire and slightly waved. Inconspicuous 8mm greenish white flowers followed by clusters of seed capsules which open to expose shining black seeds. Ternata — in threes referring to the foliage. Evergreen. 4 × 3m.

MELICYTUS

A genus of four species of trees and shrubs three endemic to New Zealand, one extending to Norfolk Island, Tonga and the Fiji Islands, named from the Greek *meli*, honey and *kytos*, a hollow container or jar, in allusion to the hollow nectaries of the flowers. Being so prevalent in natural bush the sheer beauty of Melicytus has been somewhat overlooked. Slender white stems pleasant foliage and attractive berries together with easy culture suggests that maybe such potential needs recognizing. Although slightly frost tender when young, Melicytis is easy to grow in any reasonably good, deeply worked, free-draining soil in sun or semi shade, protected from strong winds.

Violaceae. *All evergreen.*

Melicytus lanceolatus
Mahoewao
Slender spreading shrub or small tree with brownish grey bark widely distributed in lowland and mountain forests and margins south from the Bay of Islands through the South and Stewart Islands. Willow-like, oblong to lanceolate leaves to 15 × 3cm, pale green and prominently veined above, paler beneath, margins finely but bluntly toothed. Clusters of purplish tinged 4mm flowers followed by globose 6mm dark purple fruit. Lanceolatus — lanceolate or spear-shaped leaves. 3 × 3m.

Melicytus ramiflorus
Mahoe, Whiteywood
Small spreading tree abundant in lowland and mountain forests of North South Stewart and Kermadec Islands extending to Norfolk Island Tonga and Fiji. Naturally tends to form multi-stems with whitish or pale grey bark and rather brittle branchlets. Leaves lanceolate to elliptic-oblong, to 15 × 5cm, bright green, paler beneath and bluntly serrated. Small 3mm greenish yellow flowers in racemes to ten, followed by 5mm, violet to dark bluish purple berries clustered along branchlets on female trees. Ramiflorus — with branching inflorescence. 5 × 3m.

MERYTA

A genus of about 25 species of small to medium trees distributed throughout Micronesia through Vanuatu, Australia and New Zealand named from the Greek

merytos, glomerate, referring to male flowers concentrated in a head. Valued for large bold dramatic foliage and tropical effects, ideal for contemporary landscaping, patios, lawn specimens, containers etc, holding its own with many exotic species. Plant in deeply worked, organically enriched, moisture-retentive soil in full or partial sun. Suitable for coastal gardens but protect from strong wind and frost especially when young. Single-stemmed as a juvenile topped with big dramatic leaves, later branching to form a handsome broad topped specimen.

Araliaceae. *All evergreen.*

Meryta sinclairii
New Zealand Puka
New Zealand endemic species, the Puka is one of the rarest native trees found on remote offshore islands such as Three Kings, Poor Knights and Hen and Chickens, usually as a multi-branched small round-headed tree less than 6m high, hugging sheltered ravines and avoiding exposed ridges. Massive oblong-obovate glossy green leaves to 50 × 20cm, leathery, distinctly veined, margins slightly wavy. Leaves may turn bright yellow as they fall lasting well in floral arrangements. Greenish flowers in erect terminal panicles to 45cm long mid-winter followed by black shiny fleshy 13mm fruit resembling grapes. Named for Dr Sinclair RN, one time colonial secretary in New Zealand. 4 × 3m.   **204**

Meryta sinclairii 'Moonlight'
Variegated Puka
Originated in Auckland New Zealand. A most beautiful form with large glossy 30–50cm leaves with central zone of golden yellow and lime green irregularly bordered deep green. Forms a handsome multi-branched small tree superb as a feature specimen outdoors or in containers for terrace or patio. Elegant and striking evergreen foliage tree. 3.5 × 3m.   **204**

METASEQUOIA

A genus of one species from western China, named from the Greek *meta*, with and *Sequoia*, a genus to which it is related. Although now cultivated extensively throughout the world, this tree was thought to exist only in fossil form until 1941 when specimens were found in an obscure part of China. Viable seed distributed amongst arboretums in various parts of the world led to the introduction of this remarkable tree into cultivation. A handsome tree through all seasons resembling Sequoia or California Redwood but Sequoia's cones are smaller and leaves evergreen.

Grows easily and quickly thriving in deeply worked, organically enriched, free-draining, moisture-retentive soil preferably within reach of water, alongside rivers streams or dams. Mulch freely and keep moist during dry periods. Has a strong dislike for dry soil conditions, is hardy to −30°C but needs hot summers for healthy growth.

Taxodiaceae. *All deciduous.*

Metasequoia glyptostroboides
Dawn Redwood

A strong growing vigorous deciduous tree with slender pyramidal to conical form when young broadening with maturity, bark shaggy and cinnamon brown. Flattened ferny or feathery leaves, soft to the touch, bright larch green in summer, tawny-pink and old gold in autumn before falling. Elegant bare branch pattern. Glyptostroboides — to do with cone formation, *glyptos*, carved and *strobus*, cone. 12 × 6m.

Metasequoia glyptostroboides 'Sheridan Spire'

Selected form of Dawn Redwood from Canada with distinct narrow pyramidal form, semi-pendulous branches and longer finer leaves, fresh green in summer, bright orange-brown in autumn. 7 × 3.5m.

METROSIDEROS

A genus of about 50 species of trees shrubs and climbing plants distributed through Africa, Polynesia, New Zealand and Australia, named from the Greek *metra*, middle or core and *sideros*, iron, referring to the hard heart wood. A familiar species, M excelsa is commonly referred to as New Zealand Christmas Tree. Maori name *Pohutukawa*, 'drenched with spray' refers to the way these robust trees cling tenaciously to rocky cliffs and endure wild ocean storms.

Valued for floral beauty, handsome foliage and resistance to the elements. Perfect in many landscaping situations, an obvious first choice as a front line seaside plant where strong salt laden winds prevail, but equally happy in more sheltered inland gardens. Most species reasonably hardy, but juvenile leaves may need protection until well established with adult foliage. Plant in almost any sandy to heavy clay, deeply worked, organically enriched and free-draining soil in full or partial sun. Mulch freely and water during dry periods.

Highly drought resistant once established. Metrosideros normally branch heavily from ground level. Old gnarled trunks quite picturesque. Single trunk with rounded head may be encouraged with careful staking and pruning. As a screen, regular pinching or trimming maintains desired size resulting in an almost impenetrable barrier. Juvenile leaves sometimes attacked by small insects which dwell beneath the foliage and cause distortion of the upper surface. Control by spraying.

Myrtaceae. *All evergreen.*

Metrosideros excelsa
New Zealand Christmas Tree, Pohutukawa

Prominent on ocean and lake coastlines from North Cape to Poverty Bay on the east and Urenui on the west where ancient specimens abound with gnarled trunks and vivid summer displays of gorgeous blossom. Leaves elliptic to oblong, to 10 × 5cm, firm leathery deep green, white felted beneath. Orange-scarlet to deep crimson flowers comprising dense clustered 3–4cm stamens opening from powdery buds totally cover the tree for three or four weeks in mid-summer suggesting the common name of Christmas Tree. Fallen stamens lay a red carpet on the ground. Untrimmed specimens grow 5–6m in ten years under normal conditions. Easily trained to any desired dimensions. Excelsa — very tall. 3–8 × 2–5m. **202**

Metrosideros excelsa 'Aurea'
Yellow Pohutukawa

Unusual form with clean upright growth, commencing to flower at an early age. Sulphur-yellow flowers lacks the flamboyance of M excelsa, but worth growing for its botanical interest and tidy growth habit. Originally from Motiti Island, Bay of Plenty in 1940. 5 × 3.5m. **202**

Metrosideros excelsa 'Butterscotch'

Selected for golden yellow young foliage with tips tinted bronzy orange. Red blossoms mid-summer. 3 × 2.5m.

Metrosideros excelsa 'Fire Mountain'

Selected cultivar with rounded spreading habit and large heads of bright orange-scarlet pin-cushion flowers. 5 × 3.5m.

Metrosideros excelsa 'Goldfinger'
Variegated New Zealand Christmas Tree

Attractive compact grower with beautifully variegated leaves, dark green with prominent bright golden-yellow central blotch. Scarlet flowers with gold-tipped stamens contrast dramatically against a background of handsome foliage. 4 × 3m.

Metrosideros excelsa 'Lighthouse'

Compact erect bushy grower, leaves large and heavy-textured. Bright red flowers appear profusely early summer (November). Hardy and disease-resistant. Discovered by Graeme Platt growing near the lighthouse on the north-western end of Rangitoto Island. 5 × 3.5m.

Metrosideros excelsa 'Moon Maiden'
Yellow Pohutukawa

Compact rounded form, grey-green glossy foliage and compact clusters of clear sulphur yellow flowers early summer. Hardy to wind and coastal spray. Selected form of M excelsa 'Aurea'. 5 × 3.5m.

Metrosideros excelsa 'Parnell'

Large-growing, spreading form with larger than usual foliage. Smothers itself mid summer (December) with bright red flowers. Appears to be without aerial roots, although branches which touch the ground take root. Excellent for large-scale coastal planting. Originated from the immense, sprawling, 120 year-old example growing in the Parnell Rose Gardens in Auckland. 5 × 6m.

Metrosideros excelsa 'Pink Lady'

Erect grower, narrow rounded open crown, deep green glossy foliage and dense heads of carmine-pink flowers. 5 × 3.5m.

Metrosideros excelsa 'Royal Flame'

Vigorous cultivar with upright compact habit and masses of vivid glowing crimson flowers with prominent gold-tipped stamens mid-summer. Reliable and prolific. 6 × 4m.

Metrosideros excelsa 'Scarlet Pimpernel'

Small slow growing compact rounded bush with multi-stems, glossy deep green foliage, grey-green beneath and prolific displays of brilliant scarlet flowers for long periods during summer. Commences flowering at an early age. 5 × 3.5m.

Metrosideros excelsa 'Springfire'

Excellent cultivar, selected for compact growth, fresh green foliage, abundance of flower and early blooming. A specimen seen in Auckland during October and November was a mass of bright orange-red blossom, hence the name. 3–4 × 3m. **202**

Metrosideros excelsa 'Springtime'

Selected variegated cultivar. Leaves pale lemon and deep green, considerably larger than other variegated Metrosideros. Red flowers in profusion on mature plants.

Discovered by George Rainey, Auckland nurseryman. 5 × 3m.

Metrosideros kermadecensis
Kermadec Pohutukawa
Dense, more compact growing species from Raoul Island in the Kermadec group. Leaves broadly ovate to elliptic ovate, to 5 × 2cm, deep green and glabrous. Scarlet flowers sporadically through the year, lacking the short term flamboyance of M excelsa but a desirable large shrub recommended for coastal planting in exposed locations or where frosts are not severe. 5 × 3m.

Metrosideros kermadecensis 'Radiant'
Small round-headed tree with smaller deep green leaves irregularly splashed golden yellow in the centre. Flowers scarlet with gold-tipped stamens sporadically through the year. Differs from 'Sunninghill' with yellow young stems instead of red and foliage retains colour rather than losing variegation as the tree gets older. 3.5 × 2.5m.

Metrosideros kermadecensis 'Red and Gold'
Deep green leaves brightly margined golden yellow, distinctive dark red young stems and red flowers intermittently through the year. 3 × 2.5m.

Metrosideros kermadecensis 'Sunninghill'
Distinct cultivar with rounded leaves basically green with prominent central yellow splash carried on deep red young stems. New shoots orange tinted. Red flowers appear on young trees. Hardy to wind but frost tender. Originated in Sunninghill Nursery, Auckland around 1950. 3 × 2.5m.

Metrosideros kermadecensis 'Variegata'
Fine compact variegated form, green foliage broadly margined creamy yellow providing garden colour from the moment of planting. Characteristic red flowers produced from an early age together with attractive foliage make this an aristocrat among shrubs. Extremely hardy to coastal conditions and an ideal container plant. 3 × 2.5m.   **202**

Metrosideros 'Mistral'
Small erect-growing tree with characteristics halfway between the two parents. Leaves elliptic, deep green and glabrous. Brilliant deep scarlet flowers early summer a little before M excelsa. Natural hybrid of M excelsa × M robusta found on Great Barrier Island, introduced into cultivation by Auckland nurseryman Graham Platt. 5 × 3m.

Metrosideros polymorpha 'Tahiti'
Beautiful well-rounded shrubby cultivar of a Pacific Island species. Distinctive obovate to orbicular foliage to 5cm across, deep-green, coated on both surfaces with powdery grey bloom. Brilliant orange red blooms appear from mid winter through spring, sporadically at other times of the year and last much longer than M excelsa cultivars. New shoots through winter have reddish covers, pubescent almost like deer velvet as they break into leaf. Hardy in coastal conditions but intolerant of frost. Great landscaping versatility, excellent in containers. Most desirable dwarf shrub, attractive at all seasons. Polymorpha — many or variable forms. 1 × 1m.

Metrosideros robusta
Northern Rata
Interesting New Zealand species prolific in coastal lowland and hilly forests on Three Kings Islands, North Island and the north western regions of the South Island, usually commencing life as an epiphyte. Aerial roots which cling firmly to the host trunk thicken as they descend and reach the ground. Eventually the host tree dies leaving the Rata as an impressive forest giant festooned with less aggressive epiphytes. As a garden subject, M robusta grows slowly, densely clothed with olive-green foliage. After many years deep scarlet flower heads appear. 4 × 2.5m.

Metrosideros thomasii
Ohia-Lehua
Native to the Hawaiian Islands, Tahiti, Samoa and South East Polynesia growing from sea level to 3000m. Forms a bushy, multi-stemmed shrub or small tree with pubescent branchlets, young shoots light green deepening to greyish brown. Leaves elliptic to obovate-elliptic to 80 × 45mm, light green as juvenile, maturing dull deep-green, heavily pubescent at first becoming almost glabrous above, paler and pubescent beneath, firm and leathery, midrib yellowish, finely nerved, margins entire, short tip abruptly curved downward. Flowers orange-scarlet to red comprising dense clusters of 3–4cm stamens opening from powdery buds, conspicuous for long periods in winter, also through autumn and spring. Used extensively for foreshore planting. Hardy to salt-laden winds and ocean spray. Drought tolerant. Reasonably slow-growing. 3 × 2m.   **202**

Metrosideros umbellata
Southern Rata
Occasionally found in the North Island but more prevalent in the South Island, Stewart and other southern offshore islands. Forms an erect multi-branched tree with elliptic to lanceolate leaves to 75mm long. Regarded as a rare and beautiful sight as whole mountainside forests burst into brilliant blood-red bloom. Under cultivation the tree is slow growing with smaller pointed foliage and, after several decades, bright crimson flowers usually late summer. 3 × 2m.

A genus of about 45 species of evergreen shrubs and trees from south east Asia, India and Sri Lanka closely allied to Magnolias, named for Pietro Antonio Micheli, 17th–18th century Florentine botanist. Grown for good form, handsome foliage and highly fragrant flowers. Plant in deeply worked, organically enriched, free-draining, moisture-retentive neutral to alkaline soil in a warm sunny or semi-shady position safe from all but light frost. Magnoliaceae. *All evergreen.*

Michelia doltsopa
Strong growing large open branched pyramidal small tree from eastern Himalaya, south west China and eastern Tibet with neat pyramidal habit. Leaves oblong-lanceolate, to 18 × 8cm, glossy rich green, thin and leathery, covered with fine grey hair beneath. Brown furry buds appear in great quantity among the foliage near the ends of nearly every branch. Creamy white, highly perfumed, 10–15cm flowers with 12–16 petals tinged green near the base produced abundantly winter through spring. Good lawn specimen background or feature. 6 × 3m.

Michelia doltsopa 'Silver Cloud'
Delightfully fragrant, creamy white, magnolia-like blooms appearing late winter through spring in great masses. Selected for ability to flower at an early age and reliability. 4.5 × 2.5m.   **203**

Michelia figo
Port Wine Magnolia
Chinese species forming a dense multi-stemmed bush with foliage to the ground. Leaves elliptic-oblong to 10 × 5cm, deep green and lustrous. Cup-shaped flowers 3–4cm across resembling small Magnolias, ivory tinged yellow, base and margins tinted rosy-purple, with banana or rich port wine fragrance appear in great quantities amongst the foliage during spring. Exploit the rich fruity fragrance by planting near an entryway patio or bedroom window. Figo — native name in Cochin, China. 2.5 × 2m.

Michelia × foggii

Interesting hybrid from M figo × M doltsopa with characteristics intermediate between the two. Forms a large shrub or small tree with rounded, bushy habit. Leaves ovate to elliptic to 15 × 8cm, rich deep green, margins entire. Flowers to 35mm across, cream shaded rosy purple with the fruity fragrance of M figo. 4.5 × 3.5m.

MIMETES

A genus of 12 species of erect or prostrate small shrubs from South Africa named from the Greek *mimetes*, an imitator, a reference to the resemblance to other plants. Only one species in cultivation, a decorative shrub needing deeply worked, free-draining, moisture-retentive sandy soil in a well-ventilated sunny spot preferably near the coast. Mulch freely and water at ground level during dry periods. Members of the Protea family generally dislike excess water over the leaves.

Proteaceae.

Mimetes cucullata

Somewhat sprawling shrub with decumbent, densely tomentose branches well covered with oblong or oblong-lanceolate, upward curving leathery leaves to 75 × 12mm, deep green faintly margined red, pubescent at first becoming glabrous when mature. Each stem topped with terminal bracts yellow at the base gradually shading to bright red or orange near the tips borne profusely spring through midsummer. A cluster of silvery tassel-like stamens project from the base of each bract. Cucullata — hoodlike, referring to the hood-like bracts over each flower. Evergreen. 1.3 × 1.3m.

MONSTERA

A genus of about 20 species of epiphytic climbers from tropical America, possibly named from the Latin *monstrum*, a wonder or *monstrosus*, strange or wonderful, from the curious or monstrous leaves of some species. The best known species M deliciosa with odd, deeply cut and holed leaves is a valuable outdoor landscaping plant, creating dramatic and exotic effects. Grows in any reasonably warm, semi-shady, well-drained spot, such as the base of a high-branching tree, or within patios or courtyards either planted out or in containers, sheltered from severe frost. In suitable climates may be allowed to scramble as large scale bank or ground cover. Plant in deeply worked, free-draining soil. Prune severely if the plant gets out of hand.

Araceae.

Monstera deliciosa
Fruit salad plant

Native from Mexico to Panama and closely related to Philodendron. Curious plant with immense rounded deep green leaves to 90cm across, deeply lobed and holed, supported on long stout stems. Flower consists of a large central 25 × 3cm spadix, surrounded by a white spathe or bract like a giant arum lily. Spadix swells and matures to cream-coloured edible fruit with distinctive pineapple and banana flavour and aroma. With support will climb and attach itself, otherwise develops into an impressive mass of tropical looking leaf growth. Deliciosa simply means delicious. Evergreen. 2 × 3m. **203**

MORUS

A genus of about 12 species of deciduous trees and shrubs of Asiatic and North American origin named from the Latin *morus*, a mulberry tree. In many parts of the old world mulberry has been grown for centuries to feed silkworms and reputed to produce silk of better quality when fed on white mulberry leaves. As a garden tree the mulberry has picturesque form and few cultural problems, growing under most average conditions, with coastal planting reported as successful. Stake new plants securely as they quickly develop a heavy crown which may cause the tree to topple. Shorten back overzealous shoots or branches if necessary during the growth period. Deeply worked average soil in full sun. Water deeply during dry periods until established after which Morus is quite drought tolerant.

Moraceae. *All deciduous.*

Morus alba
White Mulberry

Native to central and Eastern China, a small to medium tree with rugged appearance. Leaves broadly ovate-cordate or heart-shaped to 20 × 12cm, coarsely toothed, often lobed and glossy green. Pale green flowers in cylindrical heads followed late spring by edible and sweet fruit resembling small raspberries at first greenish white, ripening pink or blackish purple. 6 × 4m.

Morus alba 'Pendula'
Weeping White Mulberry

Pendulous form which develops a weeping crown if trained on a single stem or grafted high on M alba stock, resulting in a gracefully weeping and fruiting specimen with foliage and fruit as above. 2.5 × 3m.

Morus alba 'Tatarica'
Russian Mulberry

Somewhat resembles M alba but with smaller growth habit, leaves and fruit of poorer quality. Extremely hardy. Tatarica — from central Asia. 5 × 4.

Morus nigra
Black Mulberry

Small tree from western Asia with widespread head, becoming gnarled and picturesque with age. Heart shaped leaves to 12 × 8cm, coarsely toothed, unlobed or deeply lobed, with rough texture and downy undersides. Dark blackish red 25mm fruit drop when ripe, very juicy and delicious flavour. Desirable tree with good form, but locate away from areas where fallen fruits are likely to be trampled on. Birds love them. 5 × 3m.

MUEHLENBECKIA

A genus of about 20 species of procumbent or climbing shrubs from South America, New Guinea, Australia and New Zealand named for Henri Gustave Muehlenbeck, 19th century German physician and botanist. Cultivated for its thin wiry intricate stems in delicate patterns and textures providing dense cover amongst other shrubs, for banks beds or old tree-stumps. Some species play a part in regeneration or soil stabilization. Tolerant of almost any deeply worked, free-draining soil in sun or semi-shade and hardy to sub-zero temperatures.

Polygonaceae. *All evergreen.*

Muehlenbeckia astonii

Distinctive New Zealand species, forming a dense upright shrub with numerous slender flexuous interlacing and divaricating branches with dark reddish brown bark. Leaves in clusters of 2–3, broad-obcordate or heart-shaped to 8mm across, bright green, paler beneath with a marginal fringe of fine hairs. Miniature flowers in axillary clusters of up to four followed by 3–4mm translucent succulent fruit. Slow growing, very hardy, wind-tolerant. 2 × 1.5m.

Muehlenbeckia axillaris
Creeping Wire Vine, Creeping Pohuehue
Multi-branched prostrate shrub with slender wiry reddish brown or blackish stems rooting at the nodes forming a matting or dense low climbing plant. Leaves oblong to orbicular to 10 × 10mm, dark green and glossy above, paler beneath, on slender 2–3mm petioles. Yellow-green, 4mm flowers in leaf axils early summer through autumn followed by black glossy 3mm seeds set in a white aril.

Distributed through New Zealand, New South Wales, Victoria and Tasmania, often in lowland to subalpine open grassland, dry riverbeds, rocky or gravelly places. Vigorous somewhat invasive ground cover, but underground stems easily cut with a sharp spade. Axillaris — borne in the axils. 1m × 30cm.

M Y O P O R U M

A genus of thirty species of trees and shrubs mostly from Australia others from Mauritius, Hawaii, Asia and New Zealand, named from the Greek *myo*, to shut and *poros*, opening or pore referring to prominent spots or translucent oil glands on the leaves. Useful for exposed coastal planting to provide rapid windbreaks, shade for cattle on coastal farms or temporary protection for other trees.

Generally, they require deeply worked, free-draining soil in full sun but adapt to wide-ranging soil types, extended dry periods, reasonable frost and salt-laden winds. Grows rapidly and responds to light applications of slow-release fertilizer and occasional deep watering. Heavy trimming at least every second year maintains size and shape. Naturally, Myoporum is seldom found far from the seashore.

Myoporaceae. *All evergreen.*

Myoporum insulare
Boobialla
Australian native species distributed through all southern states, forming a dense, compact small to medium shrub with glabrous, often sticky young shoots and four-angled somewhat warty stems. Leaves lanceolate to obovate tapering to the base, to 80 × 25mm, mid to dark-green, thick and fleshy. White flowers to about 10mm with central ring of purple dots borne in axillary clusters of 2–8 winter through spring, followed by white 8mm globular succulent fruit with purple markings.

Excellent screen or barrier in exposed coastal positions. Insulare — growing on an island. 3 × 2.5m

Myoporum laetum
New Zealand Ngaio
A small New Zealand native tree or large shrub found in coastal and lowland forests of the North and outlying Islands and the northern part of the South Island. Young shoots sticky, leaves lanceolate to ovate, to 100 × 35mm, bright green and glabrous, somewhat fleshy, prominent pellucid dots above, paler beneath, margins entire. Flowers 12mm across, white lightly spotted lilac carried in axillary clusters of 2–6 spring through mid summer, followed by 8mm oblong reddish purple fruit. Grows at the rate of one metre each year and effectively controls sound, wind, sun or blown sand. Laetum — bright or vivid. 4 × 3m.

Myoporum laetum 'Purpureum'
Growth and form similar to M laetum but with purplish leaves, more intense when grown in full sun. 4 × 3m.

Myoporum parvifolium
Creeping Boobialla, Creeping Myoporum
Australian native species distributed through southern states. Prostrate ground cover or rockery plant, creeping or trailing and rooting wherever branches touch moist ground providing total cover within six months. Densely covered with linear-lanceolate, bright green, thick, often warty leaves to 40 × 8mm. White or pale pink, 7mm starry flowers spotted purple, spring through autumn followed by 7mm globular yellowish white berries. Try it as a trailing container plant. Syn M humile. Parvifolium — small leafed. 20cm × 1m.

Myoporum parvifolium 'Purpureum'
Resembles M parvifolium but with a tinge of purple to the leaves. 20cm × 1m.

M Y R S I N E

A genus of about five species of trees and shrubs from Azores, China and New Zealand named from the Greek *myrsine*, myrrh or myrtle. Some species are valued for aromatic foliage. The New Zealand *Matipou* thrives in almost any reasonable free-draining soil or situation, growing quickly without fuss, often with young plants growing beneath when left undisturbed. May be trimmed to almost any form or size. Plant Toro in deeply worked, free-draining, moisture-retentive soil in

shade or partial sun. Mulch freely and keep moist during dry periods. Train early to one leader, then only to maintain good form.

Myrsinaceae. *All evergreen.*

Myrsine australis
Matipou
Widely distributed around forest margins and scrubland throughout New Zealand. Forms a compact shrub with reddish brown young branches and shoots. Leaves obovate or broad-elliptic, to 55 × 25mm, yellowish to light green with wavy crinkly margins. Small 3mm insignificant flowers summer through autumn accompanied by oval 3mm reddish to black fruit from the previous year. Australis — southern. 3 × 2m.

Myrsine salicina
Toro
Distinctive foliage flower and fruit. Often seen in coastal and lower mountain forests of New Zealand's North and South Islands. Erect growth habit with dark red or black bark. New shoots reddish brown, leaves narrow-elliptic almost linear to 17 × 3cm, dark-green with a dull gloss, distinctive veining beneath. Clusters of 3mm flowers followed by 8mm oblong blackish fruit with red or orange seeds appear along the branches beneath the foliage. Handsome specimen shrub. Salicina — willow-like. 4 × 2.5m.

M Y R T U S

A genus of about 100 species from South America, New Zealand and Southern Europe named from the Greek and Latin *myrtus*, the myrtle tree. Many species rich in fragrant oils used medicinally and in the manufacture of cosmetics. Two New Zealand species and cultivars previously listed under Lophomyrtus are reunited with the genus Myrtus. Numerous ornamental hybrids from M bullata × M obcordata, classified as M × ralphii are foliage shrubs with excellent colour texture and form, useful for colour accent among darker greens, backgrounds and cutting for indoor decoration.

Easily grown in deeply worked, free-draining, fertile soil. They grow in partial shade, but develop brighter foliage colour in full sun and high exposure and benefit from regular cutting, keeping more compact and providing a continual supply of decorative foliage for garden decor or floral arrangements.

Myrtaceae. *All evergreen.*

Myrtus bullata
New Zealand Ramarama
Found naturally in both North and South
Islands of New Zealand, inhabiting more
open parts of forest margins or clearings.
Easily distinguished by shining, blistered
or puckered, broadly ovate leaves to
50 × 30mm, bronze-green to reddish above
and reddish purple beneath. Creamy white
12mm flowers through summer followed
by dark reddish purple, 8mm berries.
Handsome garden shrub with erect and
dense habit. Bullata — with blistered or
puckered surface. 2.5 × 1.5m.

Myrtus bullata 'Matai Bay'
A selected form discovered at Matai Bay in
Pelorous Sound. Large rounded, heavily
puckered, deep brownish-green leaves. New
shoots bright mahogany red, maturing
mahogany brown during winter. Superior to
M bullata. 2.5 × 1.5m.   **203**

Myrtus communis 'Variegata'
Common Variegated Myrtle
From Mediterranean regions. Species a
densely foliaged shrub with ovate-lanceolate, dark green, glossy leaves to 50 × 15mm,
pleasantly aromatic when crushed. White
sweetly fragrant starry flowers with numerous stamens appear mid-summer, followed
by 12mm, blue-black berries. M communis
'Variegata' is a compact grower with
leathery leaves striped or margined white.
1 × 1m

Myrtus obcordata
New Zealand Pohutu
Occurs naturally in coastal and elevated
forests of both North and South Islands.
Easily recognized with green distinctive
obcordate or heart-shaped 6–12mm leaves,
and 7mm creamy white flowers through
summer, followed by 5mm bright to dark
red or violet fruit. Obcordata — inversely
heart shaped. 3 × 2m.

Myrtus × ralphii 'Astbury'
Upright grower, attractive rounded dusky
pink foliage, intensifying through winter.
White flowers. 3 × 1.5m.

Myrtus × ralphii 'Barry's Multicolor'
Compact bushy grower, new shoots pink
ish brown. Leaves broadly elliptic, heavily puckered, with irregular central zone
in several different shades of olive green
surrounded by a broad, creamy yellow
margin. 2 × 1.5m.   **203**

Myrtus × ralphii 'Gloriosa'
Bushy grower, dainty small rounded light
green leaves variegated cream and tinged
pink. 1.5m × 90cm

Myrtus × ralphii 'Ihaka'
Selected upright-growing form discovered
in Ihaka Street, Palmerston North. Medium
sized, rounded, bronzy red, puckered leaves.
Good for cutting. 2 × 1m.

Myrtus × ralphii 'Indian Chief'
Tall narrow grower, dark reddish brown
foliage, more intense mid winter and in
exposed location. 2 × 1m.

Myrtus × ralphii 'Kakapo'
Vigorous bushy upright grower, with
coppery bronze puckered leaves. Named
after the New Zealand native green parrot.
2.5 × 1.5m.

Myrtus × ralphii 'Kathryn'
Reddish purple to coppery brown broadly
ovate leaves to 3 × 2cm, heavily puckered and glossy. Intense colour in winter.
2 × 1m.   **203**

Myrtus × ralphii 'Krinkly'
Fine red-foliaged form maintaining good
colour all year, more intense during winter.
Leaves glossy and puckered. 2 × 1m.

Myrtus × ralphii 'Lilliput'
Exceptional compact dwarf grower. Dainty
rounded rich reddish brown leaves to
12 × 10mm, overlaid wine red with purple-
red veining and stems. 50 × 50cm.

Myrtus × ralphii 'Little Star'
Small rounded leaves edged red and cream
with green inner panel, colour intensifying
in winter. Exceptional dwarf foliage shrub.
Trim occasionally for best form. 50 × 50cm.

Myrtus × ralphii 'Lyndale'
Compact bushy grower with rounded leaves,
smaller and lighter coloured than M 'Kathryn', basically bronze with a hint of pink as
cooler weather approaches. Ideal foliage for
floral art. Introduced and named for Lyndale
Nurseries, Auckland. 1.5m × 90cm.

Myrtus × ralphii 'Multicolour'
Young shoots flushed rose-pink, mottled
green and greyish green with maturity,
irregularly margined creamy yellow. Compact grower. 1.5m × 90cm.

Myrtus × ralphii 'Pink Dainty'
Small dainty leaves, new shoots tinged
pink to red in winter. Ideal for picking.
2 × 1m.

Myrtus × ralphii 'Pixie'
Charming miniature form and attractive
small bronzy green foliage. Dark purple new
growth and leaf veining. Excellent in rock
or feature gardens. 50 × 50cm.

Myrtus × ralphii 'Plum Duff'
Small rounded bushy grower. Dainty
crinkled leaves in green cream pink and
purple intensifying in winter. 1.3 × 1m.

Myrtus × ralphii 'Red Dragon'
Medium grower with small pointed textured
leaves, new shoots brilliant reddish pink
maturing blackish red, intensifying through
winter. Outstanding, excellent for picking.
1.5m × 70cm.

Myrtus × ralphii 'Redwing'
Rich pink new growth, mature leaves rich
red with brilliant colour all year. Outstanding
foliage shrub more intense in exposed
situations. 2 × 1m.

Myrtus × ralphii 'Sundae'
Narrow upright slow-growing shrub.
Broadly ovate crinkly leaves to 3 × 2cm,
creamy yellow over green with pinkish red
splashes. 2 × 1m.

Myrtus × ralphii 'Traversii'
Erect-growing bush with reddish stems,
heavily puckered light-green leaves with
yellow central zone and a touch of pink. Best
in full sun. Syn M × ralphii 'Variegata'.
1.5m × 90cm.

Myrtus × ralphii 'Wild Cherry'
Upright slender grower, rich purple-red
foliage, intensifying in winter. 1.5m × 90cm.

A genus of just one species native to the
region from India to Japan named from
the Japanese title *nandin*. Belongs to the
Barberry family, quite unrelated to
Bamboo although it has a fancied resemblance. Valued for beautiful foliage, floral
and berry display. Useful in oriental or
tropical plantings, in narrow restricted
areas against fences or buildings or in
containers. Create dramatic effects with
night lighting. Plant in deeply worked,
free-draining, moisture-retentive soil in
sun or partial shade, although leaf
colouring more intense in full sun and
without excessive feeding.

In alkaline soils, correct chlorosis or
yellowing of the leaves by adding iron
sulphate. Mottling of the leaves, especially
in pygmy forms usually indicates viral
infection. A virus eradication programme
sponsored by the New Zealand Nurserymen's Association has made available
plants which are free of known virus —
labelled 'FKV'. Select these wherever

possible. **Tired plants may be rejuvenated by cutting some of the oldest canes to the ground. Evergreen in temperate climates, hardy to −15°C but may loose some leaves in winter.**

Berberidaceae. *All evergreen.*

Nandina domestica
Chinese Sacred Bamboo, Heavenly Bamboo
Chinese native grown in Japan for centuries. Has a light and airy structure of slender unbranched reddish cane-like stems and fine-textured, bipinnate leaves with numerous lanceolate to elliptic, 3–5cm leaflets in lacy pattern. New leaves tinged pink and bronzy red in spring, turning lime-green tinted rose, taking on hues of reddish purple and bronze in autumn, eventually fiery crimson. Erect to arching 40cm panicles of small creamy white or pinkish flowers late spring followed in autumn by masses of shiny red, 8–10mm berries when planted in groups for cross-pollination. Domestica — domesticated or used as a house plant. 1.8 × 1m.

Nandina domestica 'Burdens Dwarf'
Selected in the USA for bushy, compact form and dense foliage. Leaves similar to above, lime green in summer becoming orange scarlet and apricot through autumn and winter. Hardy and versatile. 80 × 60cm.

Nandina domestica 'Firepower'
Dwarf Heavenly Bamboo
Compact rounded dwarf shrub with fresh lime-green leaves in summer, changing through vivid hot-pink and fiery crimson in autumn and winter. FKV (see above). 60 × 60cm.

Nandina domestica 'Little Princess'
American selection. Semi-dwarf with dainty finely divided foliage, rich wine-purple new growths, foliage green with maturity rich orange autumn and winter. Ideal for smaller gardens or containers. 1 × 75cm.

Nandina domestica 'Pygmy'
Dwarf Heavenly Bamboo
Forms a compact rounded densely foliaged bush. Leaves lime-green at first, gradually changing through purple, crimson, orange or scarlet summer through winter. Attractive through all seasons, more intense during colder months especially plants in full sun and not overfed. Perfect for rock or feature gardens, grows without fuss with little or no maintenance. 60 × 60cm.   **204**

Nandina domestica 'Richmond'
Valuable New Zealand self-fertile introduction originally from a South Island

garden, named after the town in which it was found. Produces each winter a consistent and abundant crop of brilliant scarlet-red berries about the size of small currants, held in large pyramidal panicles above the foliage, remaining attractive and untouched by birds until late spring. Growth habit and foliage as for N domestica. 1.8 × 1m.   **204**

Nandina domestica 'Woods Dwarf'
American selection. Vigorous dwarf compact plant, young leaves lime-green changing through light yellow to apricot orange and red in autumn and winter. 75 × 50cm.

NERIUM

A genus of one species, an evergreen shrub from the Mediterranean to western China, called by the classical Greek name. The term Oleander is from the Italian *oleandro*, a reference to olive-like leaves. Free flowering Oleanders are amongst the most colourful shrubs in warm climate gardens of the world. Commencing in spring and continuing over the heat of summer they produce great masses of single or double flowers well into autumn. Their natural form is a multi-stemmed rounded shrub with smooth strong erect and flexuous branches which bend with the wind or weep gracefully under the weight of blossom.

As well as being excellent shrubs for summer colour, Oleanders make excellent wind barriers, provide mass cover on sunny banks and are perfect for containers especially where they are likely to be subjected to reflected heat from paved areas.

All cultivars have lanceolate leaves in whorls of three, tapering to a point, to 22cm long, dark green, midrib prominent, leathery and somewhat glabrous. Flowers either funnel-form, semi double or fully double borne in broad terminal cymes late spring through autumn.

All parts of the plant are highly toxic. Sap may cause skin irritations and inhalation of smoke when burning prunings must be avoided. Chewing leaves may result in sickness, but the taste is repugnant. Children should be warned of these dangers.

Neriums are sun lovers and thrive under hot coastal or inland conditions. Plant in deeply worked, organically enriched, free-draining soil. They are lime tolerant, but need protection from frost. Unpruned plants tend to become loose open and woody. Cut back to half way old

wood which has flowered to encourage new shoots from the base which may be pinched back lightly as they grow. Pull off rather than cut unwanted basal shoots. Prune to ground level plants which become too large or rangy. Growth renewal is rapid and they bloom on current year's wood.

Apocynaceae. *All evergreen.*

Nerium oleander 'Albus'
Showy heads of single white flowers. 2 × 1.5m.

Nerium oleander 'Delphine'
Deep cerise single flowers. 2 × 1.5m.   **221**

Nerium oleander 'Dr Golphin'
Deep cerise single blooms. 2 × 1.5m.   **221**

Nerium oleander 'Luteum Plenum'
Semi-double, rich cream flowers. 2 × 1.5m.

Nerium oleander 'Madonna Grandiflora'
Pure white semi-double hose-in-hose flowers. 1.5 × 1.5m.   **221**

Nerium oleander 'Mrs F Roeding'
Large salmon-orange fully double flowers in abundance on a dwarf bushy shrub. 1.5 × 1.5m.   **221**

Nerium oleander 'Petite Salmon'
Popular dwarf dense grower, dark green leaves to 12 × 2cm. Masses of salmon pink, 4cm single flowers. 90 × 90cm.   **221**

Nerium oleander 'Professor Durrand'
Clear pale yellow single blooms. 1.5 × 1.5m.

Nerium oleander 'Professor Martin'
Bright red single flowers. Extremely showy. 2 × 1.5m.

Nerium oleander 'Punctatum'
Bright pink single flowers in great abundance. The most free-blooming Oleander. 3 × 2m.   **222**

Nerium oleander 'Sorrento'
Bright yellow, fully double flowers. Free-flowering in warm, sunny conditions. 2 × 1.5m.

Nerium oleander 'Splendens'
Large deep rose pink fully double flowers. Excellent flower formation. 3 × 2m.   **222**

Nerium oleander 'Splendens Variegata'
Beautifully green and gold variegated foliage, double pink flowers. 2 × 1.5m.

NOTHOFAGUS

A genus of about forty species of deciduous and evergreen trees distributed throughout New Zealand, Australia, New Caledonia, New Guinea and temperate South America, named from the Greek *nothos*, false and *fagus*, beech. It represents the Beech family in the Southern Hemisphere. While they could be considered too large for garden use, growth is extremely slow so good use may be made of their juvenile laciness, especially amongst collections of more broad-leafed plants.

Coming from high country, Nothofagus are unable to tolerate prolonged periods of drought or wet feet. Plant in deeply worked, organically enriched, free-draining, moisture-retentive soil in full sun or partial shade such as woodland areas sheltered from prevailing wind. Water deeply and frequently during summer.

Fagaceae. *All evergreen.*

Nothofagus fusca
Red Beech
Attractive foliage tree reaching large proportions naturally, but slow growing and manageable for garden use with pruning. Found in lowland to mountain forests in the North Island of New Zealand, southwards from Te Aroha and Rotorua and throughout the South Island. Forms an erect narrow pyramidal tree with broad-ovate leaves to 5 × 3cm, bluntly toothed, slightly crinkled and waved in brownish, deep bronzy red tones, often much brighter, colour intensifying towards autumn. Foliage highly regarded for floral arrangements. Fusca — brown or dusky. 5 × 3m.

Nothofagus fusca 'Rainbow'
Smaller growing form of above. In summer, leaves margined cream, becoming bronze tinted with the onset of cooler weather, then changing through pink, finally bright cerise. Best in partial shade. Excellent foliage for floral art. 3 × 2m.

Nothofagus menziesii
Silver Beech
From lowland or mountain forests in the North Island, south from Thames and Te Aroha and throughout the South Island. Distinctive small dark green orbicular to ovate leaves to 15mm long, margins finely and bluntly toothed. Young spring growth pale green against silvery white trunk. 5 × 3m.

Nothofagus solandrii
Black Beech
Extremely decorative as a juvenile with open form, wiry stems and ovoid leaves to 13 × 7mm, glossy dark-green, margins entire, neatly arranged in two distinct rows, richly coloured during winter. Develops into a slender tree with ascending fan-like branches. Named for Daniel Solander, 18th century Swedish disciple of Linnaeus and fellow traveller with Sir Joseph Banks and Captain Cook. 5 × 3m.

Nothofagus solandrii Cliffortioides
Mountain Beech
Elegant form, small deep green ovoid leaves with curled edges and raised tip, closely set in rows. Fairly fast grower as a juvenile with graceful spreading branches and attractive foliage. Named for George Clifford, 18th century Dutch merchant banker, garden enthusiast and associate of Linnaeus. 5 × 3m.

NYMPHAEA

A genus of about forty species of waterlilies with tuberous or fleshy roots, mostly from tropical or subtropical regions of the northern hemisphere, Africa and Australia, named for *Nymphe*, water nymph of Greek mythology. Requiring little in the way of care, waterlilies and the pools in which they grow provide an irresistible feature in any garden. Given water, sunlight and fertile soil, they'll reward you with exquisite waxy blooms set against a background of luxuriant floating foliage through spring, summer and autumn.

Nymphaceae.

Nymphaea Culture
Waterlilies produce greater quantities of better and larger flowers when in maximum sunlight and warmth. Provide space for free development, rich soil for their roots and from 15–25cm of water above the crown. Pools with a minimum depth of 50cm are best, although Pygmy lilies will grow in less. As they derive little or no nourishment from water, grow them in fertile soil such as well-rotted animal manure and good loam in equal proportions well mixed with about 500g of bone-dust.

Plant tubers in substantial boxes, about 30 × 22 × 20cm, using untreated timber which lasts well when completely submerged. Don't let plants dry out prior to planting. Either keep them in water or covered with a wet sack. Plant hardy lilies horizontally with the crown just above the soil surface. Tropicals, which when dormant somewhat resemble a pinecone, are planted upright. Cover the surface with 3–4cm of sand or small pebbles to keep the soil in place and prevent fish from burrowing. The boxes are now ready for plunging.

In deep pools, use bricks or concrete blocks to raise crowns to within 15–25 cm of the surface. Place weights on boxes until saturated to prevent floating and tipping. Waterlilies may be grown in lakes or streams, planted 1.5–2m apart at a depth of 60–90cm. Enclose the roots and soil mixture in a small hessian sack, tie the top and allow to sink. They'll become naturalized and need no further attention. Always choose the sunniest location.

Planting time is from late winter through mid summer. Unlike most gardening activities, waterlily pools need little attention. After two or three years, pools may need cleaning, a task for early spring. Divide overcrowded crowns and replant in fresh soil. Possibly the only pests are aphids. At first appearance, hose them off early in the morning and fish will enjoy them. Otherwise a light summer oil spray may be used without harming plants or fish. Fish also control mosquitoes, devouring wrigglers long before they're visible to the naked eye.

Nymphaeas are in three major groupings:

Tropical lilies have blooms in blue, red, pink and white, to 25cm or more across, held above the water on long stems ideal for picking. They bloom profusely, one plant capable of bearing a hundred or more flowers over a six month season. Although tropical by name, they'll grow successfully in most regions of Australasia.

Hardy lilies mostly float their flowers on the water against a background of dense foliage. They're amongst the easiest of any plant to grow, flourishing with minimum care to produce large quantities of glorious blooms in a wide range of colours year after year.

Pygmy lilies are delightful miniatures, perfect for small pools or tubs, or in odd pockets or corners of larger pools. Generally they resemble hardy lilies, only much smaller in growth habit, foliage and flower.

Many of the following cultivars are hybrids of unknown parentage.

Nymphaea 'A E Seibert'
Tropical. Star-shaped flowers, lavender pink with central cluster of waxy yellow stamens. **223**

Nymphaea 'After Glow'
Tropical. Beautiful combination of pink, orange and yellow flowers.

Nymphaea 'Alba'
Pygmy. Pure white, 25mm flowers in abundance. Small oval leaves, purplish beneath. Excellent for tubs and also small pools.

Nymphaea 'American Beauty'
Tropical. Magnificent soft magenta flowers with central cluster of yellow stamens. Large orbicular leaves with wavy margins.

Nymphaea 'Arethusa'
Hardy. Large, globular flowers, deep wine-red in the centre shading through rose pink to light red at the tips. Prominent gold stamens.

Nymphaea 'Attraction'
Hardy. Large fragrant flowers to 25cm across, vivid red with white spots, sepals tinted pink, deep-brown stamens tipped gold. Large leaves.

Nymphaea 'Aurora'
Pygmy. Small starry flowers less than 5cm across, opening cream, deepening to apricot. Excellent for tubs and small pools.

Nymphaea 'Black Prince'
Tropical. Star-shaped, deep purple-blue flowers with golden centre and stamens. Possibly the most vigorous blue tropical.

Nymphaea 'Blue Beauty'
Tropical. Large star-shaped, deep-blue, fragrant flowers with yellow centre and stamens, violet anthers and sepals marked black. Large leaves, green spotted brown, margins waved.

Nymphaea 'Carmine Laydeker'
Pygmy. Flowers less than 7cm across, deep carmine-red concave petals, reddish stamens. Vigorous.

Nymphaea 'Clarissa'
Pygmy. Brick red flowers to 6cm across. Free-flowering. Excellent for tubs and small pools.

Nymphaea 'Comanche'
Hardy. Rose apricot at first, slowly changing to coppery red, outer petals with yellow glow, stamens bright yellow. Leaves purplish when young.

Nymphaea 'Conqueror'
Hardy. Large cup-shaped flowers with broad incurved petals, brilliant crimson red, flecked and shading to white.

Nymphaea 'Darwin'
Hardy. Fragrant, semi-double, wine-red flowers with white shading and marking.

Nymphaea 'Dentata'
Night-blooming tropical. Large white starry flowers with central golden zone and stamens, held well above the water.

Nymphaea 'Director George T Moore'
Tropical. Deepest violet-purple, 20–25cm flowers with prominent yellow central zone and purple stamens. Very free-flowering.

Nymphaea 'Escarboucle'
Hardy. Brilliant vermillion-crimson, 16cm flowers with garnet-red stamens tipped yellow. Rich spicy fragrance. Colour intensifies with maturity.

Nymphaea 'Fire Crest'
Hardy. Soft shell-pink, strongly fragrant, wide-open flowers with pointed petals and red stamens.

Nymphaea 'General Pershing'
Tropical. Large, lilac-pink, fragrant blooms held 30cm above the water. Large pinkish leaves tinted purple.

Nymphaea 'Gladstone'
Hardy. Immense, pure-white starry flowers, rich green foliage.

Nymphaea 'Golden West'
Tropical. Large starry clear pink flowers blending to golden apricot. Green foliage speckled purple.

Nymphaea 'Gonnere'
Hardy. Large cup-shaped, pure white flowers with green sepals and bright-yellow stamens. Large foliage.

Nymphaea 'Hal Miller'
Hardy. Large, pale primrose yellow flowers. Large deep-green foliage.

Nymphaea 'Helvola'
Pygmy. Small, star-shaped, vivid canary-yellow flowers less than 5cm across, orange stamens. Leaves dull-green with brown marbling.

Nymphaea 'Hermine'
Hardy. Star-shaped flowers with white petals and bright green sepals. Ovate, dark green leaves. Moderately vigorous.

Nymphaea 'Indiana'
Pygmy. Miniature apricot flowers deepening to coppery red. Olive-green leaves flecked purple. Excellent for tubs and small pools.

Nymphaea 'Jack Woods'
Tropical. Raspberry-red, fragrant flowers with golden centre and stamens. Leaves spotted brown.

Nymphaea 'James Brydon'
Hardy. Large fragrant, cup-shaped, double flowers, bright red with metallic sheen, deep orange stamens tipped yellow. Large purple-tinted leaves, often spotted dark red.

Nymphaea 'Joanne Pring'
Pygmy. Small, deepest pink flowers, paler towards the tips. Orange-yellow stamens. Excellent for tubs and small pools.

Nymphaea 'Lilac Star'
Tropical. Magnificent, lilac blue starry flowers borne profusely on long stems.

Nymphaea 'Lucida'
Hardy. Pale apricot, almost orange, 15cm starry flowers with deeper centre and orange stamens. Leaves deep green with purple variegation. Small grower but very prolific, ideal for small pools.

Nymphaea 'Lustrous'
Hardy. Large cup-shaped, soft rose pink flowers with silvery, silky sheen and canary yellow stamens. Leaves reddish brown at first, becoming deep green, margins undulating.

Nymphaea 'Margaret Randig'
Tropical. Large, rich lavender-blue, fragrant flowers with wide petals. Dark-green leaves speckled bronze.

Nymphaea 'Marliacea Carnea'
Hardy. Shell pink, fragrant flowers shading to delicate rose. Excellent for cutting.

Nymphaea 'Marliacea Chromatella'
Hardy. Clear, rich creamy yellow, medium sized flowers. Profuse bloomer. Deep-green leaves mottled brown. **223**

Nymphaea 'Mary Patricia'
Pygmy. Beautiful, peach-blossom pink miniature cup-shaped flowers. Small grower, ideal for tubs and small pools.

Nymphaea 'Meteor'
Hardy. Deep pink flowers deepening to almost crimson, sepals with reddish streaks, bright yellow stamens. Leaves green above, purplish beneath.

Nymphaea 'Mexicana'
Hardy. Rich creamy yellow, medium sized flowers with prominent yellow stamens. Foliage variegated green and purple.

Nymphaea 'Mme Wilfron Gonnere'
Hardy. Large rich pink, cup-shaped, almost double flowers, outer petals spotted deeper pink. Resembles a formal Camellia. Rich green foliage.

Nymphaea 'Mrs George H Pring'
Tropical. Star-shaped, fragrant flowers to 25cm across, white flushed cream, yellow stamens tipped white. Large brown-blotched leaves. **223**

Nymphaea 'Mrs James Hudson'
Hardy. Large, pink to wine-red flowers. Large deep green, purple-flecked foliage, vigorous grower.

Nymphaea 'Mrs Martin E Randig'
Tropical. Dark purple, fragrant flowers with pink sepals. Leaves flecked above, bronzy beneath.

Nymphaea 'Newton'
Hardy. Brilliant rose-vermillion to brick red flowers, long narrow petals and prominent orange stamens. Stands clear of water, resembling tropicals.

Nymphaea 'Paul Harriot'
Hardy. Flowers to 15cm across, clear yellow to pale copper at first, deepening to deep orange-red. Blooms slightly fragrant, held above the water. Foliage green, spotted with red on both surfaces. Lasts well when cut.

Nymphaea 'Phoebus'
Pygmy. Small flowers, at first creamy yellow striped red, maturing copper-red. Green leaves with brown and purple markings. Ideal for tubs and small pools.

Nymphaea 'Picciola'
Hardy. Large, star-shaped, crimson-red flowers to 25cm, held above the water. Reddish green foliage spotted maroon. Vigorous and prolific.

Nymphaea 'Pink Opal'
Hardy. Globose buds open to soft pink to coral red, cup-shaped double flowers held above water. Bronze tinted leaves.

Nymphaea 'Pink Pearl'
Tropical. Starry silvery pink flowers, yellow stamens tipped pink, well above the water.

Nymphaea 'Pink Sensation'
Hardy. Large 20cm, starry, rich pink flowers with oval petals, held clear of the water. Rounded foliage.

Nymphaea 'Pink Star'
Tropical. Large, pale pink, star-shaped flowers, stamens golden yellow flushed lavender. Large, light green foliage.

Nymphaea 'Princess Elizabeth'
Hardy. Clear light-pink, cup-shaped, double flowers maturing rich deep-pink, well above the water. Vigorous and free-flowering.

Nymphaea 'Red Star'
Tropical. Large star-shaped, rosy-red flowers with golden yellow stamens tipped pink. Pale green foliage reddish beneath.

Nymphaea 'Rosanna Supreme'
Hardy. Medium to large rose-pink blooms with pale golden stamens. Vigorous and free-flowering.

Nymphaea 'Rose Arey'
Hardy. Large, fragrant, star-shaped, rose-pink flowers with yellow stamens. Red-tinted leaves.

Nymphaea 'Rose Star'
Tropical. Reddish pink, star-shaped flowers, stamens pink blending to yellow in the centre. Blooms held high above the water on strong stems.

Nymphaea 'Sioux'
Hardy. Buff-yellow at first, changing through peach-pink to deep orange-red. Bronzy leaves with brown marbling.

Nymphaea 'Stellata'
Tropical. Pale-blue flowers to 12cm across, sepals light green beneath, pale blue within, numerous yellow stamens tipped blue. Blooms held well above water. Bright-green leaves to 15cm across, blotched brown above, purplish pink beneath. Stellata — star-like.

Nymphaea 'Sultan'
Hardy. Cherry-red to wine-red flowers irregularly streaked with white. Dark-green foliage. Vigorous grower.

Nymphaea 'Superba'
Hardy. Very large, pure-white, star-shaped flowers with golden stamens. Fresh-green foliage, medium grower.

Nymphaea 'Tina'
Tropical. Rich purple, star-shaped flowers shaded white in the centre, golden stamens. Blooms held well above the water.

Nymphaea 'White Laydeker'
Pygmy. Dainty, pure-white flowers with golden stamens. Ideal waterlily for small tubs.

Nymphaea 'William B Shaw'
Hardy. Large flat, creamy pink, fine-petalled flowers with central dark red zone. Large rounded leaves.

Nymphaea 'William Falconer'
Hardy. Deep ruby-red, cup-shaped flowers to 15cm across with orange-yellow stamens.

Nymphaea 'Yellow Dazzler'
Tropical. Large, flat, lemon yellow, starry blooms borne on long stems. Very large, pale golden leaves.

NYSSA

A genus of five species of deciduous trees native to North America and south east Asia, the name Nyssa meaning a water nymph referring to the swampy habitat of some species. Tupelo is an American Indian word for Nyssa. Naturally found in colonies in wetlands or swamps, with brilliant autumn leaf colours and picturesque winter outline. Excellent for planting near lakes or ponds for beautiful reflections. Plant in deeply worked, moisture-retentive neutral to alkaline soil in sun or partial shade. Tolerant of wet feet. Best planted when small as they resent root disturbance.
Nyssaceae. *All deciduous.*

Nyssa sinensis
Chinese Tupelo
Resembles N sylvatica but smaller growing and more spreading. Leaves oblong-lanceolate to 20 × 8cm, sparsely pubescent and red-tinged when young, almost glabrous with maturity. Brilliant red and yellow autumn colour, possibly outshining N sylvatica. 5 × 3m.

Nyssa sylvatica
Tupelo, Black Gum, Sour Gum
From eastern North America, one of the showiest trees for autumn colour. Slow to moderate growth rate, pyramidal when young, spreading irregular and rugged with age, lower branches often drooping. Angular branches and twigs and dark red bark present a dramatic picture against a winter sky. Dark green glossy elliptic to obovate leaves to 15 × 7cm, rich scarlet, orange and yellow in autumn even in milder areas. It is normal for leaves to be slow to appear in spring. Small greenish yellow flowers and blue black fruits of little consequence. Sylvatica — growing in woods or forests. 7 × 5m.

OCHNA

A genus of about 85 species of evergreen and semi-evergreen shrubs and trees from tropical Africa and Asia, named from the Greek *ochne,* wild pear, apparently from leaf resemblance. Grown for curious fruits, beautiful flowers and lustrous leaves. They revel in warm temperate frost-free climates and start flowering when quite small.

Plant in sun or partial shade in deeply worked, organically enriched, free-draining, moisture-retentive acid soil. Mulch freely, feed during spring and autumn and water during prolonged dry periods. Locate where the flowers and fruit may be appreciated at close range. Ochnaceae.

Ochna serrulata
Mickey Mouse Plant, Bird's Eye Bush
Fascinating South African species also known as Fun Shrub. Forms an angular twiggy open bush, bark spotted with lenticels or raised cellular pores. Young shoots bronze and very glossy, leaves narrowly elliptic to 6cm long, dark green, leathery, margins finely toothed.

Masses of greenish buds open to yellow flowers resembling buttercups. Following petal-fall, sepals turn vivid red and five or more seed-like fruits cluster around the centre, at first green later turning jet black, suggesting the name Mickey Mouse Plant. A curious plant with subtle beauty. Serrulata — with small saw-like teeth. Evergreen. 1.5 × 1m.   **222**

A genus of about 130 species of herbs, shrubs and small trees from Australia and New Zealand named for Adam Olsch-lager, 17th century botanist (latinized to olearius). Some are grown for the beauty of flower, others for foliage. Some lay claim to both. Many are maritime plants, indifferent to soil conditions, tolerant of drought and withstanding coastal exposure. Others are from alpine or sub-alpine environments and extremely hardy. Most of the following grow in almost any deeply worked, free-draining fertile soil in full sun.
Compositae. *All evergreen.*

Olearia albida
Coastal Bush Tree Daisy, Tanguru
From coastal forests and scrublands of New Zealand's North Island. Vigorous grower with erect habit, oblong to ovate-oblong leaves to 100 × 35mm, glabrous and dark green, white tomentose beneath, margins slightly waved. White daisy flowers in large panicles summer through late autumn. Good shelter or screen. Albida — whitish. 4 × 3m.

Olearia albida 'Angulata'
Found along coastal ridges of the North Island of New Zealand. Somewhat resembles O albida, but leaves smaller, to 65mm long, stiffer, leathery, yellow green above, margins strongly waved. Flowerheads smaller. A little slower growing, smaller and hardier. 3 × 2m.

Olearia arborescens
Common Tree Daisy
Of widespread distribution from East Cape south to Stewart Island, regarded as one of the most beautiful Olearias. A large shrub, branchlets angular at first rather more stocky with maturity. Leaves ovate to elliptic-ovate, to 75 × 50mm, deep green glabrous glossy above, covered with silvery tomentum beneath, margins faintly sinuate to entire. Creamy white daisy-like flowers borne profusely in rounded, axillary corymbs to 25cm across spring through mid-summer. Arborescens — woody or tree-like. 3 × 2m.

Olearia avicenniaefolia
Mangrove-leaved Olearia
Found in mountain scrubland of New Zealand's South Island at altitudes to 1000m. Forms a bushy shrub with thick, broadly lanceolate leaves to 10 × 5cm, densely buff or white tomentose beneath. Impressive flat-topped corymbs of white sweet-scented daisy flowers produced freely late spring through autumn. Useful hardy garden shrub tolerant of dry conditions. Avicenniaefolia — leaves resembling Avicennia or Mangrove. 2 × 1.5m.

Olearia cheesemanii
Streamside River Daisy
The most floriferous and beautiful of all Olearias. Forms a multi-branched shrub with oblong-lanceolate leaves to 85 × 30mm, dark green glabrous, margins wavy, pale buff satin-downy beneath. Large 20cm flattened corymbs of white 12mm daisy-flowers with yellow centre entirely cover the bush during spring, obscuring all leaves. Faded flowers quickly overtaken by new growth, but light pruning will tidy the bush. Commences to flower at an early age. Top choice amongst flowering shrubs. Inhabits lowland streams of New Zealand's two main islands between Tauranga and Westport. Named for T F Cheeseman, 20th century New Zealand botanist. 2 × 2m.

Olearia × haastii
Erect growing, hardy and floriferous, multi-branched rounded shrub. Leaves oblong to elliptic-oblong, to 30 × 10mm, dark green and glossy, leathery, glabrous above, dense white tomentum beneath, margins entire and slightly rolled. Flowers white with yellow centre, 1cm across borne in lax or compact corymbs early-mid summer. Natural hybrid of O avicenniaefolia × O moschata found in Canterbury Westland and Otago. Extremely hardy. Named for Sir Julius von Haast, 19th century explorer. 2 × 1.3m.

Olearia ilicifolius
New Zealand Holly
Attractive dense shrub found naturally from East Cape to Stewart Island growing mostly in high country. Leaves linear-oblong to lanceolate, to 10 × 2cm, tough and leathery, margins deeply waved, coarsely and sharply toothed, grey green above, yellowish or silvery tomentose beneath. White fragrant flower heads in summer of little significance, but the whole plant emits a strong musky fragrance. Best in cold partly shaded conditions with adequate moisture. Ilicifolius — with holly-like leaves. 2 × 1.5m.

Olearia macrodonta 'Minor'
Found in lower ranges of North and South Islands. Smaller version with 60 × 30mm, ovate-oblong, greyish green leaves, white felted beneath, margins coarsely toothed. White daisy-flowers with yellow centres spring through mid-summer. Hardy well-mannered shrub thriving in cold or shady locations. Macrodonta — with large teeth, referring to the leaves. 1 × 1m.

Olearia moschata
Incense Plant
Somewhat erect multi-branched shrub with branchlets leaves and flower heads covered with soft white tomentum. Distinctive closely set ovate-oblong leaves to 20 × 8mm, leathery glabrous to faintly scurfy above, heavily pubescent beneath, musky scented when brushed or bruised. White 1cm flowers with yellow centre borne in axillary corymbs of 20–30 early summer through autumn. From South Island alpine scrublands south from Arthur's Pass. Moschata — musky. 2 × 1.3m.

Olearia nummularifolia
Coin-leafed Olearia
Sub-alpine species from North and South Islands. Stiffly branched shrub of distinctive appearance with small close-set very thick saddle shaped leaves to 10 × 7mm, bright green and glabrous when young, buff or yellowish tomentose beneath, curved and twisted to reveal unusual effects of upper and lower leaf surfaces with their contrasting colours. White flowers with yellow centres early summer through autumn. Flowers attractive, but more valued for foliage. Grows in dry or exposed locations and very hardy. Nummularifolia — resembling a coin, referring to the leaves. 1 × 1m.

Olearia paniculata
Golden Ake Ake

Multi-branched shrub or small tree. Leaves elliptic-oblong to broadly ovate to 75 × 40mm, leathery, lemon-green above, greyish white tomentose beneath, conspicuous wavy margins. Inconspicuous but fragrant flowers in autumn. Excellent shelter, screen or hedge which can be trimmed to size or form. Hardy and tolerant of coastal conditions but needs good drainage. At one time referred to as Olearia forsteri and widely used as a clipped hedge. Insect attacks in milder areas restrict it to cooler southern regions. 3 × 2m.

Olearia phlogopappa 'Blue Gem'
Dusty Daisy Bush

Australian species native to New South Wales, Victoria and Tasmania. Fast growing, free flowering upright slender shrub. Greyish green oblong leaves to 4cm long, sage-like with leathery texture. Rich blue daisy-flowers with yellow centre completely cover the bush through spring. Prune heavily after flowering for growth renewal and maximum flower. Good drainage, full sun are desirable. Phlogopappa — Phlox-like pappus (bristly tuft or scales in place of calyx). Other forms — 'Pink Gem' soft pink flowers, 'White Gem' pure white flowers. 1.5 × 1m. **222**

Olearia rani
Forest Tree Daisy, Heketara

Erect shrub or small tree with branches branchlets and leaf undersides densely covered with soft off-white tomentum. Leaves broad-ovate to elliptic, to 15 × 6cm, deep green leathery glabrous prominently veined, margins coarsely toothed. Crushed leaves emit a pleasant fragrance. Creamy-white flowers with yellow centres borne profusely in branched panicles to 18cm across late winter through spring. From lowland forests and forest margins in North Island and northern South Island. 3 × 2m.

Olearia traversii
Chatham Island Ake Ake

Grows in forests and around dunes and rocks of Chatham Island. Distinguished by four-angled stems and oblong to ovate-oblong leaves to 6 × 3cm, dark green leathery and shining above, and a cladding of white silky tomentum beneath. Summer flower heads of little significance. Notable for extreme hardiness and tolerance of coastal conditions, making it a fair choice as a hedge or screen for such areas. Named for H Travers who discovered the species in 1863. 3 × 2m.

Olearia traversii 'Tweedledee'

Resembles above but with ornamental dark green leaves irregularly blotched yellow in the centre. 3 × 2m.

Olearia virgata 'Lineata'
Twiggy Tree Daisy

Forms a dense thicket of tangled slender wiry twiggy four-sided branchlets somewhat pendulous and pubescent. Leaves narrowly linear to 15 × 2mm, deep green, white felted beneath, margins rolled under. White 9mm flowers with yellow centres borne in axillary clusters spring through mid-summer. Found in swamps or damp lowland or subalpine scrub and tussock south of Thames to Stewart Island. Attractive and graceful shrub for damp or windy locations. Virgata — twiggy. Lineata — with lines or stripes. 2 × 1.5m.

OPHIOPOGON

A genus of four species of perennial herbs, natives of the East Indies and eastern Asia as far as Japan named from the Greek *ophis*, snake and *pogon*, beard. Useful landscaping plants which form tufty clumps of narrow glossy gracefully curved leaves, plus a bonus of small lily of the valley flower spikes. They form neat edges around beds and borders, can be grown individually amongst other plants or serve well as container plants. Although slow growers, they are long-term plants needing little attention for long periods, apart from occasional grooming. Easy to divide when overcrowded. Grow in deeply worked, free-draining soil, with a preference for shady or semi-shady conditions, or in full sun with adequate summer moisture.

Liliaceae. *All evergreen.*

Ophiopogon intermedius

Graceful Chinese tufted plant with linear leaves to 300 × 5mm, deep green, glossy leathery and gracefully recurving. Flowers resembling miniature lily of the valley, white often tinted lilac. Intermedius — intermediate in colour form or habit. 30 × 50cm.

Ophiopogon japonicus
Snake's Beard, Mondo Grass

Forms low tufts of narrow-linear grass-like leathery leaves to 250 × 3mm, dark blackish green and somewhat curved. Small pale lilac flowers followed by small crops of 5mm porcelain blue berries, usually hidden amongst the foliage. Long term neat edging plant. Japonicus — Japanese. 25 × 20cm.

Ophiopogon planiscapus 'Nigrescens'
Black Dragon

Small grass-like plant forming a tuft of curving leaves to 350 × 5mm, at first bright green and glossy but soon turning and remaining dark purple-black. Loose racemes of hyacinth-like white or lilac flowers, occasionally flushed pink appear through summer followed by dull blue fruit. Planiscapus — with a flat scape. Nigrescens — blackish leaves. 35 × 25cm.

OSMANTHUS

A genus of some 30 species of hardy evergreen trees and shrubs from southern USA, Middle East, China and Japan named from the Greek *osme*, fragrance and *anthos*, a flower. Valued for shiny cleanliness, leathery, holly-like leaves and richly fragrant flowers. Plant beneath a window, near doors or outdoor living areas, or grow in containers for patio or terrace to capture the spicy fragrance. Enjoys sun or partial shade, in deeply worked, free-draining, neutral to slightly acid soil with average moisture. Because it grows slowly, pruning and pinching seldom necessary.

Oleaceae. *All evergreen.*

Osmanthus × 'Burkwoodii'

Forms a bushy compact shrub with downy stems. Leaves ovate-elliptic to 3–5cm long, glossy dark-green, margins serrated. Small fragrant white flowers in axillary clusters of 5–7 late spring. Hybrid variety from O delavayi × O decorus. Syn Osmarea 'Burkwoodii. 1.8 × 1.8m.

Osmanthus delavayi

Graceful slow-growing shrub from western China with wide-spread arching branches. Ovate leaves to 3cm long, dark green glossy, margins finely serrated, minutely spotted beneath. White tubular flowers with four flaring lobes, suspended on long peduncles in axillary clusters of about eight through autumn. Flowers larger than other Osmanthus but less fragrant. Delavayi — for Abbé Jean Marie Delavay, 19th century French missionary in China who introduced numerous plants into cultivation. 1.5 × 1.5m.

Osmanthus heterophyllus
Holly Olive, Chinese Holly

Rather slow growing, erect, Japanese holly-like shrub. Leaves elliptic-oblong, to 6cm long, glossy deep-green, yellowish beneath, margins variable from entire to coarsely spine-toothed. Small white sweetly fragrant flowers borne in axillary clusters of four to six late summer, followed by 12mm blue ovate fruit. Heterophyllus — having leaves of diverse forms. 1.5 × 1m.

Osmanthus heterophyllus 'Purpureus'
Young growth at first blackish purple, maturing purple-green. More frost resistant. 1.5 × 1m.

Osmanthus heterophyllus 'Variegatus'
False Holly
Attractive holly-like spiny leaves, mid-green and bluish grey-green edged and marbled creamy white, pink-tinted when young. 1.5 × 1m.

OSTRYA

A genus of nine species of medium to large deciduous trees native to Europe, Asia and America named from the Greek *ostrys*. Closely related to Carpinus or Hornbeam, they bear ornamental clusters of hop-like fruit and display brilliant foliage colour in autumn. Grows freely in almost any good deeply worked, free-draining soil and are tolerant of sub-zero temperatures.
Carpinaceae.

Ostrya carpinifolia
Hop Hornbeam
Native to southern Europe and Asia Minor. Forms a round headed tree with ovate leaves to 10 × 5cm, lustrous deep green, prominently veined, margins double-toothed, clear yellow in autumn. Enchanting spring displays of 75 × 10mm drooping male catkins resembling Hops. Fruit 35–50mm long containing a flat bladder-like husk. Carpinifolia — with leaves like Carpinia or hornbeam. Deciduous. 10 × 8m.

OTHONNA

A genus of about 150 species of perennial herbs or small shrubs, mostly native to South Africa, named from the Greek *othone*, linen, a reference to their soft foliage. Listed species reputed to be the hardiest, tolerant of temperatures to −15°C, growing readily in deeply worked, free-draining, moderately fertile, loose-free soil in full sun. Admired for succulent leaves and an almost continual floral display.
Compositae.

Othonna cheirifolia
Succulent Daisy
Dwarf shrub with spreading branches. Leaves lanceolate-spathulate, obtusely rounded at the apex, thick and fleshy, grey-green and glaucous. Bright yellow daisy-like flowers appear through most of the year. Syn Othonnopsis cheirifolia. Cheirifolia — from the Greek *cheir*, a hand and *folia* — leaf. Evergreen. 50cm × 1m.

PARAHEBE

A genus of about thirty species of woody or partly woody dwarf shrubs from New Zealand, New Guinea and Australia named from the Greek *para*, close to and *Hebe*, from close relationship. Once included amongst Hebes or Veronicas.

Dainty, low growing or sprawling free flowering shrubs for rock gardens, near edges of pools or spilling over walls. Plant in full sun in deeply worked, free-draining average garden soil. Keep moist over dry periods or leaves may tend to brown off near the base and stems become bare. Feed and cut back occasionally to encourage growth renewal. See under Hebe for additional information about culture.
Scrophulariaceae. *All evergreen.*

Parahebe cataractae 'Delight'
The species grows alongside streams, on cliffs and rocky places in lowland and mountain areas of the North, South and Stewart Islands of New Zealand as a slender, ground hugging sub-shrub with branches taking root where they touch the ground.

The cultivar 'Delight' is a superior form with leaves ovate-lanceolate to elliptic, to 25 × 20mm, mid to dark green, paler beneath, margins slightly toothed. Flowers to 12mm across, heliotrope with central chartreuse zone ringed with purple, produced abundantly in 10cm racemes during summer. Cataractae — of a waterfall. 20 × 75cm.

Parahebe decora
Prostrate mat-forming shrub with slender woody stems often rooting at the nodes and sending up leafy erect 5cm branchlets. Leaves ovate to suborbicular, to 3 × 5cm, mid green, fleshy and glabrous, often tinged red. Flowers open bowl-shaped, white to pink often with reddish veins borne in racemes to 15 through summer. From river beds and rocky subalpine areas of New Zealand's South Island. Decora — beautiful. 10 × 60cm.

Parahebe hookeriana 'Olsenii'
Low-growing, multi-branched shrub with slender sprawling to erect branches. Closely set overlapping leaves, ovate to suborbicular, to 8 × 12mm, pale green, thick-leathery or fleshy, sparsely pubescent, margins deeply crenate or serrate. Lavender flowers in racemes to eight through summer. Found in rocky subalpine areas in the southern half of New Zealand's North Island. 10 × 60cm.

Parahebe linifolia
Small multi-branched somewhat sprawling and soft wooded shrub, slender branchlets often rooting. Closely set, linear to lanceolate leaves to 20 × 4mm, dark green and rather fleshy, paler beneath. White to pink, saucer-shaped flowers with reddish veins in racemes up to four through summer. From wet rock faces or alongside streams in subalpine areas of the South Island. Plant in moist shady spots. Linifolia — flax-leaved. 15 × 50cm.

Parahebe lyallii
Low-growing, multi-branched shrublet with woody, prostrate stems often rooting at the nodes, branches horizontal to ascending. Leaves orbicular to linear-obovate, to 8 × 10mm, reddish at first, then mid green, leathery, margins bluntly serrated or lobed. Saucer-shaped, 1cm flowers, white veined pink with blue anthers, borne profusely on slender 7cm racemes through spring and summer. Named for David Lyall, 19th century botanist and plant collector. 20 × 75cm.

Parahebe lyallii 'Baby Blue'
Compact grower, leaves attractively bronzed, masses of small blue flowers through spring and summer. Ideal front border or rockery. Syn P 'Blue Eyes'. 15 × 75cm.

Parahebe lyallii 'Pink'
Perfect companion to 'Baby Blue'. Forms a compact ground-hugging plant with green foliage flushed bronze and masses of tiny shell-pink flowers through spring and summer. 20 × 75cm.

Parahebe 'Mt Dalgety'
Prostrate sub-shrub with small, bright green foliage and abundant sprays of white flowers through summer. Ideal ground cover for use in damp sites. Discovered on Mount Dalgety in the South Island of New Zealand and introduced by Blue Mountain Nurseries, Tapanui. 25 × 75cm.

Above: Nerium oleander 'Delphine' **214**

Above: Nerium oleander 'Petite Salmon' **214**
Below: Nerium oleander 'Madonna Grandiflora' **214**

Above: Nerium oleander 'Dr Golphin' **214**
Below: Nerium oleander 'Mrs F Roeding' **214**

Above: Nerium oleander 'Punctatum' **214**

Above: Nerium oleander 'Splendens' **214**

Above: Ochna serrulata *Mickey Mouse Plant* **218**
Below: Phebalium squameum 'Illumination' **226**

Above: Olearia phlogopappa 'Pink Gem' *Dusty Daisy Bush* **219**
Below: Philadelphus 'Snowflake' **226**

Above: Nymphaea 'Marliacea Chromatella' **216**
Below: Phoenix canariensis *Canary Island Date Palm* **227**

Above: Nymphaea 'Mrs George H Pring' **217**
Below: Nymphaea 'A E Seibert' **215**

Above: Philodendron selloum **227**

Above and below: Phylica plumosa *Flannel Flower, Featherhead* **229**

Above: Phormium cookianum 'Maori Chief' **228**
Below: Phormium tenax 'Yellow Wave' **229**

P A R A N O M U S

A genus of 18 species of small erect shrubs from South Africa named from the Greek *para*, near or close to and *nomos*, meadow. A distinctive feature of the genus is one it shares with other members of the Protea family — having two different types of leaves on the same bush, known botanically as dimorphic foliage. Grown for exquisite bottlebrush-like flowers, excellent for garden display and long-lasting cut blooms. Plant in deeply worked, free-draining, soil with sand or peat moss. Grows naturally in areas of low rainfall and low humidity. Cut blooms freely and prune to shape after flowering.

Proteaceae.

Paranomus reflexus
Handsome shrub from the Humansdorp to Port Elizabeth area of south western Cape. Densely bushy with erect branches from the base. Feathery lower leaves to 8cm long, finely divided into slender lobes, pale to mid green tipped red. Onset of flowers signalled by the appearance of 30cm stems densely clothed with ovate leaves, margins entire, to 3 × 2cm, smaller towards the flower. Flowers comprise numerous slender greenish yellow tubes which reflex as they mature, resembling a stiff 12 × 8cm bottlebrush borne freely from late autumn through winter and spring. Reflexus — bent sharply backwards. Evergreen. 1.8 × 1.3m.

P A R R O T I A

A genus of one species, a slow-growing shrub or tree from northern Iran named for F W Parrott, early 19th century German naturalist and traveller. Naturally an important native forest tree where it grows tall and straight with spreading crown. As an ornamental it is valued for picturesque branch pattern, attractive flaking bark, curious flowers in spring and richly toned autumn foliage.

Plant in sun or partial shade in deeply worked, free-draining, fertile, neutral to slightly acid loam. Parrotia is hardy and withstands considerable drought and exposure. Minimal pruning is required unless training to a single trunk in which case shorten lower side branches, allowing upper branches to grow wide. Eventually lower side branches may be cut off.

Hamamelidaceae.

Parrotia persica
Persian Witch Hazel, Ironwood
One of the finest small trees for autumn colour, a slow grower with broad horizontal branch structure tending to be multi-trunked during early years. Densely foliaged with lustrous, dark green, 7–10cm ovate to obovate or diamond-shaped leaves, distinctly veined and quilted, margins unevenly and shallowly toothed, turning golden yellow, orange, rosy-pink and scarlet in autumn, more intense in areas with dry summers and cold winters. Picturesque bare branch pattern in winter. Flaking grey bark reveals white patches beneath. Clusters of tasselled flowers comprising blood-red stamens set in brown woolly bracts appear all over the tree, in early spring before the new leaves. Cut branches valuable for floral arrangements. Persica — of Persia or Iran. Deciduous. 5 × 4m.

P A U L O W N I A

A genus of about seventeen species of deciduous trees from east Asia named for Anna Paulowna, daughter of Paul 1, Czar of Russia 1795–1865. Paulownia species have been grown for centuries in China and Japan for the production of high quality timber and extremely fine paper. Suitability for forestry projects is being assessed in many western countries. With extremely rapid growth, immense leaves and beautiful flowers, they provide one of the finest ornamental shade trees. Excellent lawn or patio tree, especially if viewed from above.

Paulownia grows under average conditions, withstands moderate frosts and salty air, but appreciates being away from constant strong winds which damages the leaves. Overwintering buds may be damaged by extreme frosts in some areas but once established should be hardy to – 15°C. However young plants must have protection.

Bignoniaceae. *All deciduous.*

Paulownia elongata
Empress Tree, Money Tree
Native to China where it has been selectively cultivated for over 2500 years. A major timber tree in China and Japan, rapidly gaining favour elsewhere. Attains harvestable size in about 15 years, yielding approximately 1.5 cubic metres per stem. It is deep rooting and easily pruned with a straight, clean bole and open crown, allowing pasture or crops to grow beneath it. Forms a large tree with robust reddish brown glabrous shoots. Immense ovate and acuminate leaves, 18–36 × 8–22cm, deep green and almost glabrous above, tomentose beneath. Violet-blue, 8–10cm funnelform flowers borne in erect panicles to 35cm long during spring, followed by 33mm, ovoid capsules. Elongata — elongated. 10 × 8m.

Paulownia fargesii
Excellent species from western China. Leaves long-ovate to 21 × 14cm, margins entire, densely tomentose beneath. Fragrant trumpet-shaped, heliotrope flowers resembling foxgloves, liberally speckled dark purple in the throat, stained creamy yellow near the base, followed by 35mm ovoid capsules. Reputed to be hardier than P tomentosa. Named for Paul Guillaume Farges, French missionary and naturalist in central China (1844–1912). 10 × 8m.

Paulownia tomentosa
Umbrella Tree, Empress Tree, Princess Tree
From central and western China. Grows rapidly with a single stem to 3–4m, then develops smooth round almost horizontal branches to form a clean stout-trunked, broad spreading tree. Tropical-looking, broadly ovate leaves to 30 × 28cm, deep green, soft textured and hairy above, densely grey-woolly beneath. Larger leaves may be encouraged by annual pruning, but at the expense of flowers. In autumn, brown olive-sized flower buds form, remain closed over winter and open early spring ahead of the leaves. Violet-blue, trumpet-shaped, fragrant flowers with darker spots and yellow stripes, resembling foxgloves appear in erect 30cm pyramidal clusters followed by seed capsules about the size of a walnut which often remain until the next season's flowers. Tomentosa — densely woolly. 8 × 6m.

P E N N I S E T U M

A genus of about eighty species of annual and perennial grasses from tropical regions, named from the Latin *penna*, a feather and *seta*, a bristle, referring to the flowers. Valued for its willingness to grow in adverse conditions, ability to fill in large areas and for ornamental fluffy flower-heads. Good for rapid short term dramatic garden effects. Grows in any deeply worked, free-draining soil in full sun. Drought resistant and virtually pest free. Cut freely for indoors and remove spent heads before they go to seed. Becomes dormant in winter.

Graminae.

Pennisetum setaceum
Fountain Grass

Robust ornamental grass from tropical Africa, south west Asia and Arabia. Grows rapidly to form a dense rounded clump with narrow, arching, grassy leaves to 60cm long. Erect stems to one metre appear through summer, topped with showy coppery pink or light purplish, fuzzy flower spikes which fade to white as the flower ages. Setaceum — bristled. Syn P ruppelii. 1m × 60cm.

PHEBALIUM

A genus of about 45 species, all but one endemic in Australia, named from the Greek *phibale*, myrtle, from their similar appearance. Valued for slender erect form and handsome foliage. Phebalium requires deeply worked, free-draining, acid soil with a crumbly texture and without hard-pan subsoil. Yellowing or withering of the foliage usually indicates wet feet or excess alkalinity. Once established in suitable conditions, maintenance is minimal.

Rutaceae. *All evergreen.*

Phebalium squameum
Satin Wood

Distributed through Queensland, New South Wales, Victoria and Tasmania. Hardy erect shrub with aromatic, pale green, olive-like, narrow-lanceolate, 5–8cm leaves, covered beneath with scales to give a silvery white satiny appearance. Small white flowers of little consequence. Slender erect form and minimum maintenance has made this tree a popular choice for shelter and seclusion. Squameum — covered with scales. Plant 60cm apart for a clipped screen under two metres, or 1–1.5m apart if left untrimmed. 4 × 1m.

Phebalium squameum 'Illumination'

Upright columnar form, attractive yellow and pale green variegated, aromatic leaves. Somewhat less vigorous and with smaller dimensions but an excellent specimen and screen. Small white flowers. 3 × .60m.　　　**222**

PHELLODENDRON

A genus of ten species of tall deciduous trees from temperate and tropical eastern Asia named from the Greek *phellos*, cork and *dendron*, a tree a reference to corky bark. Grown for picturesque framework, deeply furrowed bark, aromatic and highly autumn-coloured leaves and black fruits. Hardy to –15°C, but enjoys long hot summers. Plant in an open position in full sun in deeply worked, free-draining, moisture-retentive fertile soil.
Rutaceae

Phellodendron amurense
Amur Cork Tree

From northern China and Manchuria. Develops a broad crown with wide spreading framework, trunk with pale grey, thick corky deeply grooved bark. Immense pinnate leaves to 35cm long, divided into 9–13 broadly ovate to ovate-lanceolate leaflets to 10 × 5cm, bright green spring and summer, golden yellow in autumn, glaucous beneath, becoming deciduous late summer. Silvery hairy winter buds, small yellowish green spring flowers followed on female trees by small sticky black fruits. Large handsome foliage and form resembles Ailanthus. Amurense — from the area of the Amur River on the Russian border. Deciduous. 6 × 5m.

PHILADELPHUS

A genus of about forty species of deciduous shrubs from Central and North America, Caucasus, Himalayas, China and eastern Asia, named *Philadelphus*, ancient Greek term meaning brotherly love. Commonly known as Mock Orange they are highly valued for beautiful white or cream highly fragrant flowers produced early summer after many other spring blossom shrubs have faded. Use Philadelphus for backgrounds, shrub borders especially amongst colourful spring flowering annuals, perennials or bulbs.

Plant in full sun in any reasonable deeply worked, free-draining soil. They are lime lovers and benefit from an annual dressing of bone meal or blood and bone. Watering over dry periods maintains freshness, although once established tolerant of extremes including frost. Prune each year after blooming, cutting back flowered shoots to within a few centimetres of the old wood and any surplus growths from the base.

Saxifragaceae. *All deciduous.*

Philadelphus coronarius
Sweet Mock Orange

From Southern Europe to Caucasus. Vigorous erect grower forming a multi-stemmed rounded bush with ovate leaves to 90 × 45mm, dark green, prominently veined, Margins irregularly and shallowly toothed. Creamy white cap-shaped richly scented 25mm single flowers with conspicuous yellow stamens early summer in terminal racemes up to nine. Coronarius — used for garlands. 2 × 1.5m.

Philadelphus coronarius 'Aureus'

Resembles above but with more compact habit and bright golden yellow leaves which turn lime-green during summer. 1.8 × 1.3m.

Philadelphus hybrid 'Beauclerk'

Medium compact bushy shrub with graceful arching branches. Extra large 6cm, broad-petalled, sweetly scented, milky white single flowers with light cerise central zone. Purpureo-maculatus group. 1.5 × 1m.

Philadelphus hybrid 'Belle Etoile'

Excellent compact shrub with erect habit and semi-arching branches. Delightfully fragrant, 5cm, milky white single flowers with central maroon flush borne in profusion. Purpureo-maculatus group. 2 × 1.3m.

Philadelphus hybrid 'Birchlands'

White single flowers are small, considering the large size of the bush, but produced in vast quantities to provide an outstanding spring display on arching branches. Originally from the grounds of Government House, Auckland for which it was named, and assessed for local conditions by the Auckland Regional Botanic Gardens. 3 × 2.5m

Philadelphus hybrid 'Enchantment'

Small to medium grower. Pure white, sweetly scented double flowers. 2 × 1.3m.

Philadelphus hybrid 'Frosty Morn'

Slow-growing, narrow-upright grower with twiggy branches. Exquisite ice white, orange-blossom scented, 3cm double flowers with dainty fringed petals in great masses during summer. Useful in floral decorations. Noted for its frost tolerance. 1.5 × 1m.

Philadelphus hybrid 'Manteau d'Hermine'

Choice compact and rounded dwarf grower. Fragrant creamy white double flowers early summer. Lemoinei group. 1 × 1m.

Philadelphus hybrid 'Snowflake'

American cultivar with arching branches literally weighed down with great masses of fully double snow white highly fragrant flowers in spring. × Virginalis group. 1.5 × 1m.　　　**222**

Philadelphus hybrid 'Sybille'
Superb dwarf rounded grower with graceful arching branches. Almost square, white single flowers with light purple central stain and orange blossom fragrance late summer. Purpureo-maculatus group. 1 × 1m.

Philadelphus hybrid 'Virginal'
Excellent French hybrid raised late 19th century, and possibly still the best double flowered cultivar. Strong growing shrub with sweetly fragrant 5cm pure white double flowers produced freely in terminal clusters on erect stems. Virginal means pure white. × Virginalis group. 2 × 1.5m.

Philadelphus × lemoinei
Forms a low compact shrub with peeling bark. Leaves ovate to 25 × 12mm, glabrous deep green above, sparsely bristly beneath. Pure white highly fragrant cross-shaped single 3cm flowers borne through summer in clusters of 3–7 on short side branches. Original hybrid from P coronarius × P microphyllus. 1.3 × 1m.

PHILODENDRON

A genus of 350 or more species of climbing shrubs, small trees and epiphytes mostly from tropical America, named from the Greek *phileo* to love and *dendron*, a tree. Dramatic leathery leaves in various shapes hues and sizes, bold habits and trouble free culture, make them the ultimate in indoor and outdoor decoration. While climbing species are mostly seen indoors in temperate climates, non-climbers or 'self-headers' serve well outdoors in contemporary landscape design. Use in courtyards, patios, entryways, galleries or amongst tropical plantings to create jungle effects.

Plant in loose free soil with good drainage, in warm locations free of heavy frost, shade semi-shade or full sun. Once established they are remarkably hardy withstanding light frost, strong wind and exposure to hot sun. In early stages they respond to feeding in the production of bigger bolder and deeper green leaves. Allow adequate space for unhindered development of this most useful and dramatic plant.

Araceae. *All evergreen.*

Philodendron bipinnatidifidum
This Brazilian species forms a bold plant with huge, deeply cut and lobed leaves a metre or more in length, supported on stiff stems arising from the plant at ground level to form a rosette. Mature plants produce flowers like arum lilies, comprising a large thick white spathe enclosing an erect fleshy spike of tiny flowers known as a spadix. Bipinnatidifidum — having both primary and secondary deeply divided leaf segments. 2 × 2.5m.

Philodendron selloum
Also Brazilian with lush dark green one metre bipinnate leaves similar to above but with short lobe at the tip. Juvenile leaves relatively small and without lobes, but growth rate is rapid and adult leaves soon appear. Selloum — after Friedrich Sellow, German traveller and naturalist in South America (1789–1831). 2 × 2.5m. **224**

PHOENIX

A genus of about 17 species of solitary or clustered palms from tropical Asia and Africa called by an ancient Greek name for the Date Palm. Of the two species listed, P canariensis performs well in cooler climates. Pygmy Date Palm with slower growth rate and smaller ultimate dimensions is more easily accommodated in average gardens but only in frost free locations. Excellent specimens for large lawn areas, tolerant of wide ranging climatic and cultural extremes. Good container plant. Plant in deeply-worked, free-draining fertile soil in maximum sunshine. Feed twice yearly and water frequently until established. Protect from frost when young and trim old leaves back to the main stem.

Palmaceae. *All evergreen.*

Phoenix canariensis
Canary Island Date Palm
Compact robust and stiff when young, eventually forming an impressive specimen with heavy trunk to 60cm diameter, patterned with marks left by fallen leaves. Graceful long arching pinnate leaves or fronds to 5m long form a dense canopy, slow growing at first, becoming more rapid once trunk commences to form. Planted in avenues or as single specimens, these majestic palms provide a dramatic touch to any landscape. Avoid placing close to buildings or where they may cause embarrassment in years ahead. Canariensis — of the Canary Islands. 6 × 5m. **223**

Phoenix roebelenii
Pygmy Date Palm, Miniature Date Palm
Delightful fine leafed smaller palm from Laos and Vietnam. Over many years will form a slender, rough textured trunk of one or two metres, topped by dense rounded crown of curved feathery pinnate fronds to 1.2m with about 50 pairs of 25 × 1cm deep green leaflets. A graceful plant for feature gardens, patios, entryways or galleries in frost free sunny or semi-shady outdoor areas. Ideal in conservatories or rooms with adequate light. Roebelenii — after plant collector M Roebelin. 1 × 1m.

PHORMIUM

A genus of two species, one endemic in New Zealand, the other shared with Norfolk Island, large perennial herbs with long leathery sword like leaves arranged in fans arising directly from fleshy, rhizomatous roots, named from the Greek *phormion*, a mat referring to strong fibres produced from the leaves. Phormium is a distinct and unmistakable feature of New Zealand landscape, abounding in lowland swamps throughout the country.

Highly valued in landscaping throughout the world. Simple poise gives unique character. Curious bronzy red flowers which tower above the leaves on long stems in summer are a great source of nectar for birds of all kinds. Use Phormium to accent entryways, pools, feature or rock gardens, mass-plant in beds or on banks.

They grow in any reasonable soil, tolerate extremes of heat and cold, salt air, ocean spray and damp conditions. Occasional grooming and dividing every two or three years keeps them in top form. Fancier types may need spraying for leaf spot, otherwise they demand little in the way of maintenance. Many beautiful hybrid forms and colours continue to be introduced.

Agavaceae. *All evergreen.*

Phormium cookianum
Mountain Flax
Smaller species than the more common P tenax, found from North Cape to Stewart Island, sea level to 1300m, growing on steep cliff faces and rocky promontories overlooking the ocean or growing among rocks not far from the water's edge. Variable foliage, some forms with erect leaves less than a metre, others lax and drooping to 1.5m. Easily distinguished by slightly twisted and pendulous seed pods which ripen three months later. Effective against a large rock, or mass planted on banks for erosion and weed control. Syn P colensoi. 1 × 1m.

Phormium cookianum 'Apricot Queen'
Outstanding dwarf grower, cream leaves flushed apricot when young maturing light creamy yellow, margined green and bronze. The whole leaf has an apricot flush. 75 × 75cm.

Phormium cookianum 'Bobby Dazzler'
Small grower with arching foliage, rich deep red with darker red edge. 75 × 75cm.

Phormium cookianum 'Cream Delight'
Compact grower, arching foliage, with broad cream band, narrowly striped green towards the edges, margined deep mahogany red. A sport of P tricolor. Excellent for cutting. 1 × 1m

Phormium cookianum 'Dark Delight'
Vigorous ascending broad leaves, drooping at the tips, dark chocolate brown becoming blackish bronze with age, rich dark red midrib and overtones. Good colour contrast for the garden or in floral arrangements. 1.5 × 1m.

Phormium cookianum 'Duet'
Excellent dwarf with slender, erect, green leaves broadly banded creamy white on both edges. Stiff spiky grower ideal for small feature gardens, containers etc. 60 × 60cm.

Phormium cookianum 'Emerald Gem'
Forms a bushy clump with unusual emerald-green leaves. Excellent contrast plant. 60 × 75cm.

Phormium cookianum 'Evening Glow'
Graceful arching foliage coloured rich red, edged darker red and quite glossy. Brighter red than Bobby Dazzler. Excellent dwarf grower. 75 × 75cm.

Phormium cookianum 'Gold Sword'
Broad stiff bright golden yellow leaves banded green. Sturdy appearance. 1 × 1m.

Phormium cookianum 'Greensleeves'
Attractive slender drooping leaves of medium green. Possibly the finest cultivar where plain green foliage is required. 1 × 1m.

Phormium cookianum 'Jack Spratt'
Miniature very compact grower. Erect narrow delicate reddish brown leaves. Excellent in rock gardens or containers. 30 × 30cm.

Phormium cookianum 'Limelight'
Clear green, one-coloured leaves with a hint of lime. Soft upright grower. Very disease resistant. 1.5 × 1.3m.

Phormium cookianum 'Maori Chief'
Forms a bold clump of ascending leaves which droop at the tips, in rich tones of bronze and scarlet. Syn 'Rainbow Chief'. 1.2 × 1m.   **224**

Phormium cookianum 'Maori Maiden'
Upright leaves drooping at the tips, in rich rosy salmon pink to coral red, banded with bronze margins. Syn 'Rainbow Maiden'. 1 × 1m.

Phormium cookianum 'Maori Queen'
Broad upstanding foliage gracefully curving at the tips, bronzy green with rosy red stripes. Syn 'Rainbow Queen'. 1 × 1m.

Phormium cookianum 'Maori Sunrise'
Low gracefully curving fine slender leaves, light red to orange red, margined bronze. Delicate in colour and form. Syn 'Rainbow Sunrise'. 75 × 75cm.

Phormium cookianum 'Pinkie'
Graceful arching leaves, rich pink and bronze when young, fading to cream with age. 80 × 80cm.

Phormium cookianum 'Platt's Black'
Rich dark purple-black or deep chocolate coloured leaves and compact clumping growth habit. Holds colour well. Excellent contrast amongst lighter shades. 90 × 150cm.

Phormium cookianum 'Rubrum'
Dwarf Red Flax
Dwarf compact form with dark coppery red foliage. Adds colour and texture to feature gardens, shrub borders, containers. 75 × 75cm.

Phormium cookianum 'Sundowner'
Strong erect vigorous grower with broad leaves, coppery red with pink margins fading to cream, flushed pink at maturity. 1.5 × 1m.

Phormium cookianum 'Sunset'
Medium erect grower, leaves basically bronze overlaid with pastel shades of gold and apricot pink with green stripes and margins. Highly valued for floral decorations. 1.2 × 1m.

Phormium cookianum 'Surfer'
Delightful clumping Flax, narrow waved and twisted leaves in soft bronze tones. Excellent for rock gardens, containers etc. 70 × 70cm.

Phormium cookianum 'Tricolor'
Outstanding form with broad gracefully arching leaves, rich green with broad cream edge, outlined with conspicuous red margins. 1 × 1.5m.

Phormium tenax
New Zealand Green Flax
Versatile plant of extreme vigour with rich green sword foliage to 3m long, abundant throughout New Zealand and Norfolk Island in coastal and lowland swamps. Many introductory remarks to the genus refer to this species. Tenax — strong and tough. 2 × 2m.

Phormium tenax 'Bronze Baby'
Foliage coloured bronze above, slightly glaucous beneath, usually straight or spreading with curving tips. Strong grower seen at its best when contrasted against lighter background. 75 × 75cm.

Phormium tenax 'Dazzler'
Compact grower with arching leaves, dark maroon purple, heavily striped or overlaid red and pinkish red. 75 × 75cm.

Phormium tenax 'Dusky Chief'
Forms a large mounded clump of broad arching leaves coloured bronze purple. 1.2 × 1m.

Phormium tenax 'Fanfare'
Gracefully arching leaves of darkest bronzy red with narrow crimson stripes plus a wider stripe on one side and distinct misty sheen. 1.5 × 1m.

Phormium tenax 'Firebird'
Strong erect grower with broad, deep red leaves edged vivid red. Outstanding vibrant colour and personality. 1.5 × 1m.

Phormium tenax 'Guardsman'
Vigorous erect grower, deep bronzy purple leaves striped pink broadly margined bright crimson. 1.5 × 1.5m

Phormium tenax 'Pizazz'
Excellent multi-coloured cultivar, gold leaves overlaid with a broad, orange-red central band and irregular green stripes at the margin. Very upright, bold grower. 2 × 1.3m.

Phormium tenax 'Purpureum'
Vigorous grower with smooth bronzy sword leaves, usually grown from seed resulting in many unusual and interesting variations. 1.5 × 1m.

Phormium tenax 'Radiance'
Rigid erect sword leaves, green with broad band of golden yellow, plus narrow stripes of yellow and reddish brown margins, actually appearing as a yellow leaf with a few green stripes. 1.5 × 1m.

Phormium tenax 'Tom Thumb'
Delightful little dwarf with very narrow erect leaves in bright green, margined bronzy brown. Perfect in rock or feature gardens and containers. 35 × 35cm.

Phormium tenax 'Stormy Dawn'
Dark coffee colour with central white vein, leaf outlined rich reddish brown. Strong contrast against a pale background. 1.5 × 1.3m.

Phormium tenax 'Williamsii Variegata'
Larger growing variegated form for larger areas. Robust leaves exceeding two metres long and nearly 12cm wide, gracefully curving at the tips, green with numerous pale yellow stripes, glaucous beneath. 2.5 × 2m.

Phormium tenax 'Yellow Wave'
Vigorous grower with gracefully drooping foliage, heavily variegated yellow, with increasing green zone as leaves mature. 1 × 1m. **224**

PHOTINIA

A genus of 60 species of evergreen and deciduous trees and shrubs from east and south-east Asia, Himalayas and western USA named from the Greek *photos*, light or shining, a reference to glossy foliage. Valued for impressive displays of glabrous, distinctive rich red new growth. The shrubby Photinias respond to trimming and shaping making them ideal for formal or informal landscaping, whether planted in isolation, amongst species of contrasting foliage colour or mass-planted in beds, banks or used as screens.

They are easy to grow, best in full sun for maximum colour. Plant in deeply worked, free-draining average garden soil and avoid excessive exposure to wind. Mulch freely and keep moist during prolonged dry spells. Feed with slow release balanced fertilizer early spring and autumn. Frequent tip pinching enhances colour display. Pruning mature growth encourages a further burst of colourful shoots. Equally attractive whether grown formally or informally, although most colour impact comes from plants regularly sheared.

Rosaceae. *All evergreen.*

Photinia × fraseri 'Red Robin'
New shoots deep crimson-red for long periods in spring. Mature leaves elliptic-ovate to elliptic, to 9cm long, glossy dark green, margins sharply toothed. The best known and most brilliant of cultivated Photinias. Syn P glabra 'Red Robin'. Hybrid from P serrulata × P glabra raised in Masterton, New Zealand. 2.5 × 1.5m.

Photinia × fraseri 'Robusta'
Vigorous hybrid raised in Sydney, somewhat more robust and hardy but lacking the brilliance of other cultivars. Brilliant coppery red young shoots break into spring growth earlier but become green more rapidly. Mature leaves dark green, to 10cm long, thick and leathery, margins slightly waved. Syn P glabra 'Robusta'. Robusta — strong or vigorous. 3 × 2m.

Photinia × fraseri 'Rubens'
Japanese Red Leaf
During spring and autumn this shrub covers itself with brilliant, sealing-wax red young foliage. Mature leaves resemble Red Robin, but smaller and less glossy. Clusters of fragrant creamy white blooms tinged pink mid-summer followed in winter by small black fruit. Both of little consequence and don't appear on regularly trimmed plants which of course is necessary to promote dense colourful growth. Syn P glabra 'Rubens'. 2 × 1.5m.

PHYLICA

A genus of about 150 species mainly evergreen shrubs, mostly from rocky mountain slopes in the South Western Cape areas of South Africa, named from the Greek *phyllikos*, leafy, a probable reference to the dense foliage on some species. Highly prized for flowers which although not colourful, have an elegant charm placing them in great demand for floral art. Plant in deeply worked, free-draining, moisture retentive, organically enriched lime-free acid soil in full sun, free of severe frosts and with plenty of ventilation. Reasonably drought resistant and good for coastal gardens. Prune back by about one third after flowering.

Rhamnaceae. *All evergreen.*

Phylica plumosa
Flannel Flower, Featherhead
Forms an erect evergreen shrub with downy shoots. Leaves linear-lanceolate terminating in a sharp point, to 3cm long, deep green, glabrous above, woolly beneath. Curious 5–6cm plumy flower heads surrounded by soft feathery pale yellowish or sandy green narrow pointed bracts fringed with silvery hairs which glisten in the sunlight. Flowers produced at the tip of each branchlet winter through spring and last six to eight weeks when picked. Plumosa — feathery. Syn P pubescens. 1.3 × 1m. **224**

PHYLLOCLADUS

A genus of about five species of evergreen trees from New Zealand, Tasmania, New Guinea, Malaysia and Indonesia named from the Greek *phyllon*, a leaf and *klados*, a branch in reference to flattened leaf-like branchlets known as cladodes or cladophyll. The common name Celery Pine is from the similarity of these cladodes to celery leaves. New Zealand native species, worth planting as specimens in multiple groups or amongst other trees. Not rapid growers, but perform without fuss if planted in semi-shady locations in well worked soil with adequate summer moisture. Yields a red dye, said to have been used by Maoris to add colour to their cloaks.

Phyllocladaceae. *All evergreen.*

Phyllocladus alpinus
Mountain Toa Toa
Found growing in subalpine and mountain forests in the North and South Islands south of Cape Colville and Te Aroha. A shrub or small tree with numerous short stout branches and branchlets with thin cladophylls to 2cm long deeply divided with narrow linear segments. Fine small specimen tree, very hardy and slow growing. 5 × 3m.

Phyllocladus trichomanoides
Tanekaha
Handsome trees with symmetrical outline, straight tapering trunk, light grey and smooth bark, and branches in a series of whorls. Flattened cladophylls, rich green when mature, shaped like fans, resemble the fronds of maidenhair fern. Slow-growing enough for planting in suburban gardens. Trichomanoides — resembling trichomanas the Kidney Fern. Maori name Tanekaha — virile or strong in growth. 6 × 3m.

PHYSOCARPUS

A genus of ten species of deciduous shrubs from North America and north-east Asia, named from the Greek *physa*, a bladder and *karpos*, fruit in reference to inflated seed pods. Grown for hardiness, delightful clusters of flowers and colourful autumn foliage. Plant in deeply worked,

free-draining, moisture-retentive, moderately fertile acid soil in full sun. **Thin overcrowded stems to ground level after flowering.**
Rosaceae.

Physocarpus opulifolius 'Luteus'
Golden Ninebark
Ninebark refers to the bark which separates in many thin layers. Uncommon shrub native to eastern North America. Graceful arching branches with smooth peeling bark. Leaves oval to rounded, heart-shaped at the base, margins deeply lobed and double-toothed, clear bright yellow in spring, later turning bronzy yellow. Small white flowers tinged pink with purplish stamens during summer in crowded 5cm clusters, then reddish tinted inflated pods in autumn. Effective amongst other shrubs, especially those with purple leaves for colour contrast. Opulifolius — with leaves like viburnum or guelder rose. Luteus — yellow. Deciduous. 1.5 × 1m.

PICEA

A genus of about 35 species of coniferous trees widely distributed in cooler latitudes or at high altitudes in the northern hemisphere, called by its Latin name *picea*, from *piceus*, of pitch, referring to its resinous character. The common name Spruce refers to any species of the genus Picea, possibly on account of elegant, well groomed, immaculate appearance. Picea is a large and important group of conifers, usually of elegant conical form with branches in whorls. Many cultivars are dense dwarf growers, ideal for rock or conifer gardens, some attaining no more than 60cm in a decade.
They contain a range of shapes and sizes with foliage in shades of green, blue, silver and grey. Leaves short and needle-like, arranged spirally in two ranks. Dormant buds usually conspicuous. Picea or Spruce differs from Abies or Fir in peg-like leaf-scars which make shoots and branchlets rough to the touch. Also, cones are pendulous. Spruce thrives in a variety of soils, but cannot be recommended for impoverished, shallow clay or dry soils. Cool sheltered locations with rich, deeply worked soil, ample water and occasional feeding during early growth periods.
Pinaceae. *All evergreen.*

Picea abies
Common Spruce, Norway Spruce
Found throughout northern and central Europe in forests, plains and mountains to 1800m as a stately pyramidal tree with thick, reddish brown bark, spreading branches well clothed with deep green leaves, and attractive brown winter buds. Long slender light-brown rough-textured cones. Extremely slow growing, with traditional Christmas tree appearance for many years. Needs adequate space for full development. Ideal container plant. 3 × 2m.

Picea abies 'Humilis'
Slow growing globose dwarf bush with crowded or congested branchlets. Foliage deep green, winter buds pale or yellowish brown. Good for rock gardens. Humilis — dwarfer than most of its kindred. 40 × 60cm.

Picea abies 'Nidiformis'
Bird's Nest Spruce
Slow growing dwarf form with semi-erect main branches curving outwards from the centre of the plant to leave a low depression, particularly in younger plants, resembling a bird's nest. Attractive in spring with bright fresh green shoots, at first pendulous, becoming straighter as the wood hardens. Nidiformis — nest form. 25 × 70cm.

Picea glauca 'Conica'
Dwarf Alberta Spruce
Delightful dwarf conifer found originally in the wilds near Lake Laggan, Alberta, Canada in 1904. Grows slowly to form a miniature forest tree of perfect conical or pyramidal outline with dense, short, bright green needle foliage, deepening to grey green. Excellent formal dwarf conifer for rock or feature gardens and containers. Conica — cone-shaped. 80 × 30cm.

Picea omorika
Serbian Spruce
Native to Yugoslavia where it inhabits limestone rocks beside the river Drina. Among the most beautiful and adaptable Spruces in cultivation. Quickly forms a tall graceful slender tree with relatively short, upward curving branches and drooping branchlets. Young shoots pale brown and hairy, dark green above, glaucous beneath. Cones conical and bluish black. Perfect narrow Christmas tree form. Succeeds in highly alkaline soils and dry situations and seems more resistant to pests than other Spruces. Omorika — its local name. 3 × 1.2m.

Picea pungens
Colorado Spruce
Stiff regular horizontal branches forming a positive upright broad pyramid with silver-grey needle foliage. Slow growing yet retains its juvenile beauty for many years and makes an ideal garden specimen. Pungens — ending in a sharp point, referring to the leaves. 3.5 × 2m.

Picea pungens 'Glauca'
Blue Colorado Spruce
Typical rigid horizontal branches, narrow pyramidal form densely covered with stiff needle-like rich blue-green foliage. Winter buds brown, new growth bright blue. Very hardy and drought tolerant. Colour habit and growth rate variable, as selected seedlings have been propagated in many areas under this name. Worthwhile conifer for specimen or group planting. 3 × 1.5m.

Picea pungens 'Koster'
Koster's Blue Spruce
The most beautiful form of Blue Spruce. Typical conical form with branches in distinct flattish layers and intense silver blue leaves throughout the year. Small grafted plants may take two or three years of patient training to encourage an upright leading shoot and to commence filling out. Worth the initial cost and effort to get one established. 2 × 1m.

Picea sitchensis
Sitka Spruce, Alaska Spruce
Possibly the only coastal species found from Alaska to mid-California. Moderately fast growing, broadly conical or pyramidal tree with open, slightly ascending branches and pendulous tips. Young shoots light brown and glabrous, thin rigid narrow sharply pointed leaves, green above, glaucous or silvery beneath. Used extensively in some countries as a timber tree. Sitchensis — of Sitka, Alaska. 5 × 3m.

PIERIS

A genus of about seven species of ever-green shrubs or small trees, native to east Asia, the Himalayas, eastern North America and West Indies named from the Latin *Pieris*, a Muse from Greek mythology. Highly ornamental slow growing well mannered shrubs, ornamental in leaf bud or flower any month of the year. Related to rhododendron and generally thrive in similar growing conditions.
Locate in semi-shade, avoiding afternoon sun, in deeply worked, organically enriched, free-draining, moisture-retentive acid soil conditioned with peat moss. Mulch freely to insulate and keep the roots cool and moist. Water frequently during dry spells. Ideal in association with azaleas and rhododendrons, in oriental or woodland gardens, shady borders or

entryways or wherever year round visual quality is required.
Ericaceae. *All evergreen.*

Pieris formosa 'Wakehurst'
Chinese Pieris
The species P formosa is native to south west China, Vietnam, Himalayas and Nepal. Highly regarded amongst beautiful shrubs, with brilliant fiery red young growth resembling photinia and panicles of pure white flowers. 'Wakehurst' is selected for strong vigorous growth, oblong-elliptic to oblanceolate leaves, at first brilliant red, fading to pink, maturing deep green. Glistening pearly white fragrant flowers in large cone-shaped terminal panicles in spring. Requires more shade than P japonica. Formosa — beautiful. 2 × 2m.   **234**

Pieris japonica
Lily of the Valley Bush
Introduced into cultivation from Japan around 1870 and still a popular garden shrub, although superseded by numerous cultivars. Leaves obovate to lanceolate to 100 × 30mm, new shoots bronzy pink to red, maturing dark green and lustrous, margins finely serrated. During autumn, delicate strands of greenish pink buds suspended from branch tips become reddish during winter, opening early spring into fragrant pearly white urn-shaped flowers in beautiful panicles resembling lily of the valley. Japonica — of Japan. 1.5 × 1m.

Pieris japonica 'Bert Chandler'
Young foliage salmon pink at first, becoming glossy yellow, fading through cream to white and finally rich deep green. As new growth unfolds, the bush often displays all these colours against a background of deep green, a most impressive sight. Best in dappled light. Raised in Chandlers Nurseries, Victoria, Australia. 1.3 × 1.3m.   **234**

Pieris japonica 'Christmas Cheer'
Compact tidy grower with attractive bronzy tinted young shoots. Panicles of fragrant bicolor bell-flowers, white delicately tinted deep rose at the tips. Blooms from an early age. Named in the Northern Hemisphere for December winter colour. Known in New Zealand by the name 'Tickled Pink'. 1.3 × 1.3m.   **234**

Pieris japonica 'Dorothy Wyckoff'
Slender erect compact grower. Young shoots burgundy red, maturing dark green through summer, reddish in autumn, purplish black in winter. Deep burgundy red winter buds open to fragrant pink-tinged flowers fading to white. 1.5 × 1m.

Pieris japonica 'Flamingo'
Compact rounded form, new growths rich bronzy red maturing deep green. Slightly fragrant, rosy purplish red flowers fading to deep pink. Deepest colour amongst Pieris. 1.5 × 1.3m.

Pieris japonica 'Forest Flame'
Superb compact hybrid combining the hardiness of P japonica with brilliant foliage of P formosa 'Wakehurst', resulting in oblong-oblanceolate leaves with finely serrated margins, unfolding red, changing through flamingo pink and creamy white before maturing bright green. Creamy white, pitcher-shaped flowers in large spreading panicles. 1.8 × 1.5m.

Pieris japonica 'Mountain Fire'
Medium size neat compact bush. Fiery crimson new shoots in spring maturing glossy deep green. Impressive clusters of fragrant ivory- white, somewhat larger flowers. 1.5 × 1.3m.

Pieris japonica 'Pink Delight'
Rounded compact form, coppery new shoots maturing deep green. Pink buds open to white fragrant flowers lightly tinted pink borne in long pendent racemes. 1.5 × 1.3m.

Pieris japonica 'Purity'
Neat compact grower, selected for masses of comparatively large pure white flowers in spring. 1.5 × 1m.

Pieris japonica 'Red Mill'
Vigorous compact grower with charming fiery-red new shoots maturing dark-green and attractive heads of pure white flowers. 1.8 × 1.5m.

Pieris japonica 'Scarlett O'Hara'
Slender erect form, glossy bright scarlet young shoots fading to bronze and maturing dark green. Creamy white flowers with distinctive red flecks borne on reddish stems. 1.8 × 1.3m.

Pieris japonica 'Tickled Pink'
Compact rounded form, bronzy young shoots maturing deep green. Panicles of fragrant bicolor bell-flowers, white delicately tinted deep rose at the tips. Blooms from an early age. Syn P japonica 'Christmas Cheer'. 1.3 × 1.3m.

Pieris japonica 'Variegata'
Flower and form resembles P japonica, but more compact. Smaller leaves attractively variegated silvery white. New shoots flushed pink. Flowers white. 1 × 1m.

Pieris japonica 'White Cascade'
Compact grower, coppery young shoots maturing glossy deep-green. Pure white flowers in long pendulous racemes borne profusely through spring. Syn P 'Diamante'. 1.5 × 1.3m.

Pieris japonica 'White Rim'
Resembles P japonica 'Variegata' but growth is somewhat faster. White leaf margins more clearly defined. Larger white flowers in dense panicles early spring. 1.5 × 1.3m.

Pieris ryukyuensis 'Temple Bells'
Selected cultivar of the species native to Ryukyu Retto Islands off the southern tip of Japan. Erect rounded form with tiered horizontal branches. New shoots at first light green flushed apricot-bronze becoming reddish bronze, maturing deep emerald green and glossy. Striking bell-shaped large creamy white flowers, twice the size of other forms, produced in large racemes in spring. Plant in dappled light protected from frost. 1.5 × 1.3m.

Pieris taiwanensis
Taiwan Pieris
From cool alpine regions of Taiwan. Medium, broad-spreading form. Young shoots bronze to bronze-red, maturing deep green with matt surface distinguishing it from P japonica which it otherwise resembles. Larger more erect panicles of beautiful white flowers in spring. 1.3 × 1.3m.

PIMELIA

A genus of about eighty species of small to medium woody shrubs from Australasia, named from the Greek *pimele*, fat, referring to their oily seeds. The relatively few species and cultivars generally grown are excellent dwarf shrubs with colourful long lasting floral displays. Plant in deeply worked, free-draining, organically enriched acid soil in full sun or partial shade, sheltered from frost. Prune immediately after flowering. Ideal for sunny banks or borders, and effective in massed beds.
Thymelaeaceae. *All evergreen.*

Pimelia ferruginea
Rosy Rice Flower
Dwarf rounded erect bush from Western Australia. Leaves ovate or oblong to 12mm, glossy green crowded in opposite pairs along slender stems. Rose-pink tubular flowers in almost spherical, 3–4cm terminal clusters,

mainly late spring through early summer, but intermittently through the year. Resistant to salt spray. Ferruginea — rust coloured. 1 × 1m.   **233**

Pimelia ferruginea 'Bonne Petite'
Among the most beautiful and free flowering dwarf shrubs with compact form, tidy foliage and great masses of deep reddish-pink flowers in terminal clusters spring through autumn. 70 × 70cm.   **233**

Pimelia ferruginea 'Magenta Mist'
Forms a low compact cushion with glossy deep green leaves and large 'posy' clusters of brilliant cerise-pink flowers with soft magenta hue. Offered in New Zealand as Pimelia 'My Love'. 60 × 60cm.

Pimelia prostrata
New Zealand Daphne
Small mat-forming plant found from North Cape to the Bluff on the coast or in mountains scrambling happily over rocks and flowering through summer. Minute 2–12mm, dull-green, ovate to elliptic-oblong leaves, margins often red, arranged in four neat ranks along wiry stems. Fragrant white or blue flowers in small crowded heads, followed by small white berries. Excellent for growing around or over rocks. Prostrata — lying flat on the ground but not taking root. 15cm × 1m.

Pimelia rosea
Pink Rice Flower
Erect dwarf bush from Western Australia with attractive, linear- lanceolate, 25mm leaves, rather more sparse than other species. Tubular starry rose pink flowers covered with tiny hairs, carried in 3–4cm rounded heads resembling pink daphne, produced on the tips of previous year's growth during spring. 60 × 60cm.

PINUS

A genus of about 110 species of coniferous trees and shrubs from the Arctic Circle to Central America, North Africa and south east Asia called *Pinus*, the Latin name. Besides their commercial value, Pines are useful landscaping subjects especially as juveniles. They have neat well groomed conical form and fascinating new growths resembling erect candles in contrasting colours at the ends of each branch.

Those with gnarled and rugged trunks have distinctive character. Dwarf Pines possess charm equivalent to any other low growing conifer. Cones of various shapes usually take two years to ripen, some releasing their seeds when mature. Other species keep them intact on the tree until forced open by forest fires facilitating natural regeneration.

Pines generally grow in poor soils, withstand heat, wind frost and drought. Under garden conditions, soil need not be rich, but well drained. Naturally, many grow on rocky slopes, or barren, sandy areas where fertility is low but drainage perfect. Pines have a place in contemporary landscaping, either planted or in containers. They may be shaped and improved by pruning. To slow down growth or thicken a weaker tree, cut back new growth to half way or more, when needles begin to emerge.

To train in an oriental manner, remove any branches which interfere with desired effects, shortening others and creating an upswept look by removing all downward growing twigs. Horizontal growth can be induced by cutting the main trunk back to well-placed side branches. Cascade effects may also be achieved by wiring or weighing branches. Dwarf, slow-growing species so useful in rock or feature gardens rarely require any training.

Pinaceae. *All evergreen.*

Pinus banksiana
Jackpine
Extremely hardy as it is the northernmost pine found in North America. Easily distinguished by crooked open picturesque appearance, and slender spreading branches. Occasionally gnarled and shrubby. Pairs of short needles only 3–4cm long, bright green curved and twisted. Winter buds cylindrical and resinous, young shoots yellowish green and glabrous. Named for Sir Joseph Banks. 6 × 4m.

Pinus densiflora
Japanese Red Pine
Regarded as the Japanese counterpart of Pinus sylvestris and with similar reddish bark. Needles in pairs, 5–12cm long, twisted bright blue-green or yellow green. Winter buds oblong sharply pointed and resinous. Young growth pink and bloomy at first then greenish with short hairs. Neutral or slightly acid soil. Handsome pine for informal effects, especially multi-trunked specimens. Densiflora — densely flowered. 5 × 3m.

Pinus halepensis
Aleppo Pine
Native to Mediterranean regions, found naturally in warm dry maritime areas. Attractive as a juvenile, developing dramatic rugged character after five years. Open irregular crown with numerous short ascending branches when mature. Light green needles usually in twos, 5–10cm long, slightly twisted and sparse. Cone shaped winter buds, young shoots glaucous and glabrous. Good for poor soils and arid climates. Thrives in heat drought wind and by the seashore. Halepensis — from Aleppo, northern Syria. 5 × 3m.

Pinus montezumae
Montezuma Pine
Semi-tropical species from Mexico and Guatemala with long substantial, light blue-green needles in fives to 30cm, drooping gracefully. Conical cones to 30cm, yellow reddish or dark brown. Broad, fairly dense grower with horizontal somewhat drooping branches. Not for cold temperatures. 5 × 3m.

Pinus monticola
Western White Pine
Native from northern California to British Columbia, fast growing in youth with attractive, narrow open crown, rather pyramidal with drooping branches when mature. Needles in fives, 6–10cm long, blue green, white banded beneath, fine and soft. Cones slender, 13–25cm long and light brown. Very hardy. 5 × 3m.

Pinus mugo
Dwarf Mountain Pine
Native to mountains of Spain, central Europe to the Balkans. Extremely slow grower of somewhat variable form. Ideally a low prostrate compact shrub with dense bushy habit. Usually seen as a dense or rather open mound with short curved branchlets arising from the base, completely surrounded and well covered with 4–5cm needles in pairs. Leaves stiff and bristly, dark green, sometimes curved and often shaded brown. Winter buds small round and very resinous, candle-shaped young shoots light green and glabrous. Excellent in rock gardens when featured against a large boulder. 90 × 90cm.   **235**

Pinus muricata
Bishop Pine
Native to northern Californian coast, growing rapidly with open pyramidal form when young, becoming dense rounded and irregular with age. Needles in twos, 10–15cm, dark green and crowded. Cones 5–7cm, brown, broadly oval, borne in whorls up to five. Hardy for coastal planting, tolerant of wind and salt air. Slower growing and denser in youth than P radiata. 5 × 4m.

Above: Pisonia umbellifera 'Variegata' **237**

Above: Plumeria rubra acutifolia *Tropical Frangipani* **241**

Above: Platycerium bifurcatum *Stags Horn Fern* **241**
Below: Pimelia ferruginea 'Bonne Petite' **232**

Above: Pimelia ferruginea *Rosy Rice Flower* **232**
Below: Pimelia ferruginea 'Bonne Petite' **232**

Above: Pinus patula *Jelecote Pine* **237**

Above: Pieris formosa 'Wakehurst' *Chinese Pieris* **231**
Below: Pieris japonica 'Bert Chandler' **231**

Above: Pinus roxburghii *Indian Long-Leaf Pine* **237**
Below: Pieris japonica 'Christmas Cheer' **231**

Above: Pittosporum tenuifolium 'Gold Star' **239**

Above: Pittosporum eugenoides *Lemonwood   Tarata* **238**
Below: Pinus mugo *Dwarf Mountain Pine* **232**

Above: Pittosporum tenuifolium 'Mellow Yellow' **239**
Below: Pittosporum eugenoides 'Variegata' **238**

Above: Podalyria calyptrata *Sweet Pea Bush* **242**

Above: Protea cynaroides *King Protea* **249**
Below: Protea cynaroides *King Protea* **249**

Above: Protea neriifolia 'Snowcrest' **250**
Below: Protea magnifica *Queen Protea* **250**

Pinus nigra
Austrian Black Pine
Slow to moderate grower from Europe and western Asia. Forms a dense stout pyramid with rough greyish brown or dark brown bark and branches in regular whorls. Stiff very dark green, 8–16cm needles. Oval brown cones to 8cm. Tree of strong character, very hardy tolerant of winter cold and wind including maritime conditions, growing equally well in sandy or heavy dry soils. 7 × 5m.

Pinus patula
Jelecote Pine
Elegant species native to Mexico. Forms an extremely beautiful small tree with graceful pyramidal growth habit, reddish bark and widely spaced pairs of branches which gently curve upwards. Round long pointed winter buds, young shoots glabrous and glaucous green. Bright green leaves in groups to five, 15–30cm long, hang straight down and give the tree distinctively graceful appearance. One of the fastest growing pines, quite hardy, preferring free-draining slightly acid soil and full sun. Patula — standing open or spreading. 6 × 4m. **234**

Pinus pinea
Italian Stone Pine, Umbrella Pine
From Mediterranean regions of southern Europe and Turkey. A stout bushy globe in youth, developing a thick trunk with many branches providing characteristic dense, flat topped, or umbrella head in middle age. Winter buds oval and pointed, young shoots greyish green. Rather distinctive leaves in pairs, 12–20cm long, bright green to grey green, stiff slightly twisted and sharply pointed.

Picturesque pine of distinct habit, particularly suited to sandy soils, beach gardens or coastal areas. 6 × 5m.

Pinus radiata
Monterey Pine
Native to California's central coastal area and found to thrive in moist temperate climates. Radiata pine chemically treated to varying degrees is a basic building material. Grows rapidly in youth to form a handsome symmetrical specimen. Discards lower branches with age, developing a broad top, and massive trunk with rugged deeply fissured bark. Oval resinous winter buds and glabrous, light green young shoots. Rich green needles in threes, 10–15cm long, densely crowded on branchlets. Obvious choice for forestry, farm shelter, erosion control and filling waste areas. Seldom used ornamentally, but interesting results may be obtained with pruning and training. 6 × 4m.

Pinus radiata 'Aurea'
Golden Monterey Pine
In most respects like Monterey Pine, but with golden yellow needles. As seedlings of this cultivar do not survive, grafting is the only reliable method of reproduction. 6 × 4m.

Pinus roxburghii
Indian Long Leafed Pine
Native to Himalayan foothills, forming a slender pyramid in youth with long slender light green drooping leaves in threes, 20–30cm long. Young shoots clothed with scale like leaves. Winter buds small and ovoid. Cones ovoid up 20cm long. Mature form broad-spreading with round-topped symmetrical head. 6 × 4m. **234**

Pinus strobus
Eastern White Pine
Eastern United States is the natural habitat. Symmetrical conical form with horizontal branches in regular whorls when young, later developing a rounded head. Soft blue green, 5–10cm needles in fives and slender, 7–20cm cones sometimes curved. Hardy to cold but tends to burn in windy areas. 7 × 5m.

Pinus sylvestris
Scots Pine
The only pine native to the British Isles, found in parts of northern Scotland, but widely planted for forestry purposes in other parts of the country. In youth a straight well branched pyramid, becoming irregular and picturesque with branches drooping with age. Needles in pairs from 3–10cm long, blue green or grey green, stiff and twisted. Brown, oval or cone shaped winter buds, young shoots greenish and glabrous. Young bark attractive, characteristically reddish brown. Sylvestris — of a wood or forest, growing wild. 6 × 4m.

Pinus thunbergii
Japanese Black Pine
Important timber tree in native Japan where it often occurs by the seashore. Attractive species forming a broad conical tree with stout twisted branches, becoming irregular and spreading with maturity. Winter buds ovoid, sharply pointed, silky, silvery white. Young shoots light brown ridged and glabrous. Needles in pairs to 18cm long, rigid and twisted. Hardy in dry or maritime conditions. Thunbergii — for Carl Peter Thunberg, 18th–19th century botanist. 6 × 4m.

Pinus wallichiana
Himalayan White Pine
Native to temperate Himalayas. Elegant large broad conical specimen, retaining lower branches when isolated. Winter buds resinous, young shoots glaucous and glabrous. Slender blue green drooping leaves in fives to 20cm long. Light brown banana shaped cones to 25cm. Attractive pine with graceful foliage, resin smeared buds and cones and good form. Not exceptionally hardy, but good garden feature tree. Syn P griffithii. Wallichiana — for Nathaniel Wallich, 18th–19th century botanist. 5 × 3m.

PISONIA

A genus of about 35 species of climbing to erect trees and shrubs from Australasia, South America and Hawaii named for Wilhelm Pison, 17th century Dutch naturalist. Listed species is a large leafed New Zealand native with foliage suggestive of tropical origin. Both forms, especially the variegated one are useful as bold-foliage plants indoors, outdoor patios, courtyards, entryways, woodlands gardens and containers. Plant in deeply worked, free-draining, organically enriched, moisture-retentive soil in semishady warm locations sheltered from strong wind and frost. Early tip-pruning encourages low-level branching. Prune for size control.

Nyctaginaceae. *All evergreen.*

Pisonia umbellifera
Bird Catcher Tree, Para Para
Found on Kermadec and Three Kings Islands, along the east coast of the North Island south to East Cape, also in Norfolk and Lord Howe Island and eastern Australia.

Forms a small tree with smooth glossy deep green, oblong to elliptic-oblong leaves to 35 × 15cm. Greenish funnel-shaped flowers in terminal panicles to 10cm across, followed by five-ribbed, 2–3cm fruit covered with a sweet viscid substance which adheres to the wings of small birds, either holding them captive or making them unable to fly. Syn P brunoniana. Umbellifera — furnished with umbels. 4 × 2m.

Pisonia umbellifera 'Variegata'
Perfectly shaped leaves as above, but marbled in green and grey green, broadly and irregularly margined creamy yellow suspended on sturdy upright stems. Tender-pink young shoots add a dramatic touch. Magnificent foliage plant for warm semishady frost free locations planted out or in containers. Rarely if ever produces bird-catching seed pods. 3 × 2m. **233**

PISTACIA

A genus of about nine species of trees and shrubs from southern USA, Mexico, Malesia, central Asia to Japan and Mediterranean regions, named from the Greek *pistake*, pistachio nut. Listed species an ornamental and popular shade tree with elegant foliage and good autumn colour belonging to the same genus as P vera, the species cultivated extensively in many countries for pistachio nuts.

Grows in any reasonable deeply worked, free-draining soil, even in moderately alkaline conditions. Tends to be gawky when young, but with staking may be trained to a dense and shapely shade tree. Good tree for streets, lawns, patios or in a corner. Trees of both sexes must be present for crops of nuts.

Anacardiaceae.

Pistacia chinensis
Chinese Pistache
Handsome small tree with elegant paripinnate green and glossy leaves, comprised of 10–20 lanceolate leaflets to 8 × 2cm, coloured scarlet, crimson, orange and often yellow in autumn, intense even in warmer areas. Panicles of insignificant flowers, which if pollinated produce 5mm fruit, bright red later turning dark blue. Grown mainly for the beauty of autumn foliage. Chinensis — of China. Deciduous. 6 × 5m.

PITTOSPORUM

A genus of about 200 species of evergreen trees and shrubs from New Zealand, Australia, South Africa, south and east Asia and Hawaii, named from the Greek *pitta*, pitch and *sporum*, seed, referring to the sticky seeds of most species. Grown mostly for handsome foliage, easy culture and hardiness. Excellent choice for fillers. backgrounds, privacy or shelter screens and lawn specimens. Foliage of many cultivars popular for floral decorations.

Although growing under a wide range of soil and climatic variations, plant in deeply worked, free-draining, fertile soil in full or partial sun. They respond to deep watering through dry periods and feeding in spring and autumn with a balanced fertilizer. Pinch back when young to encourage strong root system and denser growth at ground level. Prune for size.

Pittosporaceae. *All evergreen.*

Pittosporum crassifolium
Karo
New Zealand native found along forest margins or along banks of streams from North Cape to Poverty Bay. Forms a large shrub or small tree with dark brown bark. New shoots white-felted, leaves elliptic or obovate, to 75 × 24mm, dark green, glabrous, leathery, white or buff tomentose beneath, margins entire and rolled under. Flowers dark crimson to purple with yellow anthers, 12mm across, produced in small terminal clusters spring through midsummer, filling the evening air with rich fragrance. Seed capsules 2–3cm across, light grey at first, bursting open autumn and winter to reveal black shiny seeds in a sticky substance. Good coastal screen. Crassifolium — thick leafed. 3 × 2m.

Pittosporum crassifolium 'Variegatum'
Natural sport from above with similar foliage, grey-green to almost grey, heavily margined creamy white. Excellent variegated shrub, handsome throughout the year but slower in growth than Karo. 2 × 1.5m.

Pittosporum eugenoides
Lemonwood, Tarata
One of the larger-growing New Zealand Pittosporums found in lowland and sub-alpine forests of both islands. Leaves elliptic to elliptic-oblong, to 12 × 4cm, semi-glossy pale green, delicately veined, almost white midrib, margins wavy or undulating. When bruised, leaves emit a distinct lemon fragrance. Pale yellow, 12mm, richly scented flowers in large terminal sprays spring through mid summer followed by yellowish fruit, black and wrinkled when ripe in autumn. Highly desirable tree, very hardy, grows in the poorest soils and responds to pruning. Eugenoides — resembling eugenia. 5 × 3m.   **235**

Pittosporum eugenoides 'Mini Green'
Forms a compact, rounded bushy shrub. Leaves semi-glossy emerald green with undulating margins. Easily pruned or clipped smaller if desired and good for containers. Wind tolerant. 2 × 1.5m.

Pittosporum eugenoides 'Platinum'
Neat compact pyramidal growth habit, bold leaves, light silvery-green with silver-white margins carried on contrasting purple-brown stems. Extremely ornamental. Aptly named. 3 × 2m.

Pittosporum eugenoides 'Variegata'
General appearance resembles Tarata but with grey-green to pale green leaves irregularly margined creamy white. Attractive throughout the year, excellent lawn specimen and for highlighting mixed borders. Foliage sprays valued for floral decorations. 2 × 1.5m.   **235**

Pittosporum ralphii
New Zealand species from lowland forest margins and alongside forest streams throughout the North Island. Spreading shrub or small tree with dark brown or greyish bark. Branchlets, petioles, peduncles, sepals and leaf undersides covered with dense white or grey woolly tomentum. Leaves elliptic to obovate-oblong, to 12 × 5cm, dull-glossy dark green, margins entire. Flowers reddish brown, about 15mm across with five reflexed petals, carried in umbels of 3–10 spring through midsummer, followed by broadly ovoid, 2cm capsules. Somewhat resembles P crassifolium but with larger, narrower leaves and not as hardy on the coast. 4 × 3m.

Pittosporum tenuifolium
Kohuhu
New Zealand native small tree found through both islands in coastal and lowland forests except Westland. Slender erect narrow pyramidal form, branches and twigs quite black. Leaves elliptic, obovate or oblong, to 60 × 25mm, glossy pale green, paler beneath, leathery, margins undulating or wavy. Flowers bright purple at first, changing to almost black, filling the evening air with sweet fragrance spring through early summer. Woody capsules open to reveal seeds embedded in a sticky glutinous substance. One of the easiest trees to grow in almost any soil or climate sun or shade. Tenuifolium — thin-leaved. 5 × 3m.

Pittosporum tenuifolium 'Argenteum Variegatum'
Light grey-green leaves edged creamy white with contrasting blackish stems. Vigorous growth habit, but easily pruned to size and shape. 3 × 2m.

Pittosporum tenuifolium 'Black Lace'
Small wavy leaves becoming very dark almost black during cooler months. Open airy form provides lacy effects suggested in the name. Benefits from light pruning of outer tips. 2.5 × 1.5m.

Pittosporum tenuifolium subspp colensoi
Black Mapou
New Zealand species occurring in forest and scrublands south from Rotorua to Stewart Island. Rapidly forms a large shrub or small tree with dark greenish brown bark. Leaves elliptic to obovate-oblong, to 10 × 5cm, leathery, glossy deep green, pale yellowish green beneath, margins entire, apex sharply pointed. Fragrant flowers reddish purple,

about 10mm across with five reflexed petals, borne singly or in small cymes late spring and early summer, followed by 12mm seed capsules ripe in autumn. Colensoi — for W Colenso, 19th century botanist. 6 × 3m.

Pittosporum tenuifolium 'Deborah'
Distinctive cultivar with small leaves, green to grey-green broadly margined creamy white, heavily flushed pink or rosy red through the year, particularly in winter. Upright airy habit. 2 × 1.5m.

Pittosporum tenuifolium 'Deborah's Gold'
Tiny waved leaves with golden yellow central panel deepening to lime green with maturity, margins irregularly edged green. Not as robust as other Pittosporums. 2 × 1.5m.

Pittosporum tenuifolium 'Eila Keightley'
Rounded to oval foliage, fresh green irregularly variegated in the centre with yellow and yellowish green, veins and midrib cream. Changes to lime green with maturity. Dark blackish purple stems enhance the foliage. Syn P tenuifolium 'Sunburst'. 2 × 1.5m.

Pittosporum tenuifolium 'French Lace'
Forms an erect tidy shrub with lacy small to medium wavy-edged green leaves which in winter turn plum-red or olive-purple. Ideal specimen or screen. 3 × 1.5m.

Pittosporum tenuifolium 'Garnettii'
Attractive hybrid cultivar from P tenuifolium × P ralphii. Leaves ovate to elliptic, medium green beautifully variegated creamy white, flushed and spotted pink to wine red, more intensely during colder months, margins undulating. Although listed as a P tenuifolium cultivar, it bears little resemblance to the species. 2 × 1.5m.

Pittosporum tenuifolium 'Gold Star'
New leaves intense golden yellow in the centre. Mature leaves with bright gold and chartreuse central zone, midrib yellow and creamy white, undulating margins irregularly edged green. Excellent compact grower. 1.5 × 1m.   **235**

Pittosporum tenuifolium 'Green Pillar'
Attractive cultivar with distinctively rounded form and fresh green foliage. Useful landscaping shrub planted out or in conainers. 1.2 × 1m.

Pittosporum tenuifolium 'Green Ripple'
Attractively rippled bright green foliage and sturdy erect habit. Vigorous and hardy, responds to regular pruning. 3 × 1.5m.

Pittosporum tenuifolium 'Green Wave'
Neat compact growth habit, mid to dark green leaves, margins wavy. Green sport from Yellow Wave. 3 × 1.5m.

Pittosporum tenuifolium 'Irene Paterson'
Enchanting cultivar with slender black branchlets and young leaves almost completely white with faint green speckling. Background becomes light green as foliage matures, often tinged pink in winter, margins undulating. Good contrast shrub excellent for picking. 2 × 1.5m.

Pittosporum tenuifolium 'James Stirling'
Distinctive small pale green to silvery leaves rounded and slightly waved. Long slender rather stiff blackish stems sparsely clothed with foliage, perfect for floral arrangements. Narrow erect form with pleasing outline. Good silhouette against architectural background. 3 × 1.5m.

Pittosporum tenuifolium 'Katie'
Small light green slightly wavy leaves irregularly banded creamy white. Branchlets black. Vigorous, fast growing, needs regular pruning. 2.5 × 2m.

Pittosporum tenuifolium 'Limelight'
Vigorous hybrid with oval to elliptic leaves variegated with large central yellowish green zone and irregular narrow green margins carried on reddish stems. Colour deepens to chartreuse as foliage matures. Sturdy, bushy grower with good personality. 3 × 2m.

Pittosporum tenuifolium 'Marjorie Channon'
Excellent compact rounded form, leaves light green, richly margined creamy white flushed pink. Hardy, easily grown. 1.5 × 1m.

Pittosporum tenuifolium 'Mellow Yellow'
Excellent small-leaved twiggy cultivar, golden yellow, reddish markings. Outstanding shrub, prized for floral arrangements. Not for cooler areas. 3.5 × 1.5m.   **235**

Pittosporum tenuifolium 'Moonlight'
Forms a compact bush with fine, rounded, deep-green leaves highlighted in the centre with bright creamy yellow. At its brightest during spring and summer, colour fading as foliage matures. Very hardy. Developed by nurseryman Ross Stuart, South Otago. 1.5m × 90cm

Pittosporum tenuifolium 'Mountain Green'
Small to medium, rounded, closely internoded, light fresh-green leaves on erect

green branchlets. Compact bushy growth habit. 2.5 × 2m.

Pittosporum tenuifolium 'Oliver Twist'
Bushy compact grower. Leaves elliptic, medium green with prominent undulating or twisted margins. 2 × 1.3m.

Pittosporum tenuifolium 'Pixie'
Distinctive form, compact habit and miniature silvery grey leaves with wavy margins. Dense upright grower. 1.2m × 75cm.

Pittosporum tenuifolium 'Purpureum'
Young growths pale green gradually changing to bronzy green, maturing deep purple almost black. Leaves 30–45mm long, oblong to elliptic with strongly undulating margins, so dark in colour that the shrub needs to be against a lighter background or with lighter coloured foliage for its subtle beauty to be appreciated. 1.5 × 1m.

Pittosporum tenuifolium 'Rotundifolium'
Erect tall narrow shrub with 2–4cm leaves, almost round, hardly undulating, upper surface grey green broadly and irregularly margined pale greenish yellow to creamy white. Open and dainty. 2 × 1.2m.

Pittosporum tenuifolium 'Saundersii'
Almost identical to P tenuifolium 'Garnettii' the only noticeable variation between the two being denser foliage and better growth habit in Saundersii. 2 × 1.5m.

Pittosporum tenuifolium 'Silver Magic'
Rapid grower with erect habit and conspicuous blackish branchlets. Small pale green leaves with silvery white margins give the plant overall silvery appearance, flushed pink during winter. 3 × 1.5m.

Pittosporum tenuifolium 'Silver Sheen'
Tiny shimmering rounded pale silvery green leaves carried on slender ebony black stems. Excellent for floral decorations. Fast upright grower. 3 × 1.5m.

Pittosporum tenuifolium 'Stirling Gold'
Delightful slender form, tiny rounded foliage with undulating margins. Young leaves have broad central zone of pale yellow to greenish yellow and reddish midrib. As foliage ages becomes almost green with white midrib. Vigorous dainty habit. 1.5 × 1m.

Pittosporum tenuifolium 'Stirling Silver'
More vigorous form of 'Silver Magic' which has taken its place with more dense and compact habit. Has similar leaf markings. 2.5 × 2m.

Pittosporum tenuifolium 'Sunny Boy'
Upright bushy grower, leaves variegated bright green and cream. 2.5 × 1.5m.

Pittosporum tenuifolium 'Tandarra Gold'
Neat compact bushy grower with smooth slender black branchlets. Small rounded leaves prominently splashed gold in the centre, irregularly margined green. 3 × 1.5m.

Pittosporum tenuifolium 'Tiki'
Pleasing bushy small shrub with erect green-brown branchlets, leaves medium green, lighter green young shoots. 1.5 × 1m.

Pittosporum tenuifolium 'Tom Thumb'
Delightful dwarf compact grower. Glossy oval leaves with undulating margins, developing from light green through deep wine-red eventually purple-black, all colours often appearing at the same time. Good contrast amongst lighter coloured foliage. Best in full sun. Dwarf form of P tenuifolium 'Purpureum'. 75 × 75cm.

Pittosporum tenuifolium 'Trixie'
Excellent addition, selected for its dainty grey-green leaves which become bronze-tinged in winter. 2 × 1.5m.

Pittosporum tenuifolium 'Victoria'
Bushy upright grower with dark red stems. Leaves small to medium, variegated green and grey, touch of pink in winter. 2.5 × 1.5m.

Pittosporum tenuifolium 'Wai-iti'
Clear jade green oval foliage overlaid silver contrasting nicely against wine-red stems. Bushy medium grower. 2.5 × 1.5m.

Pittosporum tenuifolium 'Waimea'
Extra selected form with glossy jade-green leaves, lighter beneath on blackish brown branchlets. Compact, claimed to outshine other green foliaged forms. 2 × 1.5m.

Pittosporum tenuifolium 'Warnham Gold'
Young foliage pale light green, changing to pale creamy yellow, becoming golden yellow with maturity in autumn. Not as impressive as other golden forms. 2 × 1.5m.

Pittosporum tenuifolium 'Wendell Channon'
Small fresh green leaves with white wavy margins, flushed rose pink especially during winter. Black branchlets. Compact open habit. 1.5 × 1m.

Pittosporum tenuifolium 'Yellow Wave'
New foliage attractively waved, bright golden yellow irregularly banded green, rich green and marbled when mature. Good contrast of new and mature foliage. Compact grower, responds to pruning. 2 × 1.3m.

Pittosporum 'Variegatum'
Most pleasing. Slender erect grower always tidy with bright cheerful appearance. Greyish branchlets, elliptic to 5cm long, grey green with irregular but neat creamy white margins. Grows easily and rapidly, excellent as a specimen. The type of shrub which blends in anywhere. Often listed as a cultivar of P tenuifolium, but with obvious differences to indicate its hybrid origin. 3 × 1.5m.

PLAGIANTHUS

A genus of about 15 species confined to Australasia named from the Greek *plagios*, oblique and *anthos*, a flower, referring to asymmetrical petals. Genus includes some of the few New Zealand native deciduous trees. Grown for the effect of new leaves in spring, masses of blossom and seed capsules. Provides a handsome specimen tree where space permits. Plant in deeply worked, organically enriched, free-draining soil. Withstands exposed positions, growing strong and erect against prevailing winds. Trim off interleaving juvenile branches as the tree matures to develop a clean trunk.
    Malvaceae.

Plagianthus regius
Ribbonwood
The species is found in lowland forests of New Zealand's main islands. Inclined to be a dense bush of slender flexuous interlacing branches with small foliage as a juvenile, but forms a graceful slender small to medium sized tree with tough stringy bark as it matures. Mature leaves broad-ovate to ovate-lanceolate, to 75 × 50mm, soft-textured, margins deeply and irregularly toothed, bright green above paler beneath. Small yellowish green bell-shaped 7mm flowers in multi-flowered terminal and axillary cymes, mass produced through spring and early summer, giving an attractive lime green glow, followed by downy seed capsules ripe early autumn. Syn P betulinus. Regius — royal. Deciduous. 5 × 4m.

PLANCHONELLA

A genus of about 60 species of trees and shrubs from east Asia, western Polynesia and New Zealand named for J E Planchon, 19th century French botanist. The New Zealand species resembles species found on Lord Howe Island and Fiji. A handsome specimen tree, valued for large shining foliage and colourful fruit. Plant in deeply worked, organically enriched, free-draining soil. Requires shelter from frost but survives coastal conditions.
    Sapotaceae.

Planchonella costata
Tawapou
Found mainly along northern east areas of the North Island and adjacent offshore islands. Closely branched specimen tree with trunk to 90cm diameter. Leaves elliptic to obovate-oblong, to 10 × 5cm, glossy deep-green, prominent midrib, margins entire. Small 3–5mm delicate light green flowers followed by ellipsoid to ovoid, 25mm fruit varying in colour from green during midsummer, changing through autumn to yellow, red and purple-black when ripe. Syn P novo-zelandica. Costata — ribbed, in reference to the seeds. Evergreen. 5 × 4m.

PLATANUS

A genus of about seven species of mainly deciduous trees from North America, south west Europe, south west Asia and Indochina, named from the Greek *platanos*, oriental plane derived from *platys*, broad or flat in reference to the leaves. Plane trees, especially London Plane are important in many of the world's cities, amongst the few to survive extreme conditions of poor soil, limited moisture, sealed roots and pollution by smoke smog grime and dust. They form magnificent, maple-like trees with scaling bark and large long stalked leaves.
    Once a framework is established they can be pollarded to create a dense low canopy. This entails severe annual pruning of all current season's growth. Where space is unlimited they form handsome spreading trees for shade or shelter, perfect for large lawn areas, public or private parks, streets etc. Grows in all types of fertile, deeply worked soil with adequate moisture until established.
    Platanaceae. *All deciduous.*

Platanus × acerifolia
London Plane
Of hybrid origin from P orientalis × P occidentalis. Grows rapidly to form a round headed tree with clean smooth cream coloured bark eventually grey which peels

off in flakes. Palmate leaves, 20–25cm across with 3–5 triangular lobes, deep green and glossy which helps to clean off pollutants during rain. Rounded burr-like 25mm fruit in clusters of 2 or 3 hang like baubles summer through spring. Syn P hispanica. Acerifolia — resembling maple. 7 × 5m.

Platanus × acerifolia 'Sutternii'
Magnificent form of the London Plane with large green leaves prominently blotched and speckled creamy white. 7 × 5m.

Platanus occidentalis
Buttonwood, American Plane
Native to an area from southern Ontario, eastern USA and north east Mexico. Forms a substantial tree with ascending branches and bark peeling off in small plates. Leaves mostly three-lobed to 18cm across, lobes shallower than London Plane, margins coarsely undulating, deep green and glabrous above, tomentose beneath. Fruit clusters smoother, usually produced singly on long stalks. Occidentalis — western. 8 × 5m.

Platanus orientalis
Oriental Plane
Native to south eastern Europe and Asia Minor where natural specimens usually have shorter trunks and an immense rounded head of branches. Bark peels off in plates. Leaves deeply cut into 3–7 finger-like lobes. Seems tolerant of city pollution. A number of selected clones have been identified. Orientalis — eastern. 7 × 5m.

Platanus orientalis 'Autumn Glory'
Specially selected for the beauty and intensity of gold and orange autumn colours. Leaf pattern variable and ultimate size may be smaller than the type. 6 × 5m.

Platanus orientalis 'Digitata'
Large soft green palmate leaves deeply divided into 3–5 finger-like lobes. 6 × 5m.

PLATYCERIUM

A genus of about 18 species of epiphytic ferns, from many tropical areas named from the Greek *platys* meaning broad and *keras*, horn, referring to broad, fertile fronds of which 'stag horn' is very descriptive. Commonly seen as epiphytes on tall trees in subtropical or temperate rainforests. Unique plants in landscaping situations mounted on trunks of large trees or attached to timber structures or slabs of wood or bark in patios, shade houses or cool porch areas. Remarkably

hardy, preferring shady moist conditions, but otherwise trouble free.
Polypodiaceae.

Platycerium bifurcatum
Stag Horn Fern
From subtropical Australia, New Guinea and New Caledonia at 250–1000m. Rounded, heart or kidney-shaped sterile basal fronds like large flat scales with feathered edges support the plant and accumulate organic material on which it feeds. Fertile fronds to 1m long, usually laxly pendent and twice divided into long forks, leathery, greyish dark green with silvery reverse, thinly covered with small white hairs, produced in dense clusters. Numerous offsets at the base. Bifurcatum — forked into two almost equal stems or branches. Evergreen.   **233**

PLUMBAGO

A genus of about 15 species of shrubs and herbs from warm and tropical regions named from the Latin *plumbum*, leaden, for either of two contradictory reasons, firstly some species were thought to cure lead poisoning, or because the sap causes a greyish skin irritation. Plumbago auriculata is frequently seen in warm temperate or frost-free gardens providing a spectacle of sky-blue flowers through summer and autumn. Excellent plant for scrambling over fences, trellis, pergolas or banks, growing against walls amongst other shrubs, in a corner, or wherever it can get some kind of support.

Plant in deeply worked, free-draining, moisture-retentive, fertile soil in full sun sheltered from constant wind. Reasonably drought resistant but responds to regular watering. Best in frost free conditions, but recovers from mild damage. Prune heavily each spring, tip-prune for good form or shear when growing on supports.
Plumbaginaceae.

Plumbago auriculata
Cape Plumbago, Cape Leadwort
From Eastern Cape and Natal, scrambling over other bushes.This is a semi-climbing or rambling plant, rapidly filling blank spaces. Main leaves oblanceolate to elliptic, to 7 × 3mm, light to medium green, glabrous above, rough-textured with minute scales beneath, margins undulate. Smaller leaves in clusters of about five appear from leaf axils. Flowers bright sky-blue with five flaring petals to 30mm across backed by a slender 30mm tube in a hairy calyx, produced in terminal racemes spring through

autumn. In warmer areas they seem continually in bloom. Auriculata — having ear-shaped appendages. Evergreen. 1.5 × 1m.

Plumbago auriculata 'Alba'
Resembles above, but with masses of pure white flowers. Evergreen. 1.5 × 1m.

PLUMERIA

A genus of 8 species of shrubs or small trees from West Indies and Central America named for Charles Plumier, 17th century French monk, botanist and writer on tropical flora. Frangipani is thought to honour Marquis Frangipani, Major General under Louis XIV. Frangipani abounds in warm temperate, subtropical and tropical areas of both hemispheres, producing exquisite, highly fragrant flowers spring through autumn.

Requires frost free locations, humidity and maximum sunlight for strong growth and production of flower buds. Grows freely almost anywhere in warm temperate to tropical climates, but in cool areas they may survive against a north-facing wall, sheltered from cold winds. Plant in deeply worked, free-draining, organically enriched, moisture-retentive soil. Mulch this plant freely and keep it moist until it is well established. Ideal in containers for warm sheltered patio areas.
Apocynaceae.

Plumeria rubra acutifolia
Tropical Frangipani
Shrub or small tree with open gaunt character, stout fleshy stems and broadly elliptic leaves to 40 × 12cm, conspicuous veins and entire margins. Sweetly scented, 5–6cm flowers with five twisted petals appear in terminal clusters. Blooms of exquisite beauty in colours of white, cream, pink, red, orange and yellow continue to open over long periods spring through autumn. Rubra — red. Acutifolia — with sharply pointed leaves. Deciduous. 3 × 3m.   **233**

PODALYRIA

A genus of 25 species of South African shrubs named for Podalyrius, son of Aesculapius, skilful physician of Greek mythology. Grown for masses of fragrant pea-like flowers and downy leaves. Plant in full sun in deeply worked, free-draining fertile soil with sand gravel or peat moss, sheltered from strong wind and where frosts are not severe. Light annual pruning immediately after flowering preserves shape and vigour. Pinch back growing tips to encourage denser bush and better floral display. Be sparing with summer moisture and fertilizer.

Fabaceae. *All evergreen.*

Podalyria calyptrata
Sweet Pea Bush

From south western Cape, Table Mountain eastwards to Caledon and Bredasdorp. Large rounded shrub with elliptic, greyish green, 3–4cm leaves covered with fine silky white hairs. Pale pinkish mauve, sweetly scented flowers resembling sweet peas with two very broad, flattened upper petals about 4cm across, and a lip petal. They appear profusely amongst leaves of every branch, creating an attractive contrast spring through early summer. Last well when cut for indoors, especially if a portion of the foliage is removed. Popular shrubs for temperate gardens. Calyptrata — refers to the calyptra, hood or lid covering the flower. 2.5 × 2m. **236**

Podalyria sericea
Satin Bush

From south western Cape and peninsula regions. Charming dwarf shrub greatly admired for the silvery shiny sheen of silky down on obovate, 25mm leaves. Small lilac rose 2cm pea flowers produced between leaf axils appear in great profusion winter through spring. In warmer areas, flowers followed by silvery swollen seed pods which remain on the bush through summer. May drop some leaves during winter in cooler areas. Good in dry borders and sunny banks. Sericea — silky or covered with soft hairs. 75 × 75cm.

PODOCARPUS

A genus of about 100 species of evergreen trees and shrubs from Mexico, Central and South America, Central and South Africa, Himalayas to Japan, Australia and New Zealand, named from the Greek *pous* or *podos*, a foot and *karpos*, fruit, referring to the fleshy stalk or peduncle supporting seeds. Podocarpus have a prominent place in contemporary landscaping including excellent ground covers. Plant in full or partial sun in deeply worked, free-draining, organically enriched, moisture-retentive soil. Mulch freely and keep moist during the establishment period.

Podocarpaceae. *All evergreen.*

Podocarpus alpinus
Mountain Plum Pine

Australian native from all south east States found as prostrate mats or espaliers hugging the surfaces of rocks on exposed mountain slopes. Remarkably hardy dwarf species forming low densely branched mounds or carpets, extending slowly to 2m across. Soft but tough, dark green yew-like, linear-oblong leaves to 12 × 2mm, densely arranged on long slender arching or interlaced branches. Small 3mm seeds attached to showy red fruits or peduncles, fleshy stems of the true fruit. For rock garden, bank or ground cover. Naturally effective in erosion control. Alpinus — from high mountains. 45 × 130cm.

Podocarpus gracilior
Fern Pine

Graceful tree from Kenya, Uganda and Ethiopia, an important timber tree with long clean trunk and dense head of branches. Attractive and elegant as a juvenile with deep green glossy, linear, needle-like leaves to 10cm × 8mm, densely arranged along slender willowy branches, creating soft graceful effects. Somewhat variable but usually seen as a multi-branched shrub. Supple stems and branches may be trained upright or espaliered for dramatic effect along walls or fences. Excellent street tree, lawn or patio specimen or in containers. Gracilior — more graceful. 2 × 1.5m.

Podocarpus henkelii
Falcate Yellowwood

South African species forming a large tree with bole to 2m, charcoal-grey bark peeling in long strips, and pendent branches. Leaves narrow-lanceolate to 15cm × 9mm, glaucous green, midrib prominent beneath, falcate or curved sideways like a scythe, spirally arranged around branchlets. Fleshy peduncle, green tinged glaucous-blue with hard yellow-green seed embedded. 5 × 4m.

Podocarpus nivalis
Mountain Totara

Prostrate New Zealand native shrub found in subalpine situations from Coromandel to Southland. Forms a multi-branched prostrate or erect shrub with wide spreading branches often rooting near tips, helping to stabilize loose soil, shingle or steep alpine slopes. Leaves elliptical to oblong-ovate, to 18 × 3mm, rigid leathery, thick margined, often yellow or rust coloured, closely set and spirally arranged. Reddish fleshy seed receptacles, pleasantly sweet, occur on female plants midsummer. Vigorous plant for rock gardens, growing over large boulders or sprawling over banks. Nivalis — snow dweller. 50cm × 1m.

Podocarpus totara
Totara

Lofty New Zealand tree found naturally in lowland and mountain forests from North Cape to south east Otago. Totara forms a large tree with dense dull bronzy green, stiff, narrow leaves to 25mm long ending in a sharp needle-like point. Foliage similar during juvenile and adult stages. Stout trunk and lower limbs, rough reddish brown bark peeling off in strips. Female flowers after fertilization bear nut-like seeds on typical swollen peduncles which become red and succulent as fruit ripens in autumn. Young trees most handsome with tall pyramidal form, fine character and dense branch structure. Hardy slow growing, fits smaller gardens for decades without overcrowding. 6 × 4m.

Podocarpus totara 'Aurea'
Golden Totara

Similar growth habit and foliage to P totara but with more graceful branches, leaves softer and rich golden yellow especially in full sun. Desirable hardy golden foliage tree meriting extensive planting in all gardens. Prune to maintain shape and size. 5 × 3m.

POLYGALA

A genus of over 500 species of shrubs and herbs distributed worldwide except in Arctic zones and Australasia, named from the Greek *polys*, much and *gala*, milk, alluding to a reputation of some species to enhance the flow of milk. Only one species seems to be in general cultivation, grown for colourful spikes of pea-shaped flowers. Plant in deeply worked, free-draining, moisture-retentive fertile soil in full sun. Pinch when young and prune annually to keep compact. Useful shrub for fairly constant blooming although the colour may be hard to handle. Good for backgrounds or with other flowering plants in blue or white.

Polygalaceae.

Polygala myrtifolia 'Grandiflora'
Milkwort

A South African species forming a dense leafy shrub. Leaves elliptic-oblong or obovate, to 5cm long, light to mid green, smooth textured, margins entire. Reddish purple pea-shaped flowers with upstanding purple crest and prominent white anthers in grouped terminal clusters late winter through summer and autumn and sporadically throughout the year. Myrtifolia — myrtle-leaved. Evergreen. 2.5 × 1.5m.

POMADERRIS

A genus of about 40 species of evergreen shrubs and small trees native to Australia, Tasmania and New Zealand named from the Greek *poma*, a lid or cover and *derris*, skin, from the membranous covering of seed capsules. Grown for massed spring displays of fluffy flowers, felted foliage and easy culture.

Most Pomaderris thrive in poor coastal clay soils, dropping seed, germinating and growing freely to flowering stage in a year. Plant in deeply worked, free-draining soil, frequently pinch back tip growths. They develop rapidly and flower in great profusion. Treat P kumeraho as a short-term plant allowing natural re-seeding to provide continuity.

Rhamnaceae. *All evergreen.*

Pomaderris apetala
Tainui
From more northern coastal areas of New Zealand's North Island, Chatham Islands and Australia. Forms a large shrub with oval or oval-oblong leaves to 75 × 30mm, dull dark green, surface heavily wrinkled, margins crenulate, white or brown tomentum and conspicuous veins beneath. Clusters of 7mm greenish yellow flowers in terminal and lateral panicles late spring through to midsummer. Somewhat un-attractive as an ornamental, but useful as a fast-growing screen or shelter, hardy to frost and wind. Apetala — without petals. 4 × 2.5m.

Pomaderris kumeraho
Kumarahou, Golden Tainui
Naturally a dwarf to medium free-flowering shrub thriving on poor clay soil around lowland forests and scrubland throughout the northern half of New Zealand's North Island. Leaves oval or elliptic to 6 × 3cm, dull deep green and glabrous, margins entire, covered with white tomentum beneath. Flowers bright yellow to 7mm, borne in multi-branched corymbs or panicles to 10cm across, almost completely covering the bush through spring. Useful for dry banks, filling in waste areas or rapid filler in shrub borders. Kumeraho — from the Maori name. 1.5 × 1m.

Pomaderris phylicifolia var ericifolia
Dwarf Pomaderris
Attractive dwarf shrub occurring throughout the North Island and northern part of the South Island. Forms a prostrate to medium, multi-branched shrub with linear-elliptic leaves to 12 × 6mm, deep green, margins prominently recurved. Masses of bright creamy yellow flowers in axillary and lateral corymbs spring and early summer. Phylicifolia — leaves resembling Phylica. Ericifolia — leaves similar to those of Erica or heath. 90 × 90cm.

Pomaderris rugosa
Wrinkle-leaf Pomaderris
From northern coastal areas of New Zealand's North and offshore Islands. Attractive upright to spreading multi-branched shrub resembling P kumeraho, but with wrinkled foliage and longer flower clusters. Leaves oblong-lanceolate to elliptic, to 50 × 12mm, deep green, leathery glabrous and wrinkled, stellate-hairy beneath. Creamy yellow flowers to 4mm in elongated axillary or terminal panicles spring through mid-summer. Rugosa — rugose or wrinkled. 2.5 × 1.5m.

POPULUS

A genus of about 35 species of trees from Europe, Asia, North Africa and North America named from the Latin *populus*, poplar tree. Vigorous, rapid grower, tolerant of heavy, damp soil conditions in which many others would fail. Quickly form effective windbreaks, privacy screens, dust or noise barriers. The stately elegance of Lombardy Poplar adds much to the scenic beauty of southern New Zealand and Australia.

Many species have greedy invasive roots so careful siting is essential to avoid problems with drains, paths, lawns or small gardens. Otherwise they grow anywhere in any reasonable soil, and although tolerant of damp conditions, generally withstand long periods of drought once established.

Salicaceae. *All deciduous.*

Populus × canadensis 'Aurea'
Golden Poplar
Forms a large symmetrical tall-pyramidal specimen, providing splashes of shimmering gold from the moment leaves appear in spring through summer, autumn and well into winter. Leaves triangular to ovate, 7–10cm on long slender red-tinted petioles. Falling leaves over long periods create raking problems, but bare winter framework picturesque. Excellent colour-foliage tree where space permits. Canadensis — of Canada or north eastern USA. Syn P serotina 'Aurea'. 8 × 5m.

Populus × hybrid 'Flevo'
Vigorous rust-resistant erect growing poplar with limited open branching habit, reaching 15–18m after five years. Stems inclined to be brittle. Very fast growing and competes with nearby crops. Prefers well drained soils, prone to water stress and responds to irrigation. This tree is commonly used in orchards instead of willows. 9 × 3.5m.

Populus × hybrid 'Tasman'
Resembles P 'Flevo' but with more upright habit. Leaves larger than Lombardy Poplar, more open and widespread. Rust resistant. 9 × 3m.

Populus hybrid 'Manawatu Gold'
Hybrid cultivar from P deltoides × P canadensis 'Aurea'. Grows rapidly to a large-crowned tree with pale gold foliage. Selected for high resistance to leaf rust and Dutch Elm disease. Only moderately patalatable to possums and needs protection until established in high density possum population areas. Good alternative for farm planting, large parks and gardens. 25 × 15m.

Populus nigra 'Italica'
Lombardy Poplar, Italian Poplar
Narrow columnar tree with upward reaching branches densely covered with bright green, triangular, 5–10cm leaves, turning brilliant golden yellow in autumn, intensely brighter in colder climates. Invasive roots and immense proportions preclude planting in limited spaces, but indispensable in parks, school grounds, camping grounds, farms or orchards. Easily established from cuttings. Control Poplar Rust by spraying or choose resistant clones. 9 × 2.5m.

Populus nigra 'Lombardy Sunlight'
Resembles the erect form of Lombardy Poplar but with soft yellow-green foliage through spring and summer, intensifying to golden yellow in autumn. 8 × 2.5m.

Populus yunnanensis
Chinese Poplar
Vigorous medium sized balsam poplar from Yunnan, China, with glabrous strongly angled shoots and gummy buds. Leaves ovate to obovate-lanceolate, 7–15cm, glabrous bright green above, pale green beneath, margins crenate. Autumn colour negligible, but has pleasing appearance all year. Good screen tree giving urgently needed privacy or protection, tolerant of poor conditions. For farm planting Chinese Poplar is rust-tolerant, well suited for boundaries or sidings with wide branching habit. 8 × 5m.

POTENTILLA

A genus of about 500 species of herbaceous and shrubby perennials from temperate and cooler regions of the Northern Hemisphere named from the Latin *potens*, able, powerful, capable referring to supposed medicinal qualities. The common name *Cinquefoil* is derived from *quinque*, five and *folium*, leaf, in reference to five-part leaves and flowers of many species. Grown for extreme hardiness and long-lasting summer displays of colourful flowers.

Plant in deeply worked, free-draining, not over-rich soil, in maximum sunlight avoiding the hottest part of the day, especially plants with strong colours such as red or orange. Occasional deep watering during prolonged dry spells, otherwise they're better out of the reach of the hose. Prune early spring, cutting weak growth to ground level and vigorous growth to half way. Give old jaded plants a fresh start by cutting all growths to ground level.

Rosaceae. *All deciduous.*

Potentilla arbuscula
Low shrub from Himalayas and northern China with erect and trailing stems. Leaves have 3–5, thick, lobed, 1cm light to mid-green leaflets, white hairy beneath. Rich-yellow, 3cm flowers in lax clusters through summer and autumn. Syn P fruticosa var arbuscula. Arbuscula — resembling a small tree. 75 × 90cm.

Potentilla fruticosa 'Elizabeth'
The species has small leaves divided in five or seven, narrow leaflets. Masses of 25mm wide-open, five round-petalled flowers resembling buttercups or small single roses. Bushy shrubs, hardy in all districts, blooming cheerfully through summer and autumn. Elizabeth forms a dome-shaped bush studded with 35mm golden-yellow flowers late spring through early autumn. 1 × 1m.

Potentilla fruticosa 'Goldfinger'
Vigorous, erect growing plant bearing masses of large, bright golden-yellow flowers through summer. Hardy, floriferous and reliable. 1 × 1m.

Potentilla fruticosa 'Manchu'
Low-growing shrub or ground-cover from Manchuria with grey, silky-hairy leaves. White flowers to 25mm through summer. Attractive all year. Syn P fruticosa var mandschurica. 30 × 90cm.

Potentilla fruticosa 'Moonlight'
Vigorous bushy shrub with 4cm leaves divided into five blue-green leaflets. Soft yellow flowers, paler beneath spring through late autumn. 1 × 1m.

Potentilla fruticosa 'Mount Everest'
Upright grower, leaves with five narrow yellow-green leaflets. White flowers to 35mm across through summer. 1 × 1m.

Potentilla fruticosa 'Peaches and Cream'
Flowers open peach-pink, fading through summer to soft cream. 60 × 90cm.

Potentilla fruticosa 'Red Ace'
Bright vermillion red 35mm flowers with contrasting pale-yellow reverse. Tends to fade in strong sunlight. 75 × 120cm.

Potentilla fruticosa 'Sunset'
Low growing, lax habit. Orange-yellow to brick-red summer flowers. 50 × 90cm.

Potentilla fruticosa 'Wendonside'
Vigorous bushy shrub with large yellow flowers through summer. 1 × 1m.

PROSTANTHERA

A genus of about 50 species, mostly shrubs or subshrubs endemic to Australia, named from the Greek *prostithemi*, to append and *anthera*, anthers, in reference to small spur-like appendages on the anthers. Commonly known as Australian Mint, valued for aromatic foliage and free flowering habits. Flowers rather like flattened bells with a projecting lower lip.

Plant in any loose-free, deeply worked, free-draining soil in a sunny, open aspect. Being brittle and sometimes a little top-heavy, protect from strong wind. Prune lightly after flowering from an early age to prevent legginess. Reasonably hardy. Among the showiest and most fragrant spring flowering shrubs and although possibly short lived, worth growing in mixed shrub borders or amongst plantings of annuals bulbs or perennials.

Lamiaceae. *All evergreen.*

Prostanthera aspalathoides
Scarlet Mint Bush
Small rounded shrub from drier areas of New South Wales Victoria and South Australia. Fine, stiff, heathlike, 6mm linear leaves arranged in whorls along slender stems. Red or orange tubular flowers through spring, summer and sporadically during the year. Aspalathoides — resembling the genus Aspalathus. 75 × 100cm.

Prostanthera cuneata
Alpine Mint Bush
Semi-horizontal dwarf species widely distributed at higher altitudes in all eastern States except Queensland. Leaves small densely crowded, deep green, ovate to orbicular, cuneate or wedge-shaped at the base, leathery, to 6mm long, dotted with glands, strong minty aroma when crushed. Relatively large and conspicuous flowers white or palest mauve blotched purple inside, borne in leafy racemes through summer, almost covering the bush. Hardy, tolerating frost and snow. Cuneata — wedge-shaped, generally narrow end down. 1 × 1m.

Prostanthera cuneata 'Alpine Gold'
Resembles above but with narrow gold edge to the leaves giving the plant an attractive golden sheen. 1 × 1m.

Prostanthera incisa
Cut Leaf Mint Bush
Dainty compact dwarf from New South Wales. Leaves orbicular, conspicuously toothed and with pointed ends. Small broad-lobed, lilac or lavender flowers with contrasting deep violet calyx. Reasonably hardy. Incisa — margins deeply cut. 1.3 × 1m.

Prostanthera incisa 'Rosea'
More compact grower with dainty rounded leaves and masses of rich pink flowers in spring. 100 × 75cm.

Prostanthera nivea
Tall bushy shrub from Queensland, New South Wales and Victoria with four-angled stems. Leaves linear to 4cm, light green, margins involute or rolled inwards towards the top. Solitary 15mm snow-white flowers tinted blue appear in upper leaf axils, forming leafy 15cm racemes through spring. Nivea — snow white. 3 × 2m.

Prostanthera nivea var. induta
Erect compact grower from New South Wales with silvery grey linear leaves to 3cm long. Blue flowers blending to white borne profusely in spring. Outstanding foliage shrub and quite hardy. 2 × 1.3m.

Prostanthera ovalifolia
Oval Leaf Mint Bush
Elegant species from Queensland and New South Wales. Long arching branches with oval to ovate-lanceolate leaves, 12–15mm long, dull glaucous-green. Lavender-purple flowers in short terminal racemes, weighing down the branches in spring. Ovalifolia — oval-leaved. 2 × 1.5m.

Above: Protea neriifolia 'Silver Tips' **250**

Above: Protea magnifica 'Coronet Peak' *White Queen Protea* **250**
Below: Protea scholymocephela **250**

Above: Protea cynaroides *King Protea* **249**
Below: Protea neriifolia 'Limelight' **250**

Above: Prunus campanulata 'Superba' **252**

Above: Prunus Sato-zakura 'Kanzan' **253**
Below: Puya alpestris *Pineapple Shrub* **257**

Above: Prunus Satozakura 'Shirofugen **253**
Below: Pyracantha 'Brilliant' **257**

Above: Pseudopanax laetus **255**

Above: Pseudopanax lessonii, P crassifolius **255**
Below: Restio tetraphyllus **260**

Above: Pseudopanax lessonii 'Gold Splash' **255**
Below: Reinwardtia indica *Yellow Flax* **260**

Above: Rhododendron 'Anuschka' **261**

Above: Rhododendron 'Apricot Sherbert' **261**
Below: Rhododendron 'Buttermint' **264**

Above: Rhododendron 'Blue Diamond' **262**
Below: Rhododendron 'Buttermint' **264**

Prostanthera ovalifolia 'Variegata'
Resembles above but with leaves attractively variegated creamy yellow and green. Slower growing and more petite. 1.5 × 1m.

Prostanthera 'Poorinda Ballerina'
Erect shrub bearing masses of white flowers tinged lilac in spring. Considered to be a hybrid from P phylicifolia × P lasianthos, the latter a most adaptable species. Relatively hardy. 2 × 1.5m.

Prostanthera rhombea 'Pink Surprise'
Slender wiry shrub from New South Wales with 6mm, orbicular, sage-green aromatic leaves and masses of pink flowers in long racemes through spring. Dainty shrub with attractive leaves for rockery pockets or front borders. Rhombea — rhomboidal, diamond-shaped. 50 × 90cm.

Prostanthera rotundifolia
Rounded compact grower from New South Wales, Victoria and Tasmania. Leaves orbicular to ovate, to 10mm, dark green, paler beneath, margins finely dentate or crenate. Flowers purple violet or lilac in short loose terminal or axillary racemes through spring. Rotundifolia — with round leaves. 2 × 1.5m.

Prostanthera rotundifolia 'Rosea'
Somewhat resembles above, but more compact and with masses of clear pink flowers in spring. Considered one of the most beautiful Mint Bushes but often short-lived. Appreciates mulching or being alongside large rocks or other plants to avoid drying out in summer. 75 × 50cm.

Prostanthera saxicola var montana
Excellent spreading shrub , native to New South Wales and with dark green elliptical leaves to 12mm long. Masses of large white flowers during spring. Reliable grower, excellent ground cover or rockery subject. Saxicola — growing on rocks and mountains or pertaining to the mountains. 30cm × 1m.

PROTEA

The Protea genus is the most outstanding in the Proteaceae family. Name derived from Proteus, Greek mythological figure who, according to legend, changed into every imaginable shape to avoid capture. Proteas grow naturally only in South Africa, the majority of the 115 or so species concentrated into south western Cape areas, growing mainly in mountains which curve around the coastline from the Clanwilliam district to the region of Port Elizabeth. A few grow in the eastern ranges extending north into Natal and Transvaal, Zimbabwe and tropical Africa.

Proteas provide great quantities of magnificent blooms mainly through winter and spring, large flowerheads consisting of colourful bracts surrounding actual flowers, often referred to as stamens or anthers. Most Proteas grow naturally on mountainsides, so good drainage is one of the plant's basic requirements. They need maximum sunshine and slightly acid, loose free, not over-rich stony soil. Ideal locations are sunny banks or hillsides in open aspects with plenty of air circulation to quickly dry out foliage.

Most Proteas are hardy to light frost, withstand long periods of drought, but benefit from occasional deep watering directed at ground level rather than over foliage or flowers. Mulch lightly with peat moss or granulated bark, more to suppress weed growth than conserve moisture, thus avoiding deep cultivation which may damage surface roots. Pruning after flowering conserves energy reserves, removes unsightly seed heads, maintains good shape and encourages new growth. Don't hesitate to pick the blooms for display indoors. Use Proteas as lawn specimens, verge planting, mass planting on banks, amongst shrub borders or wherever a top rate flowering plant is called for.
Proteaceae. *All evergreen.*

Protea amplexicaulis
Spreading, low-growing plant with attractive foliage and unusual flowers. Leaves triangular to cordate, bluish-green with fine blood-red margins, stiff, leathery and almost glabrous, attached directly to stems without petioles. Young foliage deep red. Flowers hidden beneath branches and face downwards, about 7cm across with a circle of purple-black velvety bracts, creamy brown and smooth within, and dark central cone of hairy stamens sprinkled with yellow pollen. Densely covers the ground with foliage, suited to rock gardens or trailing over banks. Leaves and flowers highly valued for floral art. Amplexicaulis — stem clasping. 45 × 75cm.

Protea aurea 'Goodwood Red'
Shuttlecock Protea
New Zealand raised hybrid of the Cape Province species. Quickly forms a dense bushy shrub with glabrous ovate to oblong leaves. Buds long and pencil-like, opening to deep red shuttlecock-type flowers. Adaptable to wide-ranging soil and other conditions, tolerant of both frost and wind. 1–2 × 1.5m.

Protea 'Clark's Red'
New Zealand raised, extremely popular for garden display and cut blooms. Somewhat rangy when small, maturing to a neat bush with erect branches, densely clothed with ascending, smooth, glaucous, ovate leaves to 90 × 15mm. Smooth slender long-pointed, deep crimson buds appear early summer commencing to open midsummer. Flowerheads comprise bright cherry-red bracts in open cone formation to 9cm wide, filled with cherry-red stamens tipped with greyish wool. Valued for rich colour and quantity of bloom. 2 × 1.5m.

Protea compacta
Bot River Protea
Vigorous species with long slender branches well clothed with oblong to elliptic leaves to 120 × 25mm, leathery, minutely and invisibly pubescent, finely margined reddish orange. Flower-heads wineglass-shaped to 11 × 10cm comprising broad, translucent deep-pink velvety bracts curving inwards at the top enclosing a central mass of soft pink stamens. Blooms appear profusely at the top of each branch through autumn winter and spring. Stake and tip-prune when young to avoid a top-heavy plant. Compacta — compact or dense. 3 × 3m.

Protea cordata
Heart-Leaf Protea
Unusual species found in poor sandy soil from sea level to 850m, with underground rooting system and main stem from which arises numerous slender reddish stems with sparse, heart-shaped, leathery light green leaves and reddish veins. Young shoots pink or red. Actually grown for decorative leaves which last for weeks in floral arrangements. Stems remaining on the plant die back each year at the end of summer. During winter and spring, small brown stemless insignificant 3cm flower-heads appear at ground level or hidden beneath the soil. Requires poor sandy free-draining soil sheltered from frost. Cordata — heart-shaped. 75 × 90cm.

Protea cynaroides
King Protea
The largest of all Protea flowers, natural specimens reaching 30cm across. Forms a semi-spreading open plant with smooth, almost horizontal branches ascending near the tips. Leaves orbicular to elliptic, to 14 × 13cm, smooth leathery, with 4–18cm wiry reddish petioles or stems. Exquisite cone-shaped white-felted terminal buds

burst open to immense flower-heads comprising pointed satin-pink bracts enclosing a silky peak of hairy stamens, coming to a point in the centre. Blooms appear autumn through spring. Colour varies pale to deep pink to red. Cynaroides — resembling cynara, Globe Artichoke. 1 × 1.5m   **236**

Protea 'Franciscan Hybrid'
Forms a large bushy shrub, remaining dense and well-foliaged with minimum attention. Leaves oblong or lanceolate to 14 × 5cm, light to medium green, slightly pubescent and soft-textured. Magnificent silvery flowerheads to 15 × 10cm, comprise rich-pink bracts blending to delicate cream at the base, covered with silvery down and central flower mass shaded deep wine-red. Flowering season late winter through spring. Excellent as a garden shrub and ideal for cut blooms. Adaptable to wide-ranging soils. Possible hybrid from P compacta × P magnifica discovered near Wellington and named in 1982 to mark the 800th anniversary of the birth of St Francis of Assisi. 2 × 1.5m.

Protea grandiceps
Peach Protea
Most beautiful Protea forming a low open bush with sturdy stems covered with close-set obovate, glaucous green, leathery, red-edged upward-curving leaves to 130 × 85mm. Erect terminal flower-heads to 10cm across and 15cm deep comprising closely-set, peach or coral red bracts incurved at the top fringed with long silky white or reddish purple hairs, enclosing masses of hairy white stamens. Blooms appear late spring through midsummer. Grandiceps — large headed. 1.5 × 1.5m.

Protea lepidocarpodendron
Black Bearded Protea
Distinct Protea with subtle beauty. Easily grown medium bush with narrowly oblong leaves to 115 × 20mm, deep green with a touch of red on the margins. Slender 12cm flower-heads comprising cream or pale-green bracts tipped with heavy black fur and contrasting reddish brown overlapping outer bracts. Flowers don't open wide. Protect from frost. Lepidocarpodendron — literally 'scale fruited tree' but reason obscure. 1.5 × 1.5m.

Protea magnifica
Queen Protea
Regarded as the showiest of all proteas with immense flower heads to 15cm across, second only to the King Protea. Semi-spreading growth, leaves oblong to lanceolate, to 10 × 5cm, grey green with faint red margin, covered with soft hairs. Flower-head comprises numerous incurving rosy pink satiny bracts tipped with powder-puff down, filled with a mass of soft white hairs culminating in a pointed black woolly centre, appearing late winter through early summer. Not the easiest to grow but worth every attempt. Syn P barbigera. Magnifica — great, splendid, magnificent. 1.5 × 1.5m.   **236**

Protea magnifica 'Coronet Peak'
White Queen Protea
Immense goblet-shaped blooms with delicately shaded creamy white silky bracts tipped with white fluffy wool and snowy white soft cottony centre terminating in a black central zone. Incredible flower. Syn P magnifica 'Alba'. 1.5 × 1.5m.   **245**

Protea neriifolia
Oleander-Leaved Protea
Forms a large well groomed bush with erect stems, well covered with narrowly oblong leaves to 18 × 3cm, deep to bright green and minutely pubescent. Flower heads to 13 × 8cm, comprising pink satiny bracts curving inwards at the top, trimmed with fine black fur and a central mass of pink stamens tinged reddish purple, borne prolifically autumn through winter and into spring. Neriifolia — leaves like oleander. 2.5 × 2m.

Protea neriifolia 'Alba'
Similar form foliage and flower but with glistening creamy white bracts tinged green, trimmed with fine black fur. 2.5 × 2m.

Protea neriifolia 'Green Ice'
Magnificent flower-heads tapering towards the base, slightly incurved at the top. Bracts palest green at the base gradually shading to silvery green and tipped with fine black fur. Central cluster of woolly black stamens. 1.5 × 1.5m.

Protea neriifolia 'Limelight'
Typical neriifolia vigour. Flower-heads of creamy-lime bracts trimmed with black fur tinged purple. 2 × 2m.   **245**

Protea neriifolia 'Pink Ice'
Australian raised seedling of great merit. Rich deep-pink flower-heads with incurved tips trimmed with white fur and large central pink woolly cone. Compact bushy plant, free flowering over a long season. Hardy to −7°C, although with risk of bud blemish. New Zealand synonym P 'Sylvan Pink'. 1.5 × 1.5m.

Protea neriifolia 'Ruby Glow'
Selected richer coloured form with deep-red silky-sheened bracts tipped with black woolly 'ears'. Vigorous upright bushy grower. 1.8 × 1.8m.

Protea neriifolia 'Ruby'
Superb cultivar, well-sculptured blooms, with incurving satiny rich-watermelon pink bracts frosted white towards the tips and central zone of fine black fur. Erect grower, winter blooming, excellent for cut blooms. 2 × 2m.

Protea neriifolia 'Silver Tips'
Attractive flower-heads tapering to the base and slightly incurved at the top. Bracts bright silvery pink tipped with fine silvery-white hairs arranged like eyelashes with a tuft of black. 1.5 × 1.5m.   **245**

Protea neriifolia 'Snowcrest'
Exquisite flower-heads of soft rose pink satiny bracts tipped with snow white fur with tufts of black and soft yellow central cone. 2 × 2m.   **236**

Protea pudens
Ground Rose
Procumbent spreading shrub with trailing stems. Crowded linear grey-green leaves to 100 × 5mm. Terminal bell-shaped 8 × 6cm flower-heads comprising reddish brown to deep dusky rose bracts with central cluster of hairy white, black-tipped stamens, borne during winter on 12–20cm stems which lay on the ground. Pudens — modest or shame-faced. 40 × 100cm.

Protea punctata
Baby Protea
Forms a substantial rounded bush with obovate to oblanceolate, bluish green, thick leathery rough-textured leaves to 55 × 25mm, touched light red around the margins. Charming wide-open starry flowers comprise deep-pink petal-like bracts with a central cluster of pink stamens intermingled with creamy pink hairs autumn through winter. Excellent for floral art. Slim 65mm buds appear in great quantities. Pick just as bracts begin to open. They'll continue opening in water unlike most Proteas which remain the same after picking. Punctata — dotted with minute translucent impressions. 2.5 × 2.5m.

Protea scholymocephela
Small Green Protea
Neat little shrub with subtle charm. Forms a mass of erect slender branchlets with linear to spathulate leaves to 90 × 6mm, greyish green and smooth, tapering towards the base. Opening from small rounded buds, wide-open, somewhat flattened, 45mm flower-heads comprising smooth greenish bracts and loose central zone of creamy stamens appear autumn through early summer. This species highly valued for floral art.

Scholymocephela — from scolymus, a type of thistle and cephale, head. 1 × 1m. **245**

Protea venusta
Swartberg Protea
Hardy species found above the snowline in the Swartberg mountains of south western Cape. Low spreading plant with thick underground root and branching stems from which grow long prostrate branches to 4–5m curving upwards at the tips. Leaves oblanceolate to 65 × 20mm, bluish green, thick and leathery. Terminal flower-heads about 9cm across when open comprise ivory-white, scale-like bracts shading to deep rose pink where exposed and a central tuft of pure white, satin-like stamens tipped with white wool, prolific through summer. Ideal in a large well-drained rockery, on sloping banks etc in full sun. Venusta — handsome, charming. 1 × 5m.

PRUMNOPITYS

A genus of about ten species of coniferous trees from South America, New Zealand, eastern Australia and New Caledonia named from the Greek *prumne*, stern and *pitys*, pine. Genus isolated from Podocarpus on the basis of leaf structure, absence of an enlarged basal receptacle in the fruit, and leaves that are softer and not so sharp. See under Podocarpus for cultural details.
Podocarpaceae. *All evergreen.*

Prumnopitys ferrugineus
Miro
Handsome forest tree found throughout New Zealand, with almost black hammer-marked bark and linear dark green leaves set in two rows on branchlets resembling a yew. Male and female flowers appear on separate trees. Female flowers succeeded by attractive 2cm, bright red plum-like fruit covered when first ripe with a waxy bloom. Native pigeons overeat the fruit, get fat and lazy through over-indulgence and very thirsty from the taste and odour of turpentine. Old time Maoris exploited this by providing troughs of water complete with snares for easy capture. Slow growing and handsome in juvenile form. Ferrugineus — rust coloured. Syn Podocarpus ferrugineus. 5 × 3m.

Prumnopitys taxifolia
Matai, Black Pine
Found in lowland or hilly forests of New Zealand's North and South Islands. Close relative of P ferrugineus but differs with smaller leaves and almost black rounded

fruit. Somewhat straggly as a juvenile but handsome as it matures. Yields valuable timber with great strength, smooth even texture varying from light to deep brown. Syn Podocarpus spicatus. 4 × 3m.

PRUNUS

A genus of over 400 species mostly from temperate regions of the Northern Hemisphere and South America named from the Latin *prunus*, a plum tree. The numerous cultivated hybrids and cultivars embrace both ornamental and fruiting cherries, peaches, plums, almonds, apricots and nectarines, giving within the family almost limitless choice for beauty or utility. Only ornamental Prunus are dealt with here, all noteworthy for bare branch pattern, quantity and colour of flower and some for colourful foliage. Give them adequate room to show off their exquisite loveliness. Use to break hard lines, lighten an overdose of green, or as feature specimens.

Prunus need plenty of light and sunshine for maximum flower production, protection from late or early frost and shelter from prevailing wind especially during the flowering period. While they grow in most average garden soils, deeply worked, free-draining, organically enriched, moisture-retentive soil will ensure healthy growth. Mulch freely and keep moist during dry periods. A balanced fertilizer early spring will maintain vigour.

Rosaceae. *All deciduous except P lusitanica.*

Flowering Almonds
Flowering Almonds from central and northern China bear no resemblance to those grown for nuts. They're mostly dwarf, multi branched, spreading shrubs with closely set flowers resembling light fluffy pompon chrysanthemums. Use them in shrub borders in average conditions. Pick flowers freely for indoors and prune heavily as soon as blooming is finished.

Listed varieties — × amygdalo-persica 'Pollardii', triloba 'Plena'.

Flowering Apricots
Usually the first blossom trees to announce the arrival of spring, and could be the longest lived of flowering fruit trees, eventually developing into gnarled picturesque specimens. Pruning important for good flowering habits and form. After the first year's growth,

cut all young branches back to 15cm. Then cut back to half way each year straight after flowering.

Listed variety: mume 'The Geisha'.

Flowering Cherries
Among this group you'll find a type for every purpose — upright columns, spreaders, weepers etc, in a wide range of glorious colours. Pruning of any kind seldom necessary, but if shaping or reduction in size becomes unavoidable, carry out late summer to give wounds time to heal before winter. Grow in all types of deep well drained soil. Hybrid Japanese flowering cherries listed under the specific title *Sato-zakura*, a Group which includes cultivars of complex parentage.

Listed varieties: 'Accolade', campanulata 'Felix Jury', campanulata 'Okame', campanulata 'Pink Cloud', campanulata 'Superba', × hillieri 'Spire', incisa, lusitanica, nipponica, padus, Sato-zakura 'Amanogawa', Sato-zakura 'Ariake', Sato-zakura 'Hokusai', Sato-zakura 'Kanzan', Sato-zakura 'Kofugen', Sato-zakura 'Ojochin', Sato-zakura 'Pink Perfection', Sato-zakura 'Shimidsu Sakura', Sato-zakura 'Shiro-fugen', Sato-zakura 'Shirotae', Sato-zakura 'Taihaku', Sato-zakura 'Takasago', Sato-zakura 'Ukon', serrula, speciosa subhirtella 'Autumnalis Rosea', subhirtella 'Fukubana', × yedoensis, × yedoensis 'Awanui', × yedoensis 'Chinese Brocade'.

Weeping Cherries
Few deciduous shrubs can match the charm of weeping cherries. Their cascading blossom display is one of the most exciting spring events. Never overcrowd them but treat them as individuals. Hardy, grow in most reasonable soils, tolerate considerable moisture but prefer good drainage. Stake until root development is adequate for self support.

Listed varieties: Sato-zakura 'Kikushidare Sakura', subhirtella 'Falling Snow', subhirtella 'Pendula', × yedoensis 'Shidare Yoshino'.

Flowering Peach
Noted for intensity of colour and mass of bloom. Every branch becomes a solid mass of colour. They perform with little attention, but expect more luxuriant growth and better floral displays if stems pruned back to 20cm stubs each year after flowering. Such pruning helps prevent Leaf Curl disease, but spraying may be necessary at bud-burst stage for effective control.

Listed varieties — persica 'Cascade', persica 'Helen Borcher', persica 'Iceberg', persica 'Klara Mayer', persica 'Windle Weeping'.

Flowering Plums

Ornamental plums provide year round beauty of stem, foliage and flower, their dark coloured foliage providing dramatic colour contrasts. They grow in almost any reasonable soil and prefer full sun for maximum leaf colour. Prune old flowered stems after blossom-time and spray to control caterpillar and pear slug.

Listed varieties — × blireiana, cerasifera 'Elvins', cerasifera 'Nigra', cerasifera 'Thundercloud', cerasifera 'Wrightii'.

Prunus 'Accolade'
Flowering Cherry

Hybrid from two oriental cherries P sargentii × P subhirtella. Outstanding small tree with spreading branches and compact rounded form. Leaves green through spring and summer, orange-red in autumn. Semi-double rich-pink 4cm flowers with frilled margins mass produced in pendulous clusters early spring. 6 × 5m.

Prunus × amygdalo-persica 'Pollardii'
Pollard Almond

Vigorous hybrid from P dulcis × P persica raised in Victoria. Forms a robust tree with leaves lanceolate to 13 × 4cm, light green, margins roughly serrated. A profusion of 5cm fragrant soft rose-pink single flowers with stamens and central zone deepening to red. Branches cut in bud stage open up indoors and last a week. Tolerant of hot, dry conditions, but include when spraying peaches for Leaf Curl. Amygdalo — from the Greek for almond. Persica — of Persia. 4 × 3m.

Prunus × blireiana
Double Rose Cherry Plum

Beautiful hybrid from P cerasifera 'Atropurpurea' × P mume. Forms a graceful tree with long slender branches. Leaves oval to 6cm, bronze red or coppery purple at first, greenish bronze through summer. Fragrant, rose pink, 3cm double flowers appear profusely with the foliage in spring. Fruit very few if any. Excellent for garden display and picking for indoors. 3.5 × 2.5m.

Prunus campanulata 'Felix Jury'
Formosan Cherry, Taiwan Cherry

Small pyramidal tree with purple-brown bark, densely branched and bushy with graceful slender habit presenting an arresting sight in full bloom. Leaves elliptic to 11 × 8cm, deep green above, paler beneath, margins double-serrated. 'Felix Jury' is a hybrid from P campanulata with larger carmine-red pendent bell-flowers gracefully suspended on every branch. Blooms a little later then campanulata but early spring before leaves appear. Blossoms full of nectar

to the delight of birds. Species native to Formosa and southern Japan. Campanulata — bell shaped. 4 × 3m.

Prunus campanulata 'Okame'
Hybrid Japanese Cherry

Beautiful hybrid from P incisa × P campanulata forming a broadly ovate bush with small leaves, light green to bronze at first, deepening through summer, bright orange in autumn. Bright carmine-rose bell-shaped flowers with fringed edges, borne in pendent clusters covering leafless branches early spring. Commences blooming when quite young. Good for smaller gardens. 2.5 × 2m.

Prunus campanulata 'Pink Cloud'
Hybrid Formosan Cherry

Hybrid cultivar raised by Felix Jury forming a small neat round-headed specimen with spreading branches. Produces late winter a profusion of soft-pink single flowers with clusters of erect petaloids. 4 × 3m.

Prunus campanulata 'Superba'
Formosan Cherry

More robust grower with slightly larger brilliant claret-red bells smothering every branch late winter. 5 × 3m.   **246**

Prunus cerasifera 'Elvins'
Flowering Plum

Species includes the fruiting Cherry Plum. This ornamental cultivar originated in Victoria, Australia. Forms a bushy shrub, every branch literally smothered in spring with white tinged rose-pink flowers followed by small dark-red fruit. Cerasifera — bearing cherry-like fruit. 3 × 3m.

Prunus cerasifera 'Nigra'
Purple Leaf Cherry Plum

Leaves dark purple-black as they unfold, colour persisting through summer and autumn until they fall, leaving a tracery of black stems through winter. Stems wreathed during spring with small but pretty, single pink flowers. Amongst the finest dark foliaged trees. Perfect for dramatic contrasts. 4 × 2.5m.

Prunus cerasifera 'Thundercloud'
Purple Leaf Cherry Plum

More rounded form of 'Nigra', with dark coppery to deep smoky purple red foliage. Flowers light pink to white and with seasonal variations will produce crops of red fruit. 4 × 3m.

Prunus cerasifera 'Wrightii'
Flowering Plum

New Zealand raised hybrid displaying deeper colours of flowering almonds with bronzy cerasifera foliage. Large single

saucer-shaped flowers, brightest rose pink with prominent stamens. Foliage purple red and quite glossy. 3.5 × 2.5m.

Prunus × hillieri 'Spire'
Flowering Cherry

Hybrid species from P incisa × P sargentii. Forms a densely branched tree. New shoots red, leaves bronze in spring, richly coloured in autumn. Cultivar 'Spire' becomes a cloud of soft pink single flowers in spring. Narrow form makes it excellent for street planting. 5 × 2m.

Prunus incisa
Fuji Cherry

The Japanese species is a small tree, often with pubescent young branchlets. Leaves obovate to ovate, to 5 × 3cm, pubescent above and veins beneath, margins doubly and sharply serrated, brilliantly coloured in autumn. Pink buds open to small white single flowers produced freely very early spring, followed by 8mm ovoid purple-black fruit. Incisa — deeply and irregularly cut. 2 × 1.5m.

Prunus lusitanica
Portugal Laurel Cherry

Native to Spain and Portugal. Forms a large evergreen shrub or small tree with smooth stems and reddish branchlets. Leaves oblong-ovate to 12cm long, dark green glossy, paler beneath, margins shallowtoothed, reddish petioles or stalks. Foliage somewhat resembles Photinia serrulata. Dull white hawthorn-scented 12mm flowers in slender 15cm racemes late spring and summer, followed in autumn by 8mm conical fruits turning dark purple. Good specimen tree and quite hardy. Lusitanica — from Portugal (Lusitania). Evergreen. 5 × 4m.

Prunus mume 'The Geisha'
Japanese Apricot

Species native to southern Japan where many outstanding cultivars have been developed. Forms a rounded bush with lustrous branchlets. Leaves rounded to broadly ovate to 10cm, margins usually double serrated. Delightfully fragrant, claret rose flowers with numerous central stamens, appear profusely on bare stems mid winter. Amongst the first Prunus to flower, valuable for winter garden colour and artistic floral arrangements. 3 × 2.5m.

Prunus nipponica
Japanese Alpine Cherry

Forms a dense rounded bushy shrub with chestnut brown branches. Leaves obovate to 80 × 45mm, tapering to a long tail-like appendage, green through summer, yellow and red in autumn, margins doubly and sharply serrated, glabrous above, paler and slightly downy beneath. Buds pink, opening to 25mm, blush pink single blossoms in pendent corymbs in spring followed by 8mm, globose, purple-black fruit in autumn. 3 × 3m.

Prunus padus
Bird Cherry
Native to Europe, Western Asia, Korea and Japan. Large but tidy tree with dark brown bark, erect branches pendent at the tips and finely pubescent young branchlets becoming glabrous. Leaves obovate to elliptic, to 9 × 6cm, margins sharply serrated. White 15mm almond-scented single flowers in 12cm finely pubescent racemes in spring, followed by globose, pea-sized, black, bitter fruit. Padus — Greek name for a wild cherry. 5 × 4m.

Prunus persica 'Cascade'
Weeping Blossom Peach
Outstanding weeping tree with the same glistening ice white, fully double blossoms as Iceberg, borne on gracefully weeping stems cascading from a 2m standard. 2.5 × 1.5m.

Prunus persica 'Helen Borcher'
Flowering Peach
From America. Extra large 6cm deep-pink double blossoms. Late flowering. 3.5 × 3m.

Prunus persica 'Iceberg'
Flowering Peach
Glistening white large fully double blossoms appear in great profusion. 3.5 × 3m.

Prunus persica 'Klara Mayer'
Forms a multi-branched bush. Large double peach-pink 4cm flowers followed by pale green fruit tinted red. 3 × 2.5m.

Prunus persica 'Windle Weeping'
Natural vigorous weeping habit forming an umbrella crown and broad foliage. Masses of purplish pink semi-double, cup-shaped flowers followed by edible fruit. Stake and train from an early age. 3 × 3m.

Prunus Sato-zakura 'Amanogawa'
Upright Flowering Cherry
Small columnar tree with erect branches, often referred to as Lombardy Poplar Cherry. Young foliage greenish yellow, red and yellow in autumn. Dense clusters of fragrant, single or semi-double, pale-pink flowers with deeper margins, freely produced mid to late spring. Useful accent specimen where broader species may overcrowd. Amanogawa — milky way or celestial river. 6 × 1.3m.

Prunus Sato-zakura 'Ariake'
Somewhat resembles 'Kanzan' with upright arching branches. Leaves tinted bronze when young. Pink buds open to large single 6cm flowers, blush pink at first fading to white. Ariake — dawn. Syn P 'Candida'. 4 × 2.5m.

Prunus Sato-zakura 'Hokusai'
Flowering Cherry
Vigorous wide spreading, flat-topped tree. Leaves bronze at first, turning green through summer, orange-red in autumn. Branches covered in spring by immense clusters of large semi-double, shell-pink fragrant flowers. Hokusai — for Japanese artist Hokusai Katsu shuka. 5 × 4m.

Prunus Sato-zakura 'Kanzan'
Flowering Cherry
Narrow vase form with ascending branch structure. Leaves with short-toothed serrations, bronze in spring, green through summer, red orange and yellow in autumn. Buds maroon opening to large fully double 3–4cm, rich cyclamen-pink flowers often tinged blue, produced in large showy pendent clusters of 3–5 during spring. Floral display enhanced by coppery new leaves. Syn P Sekiyama, Kwanzan, Purpurascens. 6 × 3m. **246**

Prunus Sato-zakura 'Kiku-shidare Sakura'
Cheal's Weeping Cherry
Beautiful spring display of bright rose-pink, 3cm fully double serrated and frilled flowers in dense clusters on steeply pendulous branches which weep gracefully to the ground. Grafted on 2m stems, a mature specimen in full bloom, contrasted against green lawn or foliage a most impressive sight. Leaves lanceolate, pale green at first, darker green through summer, yellow and orange in autumn. 2.5 × 2m.

Prunus Sato-zakura 'Kofugen'
Somewhat resembles 'Kanzan' but forming a broad, flat-topped spreading crown. Rounded leaves, margins finely toothed, coppery-red when young, yellow in autumn. Large rose-pink double flowers in long pendulous clusters, profusely late spring. Syn P 'Fugenzo'. 4 × 3m.

Prunus Sato-zakura 'Ojochin'
Large Lantern Cherry
Distinguished by stout stiffly erect robust growth forming a broad rounded crown. Large broadly elliptic leaves, tough and leathery when mature, bronze at first, orange red in autumn. Flowers pink in bud, single, 5cm, blush pink, borne in long stalked clusters to eight, late spring. Ojochin — large lantern. Syn Senriko. 4.5 × 3.5m.

Prunus Sato-zakura 'Pink Perfection'
Flowering Cherry
Erect spreading vase-shaped tree. Young foliage bronze, green through summer, orange in autumn. Fully double, 45mm flowers with frilled margins, bright rosy pink in bud, opening clear pink, carried in long pendulous clusters through spring. Striking English cultivar, presumably a hybrid from Shimidsu Sakura × Kanzan with intermediate growth habit. 6 × 4m.

Prunus Sato-zakura 'Shimidsu Sakura'
Flowering Cherry
Among the most beautiful, growing into a small spreading tree with gracefully arching branches, forming a broad flattened crown. Young foliage pale bronze, green through summer, orange-red in autumn. Large 5cm fimbriated semi-double flowers, pink in bud, opening palest pink, fading pure snow white in 20cm pendulous corymbs of 5–6 late spring. Syn P Okumiyaku. Shimidsu Sakura — Moon low nearby a pine tree. 4 × 5m.

Prunus Sato-zakura 'Shiro-fugen'
Flowering Cherry
Strong growing, wide spreading flat-topped tree with tiered horizontal branches and dark brown bark. Leaves coppery bronze at first, green in summer, orange-red in autumn. Fully double flowers pink in bud, opening palest pink, becoming pure white, finally pale lavender pink with darker centre, borne prolifically in loose pendent clusters very late in spring. The latest Cherry to bloom. Shiro-fugen — white god. 5 × 5m. **246**

Prunus Sato-zakura 'Shirotae'
Mount Fuji Cherry
Forms a beautiful artistic small flat-topped tree with wide-spread tiered horizontal branches, sometimes pendulous to the ground. Leaves deeply serrated with distinctive fringed appearance, golden yellow in autumn. Large snow white single and semi-double flowers to 55mm, with hawthorn fragrance, in long drooping clusters against a background of soft-green new foliage in spring. Syn Hosokawa, Mount Fuji. Shirotae — snow white. 5 × 5m.

Prunus Sato-zakura 'Taihaku'
Great White Cherry
Reputed to be the most robust and largest flowering cherry. Forms a tall spreading tree with rounded crown, bark spotted with prominent brown lenticels. Leaves large to 20 × 12cm, reddish bronze at first, bright green through summer, golden-yellow and orange in autumn. Large single saucer-shaped, pure dazzling white, slightly fragrant, 6–7cm flowers, enhanced by rich coppery red young foliage in spring. A

spectacular white blossom tree. Syn Tai Haku. Taihaku — great white cherry. 8 × 6m.

Prunus Sato-zakura 'Takasago'
Flowering Cherry
Small slow growing spreading cherry with silky downy young foliage light green at first, bronzy green through summer, deep red in autumn. Buds unusual mushroom pink, opening to semi double, pale pink flowers in large clusters during spring. 4 × 4m.

Prunus Sato-zakura 'Ukon'
Flowering Cherry
Robust tree with stiffly erect branches in vase or funnel-form. Leaves bronze in spring, green through summer, orange red to plum red in autumn. Large 45mm semi double flowers, primrose or sulphur-yellow tinted green borne freely in large clusters amongst new foliage in spring. Ukon — yellowish. 5 × 5m.

Prunus serrula
Ornamental Cherry, Birch Bark Tree
Small vigorous species from west China, prized for glistening, polished reddish brown, mahogany-like, peeling bark. Forms a rounded tree. Leaves lanceolate to 75 × 9mm, margins finely serrated, green through summer, yellow in autumn. Small white single blossoms appear with new foliage in spring. Serrula — with small saw-like teeth. 6 × 5m.

Prunus speciosa
Oshima Cherry
Loosely branched tree with pale greyish fawn bark. Leaves elliptic-ovate to narrow obovate, to 10 × 6cm, bronzy green during the growing period, midrib and petiole sparsely pubescent at first, later glabrous. White bell-shaped to tubular fragrant flowers in lax corymbs through spring. Speciosa — showy. 5 × 4m.

Prunus subhirtella 'Autumnalis Rosea'
Pink Spring Cherry
Forms a rounded tree with widely ascending branches. Leaves ovate to lanceolate, margins deeply serrated, red yellow and orange in autumn. Semi-double almond-scented flowers, pink in bud, opening soft pink, deeper in the centre, borne intermittently in dainty clusters through winter and spring. Good for winter floral decoration. Subhirtella — somewhat hairy. 5 × 5m.

Prunus subhirtella 'Falling Snow'
White Spring Cherry
Magnificent slender weeping tree building up tiers of arching and gracefully pendent branches decked in small snowy white single blooms. Better in warm temperate areas. Early to mid season. 2.5 × 2m.

Prunus subhirtella 'Fukubana'
Spring Cherry
Striking small tree with broadly ascending branches. Buds almost red opening to semi-double deep rose-pink flowers with deeply notched petals during spring. 3 × 3m.

Prunus subhirtella 'Pendula'
Weeping Rosebud Cherry
Slender willowy arching gracefully pendent branches build up tier upon tier, becoming completely clothed with sprays of dainty, pale-pink single flowers, giving a delightful fountain or mushroom effect. Branching pattern of mature specimens resemble a miniature weeping willow. Also a deeper coloured form — P subhirtella 'Pendula Rosea' 2.5 × 2m.

Prunus triloba 'Plena'
Chinese Almond
Bushy erect low growing shrub with beautiful 25mm, multi-toned pink, double flowers, tightly packed on angular branches from base to tip. Leaves ovate or obovate to 65 × 30mm, three lobed, (triloba), irregularly and coarsely toothed. 1.3 × 1m.

Prunus × yedoensis
Yoshino Cherry, Tokyo Cherry
Hybrid species from P subhirtella × P speciosa. Small broadly upright tree with smooth bark. Leaves elliptic to 12cm long, doubly serrated, vivid green, paler beneath, orange-red in autumn. Pure white, 35mm, almond-scented single flowers in ascending racemes of 5–6 early spring followed by globose, black pea-sized fruit. Yedoensis — from Yedo (now Tokyo). 5 × 4m.

Prunus × yedoensis 'Awanui'
Hybrid Yoshino Cherry
Erect vase-form, producing great masses of large fragrant white single blossoms opening from soft-pink buds mid spring. Raised in New Plymouth, New Zealand. 5 × 8m.

Prunus × yedoensis 'Chinese Brocade'
Hybrid Yoshino Cherry
Extremely free flowering selected cultivar raised in New Zealand. Large single almond scented pearly white flowers, the edges of the petals shaded pink, opening from pink buds. 4 × 6m.

Prunus × yedoensis 'Shidare Yoshino'
Yoshino Weeping Cherry
Acclaimed for consistent year round garden performance. Grafted atop a 2.5m stem, slender branches weep gracefully to the ground, crowded in spring with white to palest pink, wide open single blossoms providing a magnificent display for weeks. Large elliptic rich green leaves clothe the structure through summer, making a natural sun umbrella. In autumn the leaves turn gold orange and red, holding well into winter. Picturesque tracery of naked branches in winter. Syn P × yedoensis 'Purpendens'. 2.5 × 2.5m.

PSEUDOPANAX

A genus of about 20 species of trees or shrubs from New Zealand, Tasmania and Chile named from the Greek *pseudo* false, and *panax*, literally having the appearance of panax. About fourteen species endemic to New Zealand. Unique form and handsome foliage have given them a prominent place in modern landscaping with types to fulfil a range of functions whether planted out or in containers.

Perfect where tall vertical plants, singly or in groups are required by entryways or to silhouette against a background of glass, brick, wood or stone. With slender stems and sparse angular foliage, Lancewood especially creates exciting garden drama. Undoubtedly better as juveniles, a stage which may last up to ten years. Generally hardy to −10°C, grow freely in sun or shade and under adverse climatic or cultural conditions. Ideally, plant in deeply worked, free-draining, fertile soil.

Araliaceae. *All evergreen.*

Pseudopanax arboreus
Five Finger
One of the more common New Zealand natives, abundant throughout lowland forests of both North and South Island. Forms a small rounded tree with open habit and spreading framework of slender stems. Large leaves on stout petioles or stalks divided into five or seven radiating oval-oblong leaflets, deep green, glossy, margins serrated. Rounded clusters of small greenish flowers, attractive to bees followed by decorative bunches of rounded black berries enjoyed by birds. Extremely hardy. Syn Neopanax arboreus. Arboreus — growing in tree-like form. 3 × 3m.

Pseudopanax chathamicus
Hoho
From lowland forests of Chatham Islands. Eventually forms a small tree with stout ascending branches and bushy crown. Juvenile leaves broad-lanceolate or oblong lanceolate, to 15 × 3cm, somewhat leathery,

margins coarsely or finely toothed, ascending or spreading, rather than deflexed as in P crassifolius. Adult leaves oblanceolate or obovate-oblong, to 20 × 4.5cm, dull and dark green above, paler beneath, veins prominent, thick and leathery, margins coarsely serrated or toothed toward the tip. Not as effective for landscaping as P crassifolius although foliage is brighter. Chathamicus — of the Chatham Islands. 4 × 1m.

Pseudopanax crassifolius
Lancewood, Horoeka
Grows naturally from North Cape to Bluff, an extraordinary plant, usually with single erect, very flexible stem from which long thin leathery leaves hang at odd angles. Juvenile leaves at first ovate or lanceolate, leathery with serrated margins. They soon attain the next stage, leaves deflexed, narrow-linear to 75 × 2cm, with prominent midrib, margins shallowly toothed, varying from reddish bronze to deep-green, occasionally with lighter blotches, light brown beneath. A plant with undamaged tip will grow erect in rocket form to three or four metres before branching.

Adults have little or no resemblance to the juvenile form, becoming round-headed with thick linear to lanceolate leaves, 8–20 × 2–4cm, dull dark-green, margins entire or serrated. Inconspicuous flowers in large terminal umbels to 30cm across, summer through autumn, followed by 5mm black shiny fruit ripe the following year.

Excellent focal point in rock or feature gardens, silhouetted against glass, brick, stone or wood. No shrub border complete without at least one. Lancewood creates garden drama either singly or in groups of varying heights. Crassifolius — thick-leaved. 4 × 1m. **247**

Pseudopanax discolor
Found in lowland forests of the North Island from Mangonui to Coromandel Peninsula and on Great and Little Barrier Islands. Forms a handsome multi-branched bushy shrub with slender branchlets. Leaves divided into three to five obovate to obovate-lanceolate, coarsely serrated leaflets to 75 × 30mm, dull yellow-green or bronze. Discolor — two different and usually distinct colours. 1.5 × 1m.

Pseudopanax discolor 'Rangatira'
The finest form, with deep old-bronze coloured foliage, most intense during colder months but attractive all year. 1.5 × 1m.

Pseudopanax ferox
Savage Lancewood
Although found in both North and South Islands the species is comparatively rare.

Similar form to Lancewood, but with denser, stiffly pendent juvenile leaves to 50cm long, pale grey with deeper blotches, distinctly lobed or toothed along the entire margin. Adult leaves have similar appearance but less than 15cm long. Flowers appearing early summer resemble Lancewood, but fruits larger and ripe in autumn. Ferox — fierce or dangerous, referring to hooked teeth of juvenile leaves. 3m × 60cm.

Pseudopanax laetus
Five Finger
Handsome New Zealand shrub found only in the North Island from Coromandel Peninsula to Taranaki. Grows rapidly to a bushy multi- branched specimen. Large leathery deep-green glossy leaves comprising 5–7 obovate leaflets to 30 × 12cm, margins narrowly serrated and with thin purple line. Petioles and midribs purplish red. Laetus — bright or pleasing. Syn Neopanax laetus. 3 × 1.5m. **247**

Pseudopanax lessonii
Houpara
Found from Three Kings Islands to Poverty Bay mainly in exposed coastal areas. Natural species seldom cultivated, replaced by hybrids from P lessonii × P crassifolius which come in a wide variety of leaf forms and colours, classified as Lessonii Hybrids. Many named cultivars are propagated, but often a batch of unnamed seedlings offers interesting variations. Named for Lesson, a French officer from d'Urville's corvette, who in 1824 discovered the plant in the Bay of Islands. **247**

The following cultivars appear with the lessonii epithet for simplicity.

Pseudopanax lessonii 'Adiantifolius'
Handsome shrub with erect stems. Distinctive glossy bright-green palmate leaves to 135 × 125mm, with 3–5 upward pointing lobes, leathery, irregularly serrated near the tips. Foliage somewhat resembles Adiantum or maidenhair fern, suggesting the specific epithet. Excellent as a garden shrub and in containers. 3 × 1m.

Pseudopanax lessonii 'Black Jack'
Upright bushy grower developing rounded crown with maturity. Leaves deepest green at first, intensifying in autumn, almost black in winter. Quite hardy and excellent in containers. 2.5 × 1.8m.

Pseudopanax lessonii 'Black Ruby'
Excellent form with three or five-lobed leaves at first bronzy green, turning rich black-red as winter approaches, retaining this colour through early summer. 1.5 × 1m.

Pseudopanax lessonii 'Copper Glow'
Somewhat resembles 'Purpureum' but with more copper-bronze winter colour. 2 × 1m.

Pseudopanax lessonii 'Cyril Watson'
Distinct low-growing cultivar with rather compact bushy habit. Sturdy branches mostly erect with two leaf forms — elliptic to narrow-ovate to 8 × 5cm, either simple or with two small lobes, shallow-serrated margins, and, broadly palmate to 14 × 16cm, with 3–5 broad lobes to midway, margins coarsely toothed and serrated. Both leaf types very thick and leathery with prominent midrib and veins, fresh-green and glossy. Young growth slightly frost tender, otherwise hardy.

Named for a long-serving staff member of New Plymouth nurserymen, Duncan and Davies. 3 × 1m.

Pseudopanax lessonii 'Gold Splash'
Extraordinary foliage shrub with erect multi-branched bushy habit. Foliage leathery, three to five-lobed, glossy, green heavily splashed bright golden yellow, appearing as yellow leaves flecked and splashed green. Outstanding variegated shrub for garden or container. Originated at the base of an old Pseudopanax lessonii stump which had been cut off at ground level. 3 × 1m. **247**

Pseudopanax lessonii 'Landscaper'
Selection from the Manawatu with medium-sized, mid-green, five-finger foliage. Excellent form for containers or planted out. 2 × 1m.

Pseudopanax lessonii 'Linearifolius'
Handsome shrub with erect, fastigiate form. Leaves divided into five segments, leaflets broad-linear or linear-oblong, to 100 × 25mm, prominent midrib, dark green above, paler beneath, margins coarsely and irregularly serrated. Foliage gives the plant a light airy appearance. 2.5 × 1m.

Pseudopanax lessonii 'Purpureum'
Small palmate three to five-lobed, shiny purple-bronze leaves, compact bushy habit. Handsome, commendable shrub arising from P lessonii × P discolor. 2.5 × 1m.

Pseudopanax lessonii 'Sabre'
Growth pattern resembles P crassifolius but faster growing and usually branching lower. Juvenile leaves to 30 × 5cm, very dark green with orange midrib, twisted and undulating, deflexed in a similar way to Lancewood. Adult leaves much shorter as the tree matures. Stiffly upright habit. Superb garden or container plant. Possible parentage P lessonii × P arboreus. 3 × 1m.

Pseudopanax lessonii 'Skyrocket'
Very upright habit and leaves resembling P Adiantifolius. Benefits from occasional hard pruning for rejuvenation. 2.5 × 1.5m

Pseudopanax lessonii 'Toru'
Neat upright rounded grower. Tri-lobed, rich green foliage. Toru — Maori three. 2 × 1m.

Pseudopanax lessonii 'Trident'
Erect shrub sparingly branched from almost ground level. Juvenile leaves in two forms, simple lanceolate, to 20 × 6cm, thick and leathery, dark-green, margins coarsely toothed, and, trident-shaped, to 25 × 15cm, light green to yellow-green, midrib and veins prominent. As the plant matures, trident-lobes less obvious, leaves eventually entire and smaller. Sturdy and reliable. 3 × 1m.

PSEUDOTSUGA

A genus of about 7 species of conifers from North America, China and Japan, named from the Greek *pseudo*, false and *tsuga*, the hemlock spruce. North American species P menziesii is claimed to be the world's most important timber tree. Best suited to cooler climates, planted in free-draining soil in sun or shade with adequate summer moisture until established.
Pinaceae.

Pseudotsuga menziesii
Oregon Douglas Fir
Native to north western America, originally discovered by Archibald Menzies and named in his honour. Found in Oregon, also northern California, Washington, British Columbia, north to Alaska. Immense specimens to 90m recorded. A stately conifer, lower branches of mature trees down-swept, and with thick corky deeply furrowed bark.

Pyramidal when young, widely grown as a Christmas tree. Needles 3–4cm long, soft densely set, dark green or blue green, sweetly fragrant when crushed, radiating in all directions from branches and twigs. Branches curve up towards the ends. Pointed wine-red buds form at each branch tip in winter, opening in spring as apple-green tassels of new growth, adding beauty to an already handsome tree. Evergreen. 10 × 6m.

PSEUDOWINTERA

New Zealand endemic genus of three species of trees and small shrubs named from the Greek *pseudo*, false and *Wintera* from its similarity to that genus. Grown for hardiness and beautiful foliage. Common name Pepper Tree arises from the pungent taste of crushed leaves. Plant in deeply worked, organically enriched, free-draining, moisture-retentive, neutral to acid soil in sun or shade. Mulch freely and water deeply during dry periods. Hardy to frost, but has a preference for shady woodland locations, but leaf colour more intense if grown in open situations.
Winteraceae. *All evergreen.*

Pseudowintera colorata
Pepper Tree, Horopito
Found in New Zealand from Hunua Ranges near Auckland and as far south as Stewart Island in lowland and alpine forests, often forming thickets after the destruction of larger trees. An erect branching shrub with elliptic-oblong leaves to 6 × 3cm, quite glabrous, yellowish green flushed pink, prominently edged and blotched dark crimson or purplish red, glaucous beneath, very peppery to the taste. The highly decorative foliage lasts a month or more in water and worth growing for this purpose alone.

Small fragrant green starry flowers are borne in spring in clusters of 2–5 in leaf axils or leaf scars, followed by small black oval berries which ripen late summer and autumn. Colorata — coloured. 3 × 2m.

Pseudowintera colorata 'Red Leopard'
Selected, slower-growing form of above. Attractive red-spotted leaves, those exposed to full sun becoming deep red entirely. 2.5 × 2m.

PSORALEA

A genus of about 130 species of shrubs or perennial herbs from North and South America and South Africa, named from the Greek *psoraleos*, scabby in reference to glandular dots resembling warts covering the plant. The listed species grows easily, becoming naturalized in mild regions, often thought to be native. Grows readily in poor, deeply worked, free draining soil, but enjoys adequate summer moisture. Tolerant of light frosts, grows in sun or partial shade. Grows at least one metre in a season, flowers when young. Prune back to half way after flowering.
Fabaceae.

Psoralea pinnata
Blue Pea
Large fast growing shrub from South Africa, attractive when well grown. Has an abundance of soft pinnate leaves with 5–11 linear, 30 × 3mm needle-like, rich dark green leaflets. Sweetly scented, 2cm, bright-blue pea flowers with white striped wings, grouped in masses amongst the leaves near the tips of each branch appear spring through summer. Hardly a spectacular shrub, but an excellent filler with a pleasant combination of foliage and flower. Pinnata — in feather-like arrangement. Evergreen. 2 × 1.5m.

PTELEA

A genus of about 11 species of shrubs and small trees from North America named from the Greek *ptelea*, elm tree, from the similarity of its fruit. Grown for picturesque form, aromatic foliage and fragrant flowers. They're related to the citrus family and their leaves have similar oil glands. Plant in deeply worked, free-draining, moisture-retentive soil in sun or partial shade. Hardy to −15°C. Slow to moderate grower, quite drought resistant once established.
Rutaceae.

Ptelea baldwinii
Wafer Ash, Hop Tree
From south west USA and Mexico. Forms a large irregularly branched shrub with white bark. Trifoliate leaves with ovate leaflets to 2cm long, pale green, margins and midrib faintly hairy when young, later glabrous. Greenish-yellow 8–12mm flowers with a fragrance you either love or hate, borne in small clusters in spring followed by oblong or almost rounded fruit with thin rounded and latticed wings. Deciduous. 3 × 3m.

PTEROCARYA

A genus of about ten species of large trees from the Caucasus to east and south-east Asia, named from the Greek *pteron*, a wing and *karyon*, a nut. Large-growing trees related to Walnut, although their long pendent catkins are more suggestive of the shrub Garrya. Wingnut grows and looks well near water, thrives in damp soils and has luxuriant tropical appearance but is hardy to −12°C. Grows rapidly in moist loamy soil by lakes or streams.
Juglandaceae. *All deciduous.*

Pterocarya fraxinifolia
Caucasian Wingnut

A large wide-spreading tree with short trunk or multi-trunks and greyish black deeply furrowed bark. Young stems olive brown, slightly pubescent at first later glabrous. Large compound leaves 20–40cm long, comprising up to 21 oval-oblong to oblong-lanceolate 8–12cm leaflets deep-green and dull, lighter with pubescent midrib beneath, with margins entire or finely toothed.

Greenish flowers in pendulous catkins to 50cm long, drape branches through summer, followed by winged fruits. Merits extensive planting in acreage gardens. Fraxinifolia — ash-like foliage. 10 × 6m.

Pterocarya stenoptera
Chinese Wingnut

Native to China. Grows rapidly with heavy wide-spreading branches. Walnut-like foliage to 40cm long, with up to 23, oval-oblong to narrow-oblong leaflets, margins finely toothed. Small one-sided nuts with erect, oblong, 2cm wings, hang in clusters to 35cm long. Forms a handsome shade tree, succeeding well in heavy, compacted, poorly aerated soil such as playgrounds. Aggressive roots a disadvantage in lawns or near areas of worked soil. Stenoptera — narrow winged. 10 × 6m.

PTEROSTYRAX

A genus of four species of trees or shrubs from Japan, China and Burma, named from the Greek *pteron*, meaning a wing and *styrax*, referring to winged seeds of one species resembling Styrax. Epaulette Tree has good form, masses of flower and fruit that persist into winter on bare branches.

Plant in deeply worked, free-draining acid soil in sun or semi-shade, preferably in an elevated position so it can be seen from beneath. Mulch freely and keep moist until well established. Prune to control shape size and density.

Styracaceae.

Pterostyrax hispida
Fragrant Epaulette Tree

Native to China and Japan. Forms either a single or multi-trunk tree with open branches, spreading at the top. Young shoots smooth, leaves somewhat resemble those of the elm, oval or obovate, to 18 × 10cm, wedge-shaped at the base, margins serrated, light green and coarse-textured above, greyish-downy beneath. White lightly fragrant flowers with fringed petals, borne in downy pendulous panicles to 25cm long followed by small grey furry, cylindric or spindle-shaped, ten-ribbed fruits in pendent clusters, persisting through winter, attractive on bare branches. Hispida — bristly. Deciduous. 6 × 3m.

PUNICA

A genus of two species of shrubs or small trees from eastern Mediterranean to Himalayas, named from the Latin *punicum* the Carthaginian apple. Pomegranate derived from the Latin *pomum*, fruit. Pomegranate fruit about the size of an orange is covered with a hard rind and contains numerous seeds enclosed in reddish juicy pulp with acid flavour. Grown in Mediterranean regions from remote antiquity, and often referred to in early Biblical writings.

Only the highly ornamental cultivars with brilliant flowers are generally cultivated in the southern hemisphere. Plant in full sun in deeply worked, free-draining, fertile, neutral to alkaline soil. Mulch freely and keep moist until the plant is established, then it is quite drought tolerant.

Punicaceae. *All deciduous.*

Punica granatum 'Nana Pleno'
Dwarf Pomegranate

Forms a charming densely twigged shrub with small narrow leaves, bronzy and glossy when they first appear. Produces great quantities of bright vermillion-orange double blooms resembling small carnations. Foliage falls in winter but usually not until new leaves ready to appear. Good for rock gardens, window boxes, containers. Granatum — many seeds, nana — dwarf, pleno — double. 60 × 60cm.

Punica granatum 'Scarlet Devil'

Vigorous bushy dwarf shrub with dense twiggy habit and an abundance of five-petalled, reddish orange single blooms during summer. Hot sunny conditions essential. 1.2 × 1m.

PUYA

A genus of about 170 species of terrestrial herbs mostly from more northern parts of South America, called by its Chilean vernacular name. The listed species is a valuable landscaping plant especially as a juvenile. Giant inflorescence on mature plants most dramatic. Puya grows easily in average well-drained soil in full sun or semi shade. Tolerant of light frost and long periods of drought. Quite maintenance free apart from occasional grooming. Effective plant for rock or feature gardens. Locate where sharp spines will not offend.

Bromeliaceae.

Puya alpestris
Pineapple Shrub

Forms a dense rosette of curled, tapering, greyish green, sword-like leaves to 70 × 25mm, margins with sharp spines, pointed apex, silvery grey beneath, somewhat resembling those of the related pineapple.

Mature plants produce spectacular inflorescence at first resembling giant asparagus stalks, and growing 3–4m high, topped with pyramidal clusters of bell-shaped, metallic greenish blue flowers accented with orange anthers. Alpetris — of the mountains. Evergreen. 1 × 1m.   **246**

PYRACANTHA

A genus of about seven, hardy evergreen species from south east Europe to China, closely related to Crataegus and Cotoneaster, named from the Greek *pyr*, fire, and *akanthos*, thorn. All species produce clusters of small white flowers on short leafy spurs, followed in autumn and winter by crowded bunches of shiny fruit like miniature apples. Suitable as espalier on sunny walls, formal or informal specimens, bank or ground cover, or fillers in public areas.

Pyracanthas ask for no special care, seeming to thrive on neglect. They are tolerant of low temperatures as well as heat and drought. Plant in full sun in deeply worked, free-draining soil. When pruning keep in mind that fruit is produced on second year wood. Cut back any branches that have berried to a well placed side shoot. Size and form may be controlled by pinching shoots and shortening long branches just before growth commences.

Rosaceae. *All evergreen.*

Pyracantha 'Brilliant'
Firethorn, Fireberry

American hybrid characterized by attractive shining green foliage, profusion of snow white flowers and abundance of brilliant scarlet, shiny fruit throughout winter. Vigorous grower. 2 × 1.5m.   **246**

Pyracantha 'Orange Glow'
Grows erect with horizontal branches. Bright green foliage, masses of creamy-white flowers followed by heavy crops of orange fruit through winter. Excellent for espalier. 2.5 × 2m.

Pyracantha 'Shawnee'
Densely branched spiny shrub of medium size, rather widespread at the base to form a loose pyramid. Every branch laden with masses of white flower, followed by an equal abundance of yellow to light-orange fruit colouring late summer, persisting through winter. 2.5 × 2m.

Pyracantha 'Tiny Tim'
Delightful compact bush with small glossy green leaves and few thorns. White flower masses succeeded by bright red berries. 1.2 × 1m.

PYRUS

A genus of about 30 species of trees and shrubs from Europe, east Asia and north Africa called *Pyrus* its Latin name. European fruiting pears belong to the Pyrus genus having arisen predominantly from the species P communis. Asian Pears or Nashi, Japanese for pear, have been developed from P pyrifolia and P ussuriensis. The two ornamental species featured below are valued for good form, handsome foliage and showy flowers. Plant in full sun in deeply worked, free-draining soil.
    Rosaceae. *All deciduous.*

Pyrus calleryana
Ornamental Pear
Chinese species. Elegant tree with strong horizontal branching pattern. Leaves broadly ovate to 8cm long, dark green, very glossy and leathery, margins scalloped, rich purplish red in autumn. Clusters of pure white 25mm flowers very early spring followed by small brown 1cm inedible fruit. Calleryana — for J Callery, a French missionary to China who collected the species. 5 × 4m.

Pyrus salicifolia 'Pendula'
Weeping Silver Pear
Gracefully pendulous form of Silver Pear from Asia Minor. Elegant weeping stems with silvery grey bark. Willow-like leaves, narrow-elliptic to 9cm long, shining silvery white at first becoming silvery green, margins sparsely toothed or entire, downy beneath. Clusters of 2cm cream to greenish white flowers in spring, followed in autumn by 2–3cm, pear-shaped brownish fruit. Effective against a dark background. Very hardy. Salicifolia — willow-like, Pendula — weeping. 3 × 2m.

QUERCUS

A genus of about 600 species of acorn-bearing trees or shrubs from North Africa, Europe, Asia and North America to western tropical South America, named from the Latin *quercus*, the Oak. The mighty Oak has always been a symbol of strength and durability. Reports of 2000 year-old veterans may be somewhat exaggerated but Oaks from five to seven centuries are by no means exceptional. They are hardy reasonably fast growing and most picturesque trees meriting extensive planting in parks, schools, farms and large public areas.
    Plant in deeply worked, free-draining, moisture-retentive, slightly acid soil, mulch freely after planting and keep moist over dry periods during establishment. Most young Oaks are extremely twiggy, often slow to elect a leader. To promote fast vertical growth, discourage the development of unwanted lower side branches by pinching out the tips.
    Fagaceae. *All deciduous.*

Quercus cerris
Turkey Oak, Mossy-Cup Oak
Handsome wide-spreading tree of noble proportions, native to Southern Europe and Asia Minor, reputed to be the fastest growing oak, mature specimens known to have attained a height of 36m with a girth of 4 or 5m. Leaves oblong to oblong-lanceolate, to 12 × 3cm, coarsely toothed or shallowly lobed, slightly rough to the touch, dark green above, downy beneath. Winter buds and acorn cupules covered with long narrow downy scales. Magnificent specimen tree. Cerris — classical Latin name for the species. 10 × 6m.

Quercus coccinea
Scarlet Oak
Beautiful North American oak, providing the most brilliant autumn colour of the whole family. Forms a stately specimen with wide-spreading irregular crown, and high, light and open branching pattern. Bark has reddish cast in winter. Broad oval or obovate, deeply lobed leaves to 12 × 12cm, each lobe with bristle-tipped teeth, glossy, dark green in summer, intense glowing scarlet in autumn, colour often persisting into winter. Acorns ovoid to 25 × 25mm enclosed to half way in a yellow-brown scaly cupule. Offers minimal competition to nearby plants. Grows in a relatively narrow space and lawn grows beneath it. Coccinea — scarlet. 7 × 5m.

Quercus incana
Bluejack Oak
Small tree from south eastern USA. Forms a narrow irregular crown with branches held at angles of 70°- 90°. Branchlets dark-grey tomentose at first. Leaves oblong to 9cm long, apex pointed and bristle-like, base rounded, two halves often irregular in outline, deep green, covered in minute hairs at first, becoming glabrous and glossy, white tomentose beneath, margins entire. Acorns ovoid or top-shaped, 15mm, enclosed in cupule to half way. Incana — hoary, quite grey. Semi-evergreen. 6 × 5m.

Quercus palustris
Pin Oak
Native to Canada and eastern United States. Pyramidal habit when young becoming more open and round-headed at maturity. Brownish grey bark, deeply fissured and ridged. Leaves obovate to 15cm, glossy, dark green, deeply cut into spine pointed lobes, brilliant scarlet yellow and reddish bronze in autumn. Lower branches tend to droop almost to the ground. By removing lower ones, those above will adopt the same weeping effect. Palustris — marsh loving. 8 × 6m.

Quercus petraea
Durmast Oak
Widely distributed Europe to western Russia. Resembles Q robur in general appearance, varying mainly in leaves and acorns. Forms a large crown with substantial trunk with grey to blackish brown, deeply furrowed bark. Broadly obovate leaves to 18 × 9cm with 4–6 pairs of even rounded lobes, glossy green and glabrous above, paler, glaucous and slightly pubescent beneath, petioles or leaf-stalks to 16mm. Clustered ovoid acorns 2–3cm long in a scaly cupule. Petraea — rock-loving. 10 × 8m.

Quercus phellos
Willow Oak
Native to eastern USA. Forms a rounded to columnar crown with smooth greyish bark tinted reddish brown. Young stems reddish brown, slightly hairy at first becoming glabrous. Distinctive willow-like oblong-lanceolate leaves to 12 × 2.5cm, dark green above, paler beneath, glabrous on both

surfaces, margins entire and slightly undulating, turning yellow or orange in autumn. Clustered 2–3cm ovoid acorns in a scaly cupule. Phellos — cork, referring to bark. 8 × 6m.

Quercus robur
English Oak, Common Oak
The classic Oak, usually found in parks and public gardens as majestic veterans, often with short trunk, greyish brown deeply fissured bark, wide-spreading head and rugged branches. Leaves oblong to obovate to 14 × 6cm, with 3 to 6 pairs of rounded lobes, glabrous dark green, paler blue-green beneath, yellow in autumn, persisting into winter. Acorns ovoid to oblong ovoid, to 25mm, carried either singly or in clusters in cupules covered with velvety scales. A tree for large open spaces. Robur — Latin for hard wood, oak, or oak-wood, signifying strength and dependability. 8 × 5m.

Quercus robur 'Concordia'
Golden Oak
Resembles Q robur but with golden-yellow leaves through spring and summer. Vivid contrast. 6 × 4m.

Quercus robur 'Cristata'
Resembles Q robur in general form. Leaves smaller, deeply lobed and curiously curled and twisted. Quite distinct. Cristata — having tassel-like tips, or crested. 5 × 4m.

Quercus robur 'Fastigiata'
Upright English Oak
Narrow erect form when young, somewhat resembling Lombardy poplar, becoming more pyramidal as the tree matures. Fastigiata — having branches close together and erect. 8 × 3m.

Quercus rubra
Red Oak
Native to eastern North America. Forms a large specimen with broad, spreading branches and round-topped crown, new leaves and petioles rich red in spring. Leaves oblong to obovate, to 22 × 15cm, with three to five pairs of sharp-pointed triangular lobes, dark green, glabrous, matt-surfaced, yellow-green beneath, dull red or yellowish brown in autumn. Ovoid, 2–3cm acorns in close-scaly cupule. Closely related to Q coccinea, differing in more horizontal primary branches, bigger leaves, shallower lobes and matt surface rather than glossy. High branching habit and open shade makes it an ideal choice for large lawns or public areas. Deep rooting enables other plants to grow beneath it. Stake and train to encourage good form. Syn Q borealis maxima. Rubra — red. 10 × 7m.

QUINTINIA

A genus of about 25 species of trees and shrubs confined to Australia, New Zealand and New Guinea named for La Quintinie, French horticulturist and author. None are well-known in cultivation. The listed species has good form and outstanding foliage colour. Quite hardy, prefers semi-shade, deeply worked soil, good drainage and adequate summer moisture.

Escalloniaceae.

Quintinia acutifolia
Westland Quintinia
Found in North and South Islands, Great and Little Barrier Islands, but more abundantly in Westland. Handsome small tree of medium growth rate. Leaves broadly obovate-elliptic to 16 × 5cm, glossy, green to purplish, paler beneath, margins slightly serrated and undulate. Juvenile leaves yellow-green to bronze-green, with purplish marbling becoming intensely coloured with cooler weather. Cooler climate brings out rich old-mahogany foliage colour. Showy white flowers in 10cm racemes appear spring through early summer. Acutifolia — with sharply pointed leaves. Evergreen. 4 × 3m.

RADERMACHERA

A genus of about 15 species of trees or shrubs from south east Asia to Indonesia named for J C M Radermacher, 18th century Dutch botanist in Java. The listed species is probably more familiar to most gardeners as a multiple-stemmed container plant with good form and dainty foliage. Mature plants bear bell or trumpet-shaped flowers resembling Bignonia to which the genus is related. Some species grow into sizeable trees.

Radermachera thrives outdoors in frost-free gardens in full sun or partial shade providing a rapid and most ornamental screen. Plant in deeply worked, free-draining, moisture retentive soil that is not over-rich. Mulch freely and keep moist during dry periods, but once established and growing freely, don't overfeed. Tip-pinch during strong growth periods to keep compact. Plants which become tall and lank may be pruned to almost ground level.

Bignoniaceae.

Radermachera sinica
China Doll
A handsome plant from China and southern Asian regions. Forms a small tree in its natural state but in cultivation is seen more as a juvenile with erect stems crowned with bipinnate leaves to 50cm long comprising numerous ovate-lanceolate dark green leaflets. Cultivated plants rarely flower, but mature specimens bear 75mm bell-shaped, deep-yellow flowers with triangular, crisped lobes through spring and summer followed by 40cm seed capsules. China Doll is a marketing name. Evergreen. 2.5 × 1m.

RAPHIOLEPIS

A genus of about 15 species of shrubs or small trees from subtropical east Asia named from the Greek *rhapis*, a needle and *lepis*, a scale, referring to awl shaped bracts. Common name Indian Hawthorn possibly arose from the relationship of Raphiolepis to Crataegus, the true hawthorn, both of which belong to the Rosaceae family. Desirable shrubs, with glossy leaves, graceful form and a profusion of beautiful flowers. A handsome permanent looking shrub.

Grow in deeply worked, free-draining, fertile soil in full sun and mulch freely. Endures periods of drought without moisture. Suitable for coastal gardens, but may be injured by severe frost. Naturally a low grower but bushier, more compact plants result from pinching tip growths each year immediately after flowering. If more open structure is desired, let them grow naturally and thin out branches occasionally. Encourage spreading by shortening vertical branches, or erect growth by pinching side shoots. If leaf-spotting occurs during prolonged cold or wet conditions or frequent overhead watering, control with a fungus spray.

Rosaceae. All evergreen.

Raphiolepis × delacourii
Indian Hawthorn
Choice low growing shrub, covering considerable ground, with the sweetest rosy pink 12mm flowers resembling apple blossom in 15cm clusters spring through autumn, followed in winter by blue-black berries. Leaves obovate, 5–7cm long, dark-green overlaid bronze, leathery, margins toothed towards the apex. Young growths shining, coppery red. Amongst the choicest dwarf shrubs. Hybrid from R indica × R umbellata raised by M Delacour, near Cannes towards the end of the 19th century. 1 × 1m.

Raphiolepis indica 'Enchantress'
Indian Hawthorn
Graceful compact cultivar of the Chinese species. Coppery red young growth, leaves lanceolate, 5–7cm, bronze-green, leathery, margins strongly serrated. Literally smothered early spring through autumn with 12–15cm, pyramidal clusters of warm rich-pink flowers. Fast growing and vigorous. Indica — literally of India, but also applied to plants from the East Indies to China. 1 × 1m.

Raphiolepis umbellata
Oriental Raphiolepis
Hardy species from Japan or Korea forming a rounded shapely bush. Young shoots covered with greyish down which quickly disappears. Leaves thick and leathery, broad-oval or obovate to 9 × 6cm, deep-green and glossy above, densely grey-woolly beneath, margins finely and bluntly toothed. Pure white, 2cm slightly fragrant flowers with pinkish centres, borne in terminal umbels during summer, followed in winter by clusters of blue-black berries. Handsome shrub for form, foliage and flower. Umbellata — Latin *umbella*, a parasol. 1.5 × 1.5m.

REINWARDTIA

A genus of one species, a delightful dwarf shrub from northern India and China named for K G K Reinwardt, 18th century director of the Leiden Botanic Garden. Valued for beautiful yellow flowers contrasted against rich green foliage. The term *flax* arises from the plant's relationship to a species of Linum, common flax of Europe, source of fibres used in the manufacture of linen. Reinwardtia is frost tender but otherwise easily grown in a sheltered, sunny or semi-shady location, under overhanging eaves, or beneath the protection of larger trees or shrubs. Plant in deeply worked, organically enriched, free-draining soil. Mulch freely and keep moist during dry periods. Excellent for winter colour.
Linaceae.

Reinwardtia indica
Yellow Flax
Delightful perennial shrub from mountains of northern India, spreading by underground roots. Slender erect stems with elliptic-obovate, 5–7cm leaves, bright green, dull-glossy, conspicuously veined, margins entire or finely serrated. Brilliant yellow 5cm, open bell-shaped flowers with five twisted petals, produced through winter and spring in terminal clusters. Individual flowers don't last long, but new ones open daily over several weeks. Indica — of India. Evergreen. 90 × 75cm.   **247**

RESTIO

A genus of about 90 species of rush-like perennial herbs with underground rhizomes from South Africa and Australia, named from the Latin *restio*, rope or cord maker. The listed species with slender erect plumy stems effective near pools, in rock gardens or shrub borders. In Australia plumes are harvested commercially, used in floral arrangements, often seen in florist shops and flower stalls. Plume Rush prefers damp sandy soil, but seems to adapt to any reasonable conditions. Plant in full sun and keep moist during dry periods.
Restionaceae.

Restio tetraphyllus
Plume Rush
Distributed through all Australian States except Western Australia. Forms a dense clump of smooth slender erect stems about a metre high, 5mm at the base and tapering gradually arising from rhizomatous roots, somewhat resembling miniature bamboo. Each node has a tightly wrapped light brown sheath and thin threadlike bright green 25mm 'leaves' emerge from each node from about half way up each stem. Tetraphyllus — four-leafed. Evergreen. 1 × 1m.   **247**

RHABDOTHAMNUS

A genus of one species, a rambling shrub endemic in New Zealand named from the Greek *rhabdos*, a rod and *thamnos*, a bush. From basically a tropical family including the popular greenhouse plant Gloxinia. R solandri is the southern-most representative. Grows naturally on the shaded side of gullies or rocky banks. In the garden, select a shady site, sheltered from frost and prevailing wind. Plant beneath larger trees or on dry shady banks. Plant in deeply worked, organically enriched, free-draining, shingly or sandy soil. Tip-prune to encourage bushiness.
Gesneriaceae.

Rhabdothamnus solandri
New Zealand Gloxinia, Taurepo
Small slender multi-branched shrub from coastal or lowland forest margins and streamsides of the Auckland province and offshore islands. Slender branchlets distinctly grey-hairy. Leaves broadly-ovate to orbicular, dark green, both surfaces covered with rough hairs, margins coarsely toothed. Flowers bell-shaped about 25mm long with five rounded wide-spreading lobes, bright orange or yellow with dark red markings, borne singly from terminals or leaf axils almost all year. Solandri — for Daniel Carl Solander, 18th century Swedish botanist. Evergreen. 1.3 × 1.3m.

RHAMNUS

A genus of about 130 species of deciduous or evergreen trees or shrubs of wide distribution in northern temperate regions, Africa and Brazil named from *Rhamnos*, Greek name for the genus. Grown for form, foliage and fruit rather than the insignificant flowers. Some species yield the purgative cascara so do not eat drupes or berries. Listed species is said to be the earliest variegated shrub in commercial production, introduced in the 17th century.

Thrives in coastal situations. Tolerant of drought and industrial pollution, but needs protection from all but light frost. Fruits prolifically in warmth and sunshine. Plant in deeply worked, free-draining, neutral to slightly alkaline soil. Cut out plain green reverting branches which may appear.
Rhamnaceae.

Rhamnus alaternus 'Argenteo-variegatus'
Italian Buckthorn
From southern Europe. Fast-growing dense thornless shrub either single or multi-stemmed. Leaves ovate to elliptic to 7 × 2.5cm, glossy and leathery, deep green marbled grey with irregular creamy white margins, margins serrated. Tiny yellowish green flowers in condensed panicles in spring followed by 6mm obovoid fruit at first red, black when ripe in autumn. Alaternus — the Latin name. Evergreen. 3 × 3m.

RHODODENDRON

Rhododendrons are amongst the world's most important groups of ornamental plants. The genus which comprises 700–800 species is distributed throughout western and southern China where about half of all known species originated, Burma, India and Papua New Guinea. Rhododendron is derived from the Greek *rhodon*, rose and *dendron*, tree. Although first introduced into England in 1656, by 1800 there were still only a dozen known species. It was not until the mid 19th century that pioneering expeditions to Himalayas revealed a wealth of exciting new discoveries.

By 1900 known species numbered around 300, but explorations to remote and mountainous regions of China and other parts of the world yielded hundreds more. Nearly eight hundred known species have been classified and no doubt more will be discovered. Around 10,000 hybrids have been named and registered and probably 2000 cultivars are currently propagated and available to gardeners around the world. The range includes tiny rockery plants to substantial trees.

Few shrubs can match the dramatic beauty of Rhododendrons in full flower. Modern hybrids offer a wide range of beautiful colours from white through pink, red, purple and blue, and from cream through apricot and orange. Most are particularly hardy, growing well throughout south eastern Australia or New Zealand, and cooler mountain areas of Queensland and New South Wales.

Occurring naturally in areas of high rainfall and moist atmosphere, better results occur with similar conditions in cultivation. Plant in deeply worked, loose-textured, free-draining acid soil with a pH of 4.5–5.5 to which peat moss, sand, leaf mould, well decayed compost, rotted sawdust or decayed straw is added. Aim to provide deep cool soil which retains summer moisture but is not waterlogged during heavy rains.

Special acid fertilizers for Rhododendrons are readily available, but apply sparingly. Vigorous growth, good general health and quantity of bloom are more dependent on correct soil conditions and atmosphere than any other factor. Rhododendrons tolerate more sunlight than is generally thought but ideally, they are happiest in a position which avoids midday sun. As a general rule, varieties with larger leaves require dappled shade in summer, best provided by tall sparse-foliaged deciduous trees.

Roots may be kept cool and moist by mulching with about 8cm of peat moss which acts as an insulator, keeping moisture in and heat out. Thrips which may cause a silvery appearance to the leaves, especially in more temperate climates may be controlled with Orthene or Pestmaster, applied at the first sign of infestation, repeated one week later.

The genus also includes Azaleas, but in the interests of simplicity, and the fact that most gardeners and nurserymen will probably always refer to Azaleas as Azaleas, they appear under their own heading. Flowering season for most Rhododendron cultivars is mid winter through mid summer, governed to some degree by climatic variations.

Mid season equates to mid spring. Dimensions also vary according to climate and growing conditions and are intended only as a rough guide.

Ericaceae. *Listed species and cultivars all evergreen.*

Rhododendron aberconwayi
Chinese. Open bell-shaped white to pale-rose flowers spotted purple. Thick elliptic leaves to 6 × 2cm. Relatively compact bush. (species) Mid season. 1.5 × 1.3m.

Rhododendron 'Alice Street'
Soft lemon-yellow, trumpet-shaped florets in shapely truss. Handsome emerald-green foliage, compact grower. ('Diane' × wardii) Mid season. 2.5 × 2m.

Rhododendron 'Alice'
Reddish in bud, opening deep-pink with lighter centres, funnel-shaped florets in tall conical trusses. Hardy, dense foliage, tolerant of considerable sunlight. (griffithianum hybrid) Mid season. 1.8 × 1.5m.

Rhododendron 'Alison Johnstone'
Golden-amber flowers flushed apricot fading to pink. Slender tubular florets in trusses of 9–10. Fine rounded bluish-green foliage, dense compact growth. Free-flowering. (yunnanense × cinnabarinum) Mid season. 1.8 × 1.5m.

Rhododendron 'Alpine Meadow'
Masses of creamy white flowers, dwarf compact grower, distinctive bristly foliage. New Zealand raised. (R leucaspis seedling.) Early. 1 × 1m.

Rhododendron 'Amor'
White flowers delicately flushed pink within, irregular pink staining on the outside. Shapely trusses of 8–10 florets. Handsome

leaves glossy lime-green at first maturing deep-green. Low bushy grower. (griersonianum × thayerianum) Late. 1.5 × 1.5m.

Rhododendron 'Anah Kruschke'
Intense reddish purple with deep purplish red flare and prominent anthers. Compact ball-shaped to conical truss of 12 florets. Compact grower, glossy deep green foliage. (ponticum × 'Purple Splendour') Mid to late season. 2.5 × 2m.

Rhododendron 'Angelo Solent Queen'
Deep-pink in bud, opening pale rose fading to white margined pink, and central green ray. Large funnel-shaped florets to 12cm in dome-shaped trusses. (griffithianum × discolor) Mid to late season. 3 × 2.5m.

Rhododendron 'Anna'
Deep-pink fading to pastel-pink, prominent wine-red eye. Frilled florets in compact trusses. Deep-green foliage. ('Norman Gill' × 'Jean Marie de Montague') Mid season. 2.5 × 2m.

Rhododendron 'Anna Rose Whitney'
Bright rose pink flowers with light brown spotting, borne prolifically in conical trusses. Vigorous, bushy, good form and foliage. (griersonianum × 'Countess of Derby') Mid season. 2.5 × 2m.

Rhododendron 'Antoon van Welie'
Large trusses of magnificent pure pink flowers with yellow centre. Very vigorous grower, handsome foliage. Surpasses 'Pink Pearl'. ('Pink Pearl' hybrid) Mid season. 1.8 × 1.5m.

Rhododendron 'Anuschka'
Bright crimson-red outside, soft-pink shaded white inside. Conical truss, compact grower. ('Sammetglut' × 'Koichiro Wada') Mid season. 2 × 1.8m.   **248**

Rhododendron 'Applause'
Florets white blending to ivory in large rounded trusses. Leaves medium size, dark green. Somewhat spreading bush. ('Catawbiense Album' × 'Adriaan Koster' × williamsianum) Mid season. 2.5 × 3m.

Rhododendron 'Apricot Sherbert'
Unusual buff-apricot with salmon reverse. Open cup-shaped florets in shapely flattened truss. Unique Rhododendron colour. ('Comstock' × 'Dido') Mid season. 1.5 × 1.5m.   **248**

Rhododendron 'April Glow'
Pale rose-pink, faintly spotted flowers in flat trusses of 7–10. Grows to a compact mound. Coppery red new growth. (williamsianum

× 'Wilgens Ruby') Early to mid season. 1 × 1m.

Rhododendron 'Arthur Bedford'
Lavender-mauve with dark-rose madder spotted flare. Dense pyramidal truss of 11–16 florets. Dense glossy foliage, purplish petioles. (possibly ponticum × mauve seedling) Mid season. 2 × 1.8m.

Rhododendron 'Arthur J Ivens'
Deep pink in bud opening delicate rose-pink with two small crimson flares. Shallow bell-shaped florets to 75mm across in lax trusses. Dome-shaped bush, young shoots tinted coppery red, leaves ovate-orbicular to 45 × 15mm. (williamsianum × houlstonii) Early to mid season. 2.5 × 2m.

Rhododendron augustinii 'Barto Blue'
Deep blue flowers borne in clusters of 3–5 at branch ends. Cultivar of the species augustinii from western China. Compact grower, small foliage. Mid season. 2.5 × 2m.

Rhododendron 'Autumn Gold'
Salmon-apricot with deeper eye. Open bell-shaped florets in loose trusses. Light green 12 × 5cm leaves. Unique Rhododendron colour. Heat tolerant in dappled shade. (discolor × 'Fabia') Mid to late. 1.8 × 1.5m

Rhododendron 'Avalanche'
Pink-flushed buds opening snow-white with contrasting red flush in the throat. Immense fragrant wide funnel-shaped florets in large trusses. Large grower, moderately hardy. (calophytum × Loderi) Early. 3.5 × 3m.

Rhododendron 'Award'
Basically white with lemon throat, margins shaded pink giving a bicolour effect. ('Anna' × 'Margaret Dunn') Mid to late. 2.5 × 2m.

Rhododendron 'Babylon'
White with red basal blotch, reverse flushed pale pink. Open trumpet-shaped florets in huge trusses. Handsome and spectacular cultivar. (calophytum × praevernum) Mid season. 2.5 × 2m.

Rhododendron 'Bacher's Gold'
Attractive bicolor, salmon pink shading to saffron-yellow, orange and crimson in the centre. Dense growing and free-flowering. ('Unknown Warrior' × 'Fabia') Mid season. 1.5 × 1.5m.

Rhododendron 'Bad Eilsen'
Glistening bright red. Florets funnel-shaped with waved and crinkled edges. Blooms freely contrasting with deep green foliage. Dwarf spreading habit. ('Essex Scarlet' × forrestii repens) 75 × 120cm.

Rhododendron 'Baden Baden'
Deep cherry red with darker centres. Excellent low growing habit with glossy deep green foliage. ('Essex Scarlet' × forrestii repens) Mid season. 60 × 120cm.

Rhododendron 'Balstrode Park'
Bright scarlet in large loose trusses. Hardy and dependable tall grower. (griffithianum hybrid × 'Sefton') Mid season. 3 × 2.5m.

Rhododendron 'Bambi'
Deep pink almost red in bud opening soft pink with yellow tinge. Compact trusses on a dwarf compact bush. Dark foliage with dense indumentum beneath. (yakushimanum × 'Fabia Tangerine') Early to mid. 1 × 1m.

Rhododendron 'Baron Philippe de Rothschild'
Deep cream bud opening soft creamy white with wine-red blotch in the throat. ('Exbury Naomi' × 'Crest') Mid to late. 3 × 2.5m.

Rhododendron 'Bashful'
Light rose pink flowers with deeper shading and reddish brown blotch. Typical dense growth habit. (yakushimanum × 'Doncaster') Mid season. 1.3 × 1.3m.

Rhododendron 'Beau Brummel'
Waxy deep blood-red flowers with black spots and prominent black anthers. Funnel-shaped florets, up to thirty in neat globular trusses. Quite spectacular. ('Essex Scarlet' × facetum) Late season. 2 × 1.8m.

Rhododendron 'Beauty of Littleworth'
Large pink buds opening to white flowers lightly speckled lavender-blue on upper petals in immense conical trusses. Vigorous, hardy and consistent once it starts to bloom. Large deep green foliage. (griffithianum × campanulatum) Mid season. 1.8 × 2m.

Rhododendron 'Beefeater'
Brilliant geranium-red flowers with sparse pale spots. Saucer-shaped florets in flat-topped, well-filled trusses. Open narrow form, long narrow foliage. (elliottii × 'Fusilier') Mid season. 1.5 × 1.2m. **265**

Rhododendron 'Belle Heller'
White flowers with golden-yellow blotch in dome to globular-shaped trusses. Tall rounded open habit. Vigorous, hardy grower. (catawbiense 'Album' × catawbiense seedling) Mid season. 2 × 1.5m.

Rhododendron 'Bernard Shaw'
Clear soft pink with darker blotches. Very large trusses in profusion. Attractive foliage, tall sturdy grower. (calophytum × 'Pink Pearl') Mid season. 3 × 2.5m.

Rhododendron 'Betsie Balcom'
Bright red flowers, red stamens. Funnel-shaped florets in full conical trusses. New shoots tinged red. Attractive foliage, dense compact grower. ('Princess Elizabeth' × 'Elizabeth') Mid season to late. 2.5 × 2m.

Rhododendron 'Betty Arrington'
Rosy pink fragrant flowers with prominent red flare borne in showy trusses. Large attractive foliage, sturdy grower. (Dexter hybrid, parentage unknown) Late. 2.5 × 2m.

Rhododendron 'Betty Wormald'
Bright pink buds open to light rose pink flowers, paler within and with light purple spotting. Widely funnel-shaped, wavy edged florets in dense trusses. Medium growth. ('George Hardy' × red garden hybrid) Mid season. 2.5 × 2m.

Rhododendron 'Bibiani'
Dark red waxy flowers with maroon spotting, bell-shaped florets in conical trusses over long periods. Hardy, upright habit. ('Moser's Maroon' × arboreum) Very early season. 3 × 2.5m.

Rhododendron 'Billy Budd'
Turkey-red, waxy flowers in dense trusses. Compact spreading habit, long leaves with wavy margins. ('Mayday' × elliottii) Mid season to late. 2 × 1.5m.

Rhododendron 'Binfield'
Clear primrose yellow with small reddish flare in the throat. Large florets in showy trusses. ('China' × 'Crest') Mid season. 2 × 1.8m.

Rhododendron 'Black Prince'
Deepest black-red. Very large florets in immense trusses. Unique. ('Romany Chai' × thomsonii) Mid season to late. 2.5 × 2m.

Rhododendron 'Blue Boy'
Violet flowers with prominent almost black triangular marking in the throat. Heavy-textured florets in large trusses borne prolifically. ('Blue Ensign' × 'Purple Splendour') Late season. 2.5 × 2m. **265**

Rhododendron 'Blue Diamond'
Rich, lavender blue flowers in tight terminal clusters. Slow growing bush with small leaves and compact spreading growth. Free flowering and showy dwarf bush, ideal for rock gardens or borders. ('Intrifast' × augustinii) Early to mid season. 1 × 1m. **248**

Rhododendron 'Blue Ensign'
Margins pale lavender-blue, paling towards the centre, prominent blackish maroon

blotch. Open trumpet-shaped frilled florets in compact globular trusses. Resembles 'Blue Peter' but with low dense habit and firmer leaves. (Ponticum hybrid) Mid season. 1.5 × 1.5m. **265**

Rhododendron 'Blue Gem'
Bright purple flowers in tiny compact trusses. Small compact plant ideal for rockery planting. (Unknown parentage) Early to mid season. 60 × 90cm.

Rhododendron 'Blue Jay'
Pale violet blue, margins pansy violet, splashed with deep-purple, spotted brown on upper lobes. Trumpet-shaped florets, compact cone-shaped trusses. Vigorous compact grower. Sun tolerant. (Ponticum hybrid) Mid season. 1.5 × 1.5m.

Rhododendron 'Blue Pacific'
Bluish purple with darker flare, medium, compact bell-shaped truss. Vigorous bushy grower, light green foliage. ('Purple Splendour' × 'Susan') Mid season to late. 2.5 × 2m.

Rhododendron 'Blue Peter'
Pale lavender-blue with purple central flare. Funnel-shaped florets with frilled margins, in compact conical trusses. Vigorous grower with erect branches. (Ponticum hybrid) Mid season. 2.5 × 2m.

Rhododendron 'Blue River'
Light lilac-violet, open faced blooms in broad upright trusses. Compact bushy grower, glossy dark green foliage. ('Van Ness Sensation' × 'Emperor de Maroc') Mid season. 2.5 × 2m.

Rhododendron 'Blue Tit'
Light greyish blue flowers in small trusses on a dense compact plant. Small dark green leaves. Very free-flowering. (impeditum × augustinii). Early to mid season. 60 × 75cm.

Rhododendron 'Boddaertianum'
Lavender pink in bud, opening white with wide crimson-purple rays in the throat. Wide funnel-shaped florets in compact rounded truss. Vigorous grower forming small tree size. (campanulatum × arboreum) Early to mid season. 3–4 × 3m.

Rhododendron 'Bow Bells'
Shapely cerise-pink buds opening clear bright pink. Open cup-shaped flowers in lax trusses borne prolifically. Attractive copper-bronze new shoots, handsome rounded leaves. Dense growth habit from ground level. Excellent against a semi-shady wall. ('Corona' × williamsianum) Early to mid season. 1 × 1m.

Rhododendron 'Brasilia'
Attractive combination of orange-yellow and pink. Saucer-shaped florets in lax trusses. (wardii hybrid) Mid season. 2 × 2m.

Rhododendron 'Bravo'
Light purplish pink shaded lighter in the centre with sparse dorsal brown spotting. Dense trusses of 11–12 florets. Handsome foliage. (catawbiense album × fortunei × arboreum griffithianum) Mid season to late. 2.5 × 2m.

Rhododendron 'Bremen'
Scarlet red flowers with small calyces in loose trusses of 12 florets. Silvery green foliage, vigorous compact plant. (haematodes × unnamed red hybrid) Mid season. 1.8 × 1.5m.

Rhododendron 'Brendon King'
Deep blood-red flowers borne prolifically in compact trusses. Prostrate dwarf grower. (Parentage unknown) Early to mid season. 60 × 90cm.

Rhododendron 'Bric-a-Brac'
Milk-white to palest pink flowers with chocolate-brown anthers. Wide-open 6cm florets in showy trusses during late winter. Small neat floriferous plant. (leucaspis × moupinense) Very early. 1 × 1m.

Rhododendron 'Brickdust'
Rose-madder shaded orange-red, appearing glowing orange-rose. Open trumpet ruffled florets in loose trusses of 6–8. Bronzy new shoots, dense glossy deep-green rounded leaves, vigorous compact plant. (williamsianum × 'Dido') Mid season. 1.3 × 1.3m.

Rhododendron 'Brigitte'
Delicate lavender pink on outer edges shading white towards the centre and distinctive olive-green flare in the throat. Open bell-shaped florets in showy trusses. (insigne × 'Mrs J G Millais') Mid season. 2 × 1.8m.

Rhododendron 'Brinny'
Bronze buds opening straw-yellow with bronze centre. Impressive trusses in an unusual colour. Light green foliage, fairly compact plant. ('Day Dream' × 'Margaret Dunn' × unnamed seedling) Mid season. 2 × 1.8m.

Rhododendron 'Broughtonii Aureum'
Soft-yellow sweetly fragrant flowers spotted orange-yellow. Buds flushed pink. Wide funnel-shaped florets in compact ball-shaped trusses borne profusely. Handsome dark-green elliptic to obovate leaves to 10cm long, paler beneath, flushed bronze in winter.

Small rounded shrub, sun and heat tolerant. (maximum × ponticum × molle) Semi-deciduous Azaleodendron. Mid season to late. 1.8 × 1.8m.

Rhododendron 'Brown Eyes'
Rich pink with prominent brown flare. Open trumpet-shaped florets in large rounded trusses. Deep green foliage, compact rounded grower. (fortunei hybrid) Mid season. 1.8 × 1.5m.

Rhododendron 'Broxens'
Royal red flowers with dominant purple blotch. Trumpet-shaped florets in globular trusses. Hardy robust plant. Mid season. 1.5 × 1.5m.

Rhododendron 'Bruce Brechtbill'
Pale pink flowers with creamy yellow throat, in rounded trusses of 10–12. Small and compact with rounded glossy foliage. Resembles Unique. (bud sport of 'Unique') Early to mid season. 1.8 × 1.5m.

Rhododendron 'Bud Flannagen'
Deep mauve flowers with dark maroon flare, in immense conical trusses. Strong grower, handsome foliage. (ponticum x) Mid season to late. 2.5 × 2m.

Rhododendron 'Bulstrode Park'
Waxy brilliant scarlet red flowers. Large florets in large loose trusses. Hardy, tall growing, consistent flowerer. (griffithianum hybrid × 'Sefton') Mid season. 3 × 2.5m.

Rhododendron 'Bumblebee'
Deep purple flowers with large almost black eye, borne in large conical trusses. Erect grower, glossy dark green foliage. ('Purple Splendour' × 'Blue Peter') Mid season. 2.5 × 2m.

Rhododendron 'Burgundy'
Glowing burgundy-red flowers in large rounded dome-shaped trusses. Unusual colour, large leathery leaves, healthy grower. ('Brittania' × 'Purple Splendour') Mid season to late. 2.5 × 2m.

Rhododendron 'Burma Road'
Salmon-apricot flowers. True apricot coloured funnel-shaped florets in loose domed trusses. Requires good growing conditions. ('Fabia Tangerine' × 'Romany Chai') Early to mid season. 2.5 × 2m.

Rhododendron 'Burning Bush'
Fiery tangerine-red, narrow bell-shaped florets in loose trusses. Low spreading compact bush impressive in full flower. (haematodes × dichroanthum) Mid season. 60 × 90cm.

Rhododendron 'Buttermint'
Orange buds opening to brilliant light yellow, lightly shaded pink on margins and reverse, fading to yellow. Loose trusses of 10–15. Dense compact grower, new leaves bronze-tinted. ('Unique' × 'Fabia' × dichroanthum) Mid season. 90 × 90cm.   **248**

Rhododendron 'Captain Jack'
Blood red open-trumpet flowers with waxy glossy sheen held in tall open trusses of about 15. Compact rounded bush, large unusual leaves with rolled margins. ('Mars' × facetum.) Mid season to late. 1.8 × 1.5m.

Rhododendron 'Carlene'
Warm golden cream flowers with pink centre, prominently striped on the reverse, borne in loose trusses of 6–8 bell-shaped florets. Bright green, rounded leaves, yellow petioles. Compact grower. ('Lems Goal' × williamsianum) Mid season. 1.3 × 1m.

Rhododendron 'Carmen'
Bright deep red, waxy bell-shaped flowers which look you in the eye, produced freely on a low, compact, bun-shaped bush. Dense emerald green foliage. Excellent dwarf Rhododendron. (didymum × forrestii repens) Mid season. 75cm × 1m.

Rhododendron 'Carolyn Grace'
Chartreuse yellow with a greenish tinge, loose rounded truss of 7–10 florets. Dense grower, glossy deep green leaves with reddish brown petiole. (wardii hybrid) Early to mid season. 1.8 × 1.5m.

Rhododendron 'Cary Ann'
Coral red, flared trumpet-shaped blooms in large conical trusses. Handsome dark green foliage. Broad compact grower. ('Carona' × 'Vulcan') Mid season. 1 × 1m.

Rhododendron 'Chapmanii Wonder'
Light lavender pink flowers almost completely covering the plant. Grows rapidly and tolerant of extremes of heat and cold. (chapmanii × dauricum album) Early to mid season. 1.8 × 1.5m.

Rhododendron 'Charlotte de Rothschild'
Delicate soft pink with wine eye and spotting, borne in large compact trusses. Grows slowly to a substantial bush. (fortunei × 'St Keverne') Mid to late season. 3 × 2.5m.

Rhododendron 'Cheer'
Soft pink flowers, tinted deeper pink with maroon flare, borne in compact rounded trusses. Medium dwarf, compact mound, glossy deep green foliage. Flowers early spring and often again in autumn. ('Cunning-

ham's White' × red catawbiense hybrid) Early to mid season. 1.3 × 1.3m.   **265**

Rhododendron 'Chikor'
Soft yellow flowers with deeper spots, flat-faced florets in trusses of 3–6. Tiny, semi-glossy leaves, bronze in winter, compact, upright dwarf bush. (chruseum × ludlowii) Early to mid season. 75 × 50cm.

Rhododendron 'Chink'
Pale chartreuse-yellow, drooping flowers in loose trusses. Erect, compact grower, new foliage attractive bronze, often reddish in winter. Semi deciduous. (keiskei × trichocladum) Mid season. 1.8 × 1.5m.

Rhododendron 'Christmas Cheer'
Rose pink in bud, opening pale pink, fading to near white. Funnel-shaped flowers, frilly edges in tight, rounded trusses. Medium compact grower, extremely hardy and early blooming, often commencing in winter. (caucasicum hybrid) Very early. 1.5 × 1.5m.

Rhododendron 'Chrysomanicum'
Rich sulphur yellow, open trumpet, 5cm flowers in loose trusses. Low compact grower, very free flowering and extremely showy. Blooms from mid winter, persisting until spring. (chrysodoron × burmanicum) Early to mid season. 1 × 1m.

Rhododendron 'CIS'
Conspicuous rich bright pink buds open orange crimson maturing to creamy apricot, hose-in-hose florets in loose trusses of 8–11, skirted with unusual large calyces. Named for C I Sersanous, Past President American Rhododendron Society. ('Loders White' × 'Fabia') Low spreading bush. Early to mid season. 1.5 × 1.5m.   **265**

Rhododendron 'Clementine Lemaire'
Bright pink flowers with yellow flare in tight rounded trusses. Medium upright grower. (Parentage unknown) Late. 1.5 × 1.5m.

Rhododendron 'Colonel Coen'
Deep purple flowers with dark spots in fully domed truss. Bushy, vigorous plant, glossy deep-green foliage. (ponticum hybrid) Mid season. 1.8 × 1.5m.

Rhododendron 'Cornubia'
Bright blood red, bell shaped flowers, in compact rounded trusses. Handsome, but sparse foliage, erect grower. (arboreum × 'Shilsonii') Early to mid season. 3 × 2.5m.

Rhododendron 'Cotton Candy'
Pastel pink with small maroon blaze in the throat, enormous flowers in large spiralling trusses to 17 florets. Robust. Handsome

thick deep green foliage. ('Marinus Koster' × 'Loderi Venus') Mid to late. 2.5 × 2m.

Rhododendron 'Countess of Haddington'
White flushed pale rose, fragrant, 10 × 8cm, trumpet-shaped flowers, in lax trusses of three or four. Open spreading grower. (ciliatum × dalhousiae) Early. 2 × 1.5m.

Rhododendron 'Cowslip'
Pale primrose yellow to cream with pale pink blush, bell-shaped flowers. Dwarf mound-shaped plant, small ovate foliage. (williamsianum × wardii) Early to mid season. 1 × 1m.

Rhododendron 'Cream Crest'
Small cup-shaped creamy yellow flowers in tight trusses of 6–8 literally smother the plant. Small attractive foliage, dwarf compact habit. (chryseum × Cilpense) Early to mid season. 1 × 1m.

Rhododendron 'Cream Glory'
Buttery creamy yellow, large florets in compact truss. Handsome rich deep green foliage. American award winner. Best in filtered sunlight. ('Comstock' × 'Cheyenne') Mid season. 2.5 × 2m.   **266**

Rhododendron 'Creamy Chiffon'
Salmon-orange buds open to pale yellow, delicately ruffled double blooms in loose trusses. Compact rounded bush, dark green foliage. Mid season. 1 × 1.2m.   **266**

Rhododendron 'Crest'
Orange buds open to clear primrose-yellow, heavily textured flowers, slightly deeper in the centre, borne in elegant trusses of 10–12 florets. Erect grower, glossy deep green foliage. One of the top yellows. (wardii × 'Lady Beesborough') Mid season. 3 × 2.5m.

Rhododendron 'Crossroads'
Cardinal red flowers of good substance in full, outstanding trusses. Medium grower, long narrow, deep green foliage covered with indumentum beneath. Stems and midrib covered with woolly hair. (strigillosum hybrid) Early to mid season. 2.5 × 2m.

Rhododendron 'Curlew'
Yellow flowers tinged green, funnel-shaped florets with flaring lobes. Tiny green foliage, dwarf compact habit, excellent for rock gardens. Free-flowering. (ludlowii × fletcherianum) Early to mid season. 50 × 75cm.

Rhododendron 'Dalkeith'
Lavender pink flowers. Compact free-flowering semi-dwarf bush. New Zealand raised. (Possibly R uniflorum × R triflorum.) Mid season. 1.5 × 1.5m.

Above: Rhododendron 'Blue Boy' **262**

Above: Rhododendron 'Cheer' **264**
Below: Rhododendron 'Blue Ensign' **262**

Above: Rhododendron 'CIS' **264**
Below: Rhododendron 'Beefeater' **262**

Above: Rhododendron 'Cream Glory' **264**

Above: Rhododendron 'Creamy Chiffon' **264**
Below: Rhododendron 'Danella' **273**

Above: Rhododendron 'Furnivals Daughter' **273**
Below: Rhododendron 'Fair Lady' **273**

Above: Rhododendron 'Frontier' **273**

Above: Rhododendron 'Goldbukett' **273**
Below: Rhododendron 'Flirt' **273**

Above: Rhododendron 'Denali' **273**
Below: Rhododendron 'Halfdan Lem' **274**

Above: Rhododendron 'Hallelujah' **274**

Above: Rhododendron 'Heart's Delight' **274**

Above: Rhododendron 'Helene Schiffner' **274**
Below: Rhododendron 'Hurricane' **274**

Above: Rhododendron 'Hotei' **274**
Below: Rhododendron 'Mary Tasker' **275**

Above: Rhododendron 'Mrs J P Lade' **276**

Below: Rhododendron 'Irresistible Impulse' **274**

Below: Rhododendron 'Lems Cameo' **275**

Above: Rhododendron 'Odee Wright' **276**

Above: Rhododendron 'Jean Marie de Montague' **274**

Above: Rhododendron 'Little White Dove' **275**
Below: Rhododendron 'Nancy Evans' **276**

Above: Rhododendron 'Mi Amor' **275**
Below: Rhododendron 'Ivan D Wood' **274**

Above: Rhododendron 'Pania' **276**

Above: Rhododendron 'Rubicon' **277**
Below: Rhododendron 'Kubla Khan' **274**

Above: Rhododendron 'Renoir' **277**

Above: Rhododendron 'Percy Wiseman' **276**
Below: Rhododendron 'President Roosevelt' **276**

Above: Rhododendron 'Repose' **277**

Above: Rhododendron 'Spring Parade' **277**

Above: Rhododendron 'Ruby Bowman' **277**
Below: Rhododendron 'Ruby Hart' **277**

Above: Rhododendron 'Sunspray' **277**
Below: Rhododendron 'Sunbeam' **277**

Rhododendron 'Danella'
White to palest cream gradually blending to a golden haze in the throat. Exquisite, fragrant lily-like flowers in lax trusses. Leathery, rough textured, dark green foliage on reddish stems. (lindleyi × nuttallii) Mid season. 3 × 2.5m. **266**

Rhododendron 'Denali'
Bright red buds open to deepest rose pink flowers in large magnificent trusses. Vigorous grower, bold dark green foliage. ('Vanessa Pastel' × 'Pink Walloper') Mid season. 3 × 2.5m. **267**

Rhododendron 'Dianne Titcomb'
White flowers margined pink in perfect trusses. Large handsome foliage, vigorous bushy grower. ('Marinus Koster' x 'Snow Queen') Mid season. 3 × 2.5m.

Rhododendron 'Dido'
Orange-pink flowers with yellow centre in lax trusses. Sturdy compact grower, handsome light green rounded foliage. (dichroanthum × decorum). Mid season. 1.8 × 1.5m.

Rhododendron 'Doc'
Rose pink flowers with deeper margin, fading to almost white, frilled florets in tight trusses. Fresh and faded flowers look well in combination. Compact.. (yakushimanum × 'Corona') Mid season. 1.3 × 1.3m.

Rhododendron 'Dopey'
Deep strawberry red glossy flowers in attractive ball-shaped trusses, margins fading to white with maturity. Low compact, bushy habit. ([facetum × 'Fabia'] × [yakushimanum × 'Fabia Tangerine']) Mid season. 1.5 × 1.5m.

Rhododendron 'Dora Ameteis'
Pure white flowers with green spots and spicy fragrance in lax trusses. Compact bushy grower, free flowering, hardy and easily grown. (carolinianum × ciliatum) Early season. 1 × 1.5m.

Rhododendron 'Dorinthia'
Clear tomato-red waxy flowers in firm trusses. Compact grower, flowers profusely. (griersonianum × 'Hiraethlyn') Early to mid season. 2.5 × 2m.

Rhododendron 'El Camino'
Deep rosy pink flowers flared red in the throat. Large open trumpet-shaped florets in large compact domed trusses. Firm wide-spreading branches, large leathery deep-green leaves. Mid season. 2 × 1.8m.

Rhododendron 'Elegans'
Bright tyrian rose with sepia blotch.

Trumpet-shaped flowers in dense, conical trusses. Extremely free flowering and hardy. Older cultivar able to grow under average garden conditions and provide spectacular floral displays. ('Altaclarense' × catawbiense) Mid season. 4 × 3m.

Rhododendron 'Elizabeth'
Rich scarlet red, trumpet-shaped, 7cm flowers, in lax trusses of 6–8. Low spreading shrub, dark green leaves. Free-flowering. (forrestii repens × griersonianum) Early to mid season. 60 × 90cm.

Rhododendron 'Elizabeth Hobbie'
Scarlet to wine red, translucent, bell-shaped flowers in loose umbels to ten. Dwarf grower, very glossy, dark green rounded foliage. ('Essex Scarlet' × forrestii repens) Early season. 60 × 90cm.

Rhododendron 'Fair Lady'
Rich rose pink, slightly paler on the lobes and deeper reverse, borne in magnificent tight compact trusses. Handsome deep green foliage. (arboreum var roseum × 'Loderi Venus') Mid season. 3 × 2.5m. **266**

Rhododendron 'Fairy Light'
Soft pink flowers with salmon throat in loose trusses. Somewhat compact bush, very free-flowering. (Lady Mar × griersonianum.) Highly rated. Mid season. 1.5 × 1.5m.

Rhododendron 'Fireman Jeff"
Bright blood red flowers with extra large red calyces, borne in trusses of 8–10. Well-branched plant, medium green foliage. Brightest blood-red of any Rhododendron. Flowers when young, and continues freely. ('Jean Marie de Montague' × 'Grosclaude') Mid season. 2.5 × 2m.

Rhododendron 'Flirt'
Red buds open to deep rosy red flowers gradually merging with white centre, borne in compact globular trusses. Compact, densely foliaged plant. ('Britannia' × yakushimanum Koichiro Wada) Mid season. 1.8 × 1.5m. **267**

Rhododendron 'Floras Boy'
Bright red, waxy flowers in large trusses. Dwarf upright grower, small glossy deep green foliage. (forrestii repens × Jean Marie de Montague) Early to mid season. 60 × 90cm.

Rhododendron 'Fragrantissimum'
Buds flushed carmine opening to white flowers flushed green within and on the outside. Broad funnel-shaped blooms with nutmeg fragrance in lax umbels of four. Medium growth habit, flexible willowy

stems. Train as a shrub, espalier or ground cover. (edgeworthii × formosum) Early to mid season. 2 × 2m.

Rhododendron 'Frontier'
Pink buds open to rich warm yellow flowers in dense trusses. Attractive foliage, very free-flowering. ('Letty Edwards × 'Crest') Mid to late season. 3 × 2.5m. **267**

Rhododendron 'Furnivals Daughter'
Bright rich pink flowers with cherry-pink flare in magnificent conical trusses. Large textured leaves, vigorous grower. ('Mrs Furnival' selfed) Mid season. 1.8 × 1.5m. **266**

Rhododendron 'Genghis Khan'
Bright scarlet red flowers with prominent calyx giving the effect of double flowers, borne in full trusses. Dense bushy plant, dark green foliage with silver indumentum beneath. ('Britannia' × 'Felix') Mid season. 2.5 × 2m.

Rhododendron 'Gertrude Schale'
Translucent blood red flowers borne profusely on a compact spreading bush. Ideal for rock gardens or front borders. (forrestii Repens × 'Prometheus') Early to mid season. 90cm × 1.3m.

Rhododendron 'Ginny Gee'
Multi-coloured semi-double flowers opening pink maturing white. Compact bush, completely covered with bloom. Exceptional. (R keiskei 'Yaku Fairy' × racemosum.) Mid season. 1 × 1.3m.

Rhododendron 'Goldbukett'
Creamy yellow flowers, carefully spotted maroon on upper lobes, in compact rounded truss. Compact grower, attractive foliage. ('Scintillation' × wardii) Early to mid season. 1.5 × 1.3m. **267**

Rhododendron 'Golden Belle'
Bright orange and yellow flowers, pink margins, large saucer-shaped florets in flat trusses. Broad, low bushy grower. (fortunei ssp discolor × 'Fabia') Mid season to late. 1.3 × 1.3m.

Rhododendron 'Gold Mohur'
Golden yellow flowers with a band of pink on the outside margin of each lobe. ('Day Dream' × 'Margaret Dunn') Mid to late. 1.5 × 1.3m.

Rhododendron 'Golden Torch'
Salmon pink in bud opening chrome yellow in firm rounded trusses. Compact bushy grower. ('Bambi' × ['Grosclaude × griersonianum]) Mid season to late. 1.3 × 1.3m.

Rhododendron 'Golden Witt'
Golden yellow waxy flowers with red speckled throat. Compact grower, handsome foliage. (scyphocalyx × seedling × ['Moonstone' × 'Adrastia']) Mid season. 1 × 1m.

Rhododendron 'Grace Seabrook'
Deep blood red, margined currant-red, borne in full dense trusses. Heavy textured foliage. Excellent red. ('Jean Marie de Montague' × strigillosum) Early to mid season. 2.5 × 2m.

Rhododendron 'Grand Slam'
Glowing florescent pink, large flared and frilled florets in large conical truss. Strong pyramidal form, large glossy deep-green foliage. Mid to late. 2 × 1.8m.

Rhododendron 'Grumpy'
Pale pink in bud opening creamy white with a tinge of pink. Dark green foliage with heavy indumentum beneath. Typical compact growth habit. (yakushimanum × unknown) Mid season. 1.3 × 1.3m

Rhododendron 'Halfdan Lem'
Bright red, thick-textured flowers, darker spotting, in immense tight trusses. Broad thick deep-green foliage. Multiple award winner. ('Jean Marie de Montague' × 'Red Loderi') Mid season. 2.5 × 2m.   **267**

Rhododendron 'Hallelujah'
Bright rose pink with minimal maroon spotting in the throat. Compact, densely foliaged plant. ('Kimberley' × 'Jean Marie de Montague') Mid season. 2.5 × 2m.   **268**

Rhododendron 'Harvest Moon'
Bright lemon-yellow flowers with reddish brown flare in rounded compact trusses. Upright habit, glossy yellow-green foliage. (campylocarpum hybrid × 'Mrs Lindsay Smith') Mid season to late. 1.5 × 1.5m.

Rhododendron 'Heart's Delight'
Vibrant light red with a smudge of white near the centre. Tight rounded truss. Handsome dark green foliage. ('Mrs A T de la Mare' × 'Britannia') Mid season to late. 2.5 × 2m.   **268**

Rhododendron 'Helene Schiffner'
Pure white flowers without spotting, opening from pale pink buds, perfect, erect domed truss. Deep green foliage. (Unknown) Mid season. 2 × 1.8m.   **268**

Rhododendron 'Honeymoon'
Chartreuse buds opening soft lemon-yellow, greenish throat with small orange blotch. Compact. Firm dark-green foliage. (R wardii 'Barto' × 'Devonshire Cream' × R wardii var croceum.) Mid season. 1.5 × 1.5m.

Rhododendron 'Hoppy'
Delicate pale lilac flowers becoming white tinged lilac. Compact, wide-spreading habit. (yakushimanum × unknown) Mid season. 1 × 1.5m.

Rhododendron 'Hotei'
Deep canary yellow, well defined calyx, compact rounded truss. Dense compact grower, small mid-green foliage. ('Goldsworth Orange' × souliei-wardii) Mid season. 1.5 × 1.3m.   **268**

Rhododendron 'Hurricane'
Bright rose pink flowers with deep red flare, in large conical trusses. Vigorous, compact growth. ('Mrs Furnival' × 'Anna Rose Whitney') Mid season. 1.5 × 1.5m.   **268**

Rhododendron 'Hydon Hunter'
Reddish purple flowers, fading almost to white in the centre, spotted orange-yellow in the throat. Dense dome-shaped trusses. Compact, erect growth habit. (yakushimanum × 'Springbok') Mid season. 1.3 × 1m.

Rhododendron 'Igtham Yellow' #2
Soft lemon-yellow flowers with small mustard blotch in the throat. Medium compact grower, handsome foliage. ('Naomi' × wardii) Early to mid season. 2.5 × 2m.

Rhododendron 'Ina Hair'
Apricot pink fading to cream, borne in magnificent erect trusses. Large-growing specimen, immense broadly elliptic leaves. (Macabeanum hybrid.) Mid season. 3 × 3m.

Rhododendron 'Indiana'
Orange-red flowers speckled dark red in compact trusses. Handsome, glossy deep green leaves, amongst the best foliage for Rhododendrons. (dicroanthum ssp scyphocalyx × kyawii) Mid season to late. 1 × 1m.

Rhododendron 'Irresistible Impulse'
Deep reddish purple with purple-black spotted blotch on upper lobe. Large tight truss. Rich green leathery leaves. ('Mars' × 'Purple Splendour') Mid season to late. 2.5 × 2m.   **269**

Rhododendron 'Isabel Pierce'
Cardinal red buds open rosy red, fading to neyron-rose with deeper pink margins and prominent wine blotch, spotting and striping, top lobe recurving. Immense trusses. Robust grower, glossy deep green leaves with yellow midrib. ('Anna' × 'Lem's Goal') Mid season. 3 × 2.5m.

Rhododendron 'Ivan D Wood'
Peach pink in bud, opening delicate soft pink with deeper pink flushes, blending to lemon centre and gold eye, borne in compact rounded trusses. Strong growing and very floriferous. ('King of Shrubs' × 'Fawn') Mid season. 3 × 2.5m.   **270**

Rhododendron 'Ivanhoe'
Brilliant orange scarlet, funnel shaped flowers with deeper central markings in flat topped trusses. Tall shrub with somewhat loose habit. ('Chanticleer' × griersonianum) Mid season. 2.5 × 2m.

Rhododendron 'Janet Blair'
Light pink, white throat with green flare, frilled, open trumpet-shaped florets in rounded open truss. Compact spreading bush, glossy deep green foliage. Mid to late. 1.5 × 1.8.

Rhododendron 'Jean Marie de Montague'
Crimson-scarlet flowers in full rounded trusses. Recognized as one of the finest reds. Thick heavy foliage, slow-growing, compact bushy shrub. (griffithianum hybrid) Mid season. 3 × 2.5m.   **270**

Rhododendron 'Jingle Bells'
Scarlet buds opening golden-orange blending to salmon pink margins, fading to yellow with reddish throat. Bell-shaped, frilled florets in loose trusses. Tidy, low compact habit. ('Fabia' × 'Ole Olsen') Mid season. 1.3 × 1.3m.

Rhododendron 'Johnny Bender'
Intense currant-red flowers with darker spotting, ball-shaped trusses of 5–8 florets. Glossy dark green, heavily textured foliage. ('Jean Marie de Montague' × 'Indiana') Mid season. 1.5 × 1.5m.

Rhododendron 'Kaponga'
Scarlet-red flowers in large compact ball trusses. Erect grower. dark green foliage with silvery reverse. ('Ivery's Scarlet' × arboreum) Very early. 2.5 × 2m.

Rhododendron 'Kirsty'
Basically white, flushed and spotted with purple on upper petal and outside flower. (Adenophorum Group) Mid season. 1.5 × 1.5m.

Rhododendron 'Kubla Khan'
Combination of salmon pink, orange and red with creamy hue in the centre and prominent maroon flare on upper lobe. Compact conical trusses. Large mossy-green foliage. ('Britannia' × 'Goldsworth Orange') Mid season to late. 2.5 × 2m.   **271**

Rhododendron 'Lady Clementine Mitford'
Delicate soft peach-pink. Foliage appears to be sprinkled with silver. (Maximum hybrid) Mid season. 1.5 × 1.5m.

Rhododendron 'Lady Dorothy Ella'
Large deep cream fragrant flowers, deeper yellow throat. Somewhat open grower. (lindleyi × nuttallii) Mid season. 3 × 2.5m.

Rhododendron 'Lalique'
Deep pink in bud, opening white tinged delicate pink and lilac. Frilled florets in compact conical trusses. Vigorous grower, handsome deep green foliage. ('Loderi' or griffithianum hybrid) Early to mid season. 3 × 2.5m.

Rhododendron 'Lamplighter'
Light red flowers with sparkling salmon glow, dense conical trusses. Compact rounded plant, medium green foliage. ('Britannia' × 'Madam J Chauvin). Mid season. 1.8 × 1.5m.

Rhododendron 'Lascaux'
Buds a blend of red and orange, opening barium yellow with crimson blotch at the base of the throat. Compact grower. ('Fabia' × wardii) Mid season to late. 2.5 × 2m.

Rhododendron 'Lavender Girl'
Deep lavender buds open to pale-lavender fragrant flowers margined rosy mauve, paler in the centre and with golden-brown spotting. Dense domed trusses. Vigorous grower, handsome glossy foliage. (fortuneii × 'Lady Grey Egerton') Mid season. 2.5 × 2m.

Rhododendron 'Lemon Ice'
White flowers with a hint of yellow. Hardy compact grower, tolerant of some exposure. (ponticum hybrid). Mid season to late. 1.8 × 1.5m.

Rhododendron 'Lemon Lodge'
Soft yellow in bud opening cream with yellow centre. Large well-shaped truss. Free flowering, bushy grower, attractive foliage. ('Prelude' seedling) Mid season. 2.5 × 2m.

Rhododendron 'Lemon Mist'
Bright greenish yellow flowers. Compact grower, small foliage free-flowering. Early to mid season. 50 × 90cm.

Rhododendron 'Lems Cameo'
Bright pink to red buds open to delicate-apricot, cream and pink flowers. Beautiful frilled florets in magnificent rounded trusses. Good effect of colourful buds interspersed with opened flowers. Foliage deep green and glossy. An aristocrat. ('Didi' × 'Anna') Mid season. 2.5 × 2m.   **269**

Rhododendron 'Lems Monarch'
Deep pink margins shading through paler pink to almost white in the centre. Large compact conical trusses. Excellent flower and foliage. ('Anna' × 'Marinus Koster') Mid season. 3 × 2.5m.

Rhododendron 'Leo'
Dark red waxy florets in tight conical trusses. Amongst the best red Rhododendrons. Excellent shrubby grower, dark green foliage. ('Britannia' × elliottii) Mid season to late. 2.5 × 2m.

Rhododendron 'Lily'
Blush pink in bud opening white with creamy yellow throat. Flared trumpet-shaped flowers. Vigorous grower. Mid season. 1.8 × 1.5m.

Rhododendron 'Little White Dove'
Pink in bud opening purest white in small compact trusses of 10–12 florets. Compact grower, handsome glossy mid green foliage. (fortunei × yakushimanum) Mid season. 1.3 × 1.3m.   **270**

Rhododendron 'Loderi
A group of hybrid Rhododendrons from R griffithianum × R fortuneii most of which prefer woodland conditions where they grow strongly into large shrubs or small trees with dense foliage. Loderi hybrids are renown for massive trusses of large trumpet-shaped, sweetly fragrant flowers.

Rhododendron 'Loderi Fairyland'
Pink in bud opening almost pure white, sweetly fragrant florets in immense trusses. Typical large Loderi foliage and growth habit. Early to mid season. 3.5 × 3m.

Rhododendron 'Loderi King George'
Very soft pink in bud opening to pure white. Large lily-like, fragrant florets to 16cm across with as many as ten in a truss. Early to mid season. 3 × 2.5m.

Rhododendron 'Loderi Patience'
Mauve pink in bud, opening soft pink in large trusses. Early to mid season. 3.5 × 3m.

Rhododendron 'Loderi Pink Diamond'
Deep pink in bud opens shell-pink with deeper markings. Fragrant, lily-like, trumpet shaped florets to 12cm across, in enormous trusses. An aristocrat. Mid season. 3 × 2.5m.

Rhododendron 'Loderi Pink Topaz'
Soft pink with basal flash of green inside the flower. Early to mid-season. 1.5 × 1.5m.

Rhododendron 'Loderi Venus'
Possibly the deepest pink Loderi and strongly fragrant. Early to mid season. 3.5 × 3m.

Rhododendron 'Loders White'
Pink candelabra buds open to slightly fragrant white flowers with a hint of pink borne in huge trusses. Free-flowering, vigorous grower. (arboreum album × griffithianum) 2.5 × 2m.

Rhododendron 'Lucky Strike'
Deep salmon pink, heavy-textured florets in dense rounded trusses. Free flowering, extends the season. Best in partial shade. (griersonianum × 'Countess of Derby') Late season. 2.5 × 2m.

Rhododendron 'Markeeta's Prize'
Brilliant rosy red flowers with a few darker spots, heavy textured florets in immense trusses. Vigorous, sturdy erect bush, with large dark green foliage. ('Loderi Venus' × 'Anna') Mid season. 3.5 × 3m.   **290**

Rhododendron 'Mars'
Deepest red waxy flowers with contrasting white anthers in large conical trusses. Deep green ribbed foliage. (griffithianum hybrid) Mid season to late. 2 × 1.8m.

Rhododendron 'Mary Tasker'
Warm-pink buds open to delicate mushroom pink, delicately blending to cream in the throat with small red eye. Compact rounded trusses. Excellent mid green foliage. (racemosum × keiskei) Mid season. 3 × 2.5m.   **268**

Rhododendron 'Medusa'
Deep brick-orange in the throat with brown specks, blending to mandarin-red around the lobes. Attractive trumpet-shaped florets with flaring lobes, borne in loose trusses. Dense rounded bush, leaves deep green with fawn indumentum beneath. (scyphocalyx × griersonianum) Mid season. 2 × 1.5m.   **289**

Rhododendron 'Merle Lee'
Deep pink, shaded darker round the margins and glowing wine eye. Large wide florets in compact trusses. Vigorous open grower. ('Azor' selfed) Mid season. 2.5 × 2m.

Rhododendron 'Mi Amor'
Magnificent lily-like florets to 15cm across, pure white with a blush of yellow in the throat, exquisite fragrance, set in trusses of about five. Tall erect grower, large dark green leathery leaves. (lindleyi × nuttallii) Mid season. 2.5 × 2m.   **270**

Rhododendron 'Michael's Pride'
Lime-green buds open to deep creamy yellow, fragrant lily-shaped or tubular flowers. Medium grower, new leaves attractive bronze colour. (burmanicum × dalhousiae) Mid season. 2.5 × 2m.

Rhododendron 'Mission Bells'
Bright rose-pink sightly fragrant flowers. Compact grower, glossy deep green foliage. Quite sun tolerant. (orbiculare × williamsianum) Mid season. 1 × 1m.

Rhododendron 'Molly Ann'
Beautiful shade of rose pink, thick-textured florets in small erect trusses. Dense compact habit, rounded leaves. ('Elizabeth' × unknown) Early to mid season. 1.3 × 1.3m.

Rhododendron 'Morning Cloud'
White flowers flushed pale lavender-pink, paler in the throat, fading to cream borne in rounded trusses. Dark green foliage, compact dwarf grower. (yakushimanum × 'Springbok') Mid season. 1 × 1.3m.

Rhododendron 'Mount Everest'
Pure white flowers with reddish brown flare. Large conical truss. Hardy and reliable. (campanulatum × griffithianum) Mid season to late. 2.5 × 2m.

Rhododendron 'Mrs A T de la Mere'
Rose pink in bud opening to pure white, slightly fragrant flowers, spotted greenish yellow in the throat, borne in large dome-shaped trusses. Hardy, free flowering. ('Sir Chas Butler' × halepeanum) Mid season. 2.5 × 2m.

Rhododendron 'Mrs G W Leak'
Clear light rose pink flowers with prominent reddish brown flare in the throat extending well into upper lobes. Excellent compact conical trusses. Medium growth habit and hardy. ('Coombe Royal' × Chevalier Felix de Sauvage') Early to mid season. 2.5 × 2m.

Rhododendron 'Mrs J P Lade'
Smoky lavender mauve, large bell-shaped florets in large heavy trusses. Medium grower, vigorous bush with fresh looking foliage. Hardy, easy to grow and free flowering. (Unknown) Mid season. 1.8 × 1.5m. **269**

Rhododendron 'Nancy Evans'
Orange-red buds opening to rich amber-yellow flowers with enlarged calyx. Frilly florets in ball-shaped trusses almost cover the plant. Compact grower, young leaves bronze becoming glossy deep green. ('Hotei' × 'Lem's Cameo') Mid season. 1.5 × 1.5m. **270**

Rhododendron 'Naomi Exbury'
Pastel pink to lilac blending to shades of yellow-apricot. Fragrant, wide-spreading trumpet-shaped florets in large shapely trusses. Compact rounded plant. ('Aurora × fortunei) Early to mid-season. 1.3 × 1.3m.

Rhododendron 'Naomi Nautilus'
Rose-pink flush pale orange with pale greenish yellow eye, fragrant frilled flowers. ('Aurora' × fortunei) Mid season. 3 × 2.5m.

Rhododendron 'Noyo Chief'
Translucent-red flowers in rounded trusses. Grown also for handsome leaves, elliptic, glossy dark green with prominent veins and midrib, covered with fawn tomentum beneath, petioles red. (arboreum ssp. nilagiricum hybrid) Mid season. 2.5 × 2m.

Rhododendron 'Odee Wright'
Waxy yellow flowers with tinges of green and apricot. Glossy or waxy dark-green foliage. Most ornamental compact rounded plant. ('Idealist' × 'Mrs Betty Robertson') Mid season. 1.3 × 1.3m. **270**

Rhododendron 'Old Copper'
Rich coppery orange, large wide-flaring trumpet-shaped florets in lax trusses. Medium bushy upright grower, tolerant of warmer climates. ('Vulcan' × 'Fabia') Late season. 2.5 × 2m.

Rhododendron 'Ostbos Low Yellow'
Apricot pink buds opening to apricot, cream and soft yellow flowers in loose trusses. Flowers freely when young, forming a compact bush with dark green foliage. (Possibly a 'Fabia' hybrid') Mid season. 1.3 × 1.3m.

Rhododendron 'Pania'
Deep pink buds open to delicate pink flowers, gradually blending to cream in the centre with few tan spots on the upper lobe. Beautiful trusses. Blooms prolifically. (Probably dichroanthum hybrid) Early to mid season. 2.5 × 2m. **271**

Rhododendron 'Paprika Spiced'
Pale creamy yellow flowers highlighted with a profusion of salmon-orange spots. Compact ball-shaped trusses. Compact rounded plant, moss-green foliage. ('Hotei' × 'Tropicana') Mid season. 1 × 1m.

Rhododendron 'Parisienne'
Sulphur yellow in bud opening pale yellow. Open bell-shaped florets in loose trusses. Low spreading habit, extremely floriferous. (burmanicum × valentinianum) Early to mid season. 1.3 × 1.3m.

Rhododendron 'Patty Bee'
Lemon yellow flowers in tight trusses. Forms a dwarf compact mound covered with bloom. (R keiskei 'Yaku Fairy' × fletcherianum) Mid season. 60 × 90cm.

Rhododendron 'Percy Wiseman'
Multi-coloured flowers peach pink and cream, fading to creamy throat and greenish brown flare. Compact rounded truss. Vigorous compact grower, glossy dark green foliage. Free-flowering. (yakushimanum × 'Fabia Tangerine') Mid season. 1 × 1.3m. **271**

Rhododendron 'Pink Cherub'
White flowers flushed pink, dense rounded trusses. Vigorous erect compact grower. (yakushimanum × 'Doncaster') Mid season. 1.3 × 1m.

Rhododendron 'Pink Twins'
Deep pink buds open to a unique shade of pink, hose-in-hose florets. Emerald-green leaves contrasting with yellow stems and petioles. (catawbiense × haematodes) Mid season to late. 2.5 × 2m.

Rhododendron 'Platinum Pearl'
Delicate pale pink with dark rose basal flare. Large flared trumpet-shaped florets, immense compact rounded truss. Vigorous grower, erect rounded compact form, large jade-green foliage. Mid season to late. 2.5 × 2m.

Rhododendron 'President Roosevelt'
Rich rosy red margins merging to white in the centre. Frilly florets in tall conical trusses. Attractive leaves, variegated deep yellow and green. Vigorous, beautiful in form, foliage and flower. (sport from limbatum) Early season. 2.5 × 2m. **271**

Rhododendron 'Ptarmigan'
Pure white, thin-textured flowers borne profusely on dwarf compact plant with small dark foliage. (orthocladum var microleucum × leucaspis) Early to mid season. 30 × 90cm.

Rhododendron 'Purple Gem'
Light purple flowers in a profusion of small trusses. Dwarf compact, bushy habit, scaly new foliage. (fastigiatum × carolinianum) Early to mid season. 60 × 90cm.

Rhododendron 'Purple Lace'
Large buds open to dark royal purple flowers with faint white smudge. Large lacy florets in compact shapely trusses. Handsome glossy leaves, compact bushy grower. ('Britannia' × Purple Splendour') Mid to late season. 2.5 × 2m.

Rhododendron 'Purple Splendour'
Darkest purple flowers with darker central flare and yellow anthers. Ruffled florets in compact rounded trusses. Sturdy compact leafy plant. Among the finest in this colour. (ponticum hybrid) Late season. 2.5 × 2m.

Rhododendron 'Rainbow'
White flowers margined deep pink. Vigorous upright grower, glossy, textured foliage. (hardy hybrid × griffithianum) Mid season. 3 × 3m.

Rhododendron 'Red Eye'
Deep reddish purple with olive-green eye, gradually changing to red. Hardy and dependable. Medium compact grower. ('Anna Kruschke' × 'Purple Splendour') Mid season to late. 2.5 × 2m.

Rhododendron 'Red Olympia'
Beautiful dark red, heavily spotted black. Open cup-shaped florets in large wide dome-shaped truss. Narrow erect grower, large glossy dark-green foliage. ('Anna' × 'Fusilier') Mid season. 2 × 1.3m.   **289**

Rhododendron 'Renoir'
Bright red buds opening light pink in the centre with deeper pink margins and a maroon flare in the throat, borne prolifically in compact trusses. Compact grower, suitable for training as a standard. (Pauline × yakushimanum) Mid season. 1.3 × 1.3m.   **271**

Rhododendron 'Repose'
Magnificent deep cream fading to white with chartreuse flare in the throat. Large florets in a compact rounded truss. Slow growing. (lacteum × discolor) Mid season. 3 × 2.5m.   **272**

Rhododendron 'Reve Rose'
Salmon rose flowers freely produced in loose trusses on a neat rounded compact bush. Coppery young foliage maturing bright green. (forrestii repens × 'Bowbells') Early to mid season. 75 × 90cm.

Rhododendron 'Ring of Fire'
Deep golden yellow flowers margined with a ring of vibrant orange red. Small to medium compact grower, attractive foliage. ('Darigold' × 'Idealist'). Mid to late season. 2.5 × 2m.

Rhododendron 'Rubicon'
Glistening cardinal-red flowers spotted black on upper lobe. Large open bell-shaped florets in impressive compact trusses. Glossy deep green foliage, upright compact grower. ('Noyo Chief' × Kilimanjaro) Mid season to late. 1.3 × 1.3m.   **271**

Rhododendron 'Ruby Bowman'
Rose pink shaded deep wine-red in the centre. Compact long-lasting trusses. (R fortunei × 'Lady Bligh') Mid season. 1.3 × 1.3m.   **272**

Rhododendron 'Ruby Hart'
Deep blood red, heavy wax-textured flowers in lax trusses of 4–6 florets. Compact grower, dark green glossy foliage. Sun tolerant. ('Carmen' × 'Elizabeth') Early to mid season. 75 × 90cm.   **272**

Rhododendron 'Saffron Queen'
Saffron yellow to sulphur yellow, 4cm flaring trumpet-shaped florets in lax trusses. Narrow glossy leaves, open growth pattern. (xanthostephanum × burmanicum) Mid season. 1.5 × 1.5m.

Rhododendron 'Sapphire'
Light purplish blue, with 4–5 florets in loose trusses. Very compact plant, small 'dusty' green leaves. ('Blue Tit' × impeditum) Early to mid season. 90 × 90cm.

Rhododendron 'Scarlet Wonder'
Brilliant scarlet-red, frilly bell-shaped florets of good substance in lax trusses of 4–6. Compact grower, glossy foliage, tolerant of heat and cold. ('Elizabeth Hobbie' seedling) Mid season. 90 × 90cm.

Rhododendron 'Scintillation'
Pastel pink flowers with bronze flare. Florets with good substance in full rounded trusses. Vigorous grower, dark glossy foliage, plant with good form. (possibly fortunei hybrid) Early to mid season. 1.5 × 1.5m.

Rhododendron 'Seta'
Light pink with deeper pink candy stripe on reverse. Narrow tubular florets in lax umbels in profusion. Free-flowering early in the season. (spinuliferum × moupinense). Early season. 1.30 × 1.30m.

Rhododendron 'Seven Stars'
Reddish purple buds open to palest pink, almost white flowers with delicate fragrance, flushed purple-red outside. Long-lasting, ball-shaped trusses of 12–15 florets. Dull deep-green recurving foliage. (Loderi Sir Joseph Hooker × yakushimanum) Mid season. 1.3 × 1.3m.

Rhododendron 'Shamrock'
Pale-green and yellow buds open to chartreuse tinged green flowers with minimal darker spots, borne in trusses of 7–9 florets. Compact spreading plant, rounded glossy deep green foliage. (keiskei dwarf × hanceanum nanum) Early season. 60 × 90cm.

Rhododendron 'Silver Edge'
Lavender with light orange flare. Attractive deep green leaves margined creamy white. Hardy vigorous grower. (Syn ponticum 'Silver Edge') Mid season. 2.5 × 2m.

Rhododendron 'Sleepy'
Delicate soft lavender mauve flowers fading to white. Compact bushy grower. (yakushimanum × 'Doncaster' selfed) Mid season. 1.3 × 1.3m

Rhododendron 'Spring Parade'
Clear rosy red with distinctive creamy anthers, borne profusely in compact conical trusses. Vigorous compact grower, unusual recurving leaves. (red catawbiense hybrid × 'Cunningham's White') Mid season. 2.5 × 2m.   **272**

Rhododendron 'Sugar Pink'
Clear bright pink in tall compact trusses. Large smooth deep green foliage. (['Fawn' × Queen O'the May] × 'Trude Webster') Mid season. 3 × 2.5m.

Rhododendron 'Sunbeam'
Light brown buds open to blend of pink and lemon, melting into apricot-orange margins. Large florets in compact trusses. Most unusual colour in Rhododendrons. ('Jalisco' × 'Dido') Mid season. 1.5 × 1.5m.   **272**

Rhododendron 'Sunspray'
Pure golden yellow flowers, large florets in lax trusses. Large attractive foliage. ('Alice Franklin' × 'Crest') Mid season. 3 × 2.5m.   **272**

Rhododendron 'Surrey Heath'
Rose-pink flowers with creamy yellow centre, slightly spotted orange. Flowers fade with two-toned effect. Compact rounded trusses. Compact spreading mound, long narrow leaves covered with white tomentum when young. Mature leaves without indumentum. (['facetum × 'Fabia'] × [yakushimanum × 'Britannia']) Mid season. 1.3 × 1.3m.

Rhododendron 'Susan'
Delicate lavender-blue flowers with maroon flare on upper lobe, borne in compact rounded trusses. Slow-growing, compact habit. Exquisite. (campanulatum × fortunei) Mid season. 2.5 × 2m.   **289**

Rhododendron 'Taurus'
Vibrant flowers in cherry-red, orient-red with turkey-red throat spotted black borne in globular trusses. Sturdy erect plant, thick textured deep green foliage. (Jean Marie de Montague × strigillosum) Early to mid season. 1.8 × 1.5m.

Rhododendron 'Ted's Orchid Sunset'
Lilac to orchid-pink flowers with radiating central zone of golden-yellow and rust-brown flare, borne in full rounded trusses. Dark green, ribbed and recurved leaves with reddish stems and petioles. ('Purple Splendour' × Mrs Donald Graham') Mid season. 2.5 × 2m.

Rhododendron 'Titian Beauty'
Venetian red flowers in small compact trusses. Neat compact grower with small foliage. ([facetum × 'Fabia Tangerine'] × 'Fabia' × yakushimanum) Mid season to late. 1.3 × 1.3m.

Rhododendron 'Trewithan Orange'
Translucent, tangerine-orange, pendent bell or trumpet-shaped florets in small trusses. Erect grower. ('Full House' × concatenans) Mid season. 1.5 × 1.5m.

Rhododendron 'Trude Webster'
Clear deep pink flowers, fading to almost white, held in large conical trusses of beautiful frilled florets. Vigorous grower, with large broad rich green slightly twisted foliage. ('Countess of Derby' selfed), forming a compact bush with large wide leaves. Mid season. 1.5m.

Rhododendron 'Unique'
Bright pink buds opening cream with pink tinge borne in compact rounded trusses. Compact, rounded, free-flowering plant. (campylocarpum hybrid) Early season. 2.5 × 2m.   **289**

Rhododendron 'Van Nes Sensation'
Lilac-pink buds open to pale lilac or orchid pink, slightly fragrant flowers with lemon eye and reddish spotting, borne in large dome-shaped trusses. Large, dark green foliage. Prefers semi-shade as flowers fade to white in sun. (fortunei 'Mrs Butler' × halopeanum) Early to mid season. 3 × 2.5m.   **290**

Rhododendron 'Virginia Richards'
Deep pink buds open pale yellow with pink overlay, turning deep yellow with crimson flare in the throat, borne in conical trusses of 10–12 florets. Deep green heavily veined foliage. ([wardii × 'F C Puddle'] × Mrs Betty Robertson) Mid season. 2.5 × 2m.

Rhododendron 'Vulcan's Flame'
Fiery blood-red, open trumpet-shaped florets in rounded trusses. Medium compact grower, blooms consistently. (R griersonianum × 'Mars') Mid to late. 1.5 × 1.5m.

Rhododendron 'White Gold'
Pure white flowers with prominent golden-yellow flare on the upper lobe intensifying to orange in the throat. Vigorous compact grower, extremely floriferous. ('Mrs J G Millais' × 'Cheyenne') Mid season to late. 2.5 × 2m.   **289**

Rhododendron 'Whitney Orange'
Apricot-orange in the centre blending to deeper orange at the margins. Low-growing habit with decumbent branches. (possibly dichroanthum hybrid) Mid season to late. 1.5 × 1.5m.

Rhododendron 'Whitney's Late Orange'
Resembles above but deeper orange shadings and flowers later in the season when most Rhododendrons have finished. (possibly dichroanthum hybrid) Late season. 1.5 × 1.5m.

Rhododendron 'Winsome'
Rosy red in bud opening glowing cerise pink. Funnel shaped, wavy edged flowers in loose pendent racemes in great profusion. Coppery young growths maturing dark green. Compact vigorous grower. ('Hummingbird' × griersonianum) Mid season. 1.3 × 1.3m.   **289**

Rhododendron yakushimanum
Buds rose pink, opening apricot pink, maturing white. Bell-shaped florets in compact trusses smother the whole bush. Compact dome-shaped bush, young shoots covered with soft white down. Ovate leaves with recurving margins, dark glossy green above, densely brown felted beneath. Found on windy, rain drenched mountain peaks of Japanese Yakushima Island. Excellent rock garden plant. A parent of numerous hybrids. Mid season. 1.3 × 1.3m.

Rhododendron yakushimanum 'Koichiro Wada'
Rose pink in bud opening pale apple-blossom pink fading to white, medium rounded truss. Dwarf compact grower, handsome foliage, heavily brown-tomentose beneath. Parent of numerous dwarf hybrids but still highly rated. Mid season. 1 × 1m.

RHODODENDRON READY REFERENCE

Blue, mauve and purple
'Anah Kruschke'
'Arthur Bedford'
augustinii 'Barto Blue'
'Blue Boy'
'Blue Diamond'
'Blue Ensign'
'Blue Gem'
'Blue Jay'
'Blue Pacific'
'Blue Peter'
'Blue River'
'Blue Tit'
'Bud Flannagen'
'Bumblebee'
'Chapmanii Wonder'
'Colonel Coen'
'Lavender Girl'

'Mrs J P Lade'
'Purple Gem'
'Purple Lace'
'Purple Splendour'
'Sapphire'
'Silver Edge'
'Susan'

Orange and apricot
'Alison Johnstone'
'Apricot Sherbert'
'Autumn Gold'
'Bacher's Gold'
'Brinny'
'Burma Road'
'CIS'
'Dido'
'Jingle Bells'

'Kubla Khan'
'Medusa'
'Old Copper'
'Ostbos Low Yellow'
'Ring of Fire'
'Trewithan Orange'
'Whitney Orange'
'Whitney's Late Orange'

Pink
'Alice'
'Anna Rose Whitney'
'Anna'
'Antoon van Weelie'
'April Glow'
'Arthur J Ivens'
'Bambi'
'Bashful'

'Bernard Shaw'
'Betty Arrington'
'Betty Wormald'
'Bow Bells'
'Bravo'
'Brickdust'
'Brigitte'
'Brown Eyes'
'Bruce Brechtbill'
'Charlotte de Rothschild'
'Cheer'
'Christmas Cheer'
'Clementine Lemaire'
'Cotton Candy'
'Dalkeith'
'Denali'
'Doc'
'El Camino'

'Elegans'
'Fair Lady'
'Fairy Light'
'Furnivals Daughter'
'Grand Slam'
'Hallelujah'
'Hurricane'
'Ivan D Wood'
'Janet Blair'
'Lady Clementine Mitford'
'Lems Cameo'
'Lems Monarch'
'Loderi Patience'
'Loderi Pink Diamond'
'Loderi Pink Topaz'
'Loderi Venus'
'Lucky Strike'
'Mary Tasker'
'Merle Lee'
'Mission Bells'
'Molly Ann'
'Mrs G W Leak'
'Naomi Exbury'
'Naomi Nautilus'
'Pania' pix
'Percy Wiseman'
'Pink Cherub'
'Pink Twins'
'Platinum Pearl'
'Renoir'
'Reve Rose'
'Ruby Bowman'
'Scintillation'
'Seta'
'Seven Stars'
'Sugar Pink'
'Sunbeam'
'Surrey Heath'
'Ted's Orchid Sunset'
'Trude Webster'
'Van Ness Sensation'

Red
'Anuschka'
'Bad Eilsen'
'Baden Baden'
'Balstrode Park'
'Beau Brummel'
'Beefeater'
'Betsie Balcom'
'Bibiani'
'Billy Budd'
'Black Prince'
'Bremen'
'Brendon King'
'Broxens'
'Bulstrode Park'
'Burgundy'
'Burning Bush'
'Captain Jack'
'Carmen'
'Cary Ann'
'Cornubia'
'Crossroads'

'Dopey'
'Dorinthia'
'Elizabeth Hobbie'
'Elizabeth'
'Fireman Jeff'
'Flirt'
'Floras Boy'
'Genghis Khan'
'Gertrude Schale'
'Grace Seabrook'
'Halfdan Lem'
'Heart's Delight'
'Hydon Hunter'
'Indiana'
'Irresistible Impulse'
'Isabel Pierce'
'Ivanhoe'
'Jean Marie de Montague'
'Johnny Bender'
'Kaponga'
'Lamplighter'
'Leo'
'Markeeta's Prize'
'Mars'
'Noyo Chief'
'President Roosevelt'
'Red Eye'
'Red Olympia'
'Rubicon'
'Ruby Hart'
'Scarlet Wonder'
'Spring Parade'
'Taurus'
'Titian Beauty'
'Vulcan's Flame'
'Winsome'

White and cream
aberconwayi
'Alpine Meadow'
'Amor'
'Angelo Solent Queen'
'Applause'
'Avalanche'
'Award'
'Babylon'
'Baron Philippe de Rothschild'
'Beauty of Littleworth'
'Belle Heller'
'Boddaertianum'
'Countess of Haddington'
'Danella'
'Dianne Titcomb'
'Dora Ameteis'
'Fragrantissimum'
'Ginny Gee'
'Grumpy'
'Helene Schiffner'
'Hoppy'
'Kirsty'
'Lalique'
'Lemon Ice'
'Lily'
'Little White Dove'

'Loderi Fairyland'
'Loderi King George'
'Loders White'
'Mi Amor'
'Morning Cloud'
'Mount Everest'
'Mrs A T de la Mere'
'Ptarmigan'
'Rainbow'
'Repose'
'Sleepy'
'White Gold'
yakushimanum
yakushimanum 'Koichiro
    Wada'

Yellow and lemon
'Alice Street'
'Binfield'
'Brasilia'
'Broughtonii Aureum'
'Buttermint'
'Carlene'
'Carolyn Grace'
'Chikor'
'Chink'
'Chrysomanicum'
'Cowslip'
'Cream Crest'
'Cream Glory'
'Creamy Chiffon'
'Crest'
'Curlew'
'Frontier'
'Gold Mohur'
'Goldbukett'
'Golden Belle'
'Golden Torch'
'Golden Witt'
'Harvest Moon'
'Honeymoon'
'Hotei'
'Igtham Yellow' #2
'Ina Hair'
'Lady Dorothy Ella'
'Lascaux'
'Lemon Lodge'
'Lemon Mist'
'Michael's Pride'
'Nancy Evans'
'Odee Wright'
'Paprika Spiced'
'Parisienne'
'Patty Bee'
'Saffron Queen'
'Shamrock'
'Sunspray'
'Unique'
'Virginia Richards'

Dwarf and small-growing
(to 1.5m)
aberconwayi
'Alpine Meadow'

'Amor'
'Apricot Sherbert'
'April Glow'
'Bacher's Gold'
'Baden Baden'
'Bambi'
'Bashful'
'Beefeater'
'Blue Diamond'
'Blue Gem'
'Blue Jay'
'Blue Tit'
'Bow Bells'
'Brendon King'
'Bric-a-Brac'
'Brickdust'
'Broxens'
'Burning Bush'
'Buttermint'
'Carlene'
'Carmen'
'Cary Ann'
'Cheer'
'Chikor'
'Christmas Cheer'
'Chrysomanicum'
'CIS'
'Clementine Lemaire'
'Cowslip'
'Cream Crest'
'Creamy Chiffon'
'Curlew'
'Dalkeith'
'Doc'
'Dopey'
'Dora Ameteis'
'Elizabeth'
'Elizabeth Hobbie'
'Fairy Light'
'Floras Boy'
'Gertrude Schale'
'Ginny Gee'
'Gold Mohur'
'Goldbukett'
'Golden Belle'
'Golden Torch'
'Golden Witt'
'Grumpy'
'Harvest Moon'
'Honeymoon'
'Hoppy'
'Hotei'
'Hurricane'
'Hydon Hunter'
'Indiana'
'Janet Blair'
'Jingle Bells'
'Johnny Bender'
'Kirsty'
'Lady Clementine Mitford'
'Lemon Mist'
'Little White Dove'
'Mission Bells'
'Molly Ann'

'Morning Cloud'	'Pink Cherub'	'Sapphire'	'Titian Beauty'
'Nancy Evans'	'Ptarmigan'	'Scarlet Wonder'	'Trewithan Orange'
'Naomi Exbury'	'Purple Gem'	'Scintillation'	'Trude Webster'
'Odee Wright'	'Renoir'	'Seta'	'Vulcan's Flame'
'Ostbos Low Yellow'	'Reve Rose'	'Seven Stars'	'Whitney Orange'
'Paprika Spiced'	'Rubicon'	'Shamrock'	'Whitney's Late Orange'
'Parisienne'	'Ruby Bowman'	'Sleepy'	'Winsome'
'Patty Bee'	'Ruby Hart'	'Sunbeam'	yakushimanum
'Percy Wiseman'	'Saffron Queen'	'Surrey Heath'	yakushimanum 'Koichiro Wada'

RHODODENDRON
VIREYA

Vireya or tropical Rhododendrons occur naturally in an area ranging from northern Australia through New Guinea, Indonesia and Malaysia to south east Asia growing at 2–3000 metres above sea level in an environment which gives them filtered sunlight, warm midday temperatures, frequent moist cloud cover and night temperatures to almost zero. Growing near the equator where day length is relatively constant, most species flower at irregular intervals, often several times a year.

These highly coloured Rhododendrons are semi-epiphytic, happier to be perched high up in tree branches than growing on the forest floor. Sometimes they're found in rock crevices along with other plants which enjoy similar conditions. All species have lepidote leaves — covered with tiny scurfy scales. Extensive hybridizing has made available scores of beautiful cultivars in vivid shades or red, orange, yellow and pink.

Because of their epiphytic nature, Vireyas don't have extensive root systems and may not always take kindly to being allowed excessive root space in over-rich soil conditions. Group planting either with their own kind or with other plants which quickly fill the soil with competing roots, or planting within the rooting systems of large deciduous trees seems to suit them best. They also take kindly to the restriction of containers of moderate size.

Grow in loose-textured, free-draining, moisture-retentive acid soil. Apply weak soluble liquid fertilizer or light applications of controlled-release fertilizer such as Osmocote once or twice a year. Vireyas need good light but do not like continual exposure to strong sunlight. Give them adequate ventilation but protection from constant strong wind. Excellent for frost-free gardens. A whole bed of Vireya Rhododendrons would really be a magnificent feature. Average height and width 1–1.5m. Vireyas bloom 2–3 times each year, autumn through winter and spring through early summer.
Ericaceae. *All evergreen.*

Rhododendron vireya 'Aurigeranium'
Magnificent blend of orange and yellow tones, large open-faced florets in loose trusses. Purer yellow in winter.

Rhododendron vireya 'Brightly'
Brilliant orange-red, medium sized flowers. Compact grower, dark green foliage.

Rhododendron vireya 'Cameo Spice'
Creamy yellow flushed apricot pink, sweetly fragrant, large open trumpet-shaped florets in open trusses. Bold felted foliage.   **290**

Rhododendron vireya 'Candy'
Soft pale pink tubular to trumpet flowers in loose trusses. Small to medium grower, bright green foliage.

Rhododendron vireya 'Carillon Bells'
Rich pink bell-shaped flowers almost always in bloom. Small grower, lush foliage.

Rhododendron vireya 'Clare Rouse'
Yellow-orange with orange-red lobes, medium to large, bell-shaped to tubular flowers.

Rhododendron vireya 'Commonae'
Interesting type with foliage resembling Azalea. Three distinct forms with clusters of bell-shaped flowers in cream, pink or red.

Rhododendron vireya 'Coral Chimes'
Delightful pink bell-shaped flowers almost smother the plant. Dainty small foliage. Small grower, also suitable for hanging baskets.

Rhododendron vireya 'Coral Flare'
Vivid coral pink in spectacular trusses. Medium sized, spreading grower.

Rhododendron vireya 'Cordial Orange'
Bright orange tubular flowers and unusual needle-like foliage.

Rhododendron vireya 'Craig Faragher'
Soft pink, small tubular to bell-shaped flowers, small foliage and growth habit. Suitable for hanging baskets.

Rhododendron vireya 'Cristo Rey'
Vivid orange lobes merging to yellow in the throat. Vigorous erect grower.

Rhododendron vireya 'Dawn Chorus'
Lobes edged apricot blending to cream in the throat, borne in medium firm trusses. Neat tidy grower.

Rhododendron vireya 'Dr Herman Sleumer'
Beautiful, fragrant, medium sized flowers in loose trusses, pink with cream throat.

Rhododendron vireya 'Fireplum'
Wine-red or plum-red, medium bell-shaped flowers. Distinctive colouring amongst Vireyas.

Rhododendron vireya 'First Light'
Vivid pink, trumpet-shaped florets in loose trusses. Bright green, glossy foliage, compact medium grower.

Rhododendron vireya 'Flamenco Dancer'
Bright golden yellow flowers, margins suffused apricot-orange, with 15–20 flaring trumpet-shaped florets in firm rounded trusses. This cultivar smothers itself in bloom. Compact grower, glossy deep green foliage.   **290**

Rhododendron vireya 'Gilded Sunrise'
Brilliant clear yellow, large trumpet-shaped florets held in loose trusses of 7–9. Erect and open growth, with glossy deep green foliage.   **290**

Rhododendron vireya 'Gold Bells'
Soft golden yellow shadings, sometimes tinted apricot. Small to medium upright grower.

Rhododendron vireya 'Golden Charm'
Creamy-yellow flowers blending to orange-red borne profusely in large trusses. Attractive coppery bronze foliage.   **291**

Rhododendron vireya 'Greer's Pink'
Exquisite pastel pink flowers in loose trusses almost smother the entire plant.

Rhododendron vireya 'Haloed Gold'
Golden-yellow frilled florets carefully margined with thin orange line. Large trusses.

Rhododendron vireya 'Helwigii'
Deep blood red waxy textured flowers in loose trusses. Bold foliage.

Rhododendron vireya 'Herzogii'
Unusual species, white, fragrant, tubular flowers in clusters. Bold foliage.

Rhododendron vireya 'Hot Tropic'
Large, bright orange-red flowers in loose erect trusses.

Rhododendron vireya 'Hugh Redgrove'
Bright orange scarlet trumpet flowers in trusses to fourteen. Handsome, bronzed foliage.

Rhododendron vireya 'Jasminiflorum var Punctatum'
Pink flushed, tubular, strongly fragrant flowers. Salver-shaped foliage. Smaller grower, suitable for hanging baskets.

Rhododendron vireya 'jasminiflorum'
Sweetly fragrant, jasmine-like, white trumpet flowers in loose trusses. Small, erect multi branched bush.

Rhododendron vireya 'Java Light'
Brilliant orange to flame-red, large trumpet-shaped florets in rounded compact trusses. Upright bushy grower, glossy bright green foliage. **291**

Rhododendron vireya 'javanicum'
Soft orange, deepening to bright orange, with yellow shadings, large funnel-shaped florets in large rounded trusses. Attractive glossy, emerald-green foliage.

Rhododendron vireya 'Kisses'
Rich pink flowers blending to cream in the throat and cream reverse. Contrasting red anthers. **291**

Rhododendron vireya 'koneri'
Large creamy white trumpet flowers in trusses of up to eight.

Rhododendron vireya 'laetum'
Deep yellow, suffused salmon, red-tipped anthers, large fragrant funnel-shaped florets, compact trusses. Erect open grower, attractive foliage. **292**

Rhododendron vireya 'Liberty Bar'
Coral pink flowers in large trusses. Sturdy growing bush.

Rhododendron vireya 'Littlest Angel'
Small bell-shaped, cardinal red flowers. Compact, low-growing bushy plant to 30cm.

Rhododendron vireya 'Lochae'
Soft rosy red tinted scarlet, small tubular bell-shaped florets in loose trusses. Erect bushy grower, glossy bright green foliage.

Rhododendron vireya 'Loranthifolium'
Pure white, long tubular to trumpet-shaped flowers with five wide-flaring lobes, borne in loose trusses. **292**

Rhododendron vireya 'Lulu'
Apricot flowers blending to creamy yellow in the throat. Beautiful medium-size truss.

Rhododendron vireya 'Macgregoriae'
Yellow to orange shaded flowers, medium funnel-shaped florets in large rounded trusses. Vigorous upright bushy grower, glossy bright green foliage.

Rhododendron vireya 'Macgregoriae × Retivenium'
Rich golden-yellow flower in impressive trusses up to 20 florets. Deep green foliage.

Rhododendron vireya 'Narnia'
Waxy orange-red lobes blending to golden yellow in the throat. Resembles Tropic Glow but with larger, bolder trusses.

Rhododendron vireya 'Ne Plus Ultra'
Glowing bright scarlet-red flowers in large open trusses. Glossy deep green foliage.

Rhododendron vireya 'Niugini Firebird'
Spectacular, large orange-red flowers. Impressive in full bloom.

Rhododendron vireya 'Orbiculare'
Bell-shaped, rose pink unspotted, fragrant flowers. Leaves orbicular to salver form. Best in partial shade.

Rhododendron vireya 'Oriana'
Yellow, medium sized flowers suffused orange borne profusely in loose trusses.

Rhododendron vireya 'Pendance'
Attractive white flowers with the faintest pink glow, borne in large full trusses. Medium, bushy grower. **292**

Rhododendron vireya 'Phaeochitum'
Soft pink, curved tubular flowers with flared lobes. Young shoots covered with rusty brown hairs.

Rhododendron vireya 'Pindi Pearl'
Creamy apricot fragrant flowers in large open trusses. Bold foliage.

Rhododendron vireya 'Pink Delight'
Rich satiny pink, long-tubed trumpet flowers in loose trusses of 5–7 florets. Vigorous upright bushy grower.

Rhododendron vireya 'Polyanthemum'
Bright pinkish orange, strongly fragrant flowers. Young shoots reddish brown and furry, becoming glabrous green when mature.

Rhododendron vireya 'Popcorn'
Creamy white flowers in large trees of 10–14 florets. Light green foliage.

Rhododendron vireya 'Princess Alexandra'
Pale pink, waxy, slightly fragrant flowers fading to white. Compact grower.

Rhododendron vireya 'Red Rooster'
Distinctive, bright orange-red flowers. Medium sized grower.

Rhododendron vireya 'Retivenium × Tropic Glow'
Brilliant yellow flowers suffused orange, intensifying around the margins. Large open trusses, dark green foliage.

Rhododendron vireya 'Rob's Favourite'
Rich watermelon pink to salmon-red flowers in loose trusses. Open spreading grower.

Rhododendron vireya 'Saint Valentine'
Brilliant, deep-scarlet red. pendent bell-shaped flowers produced freely. Dwarf grower to 75cm, suitable for rock gardens, containers or hanging baskets.

Rhododendron vireya 'Scarlet Beauty'
Impressive orange-red flowers blending to orange-buff in the throat. Dark green foliage.

Rhododendron vireya 'Silken Shimmer'
Clear pink, fragrant silky flowers in large open trusses. Bold felted foliage.

Rhododendron vireya 'Silver Thimble'
White flowers blushed pink with deeper pink throat. Small foliage, open erect grower to 60cm.

Rhododendron vireya 'Simbu Sunset'
Yellow in bud opening orange with yellow throat, shading to red at the margins, large open trumpet flowers in rounded compact trusses. Vigorous grower, bold, glossy mid-green foliage. **291**

Rhododendron vireya 'Souvenir de J H Mangles'

Vivid, iridescent coral-rose pink in impressive loose trusses. Handsome foliage and shapely bush.

Rhododendron vireya 'Star Posy'

Clear pink with reddish veins, red throat and anthers, borne in large open trusses. Bushy growth.   **292**

Rhododendron vireya 'Stenophyllum'

Waxy, deep-orange open-faced flowers. Unusual narrow needle-like foliage. Best in semi-shade. Smaller grower, good for hanging baskets.

Rhododendron vireya 'Suaveolens'

Pure white, highly fragrant, tubular flowers with starry flaring lobes. Handsome ovate foliage. Best in semi-shade.

Rhododendron vireya 'Sunny Splendour'

Vivid golden-yellow, large flared bell-shaped flowers in rounded trusses with deep-red pedicels. Medium bushy, upright grower, deep green foliage.

Rhododendron vireya 'Sunny'

Buttercup yellow flowers shaded pink, in rounded trusses. Free-flowering.

Rhododendron vireya 'Sweet Wendy'

Creamy apricot, sweetly fragrant flowers flushed pink. Strong upright grower.   **292**

Rhododendron vireya 'Tango Time'

Bright tangerine-orange, small bell-shaped flowers, freely produced in compact trusses. Small to medium upright grower. Small, rich green glossy foliage.

Rhododendron vireya 'Tiffany Rose'

Deep rosy red, bell-shaped flowers shading to pink. Free-flowering.

Rhododendron vireya 'Tropic Glow'

Bright orange-red with yellow throat, medium to small open-faced florets in rounded compact trusses. Medium upright grower, glossy, mid-green foliage. Very free flowering and popular.   **291**

Rhododendron vireya 'Tropic Glow × Lochae'

Vivid salmon-red flowers with black anthers. Shapely bush, blooming well during winter.

Rhododendron vireya 'Tropic Tango'

Apricot flowers suffused orange. Large trusses on compact bush.

Rhododendron vireya 'Tuba'

Pale pink, tubular, 75mm, fragrant flowers with white, starry, flaring lobes. Strong growing, shapely bush.

Rhododendron vireya 'Wattlebird'

Vivid bright yellow. Up to 15 large florets in loose trusses. Excellent, reliable.   **292**

RHODOLEIA

A genus of about 7 species of small trees from southern China to Sumatra named from the Greek *rhodon*, rose and *leios*, smooth, in reference to rose-like flowers and stems without thorns. At first glance it could be mistaken for a Rhododendron or Camellia but actually belongs to the witch-hazel family. Listed species is a beautiful tree for form, foliage and flower, discovered by Captain Champion in Hong Kong in 1848 and now widely distributed throughout the warm-temperate world. Grows in humid frost-free locations, sheltered from cold winds in a warm sunny spot in deeply worked, free draining, organically enriched acid soil. Mulch freely and keep moist in dry periods.

Hamamelidaceae.

Rhodoleia championii
Silk Rose

Forms a glabrous tree with knobbly branches covered with smooth blue-green bark, slightly reddish on the sunny side. Elliptic-obovate, bright-green, smooth and thick leathery leaves to 9cm long, finely pubescent and silvery beneath, margins entire. Foliage from the previous year crowds toward the ends of each branch. Flowerheads appear from leaf axils, clusters of 5–10 flowers without petals, each with ten stamens, surrounded by overlapping brown, gold, pink, and white scales or bracts. Each cluster encircled by 15–20 rose-pink petaloid bracts. Up to ten of these exquisite inflorescences each about 5–7cm across are borne at the end of each branchlet late winter early spring, supported on recurving petioles which hold them clear of the leaves facing downwards. Championii — see above. Evergreen. 6 × 5m.

RHOPALOSTYLIS

A genus of three species of solitary palms from New Zealand, Chatham, Norfolk and Kermadec Islands, named from the Greek *rhopalon*, a club, and *stylis*, a small pillar or column, referring to the club shaped spadix. The southern-most representative of the Palm family, most others being tropic-dwellers.

Being shady bush dwellers, Nikau likes to be amongst other trees or shrubs in a shady woodland situations, planted in deeply worked soil, conditioned and mulched with peat moss. Excellent palms for garden or containers, tolerant of sun, wind, and coastal conditions but keep sheltered and moist when young. Compares favourably with some of the more tropical palms. Plant in clumps of at least three. Slow growing and easily accommodated.

Palmaceae. *All evergreen.*

Rhopalostylis baueri
Norfolk Palm

Native to Norfolk Island. Forms a closely ringed greyish trunk with short plump crownshaft to 50cm topped with stiff deep-green pinnate leaves with linear to lanceolate leaflets or pinnae to 60 × 4.5cm. Branched inflorescence to 60cm long from below the crownshaft with white flowers followed by 15mm reddish fruit. Somewhat more bold, wide-spreading and deeper green than the New Zealand Nikau. Baueri — for Ferdinand Bauer, botanical explorer. 6 × 5m.

Rhopalostylis cheesemanii
Kermadec Nikau Palm

From Kermadec Islands, closely related to R sapida and with generally similar appearance. Differs mainly in larger inflorescence somewhat larger fruit, darker seeds and distinct hilum, the scar or mark indicating the point of attachment in the seed. 3 × 1.5m.

Rhopalostylis sapida
Nikau Palm, Shaving Brush Palm

Abundant through forested areas of the North Island and south to Akaroa Harbour and Greymouth. Elegant and graceful palm with straight, smooth slender stems to 8m with close annular rings, the scars left by fallen leaves. Crowned with pinnate or feather-like rich-green leaves to 3m long, comprising linear or lanceolate leaflets to 90 × 1.5cm, margins reflexed. Leaves stand almost upright from a bulging crownshaft.

Stem crownshaft and flaring crown suggest the common name. Detached leaf bases large enough for a child to sit in. Branched inflorescence appears below the crownshaft developing from a large club-shaped spathe or spadix. Lilac to cream flower clusters to 60cm long, appear through summer followed by 10mm fruits ripe through autumn three years later. Sapida — with a pleasant taste. 4 × 1.5m.

RIBES

A genus of about 150 species of deciduous and evergreen shrubs distributed through temperate regions of the Northern Hemisphere, named from Arabic or Persian *ribas*, acid tasting, given by early Arabian physicians to a species of rhubarb and erroneously applied to currants. The genus includes fruiting currants and gooseberries. Ornamental Ribes are grown for attractive flowers. Plant in deeply worked, well-drained, moisture-retentive, moderately fertile soil in full sun. Hardy to –20°C. Remove completely about 25% of flowered stems after flowering and trim the remainder. Flowers borne on previous year's wood. Grossulariaceae. *All deciduous.*

Ribes odoratum
Buffalo Currant, Clove Currant
Native to central USA. Small to medium shrub with open erect habit and oval-rounded 3–5 lobed leaves to 8cm, glabrous, deep-green, richly coloured in autumn, margins coarsely toothed. Large golden-yellow clove-scented tubular flowers to 15mm long, lobes to 8mm across, borne in lax racemes during spring followed by 1cm globose glossy black fruit. Odoratum — fragrant. 2 × 1.5m.

Ribes sanguineum
Flowering Currant, Pink Winter Currant
Spectacular and hardy , from coastal ranges, California to British Columbia. Branches upright, reddish brown and softly downy. Palmate maple-like leaves with cordate base, 3–5 lobed, dark-green and slightly downy, white-felted beneath, well coloured in autumn. The whole bush becomes alive with colour from early spring as small deep- rose pink flowers appear from every branch in pendent racemes of 10–30. Blue-black fruit with whitish bloom often follow the flowers. Sanguineum — blood red. 1.5 × 1m.

Ribes sanguineum 'King Edward VII'
More compact form of R sanguineum with intense crimson-red flowers. 1 × 1m.

ROBINIA

A genus of some 20 species of deciduous trees and shrubs from wilder regions of USA and Mexico, named for Jean Robin of Paris, 16th century gardener and herbalist to Henri IV and Louis XIII. Ornamental cultivars of R pseudoacacia have a light airy appearance especially 'Frisia' with bright golden-yellow ferny foliage. Fast growing, hardy to –20°C, tolerant of heat drought and pollution. Plant in average deeply worked, free-draining soil. Early training and staking recommended. Prune to shape.
Leguminosae. *All deciduous.*

Robinia pseudoacacia
Black Locust, False Acacia
Rapid grower with open sparse framework, deeply furrowed brownish bark and branchlets, studded with spiny stipules. Pinnate leaves to 25cm with 9–19, elliptic to ovate 25–50mm leaflets in opposite pairs. White slightly fragrant 20–25mm flowers in pendent racemes early summer, attractive to bees. Smooth brown beanlike 10cm pods remain through winter. Hardly a species for suburban gardens, but valuable on farms, for erosion control with spreading suckering roots, tolerance to drought, thorns which make it stockproof and durable timber. Pseudoacacia — false acacia. 15 × 8m.

Robinia pseudoacacia 'Casque Rouge'
More in keeping with home garden landscaping, this selected cultivar forms a small to medium, open, round-headed tree with black bark and soft mid-green, pinnate leaves. Short racemes of lilac-pink pea-shaped flowers late spring. 5 × 5m.

Robinia pseudoacacia 'Frisia'
Beautiful Dutch selection, one of the most brilliant yellow-foliaged trees. Forms a neat rounded head on a straight sturdy trunk. New growth nearly orange, maturing rich golden-yellow, spring through autumn. Spectacular small tree, quite manageable in smaller gardens. Contrasts nicely against a dark background and blends well with other spring colour-foliaged species. Frisia — of Friesland. 5 × 5m.

Robinia pseudoacacia 'Tortuosa'
Picturesque slow-growing small tree with short contorted or twisted branches often with pendent tips. 4 × 3m.

RONDELETIA

A genus of about 150 species of evergreen shrubs from Central to South America and Polynesia named for Guillaume Rondelet, 16th century French physician and naturalist. Grown for colourful flowers borne freely over long periods.

Listed species a little frost tender, but grows well against sunny or semi shady walls with protection from overhanging eaves, and good in containers. Plant in deeply worked, free-draining, organically enriched acid soil with peat moss. Mulch freely, feed occasionally and water well over dry periods. Pinch when young for compact form, remove spent flowers.
Rubiaceae.

Rondeletia amoena
Mexican Viburnum
Neat rounded but open-branched shrub. Leaves ovate or elliptic to oblong to 15 × 10cm, glossy olive-green, deeply veined, margins entire finely pubescent beneath. Small rich salmon-pink tubular flowers with yellow throat, borne in tight terminal clusters resembling viburnum almost cover the bush mid winter through spring and into summer. Long stems ideal for picking, blooms last well in water. Rated one of the most beautiful dwarf flowering shrubs, worthy of a place in every garden. Amoena — pleasing. Evergreen. 1.5 × 1m.

ROSMARINUS

Genus of two species of evergreen shrubs from southern Europe and North Africa named from the Latin *ros*, dew or moisture and *marinus* of the sea. Aromatic shrubs cultivated for centuries in western European gardens. Oil distilled from the leaves of R officinalis an important constituent of Eau de Cologne, and also has important culinary uses. Rosemary endures hot sun and poor soil but needs good drainage. Hardy to –10°C, intolerant of wet feet and withstands considerable drought once established. Feeding and watering rarely necessary. Frequent tip pinching controls growth when small. Older plants may be lightly pruned. There are types for dry borders, clipped hedges, ground or bank cover or wall spillers.
Labiatae. *All evergreen.*

Rosmarinus officinalis
Common Rosemary
Native to southern Europe and Asia Minor. Rugged upright growing shrub with linear aromatic leaves to 40 × 6mm, dark green above, greyish white beneath, margins rolled under. Blue flowers appear early summer in numerous axillary clusters along branches from the previous year. Serves well as a neat compact shrub or low division hedge, and a valuable herb. Officinalis — sold in shops, used of medicinal or other plants. 1.30 × 1m.

Rosmarinus officinalis 'Collingwood Ingram'

Semi prostrate form with gracefully curving branches, good for taller bank or ground cover where more informal or branching effects and high colour is desired. Flowers rich bright blue-violet. Syn 'Blue Lagoon' and 'Benenden Blue'. 60cm × 1.3m.

Rosmarinus officinalis 'Lockwood de Forest'

Resembles 'Prostratus' but with lighter, bright-green foliage and richer blue flowers. 30cm × 2m.

Rosmarinus officinalis 'Prostrata'
Dwarf Rosemary

Graceful low growing plant forming prostrate mats studded with light blue flowers in clusters. Good for rapid bank or ground cover, draping over walls or rocks, growing alongside paths or steps, in containers or window boxes. Syn R lavendulaceus. 30cm × 2m.

Rosmarinus officinalis 'Tuscan Blue'

Selected form with narrow rich-green foliage and deep violet-blue flowers. Rigid upright branches grow directly from the base. 1.8 × 1m.

ROYENA

A genus of fifteen species of trees or shrubs from tropical regions of the Northern Hemisphere named for Adrian van Royen, 18th century professor of botany at Leyden. Belongs to the ebony family of which some species yield a very hard and heavy wood, used for knife handles, piano keys, chessmen etc. Persimmon is also in this family. Listed species grown mainly for the beauty of its foliage. Provides a useful permanent evergreen background shrub or screen in warm districts. Plant in deeply worked, free-draining soil in full sun. Endures hard and dry conditions.
Ebenaceae.

Royena lucida
African Snowdrop Bush

A handsome South African shrub with downy shoots. Leaves elliptic-ovate to 5cm long, leathery, highly polished, bronzy green when young, maturing rich green, margins slightly waved. Pale yellow to white solitary, axillary flowers with reflexed lobes on 25mm petioles followed by 25mm ovoid to subglobose red or purple fruits, fleshy when ripe. Excellent slow-growing neat compact

shrub, admired for glossy, reddish new growth. Lucida — clear or shining. Evergreen. 1.5 × 1m.   **301**

RULINGIA

A genus of about 20 low-growing and taller shrubs mostly from Australia, one from Madagascar, named for Dr Rueling, 18th century German botanist. Listed species a delightful mat-forming plant with attractive stems, leaves and masses of starry flowers. Plant in full sun in deeply worked, free-draining sandy or friable-clay soil. Frost tolerant, grows near the coast in protected positions. Rockery, ground or bank cover.
Sterculiaceae.

Rulingia hermanniifolia
Wrinkled Kerrawang, Dwarf Kerrawang

Delightful spreading shrub from New South Wales with reddish brown woolly stems. Leaves lanceolate, 3–5cm long, glossy, rich deep green, prominently puckered or wrinkled, margins serrated and wavy. Pale-pink star-shaped flowers with reddish central markings appear through spring in crowded axillary and terminal corymbs followed by reddish brown bristly capsules, valued in dried arrangements. Hermanniifolia — leaves resembling Hermannia. Evergreen. 30cm × 1.5m.

RUSCUS

A genus of about six species of shrubby herbs from the Azores, Madeira and Western Europe to the Caspian Sea, named from Latin meaning butcher's broom (butchers used a bunch of stiff growth to sweep their meat blocks). Listed species grown for unusual cladode foliage and brilliant red fruit. Seed-grown, plants unreliable berry producers and need planting in groups for cross pollination. A hermaphrodite form known as Wheeler's variety is recommended. Useful for dry shady places in most soil types, thriving to perfection in the dense shade of large deciduous trees where few other plants would grow.
Ruscaceae. *All evergreen.*

Ruscus aculeatus
Butcher's Broom

Hardy Mediterranean species spreading by underground stems. Forms a thick clump of

slender green flexible stems, densely covered on the upper portion with 2cm, dark-green, spine-tipped, triangular cladodes which carry out the function of leaves. Has the remarkable habit of producing small 6mm greenish white flowers in spring, followed by decorative 12mm bright sealing-wax red berries attached to the centre of each cladode. Untouched by birds, they provide excellent winter decoration in the garden or cut for indoors. Aculeatus — armed with prickles. 1 × 1m.

Ruscus aculeatus 'Wheelers Variety'

Selected hermaphrodite form clothed with dark green, sharp spikey leaves. Small white flowers in spring followed by 1cm, glossy bright red berries. More reliable for berry production. 1 × 1m.

RUSSELIA

A genus of about fifty species of sub-shrubs native to Mexico, Cuba and tropical America named for Dr Alexander Russell, 18th century naturalist and author. Listed species valued for rush-like stems and foliage and masses of brilliant flowers over a long season. Plant in full sun or partial shade in deeply worked, free-draining, moderately rich soil in frost free locations. Tends to grow from underground stems and soon builds substantial colonies, but is easy to control.
Scrophulariaceae.

Russelia equisetiformis
Coral Bush

Native to Mexico. Low-growing shrub with slender rush-like almost leafless gracefully curving branches, carrying loose racemes of scarlet 25mm, tubular flowers, blooming freely late spring through autumn. Useful for larger rock gardens, trailing over banks or walls, front borders or hanging baskets. Rarely without flower. Syn R juncea. Equisetiformis — resembling a horse's tail. Evergreen. 90cm × 1m.   **301**

RUTA

A genus of 60 species of aromatic woody perennial herbs distributed from Canary Islands through the Mediterranean region to eastern Siberia named from the Latin *ruta*, the herb rue, or bitterness. R gravoelens or Rue has been cultivated for many centuries for its legend, medicinal value and as a spice. Whole plant dotted with oil glands which make the leaves translucent and emit its pungent aroma. Rue leaves are used in salads and other dishes. As far back as the 12th century Rue was recommended as an eye compress and is probably still used for various conditions.

As an ornamental it has fine greyish leaves and yellow flowers and worthy of a place in mixed borders. Plant in deeply worked, free-draining, alkaline soil in full sun and minimal water. Prune back to old wood early spring to keep the plant compact. Grows freely from seed for easy replacement.

Rutaceae.

Ruta graveolens 'Jackman's Blue'
Rue, Herb of Grace
Native to southern Europe. A sub-shrub or perennial herb growing quickly to 60–90cm. Ferny aromatic leaves usually bipinnate with numerous narrowly oblong to obovate segments, glabrous, blue-green, distinctly glaucous, held erect on long petioles. Mustard-yellow flowers somewhat resembling buttercups borne in terminal corymbs on long stems through warmer months followed by decorative brown capsules. Graveolens — heavily scented. 75 × 75cm.

SALIX

A genus of about 300 species, confined to cooler latitudes and altitudes of the Northern Hemisphere, varying in form from tiny creeping alpines to large noble trees, named from the Latin *salix*, the Willow. Weeping Willow provides graceful waterside threads. Other species have colourful or curiously contorted stems or catkin covered branches good for floral decoration. Where privacy or protection from sun or wind is needed urgently, willows rapidly cover the situation, and in doing so demand little in the way of special soil conditions or care.

Tenacious roots keep a foothold on any soils likely to erode. They enjoy dwelling beside streams or open drains and may if necessary, settle for the nearest pipe drain, which they soon block with fine roots to satisfy an insatiable thirst. For this reason, when planting willows, keep them at a safe distance from drainage systems of any kind.

Salicaceae. *All deciduous except S × humboldtiana.*

Salix babylonica
Babylon Weeping Willow
Native of China but cultivated for centuries in Europe, North Africa and western Asia. Gracefully attractive tree with widespread head of long slender pendulous polished brown branches drooping to the ground. Leaves linear-lanceolate to 16 × 1.5cm, deep-green above, blue-grey beneath, margins entire. Slender catkins appear with young foliage in spring. The ancient city from which this willow takes its name has long been the scene of desolation. 9 × 9m.

Salix caprea 'Pendula'
Kilmarnock Willow
Salix caprea, known as Pussy Willow is rarely planted in gardens because of its notoriety as a ground robber. Kilmarnock Willow is a small umbrella-like female form with slender, stiffly pendulous branches. Leaves broadly elliptic-obovate, dark green and glabrous above, grey-green and hairy beneath. Usually grafted on top of a suitable rootstock. Caprea — of goats. 2 × 2m.

Salix × chrysocoma
Golden Weeping Willow
Most beautiful large weeping tree, a delightful study of form, colour and texture. Medium wide-spreading tree with vigorous arching branches, terminating in slender golden-yellow polished branchlets weeping gracefully to the ground, clothed with light-green, lanceolate leaves. Leaning over a pool or planted by itself, it makes its presence obvious from the moment of planting. Stake when young to encourage a clean stem and high branching habit, and be mindful of aggressive roots. Syn S vitellina 'Pendula'. Chrysocoma — golden hair. 8 × 8m.

Salix × humboldtiana
Upright Willow
Native to Mexico, central and southern America. Tall narrow tapering form resembling Lombardy Poplar. Fine erect chestnut-brown branches and twigs, leaves linear or linear-lanceolate to 15cm long, bright green, gracefully drooping. Almost evergreen in milder winters, grows rapidly sometimes 2m or more in a season. Plant in deeply worked, free draining soil, protect from heavy frost, give adequate summer moisture especially when young. Excellent tall screen for narrow spaces, large accent tree against tall buildings, amongst mixed plantings or well sited lawn specimen. Syn S chilensis. Semi evergreen. 8 × 1.5m.

Salix irrorata
Arizona Willow
From south west USA. Vigorous medium shrub, long young shoots green at first becoming smooth and purple-yellow covered with waxy white bloom, a feature in winter. Leaves lanceolate or oblong-lanceolate to 10cm long, glossy green above, glaucous beneath, margins entire to finely serrated. Male catkins with brick-red anthers becoming yellow, borne on bare stems ahead of the leaves. Irrorata — dew-sprinkled, or minutely spotted. 3 × 2.5m.

Salix matsudana 'Tortuosa'
Corkscrew Willow, Peking Willow
From China, Manchuria and Korea where it grows in dry areas with low summer rainfall. Curiously twisted stems obvious from the first bursts of spring growth, but show to greatest effect when leaves have fallen, revealing a multitude of spiralling, corkscrewed branches ascending to the sky. Vigorous grower, providing a privacy or protection screen in little more than 12 months. The bare twigs of this species are in keen demand for dramatic floral art. Allow for rather soil-robbing root system. Matsudana — oriental, tortuosa — irregular, twisted or meandering mode of growth. 6 × 4m.

Salix purpurea 'Pendula'
Purple Weeping Willow
Native to Europe and central Asia. Attractive and graceful form with long slender willowy pendulous branches, shiny and often purple when young, at its best when trained as a tall standard to form a small weeping tree. Leaves lanceolate-oblong, to 10 × 3cm, dull green above, paler or glaucous beneath. From late winter each bare branch studded with large, purple red catkins before the leaves appear, highly valued for delightful winter floral arrangements. Cut stems in bud and watch the catkins unfold. 2 × 2m.

SAMBUCUS

A genus of about 25 species of shrubs trees and herbs from the Northern Hemisphere, east and north-west Africa, South America, eastern Australia and Tasmania named from the Latin *sambuca*, a harp. Although not at all showy in flower, many species have attractive foliage and fruit. Grow in deeply worked, fertile soil in full sun, sheltered from wind. Prune hard, almost to ground level each winter to keep them dense and shrubby. New shoots grow freely from the base. Completely hardy. Excellent background.

Caprifoliaceae.

Sambucus nigra 'Aurea'
Golden Elder
The species S nigra from Europe, western Asia and North Africa is known as Black Elder. Bears white flowers and black berries, with therapeutic properties. S nigra 'Aurea' is the golden leafed form, a robust showy shrub with rugged fissured bark and pinnate leaves, bright butter yellow at first, intensifying through summer and autumn. Flattened heads of creamy white, sweetly fragrant blossoms, followed by bunches of small black shining fruit. Nigra — black. Deciduous. 4 × 3m.

A genus of about eighteen species of aromatic small shrubs or perennials from Mediterranean regions named from the Latin *sanctus linum*, holy flax. Valued for attractive ferny silvery-grey foliage, yellow flowers and ability to thrive in dry limy soils in drought conditions. The listed species prefers light sandy soil and full sun. Dislikes rich soil or damp water-logged conditions, otherwise quite hardy. Good foreground plant in hot dry gardens, rock gardens, sunny banks etc. Keep compact by clipping twice yearly.
Asteraceae.

Santolina chamaecyparissus
Lavender Cotton
Charming dwarf plant from Southern France. Forms a compact shrublet with aromatic, silver-white, finely divided foliage on densely white-tomentose, twiggy stems. Unchecked, thin brittle branchlets grow to a metre long, lying on the ground in willowy manner, each tip bearing bright yellow, 2cm button flowers in summer. Silvery white foliage rarely seen in other plants. Chamaecyparissus — dwarf cypress-like foliage and appearance. Evergreen. 50cm × 1m.

A genus of 11 species of slow-growing hardy shrubs, natives of south east Asia, western China and Himalayas, named from the Greek *sarkos*, flesh and *kokkos* a berry, referring to fleshy fruits. Valued for attractive lush green foliage, fragrant winter flowers and autumn fruit. Useful shrub for shaded areas in entryways, beneath low branching trees, between buildings or against shady walls. With-stands dry cold and draughty conditions. Plant in deeply worked, organically enriched, free-draining, neutral to acid soil. Keep moist until established.
Buxaceae.

Sarcococca ruscifolia
Christmas Box
Curious shrub from western China. Spreads by underground stems, forming a neat dwarf clump of branched vertical shoots. Leaves ovate to broadly ovate, to 55 × 35mm, dark-green, quite stiff and sharply pointed. Produces small fragrant white flowers in winter followed by 6mm crimson red berries often hidden amongst the foliage. Best planted in groups for cross-pollination. Ruscifolia — similar foliage to ruscus, butcher's broom. Evergreen. 1m × 60cm.

A genus of over 700 species of shrubs, small trees or vines found in tropical and subtropical regions of the world, named for J C Scheffler, 19th century botanist of Danzig. A handsome group with palmately compound leaves, providing some of the most dramatic foliage plants for garden or indoor decor. Frequently used as indoor plants in cool temperate climates, also thriving in outdoor locations in frost-free areas when grown against sunny walls with good drainage.

Plant in deeply worked, organically enriched, free-draining soil. Mulch freely and keep moist during dry periods. Excellent for entryways, striking tropical effects near swimming pools, long term container plants etc. Occasional tip-pinching prevents legginess. Over-grown plants may be cut almost to ground level and soon recover. As roots of S actino-phylla may become invasive, careful siting is recommended.
Araliaceae. *All evergreen.*

Schefflera actinophylla
Queensland Umbrella Tree
Striking plant from Queensland and Northern Territory, valued in milder areas for creating tropical effects. Develops straight upright non-branching stems with large palmate leaves directly attached. Leaflets 7–16, ovate to elliptic, to 30 × 10cm, glossy deep green, radiating like umbrella ribs and carried on a long petiole or stalk.

Mature plants bear curious terminal arrangements of deep red, honey-laden flowers in narrow clusters, spreading horizontally in octopus fashion. Syn Brassaia actinophylla. Actinophylla — from the Greek *aktinotus*, furnished with rays, *phyllon*, a leaf. 5 × 2.5m.

Schefflera arboricola
Hawaiian Elf Schefflera
Native to southern China and Vietnam. Somewhat resembles Umbrella Plant but with smaller growth habit and foliage. Naturally an epiphyte or woody climbing vine, but seen more as a scrambling shrub in cultivation. Compound leaves arranged in a radiating circle of 7–11 obovate leaflets to 11 × 4.5cm, glossy dark green, margins entire. Yellowish flowers in flattened, 30cm umbels, bronze when mature, followed by clusters of ovoid, 5mm orange fruit becoming black. Can reach 4m outdoors with equal spread, but easily pruned to size and form. Stems planted at an angle continue to grow in that direction making interesting effects. Arboricola — growing tree-like. 4 × 2.5m.   **301**

Schefflera digitata
New Zealand Patete
The sole New Zealand species found in damp places in lowland and subalpine forests throughout New Zealand. Forms a small spreading tree. Compound leaves with 3–9 deep green obovate-lanceolate leaflets to 20 × 7.5cm, margins finely and sharply serrated. Small greenish flowers in wide panicles to 30cm across appear below the leaves through summer followed by purplish black berries ripening autumn the following year. Prefers cool roots, reasonable drainage, shade or semi shade and adequate deep moisture during dry periods. Digitata — like an open hand with divisions arising from one point. 3 × 2.5m.

Schefflera elegantissima
False Aralia
Interesting species from Vanuatu and New Caledonia. Young plants form a colony of slender straight and smooth stems mottled black and white. Juvenile leaves divided fanwise into 5–10 narrow leaflets, 10–25 × 1cm, with notched margins, slender points, prominent pinkish midrib, dark green above, almost black with white midrib beneath. Mature leaves large, about 30 × 8cm, usually deep-green, leathery and coarsely toothed. Erect sparsely foliaged plant making a delicate lacy silhouette. Denser plants result from pinching out terminal shoots. Sun or partial shade, sheltered from strong winds. Deeply worked, free-draining soil. Excellent feature plant against a lighter background revealing its delicate tracery. Syn Dizygotheca. Elegantissima — very elegant. 2.5 × 1.5m.   **301**

Schefflera heptaphylla 'Hong Kong Bicolor'
Variegated Schefflera

Native to east Asia from Japan to Thailand, and the Philippines. With the support of other forest trees the species may reach to 25m with 8cm trunk. Cultivar known as Hong Kong Bicolor is a vigorous plant with numerous slender yellowish-green 2–3m stems, either erect or spreading, well-furnish with compound leaves to 20 × 20cm with 15cm petioles. Leaves usually comprise ten radiating linear-lanceolate leaflets to 12 × 3cm, attractively variegated deep green and yellow, some entirely yellow others green. Brighter colour in full sun. Foliage excellent for floral decorations. Syn S octophylla 'Hong Kong Bicolor'. Heptaphylla — seven-leaved. 2 × 2m.   **301**

SCHINUS

A genus of about thirty species of trees and shrubs from South America, Uruguay to Mexico named from the Greek *schinos*, the mastic tree, some species yielding resinous juices. Common name Pepper Tree is given for the pungent red drupes although they're not used in the production of pepper. Culinary pepper is produced from Piper nigrum from east India and Malaysia. The listed species are grown for elegant form and prolific crops of red drupes.

They grow in any reasonable deeply worked, free-draining soil, tolerate extreme drought and poor drainage once established and withstand light frost. Stake feed and water young plants and prune for high branching if space beneath is to be utilized. Allow enough room for full development.

Anacardiaceae. *All evergreen.*

Schinus molle
Pepper Tree, Peruvian Mastic Tree

Long established in mild areas as a popular wide spreading shade or screen tree with handsome foliage, picturesque trunk and branches. Bark on trunk and heavy limbs light-brown and rough, gnarled with knots and burls. Bright green, pinnate leaves to 30cm long, with 19–41 lanceolate 2–3cm leaflets suspended on graceful willowy branches. Numerous tiny pale-yellow flowers in drooping 10–15cm clusters through summer, succeeded by pendent clusters of rosy red berries in autumn and winter. Molle — from the Peruvian name Mulli. 6 × 5m.   **301**

Schinus terebinthifolius
Brazilian Pepper Tree

More open and rigid than S molle, attractive as a single-trunk specimen with umbrella crown or multi-stem tree. Leaves pinnate, 10–17cm long, divided into 5–13 oval-lanceolate to obovate, 3–6cm dark-green leaflets, often with reddish midrib. Small white flowers in summer followed by showy bright-red fruit autumn and winter, with sharp flavour and attractive to birds. Popular for Christmas decoration in the Northern Hemisphere. Terebinthifolius — leaf-design resembling its relative the terebinth tree Pistacia terebinthus. 6 × 5m.

SCIADOPITYS

A genus of one species, a monoecious conifer from Japan, named from the Greek *skiados*, an umbel and *pitys*, fir tree, referring to leaves in spreading whorls resembling the ribs of an umbrella. Grown for neat and dramatic appearance, ideal for creating oriental effects in rock or feature gardens, containers or bonzai. Plant in deeply worked, organically enriched, free-draining soil with pH in the range of 4–7, in cool moist or semi-shady locations. Pruning seldom necessary. Avoid damage to main central stem.

Sciadopityaceae.

Sciadopitys verticillata
Japanese Umbrella Pine

Unique and rare Japanese native forest tree growing at 600–1000m and reaching heights of 20–40m. Extremely slow growing, cultivated plants rarely exceeding 2m after several decades. As a juvenile it forms a neat pyramidal tree with symmetrical, horizontal branches in whorls. Young shoots and leaves smooth and green at first, changing to light brown. Sciadopitys is dimorphic — has two distinct foliage types. Small scale-like triangular leaves scattered along its branches, and whorls of 30–40 firm, fleshy, narrow, flattened, 8–15cm needles radiating from the centre like ribs of an umbrella at the ends of branches and twigs. Woody 7–12cm cones on mature specimens. Verticillata — in whorls. Evergreen. 1.5 × 1m.

SEQUOIA

A genus of one species, a large monoecious coniferous tree native to western USA from California to Oregon, named for

Sequoiah, creator of the Cherokee alphabet in 1821, son of a trader and American Indian girl, born at a village by the Cherokee river and reared as a full-blooded Indian. With stately pyramidal form, this is one of the most handsome large conifers. Has the distinction of being the world's tallest recorded tree, known as 'Founders Tree', measured at 111m. Redwoods are notable for their longevity, and growth rings found in fallen giants have indicated a span of 2200 years.

A good landscaping tree where space permits, relatively fast growing, almost pest free, always fresh looking and with pleasant fragrance. Plant in deeply worked, free-draining soil in full sun or semi-shade, water adequately through dry periods.

Taxodiaceae. *All evergreen.*

Sequoia sempervirens
Californian Redwood

The majestic Redwood is native to California and Oregon, growing on the seaward side of the coastal mountain range. Straight shapely trunks clothed in thick spongy reddish brown bark, branches carried horizontally with slightly ascending tips. Dimorphic leaves — scale-like 6mm, arranged spirally on long shoots, and linear-lanceolate 6–20mm deep-green to blue-grey, arranged in two opposite ranks. Sempervirens — evergreen. 8 × 4m.

Sequoia sempervirens 'Filoli'

Selection from Saratoga Horticultural Foundation of California. Attractive semi-weeping form with silvery grey-blue finely textured foliage, almost the colouring of Kosters Blue Spruce. Glaucous pistillate cones an added attraction. Fine pyramidal specimen, but needs careful training as a juvenile to establish good form. 6 × 4m.

Sequoia sempervirens 'Soquel'

Selected for fine-textured slightly bluish green foliage. Horizontal branches turn up at the tips. 8 × 4m.

SEQUOIADENDRON

A genus of one species, a monoecious conifer from western North America named from *sequoia* and the Greek *dendron*, a tree. A veritable giant among trees. In California's Sequoia National Park the tree known as 'General Sherman' measures 100m in height with a base diameter of 12m, claimed by some to be the world's largest living thing. Accurate age assessment of trees of this calibre isn't easy, but estimates range from 500 to 1500 to 4000 years. Although exceeded in height by its close relative Sequoia sempervirens, both species share worldwide fame. Possibly easier to grow and more tolerant of cold, dry conditions.

Taxodiaceae.

Sequoiadendron giganteum
Big Tree

Differs from Californian Redwood in a number of ways. Foliage denser or more bushy, grey green in colour, branchlets sheathed in short scale-like overlapping sharply pointed leaves making it rather prickly to reach into. Cones 5–9cm long, dark reddish brown. Bark similar, but Big Tree's tall pyramidal form tends to be more compact. Often incorrectly listed as Sequoia gigantea. Evergreen. 8 × 4m.

SERISSA

A genus of one species, an evergreen shrub from south east Asia called by its East Indian name. Modest shrubs related to Gardenia, grown for a profusion of flowers and lustrous leaves. Although bruised leaves give off an unpleasant smell, Serissa is a delightful bush to have around.

Easily grown, reasonably hardy and performs without fuss in most sunny locations in deeply worked, free-draining, neutral soil. This shrub is good for mass planting, low fillers, dwarf screen, rock gardens etc. Responds to clipping after flowering.

Rubiaceae.

Serissa foetida
Smelly Serissa

A desirable shrub which seems to rise above its unfortunate name. A dense multi-branched twiggy plant with purplish black branchlets. Leaves ovate to 20 × 8mm, deep green and leathery, foetid when crushed. Delightful starry, mauve shaded white flowers with three-lobed petals to 12mm across, mass-produced in leaf axils almost all year through, especially spring through autumn. Foetida — bad smelling.

Other excellent forms include the double-flowered **S foetida 'Flore Pleno'**, **S foetida 'Variegata'** with gold edged leaves, and the floriferous pure white **S foetida 'Snowflake'**. Evergreen. 60 × 60cm.

SOPHORA

A genus of about fifty species of trees shrubs and woody herbs from subtropical and temperate regions of the world named from the Arabic *sophera* a leguminous tree. New Zealand endemic species known as Kowhai is the national flower. With attractive ferny foliage and brilliant yellow nectar-rich flowers, it has become popular in many countries of the world. Grows naturally in open forests, along forest margins, on coastlines, river banks and damp or rocky places.

Plant in full sun or partial shade in deeply worked, organically enriched, free-draining, moisture-retentive soil sheltered from cold drying winds. Numerous cultivars of varying size have appeared providing a wide choice for many landscaping functions.

Leguminosae.

Sophora japonica
Japanese Pagoda Tree

Native to China and Korea. Grows moderately to 6m, then slowly forms a broad-topped tree to 12m with almost equal spread. Young wood dark grey-green and smooth, older branches gradually become rugged and corrugated, somewhat resembling an oak. Pinnate leaves 15–25cm long, with 9–17, ovate or ovate-lanceolate dark-green leaflets to 5 × 2cm. Creamy white, 12mm flowers borne in 15–25cm terminal clusters late summer through autumn, followed by 5–9cm capsules, narrowed between large seeds resembling a bead necklace. Ideal lawn shade tree. Japonica — of Japan. Deciduous. 6 × 5m.

Sophora japonica 'Pendula'

Unique and picturesque weeping form with stiffly drooping branches cascading to the ground. More effective when grafted on 2–3m standards. Deciduous. 3 × 2m.

Sophora microphylla

Widespread New Zealand species seen throughout the North Island, South Island and Chatham Islands. Distinguished from S tetraptera by smaller leaflets, usually less than 10mm long and the tangled juvenile growth which may persist for many years before assuming maturity and commencing to bloom. Older specimens form a medium tree to 12m with 30–60cm trunk, branches either spreading or gracefully drooping.

The golden-yellow, tubular, 45mm nectar-filled flowers in pendulous racemes appear in massed displays during spring, painting whole hillsides in golden hues to the delight of both flower lovers and native birds which greedily tear into the petals rather than extracting the nectar from the mouth of each flower. Although natural specimens provide magnificent floral displays, it is the numerous selected cultivars that are more frequently planted. Microphylla — small leaves. Semi-evergreen. 5 × 3m.

Sophora microphylla 'Chevalier'

Selected finer-foliaged form with compact bushy habit and bright golden-yellow flowers through spring. Semi-evergreen. 2.5 × 1.8m.

Sophora microphylla 'Dragon's Gold'

Excellent compact bushy cultivar with pinnate, fine-textured, bright-green leaves. Showy displays of lemon-yellow flowers borne in clustered racemes winter through early summer. Reliable and easy to grow. Semi-evergreen. 1 × 1m.

Sophora microphylla 'Earlygold'

Selected dwarf cultivar with a compact rounded form and lemon yellow flowers commencing to appear in early winter depending on the area, and continuing through early summer. Flowers not prolific, but the early start and long flowering period has made it popular. Semi-evergreen. 1.2 × 1m.

Sophora microphylla 'Goldies Mantle'

Selected weeping kowhai with graceful arching pendulous branches producing clusters of golden flowers in shower effect. Stake when young to encourage a central leader. Semi-evergreen. 3 × 1.5m.

Sophora microphylla 'Goldilocks'

Small neat upright irregular vase-shaped tree with silvery grey bark. Dainty rich deep-green foliage. Rich-yellow, funnel-shaped tubular flowers held in dark-brown velvety calyces. Semi-evergreen. 3 × 3m.

Sophora microphylla 'Longicarinata'

A distinct Kowhai found naturally on the limestone rocks of the Takaka district, in the north west South Island. Characterized by smaller dimensions, slender growth habit, tiny leaflets and slightly larger but paler flowers. Fresh green leaves, 8–15cm long, divided into 20–40 pairs of 3–4mm leaflets. Pale-yellow flowers 4–5cm long borne in racemes up to six through spring, followed by almost seedless pods. Has no trace of tangled juvenile growth. Longicarinata — long keel of the flower. Semi-evergreen. 3 × 2m.

Above: Rhododendron 'Unique' **278**

Above: Rhododendron 'Red Olympia' **277**

Above: Rhododendron 'Susan' **277**
Below: Rhododendron 'White Gold' **278**

Above: Rhododendron 'Winsome' **278**
Below: Rhododendron 'Medusa' **275**

Above: Rhododendron vireya 'Flamenco Dancer' **280**

Above: Rhododendron vireya 'Cameo Spice' **280**
Below: Rhododendron 'Van Nes Sensation' **278**

Above: Rhododendron 'Markeeta's Prize' **275**
Below: Rhododendron vireya 'Gilded Sunrise' **280**

Above: Rhododendron vireya 'Golden Charm' **280**

Above: Rhododendron vireya 'Java Light' **281**
Below: Rhododendron vireya 'Tropic Glow' **282**

Above: Rhododendron vireya 'Simbu Sunset' **281**
Below: Rhododendron vireya 'Kisses' **281**

Above: Rhododendron vireya 'Star Posy' **282**

Above: Rhododendron vireya 'Wattlebird' **282**

Above: Rhododendron vireya 'Pendance' **281**
Below: Rhododendron vireya 'laetum' **281**

Above: Rhododendron vireya 'Sweet Wendy' **282**
Below: Rhododendron vireya 'Loranthifolium' **281**

Sophora microphylla 'Te Atatu Gold'

Excellent selected form, willowy when young, growing slowly with upright habit. Foliage smaller than S microphylla. Rich golden yellow flowers borne in large clusters from early spring. Blooms from an early age and entirely smothers the tree in flower for many weeks. Discovered and developed by Dawn Rothay Nursery at Te Atatu, Auckland. Semi-evergreen. 3 × 1.8m.

Sophora prostrata

Distinct easily recognized species found in grassland and rocky outcrops in lowland and mountain regions, east of the Main Divide, from Marlborough to South Canterbury. Often seen as a dense hummock to 60cm high on which a person could stand without making an impression. In more protected locations may be more erect and less tangled reaching 1.5m or more. Sparse small olive green leaves 8–20mm long in 2–4 pairs on zigzagging branchlets. In the garden, a somewhat tangled wiry shrub, with yellow and orange flowers, more or less hidden amongst the branches. Plants grown from seed quite variable and sometimes disappointing. Careful selection could lead to admirable garden shrubs. Evergreen. 1 × 1m.

Sophora prostrata 'Little Baby'

Bushy low-growing dwarf shrub, with twiggy zig-zag interlacing branches. Tiny oval olive-green leaves on rust-brown branchlets. Flowers cigar-shaped with narrow keel, deep mustard-yellow blooms. Reports indicate no apparent variation from S prostrata. Evergreen. 1 × 1m.

Sophora tetraptera
New Zealand Kowhai

Found beside North Island streams, on forest margins, in lowland and hill country from sea level to 500m, north of East Cape and Ruahine Ranges. Pinnate leaves from 8–16cm with 10–20 pairs of 25–35mm leaflets. Without tangled juvenile growth of S microphylla, it commences to bloom earlier bearing golden yellow flowers in 4–10 flowered racemes through spring. A slender small tree with airy graceful habit. Tetraptera — having four wings in reference to the flowers. Evergreen. 4.5 × 3m. **301**

Sophora tetraptera 'Gnome'

Slow growing, commencing to bloom when only 30cm high, making a shrub under 2.5m after three decades. Forms an erect stiffly branched, bushy shrub with greyish green, 8–10cm pinnate leaves, divided into five or ten pairs of leaflets. Extra large buttercup-yellow flowers produced in racemes of two to six, less profusely than others. Interesting and worthwhile shrub. Evergreen. 1 × 1m.

SORBUS

A genus of up to 100 species ranging from dwarf shrubs to large trees from Europe and Asia named from the Latin *sorbum*, service berry, applied to Sorbus domestica. Grows naturally in mountainous regions or damp habitats, many from upper altitudes of Sino-Himalayas. Sorbus have attractive flowers, but are grown mainly for richly coloured autumn leaves and heavy crops of fruit. Perform well in cool temperate regions with dry autumns and cold winters for good bud production. Plant in full sun in deeply worked, free draining, moisture-retentive, neutral to slightly acid soil. Mulch freely and keep moist through dry periods. Pruning seldom necessary beyond initial training and preserving good form.
   Rosaceae. *All deciduous.*

Sorbus aria
Whitebeam

Small to medium tree often with multiple stems and broadly conical crown. New shoots and buds grey-felted, becoming olive-brown and glabrous. Leaves simple, elliptic-ovate, 8–12cm long, leathery, greyish-white with woolly indumentum at first becoming bright green, white-felted beneath, margins shallow-toothed, turning gold and russet in autumn. White 15mm flowers in branched corymbs followed by rounded 10–12mm orange-red fruit with powdery coating, coinciding with autumn foliage. Tolerates maritime conditions and industrial pollution. Aria — ancient name for Whitebeam. 5 × 4m.

Sorbus aria 'Lutescens'
Golden Whitebeam

Notable tree with dense, compact, conical crown becoming broader with maturity. Leaves covered with pale creamy-yellow tomentum through spring, later becoming grey-green with white tomentum beneath. Impressive spring foliage display. Lutescens — yellowish. 4 × 2m.

Sorbus aucuparia
Mountain Ash, Rowan Tree

Erect European tree with sharply ascending branches, forming a dense oval or rounded crown. Pinnate leaves to 20cm with 9–15 oblong-lanceolate leaflets to 6cm, dull-green and glabrous, grey-green and slightly hairy beneath, margins roughly serrated, yellow or rusty in autumn. White flowers in 15cm corymbs late spring, succeeded by masses of rounded orange-scarlet or bright-red,

75mm fruit in large clusters persisting late-summer almost through spring. Fruit attractive to birds, hence the epithet *aucuparia* — from the Greek *avis*, bird and *capere*, to catch. 6 × 4m.

Sorbus aucuparia 'Edulis'

Strong growing hardy tree, with larger longer and broader leaves than the species, almost glabrous, nearly entire, serrated in the centre. Larger 10mm fruits in heavier bunches, reputed to be edible but with acid flavour, useful in preserves. 5 × 4m.

Sorbus aucuparia 'Kirsten Pink'

Excellent shrubby grower with branches literally weighed down from early autumn with clusters of deep rose-pink fruit. 5 × 3m.

Sorbus aucuparia 'Scarlet King'

Upright growing, hybrid form of Mountain Ash, grey green foliage, contrasts attractively with large bunches of vivid scarlet, oval fruit through summer and autumn. 5 × 2m.

Sorbus cashmeriana
Kashmir Mountain Ash

Beautiful small tree of open habit from the Kashmir region. Leaves pinnate with 15–19 oval-elliptic, 2–3cm leaflets dark green and glabrous above, paler beneath, margins roughly serrated near the apex. Flowers to 15mm, deep-pink in bud, opening pinkish white followed by glistening-white 18mm globular fruit resembling marbles in loose drooping clusters, remaining long after leaves have fallen. 6 × 4m.

Sorbus discolor

From northern China. Forms a small tree with open crown of ascending branches. Leaves pinnate with 11–15 oblong-lanceolate, 3–8cm leaflets, dark green and delicately veined above, blue-green beneath, margins deeply serrated, glowing red in autumn. White flowers in clusters of 10–14 appear early spring followed by globose, 6–7mm, yellowish-white fruit, often tinged pink. Discolor — of two different colours. 4 × 3m.

Sorbus hupehensis
Hupeh Mountain Ash

Handsome species from west Hupeh, China. Develops a bold compact head of ascending purple-brown branches. Large pinnate leaves with 13–17 elliptic-oblong leaflets to 5cm, bluish green above, grey-green beneath, margins sharply toothed at the apex. Small yellowish white flowers in lax corymbs. Globose 6–8mm white fruit prominently tinged pink in loose drooping clusters, persisting into winter. 6 × 4m.

Sorbus insignis 'Ghose'

From Himalayas. Forms a small upright tree with sturdy, stiffly ascending branches. Leaves pinnate to 30cm long, comprising 15–19 elliptic-oblong leaflets to 10cm long, dull dark-green above, silvery beneath, midrib rusty pubescent, margins sharply serrated. Small rosy red autumn fruits borne in densely packed clusters remaining well through winter. 4 × 3m.

Sorbus koehneana

Erect small tree or large shrub with erect habit. Pinnate leaves with 17–25 oblong to ovate, 2–3cm bright-green leaflets, grey-green beneath, margins sharply toothed. White 1cm flowers in 5–8cm corymbs followed by porcelain-white 7mm globose fruit with red stalks in slender drooping clusters. Of Chinese origin. Named for Bernard Adalbert Emil Koehne (1848–1918). 3 × 2m.

Sorbus poteriifolia

Magnificent slow-growing Chinese species forming a small tree with sharply ascending purplish brown branches. Pinnate leaves to 10cm long comprising 9–19, elliptic, 1–2cm leaflets dark green, paler beneath, downy on both surfaces, margins sharply serrated. Attractive deep-pink globose fruit in large loose bunches. Poteriifolia — leaves resembling Poterium. 5 × 4m.

Sorbus reducta
Dwarf Rowan

Dwarf shrub from western China and Burma. Forms thickets of slender erect stems from underground suckers. Pinnate leaves to 10cm long, with 9–15 ovate to elliptic, 15–25mm leaflets, green and slightly downy above, glabrous beneath, margins sharply serrated, bronze, orange and reddish purple in autumn. Sparse white flowers in terminal corymbs followed by 6mm globose carmine fruit in autumn. Reducta — reduced or dwarf. Rare and unusual. 60 × 90cm.

Sorbus scalaris

Small tree from western China. Wide-spreading branches and attractive foliage. Pinnate leaves to 20cm long comprising 21–37 narrowly oblong leaflets, glossy dark green above, grey-felted beneath, margins slightly toothed at the apex, turning rich reddish purple in autumn. Dull white flowers in 14cm branched clusters followed by 5–6cm globose bright red fruit in flattened heads. Scalaris — ladder-like, referring to the leaves. 5 × 4m.

Sorbus vilmorinii
Vilmorin Mountain Ash

Handsome Chinese small tree or large shrub with elegant spreading habit. Fernlike pinnate leaves to 12cm long often held in clusters, each comprising 11–31 elliptic leaflets to 25mm, glabrous above, grey-green beneath, margins serrated at the apex, red and purple in autumn. Fruit in loose drooping clusters, rosy red at first, changing pink to white flushed rose. Named for French nurseryman Maurice Vilmorin. 3 × 2.5m.

SPIRAEA

A genus of about 80 species of deciduous shrubs, mostly from North America, eastern and central Asia named from the Greek *speiraira*, a plant used for garlands. Popular in the cooler regions of Europe and the United States where many species and hybrid cultivars are cultivated for wealth of bloom, graceful habit and pleasing foliage. Use as fillers, to soften hard lines of more formal plants. They emphasize the colour of spring flowering bulbs or annuals planted beneath them and provide delightful cut blooms for floral arrangements.

Plant in deeply worked, free-draining, moisture-retentive moderately fertile soil in full sun or partial shade. Most cultivated Spiraea hardy to –15°C, easy to grow and require little maintenance apart from thinning and pruning. Spring flowering Spiraeas may be pruned after flowering, to remove faded blossoms and encourage strong growth from beneath the flowered portion. Summer flowering kinds which flower on current season's wood may be pruned to 10cm of ground early spring.

Rosaceae. *All deciduous.*

Spiraea arguta
Bridal Wreath, Garland Spiraea

One of the most free flowering and effective early Spiraeas. Spreading shrub with gracefully arching branches. Leaves oblanceolate to 40 × 13mm, glabrous and bright green above, margins coarsely and biserrately toothed, undersides downy at first, orange-yellow autumn colour in cooler districts. Snow white 8mm flowers in crowded corymbs borne profusely on the upper side of slender branches through spring. Arguta — sharply toothed or notched. 1.5 × 1m.

Spiraea cantoniensis 'Lanceata'
Reeves Spiraea

Chinese native species, a wide-spreading graceful shrub with slender arching and glabrous branches. Leaves lanceolate to 60 × 20mm, green and glabrous above, bluish green with prominent veins beneath, red in autumn, margins deeply toothed or three-lobed. Pure white, 9mm double flowers resembling multi-petalled miniature roses, borne profusely in rounded corymbs along arching stems early summer. Syn S cantoniensis 'Flore-pleno'. 1.5 × 1m.

Spiraea japonica 'Albiflora'
Japanese Spiraea

Japanese species. Dwarf, compact shrub with angular, glabrous shoots and lanceolate to ovate pale-green leaves, glaucous beneath, and coarsely toothed margins. White flowers in dense terminal corymbs borne prolifically through summer on current season's growth. Excellent front row shrub. Albiflora — white flowered. 60 × 75cm.

Spiraea japonica 'Alpina'

A low flat mound, with bright rose-pink flowers in small heads. Bright autumn leaf colour. Alpina — of mountains. 50 × 90cm.

Spiraea japonica 'Anthony Waterer'
Red Spiraea

Compact shrub with lanceolate to ovate deep-green leaves variegated yellow, occasionally completely yellow, with a touch of pink in new growth. Attractive carmine red flowers in flat corymbs heads early summer through autumn. 1 × 1m. **301**

Spiraea japonica 'Bullata'

Slow-growing dwarf compact shrub. Small broadly ovate dark olive-green leaves coarsely serrated and crinkled. Crimson-rose flowers in flat-topped corymbs through summer. Bullata — blistered or puckered leaves. 60 × 75cm.

Spiraea japonica 'Cristata'

Compact, leaves deep green, margins coarsely serrated and twisted somewhat resembling parsley. Occasionally sends up creamy pink new shoots. Bright rosy red flowers in flat corymbs through summer. Cristata — with tassel-like or crested tips. 1 × 1m.

Spiraea japonica 'Gold Flame'

Closely resembles Anthony Waterer. Leaves tinted rich bronze-red at first, yellow as they develop, intensifying to coppery-red and orange with reddish tinges in autumn. Bright red flowers in flat corymbs midsummer through autumn. 1 × 1m. **301**

Spiraea japonica 'Gold Mound'

Neat, low-growing, dome-shaped plant resembling 'Gold Flame' but with clear butter-yellow foliage through spring and summer intensifying to orange-red in autumn. Shows no tendency to revert to green foliage. 75 × 90cm.

Spiraea nipponica 'Snowmound'

Japanese native shrub forming a dense mound with compact upright growth. Leaves broadly obovate to elliptic, to 28 × 15mm, blue-green above, lighter beneath, margins with a few rounded teeth at the apex. The white flowers in small rounded corymbs entirely smother the bush throughout the summer suggesting the plant's common name. 1 × 1m. **302**

Spiraea 'Pink Ice'

Cultivar of uncertain origin. Dense, compact dwarf bush. Young shoots pale pink at first, becoming creamy white and maturing green with creamy-white frosting. Hardy, especially suited to cooler climates. 1 × 1m.

Spiraea prunifolia
Bridal Wreath Spiraea

East China, Korea and Taiwan. Upright bushy shrub with long slender gracefully arching branches. Leaves obovate to 45 × 20mm, bright green above, downy grey beneath, margins evenly toothed, orange and red in autumn. Pure white 1cm double flowers held on slender 2cm pedicels in tight clusters of 3–6 along every branch through spring. Prunifolia — leaves resembling plum. 1.5 × 1.3m

Spiraea thunbergii

Dense shrub with slender, angled, wiry, bright green stems. Leaves linear-lanceolate to 40 × 7mm, pale green, glabrous or very finely pubescent, margins sparsely but sharply serrated. Pure white 8mm flowers in clusters of 2–5 closely set in wreath-like manner on gracefully nodding branchlets in the very early spring. Thunbergii — named for Carl Peter Thunberg, an 18th century Dutch botanist. 1.5 × 1.5m.

Spiraea trichocarpa

Korean species. Forms a bushy shrub with rigid spreading branches and glabrous angular shoots. Leaves oblong to lanceolate, to 65 × 25mm, vivid green, margins entire or with few teeth at the apex, brilliant scarlet in autumn. White 9mm flowers borne in rounded 5cm corymbs at the ends of each leafy twig forming long graceful sprays in summer followed by pubescent fruit. Trichocarpa — hairy fruited. 1.5 × 1.5m.

STACHYURUS

A genus of ten species of hardy deciduous shrubs native to Japan, China and Himalayas, named from the Greek *stachys*, a spike and *oura*, a tail, referring to the shape of the floral racemes. Listed species admired for impressive floral displays late-winter through early spring. Attractive when contrasted against a dark background or worked in with other shrubs. Suitable for training fanwise against a sunny wall. Ornamental at all seasons and perfect for floral art.

Plant in deeply worked, organically enriched, free-draining, neutral to slightly acid soil in sun or semi-shade. Mulch freely and water occasionally through dry periods. Regular pruning rarely necessary, but cut out dead-wood and thin weak or overcrowded stems to ground level after flowering. A low-maintenance, worthwhile shrub.

Stachyuraceae.

Stachyurus praecox
Early Spiketail

Irresistible Japanese shrub with slender spreading glabrous reddish brown stems. Leaves ovate to ovate-lanceolate, to 14cm long, bright green, margins toothed, tapered to a sharp point, red and yellow in autumn. Buds begin to form late autumn opening to bell-shaped, 8mm, pale chartreuse-yellow flowers, appearing from each leaf bud late winter through spring in pendent racemes of fifteen to twenty. Floral display lasts for several weeks, becoming interspersed with shiny coppery brown spring foliage. Globose, 8mm greenish yellow fruits tinged red appear in summer on mature bushes. Praecox — early. Deciduous. 2.5 × 2m.

STENOCARPUS

A genus of about 22 species of evergreen trees and shrubs from Australia, Malaysia and New Caledonia, named from the Greek *stenos*, narrow and *karpos*, fruit, referring to almost flat follicles or seed capsules. Stenocarpus sinuatus is widely planted for good form, handsome foliage and impressive flowers. Select cutting-grown plants which bloom earlier as seedlings may take a decade to commence flowering. Attractive form and foliage, effective from the moment of planting. Flowers are a bonus. Easily managed tree for average gardens.

Plant in deeply worked, free-draining, moderately fertile acid soil in a warm sunny location. Protect from frost and water occasionally during dry periods until established. Start training early for single trunk and adequate headroom. May be trained into almost any desired shape. Excellent lawn tree, near patios or swimming pools. Leaf drop not a problem. Good container plant. Proteaceae.

Stenocarpus sinuatus
Firewheel Tree

Substantial tree from coastal Queensland rain forests. Forms a slender specimen with clean trunk and almost vertical branches. New shoots bronze-tinted. Handsome juvenile leaves pinnately and deeply lobed 20–30cm long, deep green, leathery and glossy, margins slightly waved. Adult leaves obovate to oblanceolate with entire margins. Bright orange-red flowers arranged in 7cm whorls, radiating from a central point like spokes of a wheel, mass produced amongst the leaves late summer and autumn, remaining on the tree well into winter. Sinuatus — with a wavy margin. Evergreen. 6 × 4m. **302**

STEWARTIA

A genus of nine species of deciduous trees and shrubs from eastern North America and eastern Asia, named for John Stuart, 18th century Earl of Bute, zealous patron of horticulture. Stewartia is related to Camellia. Occurs naturally in semi-shady conditions in moist woodland. Highly valued for lengthy floral displays, picturesque bare branches and bark and handsome foliage spring through fall. Perfect choice for woodland gardens or cool shady locations as a single specimen or worked in with other shade-lovers.

Best in semi-shade in deeply worked, organically enriched, free-draining, moisture-retentive, lime-free soil conditioned and mulched with peat moss. They enjoy adequate summer moisture and resent being moved once established.

Theaceae. *All deciduous.*

Stewartia pseudocamellia
Japanese Stewartia

Japanese species forming a small tree or large shrub of open habit, exhibiting distinctive bare branch pattern in winter, attractive dark red bark flaking in large sheets. Leaves elliptic-lanceolate to obovate, 5–9cm long, margins sparsely toothed, sometimes silky beneath, yellow, orange, bright red or purple in autumn. Saucer-shaped, pure white, silky flowers with orange yellow anthers, 5–6cm across resembling single camellias freely produced in summer. Blooms quickly fade, but produced in continuous succession over several weeks. Pseudocamellia — appears as a camellia. 4 × 3m.

Stewartia sinensis

Chinese species. Small tree or multi-stemmed shrub. Mature trees have yellowy or sandstone bark which peels in broad sheets in autumn to expose smooth greyish purple-brown trunk. Leaves ovate or ovate-oblong, quite downy at first becoming glossy deep green, vivid red in autumn, margins serrated. Cup-shaped 4–5cm fragrant white flowers with yellow anthers. Sinensis — of China. 3.5 × 3m.

STRELITZIA

A genus of four species of perennial herbs native to subtropical South Africa, named for Charlotte of Mecklenburg-Strelitz who in 1761 became Queen of George III. Most gardeners are familiar with S reginae, commonly known as Bird of Paradise. Banana-like leaves and flamboyant flowers give them prominence as exotic feature plants for warm temperate and subtropical areas. Bird of Paradise can be worked in almost any sunny garden. Excellent for landscaping near pools. They drop no litter and withstand considerable abuse.

Plant in deeply worked, free draining, organically enriched, moisture-retentive soil in warm sunny locations. Against a wall, in the shelter of a patio or pool enclosure is ideal. Frosts may not kill, but damage forming flower buds. Water generously when young, drought tolerant once established. Apply well-balanced fertilizer twice yearly, otherwise periodic grooming is the only maintenance. Seed-grown plants may take seven years before blooming, but then produce every year through spring, summer and autumn. Plants from divisions bloom the first season from planting.

Streliziaceae. *All evergreen.*

Strelitzia nicolai
Blue and White Strelitzia
Although referred to as Giant Bird of Paradise, it is quite unlike S regina. Grown more for sheer bulk and banana-like leaves than floral display. Forms a massive clump of many woody stems to 9m. Leaves oblong or ovate-oblong to 2m × 80cm, grey green, leathery, arranged fanlike on vertical or curving petioles to 2m long. Mature foliage tends to split like banana leaves. Flowers with white sepals and light-blue petals emerge from a reddish purple spathe to 45cm long, spring or early summer. Named for Nicholas, 19th century Emperor of Russia. 6 × 3m.

Strelitzia reginae
Bird of Paradise
Almost trunkless perennial with giant oblong-lanceolate, greyish green leaves to 70 × 30cm, margins entire, carried on long petioles or stalks to 1m long. Flowers with interesting structure resembling tropical birds. Hard, pointed, beak-like green and pink sheath to 20cm long from which flowers emerge is called the spathe, held at an angle suggestive of a bird's head. Flowers flick up one at a time consisting of brilliant orange sepals and brilliant blue petals standing erect like a crest. Spectacular blooms held on strong stiff stems, last for long periods, valued for garden display and indoor decoration. 1.5 × 1.5m.   **302**

STREPTOSOLEN

A genus of one species, a floriferous shrub from Colombia and Peru, named from the Greek *streptos*, twisted and *solen*, pipe or tube, referring to the twist in the corolla tube. In warm temperate and subtropical gardens, Streptosolen provides magnificent displays of brilliant orange flowers through spring and summer. Has somewhat rambling style. May be trained as a bush, against a trellis or bank, spilling over a wall or grown in a hanging basket. Plant in full sun in deeply worked, free draining, organically enriched soil. Protect from frost, and water occasionally during dry spells. Prune lightly each year to keep compact and preserve vigour.

Solanaceae.

Streptosolen jamesonii
Orange Browallia, Marmalade Bush
A scandent shrub with slender wiry stems. Leaves ovate to elliptic, to 5cm long, deep green, glossy, prominently ribbed, margins entire. Flowers open trumpet-shaped with five uneven lobes, 2cm across, brilliant orange or yellow, produced in compact terminal clusters spring through autumn. Grows rapidly, commences to flower soon after planting and in suitable conditions is smothered with spectacular orange flowers almost all year. Named for Dr William Jameson, 19th century professor of botany in Quito. Evergreen. 1.5 × 1.5m.   **302**

STROBILANTHES

A genus of about 250 species of perennials and low shrubs from south east Asia and North Africa, named from the Greek *strobilos*, a cone and *anthos*, a flower, descriptive of the inflorescence. Valued for colourful foliage and floral display. The listed species has remarkably dark leaves and mauve flowers providing excellent contrast amongst shrubs, annuals or perennials. Plant in full sun or partial shade in deeply worked, free-draining, moderately fertile soil, sheltered from strong wind. Prune to half way early spring.

Acanthaceae

Strobilanthes anisophyllus
Goldfussia
Low growing bushy shrub from Assam with numerous erect blackish stems. Willow-like lanceolate leaves to 8cm long, glossy purple-black, margins entire, opposite and of unequal size. Curved-tubular, 20mm light lavender-blue flowers in sparse clusters along each stem spring through autumn. Anisophyllus — opposite leaves of unequal size. Evergreen. 1 × .75m.

STYRAX

A genus of about 100 species of evergreen and deciduous trees and shrubs from Asia, USA and south east Europe, called Styrax the classical Greek name. Admired for fragrant bell-shaped blossoms which dangle below the leaves, good reason to locate in an elevated position so the flowers may be appreciated from beneath.

Plant in deeply worked, free-draining, organically-enriched, moisture-retentive, neutral to acid soil in full or partial sun. Naturally from woodland streamsides or swampland. Styrax resents hot dry conditions preferring to grow in association with other trees. Mulch freely and keep moist during dry periods. Hardy to −15°C. Prune when young to control shape, removing lower branches. Tends to grow shrubby if left to itself.

Styracaceae.

Styrax japonica
Japanese Snowdrop Tree
Very beautiful small tree from China and Japan with slender trunk and widespread fanlike branch structure, often pendent at the tips. Leaves elliptic-oblong to 8 × 4cm, dark glossy green, margins finely scalloped, red or yellow in autumn. Delightful pendulous clusters of white, mildly fragrant, 20mm bell-shaped flowers with prominent yellow stamens resembling snowdrops hang gracefully beneath the branches late spring

through mid-summer. Leaves angle upwards creating effective green and white layers with the blossoms. Japonica — of Japan. Deciduous. 4 × 3m.

SYMPHORICARPUS

A genus of about eighteen species of shrubs from North America and western China related to honeysuckle, named from the Greek *symphorein*, bear together, and *carpos*, fruit, referring to clustered fruit. Extremely hardy, most species tolerant of urban pollution, coastal conditions and temperatures to –25°C. Grown for prolific crops of long persisting fruit. Useful for screens in cold climates. S albus useful for stabilizing soil on banks or slopes with its strongly suckering roots. Plant in deeply worked, free-draining soil in sun or partial shade. Prune to remove weak or overcrowded shoots late winter. Caprifoliaceae. *All deciduous.*

Symphoricarpus albus
Snowberry, Waxberry
Native to western USA, California to Alaska. Forms a multi-stemmed shrub with slender shoots and suckering roots. Leaves oval-oblong to 5cm long, dark green, paler and fine-downy beneath, margins coarsely and irregularly cut as if torn. Pink bell-shaped 7mm flowers in 4cm clusters in summer followed in winter by masses of snow-white, 12mm globose or ovoid fruit. Albus — white. 1.8 × 1.3m.

Symphoricarpus orbiculatus 'Variegatus'
Coral Berry
Graceful variegated berry shrub from eastern United States with thin downy stems. Leaves oval or ovate to 3 × 2cm, dull dark green, irregularly margined yellow. Ivory bell-shaped flowers flushed pale-pink in summer and autumn followed by ovoid-globose 6mm greyish-white fruit maturing purplish-rose. Locate in full sun, as it may revert to green in shade. Orbiculatus — round and flat, or disc shaped. 1.5 × 1m.

SYRINGA

A genus of about 20 species of shrubs and small trees from east Asia and south eastern Europe named from the Greek *syrinx*, a pipe or tube, a reference to hollow stems. Although Lilacs have charmed garden lovers for centuries, continual selection and hybridization has resulted in even higher quality blooms and greater depth of colour without losing their enchanting fragrance.

Blend Lilacs amongst other shrubs where their colourful and fragrant blooms may be appreciated through spring without the somewhat sparse bush being too prominent for the rest of the year. Hardy, fast growing and free flowering, performing best in areas with cold winters. Many of the following are hybrids of S vulgaris × S oblata from breeders in France and California, selected for depth of colour, truss size, intense fragrance and reliability.

Plant in full or partial sun in deeply worked, free-draining, moisture-retentive, neutral to alkaline soils which doesn't bake hard in summer. They love alkaline conditions, responding to annual dressings of lime and balanced fertilizer scattered within the drip line. Mulch freely and provide infrequent deep watering through dry periods. Prune by removing old flowered wood immediately after flowering. All are spring flowering and grow to about 2.5 × 1.5m. Oleaceae. *All deciduous.*

Syringa hybrid 'Alice Eastwood'
Buds claret purple, opening to cyclamen pink double blooms. Slender well-formed trusses.

Syringa hybrid 'Belle de Nancy'
Large panicles of double flowers, purple red in bud, opening lilac pink.

Syringa hybrid 'Charles Joly'
Dark purplish red double blooms, late spring. Reliable and popular.

Syringa hybrid 'Clarkes Giant'
Rosy mauve in bud, opening to clear lilac single blooms. Large florets and giant spike to 30cm long.

Syringa hybrid 'Congo'
Rich lilac-red single flowers, large panicles.

Syringa hybrid 'Esther Staley'
Buds red, opening to moderately large, soft rose pink single flowers. Very free flowering

Syringa hybrid 'General Pershing'
Long panicles of double purplish violet flowers.

Syringa hybrid 'Katherine Havemeyer'
Purple lavender, shading to pale lilac pink double blooms, borne in broad compact panicles. **303**

Syringa hybrid 'Madame Lemoine'
Fragrant creamy white double flowers in large trusses.

Syringa hybrid 'Marechal Foch'
Large single bright carmine rose flowers in broad open panicles.

Syringa hybrid 'Primrose'
Small dense panicles of pale primrose yellow flowers.

Syringa hybrid 'Princesse Clementine'
Double flowers, creamy yellow in bud, opening white. Very floriferous.

Syringa hybrid 'Purple Heart'
Rich purple buds, opening to double purplish pink flowers. Dainty open truss.

Syringa hybrid 'Sensation'
Large heads of reddish purple florets, each petal boldly edged white. Unusual and striking lilac.

Syringa hybrid 'Souvenir de Louis Spaeth'
Large trusses of wine red single flowers. Popular and consistent.

Syringa × josiflexa 'Bellicent'
Medium to large shrub with fine deep green foliage. Produces masses of fragrant clear rose pink, single flowers in large open plume-like panicles.

Syringa laciniata
Cut Leaf Lilac
From western China. Juvenile leaves pinnate or finely cut into 3–9 lobes. Adult leaves simple. Deep lilac buds open to faded mauve fragrant flowers with violet centre 7cm loose axillary racemes. Often listed by the incorrect name S afghanica. Laciniata — slashed into narrow divisions.

Syringa patula
Korean Lilac
Neat rounded habit, young branches flushed purple. Leaves ovate or lanceolate to 8cm long, velvety green, minutely downy, paler and pubescent beneath. Fragrant flowers, lilac outside, white within borne in paired terminal panicles late spring. Syn S velutina. Patula — spreading.

Syringa pekinensis
From northern China. Forms a gracefully arching small tree. Leaves ovate-lanceolate to 10cm long, deep green and glabrous above, faintly glaucous beneath. Creamy-white, privet-scented flowers borne in paired, loose, 15cm panicles late spring. 4 × 3m.

SYZYGIUM

A genus of between 400 and 500 species of evergreen trees or shrubs from central and South America, south east Asia, Indonesia and Australia named from the Greek *suzugos*, joined, referring to paired leaves and branchlets of a Jamaican species for which the name was originally used. The genus includes a number of handsome landscaping specimens with handsome glossy foliage, highly coloured new growth, fascinating flowers and luscious fruits.

The listed species is a rapid grower in warm temperate climates. Grows in almost any deeply worked, free-draining, moisture-retentive soil in full or partial sun, protected from frost especially when young. Apply a balanced fertilizer early spring and autumn. Excellent as a specimen shade or screen tree and good in containers. Scale insects may cause surface blisters on the leaves. Control with summer oil.

Myrtaceae. *All evergreen.*

Syzygium australe
Australian Rose Apple, Brush Cherry
Handsome tree from rainforests of Queensland and New South Wales. Attractive glistening coppery brown new shoots. Leaves elliptic to obovate, to 8cm long, rich green glossy, margins entire, carried on gracefully pendulous branches. An abundance of white, fluffy, myrtle-like flowers with yellow stamens in summer followed by heavy crops of glossy, 25mm, oval, rosy purple berries resembling bunches of grapes, persisting through winter. May be made into jam or eaten fresh. Australe — southern. Syn Eugenia australis, Syzygium paniculata. 7 × 5m.

Sysygium australe 'Variegata'
Similar to above. Leaves somewhat curled, deep green with an irregular margin of creamy yellow. 5 × 4m.

TAMARIX

A genus of about 50 species of shrubs or small trees widely distributed throughout western Europe and Mediterranean regions to east Asia and India where they abound along sea coasts, inland saline areas or in conditions of extreme drought and heat. Tamarix is an old Latin name.

All have graceful slender branches, fine ferny foliage and plumy pink flowers and provide softening effects and a spectacular splashes of colour to any landscape. Use them as specimens, informal screens, backgrounds etc.

Although tolerant of sun, salt spray, wind and drought and grow in most soil types apart from shallow clay, they revel in the easy lifestyle of average garden conditions. Pruning is important to prevent legginess. Varieties which flower on current years growth need pruning late winter. Those flowering on previous year's wood may be pruned immediately after flowering. Young plants often lack a strong rooting system. Cut them back to about 30cm from ground level at planting time.

Tamaricaceae. *All deciduous.*

Tamarix juniperina
Juniper Tamarix
From northern China and Manchuria. Large shrub or small tree with dense habit and slender rich-brown branches clothed with distinctive pale-green feathery foliage. Bright-pink flowers in great masses of 35mm clusters appear mid to late spring before the leaves on shoots of the previous year. Extremely hardy, prune immediately after flowering. Juniperina — with leaves resembling Juniper. 3 × 3m.

Tamarix pentandra
Salt Cedar
Native to south east Europe. Forms a spreading feathery shrub or small tree with long slender plumose branches. Young shoots usually purplish. Tiny lanceolate scale-like leaves, crowded and rather glaucous. Small rosy pink flowers in cylindrical racemes, 3–5cm long, borne profusely on current season's growth through late summer, the whole bush becoming a feathery mass of rose-pink blossom intermingled with light blue-green foliage.

Amongst the finest late flowering shrubs. Regular pruning to almost ground level each winter will keep it low and vigorous as well as encouraging maximum bloom. Unpruned it becomes a rangy bush with highly competitive root system. Pentandra — with five stamens. 3 × 2m.   **303**

Tamarix pentandra 'Rubra'
Selected form with dainty grey-green foliage and plumes of deeper rose pink flowers. 3 × 2m.

Tamarix ramosissima 'Pink Cascade'
The species is distributed through eastern Europe to central and eastern Asia. Forms a large shrub or small tree with slender erect branches and reddish brown bark. Awl-shaped lanceolate blue-green leaves. Plumes of rich-pink blossom clothe every branch through summer. Ramosissima — much-branched. 3 × 2m.

TASMANNIA

At one time included in the genus Drimys, the six Australian shrubby species now classified under Tasmannia — of Tasmania. Drimys are from South America. The common name Pepper Bush is given for the pungent flavour of the fruit, seeds and foliage. Many species have year-round beauty with good form, highly coloured stems, handsome aromatic leaves and fragrant flowers. Plant in partial to full shade in deeply worked, free-draining organically enriched, moisture-retentive, lime-free soil.

Winteraceae

Tasmannia lanceolata
Mountain Pepper
Found at high altitudes in south east Australia. Forms a rounded or conical shrub with obscurely angled, bright-red to purple-red branchlets. Leaves narrow-lanceolate to elliptic, to 70 × 24mm, deep-green, somewhat leathery and glossy, margins entire. Terminal clusters of 12mm, creamy white flowers with 2–8 narrow petals in summer, followed by black fruit. All parts of the plant have a hot peppery taste. Dried fruit sometimes used as a condiment. Syn Drimys lanceolata. Lanceolata — spear shaped leaves. Evergreen. 2 × 2m.

TAXODIUM

A genus of three species of deciduous coniferous trees inhabiting river and lake margins of North America and highland Mexico, named from Taxus, the yew and the Greek *eidos*, resemblance, from the similarity of leaves to Taxus. Known as Swamp Cypress, they enjoy dwelling alongside flooding rivers often with their roots in brackish water. Aged specimens distinguished by heavily buttressed trunks and grotesque woody projections to 2m high and 30cm across known as Cypress Knees or pneumatophores — structures of spongy tissue thought to assist the aeration of submerged roots.

Regardless of aquatic tendencies,

Taxodium will grow in ordinary garden conditions. Plant in deeply worked, organically enriched, moisture-retentive soil. But because established specimens thrive in water to 60cm deep, it is the perfect choice to plant alongside streams, ponds or lakes, or as an outstanding specimen tree for wet, problem areas. Hardy in all but the coldest mountain areas, and quite disease free. Prune only to remove dead wood or for shape.
Taxodiaceae. *All deciduous.*

Taxodium ascendens 'Nutans'
Pond Cypress
Native to south eastern United States. Beautiful and graceful columnar tree with billowy, nodding laterals and awl-shaped, soft green, adpressed foliage. Attractive in spring with soft-green new shoots, and in autumn when foliage becomes rich rusty brown. Ascendens — rising upwards in sloping fashion. Nutans — nodding. 5 × 3m.

Taxodium distichum
Swamp Cypress, Bald Cypress
Beautiful tree from southern United States where it abounds in rivers and coastal swamp areas, a dominant feature of the famous Everglades of Florida. Forms a large tree with fibrous, reddish brown bark and strongly buttressed trunk tapering widely at the base. Natural 30m specimens are broad topped, but middle aged examples pyramidal and very shapely. Beautiful ferny and feathery young growths, soft-green or glaucous-green, change to brownish green, then assume a rich golden brown or chestnut colour prior to falling. Distichum — in two ranks. 7 × 4m.

Taxodium mucronatum
Mexican Swamp Cypress, Montezuma Cypress
A natural giant, one specimen in Mexico claimed to be the oldest living tree with a girth of nearly 36m. Rapid grower when young with strongly weeping branches and long slender, pendent shoots which fall in the second year. Long, narrow and warty cones distinguish this species from T distichum and it is not as hardy. Rich bronze autumn colour. Not as hardy as Mucronatum — pointed. Semi-deciduous. 5 × 4m.

TAXUS

A genus of about ten recorded species from North America, south east Asia, China, Japan and Europe called by its ancient Latin name for Yew. 1000 year old specimens recorded with trunks measuring at least 5m at the base. Famous yew hedges around some of England's stately homes still in good shape after centuries of close trimming, together with fine topiaries. Perfect for formal planting, singly, in balanced groups, or containers.

Taxus are slow-growing long-term plants, preferring to grow in deeply worked, neutral soil with good drainage, adequate moisture when young, full sun or partial shade. Quite drought tolerant once established, but occasionally hose leaves during hot dry summers to wash off spider mites or other small pests.
Taxaceae. *All evergreen.*

Taxus baccata
Common Yew, English Yew
Medium densely branched tree with rounded crown and reddish brown bark. Leaves linear to 40 × 3mm, almost black-green and glossy. Has given rise to numerous ornamental forms varying in size shape and colour. Female trees when pollinated bear fleshy, scarlet, cup-shaped, single seeded fruit. Seeds are said to be poisonous. Baccata — fruits with pulpy texture. 3 × 2m.

Taxus baccata 'Fastigiata'
Irish Yew
Possibly the best known and most popular, a female clone with erect columnar growth, slowly forming a narrow upright column of closely packed branches. Radially arranged, stiff, narrow, 25mm, blackish green leaves. Appears very trim and sedate, useful as long term, formal sentinels. Slow growing with few cultural problems. Fastigiata — erect branches close together to form a column. 2.5m × 50cm.

Taxus baccata 'Fastigiata Aurea'
Slower growing, similar strict upright form and golden yellow foliage, especially new spring shoots. Holds colour through the year. 1.5m × 50cm.

TECOMARIA

A genus of one species, an erect or somewhat scrambling shrub from South Africa, named from its resemblance to Tecoma, a close relative. Highly valued as an ornamental shrub in subtropical climates where it blooms for a greater part of the year. More often seen as a formal clipped hedge in temperate frost-free regions. Merits recognition as a colourful free-flowering shrub where temperatures remain above –2°C.

Plant in deeply worked, free-draining, fertile soil in full sun. Tolerant of sun, heat, salt air and considerable drought. May be trained to any desired form, even as a climber on trellis, or encouraged to scramble over sunny banks. Constant close clipping inhibits flower development.
Bignoniaceae.

Tecomaria capensis
Cape Honeysuckle
From South Africa to tropical Africa. Rambling shrub with numerous slender stems arising from ground level. Pinnate leaves with 2–5 pairs of elliptic-ovate to orbicular leaflets to 25 × 25mm, shining deep- green, margins serrated. Curved trumpet flowers to 5cm long with flaring lobes and protruding anthers, bright orange-scarlet outside, paler within, borne in erect terminal racemes through summer and autumn. Capensis — from the Cape. Evergreen. 2 × 1.5m.

TELOPEA

A genus of four species of evergreen shrubs, confined to New South Wales, Victoria and Tasmania named from the Greek *telopos*, seen from afar, in reference to the highly visible crimson blooms of T speciosissima, floral emblem of the State of New South Wales. The Aboriginal name *Waratah* also means 'seen from afar'. Quite demanding in cultural requirements, but a most spectacular shrub where conditions suit. Numerous hybrids have been selected for vigour, flower size and colour and grown with considerable success for commercial cut-flower production in New Zealand, Victoria, New South Wales and Hawaii. Telopea is an outstanding shrub, worth every effort to grow at least one.

Plant in deeply worked, free draining, organically enriched, moisture-retentive, volcanic, sandy or stony, slightly acid soil. Locate in full sun or partial shade, mulch freely and water sparingly during the first spring and summer. Provide shelter from strong wind. Hardy to –5°C. Meagre dressings of slow-release fertilizer encourages healthy growth. Pinch out tip growths of young plants to encourage root development and flowering stems. Don't hesitate to cut blooms with long stems for indoors and after flowering, cut old flowered stems back to half way.
Proteaceae. *All evergreen.*

Telopea oreades
Victorian Waratah
Known also as Gippsland Waratah. Found naturally as a multi-branched small tree to 12m high, but semi-erect large shrub under garden conditions. Handsome leaves, oblanceolate to obovate, to 20cm long, grey-green, leathery and smooth, margins entire. Light red flower heads 7–10cm across, comprising twenty or more incurved tubes backed by pink or greenish bracts, borne at the tip of each stem spring through early summer. Not as spectacular as its New South Wales counterpart but an excellent large shrub in its own right. 4 × 2.5m.

Telopea speciosissima
New South Wales Waratah
One of Australia's most famous wildflowers, floral emblem of New South Wales. Erect growing shrub with numerous robust stems arising from a woody root known as a lignotuber. Leaves narrow obovate, to 25cm long, deep green to yellowish green with prominent network of veins, margins entire or slightly toothed. Spectacular brilliant coral red or crimson scarlet, globular or ovoid flower heads to 15cm across, comprising up to 100 incurved tubes or flowers surrounded by a ring of pointed, crimson bracts. Blooms appear spring through early summer on strong straight stems, lasting several weeks as cut flowers. Numerous selected clones in cultivation. Speciosissima — most beautiful. 3 × 2m.   **303**

Telopea speciosissima 'Burgundy'
Vigorous upright growing plant producing brilliant burgundy red flowers. 3 × 2m.

Telopea speciosissima 'Fireglow'
Compact dome-shaped flowerheads in deep glowing crimson, white-tipped stamens. Narrow pointed bracts prominently reflexed. 2.5 × 2m.

T E T R A T H E C A

A genus of about 40 species of small shrubs endemic in Australia named from the Greek *tetra*, four and *theke*, case or container, from the construction of the anthers. Delightful in their natural habitat, usually found in the dappled shade of taller shrubs or trees going under the common name of Pink Bells or Black-eyed Susan from small dark spots concealed in the centre of each flower.

Plant in deeply worked, free-draining, moisture-retentive, sandy-clay soil in partial shade or where they avoid the hottest midday sun. They enjoy cool roots so mulch freely and water during dry periods. Ideal rockery or border plant, singly or in groups.

Tremandraceae.

Tetratheca thymifolia
Pink Bells
Found in Queensland, New South Wales and Victoria. Delightful low-growing rounded shrublet with downy or bristly shoots and leaves. Leaves in whorls of 3 ovate-lanceolate to 10 × 4mm, deep green glossy, margins recurved. Deep rose-pink, 1cm, drooping flowers with four oval petals and a dark central spot hidden inside, mass produced through spring. Thymifolia — leaves resembling thyme. Evergreen. 50 × 60cm.

T E U C R I U M

A genus in excess of 300 species of wide distribution, especially from Mediterranean regions to western Asia, named from the Greek *teukrion*, possibly from king Teucer of Troy, said to have used the plant medicinally. Useful plants for grey or silvery foliage and stems, easy culture and willingness to grow in calcareous soils. Teucriums are reasonably hardy, enjoy hot, dry, sunny locations, and withstand coastal exposure. Plant in deeply worked, free-draining soil in average conditions without waterlogging. The two listed species may be clipped or sheared into formal shapes.

Lamiaceae. *All evergreen.*

Teucrium chamaedrys
Wall Germander
Low-growing hairy soft-wooded European native shrub with numerous upright stems, arising from underground rhizomatous roots. Leaves ovate to oblong, to 4 × 2cm, pubescent especially beneath, margins notched, toothed or lobed. Rose-pink, 2cm flowers with lower lip spotted white and red, produced in terminal spikes summer to autumn. Bank or ground cover, foregrounds, edging or low division hedges. Shear once or twice yearly. Chamaedrys — dwarf. 30 × 75cm.

Teucrium fruticans
Silver Germander
Western Mediterranean. Forms a loose shrub with four-angled, white tomentose stems. Leaves ovate to lanceolate, to 22 × 6mm, grey-green and glabrous above, silvery white beneath, margins entire. Lavender blue flowers, 2cm across, in loose terminal racemes almost the year through. Useful as informal hedge or screen, formal clipped specimens, backgrounds or contrast. Feed occasionally, pinch back long shoots during the growth period. A darker blue form is cultivated known as T fruticans 'Azureum'. Fruticans — shrubby or bushy. 1.5 × 1.5m.

T H R Y P T O M E N E

A genus of about thirty species of shrubs mostly from Western Australia, others from Victoria and Queensland named from the Greek *thrypto*, to break in pieces, probably from the flowers of some species which fall readily. Delightful free-flowering dwarf shrubs with dainty foliage and fragrant flowers in graceful sprays, excellent for garden display or picking for indoors. Grow Thryptomene in full sun or partial shade in deeply worked, free-draining, lime free, acid soil conditioned and mulched with peat moss. Prune heavily after flowering. Hardy in all but the coldest areas.

Myrtaceae. *All evergreen.*

Thryptomene calycina
Grampians Heath Myrtle
From the Victorian Grampians and other parts of western Victoria, growing abundantly on rocky mountain slopes. Forms a shapely bush with erect branches and small, flat, oblong, 8–12mm aromatic leaves. Pink buds open to white, starry, scalloped flowers, 3–6mm wide, with reddish eye borne so freely in winter and early spring they appear to be draped with snow. As flowers fade, reddened calyces effectively extend the flowering season. Perfect garden shrub and cut flower variety. Calycina — calyx-like. 1.5 × 1m.   **303**

Thryptomene calycina 'Pink'
Excellent selection with erect, open habit, noted for bright pink buds which open lighter pink, deepening to pinkish red with maturity, blooming autumn through spring. 1 × 1m.

Thryptomene calycina 'Taylor's White'
Erect compact grower, covered with greenish white buds early winter, opening to delicate pink flowers late winter through spring. 1 × 1m.

Thryptomene denticulata
Small compact plant from Western Australia with arching branches and dense heath-like leaves. Masses of mauve-blue flowers in small sprays cover branches through autumn. Excellent for picking. Full or partial sun. Denticulata — slightly toothed. 1 × 1m.

Above: Royena lucida *African Snowdrop Bush* **284**

Above: Russelia equisetiformis *Coral Bush* **284**

Above: Schefflera arboricola *Hawaiian Elf Schefflera* **286**

Above: Schefflera elegantissima **286**
Below: Sophora tetraptera **293**

Above: Schefflera heptaphylla 'Hong Kong Bicolor' **287**
Below: Spiraea japonica 'Anthony Waterer' **294**

Above: Schinus molle *Pepper Tree* **287**
Below: Spiraea japonica 'Gold Flame' **294**

Above: Spiraea nipponica 'Snowmound' **295**

Above: Stenocarpus sinuatus *Firewheel Tree* **295**
Below: Strelitzia reginae *Bird of Paradise* **296**

Above: Streptosolen jamesonii *Orange Browallia* **296**
Below: Thuja orientalis 'Beverleyensis' *Column Arborvitae* **305**

Above: Tamarix pentandra *Salt Cedar* **298**

Above: Tibouchina granulosa **306**
Below: Tibouchina organensis **306**

Above: Telopea speciosissima *New South Wales Waratah* **300**
Below: Thryptomene calycina **300**   Below: Syringa 'Katherine Havemeyer' **297**

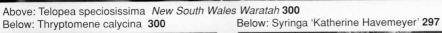

Above: Tibouchina lepidota 'Alstonville' **306**

Above: Viburnum opulus 'Sterile' *Snowball Tree* **310**

Above: Viburnum plicatum tomentosum **310**
Below: Virgilia divaricata *Keurboom* **311**

Above and below: Viburnum plicatum 'Roseace' **310**

Thryptomene saxicola 'Paynei'
Presumed to be an improved form of T saxicola but according to Wrigley & Fagg the name is best forgotten as many naturally occurring clones show equal merit. Hardy, fast growing, commencing its long flowering season mid winter and continuing well into spring with an abundance of small, soft pink flowers. Saxicola — growing in rocks. 1 × 1m.

Thryptomene saxicola 'Pink Lace'
Selected for neat habit, fine, light-green foliage and vibrant deep-pink flowers which cover the plant winter through spring. Excellent hardy shrub. 1 × 1m.

Thryptomene saxicola 'Rosea'
Rock Heath Myrtle
Excellent species from Western Australia with graceful, weeping growth habit, long slender stems and densely set, tiny narrow leaves. Great masses of dainty pink flowers provide a delightful display for several months from mid winter. 1 × 1m.

THUJA

A genus of five species of coniferous trees from North America, China and Japan, named from the Greek *thuia*, a kind of juniper. The common name *Arborvitae* means 'Tree of Life'. Most garden varieties are cultivars of Thuja occidentalis the American or Western Arborvitae or Thuja orientalis, the eastern or Chinese form. American species occur from Nova Scotia in the north to Tennessee in the south.

Although variable, western species have conical form with spreading branches, flattened spray-like branchlets, dark green leaves with paler undersides and conspicuous oil glands distinctively fragrant when crushed. Orientalis or eastern species generally have more rounded form, with either erect or upward curving branches and branchlets. The small green leaves in flattened sprays are the same colour on both sides, are less aromatic and are carried in a vertical plane.

Thujas are dependable, very versatile and highly ornamental. Appearance somewhat resembles chamaecyparis, but are generally more tolerant of adverse growing conditions. They are neat and restrained, never surprising or dramatic, but perform quietly without heavy demands of care and attention. Plant Thujas in average garden conditions, in sun or semi shade, deeply worked, free-draining soil. Protect some of the finer forms from strong burning winds. If shaping is necessary, thin from within rather than shear.

Pinaceae. *All evergreen.*

Thuja occidentalis 'Caespitosa'
Caespitosa means growing in dense clumps and that is just what this tiny arborvitae does. Remains a compact little cushion or bun of closely packed, mid-green, flattened foliage for years. Fills out faster when young. Perfect for rock or feature gardens. 30 × 50cm.

Thuja occidentalis 'Ericoides'
Heath Arborvitae
Dwarf compact rounded or pyramidal bush, rarely more than 1m high. Short twiggy branches densely covered with soft, dull green, heath-like leaves, turning walnut brown in winter. Good for formal planting or colour contrast. Ericoides — resembling heath or erica. 75 × 75cm.

Thuja occidentalis 'Pyramidalis'
Pyramid Arborvitae
Erect narrow pyramidal outline when young, developing more of a column with age. Deep green foliage in short compact flattened sprays, slightly twisted and lacy. One of the finest formal columnar shrubs with rapid development and great reliability. Good formal specimen, driveway sentinels, along a fence or as a focal point in groups of conifers or other shrubs. 2.5m × 75cm.

Thuja occidentalis 'Rheingold'
Distinguished by brilliant foliage colour and two foliage types appearing at one time — fine plumy juvenile leaves and adult foliage sprays. Grows slowly in globose or low pyramidal form, lower branches hugging the ground. Foliage in shades of cream, yellow, gold, bronze and pink through spring and summer, the gold and bronze intensifying through autumn and winter, giving warmth and colour seldom seen in conifers. Erect shoots may be removed to keep the plant low and compact. Allowed to grow, it eventually forms a handsome specimen with numerous pyramidal branches of varying dimensions. Easy to grow almost anywhere. 75cm × 1m.

Thuja occidentalis 'Vervaeneana'
Large growing conifer of dense pyramidal form with crowded foliage sprays, quite pendulous at the tips. Spring and summer colour bright gold, fading as winter approaches. Becomes quite brown in extreme cold. Lawn specimen, screen or background. 3.5 × 2m.

Thuja occidentalis 'Wareana Lutescens'
Compact grower with broad pyramidal outline. Attractive and informal foliage sprays, light yellow-green for most of the year, brightest during spring and summer, becoming bronze tinted over winter. Unusual colouring among Thujas. 2.5 × 1.5m.

Thuja orientalis 'Aurea Nana'
Dense globular to oval shape with miniature bookleaf foliage sprays which in spring and summer are pure creamy yellow, literally glowing as if illuminated. During autumn and winter foliage is rich green. Irresistible for rock or feature gardens. Protect from burning winds. 1m × 60cm.

Thuja orientalis 'Beverleyensis'
Column Arborvitae
Forms a narrow compact column, tips of each branchlet golden-yellow. Stately appearance, vivid colour in full sun. Originated in California and named for Beverly Hills. 3 × 1m. **302**

Thuja orientalis 'Juniperoides'
Dense, rounded shrub of somewhat lax habit with soft, plumy, juvenile foliage, grey green in summer, turning rich purple grey in winter. Protect from strong winds. 1.5 × 1m.

Thuja orientalis 'Meldensis'
Forms a neat rounded densely foliaged bush with fine crisp appearance, soft grey-green at most times, changing to purplish brown in winter. Good companion for Juniperoides and Rosedalis. 1m × 50cm.

Thuja orientalis 'Rosedalis'
Compact globular dwarf with fine soft foliage. Changes colour three times a year, canary yellow in spring, sea green in summer and glaucous plum-purple in winter. Quite outstanding. 75 × 75cm.

Thuja orientalis 'Westmont'
Re-selected form of Aurea Nana, with closer growth habit and compacted branch tips, which throughout spring and autumn are brilliant lemon yellow, changing to bronze during winter and fading to green as spring approaches. Needs no trimming to maintain its upright, broadly conical form. 80 × 50cm.

Thuja plicata
Western Red Cedar
Well known conifer with rigid bookleaf sprays of deep green foliage resembling Lawson Cypress. Rapidly provides an effective and permanent screen for privacy and protection, very easy to maintain,

requiring a minimum of trimming. Resistant to cypress canker. Excellent shelter from 2–8m. Plant 1 to 1.5m apart.

Thuja plicata 'Old Gold'

Large pyramidal shrub with golden yellow foliage, held on cinnamon coloured stems. Turns burnished gold in winter. Makes an attractive specimen and excellent for boundary planting. 3 × 1.5m.

Thuja plicata 'Stoneham Gold'

Attractive slow growing conifer with typical Western Red Cedar foliage, closely arranged in compact, upward facing sprays. New growth bright orange-yellow on upper and outer edges throughout the growing season. Young stems orange brown. Inner foliage green. 1m × 50cm.

THUJOPSIS

A genus of one Japanese species named from *thuja* and the Greek *opsis*, resembling thuja. Readily distinguished from Thuja with broader and flatter branchlets and larger leaves. Seems to thrive in most soil types including shallow alkaline ground provided drainage is adequate. Locate where its fascinating foliage detail can be appreciated.
Pinaceae. *All evergreen.*

Thujopsis dolobrata
Deer Horn Thuja
Heavy open flattened foliage sprays, branching like deer antlers, appearing in juvenile form like a giant species of moss. Foliage colour shining deep green with conspicuous silvery reverse. Dolobrata — hatchet shaped. 2.5 × 2m.

Thujopsis dolobrata 'Nana'
Compact dwarf forming a spreading flat topped bush with smaller rich-green leaves and branchlets. Smaller in all parts. 75 × 75cm.

Thujopsis dolobrata 'Variegata'
Vigorous form with distinct patches of creamy white scattered through the foliage. 2.5 × 2m.

TIBOUCHINA

A large genus of over 350 species of shrubs, subshrubs and herbs from tropical South America, particularly Brazil.

Pronounced tib-o-kina, Tibouchina is derived from the native name in Guyana. Rich purple flowers and green velvet leaves are familiar features. Although only about six species and their cultivars are cultivated, they're amongst the most spectacular flowering shrubs, becoming a total mass of vivid colour through summer and autumn and often again in spring.

They love sun and heat and need to be located away from strong winds and protected from all but light frosts. Plant in deeply worked, free-draining, moisture-retentive, rich acid soil. Mulch freely and keep moist during dry periods. Encourage compact form by pinching back young tip growths and by pruning after each flowering. Feed with balanced fertilizer early spring and autumn.
Melastomataceae. *All evergreen.*

Tibouchina granulosa
Grows rapidly to form a large rounded bushy shrub with thick woody upright stems. Leaves lanceolate to oblong-ovate to 20cm long, dark green, deeply veined, leathery and coarse-textured. Rosy purple, 6–8cm flowers with five narrow petals and central cluster of spidery anthers, carried above the foliage in erect pyramidal clusters of 7–10 completely covering the bush for several weeks autumn through early winter and again in spring. Performs vigorously in frost free locations. Granulosa — appearing as though covered with minute grains. 4 × 3m.   **303**

Tibouchina heteromalla
Glory Bush
Small to medium shrub from Brazil. Leaves broadly ovate to cordate, mid green with seven prominent veins, covered with fine silky hairs, margins entire. Buds and petioles reddish and velvety. Rich purplish-violet 4cm flowers with central cluster of cream anthers borne in erect terminal racemes. Heteromalla — diversely hairy. 1.3 × 1m.

Tibouchina lepidota 'Alstonville'
From Colombia. A shrubby, free-branching shrub with four-angled or square stems forming a neat rounded bush. Leaves lanceolate-ovate to 12 × 5cm, mid-green, semi-glossy, five prominent lateral veins especially beneath, densely covered above with minute hair-like scales. Deep purple, 5–7cm flowers with central cluster of spidery anthers borne in dense terminal clusters for several weeks summer through autumn and again in spring, literally covering the bush. For warm-temperate and subtropical climates. Popular cultivar, named for the

northern New South Wales town where it flourishes. Lepidota — covered with small scales. 2.5 × 2.5m.   **304**

Tibouchina lepidota 'Alstonville Variegata'
A green and yellow variegated leaf form of the above. 2.5 × 2.5m.

Tibouchina organensis
Princess Flower, Purple Glory Bush
Dense compact bush with attractive foliage. Leaves elliptic 10–15cm long, dark green with rough velvet texture, 3–5 prominent veins, margins entire with thin red line. Some leaves turn reddish orange in autumn and winter. Plump red velvety buds open to immense rich royal purple, 10–12cm, five petalled glistening flowers with central cluster of spidery anthers, late autumn through winter and spring. Organensis — referring to Organ Mountains in Brazil. 1.5 × 1m.   **303**

Tibouchina urvilleana 'Edwardsii'
Brazilian Glory Bush
Native to Brazil where it grows rapidly to a sizeable shrub or small tree. Rounded bush with smooth light brown, picturesque trunk, rather brittle branches and four-angled, fine hairy young branchlets. Leaves ovate to elliptic, 7–12cm, deep green and velvety. Rich royal purple, five petalled, 6–8cm, single flowers with curled anthers produced in terminal racemes, opening from plump velvety buds mainly summer through autumn and sporadically through the year. Named for Jules Sebastian d'Urville, early 19th century French naval officer. 2.5 × 2m.

TILIA

A genus of about 45 species of medium to large deciduous trees from cool to temperate regions of North America, Europe and Asia, named from the Latin *tilia*, linden or lime tree. Lime or Linden is a familiar avenue or street tree in Europe, their tolerance of regular heavy pruning making them admirable for the purpose. Tilias which grow to mighty trees with heavy buttressed trunks, often surrounded by suckers also feature in many parks and large gardens. Masses of small sweetly fragrant flowers and ornamental leaves.

Lindens grow at a slow to moderate rate in fertile, free-draining, alkaline to neutral or slightly acid soil in areas of high rainfall. They enjoy hot summers and cold winters, dislike either very dry or very wet

soil conditions and are best in association with other trees such as in woodlands for protection from wind. Plant in rich soil and water frequently during dry periods. Stake and train young trees, but once established need only corrective pruning.
Tiliaceae. *All deciduous.*

Tilia americana
American Linden, Basswood
From eastern and central USA. Forms a substantial tree with straight trunk, dense compact narrow crown and deeply furrowed corky bark. Young branches green and glabrous. Leaves broadly ovate or heart-shaped to 15 × 10cm, dull dark green, margins coarsely serrated. Small yellowish white, fragrant flowers in pendulous cymes of 6–15 in summer followed by smooth globose tomentose fruit. 15 × 8m.

Tilia cordata
Small-Leaved Lime
Widely distributed through England, Spain, Scandinavia, western Russia and south Caucasus. Naturally a tree to 40m, less in cultivation with dense pyramidal form. Leaves nearly orbicular, to 7 × 7cm, glossy dark green and glabrous, glaucescent or silvery beneath, margins finely serrated. Pale yellow fragrant flowers in pendulous to semi-erect cymes of 5–7 through summer, followed by globose, grey-tomentose fruit. 15 × 8m.

Tilia platyphyllos
Broad Leaf Lime
Native to central and southern Europe, northern France and south west Sweden. Large vigorous species, rounded form, trunk with rough grey fissured bark, young shoots reddish brown and downy. Leaves orbicular-ovate or heart-shaped, to 11 × 10, dull dark green above, paler and pubescent beneath, margins sharply serrated. Pale yellow flowers in threes early to mid summer, followed by pear-shaped, five ribbed fruit. Will sucker, but less than Common Lime. Platyphyllos — broad-leaved. 20 × 10m.

Tilia tomentosa
Silver Lime
From south east Europe to Asia Minor. Robust tree with erect branches, dense ovoid-conical crown, more dome-shaped or broadly pyramidal with maturity. Young shoots grey-tomentose. Leaves orbicular with cordate base, to 11 × 10cm, dark green above, silver-grey tomentose beneath, margins coarsely serrated or rarely partially lobed, effective when shimmering in the breeze. Lime-green to dull white flowers in pendulous cymes of 5–10 in spring, followed by rough, ovoid, 8mm fruit. 15 × 8m.

Tilia × vulgaris
European Linden, Common Lime
Hybrid species T cordata × T platyphyllos. Large vigorous tree with broad conical crown and suckering habit. Leaves broadly ovate or heart shaped, to 9 × 8cm, dark green and glabrous above, paler and tufted beneath, margins sharply serrated. Small fragrant lime-green flowers, hidden in new leaves in spring, secrete an abundance of nectar attractive to bees and an important source of honey. Syn Tilia × europaea. 20 × 10m.

TOXICODENDRON

A genus of about 9 species of trees shrubs or climbers from North America to northern South America, named from the Greek *toxicos*, toxic and *dendron*, tree. Once classified as Rhus succedaneum, the listed species is a spectacular autumn colour tree, but like many of its relatives, has poisonous properties which cause skin allergies through the slightest contact with cut or damaged leaves or branches. Locate away from lawns or walkways where people are least likely to touch it. Plant in deeply worked, free-draining soil. Useful as a background or amongst other trees for dramatic colour contrast. Avoid any contact with bare skin when planting, pruning or working nearby.
Anacardiaceae

Toxicodendron succedaneum
Sumach, Wax Tree
Native to China, Japan and Himalayas. Grows rapidly to form a small open sparsely branched tree. Pinnate leaves to 30cm long with 9–15 elliptic-oblong, 6–12cm leaflets, glossy medium green, often with a purplish tint, margins entire, orange scarlet to blazing red for long periods in autumn. The whole tree becomes ablaze with colour. Yellow flowers in 9–12cm axillary panicles followed on female trees by crowded clusters of kidney-shaped pale yellow inedible fruit, a source of wax once used in Japan in the manufacture of candles. Syn Rhus succedaneum. Deciduous. 5 × 4m.

TRACHYCARPUS

A genus of six species of solitary or clustering palms from the Himalayas, northern Thailand and China, named from the Greek *trachys* rough, and *karpos*, fruit, in reference to the fruit of some species. Attractive palms occurring in alpine regions to 2400m, hardy enough to withstand light snowfalls. Listed species is popular for cooler climates thriving with minimum care and attention.

Plant in deeply worked, free-draining soil in full or partial sun. Prefers rich heavy clay soil, dislikes waterlogged conditions and constant strong winds which damage the leaves. Responds to feeding and watering but really performs without fuss. Useful palm of moderate size and hardiness for feature planting in gardens or containers.
Aracaceae

Trachycarpus fortunei
Fan Leaf Palm, Windmill Palm
Elegant solitary palm native to China. Grows moderately with dark trunk, usually thicker towards the top, the upper part covered with dense, hairy-looking fibres from fallen leaf sheaths. Fan-shaped leaves to 125 × 85cm, divided into many slender sword-like deep green and glossy segments, greyish beneath, carried on 90m petioles armed with fine sharp teeth. Small inflorescence from among lower leaves with fragrant yellow flowers, followed by bluish kidney-shaped 12mm fruit. Named for Robert Fortune, 19th century Scottish horticulturist and collector of Chinese plants. Evergreen. 4 × 3m.

TRISTANIOPSIS

A genus of about 30 species of trees and shrubs from Australia, New Caledonia, New Guinea, Indonesia, Malaysia, Burma and Thailand, named from *Tristania* and the Greek *opsis*, resembling. Listed species found naturally along streams and in rainforests in eastern Victoria, New South Wales and Queensland. Mature examples to 20m high with buttressed trunks festooned with epiphytes are not uncommon. As a garden subject, the tree is slow growing, densely shrubby when young, attains about 3m high in five years and provides delightful floral displays.

Plant in deeply worked, free-draining, organically enriched, moisture-retentive soil in full sun or in dappled shade of open mature trees. Mulch freely and keep moist in dry periods. Occasional tip-pinching will maintain a shrubby bush or tree form is easily obtained by selective pruning. Tolerant of considerable moisture and hardy to infrequent light frost. Ideal street or avenue street, lawn specimen, background, screen or container plant.
Myrtaceae.

Tristaniopsis laurina
Kanooka, Water Gum
Compact branching habit, young branches mahogany brown, later peeling to reveal satiny grey bark. Leaves narrowly oblanceolate to 14cm long, yellowish green at first becoming dark green, quite glossy, greyish white beneath, margins entire, a few turning reddish orange in autumn and winter. Yellow 1cm fragrant flowers with five rounded, widely spaced petals, clustered in compact terminal axillary cymes of 7–15 late spring through mid summer, interspersed with leaves. Syn Tristania laurina. Laurina — resembling laurus, true laurel or bay tree. Evergreen. 5 × 3m.

A genus of 5–15 species of shrubs from the Americas named from *uni* a native Chilean term, distinguished from other Chilean Myrtaceae by nodding flowers and stamens shorter than the petals. Although long referred to as cranberry, Ugni is not the true American cranberry. It is *Vaccinium macrocarpon*, extensively cultivated in the USA. Ugni grows into an attractive shrubby plant with pleasant-tasting fruit. Locate near patios or paths or as a low garden division where its fruit and fragrance can be fully appreciated.
Myrtaceae.

Ugni molinae
Chilean Guava
Forms a compact stiffly erect plant with faint white pubescence on twigs and new shoots. Leaves ovate, lanceolate or elliptic to 35 × 20mm, dark green, bronze-tinted, leathery, whitish beneath, margins entire and slightly rolled under. White flowers tinted rose with almost round fleshy 5–8mm petals enclosing a cluster of 2–4mm stamens late spring through early summer, followed by edible, reddish purple, 12mm fruit with the aroma of baking apples. Eat them fresh or in preserves. Syn Myrtus ugni. Named for Juan Ignacio Molina, (1740–1829), writer on Chile's natural history. Evergreen. 1.3m × 75cm.

A genus of about 45 species of large deciduous trees or shrubs, from temperate regions of northern Mexico and central Asia named from the Latin *ulmus*, the elm. The elm family includes some of the noblest and most ornamental trees. Golden and variegated leaf forms especially make a worthwhile colour contribution for a greater part of the year, while weeping and horizontal types are picturesque, graceful and valuable for the shade they provide.

While Elms are indifferent to soil conditions, they need to be planted in reasonably good, deeply worked ground and kept moist during establishment. Stake young trees securely especially standard forms, although once strongly rooted they withstand more persistent winds without damage than many other deciduous trees. Ulmus have aggressive surface root systems and need careful placement.

Ulmaceae. *All deciduous.*

Ulmus carpinifolia 'Variegata'
Smooth Variegated Elm
Beautiful tree with graceful, open, pyramidal habit and often pendulous shoots. Leaves obliquely oval or ovate, to 10 × 5cm, uneven at the base, margins finely serrated, glabrous deep green, densely mottled or speckled white, giving a silvery grey effect. Valuable variegated specimen tree, more tolerant of wind and poor conditions than many deciduous trees. Carpinifolia — leaves resembling carpinus, the hornbeam. 6 × 5m.

Ulmus glabra
Scotch Elm, Wych Elm
Native to Britain, Europe, north and west Asia. Large tree developing a dome-shaped crown with spreading branches, arching or pendulous at the extremities. Leaves oval to obovate, to 16 × 13cm, often three-lobed at the apex, dull green and rough, downy and lighter beneath, margins coarsely and doubly serrated. Purplish red tufted flowers in clusters on bare branches high in the crown followed by showy yellowish green papery winged seeds during spring. Suitable for exposed inland or coastal situations. Used widely for grafting because of non-suckering habit. Glabra — without hairs. 9 × 6m.

Ulmus glabra 'Horizontalis'
Horizontal Elm
Foliage and general appearance resemble weeping elm. Normally grafted on 2.5 to 3m standards from which smooth, straight branches and branchlets grow horizontally. Continually spreading sideways, it needs adequate space for natural development. Easily trained for full head room. Old specimens reported to have a circumference of 60m, but this would be rare. Normally a diameter of 3–4m may be attained after ten years. Serves well as a shade tree. 3 × 4m.

Ulmus glabra 'Lutescens'
Golden Elm
Forms a magnificent round-headed specimen with smooth, light brown branches and branchlets, densely covered with rich golden-yellow foliage spring through autumn. Leaves ovate to orbicular 10 × 8cm, base uneven, irregularly serrated, distinctly corrugated, artistically curved, emerging lime-green deepening to golden bronze. Train either with low branching multi-stems, or as high branched specimens. Amongst the most attractive deciduous trees. Syn U procera 'Louis van Houtte'. Lutescens — yellowish or becoming yellow. 6 × 5m.   **313**

Ulmus glabra 'Pendula'
Weeping Elm, Camperdown Elm
Normally grafted on 2.5m standards with smooth, gracefully pendulous branches and branchlets reaching to the ground, forming a globose or dome-shaped head. Heavily foliaged with deep green, obovate, coarsely double-serrated leaves to 16 × 13cm, pubescent beneath. Provides a perfect natural 'umbrella' to 4m across. One known example serves as a dressing room beside a swimming pool. No blossom or autumn colour, but a permanent tree with impressive good looks throughout the year. 3 × 3m.

Ulmus × hollandica
Dutch Elm
Embraces a number of variable natural hybrids of U glabra × U carpinifolia distributed throughout Germany, Holland, Belgium and France. Hollandica — of Holland.

Ulmus × hollandica 'Wredei'
Dwarf Golden Elm
Narrowly conical or pyramidal tree with crowded, broadly ovate, doubly-serrated, golden yellow leaves. 3 × 2m.

Ulmus lobel
Upright Elm
Vigorous hybrid elm with striking upright growth habit. New shoots do not appear until late spring, but otherwise an excellent cultivar, resistant to Dutch Elm disease and fairly tolerant of seas breezes. Hybrid from U glabra 'Exoniensis' × U wallichiana × U carpinifolia. 10 × 3m.

Ulmus parvifolia
Chinese Elm, Lacebark
From China, Korea and Japan, described as one of the most splendid elms with the poise of a graceful Nothofagus. Forms a rounded or globose crown with gracefully pendulous branches, slender trunk and smooth bark peeling in rounded flakes. Leaves elliptic, ovate or obovate, to 5 × 3cm, bright green,

often rough or leathery, paler beneath, margins serrated. Foliage assumes reddish autumn tints in cooler regions where the tree is deciduous. Stake and train young trees for good form. Hardy, tolerant of most climates and conditions. Semi-evergreen. 6 × 4m.

Ulmus parvifolia 'Frosty'
Charming slow growing shrubby form of Chinese Elm with smaller, neatly arranged, fine-textured fresh green leaves with fascinating fringed and white serrated margins. 2 × 1.5m.

Ulmus procera 'Argenteo Variegata'
English Silver Leaf Elm
The magnificent English Elm forms a stout erect trunk with thick bark furrowed into ridges with distinct branch grouping carrying billowing clouds of foliage. Rounded ovate leaves to 7cm long, rough but glabrous, hairy beneath, margins roughly serrated, green, peppered and stippled silvery grey and white. Procera — tall. Argenteo — silvery. 7 × 5m.

Ulmus procera 'Louis van Houtte'
Small Leaf Golden Elm
Smaller and more intense golden-yellow spring foliage, becoming yellow tinged green through summer. Not to be confused with U glabra 'Lutescens', traditionally known as Golden Elm. 6 × 5m.

Ulmus pumila 'Den Haag'
Siberian Elm
Hardy species, selected for resistance to Dutch elm disease. Forms a loose open crown. New foliage creamy white, turning lime green, finally green. Leaves ovate or ovate-lanceolate, 2–7cm long, glabrous above, pubescent beneath becoming glabrous, margins serrated. Winged papery seeds disperse over a wide area. Endures cold, heat, drought, wind and poor soil. Stems brittle, crotches weak, root system aggressive although this may be a plus in erosion control. Pumila — dwarf. 6 × 6m.

VIBURNUM

A genus of about 150 species of shrubs and small trees distributed throughout the temperate Northern Hemisphere reaching into Malaysia and South America, named from the Latin term for the Wayfaring Tree, Viburnum lantana. Many species highly ornamental, exhibiting good form, handsome foliage, fragrant flowers and colourful fruit. Deserve to be high on the selection list of choice shrubs.

With few exceptions Viburnums are hardy to sub-zero temperatures and tolerate alkaline or acid soils, preferring heavy, rich free-draining, moisture-retentive loam in sun or partial shade. Prune for good shape and to prevent legginess. Leaves allergic to sulphur sprays or dust, causing black patches to develop, although without permanent damage.
Caprifoliaceae.

Viburnum × bodnantense 'Dawn'
Hybrid shrub from V farreri × V grandiflorum. Medium to large, strong well-branched upright grower. Leaves lanceolate to obovate to 10cm long, firmly textured, deeply veined, margins serrated, deep scarlet in autumn. Sweetly fragrant flowers, rich rose-red at first, fading to white with a strong flush of pink, borne in loose 7cm clusters over long periods autumn through winter. Excellent hardy winter-flowering shrub. Raised at Bodnant for which it is named. Deciduous. 2 × 1.8m.

Viburnum × burkwoodii
Beautiful hybrid from the deciduous Korean species V carlesii × V utile, evergreen species from central China. Medium-size, sparsely foliaged shrub, taller than V carlesii from which it has inherited fragrant, 9cm clusters of white flowers opening from pink buds over four months from mid-winter. Leaves ovate to elliptic to 10 × 4.5cm, glossy dark green and rough-textured above pale brown and woolly beneath, margins sparsely toothed, some richly coloured autumn and winter. Somewhat straggly when young, becoming dense with maturity. Evergreen. 1.5 × 1m.

Viburnum × burkwoodii 'Anne Russell'
Beautiful hybrid from V burkwoodii × V carlesii. Richly fragrant, waxy white flowers opening from pink tinged buds borne profusely in globose corymbs. Semi-evergreen. 1.5 × 1m.

Viburnum × burkwoodii 'Fulbrook'
Delightful hybrid from V carlesii × V burkwoodii, resulting in a medium sized shrub with large conical clusters of sweetly scented flowers, pink in bud and opening pure white, slightly later than 'Anne Russell'. Deciduous. 2.5 × 2m.

Viburnum × carlcephalum
Fragrant Snowball
Excellent hybrid from V carlesii × V macrocephalum from which it is named. Forms a medium-sized compact shrub with leaves resembling V carlesii but larger to 12cm, quite glossy, tinged red in autumn.

Buds tinted red, opening to long lasting waxy-white, fragrant flowers borne profusely in dense 15cm clusters, spring through early summer. Outstanding shrub, as showy as the snowball tree, but with fragrance. Semi-deciduous. 1.5 × 1m.

Viburnum carlesii
Korean Viburnum
Native to Korea and Japan. Medium-sized rounded shrub valued for sweet fragrance and easy culture. Leaves broadly ovate to 9 × 6.5cm, dull green and downy above, grey-green and woolly beneath, often coloured in autumn. Pure white, 12mm, starry flowers with sweet, daphne-like fragrance, opening from pale pink buds, borne in 6–8cm rounded clusters, in spring followed by 65mm ovoid black fruits. Hardy shrub, even in coastal gardens. Named for W R Carles, British Consul in China, who collected the species in Korea in 1889. Deciduous. 1.5 × 1.5m.

Viburnum carlesii 'Aurora'
Outstanding. Leaves light-green at first often becoming flushed copper. Flower buds red, opening pink and sweetly fragrant. Highly recommended. Deciduous. 2 × 1.5m.

Viburnum davidii
Delightful Chinese native. Compact habit, forming a low, wide-spreading mound providing excellent ground cover. Leaves narrow-oval to obovate, to 15 × 6.5cm, leathery, dark green above, paler beneath. Flowers in 75mm terminal clusters, opening white from dull pinkish-red buds. Flowers not so showy, but bright electric-blue, narrow-ovoid, 6mm fruit a feature during winter. Both sexes required for berry production, so plant several if raised from seed. Male and female forms preferable if available. Foundation or foreground, ground or bank cover. Named for Abbé Armand David, 19th century French missionary and plant collector in China. Evergreen. 75cm × 1m.

Viburnum 'Eskimo'
Excellent compact, slow-growing American cultivar. Handsome leaves elliptic to 6 × 2cm, glossy bright green, margins scarcely serrated. Fragrant ivory-white 12mm tubular flowers in 8cm snowball-like heads crowd the branches spring through early summer. Extremely showy shrub easily accommodated in suburban gardens. Semi-evergreen. 1.3 × 1.3m.

Viburnum japonicum
Japanese Viburnum
Dense, bushy Japanese shrub with luxurious evergreen foliage. Leaves ovate, rounded or

obovate to 15 × 14cm, bronzy when young, deeply veined, glossy deep green above, paler and dark spotted beneath. Rounded clusters of small white fragrant flowers in spring. Mature plants bear sparse clusters of small scarlet berries in suitable conditions. Good bulky filler or background in shady or semi-shady locations. Evergreen. 1.5 × 1.3m.

Viburnum × juddii
Hybrid of Japanese Viburnum bitchiuense and V carlesii. Forms a beautiful small to medium bushy shrub, freely producing sweetly fragrant pink flowers in terminal clusters. More spreading, bushier and stronger-growing than V carlesii, otherwise similar. Raised by William Judd in 1920 and named in his honour. Deciduous. 1.5 × 1m.

Viburnum macrocephalum
Giant Chinese Snowball
Magnificent flowering shrub with broad rounded habit. Leaves ovate oval or oblong to 10 × 6.5cm, dull green with scattered pubescence above, woolly beneath. Spectacular globose 15–20cm flowerheads comprising apple-green 3cm sterile florets gradually becoming pure white, literally cover the bush late spring. Spectacular specimen or border shrub. Almost evergreen in warm temperate conditions, deciduous in cooler regions. Macrocephalum — large headed. Semi-evergreen. 2.5 × 2m.

Viburnum odoratissimum 'Emerald Lustre'
Sweet Viburnum
Species native to India, Burma, China, Japan and Philippines. Young shoots orange tinted. Leaves bright lustrous green, 8–20cm, ovate to obovate, with leathery varnished appearance. Small white slightly fragrant flowers in 8–15cm conical clusters appear late spring, followed by oblong-ovoid, 10 × 5mm fruit, red at first ripening black. Valued for bold foliage effects. Fast-growing shrub for warmer areas. Odoratissimum — very fragrant. Evergreen. 4 × 3m.

Viburnum opulus
Guelder Rose, European Cranberry
An old-fashioned shrub with irresistible charm, native to Europe, north west Africa, central Asia and Asia Minor. Forms an open thicket with erect stems. Maple-like leaves to 10 × 10cm with 3–5 lobes, dark green and glabrous above, woolly beneath, margins coarsely and irregularly toothed, rich wine-red in autumn, especially in cooler climates. White fertile flowers surrounded by white ray florets, resembling lace-cap hydrangeas,

borne in flattened corymbs through summer, followed by glistening red translucent 9mm globose fruit in autumn and winter. Opulus — Latin term for a kind of Maple. Deciduous. 4 × 3m.

Viburnum opulus 'Compactum'
Smaller form of above, dense, compact habit, commencing to fruit when young. Heavy crops of shiny red berries autumn through winter. Deciduous. 1.3 × 1m.

Viburnum opulus 'Sterile'
Snowball Tree
Forms an open, graceful, robust plant with strong pithy shoots. Three to five-lobed, maple like, deep green leaves, 5–10cm long, coarsely toothed and downy beneath, intense purple in autumn. Produces an abundance of sterile, white, green-tinted, 7cm globular 'snowball' flower clusters, sometimes with a tinge of pink, mass-produced through spring, but no berries. Easy to grow and perfectly hardy. Deciduous. 3 × 2m.   **304**

Viburnum opulus 'Xanthocarpum'
Attractive white lacecap flowers in spring followed by fruit at first bright green, ripening clear golden-yellow, becoming darker and quite translucent. Xanthocarpum — yellow fruited. Deciduous. 2.5 × 2m.

Viburnum plicatum 'Lanarth'
Fine vigorous form, arranging its branches in tiered layers, decked in spring with showy heads of creamy fertile flowers, surrounded by large ray florets, resembling a white lacecap hydrangea. Deciduous. 3 × 2.5m.

Viburnum plicatum 'Mariesii'
Superb selected form with more tabulate branching arrangement. With slightly larger ray florets and great abundance of flower the bush appears to be laden with snow. Deciduous. 2.5 × 2.5m.

Viburnum plicatum 'Pink Beauty'
Selection from V p tomentosum, rounded growth habit and branches in layers, bearing a profusion of white flowers in flattish heads, becoming pink as they mature. Syn V p tomentosum 'Roseum'. Deciduous. 2 × 2m.

Viburnum plicatum 'Roseace'
Dwarf Pink Snowball Bush
Outstanding ornamental shrub with attractive foliage and flower. Leaves elliptic to 12 × 6cm, dark green flushed bronze-purple, leathery, prominently veined and crinkled, margins finely serrated. Charming rounded 'snowball' heads of creamy flowers, delicately flushed light rose pink intensifying as they mature. Compact bushy habit. Deciduous. 1.5 × 1.5m.   **304**

Viburnum plicatum tomentosum
Doublefile Viburnum
Native to China, Japan and Formosa. Wide-spreading, medium shrub with distinctive branching mode. Almost horizontal branches suspended in layers, creating an oriental, tiered effect. Elliptic, 5–10cm leaves, bright green, sharply toothed, distinctively pleated, often tinted in autumn. Small, creamy white, fertile flowers in 7–10cm umbels surrounded by conspicuous, 2–3cm white ray florets in lace cap effect, borne in double rows through late spring, appearing snow-covered. Red berries follow but not always profusely. Plicatum — pleated, tomentosum — woolly, referring to the foliage. Deciduous. 2.5 × 2.5m.   **304**

Viburnum rhytidophyllum 'Aldenhamensis'
Leather Leaf Viburnum
Exclusive Chinese species, amongst the most beautiful foliage shrubs, highly valued for floral art. Leaves ovate-oblong to 20 × 7cm, deeply veined and wrinkled, rich deep-green, the high spots dusted with gold, undersurface bronzy grey felted, suspended at an angle on semi-erect branches. Dull greenish white flowers in early summer develop into shining, scarlet red berries in winter. Heat, sun or semi shade and plenty of summer moisture. Rhytidophyllum — with wrinkled leaves. Aldenhamensis — for Aldenham, notable garden on the outskirts of London. Evergreen. 2 × 1.5m.

Viburnum setigerum
Attractive Chinese shrub with lax open habit, handsome leaves, beautiful flowers and colourful fruit. Leaves ovate-lanceolate to 15 × 6.5cm, slender-pointed, margins sharply toothed, dark-green above, paler and glabrous beneath except for long pubescence on the veins. Autumn colour progresses from metallic reddish blue, through shades of green to orange yellow. Pure white, 7mm flowers in 5cm cymes in early summer, followed by impressive clusters of 12mm, ovoid, orange-yellow fruit becoming brilliant red in autumn. Setigerum — bristly. Deciduous. 1.5 × 1.5m.

Viburnum tinus
Laurustinus
Native to southern Europe and North Africa. Multi-branched evergreen shrub of dense rounded form, with wine-red new stems. Leaves narrow-ovate to oblong, to 10 × 4cm, glossy dark green, luxuriant, leathery, paler beneath, margins entire. Small white slightly fragrant flowers, opening from pink buds in tight flattened clusters, late autumn through early spring, followed by 7mm metallic-blue ovoid berries, lasting through summer,

eventually turning black. Good winter-flowering shrub, tolerant of shade or full sun and thrives on the coast. Dense foliage to ground level, good for hedges, screens or clipping to shape. Tinus — from the Latin *laurustinus*. Evergreen. 2 × 1.5m.

Viburnum tinus 'Bewleys Variegated'
Resembles above, but dense bushy habit, leaves glossy pale-green deeply margined bright creamy yellow. Clusters of small white tinged pink flowers late autumn through early spring. Evergreen. 2 × 1.5m.

Viburnum tinus 'Eve Price'
Selected dense compact form with smaller leaves. Carmine-red buds open to white tinged pink flowers winter through early spring. Hardy and popular shrub. Evergreen. 1.5 × 1.3m.

Viburnum tinus 'Lucidum'
Vigorous form with open habit and glabrous shoots. Glossy green leaves larger than V tinus. Also flower heads larger. Lucidum — bright, shining. Evergreen. 2 × 1.5m.

Viburnum trilobum
American Cranberry Viburnum
North American native species resembling V opulus, but with foliage usually hairless, serrations more irregular, veining less pronounced and colour deeper green. Leaves maple-shaped to 12cm long, broadly ovate with three lobes, light green above, irregularly serrated, sometimes entire, paler beneath, carmine-red in autumn. Creamy white flowers in 10cm cymes, spring through summer followed by large clusters of translucent, bright-red, 9mm, subglobose, cranberry-like fruit. Fruit contrasts nicely against foliage, persisting into winter after leaf fall. Easy to grow, crops prolifically, excellent berry shrub for garden display or picking for indoors. Trilobum — three lobed. Deciduous. 3 × 2.5m.

A genus of two species of small trees from South Africa named for Latin poet Virgil. Of two similar species, V divaricata is more desirable. A tree in full bloom is quite an arresting sight and attracts hordes of birds. Life expectancy is about 15 years, but it grows rapidly, commences to flower within two years of planting and provides a consistent display each spring and early summer. Ideal for fast screening, street trees or lawn specimens.

Virgilias grow easily, preferring deeply worked, but not over-rich, free-draining soil in full sun, sheltered from strong wind. Shallow-rooted, they may blow over if unprotected. Deep watering at first will encourage the roots to go down, but once established, they're amazingly drought tolerant and flower more profusely when grown hard. Tip-pinch frequently to encourage greater density. Remove lower branches to allow underplanting. Protect over the first winter, but once established can handle temperatures to –5°C.
Leguminosae. *All evergreen.*

Virgilia divaricata
Keurboom
Luxuriant grower with dense growth habit, forming an ornamental round-headed tree with branches spreading to the ground. Feathery pinnate leaves to 20 × 7cm, with up to 13 pairs of narrowly oblong, deep green and smooth leaflets, paler beneath. Bright mauve-pink, pea shaped, sweetly scented, 12mm flowers in dense axillary racemes literally cover the tree late spring through early summer. Highly recommended tree for average garden purposes. Divaricata — spreading growth. Keurboom — Dutch for choice tree. 5 × 4m. **304**

Virgilia oroboides
Forms a rounded multi-branched small tree with reddish downy young shoots. Pinnate leaves to 20cm long with 6–10 pairs of linear-oblong, leathery deep green, 25mm leaflets, paler and tomentose beneath. Rosy mauve, fragrant pea shaped flowers in axillary clusters of seven to twelve, early summer through autumn. Oroboides — resembling orobos, a kind of vetch. 5 × 4m.

A genus of about 250 species of trees and shrubs widespread in many tropical or subtropical regions, called by the ancient Latin name used by Pliny for the species *Vitex agnus-castus*. The listed species, Chaste Tree, is valued for aromatic leaves and fragrant flowers. Grows in various free-draining soil types and prefers maximum summer heat for quantity and richness of bloom. Easy to grow, valuable in mixed shrub borders for summer colour.

The New Zealand Puriri requires moderate shelter when young and makes good progress in rich, deeply worked, free-draining, moisture-retentive soil. Mulch freely and keep moist until established. Hardy to possibly –5°C, but tolerant of wind and coastal exposure. Suited to large areas such as school grounds, parks, farms and public gardens.
Verbenaceae.

Vitex agnus-castus
Chaste Tree
Southern Europe. Desirable shrub for foliage and flower, forming a broad twiggy shrub with multiple stems and purplish young shoots. Compound leaves divided fanwise into 5–7 narrowly elliptic, thin and papery leaflets to 11 × 2cm, dark grey-green above, lighter grey beneath, margins entire. Fragrant, lavender blue or lilac flowers in erect pyramidal panicles to 30cm long, appear all over the bush throughout summer and autumn followed by 3mm, subglobose fruit. Agnus — Latin for lamb, castus — clean, chaste or pure, referring back to medieval superstitions that the fruits had an aphrodisiac qualities. Deciduous. 2.5 × 2m.

Vitex lucens
New Zealand Puriri
First discovered in Tolaga Bay in 1769, the tree has in past days been valued for strong and durable timber used extensively for railway sleepers, fence posts, house blocks and bridges. Mature specimens develop a trunk to 1.5m diameter. Maintains shrubby form for several years, later developing a round-headed tree. Compound leaves with 3–5 elliptic-oblong to obovate leaflets to 12 × 5cm, glabrous, dark green and glossy, paler beneath, margins entire. Cup-shaped, dull-red, 25mm flowers in axillary panicles, followed by bright orange red, globose, 2cm drupes. Lucens — bright, shining or clear. Evergreen. 6 × 5m.

A genus of about 10 species of deciduous shrubs from east Asia named for the 18th century German botanist, Christian E von Weigel. Valued for profuse displays of funnel-shaped flowers resembling those of the foxglove produced in great clusters on long, arching branches through spring and early summer. Excellent summer screens, colour accent in shrub borders, or underplanted with annuals or spring flowering bulbs. Also attractive when trained as a standard specimen.

Extremely hardy, adaptable to almost any conditions including summer drought, poor soil and wind exposure. Plant in deeply worked, free-draining, moderately rich soil in full sun. They call for no special care other than pruning

each year after flowering to maintain a shapely compact bush. Prune flowered stems to unflowered side branches, leaving only one or two to each stem. Cut some of the oldest stems to ground level, and thin new basal shoots to a few of the most vigorous. Rapid growth recovery.
Caprifoliaceae. *All deciduous.*

Weigela florida
Old fashioned but beautiful shrub, native to Japan, Korea, northern China and Manchuria. Medium shrub with long arching stems. Leaves ovate-oblong to obovate, to 10 × 4cm, deep green, matt surface, margins toothed, hairy veins beneath. Graceful branches literally weighed down late spring and early summer with clusters of trumpet or funnel shaped, deep rose pink, 3cm flowers. Parent of numerous attractive hybrid cultivars. Florida — blossoming, flowery, or rich in flowers. 2 × 1.5m.

Weigela florida 'Eva Rathke'
Old favourite hybrid, slower growing and more compact, bearing masses of deep crimson flowers with straw coloured anthers for long periods late spring and early summer. 1.3 × 1.3m.

Weigela florida 'Evita'
Forms a broad compact bush literally smothered with deep red flowers through spring. 60 × 90cm.   313

Weigela florida 'Foliis Purpureis'
Slow-growing, compact dwarf, leaves dark green flushed reddish purple-maroon, flowers dark pink. Foliis Purpureis — purple leaved 1.5 × 1.3m.

Weigela florida 'Grace Warden'
Compact grower with gracefully arching branches clothed during spring with deep rose pink bell flowers. 1.5 × 1.5m.

Weigela florida 'Minuet'
Canadian cultivar. Dwarf compact bushy habit, leaves dark-green tinted purple late summer. Fragrant flowers, dark rose corolla tube, lobes shaded lilac, yellow in the throat. Free-flowering early spring. 75 × 75cm.

Weigela florida 'Newport Red'
Superb form, more erect growing than Eva Rathke, with larger, bright crimson-red blossoms. One of the best reds. 1.5 × 1m.

Weigela florida 'Rosabella'
Rather stiff open habit. Large, deep rose-pink flowers with short open tube borne profusely early spring. Among the best. Hybrid from 'Eva Rathke' × 'Newport Red'. 1.5 × 1.5m.

Weigela florida 'Snowflake'
Distinctive light green foliage, vigorous bushy habit and masses of snow-white bell-shaped flowers mid spring. 2.5 × 2m.

Weigela florida 'Variegata'
Light green leaves with broad yellow margins, on slender arching branches. Colourful foliage combined with massed clusters of light pink flowers opening from reddish buds most effective for long periods in spring. Quite irresistible for garden display and picking for indoors. Merits extensive planting. 1.5 × 1.3m.   313

WEINMANNIA

A genus of about 150 species of trees and shrubs from Malaysia, Madagascar, tropical South America, Polynesia, Melanesia and New Zealand, named for Johann W Weinmann, 18th century German chemist and author. Listed species valued for its great hardiness and easy culture, handsome foliage and profuse floral display. Hardy under most conditions and grows in almost any reasonable soil. Plant in deeply worked, free-draining soil, mulch heavily and water in dry periods until well established. Cunoniaceae.

Weinmannia racemosa
New Zealand Kamahi
One of two New Zealand species, naturally a medium forest tree abundant in lowland to mountain forests in the lower North Island, South Island and Stewart Island, from sea level to 1000m. Grows slowly, being seen as a handsome shrub over all seasons for many years, especially its bright reddish brown juvenile leaves often cut for indoor decoration. Adult leaves oblong-lanceolate, to 10 × 4cm, leathery, dark green and glossy, paler beneath, margins coarsely and bluntly serrated. White fluffy flowers in erect, 11cm racemes or tapered spikes suggestive of Hebe or Bottlebrush, attractive spring through mid-summer. Racemosa — with flowers in racemes. Evergreen. 3 × 2m.

WESTRINGIA

A genus of about 25 species of shrubs, all native to Australia, named for J P Westring, 18th–19th century botanist and physician to the King of Sweden. Relatively few in cultivation, all valued for low maintenance, good appearance under adverse conditions, neat foliage and flower. Useful for filling large areas, screens or hedges. The species listed grow in virtually any deeply worked, free-draining soil in full or partial sun. Extremely hardy shrub for coastal planting, tolerant of exposure to salt spray and strong wind. Also a useful long-term, low-maintenance, landscaping plant in less rigorous conditions.
Labiatae. *All evergreen.*

Westringia angustifolia
Tasmanian species. Vigorous shrub with stiff stems, small linear leaves curved sideways like a scythe, carried erect in whorls of 3–4. Flowers white to lilac, flecked yellow or red borne solitary in leaf axils. Angustifolia — having narrow leaves. 1.8 × 1.3m.

Westringia brevifolia
Australian Rosemary
Rounded shrub from Tasmania. Leaves elliptic, 1cm long, rosemary-like, arranged in whorls of four. Pale bluish-mauve flowers in winter and spring. Neat plant which seems to thrive in most temperate regions, soils or aspects. Brevifolia — short leafed. 1 × 1m.

Westringia fruticosa
Coastal Rosemary
Extremely hardy compact plant with dense rosemary-like foliage, forming a dense twiggy bush. Leaves broadly linear to 25 × 3mm, leathery deep green and glabrous, silvery grey beneath. White to pale mauve flowers spotted purple, borne in leaf axils late winter through summer. Fruticosa — shrubby or bushy. 1.5 × 1.5m.

Westringia fruticosa 'Morning Light'
Delightful variegated form of this popular shrub. Crowded deep green leaves, margined with a band of cream. Sparse white or palest mauve flowers with spotted throats through spring. More petite and compact than fruticosa. 60cm × 1.3m.

Westringia 'Highlight'
Attractive variegated form of the Australian hybrid W 'Wynyabbie Gem'. A compact rounded shrub with mid-green leaves margined creamy yellow. Dainty mauve-blue flowers appear late spring through summer. 80 × 80cm.   313

Westringia 'Wynyabbie Gem'
Hybrid cultivar from W fruticosa × W eremicola. Hardy compact bushy shrub with linear, deep green, 20 × 1mm leaves in whorls of four. Bluish mauve flowers in small axillary clusters appear through most of the year. 1.3 × 1.5m.

Above: Westringia 'Highlight' **312**

Above: Yucca filamentosa 'Variegata' **317**

Above: Ulmus glabra 'Lutescens' *Golden Elm* **308**
Below: Xeronema callistemon *Poor Knights Lily* **317**

Above: Weigela florida 'Evita' **312**
Below: Weigela florida 'Variegata' **312**

Above: Bougainvillea 'Limberlost Beauty **319**

Above: Bougainvillea 'Scarlett O'Hara' **320**
Below: B 'Hawaiian Orange' **319**

Below: Bougainvillea 'Klong Fire' **319**

Above: Bougainvillea 'Pagoda Pink' **319**
Below: Bougainvillea 'Snow Cap' **320**

Above: Bougainvillea 'Thai Gold' **320**

Above: Bougainvillea glabra 'Magnifica' **319**
Below: Clematis montana 'Snowflake' **322**

Above: Clematis montana 'Rubens' **322**
Below: Clematis montana 'Tetrarose' **322**

Below: Clematis hybrid 'Gipsy Queen' **324**

Above: Clematis hybrid 'Lawsoniana' **324**

Above: Clematis hybrid 'Madame le Coultre' **324**
Below: Clematis hybrid 'Sir Garnet Wolseley' **324**

Above: Clematis hybrid 'Lord Neville' **324**

Above: Clematis hybrid 'Nellie Moser' **324**
Below: Clematis hybrid 'Ville de Lyon' **324**

XERONEMA

A genus of two species of perennial herbs from New Caledonia and Poor Knights Islands of New Zealand, named from the Greek *xeros*, dry and *nema*, a stringy thread or fibre. Beautiful, extremely rare New Zealand native plant with sword-like foliage and brilliant flowers. Growing naturally under conditions of extreme exposure, it isn't a plant to be coddled, preferring a light open position, its tough leaves tolerant of strong wind or ocean spray.

Plant in deeply worked, free-draining, fibrous, gravelly or sandy soil. Water deeply during dry periods and feed occasionally with liquid fertilizer. Possibly best grown in large containers with perfect drainage, located against a wall which receives morning sun and protection from frost. Strong midday or afternoon sunlight may cause leaf scorch.
Liliaceae.

Xeronema callistemon
Poor Knights Lily
Originally found on Poor Knights Islands, about 25kms off New Zealand's Northland coast. Large tufted perennial herb with sword-like, bright green leaves to 100 × 5cm, resembling flax or bearded iris, carried in two-ranked crowns. Stems to 90cm long emerge from the centre of each leaf fan, bearing gently curving 'brush' flowers to 35 × 5cm comprising masses of coral-red stamens, tipped with bright yellow anthers. Mature plants build on mounds of stringy fibre formed by the bases of old leaves. Callistemon — beautiful stamens. Evergreen. 1m × 75cm.   **313**

YUCCA

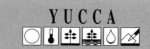

A genus of about 40 species of perennial herbs or trees from Texas, California, Mexico Central America and the West Indies, named from *Yuca*, Caribbean term for Manihot esculenta. Yucca has stiff, sword-shaped leaves attached directly to woody stems, and flowers rising in large clusters above the leaves.

Being desert plants they take considerable drought once established, but most species accept garden watering. Plant in deeply worked, free-draining, light-textured sandy soil in full sun. Good seaside plants. Dramatic landscaping subjects, ideal for grouping with agaves, cordylines, cactus and broader foliage plants for dramatic effects. Locate those with sharp pointed leaves where they're unlikely to cause offence.
Agavaceae. *All evergreen.*

Yucca filamentosa
Adam's Needle
Native to south eastern USA. Almost stemless plant forming dense clumps of spreading or erect, stiff tapering, slightly glaucous leaves to 75 × 10cm, margins inrolled near the apex, curly silvery-white filaments towards the base. Creamy white, 5cm, pendent, bell-shaped flowers borne in conical panicles on erect 1–1.5m stems through summer. Quite young plants produce flowers. Filamentosa — furnished with filaments or threads. 1.5 × 1m.

Yucca filamentosa 'Bright Edge'
Ornamental cultivar with stiff, erect emerald-green leaves broadly margined rich yellow. Creamy white bell-shaped flowers borne on compact spikes late summer. Excellent feature or accent plant in the garden or containers. 75 × 90cm.

Yucca filamentosa 'Variegata'
Low-growing plant, leaves erect or semi-pendulous, variegated green and cream flushed pink. Margins with silvery thread-like filaments. 75 × 90cm.   **313**

Yucca filifera 'Garland Gold'
Low-growing, leaves mid-green with broad, central golden band, linear-oblanceolate to 55 × 4cm, fleshy and flexible, outer leaves reflexing downwards from the centre, margins with long silvery fibres. Fragrant ivory-white bell flowers borne in long spikes in summer. Syn Y flaccida 'Garland Gold'. Filifera — thread-bearing. 60 × 75cm.

Yucca filifera 'Ivory'
Ornamental stemless plant forming a rosette of fleshy, soft green leaves, edged with loose silvery thread-like fibres along the edges. Large creamy white bell-flowers, lightly fragrant in the evening, crowded on spikes to 1.3m tall through late summer. 75 × 75cm.

Yucca glauca
Small Soapweed
From the south central areas of USA. Low-growing, short stemmed species, forming a rosette of narrow-linear, greyish leaves to 60 × 5cm, margins greyish white and slightly filiferous with straight threads. Greenish white, 6cm bell-shaped flowers produced in narrow erect racemes to 1m tall through summer. Glauca — leaves with fine whitish bloom. 60 × 75cm.

ZELKOVA

A genus of about five smooth barked trees related to the elm, from Caucasus, east Asia, Taiwan and Japan, called by the Caucasian name for one of the species. Admired for good form, handsome leaves and bright autumn colour.

Plant in deeply worked, free-draining, moisture-retentive loamy soil. Early training is important to develop a strong leading shoot and gain headroom. Shorten any excessively long pendulous branches to encourage side growths, and remove competing branches to allow full development of the strongest limbs. Deep summer watering encourages roots to go down. Worthwhile shade tree for larger lawns, farms, school grounds, parks etc.
Ulmaceae.

Zelkova serrata
Japanese Zelkova, Saw-Leaf Zelkova
Native to Japan, Korea and China. Forms an elegant goblet-shaped, medium sized tree with sharply ascending branches curving outward at the tips. Smooth grey-white bark, branchlets tinged purplish grey. Leaves oblong-elliptic to 75 × 30cm, pale green and slightly pubescent above, pale green and lustrous beneath, margins sharply toothed, yellow, dark red or reddish brown in autumn. Serrata — saw-toothed margins. Deciduous. 8 × 6m.

CLIMBING PLANTS AND VINES

Many cultivated climbing plants from tropical and temperate forests of the world, bring with them an exuberance and appeal quite unequalled in other plant forms. There are bold-textured vines, others have delicate laciness. Some cling, twine or scramble, while others merely lean against their support or run over the ground. And they come in a kaleidoscope of brilliant colours.

Climbing plants are more than something to cover ugliness. Grown on walls, patios, fences, archways or trellis or pergolas their graceful tracery softens architectural lines without taking excessive ground space to achieve their objectives. Ornamental vines are a vital ingredient in any landscape design both functional and for the creation of beauty.

ACTINIDIA

A genus of about 40 species from east Asia named from the Greek *aktis*, a ray, in allusion to the styles which radiate like the spokes of a wheel. Most notable is Actinidia deliciosa, once known as A chinensis. Orchards worldwide cover tens of thousands of hectares and produce enormous quantities of nutritious fruit, marketed as *Kiwifruit*. Demand continues to escalate as more and more people discover its health-giving qualities.

Actinidia is a useful ornamental, with the bonus of vine-ripened fruit. The vine is vigorous but easy to manage and train over pergolas, patio roofs, trellis screens, against walls or fences or allowed to scramble through old trees. Both male and female vines are needed for fruit production, but pollen from one male will pollinate up to four or five female vines.

Plant in rich, deeply worked, free-draining, moisture retentive soil with adequate moisture during dry periods. Unpruned, Actinida becomes a mass of twining stems, resulting in poor crops of inferior quality. Establish a framework suited to the chosen support over the first three years. It is then a matter of selecting and tying down strong canes which will flower in the spring and produce fruit over the following winter. Old fruited canes are cut off each year. Feed with balanced fertilizer early spring.

Actinidiaceae.

Actinidia deliciosa
Kiwi Fruit, Chinese Gooseberry

Vigorous climbing shrub of Chinese origin. Young shoots covered with red pubescence. Leaves cordate to 20cm across, semi-glossy deep green, leathery, prominently veined, densely hairy beneath, margins entire, petioles reddish brown to 8cm long. Creamy-white flowers to 4cm across turn yellow before petal-fall borne in clusters on axillary branches in spring. Fruit oblong-globose, 8–10cm, brown, covered with fine fuzzy hairs, green flesh with myriads of tiny black seeds. When fully ripe, the fruit has a unique and delicious flavour. As an ornamental, foliage has subtle colour appeal. Masses of creamy yellow flowers in spring are attractive. Cultivar 'Haywood' recommended for heavy crops of large fruit. Deciduous.

AKEBIA

A genus of about five species of twining plants from Japan, China and Korea named from the Japanese *akebi*. Grown for rapid coverage of tree stumps, old sheds or other unsightly objects, handsome foliage and quaint purplish chocolate flowers. Plant in any reasonable deeply worked, free-draining soil in sun or shade. Needs support and heavy annual pruning, even to ground level. Good choice where rapid coverage and subdued colour is needed. May become invasive in rich soil.

Lardizabalaceae.

Akebia quinata
Five Leaf Akebia

Native to Japan, China and Korea. Grows rapidly to 4m or more in mild regions, somewhat slower in cooler climates. Leaves divided into five glabrous deep green, oblong or ovate, 3–5cm leaflets, notched at the tip, blue-green beneath, margins entire. Flowers purplish chocolate, goblet-shaped to 2–3cm across, strongly vanilla scented, male and female flowers in the same cluster, borne in pendent racemes through spring. Flowers quaint rather than showy, sometimes followed by 5–10cm, ovoid-oblong, edible fruit, somewhat resembling a purple sausage containing numerous black seeds embedded in white pulp. Quinata — in fives. Evergreen in mild climates, deciduous elsewhere.

BERBERIDOPSIS

A genus of one species, scrambling evergreen climbing plant from Chile named from *Berberis* and the Greek *opsis*, like, from the resemblance of its foliage to some Berberis species. Handsome foliage and long-lasting, brightly coloured flowers. Hardy to −10°C, but should be protected from strong winds. Ideal in woodland conditions with dappled light. Plant in cool deeply worked, free-draining, organically enriched, moisture retentive, lime-free acid soil. Mulch freely and keep moist during dry periods.

Flacourtiaceae.

Berberidopsis corallina
Chilean Coral Vine

Scandent shrub or climbing plant from temperate, moist coastal woodland areas of Chile. Leaves oblong-cordate, to 75 × 35mm, dull to glossy, dark green, leathery, margins spine-toothed, glaucous beneath. Globose, fuchsia-like, 17mm, coral-red to crimson flowers, produced in drooping terminal racemes through summer and autumn. Corallina — coral red. Evergreen.

BILLARDIERA

A genus of about 25 species of Australian endemic plants, named for J J de Labillardiere, 18th–19th century French botanist. Slender climbing plants, valued for showy flowers and fleshy, colourful fruit. Relatively few species widely cultivated. Found naturally in moist sheltered forests and prefers to be grown in deeply worked, free-draining, moisture-retentive soil in semi-shade although tolerates full sun. Mulch freely and keep moist during dry periods. Effective amongst other climbing plants or shrubs and suitable as a pot plant for indoors.

Pittosporaceae.

Billardiera longiflora
Purple Apple Berry

From New South Wales, Victoria and Tasmania. Attractive twiner with slender stems and glabrous young shoots. Leaves linear to narrow-lanceolate, to 50 × 5mm, dark green, semi-glossy, often tinged purple, margins entire. Bright greenish yellow, tubular to bell-shaped, 2–3cm flowers, tinged purple, borne singly from short terminating branchlets on long slender pedicels through spring, followed by oblong 2 × 1cm, shiny, bright purple-blue fruit, late autumn through winter. Evergreen.

BOUGAINVILLEA

A genus of about eighteen species of shrubs, vines or small trees from tropical and subtropical South America, named for Louis Antoine de Bougainville, sailor and explorer who commanded the French ship *Bordeuse*. It was Philibert Commerson, a French botanist who sailed around the world on this ship (1766–1769), who first found and described the genus in Rio de Janeiro.

Bougainvillea is amongst the showiest, strongest growing and most popular tropical vine in cultivation, providing a spectacle of dazzling colour for very long periods. It is the mass of brilliant bracts around the flower which affords such flamboyance. Actual flowers are tiny and insignificant. They attracts hordes of beautiful butterflies and other insects, though not to be reckoned as pests as none of them seem to feed on Bougainvillea during the laval stages.

Planted on the sunny side of a fence, pergola, trellis or old tree, they make tremendous growth, and if allowed, completely cover the support with a mass of wiry stems and tropical colour. Try some of the dwarf cultivars in containers or hanging baskets or as a free-standing specimen. There are forms for almost any purpose. They can be pruned and trained to do just what you require. Some produce several bursts of bloom throughout the year.

Bougainvillea needs a location with maximum sunlight, sheltered from persistent cold wind, rich, deeply worked soil with good drainage. Take care not to disturb the roots when planting. Mulching will help maintain moisture, insulate the roots from excessive heat and suppress weed growth. Water frequently during dry periods. Lightly prune after flowering and feed with a slow-release fertilizer.

Numerous cultivars appear in cultivation having arisen from the species B glabra, B peruviana and B spectabilis. Of those listed, the hardiest is B glabra 'Magnifica' which once established, survives considerable frost. Others require varying degrees of protection, although some have proved surprisingly tolerant of extremes. Maximum sunlight, warm conditions and good drainage are basic essentials.

Nyctaginaceae. *All semi-evergreen.*

Bougainvillea 'Apple Blossom'

Large rounded and smooth dark-green leaves and medium thorns. Cascading branches massed with medium-size, pure white bracts flushed pink in cooler conditions. Decorative but not the most prolific. Syn 'Jamaica White'.

Bougainvillea glabra 'Magnifica'

Extremely vigorous climber scrambling to great heights if left unpruned. Leaves ovate to elliptic to 12 × 6cm, deep green, glabrous, semi-glossy, margins entire, thorns long and straight. Becomes a total mass of brilliant glowing-magenta, ovate bracts with prominent creamy flowers borne in large trusses summer through autumn. Syn magnifica 'Traillii'. **315**

Bougainvillea glabra 'Sanderiana Variegata'

Bushy compact grower, small pointed cream and green variegated foliage. Small lilac-mauve to light magenta single flowers.

Bougainvillea 'Hawaiian Orange'

Large, dark-green, rounded foliage, erect habit, medium thorns. Showy trusses of single, apricot-orange to amber bracts, inconspicuous creamy flowers. Robust and worthwhile. Syn 'Mrs McLean'. **314**

Bougainvillea 'Hawaiian Yellow'

Strong erect grower, large, dark-green rounded foliage, medium stocky thorns. Large, bright-yellow single flowers. Blooms several times yearly in suitable climates. Syn 'Lady Mary Baring'.

Bougainvillea 'Killie Campbell'

Vigorous grower, flowering branches somewhat pendulous. Leaves ovate to lanceolate, dark green, waxy, margins wavy, quite long petioles, numerous long stout spines. Large thin-textured, ruffled bracts, rust-brown as they open, changing through orange scarlet to magenta purple. Prominent large white flowers. Incredible effects as these vivid colours appear on a succession of flowering stems at the same time. Spectacular climber for warm outdoor situations or containers.

Bougainvillea 'Klong Fire'

Vigorous, compact climber. Leaves large, rounded, dark green. Double bracts at first intense carmine-red, maturing ruby red, in crowded, long-lasting trusses throughout the year. Syn Carmencita. **314**

Bougainvillea 'Limberlost Beauty'

Vigorous but compact grower, rounded, mid-green leaves, medium thorns. Gorgeous double bracts basically creamy white, tipped and flushed magenta, almost continually in bloom. Colour more intense in cooler conditions. Syn 'Bridal Bouquet'. **314**

Bougainvillea 'Pagoda Pink'

Moderate growth habit, foliage rounded, mid to deep green, straight medium spines. Large trusses of lilac-pink double bracts in recurring displays throughout the year. Colour becomes more intense with maturity. Syn 'Pink Champagne'. **314**

Bougainvillea 'Raspberry Ice'

Compact, bushy grower, leaves beautifully variegated cream and greyish-green, young shoots tinted reddish. Showy carmine-red, ovate bracts with prominent white flower borne in impressive, graceful trusses. Excellent for walls, trellis, containers or hanging baskets. Syn 'Tropic Rainbow'.

Bougainvillea 'Scarlett O'Hara'

Vigorous grower producing strong, lax upright stems, young canes dark wine red and faintly pubescent. Large, rounded, dark green leathery leaves. Almost rounded bracts, at first dark red shaded orange, maturing rich scarlet red with prominent cream flowers, creating a blaze of dazzling colour through much of the year.　　**314**

Bougainvillea 'Smarty Pants'

Unusual erect grower with short internodes causing a crowded effect of small leathery leaves and small closely packed, magenta red bracts. Small white flowers. Quite a novelty, but needs frequent pruning to encourage multiple stems and remain compact.

Bougainvillea 'Snow Cap'

Large, ovate bracts, some deep pink, some white, others multi-coloured, borne in periodic bursts of riotous colour through the year. Large, medium-green, broadly ovate leaves. Syn 'Mary Palmer'.　　**314**

Bougainvillea 'Thai Gold'

Vigorous grower, numerous erect stems, dark green, ovate leaves. Medium-size double bracts in crowded clusters of 30–50, burnt-orange at first, outer bracts maturing salmon pink to carmine, inner bracts persisting bright orange for long periods. Ideal for containers or small-scale garden decoration. Prune to shape, cut off old bracts which tend to stay on the bush. Syn 'Doubloon'.　　**315**

CAMPSIS

A genus of two species of vines or climbing plants from east Asia and North America, named from the Greek *kampe*, something bent, referring to curved stamens. Even though some species are seen as aggressive weeds in their moist woodland native setting, as garden plants they're admired for brilliant trumpet flowers over long periods and considerable hardiness. They climb by aerial roots and cling to most building surfaces.

Plant in deeply worked, free-draining soil in full sun and don't overfeed. Campsis is tolerant of most climatic conditions and is not disturbed by salt laden winds. Mature plants may be heavily pruned each year to maintain control. Cut back to within 2–3 buds of the main framework. Avoid deep cultivation as each severed root produces another plant. Ideal climber for rapid screening on a large scale, covering old trees or fences.

Bignoniaceae. *All deciduous.*

Campsis grandiflora
Chinese Trumpet Vine

Climbing shrub from central and eastern China. Rapidly forms heavy, woody growth with few or no aerial rootlets. Pinnate leaves with 7–13 ovate-elliptic leaflets, deep green and glabrous above, margins strongly serrated. Funnel-form flowers with 4cm tube opening to five rounded lobes, 45mm across at the mouth, light orange outside, pinkish-orange within, borne in loose panicles through summer and autumn. Grandiflora — large flowered.

Campsis radicans 'Flava'
Yellow Trumpet

The species is native to eastern United States. A vigorous grower which attaches itself tenaciously to supports by means of ivy-like, aerial roots. Leaves pinnate, comprising 9–11 ovate to elliptic, 6cm leaflets, glossy pale-green above, hairy veined beneath, margins serrated. Rich golden yellow funnel-shaped, 5–8cm flowers with five flaring lobes borne through summer in lax terminal clusters of six to twelve. Radicans — with rooting stems. Flava — pure yellow.

Campsis × tagliabuana 'Guilfoylei'
Trumpet Vine

A hybrid from the Asian species C grandiflora × American species C radicans resulting in a shrubby climber intermediate between the two. Leaves pinnate to 35cm long, comprising 7–11 narrow-ovate leaflets to 80 × 45mm, deep green, glossy, margins serrated. This Australian cultivar produces large orange-red trumpet-flowers in loose panicles of 8–12 through late summer and autumn. Named for the Tagliabue brothers, celebrated Italian gardeners.

CELASTRUS

A genus of about 30 species of deciduous, often scandent or twining shrubs from Africa, America, Australia, Asia and the Pacific named from the Greek *kelastros*. Grown for abundant crops of colourful autumn fruits, decorative on the vine for long periods and which may be cut and dried for indoors. Grows rampantly over old stumps or into trees whether dead or alive. Hardy to −15°C and happy in full sun or semi-shade. Plant in average deeply worked, free-draining soil in a spot where invasive root suckers won't be a problem. Prune regularly for size control, removing fruited branches after cropping and pinching tip growths during summer.
　　Celastraceae

Celastrus scandens
American Bittersweet

Vigorous North American native, a scandent or climbing shrub thriving under almost any conditions. Leaves ovate-oblong, to 10cm long, glabrous, margins finely toothed, rich golden-yellow in autumn. Small yellowish flowers in terminal racemes, unisexual or bisexual, followed in autumn by globose, 8mm, orange-yellow fruits in clusters of 10–12. Fruit splits open to reveal brilliant red seeds persisting well into winter. Although considered hermaphroditic, group planting seems to improve berrying. Deciduous.

CLEMATIS

A genus of about 200 species of climbing plants or woody perennials widely distributed through temperate regions of both Hemispheres, named from the Greek *clema*, a tendril. Masses of beautiful flowers in gorgeous colours over long periods place them among garden favourites. The seed vessels of some are almost as delightful as their flowers, useful in floral arrangements. All Clematis grow rapidly and need the support of trellis, wires or fences and generally like to have roots shaded from direct sunlight and stems in full sun.

Plant in rich, loose-textured, deeply worked, free-draining, neutral to slightly acid or slightly alkaline soil conditioned with peat moss, sand or fine scoria. Plant with the top of the root ball at least 5cm below the surface. Mulch with peat moss during summer to conserve moisture, insulate roots from heat and preserve moisture during dry periods. Watch for slugs which relish tender young shoots, especially large-flowered hybrids and C paniculata. Clematis montana and other species are relatively hardy under average garden conditions, demanding little in the way of extra care or pruning.

Varieties marked 'Minimal pruning' produce flowers on wood ripened the preceding year and require no pruning. Just remove dead or unsightly stems when flowering is finished, or before new shoots emerge in August. Other varieties may be cut back as required.

Ranunculaceae. *Deciduous unless marked otherwise.*

Clematis afoliata
Leafless Clematis
Curious New Zealand native found clambering over rocks or bushes in open places from Hawke's Bay to Southland. Semi-scandent plant forming a mass of slender, green, wire-like, grooved, glabrous, almost leafless stems. Small ovate or triangular leaves may be present on young stems or in shade. Yellowish green, four-petalled flowers to 60mm across with strong Boronia fragrance appear at each node along bare stems through spring, followed by fluffy seed capsules. Minimal pruning. Afoliata — without leaves.

Clematis alpina
Alpine Virgin Flower
Beautiful hardy vine from Europe and Asia with slender twining stems. Leaves to 15cm comprising nine ovate-lanceolate leaflets to 50 × 15mm, margins coarsely toothed. Delightful pendulous bell or lantern-shaped, clear satiny-blue flowers, to 4cm across with central tuft of white spoon-shaped staminoides, borne in great masses on slender solitary stems through spring, followed in autumn by silky seed heads. Prefers cool shade. Perfect scrambler over low walls, large rocks, old tree stumps or such places. Minimal pruning for C alpina or cultivars. Alpina — mountain dweller.

Clematis alpina 'Frances Rivis'
Robust and floriferous clone with larger flowers to 5cm, rich sky blue with central cluster of white staminoides through spring. Syn 'Blue Giant'.

Clematis alpina 'Helsingborg'
Deep purple flowers with dark-purple petaloid stamens through spring.

Clematis alpina 'Pamela Jackman'
Large dark azure-blue flowers to 8cm across, central staminoides white tinted blue through spring.

Clematis alpina 'Ruby'
Soft rosy-red four-petalled flowers, cream staminoides. Spring flowering.

Clematis alpina 'White Moth'
Exquisite pure white fully double flowers through spring.

Clematis alpina 'Willy'
Lantern-shaped, white to pale pink flowers, deeper pink at the base, early spring.

Clematis armandii 'Snowdrift'
Native to central and western China. Vigorous evergreen climber, young stems covered with minute woolly hairs, new leaves copper tinted. Leaves trifoliate, leaflets oblong-lanceolate to ovate, to 15 × 6.5cm, tough and leathery, glabrous, glossy rich-green, prominently veined. Waxy pure white, highly fragrant, 7cm flowers borne on drooping stalks in large branched clusters early spring. Ideal on warm sunny walls, on banks or up a tree. Once established prune after flowering to prevent tangling and prevent build up of unwanted stems. Armandii — named for 19th century French missionary Armand David. Evergreen.

Clematis brachiata
Travellers Joy
Tall woody South African climber, attaching itself by leaf-stalks. Leaves tri or five-foliate, leaflets oblanceolate to elliptic, mid-green, prominently veined, margins deeply lobed. Small greenish white flowers to 25mm with cluster of yellow anthers, borne prolifically in axillary clusters late summer through autumn followed by fluffy white seed heads. Minimal pruning. Brachiata — branched at right angles.

Clematis chinensis
Chinese Clematis
Native to central and western China. Strong climber, stems ribbed and sparsely covered with tiny hairs. Pinnate leaves with five ovate or cordate leaflets to 75mm, glabrous, midrib slightly hairy. Creamy white flowers to 2cm borne in multi-flowered panicles through late spring early summer, followed by fine white pubescent seed heads. Minimal pruning.

Clematis cirrhosa
From southern Europe, Asia Minor and Mediterranean. Evergreen climber with grooved or smooth stems, pubescent when young. Leaves variable, simple, or trilobed, to 5cm long, deep green and very glossy above, finely pubescent beneath, margins coarsely toothed. Broad bell-shaped, yellowish-white flowers to 7cm across, with central anthers, petals woolly on the outside, borne profusely late winter early spring, followed by silky seed heads. Minimal pruning. Cirrhosa — with tendrils, leaf-stalks function as tendrils. Evergreen.

Clematis cirrhosa balearica
Fern Leaved Clematis
Exquisite slender climber from the Balearic Islands. Attractive leaves divided into numerous fern-like segments, bronze-tinted through winter. Creamy yellow, 4–5cm flowers spotted and flecked reddish maroon within, borne on slender pedicels winter and early spring. Minimal pruning. Balearica — native state. Evergreen.

Clematis × durandii
Excellent hybrid from C integrifolia × C jackmanii. Sturdy, semi-scandent herbaceous or shrubby plant with robust stems to 1.8m. Leaves ovate to 15 × 8cm, glossy green, glabrous, prominently veined. Deep violet-blue flowers to 11cm across, petals slightly waved, central cluster of yellow stamens, borne in groups of three through summer and autumn. Minimal pruning.

Clematis × eriostemon
French hybrid from C integrifolia × C viticella. Sprawling, semi-woody or herbaceous non-climbing plant with grooved, slightly pubescent stems to 3m. Pinnate leaves with seven elliptic leaflets, deep green, margins entire except for slightly lobed terminal leaflet. Dark-violet to lavender bell-shaped, slightly fragrant flowers with reflexed, spatula-shaped, prominently veined petals, borne in terminal groups of 1–3 through summer, followed by woolly seed heads. Eriostemon — woolly stamens. Prune hard after flowering.

Clematis fargesii
Vigorous Chinese climber. Young shoots purple, covered with short woolly hair and prominently ribbed. Leaves bipinnate, to 23cm long, 5–7 ovate leaflets to 5 × 4cm, dull green, margins deeply, irregularly and coarsely serrated. Pure white flowers to 65mm across, yellowish and woolly outside, pale yellow anthers, borne in groups through summer and autumn. Named for Paul Farges, 19th century French missionary and naturalist in central China. Prune hard after flowering.

Clematis flammula
Distributed through southern Europe, North Africa, Syria, Iran and Turkey. Hardy, easily grown and most floriferous species forming a tangle of glabrous stems. Leaves with 3–5 narrow-lanceolate to rounded leaflets, bright green, glabrous and leathery, margins entire or tri-lobed. Starry, pure white, highly fragrant flowers to 25mm across, mass produced in multi-flowered, 30cm panicles through summer and autumn, followed by hairy seed heads. Prune hard after flowering. Flammula — a small flame, possibly alluding to a burning taste.

Clematis florida 'Alba Plena'
Native to China and Japan. Excellent medium climber with tough wiry stems. Ternate leaves to 12cm across, with nine 5cm, ovate to lanceolate leaflets, glossy deep green above, pubescent beneath, margins entire or coarsely serrated. Double flowers, white flushed green, sepals striped green outside, borne profusely through summer

and autumn. Minimal pruning. Florida — rich in flower, alba — white, plena — double. Semi-evergreen.

Clematis florida 'Bicolor'

Most beautiful and desirable cultivar. Creamy white, 8cm, five-petalled flowers, striped green beneath each petal, and conspicuous cluster of purple staminodes forming an anemone centre, borne singly in great profusion through summer and autumn. Minimal pruning. Semi-evergreen.

Clematis foetida
Scented Clematis

Charming, free-flowering, spreading New Zealand native which rambles over scrub along forest margins throughout the North and South Islands. Leaves tri-foliate to 75mm across, with ovate to broadly ovate leaflets to 55 × 35mm, dark green above, paler beneath, leathery, margins entire, deeply waved or lobed. Yellow-green, strongly lemon-scented, starry flowers to 25mm across, borne profusely in large axillary panicles through spring. Strongly fragrant, but not foetid. Minimal pruning. Foetida — bad smelling. Evergreen.

Clematis forsteri
Small Clematis, Puataua

New Zealand species found in lowland forests and scrub throughout the North Island. Small slender vine, leaves trifoliate to 16 × 14cm, leaflets lanceolate to broadly ovate, to 7cm long, bright green, leathery, margins entire or slightly crenate. White, starry flowers in axillary clusters of 2–6, mass produced in spring followed by greenish white woolly seed heads. Minimal pruning. Evergreen.

Clematis grewiifolia

Native to Himalayas and Burma. Medium climber with woolly, densely matted stems. Pinnate leaves with 3–5 broadly ovate leaflets to 10cm long, densely woolly, margins deeply lobed or serrated. Broadly bell-shaped, tawny-yellow, 4cm flowers, pubescent within, tomentose on the outside, borne in multi-flowered panicles through winter. Minimal pruning. Grewiifolia — leaves resembling Grewia. Evergreen.

Clematis heracleifolia

Native to central and northern China. Perennial herb with woody base, erect, reddish brown, woolly stems to 1.5m. Trifoliate leaves with rounded-ovate leaflets to 65 × 65mm, margins irregularly and sparsely serrated, terminal leaflet twice the size. Soft blue, tubular, 25mm flowers with reflexed lobes, resembling hyacinth, produced in axillary clusters summer

through autumn. Prune hard after flowering. Useful in shrub borders. Heracleifolia — leaves resembling the genus Heracleum.

Clematis integrifolia

Native to central Europe, south west Russia and Asia. Erect herbaceous plant, reddish brown stems to 1m with white pubescence. Leaves simple ovate-lanceolate to 9 × 5cm, green, glabrous above, pubescent beneath, prominently veined, margins entire. Dark violet or blue, flat, four-petalled flowers to 10cm across with central cluster of woolly yellow filaments in summer and autumn. Prune hard after flowering. Useful in shrub borders. Integrifolia — entire leaves.

Clematis japonica

Native to Japan. Scandent, downy shrubby growth. Leaves ternate, leaflets to 8cm long, almost glabrous, margins coarsely toothed. Nodding bell or urn-shaped, 3cm, purple-red to maroon or reddish brown flowers with fleshy sepals through summer. Minimal pruning. Japonica — of Japan.

Clematis × jouiniana

From C heracleifolia davidiana × C vitalba. Extremely vigorous, rambling, woody based shrubby climber with strongly ribbed stems to 3–4m. Leaves 3–5 foliate, ovate leaflets to 10cm, faintly pubescent, margins coarsely toothed. Fragrant, 3cm flowers, ivory white, becoming opal, deepening to lilac or sky-blue, resembling hyacinth, borne in terminal and axillary panicles late summer and autumn. Prune hard after flowering. Jouiniana — after E Jouin of Simon-Louis nursery, France. Semi-evergreen.

Clematis × macropetala

Native to northern China, Siberia and Mongolia. Charming, slender, easily grown climber. Handsome leaves to 15cm across, nine leaflets, ovate to lanceolate to 4 × 2cm, deep green, margins coarsely serrated.

Violet blue, semi-double flowers to 6cm across comprising dense cluster of paler blue staminodes enclosed in four outer sepals, borne on long pendent petioles through spring. Silky seed heads become grey and fluffy. Minimal pruning. Macropetala — with large petals.

Clematis × macropetala 'Blue Lagoon'

Deep-blue double flowers to 5cm across borne on pendent petioles through spring. Minimal pruning. Syn 'Maidwell Hall'.

Clematis × macropetala 'Markham's Pink'

Beautiful cultivar, double flowers in delicate shade of strawberry pink. Minimal pruning. Syn 'Markhamii'.

Clematis montana
Anemone Clematis

Native to Himalayas and China. Extremely hardy, vigorous and fast growing. Quickly forms a mass of intertwining stems. Tri-foliate leaves divided into three ovate-lanceolate, 10cm leaflets, deep green becoming bronze in cooler conditions, margins coarsely serrated. Pure white, four petalled, anemone-like flowers, 4–6cm across, mass produced early spring, persisting for several weeks.

The species and numerous cultivars cover virtually everything in their path, ideal for covering old stumps, trees or buildings, or providing fast and colourful coverage on fences or trellis. Prune lightly for size control as required. Montana — pertaining to mountains.

Clematis montana 'Elizabeth'

Large, soft pink flowers with yellow stamens and faint vanilla fragrance, mass produced in spring.

Clematis montana 'Freda'

Less vigorous cultivar, leaves bronze, cherry-pink flowers with sepals edged crimson.

Clematis montana 'Marjorie'

Vigorous grower, semi-double flowers, creamy pink tinted orange with petal-like salmon-pink staminodes.

Clematis montana 'Rubens'
Pink Anemone Clematis

New leaves reddish at first, green when mature. Breathtaking floral display as myriads of 5cm, four-petalled, rich pink flowers, shaped like a cross, appear for long periods in spring.   **315**

Clematis montana 'Snowflake'

Large snowy white blooms with yellow stamens, mass produced as leaves unfold in spring.   **315**

Clematis montana 'Tetrarose'

Vigorous, with bronzy green foliage. Soft lilac-rose pink flowers to 75mm across with central cluster of creamy yellow stamens totally cover the vine in spring. Largest flowers in the montana group.   **315**

Clematis montana 'Wilsonii'

Small cream fragrant flowers with twisted sepals and conspicuous yellow stamens, mass produced late spring.

Clematis napaulensis

Native to south western China. Vigorous, semi-evergreen climber, young stems grooved and grey. Leaves 3–5 foliolate, leaflets oval-lanceolate to 9 × 4cm, terminal largest, glabrous, margins entire or sparsely dentate. Narrow bell-shaped, 25mm lemon-yellow flowers with purple anthers, borne in axillary clusters of 6–10 through winter, followed by white woolly seed clusters. Napaulensis — of Nepal. Minimal pruning. Evergreen.

Clematis orientalis
Orange-Peel Clematis
Vigorous species from northern Asia to Himalayas. Rapidly forms a tangled mass of slender ribbed shoots, densely clothed with dainty, finely cut, soft grey-green pinnate leaves. Orange-yellow, slightly fragrant, nodding bell-shaped, 5cm flowers with conspicuous brown stamens, held on solitary, slender stalks followed by silky seed heads. Four remarkably thick sepals suggest the common name. Prune to half way after flowering. Orientalis — eastern.

Clematis paniculata
New Zealand Clematis, Puawhananga
Vigorous climber occurring in lowland forests throughout New Zealand, climbing 10m to the tops of trees, with woody main stems to 10cm diameter. Trifoliate leaves on 45mm petioles, leaflets broadly ovate to oblong-ovate, to 10 × 5cm, dark green, glossy and leathery, paler beneath, margins entire, toothed or lobed. Heralds the arrival of spring with myriads of mildly fragrant, pure white flowers to 10cm across, borne in large panicles of a hundred or more through spring and into early summer, followed by fluffy, silvery seed heads. Paniculata — flowers in panicles. Minimal pruning. Evergreen.

Clematis petriei
From the South Island of New Zealand. Rambling vine with numerous slender stems, pubescent when young, quite intertwined as they scramble over small trees or rocks. Leaves trifoliate on slender 45mm petioles, leaflets ovate-oblong to 30 × 22mm, bright green above, paler beneath, tough and leathery, entire or bluntly toothed. Strongly fragrant, yellow-green flowers to 45mm diameter with greenish filaments, borne profusely in small axillary panicles through spring followed by dark red, plumose seed heads. Named for Donald Petrie (1846–1925) NZ teacher and amateur plantsman. Minimal pruning. Evergreen.

Clematis rehderiana
Nodding Virgin Flower
Charming species from western China. Strong growing scandent, woody climber. Pinnate leaves to 23cm long, leaflets 7–9, broadly ovate, to 75 × 50mm, dark green, prominently veined, margins coarsely toothed or lobed. Delightful, pendulous, bell-shaped, soft primrose-yellow to pale green, 2cm flowers with wild-cowslip fragrance borne profusely in 23cm panicles late summer through autumn. Named for American botanist, Alfred Rehder (1863–1949). Minimal pruning.

Clematis tangutica
Golden Clematis
Vigorous, Chinese native climber, with slender twining stems rapidly covering its support. Pinnate or bipinnate leaves, leaflets oblong to lanceolate to 8cm long, bright green, margins irregularly toothed or lobed. Rich yellow, sweetly fragrant, 4–5cm bell or lantern-shaped flowers resembling small nodding lanterns, borne prolifically on long downy stalks summer through autumn. Prolonged flowering sees a succession of flowers intermingled with silky, silvery grey, seed heads. Good for spilling over walls, large boulders, banks or twining through wires or trellis. Prune hard after flowering.

Clematis texensis 'Duchess of Albany'
Species native to Texas and south west USA. A scandent climber to 2–3m, pinnate leaves with 3–5 ovate to rounded, 8cm leaflets, bluish green, glabrous, entire or lobed, and small thorny tips. 'Duchess of Albany' bears 5–8cm, deep-pink, tubular or tulip-shaped flowers with deeper pink bars January through March. C texensis cultivars need hard pruning to 2–3 basal buds after flowering. Texensis — of Texas.

Clematis texensis 'Etoile Rose'
Pendent, bell-shaped, cerise-pink flowers, silver margins, to 5cm across, December to February. Best viewed from beneath.

Clematis texensis 'Gravetye Beauty'
Small, ruby-red, tulip-shaped flowers, January through March.

Clematis texensis 'Sir Trevor Lawrence'
Small, luminous red, tubular to tulip-shaped flowers with purple margins, January through March.

Clematis viticella 'Abundance'
Native to southern Europe and western Asia. Leaves pinnate, often with three deeply lobed leaflets. The cultivar 'Abundance' bears masses of 5–7cm, wine-red to mauve-red open flowers January through March. C viticella cultivars need hard pruning to 2–3 basal buds after flowering. Viticella — diminutive of Vitis, Latin for grapevine.

Clematis viticella 'Alba Luxurians'
Small, 5–7cm creamy white, green tinted flowers, sepals twisted, dark stamens. January through March.

Clematis viticella 'Etoile Violette'
Deep violet-purple, 10cm flowers with prominent yellow stamens, mass produced January through March.

Clematis viticella 'Madame Julia Correvon'
Small, 5–7cm, deep wine red flowers with four twisted and recurving sepals, produced freely January through March.

Clematis viticella 'Royal Velours'
Small, 5–7cm, magenta-purple flowers with black anthers, borne prolifically January through March.

Clematis viticella 'Venosa Violacea'
Medium, 10–12cm, deep purple flowers with white veins, January through March.

CLEMATIS LARGE-FLOWERED HYBRIDS

The magnificent large flowered clematis cultivars in shades of red, pink, blue or white are the result of considerable hybridizing carried out since the 19th century. Many of the original hybrids are still cultivated today. A small representation of the hundreds available are listed below.

Correct pruning is important. During the first spring after planting, prune all large-flowered clematis back to the lowest pair of vigorous buds to encourage stronger growth, more profuse branching and better flower production.

Varieties which bear flowers on the current season's growth become untidy if not pruned. Some of the following descriptions say to 'Prune hard'. This means that after flowering, (or no later than August), each stem may be cut back to the lowest two or three buds from the ground.

Those marked 'Light Trim' produce flowers on wood ripened over the preceding year and need no pruning at all. Just remove any dead or unsightly stems when flowering is over, or before new shoots emerge in August.

All deciduous.

Flower sizes
Medium: 10–15cm
Large: 15–20c
Extra large: 20–25cm

Clematis hybrid 'Allanah'
Large, deepest ruby flowers, white stamens, dark anthers, spaced sepals resemble a wheel. December-March. Light trim.

Clematis hybrid 'Asao'
Large, deep pink flowers, deepening towards the margins, prominent veins. November, December and March. Light trim.

Clematis hybrid 'Barbara Jackman'
Medium to large flowers, pale mauve-blue with deep wine-red central bars on each sepal and lemon yellow stamens. November, December and March. Light trim.

Clematis hybrid 'Blue Belle'
Medium, dark smokey blue flowers, white stamens. December, March. Light trim.

Clematis hybrid 'Daniel Deronda'
Large to extra large, single or semi-double deep blue flowers with paler central markings on each sepal and ivory stamens. December, March. Light trim.

Clematis hybrid 'Dr Ruppell'
Large, rich pink flowers with broad red central bar. Exquisite colouring and free-flowering. November, December and March. Light trim.

Clematis hybrid 'Duchess of Edinburgh'
Medium, fully double, rosette-shape, milky white flowers, delicately tinged green. November, December and March. Light trim.

Clematis hybrid 'Duchess of Sutherland'
Medium to large, carmine-red flowers with paler bar and creamy yellow stamens. December to February. Light trim.

Clematis hybrid 'Elsa Spath'
Large, deepest blue flowers shaded purple, reddish anthers. November, December and March. Syn C 'Xerxes'. Light trim.

Clematis hybrid 'Ernest Markham'
Medium, deep petunia-red flowers, slightly ruffled, with overlapping petals. November, December and March. Prune hard.

Clematis hybrid 'Gipsy Queen'
Medium to large, dark violet-purple, velvety flowers, dark red anthers. December to March. Prune hard.   **315**

Clematis hybrid 'Guiding Star'
Large, deep violet-purple flowers. December to March. Prune hard.

Clematis hybrid 'H F Young'
Large, wedgewood-blue flowers, overlapping petals, creamy yellow stamens. Magnificent blue Clematis. November, December and March. Light trim.

Clematis hybrid 'Hagley Hybrid'
Medium, shell-pink flowers in profusion December to March. Prune hard.

Clematis hybrid 'Haku Ookan'
Medium, violet-blue flowers with a crown of creamy yellow stamens. November, December and March. Prune hard.

Clematis hybrid 'Henryi'
Large or extra large, pure creamy white flowers, brown anthers. November, December and March. Light trim.

Clematis hybrid 'Horn of Plenty'
Large, rosy mauve flowers with darker central bars. November, December and March. Light trim.

Clematis hybrid 'Jackmanii'
Medium to large, rich purple flowers, green stamens. Blooms continually December to March. Prune hard.

Clematis hybrid 'John Paul II'
Medium, creamy white tinted pink, broad crinkled petals. December to March. Light trim.

Clematis hybrid 'Kathleen Wheeler'
Extra large, plum-mauve with deeper central bars, golden yellow stamens. November and February. Light trim.

Clematis hybrid 'Lady Londesborough'
Medium to large, clear lavender flowers. Early blooming, October, November and February. Light trim.

Clematis hybrid 'Lasurstern'
Large to extra large, deepest blue flowers, creamy yellow stamens. November, December and March. Light trim.

Clematis hybrid 'Lawsoniana'
Extra large, lavender-blue tinted rose flowers, narrow, deeper lavender bars. Light trim.   **316**

Clematis hybrid 'Lord Neville'
Large, intense deep blue flowers, overlapping, crimped and wavy sepals. November, December and March. Light trim.   **316**

Clematis hybrid 'Madame le Coultre'
Large, broad petalled, pure white blooms, creamy yellow stamens. Vigorous grower and free flowering. November, December

and March. Syn 'Marie Boiselott'. Light trim.   **316**

Clematis hybrid 'Mrs N Thompson'
Medium to large, flowers, deep blue around the margins, blending to a vivid scarlet central bar, open waved sepals. Quite outstanding. October to November and February to March. Light trim.

Clematis hybrid 'Nelly Moser'
Large flowers, margins white with palest lavender shading, blending into vivid carmine central bars. November, December and March. Light trim.   **316**

Clematis hybrid 'Pink Fantasy'
Large, shell-pink flowers with shallow, deep red bars. December to February. Prune hard.

Clematis hybrid 'Ramona'
Large, lavender-blue, brown stamens. November, December and March. Light trim.

Clematis hybrid 'Rouge Cardinal'
Medium to large, glowing crimson, velvety flowers, light-brown stamens. Free-flowering. December to February. Prune hard.

Clematis hybrid 'Scartho Gem'
Medium to large rose pink flowers with deep pink bars. November, December and March. Light trim.

Clematis hybrid 'Silver Moon'
Large, greyish lavender to mauve or 'mother of pearl' grey, yellow stamens. Unusual and attractive. November, December and March. Light trim.

Clematis hybrid 'Sir Garnet Wolseley'
Large, bright blue flowers with faint rosy-purple glow. October, November and February. Light trim.   **316**

Clematis hybrid 'The President'
Large, deepest purple-blue, darker stamens borne freely November to March. Light trim.

Clematis hybrid 'Ville de Lyon'
Large, carmine red flowers with crimson markings, golden stamens. December to March. Prune hard.   **316**

Clematis hybrid 'Violet Elizabeth'
Medium to large, mauve-pink, both double and single flowers. November, December and March. Light trim.

Clematis hybrid 'Vyvyan Pennell'
Large, lavender and violet-mauve, double or semi-double flowers, light yellow stamens. November, December, March. Light trim.

CONVOLVULUS

A genus of about 250 species of perennial or annual climbers, scandent shrubs or herbs from temperate and subtropical regions, named from the Latin *convolvo*, to roll together or intertwine. Like Ipomoea their close relatives, they are admired for a profusion of funnel-shaped flowers which open fresh in the sunlight of each new day. Listed species an excellent ground cover or scandent shrub for covering rocks or banks, draping over walls, growing in window boxes or containers. Plant in full sun in deeply worked, free-draining, average soil.
   Convolvulaceae.

Convolvulus sabatius
Ground Morning Glory, Morocco Glorybind
Native from Italy and North Africa. Shrubby perennial plant, slender ascending or trailing, lightly pubescent stems. Leaves oblong to orbicular, 15–35mm long, grey-green, soft and hairy, margins entire. Lavender-blue, 25mm, wide open, funnel-shaped flowers with paler throat borne in great profusion through summer. Syn C mauritanicus. Sabatius — of Savona (Sabbatia) northern Italy. Evergreen. 45 × 90cm.   **333**

DISTICTIS

A genus of nine species of climbing plants from Mexico and West Indies, named from the Greek *dis*, two and *stiktos*, spotted, referring to two rows of flattened seeds appearing as spots in an open capsule. Mexican Blood Flower, reclass-ified from Phaedranthus buccinatorius, is admired for clusters of brilliant flowers, claimed to be the most showy of the Bignonia family. In warm sunny locations it will cover walls, fences, trees or buildings with a dense mantle of foliage and magnificent floral displays through-out the year. Plant in deeply worked, free-draining, fertile soil in full sun, sheltered from strong wind and frost.
   Bignoniaceae

Distictis buccinatoria
Mexican Blood Flower
A rampant grower from central Mexico, climbing to considerable heights by tendrils. Leaves bifoliate, leaflets ovate-lanceolate to 10cm long, mid green and glabrous above,

minutely white-scaly beneath, margins entire, slightly waved. Funnel-form, slightly curved, 10cm flowers with flaring deep rosy crimson lobes, orange yellow in the throat and outside, borne in terminal racemes mainly through summer and warmer seasons of the year. Extremely showy, worthy of extensive planting. Syn Phaedranthus buccinatorius.

FICUS

One of the largest genera in the plant kingdom with over 800 species of trees, shrubs and climbers distributed through-out the world's tropics and subtropics. Listed species are climbing or creeping figs clinging tenaciously to stone, concrete, wood, brick etc.
   Slender stems grow upward and outward in slow curves, embroidering as they go with tough leaves in various shades of green according to development. As the vine ages, fruiting branches bear leaves of a larger scale. Ficus provides total greenery cover for walls or founda-tions of buildings. Although from warmer climates the protection afforded by walls on which they grow allows them to be grown in cooler areas. They prefer cool shady conditions rather than hot, dry aspects. Plant in deeply worked, free-draining, fertile soil. Sometimes reluctant to get started, but rampant once growth begins. Trim as required.
   Moraceae. *All evergreen.*

Ficus pumila
Creeping Fig
Native to China and Japan. Unrecognizable as a fig until fruit begins to appear in its mature state. The early growths, which attach to almost any surface by means of barnacle-like suckers and form intricate stem patterns give little indication of ultimate character. Juvenile heart-shaped leaves, rough-textured, 2cm across. Adult stems become thicker and stubby, leaves oblong to elliptic-ovate, to 10cm long, glossy, deep green, leathery, margins entire. As a cover for low walls or foundations, Ficus pumila is without doubt the best evergreen of its type. Occasional trimming encourages the retention of juvenile character for many years. Pumila — dwarf.

Ficus pumila 'Minima'
Smaller, more petite form with juvenile leaves about 10mm across. Good for smaller areas where control of the larger form may prove difficult.   **333**

GELSEMIUM

A genus of three species of twining plants from central America and south east Asia, named from the Latin *gelsomino*, a jasmine. Listed species a modest plant with handsome foliage and fragrant flowers carried over long seasons. Grows freely, but doesn't seem to get out of hand. Easily contained on light trellis against walls, as framework for a doorway, along fences or allowed to scramble over banks etc. Plant in sun or semi shade, in deeply worked, free-draining, fertile soil.
   Loganiaceae. *All evergreen.*

Gelsemium sempervirens
Carolina Jessamine
Native to southern USA, State Flower of South Carolina. A delightful climber and twiner with glossy, warm-green, ovate-lanceolate, 3–10cm leaves, margins entire. A profusion of sweetly fragrant, bright yellow, five-lobed, funnel-shaped, 3–4cm flowers borne early spring through mid-summer in clusters of up to six. Associates well with Hardenbergia. Sempervirens — evergreen. Jessamine is another way of saying jasmine, although there's no relation-ship with Jasminum.

Gelsemium sempervirens 'Plena'
Similar to above, a slender twining vine, with fragrant, bell shaped, distinctly double, golden yellow flowers.

HARDENBERGIA

A genus of three Australian endemic species named for the 19th century Franziska Countess von Hardenberg. Evergreen shrubby vines with moderate growth rate and masses of flower cover-age late winter and spring. Naturally tends to scramble over rocks and banks, but with support provides rapid screening on trellis, pergolas, patio or carport walls. Maintains neater form if pruned heavily, to almost ground level after flowering. Spray periodically for caterpillars. Plant in deeply worked, free-draining, fertile soil in full sun or partial shade.
   Papilionaceae. *All evergreen.*

Hardenbergia comptoniana
West Australian Coral Pea
Found in the south west corner of Western Australia in jarrah and karri forests and

coastal plains. Distinguished by trifoliate leaves with linear-lanceolate to broadly ovate leaflets to 15 × 7cm, dark green, margins entire. Purplish-blue, 1cm pea shaped flowers marked with two greenish white spots, borne profusely in pendulous, crowded racemes late winter through spring. Named for Mary Compton, First Marchioness of Northampton.

Hardenbergia violacea
Purple Coral Pea
Favourite Australian wildflower found through eastern States and South Australia as a wiry stemmed, scrambling plant, forming purple garlands on hillsides or banks, occasionally ascending tree trunks. Leaves simple, narrow ovate to ovate-lanceolate, to 12 × 5cm, deep green, leathery, net-veined, margins entire. Purple or violet, pea-shaped flowers borne in profuse axillary or terminal panicles late winter through spring. Blooms profusely from an early age. Prune severely to almost ground level each second year. Violacea — violet coloured.

Hardenbergia violacea 'Alba'
White Coral Pea
Masses of pure white, pea-shaped flowers in dense racemes.

Hardenbergia violacea 'Happy Wanderer'
Extremely vigorous form with larger leaves. Masses of mauve-purple pea-shaped flowers in large panicles. Commences to bloom earlier and has a longer flowering season. Most desirable climber.   **333**

Hardenbergia violacea 'Rosea'
Pink Coral Pea
Masses of rose pink, pea-shaped flowers in dense racemes.

HEDERA

A genus of 11 species of climbing or trailing plants from Europe, Asia and North Africa called *Hedera*, ancient Latin name for Ivy. Small but familiar genus of evergreen climbers, attaching by means of twining stems and aerial roots. Among the best of self-clinging evergreens, thriving in almost any conditions, climbing unaided to great heights, or scrambling as total ground cover in situations where even grass would not survive. There's no end of leaf forms and colours.

Best in shade or semi shade, in rich moist soil. Ivies serve well on fences, archways, screens, wall cover or ground cover, growing vigorously, holding tenaciously and effectively controlling erosion. A group of plants keen to be extensively exploited, promising good service with minimum care. Numerous fine or bold-leaf ivies are cultivated. Rather than attempt to describe them, personal selection and comparison is recommended.

Araliaceae. *Evergreen.*

HIBBERTIA

A genus of over 150 species of scandent shrubs or twiners from Australia, New Guinea, New Caledonia, Fiji and Madagascar, named for George Hibbert, 18th–19th century distinguished patron of botany. The listed species is a showy, yellow-flowered climber, good for trellis, terrace or patio, either planted out or in containers. Adaptable to a number of cultural situations including exposure to salt-laden winds. Has been used to stabilize coastal sand dunes. Plant in full or partial sun in free-draining soil, sheltered from heavy frosts.

Dilleniaceae.

Hibbertia scandens
Guinea Gold Vine
Found in New South Wales, Queensland and Northern Territory on coastal dunes or forest areas. Fast growing scrambler or climber. Handsome leaves, obovate to ovate-elliptic, to 9 × 3cm, fine-hairy, heavy textured and dull green above, silky hairy beneath, margins entire. Pale yellow to bright yellow solitary flowers to 7cm across resembling a small single camellia produced sporadically through the year. Slightly unpleasant odour is offensive only at close range. Scandens — climbing. Evergreen.

HYDRANGEA

Genus introduced in the tree and shrub section of this book where shrubby species are featured. The unusual climbing form listed below is for planting on shady walls or similar locations which avoid sun where it clings firmly by means of aerial rootlets and grows to large proportions. Without support it forms itself into a tight, bushy shrub.

Hydrangeaceae.

Hydrangea petiolaris
Climbing Hydrangea
Strong growing, self clinging species from Japan, Russia, Korea and Taiwan. Leaves ovate-rounded to 11 × 8cm, abruptly pointed and finely toothed. Flower heads in open clusters, 15–25cm across, consist of numerous, dull-white, small fertile flowers, surrounded by a few white, 4cm, four-sepalled, long-stalked sterile florets, late spring through summer. Petiolaris — furnished with long petioles or leaf-stalks. Deciduous.

JASMINUM

A genus of more than 200 species of twining or scandent shrubs from tropical and subtropical regions called by the Latinized version of the Persian *yasmin*. Jasmine has a longstanding reputation for sweet fragrance, not that all species are scented. Even some unrelated plants are referred to as jasmine or jessamine. Some are used in the manufacture of perfume in southern France. Jasmine is generally easy to grow, performing under average garden conditions in sun or partial shade. Withstand heavy pruning and benefit from frequent pinching for shaping and control.

Oleaceae.

Jasminum azoricum
Azores Jasmine
Native to Azores Islands in the eastern Atlantic. Beautiful twiner with round, smooth stems, trifoliate leaves, leaflets ovate, deep green, glossy, margins entire. Pure white, sweetly scented, 4–5 petalled flowers resembling orange blossom, borne in large clusters late summer through autumn, in fact, the plant is rarely without bloom. Requires protection at first, but once established withstands considerable winter cold. Azoricum — of the Azores. Evergreen.

Jasminum beesianum
Bee's Jasmine
Native to western China. Vigorous scandent or sprawling shrub, developing a tangle of slender, grooved, slightly downy 3–4m stems. Leaves simple ovate-lanceolate, to 5cm long, tapering to a long point, dull olive-green, slightly downy, margins entire. Fragrant, deep rose pink to velvet red, 1cm flowers in cymes of three in early summer, followed by heavy crops of shining black berries persisting into winter. Named for Bees nursery of Cheshire who sponsored its introduction from China. Deciduous.

Jasminum humile 'Revolutum'
Italian Yellow Jasmine
Shrubby form from Middle East, Burma and China. Robust glabrous shrub, leaves compound with 3–7, ovate-lanceolate leaflets to 4cm, deep green, margins entire. Bright yellow, slightly fragrant flowers to 25mm diameter, in flat or domed clusters through summer. Humile — low-growing. Revolutum — rolled back leaf margins. Evergreen. 1.5 × 1.5m. **333**

Jasminum mesneyi
Primrose Jasmine
Beautiful species with square stems and opposite, trifoliate, rich deep-green leaves to 8cm long. Bright lemon-yellow, single or semi double flowers to 4cm across, without fragrance, borne singly throughout the plant during winter and spring with a few in summer. More of a rambling shrub with vigorous, long arching branches, best trained in waterfall fashion, caught firmly at the desired height and allowed to spill over. Train as a free standing shrub, or encourage to cover pergolas, large walls, trellis or banks. Introduced into England from south western China in 1900. Named for William Mesny, general in the Chinese Imperial Army. Syn J primulinum. Evergreen.

Jasminum nudiflorum
Winter Jasmine
Native to western China. Rambling viny shrub with slender, willowy, pendent, four-angled, 3–4m branches. Leaves with three oval-oblong, 1–3cm, glossy dark green, glabrous leaflets. Bright yellow, six-lobed, 3cm flowers borne singly along naked green stems through winter and early spring before the leaves unfold. Beautiful, vigorous, hardy and tolerant of extremes. Nudiflorum — flowering on naked stems. Deciduous.

Jasminum officinale 'Aureum'
Variegated Common Jasmine
Native to an area extending from Iran to China. Vigorous scandent or twining plant with slender, square-section, 4–5m stems. Pinnate leaves with 5–9 elliptic, 1–6cm leaflets effectively variegated and suffused green and yellow. Fragrant, 25mm flowers, pinkish in bud, opening pure white borne in clustered terminal cymes summer through early autumn. Officinale — sold in shops, applied to plants with real or supposed medicinal properties. Leaves may fall in cooler districts, but evergreen in mild winters. Deciduous.

Jasminum parkerii
Dwarf Jasmine
From western Himalayas. Dwarf shrubby form with twiggy, tufted growth habit. Leaves to 25mm long with 3–5 ovate-acuminate, 6mm bright green leaflets. Small, 15mm yellow flowers without fragrance borne singly or in pairs in summer. Good for rock gardens, containers. Named for botanist Richard N Parker. Evergreen. 30 × 60cm.

Jasminum polyanthum
Chinese Jasmine
Vigorous Chinese twining plant soon building up a mass of twiggy growth. Leaves with 5–7 lanceolate leaflets, at first bronzy, maturing deep green. Large clusters of carmine red buds open to fragrant flowers, pure white within, pale rose on the outside. They are borne freely from late winter through to summer. Strong climber or rampant ground or bank cover. Slightly frost tender, but otherwise an enthusiastic performer in most soils and situations. Evergreen.

Jasminum polyanthum 'Cream Glory'
Variegated Chinese Jasmine
General habit, flower and foliage fairly typical of the species, but leaves attractively variegated with prominent creamy white margins. Not as rampant in growth as the species making it an excellent vine for trellis or pergola and a most colourful plant in hanging baskets. Discovered and developed by Blue Mountain Nurseries, Tapanui, New Zealand.

Jasminum × stephanese
Chinese Jasmine
Rare hybrid of J officinale × J beesianum. Vigorous twining climber. Olive-green leaves, simple or 3–5 lobed. The soft pink flowers have a pleasing fragrance and are borne in small clusters through late spring and early summer. Evergreen in all but cold winters.

LAPAGERIA

A genus of one species, an evergreen climbing plant from Chile, named for Empress Josephine Tascher de la Pagerie, Napoleon Bonaparte's wife and patron of gardening. Among the most beautiful of flowering climbers and Chile's national flower.

Prefers the protection of a partially shaded and sheltered wall, with roots in cool, deeply worked, free-draining, organically enriched, moisture-retentive, lime-free, acid soil, conditioned and mulched with peat moss. Enjoys high humidity, moderate summer temperatures and minimal exposure to strong sunlight. Although the desire of many gardeners, it isn't an easy plant to grow and often difficult to obtain.

Philesiaceae.

Lapageria rosea
Chilean Bellflower, Chile Bells
An aristocrat among climbing plants, spreading by underground stolons. Slender, wiry, twining stems. Leaves ovate or ovate-lanceolate to subcordate, to 12 × 2.5cm, glossy dark-green, leathery, margins entire. Long bell-shaped, rosy crimson, white spotted, waxy, 7–8cm flowers, borne singly or in pendulous clusters from axils of the upper leaves, summer through autumn. Evergreen.

LONICERA

A genus of about 180 species of shrubs and climbers widely distributed throughout the Northern Hemisphere, named for the 16th century German naturalist Adam Lonitzer. The Climbing Honeysuckles include among them some excellent twining plants, not only beautiful but also able to perform well under adverse conditions. They are adaptable to trellis, ramble over bushes or tree stumps, or serve as bank cover or ground cover. Plant these Honeysuckles in sun or partial shade in deeply worked, free-draining, reasonably fertile soil.

Caprifoliaceae.

Lonicera × brownii 'Dropmore Scarlet'
Scarlet Honeysuckle
Canadian hybrid from L sempervirens × L hirsuta. Hardy scandent grower. Leaves elliptic, blue-green, slightly pubescent beneath, margins entire, uppermost pairs connate or fused together at the base. The long, narrow, tubular or trumpet-shaped, bright scarlet flowers are borne in clusters midsummer through autumn. Semi evergreen.

Lonicera × heckrotii 'Gold Flame'
A shrubby grower with scandent, lax spreading branches. Leaves oblong or elliptic to 6cm long, mid-green above, glaucous beneath, margins entire, uppermost pairs connate or fused together at the base. Fragrant, 4–5cm flowers, brilliant rich-pink outside, golden yellow inside, borne freely in terminal whorls through summer and autumn. Of hybrid origin — L sempervirens × L americana. Evergreen.

Lonicera japonica 'Halliana'
Hall's Honeysuckle

Extremely hardy and vigorous climber, native to Japan, Korea and China. Leaves oblong to ovate-elliptic, to 8 × 3cm, rich green, pubescent when young. Pure white fragrant flowers, often tinted red, and becoming yellow with age, upper lip deeply divided. Named after Dr George Hall, 19th century American plant collector. Evergreen.

Lonicera japonica 'Repens'
Japanese Honeysuckle

Stems usually deep purple-red. Leaves ovate-elliptic, deep green flushed purple, purple petioles and veins beneath. Fragrant flowers white within, flushed reddish purple on the outside. Evergreen.

Lonicera periclymenum 'Belgica'
Early Dutch Honeysuckle

Scrambling and twisting climber with elliptic-oblong, glabrous, thickish leaves. Fragrant, tubular flowers, deep rose-pink to purple in bud, opening purple-red outside, with contrasting pale creamy white reflexing lobes, borne profusely in whorls summer and autumn. Periclymenum — from the Greek term for honeysuckle. Belgica — of the Netherlands as a whole, or of Belgium. Evergreen in mild winters, deciduous elsewhere.　**333**

Lonicera periclymenum 'Winchester'

Hardy vigorous vine, leaves deep green with bluish cast. Trumpet-shaped flowers, rich wine red flushed purple outside, soft apricot-orange within., borne in large clusters summer through autumn. This plant may be grown into a bush form by pinching long shoots as they appear. Evergreen in mild areas.

Lonicera sempervirens 'Sulphurea'
Trumpet Honeysuckle

Vigorous climber, handsome, oval to obovate, rich green to bluish leaves, slightly downy beneath, uppermost pairs connate or fused together to form an almost circular disc. Fragrant, bright yellow, narrow-trumpet, 4–5cm flowers carried in loose axillary whorls spring and summer, followed by bright red fruit. Semi-evergreen to evergreen according to climate.

Lonicera × tellemanniana

Hybrid from L sempervirens × L tragophylla. Vigorous scandent grower, brilliant flowered. Leaves ovate to oblong, to 10cm long, deep green above, thickly frosted with white bloom beneath, upper pair fused into an elliptic disc. Tubular 45mm flowers with flaring lobes, yellowish coppery orange flushed red at the tips, deeper within, borne in large terminal clusters through summer. Prefers almost full shade. Deciduous.

MACFADYENA

A genus of 3–4 species of climbing vines from south east USA named for 19th century Scottish botanist and author James MacFadyen.

The listed species is a vigorous liane admired for masses of bright yellow flowers. Although recommended for frost-free locations, it has apparently survived temperatures of –7°C. Plant against a sunny wall in deeply worked, free-draining, fertile soil. Worthy of a prominent place in the garden. Useful for covering fences, pergolas, unsightly trees or buildings in warm locations.

Bignoniaceae.

Macfadyena unguis-cati
Cat Claw Vine

Native to tropical America, Mexico, West Indies to Argentina. Vigorous climber with slender stems reaching to 4m. Juvenile leaves narrow-ovate to lanceolate, to 20 × 8mm. Adult leaves narrow-ovate to ovate, to 16 × 7cm, held in pairs, equipped with three tendrils resembling cat's claws which cling tenaciously to any support within reach. Trumpet-shaped flowers with spreading lobes to 10cm across, bright golden yellow lined orange, virtually cover the entire plant spring and early summer. Syn Doxantha. Unguis — Latin term for claw. Evergreen.

MANDEVILLA

A genus of about 120 species of tuberous climbing plants, perennial herbs or subshrubs with milky sap from Central and South America, named for Henry J Mandeville, 19th century British Minister in Buenos Aires. Beautiful climbing or semi-shrubby plants from tropical or subtropical regions which enjoy warmth, sunlight, adequate moisture and sharp drainage. Growing in favourable conditions, these charming plants will continue to bloom almost the year through.

While they require open-textured, moderately fertile, free-draining soil, they seem happiest with their roots somewhat restricted either by growing in competition with neighboring plants or confined to a container. Feed sparingly with slow-release fertilizer or liquid plant food. Keep constantly moist during dry periods. May survive outdoors in temperate climates against a sunny wall, fully sheltered from frost and excessive winter moisture. Otherwise, grow in containers in a sunny, sheltered but airy corner. Needs the support of frame or trellis. Pinch young shoots to induce bushiness. Watch for aphid attacks.

Apocynaceae.

Mandevilla laxa
Chilean Jasmine

Native to Argentina. Rapid-growing vine with slender finely warty, wiry stems. Leaves cordate-oblong to 7cm long, dull deep-green with bronzy cast above, purplish or grey-green beneath, margins entire. Tufts of white down appear in the axils. Gardenia-scented, ivory-white, wide-flaring, 5cm trumpet flowers borne in clusters from leaf axils during summer. Exploit its rich fragrance by growing near windows or outdoor living areas. Syn M suaveolens. Laxa — loose-flowered. Semi-deciduous.

Mandevilla sanderi 'Rosea'
Brazilian Jasmine

Selected clone of the Brazilian species. At first appears quite shrubby, but eventually climbs to 2m or more. Slender wiry stems, leaves oval to orbicular, to 75 × 60mm, glossy, deep green, paler beneath, margins entire. Flowers funnel or trumpet shaped, 7cm across, with five wide-flaring lobes, rich warm pink, deepening towards the centre and conspicuous yellow throat. Flowers produced on axillary stems, continuing to open from terminal buds from mid winter almost the year through. Commences to flower at an early age.

Named for the Sander nursery of St Albans and Bruges. Cultivar **'Red Riding Hood'** resembles above but with bright red flowers. **'My Fair Lady'** has pale pink buds, opening white with yellow throat. Grown in vast quantities for patio or indoor flowering pot plants. Evergreen.　**334**

Mandevilla splendens 'Alice du Pont'

Charming and vigorous Brazilian twining species. Slender stems become entangled with each other. Opposite leaves oval to orbicular to 15 × 10cm, glossy dark-green, with numerous sunken veins making the surface leathery and puckered, prominent midrib, paler beneath, margins entire. Magnificent, mildly fragrant, funnel-shaped, deep rose pink flowers with five lobes to 10cm across, intensifying in the center, and yellow deep in the throat. The flowers are borne on axillary stems and progressively open from terminal buds spring through autumn. Splendens — splendid. Evergreen.   **334**

MANETTIA

A genus of about 80 species of shrubs, herbs or climbers from tropical America, named for Xavier Manetti, 18th century prefect of Florence Botanic Gardens. Listed species is a beautiful plant, quite uninvasive, perfect where a small scale climber is called for. Or, it may be grown among more vigorous plants which allows it a share of sunlight but protects from frost. Plant in full or partial sun in deeply worked, free-draining, fertile soil.
Rubiaceae.

Manettia luteo-rubra
Brazilian Fire Cracker
A dainty climber from Brazil. Slender strongly twining, intricately branched, coarsely pubescent, pale green, somewhat sticky stems. Leaves ovate to ovate-lanceolate, deep green, semi-glossy, margins entire. Solitary, tubular, 2–3cm woolly flowers with four slightly flared lobes, bright scarlet in the lower portion, tipped yellow and within, providing a display almost the year through. Syn M bicolor. Luteo — yellow, rubra — red. Evergreen.

METROSIDEROS

Introduction to the genus appears in the Tree and Shrub section of this book. Climbing relatives of the Pohutukawa, among the showiest of New Zealand's native plants, providing cover for cool banks, ponga walls, brick, stone, concrete or wood. Prefers cool, moist, semi shady locations sheltered from heavy frost, planted in deeply worked, free-draining, moisture-retentive, fertile soil.
Myrtaceae. *All evergreen.*

Metrosideros carminea
Akakura, Carmine Rata
Robust climber found in lowland coastal forests from Mangonui to East Cape and Taranaki. It will cling to almost any substance by means of aerial roots, establishing a network of slender stems. Juvenile leaves nearly orbicular, to 15mm diameter, glossy deep green, maturing to elliptic to broadly ovate, to 35 × 20mm, glossy deep green, leathery, paler beneath, margins entire. Deep carmine-rose flowers with contrasting yellow centre, borne in terminal compound cymes covering the entire plant spring through early summer. Carminea — meaning carmine.   **333**

Metrosideros carminea 'Carousel'
Foliage small, glossy, deep green, attractively margined golden yellow. Carmine-red flowers with brilliant golden stamens interspersed with colourful leaves spring through early summer. Excellent dwarf shrub, outstanding whether or not in bloom. A selection from an adult form of M carminea. Being vegetatively propagated from mature growth it is non-climbing, forming a compact mounding shrub. Frost tender. Prune lightly after flowering. 80 × 110cm.

Metrosideros carminea 'Ferris Wheel'
Forms a rounded, compact shrub, small, oval, glossy deep green foliage. Bright carmine red flowers with golden stamens borne profusely spring through early summer. Good companion plant for 'Carousel' and excellent in containers. Developed from mature growth of M carminea. 90 × 110cm.

Metrosideros fulgens
Aka
Found in coastal forests in the North Island and northern reaches of the South Island, often scrambling over old logs or banks. A vigorous multi-branched liane, mature specimens with 10cm main stems reaching to 12m high, bark peeling in large flakes. Leaves elliptic-oblong to 75 × 25mm, glossy green, leathery and glabrous above, paler beneath, margins entire. Flowers orange-red to scarlet in terminal cymes, borne either profusely or sparsely according to parentage. Useful for covering tree trunks, walls etc.

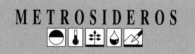

PANDOREA

A genus of six species of ornamental climbing plants from Australia, New Guinea, eastern Melesia and New Caledonia, named from the goddess Pandora of Greek mythology. With handsome leaves and beautiful flowers over long seasons, the listed species are desirable climbers for trellis, pergolas, patios, archways or fences. Plant in deeply worked, free-draining, organically enriched soil in full or partial sun sheltered from cold winds.
Bignoniaceae. *All evergreen.*

Pandorea jasminoides
Bower of Beauty
Vigorous twining plant with slender stems. Pinnate leaves with 4–9 ovate-lanceolate leaflets, glossy deep green, margins entire. Flowers trumpet-shaped with five wide-flaring lobes 4–5cm diameter, white to pale pink with maroon throat, borne in clusters of 4–8 through summer and autumn. Jasminoides — foliage with a resemblance to jasmine.

Pandorea jasminoides 'Alba'
Beautiful clusters of open-mouthed, pure milky white trumpet flowers borne in clusters of 4–8 through summer and into autumn.

Pandorea jasminoides 'Charisma'
Variegated Bower of Beauty
Combines the charm of creamy yellow and dark green variegated leaves with characteristic wide-flaring, pale pink trumpet flowers with maroon throat borne in clusters of four to eight throughout summer and into autumn.

Pandorea jasminoides 'Lady Di'
White Bower of Beauty
Similar handsome foliage and form. Creamy white, 4–5cm flared-trumpet flowers with delicate chartreuse-yellow shading in the throat, borne in clusters of 4–8 through summer and autumn.

Pandorea jasminoides 'Rosea Superba'
Selected form with larger soft pink flowers with contrasting maroon-crimson throat borne in clusters of 4–8 through summer and autumn. Amongst the most popular climbing plants.   **334**

Pandorea pandorana
Wonga-Wonga Vine
Native to a wide area of Australia's eastern States from Tasmania to Queensland and New Guinea. Vigorous climber with rope-like stems. Young leaves rich bronze and fernlike. Pinnate leaves, usually with 6 pairs of ovate-lanceolate leaflets to 10 × 6cm, terminal largest, glossy deep green, glabrous, margins entire. Fragrant, 2cm tubular to bell-shaped, slightly curved flowers, creamy white with purple markings in the throat, borne in crowded panicles late winter through spring. Somewhat hardier than P jasminoides.   **336**

Pandorea pandorana 'Golden Showers'
Golden Wonga-Wonga Vine
Resembles above but with crowded clusters of soft golden yellow tubular flowers which are borne in profusion late winter through spring.

Pandorea pandorana 'Ruby Heart'
Selected form of Wonga-Wonga Vine, flower rich cream, spotted and marked ruby-purple within, mass produced in crowded panicles late winter through spring.

Pandorea pandorana 'Snow Bells'
White Wonga Vine
Dainty pure-white bell flowers in long clustered racemes.

PARTHENOCISSUS

A genus of about ten species of woody vines from North America, east Asia and Himalayas named from the Greek *parthenos*, virgin and *kissos*, ivy, a way of saying Virginian Creeper. Grown for brilliant foliage and sturdy growth. Covers buildings, walls, or large trees. All species will grow in sub-zero temperatures in any reasonable, free-draining soil.
Vitaceae. *All deciduous.*

Parthenocissus quinquefolia
Virginian Creeper
Native to eastern United States where it reaches the tops of lofty trees in its natural state.

Climbs vigorously, slender stems supported by branched tendrils with terminal adhesive discs. Leaves with 3–5 elliptic to obovate leaflets, to 10 × 6cm, dull green above, paler beneath, rich crimson in autumn, margins sharply serrated. Insignificant flowers followed by globose, 6mm, blue-black fruits. Once established, Virginia Creeper grows with cheerful abandon its stems reaching out to any handy support. Benefits from an annual trim. Quinquefolia — five-leafed.

Parthenocissus tricuspidata 'Beverley Brook'
Excellent vigorous cultivar selected for smaller, three-lobed glossy green leaves becoming brilliant fiery-red in autumn.

Parthenocissus tricuspidata 'Veitchi'
Japanese Ivy
This rapid-growing creeper from Japan can take hold and cover the facade of large masonry or brick buildings in just a few years. It holds tenaciously to the smoothest surface by means of small suction cups at the end of each tendril. Leaves orbicular to triangular, three-lobed, coarsely crenate, 10–20cm diameter, bronze-purple at first, later becoming deep green, rich crimson orange and yellow in autumn. The fallen leaves reveal interesting branch and stem patterns.

Tricuspidata — three-pointed leaves. Introduced from Japan into England in 1862 by nurseryman J G Veitch and named in his honour.

PASSIFLORA

A genus of about 500 species of vines, scandent shrubs, herbs or small trees from tropical America, Asia, Australia and Polynesia, named from the Latin *passio*, passion and *flos*, a flower, originally used by early Spanish priests in South America who saw in the flower a fancied resemblance to the instruments of the Crucifixion. Cultivated species are mostly vines, many providing the dual purpose of showy flowers and tasty fruit.

They climb by tendrils, building up a tangled mass of densely foliaged stems. Annual pruning of excess growth maintains control and encourages a healthier and more attractive plant. Use on trellis, fences, walls, pergolas or bank cover. Plant in deeply worked, free-draining, organically enriched, moisture-retentive soil in full sun. Provide summer moisture and shelter from frost.
Passifloraceae. *All evergreen.*

Passiflora edulis
Purple Passionfruit
Native to tropical South America. Although the well known purple-fruited passionfruit is grown more for fruit than ornament, its heavily crinkled, glossy, rich green foliage does provide total cover on trellis, walls or fences, along with a harvest of fruit. Grafted plants recommended as a precaution against collar rot which commonly causes sudden collapse of an apparently healthy and thriving plant.

Passiflora 'Eynsford Gem'
Hybrid from P caerulea × P racemosa. Elegant, small-growing, non-fruiting vine with twining stems to about 2m. Leaves, trilobed to 12cm across, deep green, leathery, margins curved upwards. Deep-red buds open to soft mauve pink, 7cm flowers with a complex arrangement of anthers and stamens set in a maroon central zone, borne profusely through summer.

Passiflora mollissima
Pink Banana Passion
Rampant grower from Venezuela, Colombia, Peru and Bolivia. Leaves trilobed deeply cut into ovate lobes, deep green, softly pubescent above, tomentose beneath, margins finely serrated. Light pink, 7cm, pendent flowers, followed by edible, yellow, oblong-ovoid, 8 × 3cm edible fruit. Extremely fast growing, useful for rapid cover in warm areas. Mollissima — meaning very soft.

Passiflora coccinea
Red Passion Flower
Brilliant coloured species from tropical South America. Grows rampantly in warm, frost-free climates. Leaves oblong to suborbicular, to 14 × 7cm, dark green, minutely pubescent above, tomentose beneath, margins serrated or finely lobed. Bright scarlet, 10cm flowers with yellow reverse, through summer and autumn, followed by ovoid, 5cm orange or yellow fruit. Plant against a sheltered north wall. Prune often to maintain size and neatness. Coccinea — scarlet.

PETREA

A genus of about 30 species of climbing plants, shrubs or small trees from tropical America and Mexico, named for Lord Robert James Petra, 18th century patron of botany and horticulture. When ideally situated, Petrea volubilis with handsome deep green foliage and masses of blue starry flowers is one of the most eye-catching climbing plants.

Locate in full sun in sheltered frost-free areas, against an east or north facing wall with strong light. Plant in deeply worked, free-draining, organically enriched, moisture-retentive soil. Keep moist during dry periods.
Verbenaceae.

Petrea volubilis
Purple Wreath
Magnificent evergreen vine from Mexico and Central America. Slender pale brown to ashen-grey twining stems and branchlets. Leaves in opposite pairs with adjacent pairs at right angles, oblong-elliptic, to 20 × 10cm, deep green, leathery and rough as sandpaper above, lighter and pubescent beneath, margins entire. Individual flowers consist of five lavender-purple, 12 × 3mm sepals set like stars in a lighter blue calyx. Myriads of these delightful blooms borne in graceful drooping racemes to 30cm long, virtually enveloping the entire plant. Calyces persist for several weeks, eventually becoming dry and falling to serve as wings for seed dispersal. Volubilis — meaning twining. Evergreen.   **335**

PODRANEA

A genus of two species of climbing plants from South Africa, named from an anagram of Pandorea to which it is related. Listed species a rampant liane, rapidly sending out long waving branches and flowering during the first summer, eventually becoming a total mass of showy flowers. Useful for covering trellis, buildings, walls and fences. Good fast coverage where a large scale climber is called for. Needs a warm sunny location, away from heavy frost when young, although quite frost hardy when mature. Plant in any reasonable, free-draining, fertile soil. Prune late winter to keep the plant within bounds.
Bignoniaceae

Podranea ricasoliana
Port St John Creeper
Native to South Africa, from Pondoland around Port St Johns. Builds a strong woody base with greyish, deeply fissured bark from which it sends up a multitude of slender, twining stems. Leaves pinnate with 5–11 ovate leaflets to 5cm long, glossy deep green, margins slightly serrated. Trumpet-shaped flowers with five flaring lobes, bright shell pink with narrow red stripes, borne in crowded terminal panicles carried above the foliage and almost covering the whole plant through summer and autumn. Named for Vincenzo Ricasoli, 19th century Italian general and patron of horticulture. Evergreen. **336**

PYROSTEGIA

A genus of about 4 species of climbing plants from tropical America, named from the Greek *pyr*, fire, and *stege*, roof, in reference to the colour and formation of the flower. Pyrostegia venusta brings a gleam of colour to the garden during winter when other flowering plants are scarce, the display lasting many weeks, often into spring. Plant in maximum sunshine in deeply worked, free-draining, organically enriched soil. Protect from frost when young, but recovers from light damage once established. Use on trellis, pergolas, patios, balustrades, walls, fences, etc, wherever it gets maximum heat and sun. Prune for size control as required.
Bignoniaceae.

Pyrostegia venusta
Flame Vine
This gorgeous plant from Brazil, Paraguay, Bolivia and Argentina is among the world's most beautiful climbers. Climbs vigorously with numerous slender stems, attaching by strong tendrils. Leaves bifoliate or trifoliate, leaflets ovate to oblong-lanceolate, to 10 × 5cm, semi-glossy deep green, papery or leathery, margins entire. Flaming orange, slightly curved, pendulous tubular flowers to 7cm long with four flaring lobes borne in crowded terminal clusters, cover the plant through winter. Venusta — handsome or charming. Evergreen. **335**

RHODOCHITON

A genus of about three species of Mexican climbing herbs, named from the Greek *rhodo*, red and *chiton*, a cloak, referring to the large enveloping calyx. Listed species grown for spectacular flowers which in suitable conditions appear almost the year through. A tender frost sensitive plant requiring sunny, sheltered locations, planted in deeply worked, free-draining, organically enriched, light sandy soil. Grows freely from seed, usually treated as an annual, flowering the first season. Ideal for sunny walls or trained on a wire or bamboo frame. Try in containers or hanging baskets.
Scrophulariaceae.

Rhodochiton atrosanguinium
Purple Bells
Rapid growing twining plant from Mexico with numerous slender stems to 3m, attaching itself to the nearest support by means of clasping peduncles or pedicels. Leaves cordate or heart-shaped to 75mm across, deep green, prominently veined, margins minutely serrated, twining petiole to 80mm. Pendulous flowers consisting of a lantern-like calyx with five pointed, pinkish red lobes, and protruding, blood-red to purple-black, 65mm, tubular corolla with five inflated lobes. Calyx persists after pollination, followed by globose or oblong seed capsules. Atrosanguineum — dark blood red. Deciduous.

SCHIZOPHRAGMA

A genus of four species of climbing or creeping shrubs from Himalayas, Taiwan and Japan named from the Greek *schizo*,

to divide and *phragma*, a fence or screen, in reference to the fruit which ruptures and separates between the ribs. Related to Hydrangea and with similar appearance, grown for lush foliage and long summer floral displays. Regarded as one of the finest climbers for cool temperate climates. Best in a warm sunny location in deeply worked, free-draining, moisture-retentive soil with the support of a wall, large trees or old stumps etc.
Hydrangeaceae.

Schizophragma hydrangeoides
Japanese Hydrangea Vine
From alpine woodlands of Japan and Korea. A strong climber to 10m, stems buff and downy at first, becoming light greyish brown and glabrous establish a framework, attached by short adhesive aerial roots. Though slow at first eventually provides total coverage. Leaves resemble Hydrangea, broadly ovate, to 12cm long, pale to mid-green above, silvery green beneath, margins coarsely toothed. Flat-topped, ivory white inflorescence to 15–20cm across, comprising numerous small fertile flowers surrounded by 10–12 sterile florets with one enlarged outer sepal to 35mm, borne profusely through summer. Hydrangeoides — resembling Hydrangea. Deciduous.

SOLANDRA

A genus of 8 species of climbing, woody shrubs or vines from tropical America, named for Daniel C Solander, notable 18th century botanist. Admired for their bold stems foliage and flowers, impressive climbers against a warm sunny wall in frost-free locations. Plant in deeply worked, free-draining, organically enriched, moisture-retentive soil. Mulch freely and keep moist during dry periods. Established plants may survive only light frosts, but are reasonably tolerant of salt spray and wind, especially S maxima. Use as large scale cover on walls, pergolas, patios, swimming pool fences etc. Prune after flowering, tip-pinch to encourage lateral growth and more flower.
Solanaceae. *All evergreen.*

Solandra grandiflora
Chalice Vine
Bold climbing plant from the West Indies clambering to 6m or more. Leaves elliptic-oblong to obovate, to 17cm long, glossy deep green, leathery, margins entire. Bold club-shaped buds open to fragrant, chalice-shaped flowers to 24cm long, at first greenish white

with thin purplish stripes in the throat, becoming yellowish brown, corolla lobes frilled and reflexed. Less hardy than S maxima. Syn S nitida. Grandiflora — large flowered.

Solandra maxima
Cup of Gold, Golden Chalice
Native from Mexico to Colombia and Venezuela. Bold vine with heavy, arching, sappy branches. Leaves elliptic to 15cm, glossy deep green, margins entire. Rich yellow, chalice or cup-shaped flowers to 18 × 15cm with five purplish-brown lines in the throat, contracted into a narrow tube at the base. Flowers with mellow fragrance suggestive of coconut or ripe apricots appear through spring and summer. Maxima — the largest.

SOLANUM

A genus of about 1400 species of shrubs, trees, herbs and vines, many from tropical America including vital food crops such as S tuberosum, the potato, called *Solanum* the Latin name. Climbing species rapidly cover walls, trellis or pergolas, providing a wealth of bloom for long periods. Grow in warm frost-free locations in sun or partial shade in deeply worked, free-draining, organically enriched soil. Prune heavily for size, neatness and growth renewal.

Solanaceae.

Solanum jasminoides
Potato Vine
Fast growing, Brazilian twiner with numerous slender arching stems to 3m. Leaves with 3–5 ovate leaflets to 4–8cm, deep green often tinged purple, margins entire. White flowers with a hint of purple, about 2cm across with 5 sepals and central spot of yellow stamens in terminal and axillary racemes of about 10 almost all year but heaviest in spring. Jasminoides — resembling jasmine. Evergreen in mild climates.

Solanum seaforthianum
Brazilian Nightshade
South American scandent shrub or gentle climber with smooth stems to 6m. Leaves broadly elliptic to 10 × 8cm, either entire or pinnately divided into 3–5 ovate leaflets. Light blue to violet, star shaped, 25mm flowers with prominent orange stamens, borne in large drooping clusters through spring and summer, followed by scarlet, 8–10mm fruits attractive to birds. Beautiful climber for warm locations, sun or shade.

Named for Lord Seaforth who introduced it into USA. Evergreen in mild climates.

Solanum wendlandii
Blue Potato Vine, Costa Rican Nightshade
Strikingly beautiful vine from Costa Rica for areas substantially free of frost. Grows rapidly to 5m, somewhat fleshy stems sparsely covered with short hooked spines. Leaves variable, 10–25cm long, bright green and luxuriant, either simple or pinnate with 8–12 ovate to oblong lobes. Flowers frilled and ruffled, to 5cm across, lilac blue or mauve, with contrasting yellow centre, borne in large clusters through spring and summer. Magnificent floral display. Named for German botanist, Hermann Wendland. Deciduous.

SOLLYA

A genus of three species, Australian climbing plants or scandent shrubs, named for R H Solly, 18th–19th century English plant physiologist. Listed species an easily-grown, elegant twiner, admired for graceful nodding bell-shaped flowers, useful for training along fences, covering old stumps or trailing over walls or banks, or in containers, especially where its subtle beauty may be appreciated at close range. Plant in full or partial sun in deeply worked, free-draining, organically enriched, moisture-retentive soil. Tolerant of zero temperatures and considerable drought, but grows better with occasional summer watering.

Pittosporaceae.

Sollya heterophylla
Australian Bluebell, Bluebell Creeper
Loose spreading shrub from Western Australia, tending to grow bushy, but if given support and training will reach about 2m. Slender wiry brownish stems, leaves linear-oblong to oblanceolate to 3–5cm long, glossy deep green, margins entire. Brilliant blue, 12mm, nodding bell- shaped flowers borne in axillary cymes through summer and autumn, followed by metallic-blue fruit. Also a pink-flowered form. Heterophylla — diversely leaved. Evergreen.

STAUNTONIA

A genus of about 16 species of evergreen twining shrubs from Burma to Taiwan and Japan, named for Sir George

C Staunton, 18th century Irish naturalist and traveller in China. Staunton Vine is admired for its fragrant flowers and the attractive edible fruit, which resemble plums. A hardy evergreen climber growing in extremes of heat and cold. Plant in deeply worked, sandy or peaty, free-draining, organically enriched, moisture-retentive soil, preferably in moist shady locations.

Lardizabalaceae.

Stauntonia hexaphylla
Japanese Staunton Vine
Rare species from the mountains of Taiwan and Japan. Vigorous twining stems to 6m. Leaves with 3–7 ovate to elliptic leaflets to 14cm long, glossy dark green, leathery, margins entire, often assuming deep bronze shades. Fragrant, ivory-white, violet-tinted, 2cm, bell-shaped flowers borne in loose clusters through summer. Female plants bear soft purplish rose, 3–5cm egg-shaped fruit with a sweet white pulp. Hexaphylla — six leaved. Evergreen.

STEPHANOTIS

A genus of five species of evergreen twining shrubs from the Old World tropics named from the Greek *stephanos*, a crown and *otis*, an ear, in reference to auricles in the staminal crown. Listed species grown for its exquisite, waxy, perfumed flowers often seen in bridal bouquets.

Vigorous climber in sheltered, frost free spots, ideal for glasshouse, patio, entryway, sunporch or against walls, planted or in containers. Plant in deeply worked, free-draining, organically enriched, moisture-retentive soil, with roots in shade and tops in filtered sun. Mulch freely and keep moist during dry periods.

Asclepiadaceae.

Stephanotis floribunda
Madagascar Jasmine, Wax Flower
Beautiful, glabrous evergreen climber from Madagascar, also known as Corsage Vine. Climbs by twisting stems around the nearest support. Leaves oval to oblong-elliptic, to 15cm long, glossy dark green, prominent midrib, leathery, margins entire. Delightfully fragrant, waxy, pure white, 6cm, trumpet-shaped flowers with five flaring lobes, borne in clusters of 8–10 late spring through early autumn. Purity, fragrance and lasting quality makes Stephanotis a favourite for floral arrangements. Floribunda — free-flowering. Evergreen.

Above: Hardenbergia violacea 'Happy Wanderer' **326**

Above: Ficus pumila 'Minima' **325**

Above: Convolvulus sabatius *Ground Morning Glory* **325**
Below: Metrosideros carminea *Akakura Carmine Rata* **329**

Above: Jasminum humile 'Revolutum' *Italian Yellow Jasmine* **327**
Below: Lonicera periclymenum 'Belgica' **328**

Above: Mandevilla sanderi 'Rosea' *Brazilian Jasmine* **328**

Above: Mandevilla sanderi 'Rosea' *Brazilian Jasmine* **328**
Below: Mandevilla splendens 'Alice du Pont' **328**

Above: Mandevilla sanderi 'Red Riding Hood' **328**
Below: Pandorea jasminoides 'Rosea Superba' **329**

Above: Petrea volubilis *Purple Wreath* **330**

Above: Petrea volubilis *Purple Wreath* **330**
Below: Pyrostegia venusta *Flame Vine* **331**

Above: Pyrostegia venusta *Flame Vine* **331**
Below: Thunbergia grandiflora *Sky Flower Bengal Clock Vine* **337**

Thunbergia mysorensis 'Lady's Slipper' 337

Above and below: Podranea ricasoliana *Port St John Creeper* **331**

Above: Wisteria sinensis *Chinese Wisteria* **338**
Below: Pandorea pandorana *Wonga-Wonga Vine* **329**

TECOMANTHE

A genus of about five species of climbing or scandent plants from New Guinea, Moluccas, Queensland, and Three Kings Island just north of New Zealand, named from its close relative, Tecoma and the Greek *anthe*, flower. Listed species admired for high-gloss foliage and clusters of creamy-green, foxglove-like flowers. Plant in sun or semi-shade in deeply worked, free-draining, organically enriched, moisture-retentive soil. Thrives in coastal conditions in semi-shade but needs protection in temperatures below 3°C.

Bignoniaceae.

Tecomanthe speciosa

A strong woody climber discovered in the Three Kings Islands in 1945. Leaves to 30cm with two pairs of ovate to oblong-lanceolate leaflets to 12 × 7cm, glossy dark green, leathery, margins entire. Flowers slightly curved, tubular or trumpet-shaped to 45mm long with flaring lobes, creamy white to pale lemon-yellow, tinged green, borne in crowded panicles on wood from the previous year through winter and in early spring. Speciosa — showy. Evergreen.

THUNBERGIA

A genus of about 100 species of twining or scandent plants from tropical and South Africa, Madagascar and tropical Asia. The genus is named for Dr Karl Peter Thunberg, (1743–1822), botanist and plant collector.

Thunbergias are noted for their flamboyant flowers. They grow rapidly with little attention in deeply worked, free-draining soil, located in maximum sunlight and away from frost.

Acanthaceae. *All evergreen.*

Thunbergia alata
Black Eyed Susan Vine

Vigorous South African plant, quickly building a dense mass of slender hairy stems. Leaves ovate-elliptic to cordate, to 75mm long, deep green, rough-textured, margins lightly toothed. Open-faced, 35mm flowers with five sepals, vivid orange with jet-black eye, borne freely during warmer periods of the year. Useful for covering walls, window boxes, hanging baskets, bank or ground cover. Alata — winged.

Thunbergia coccinea
Scarlet Clock Vine

Native to India and Burma. Tender, wide-spreading climber. Leaves narrowly ovate-elliptic to 15 × 7cm long, green above, somewhat glaucous beneath thick and leathery, palmately nerved, margins toothed. Tubular, 25mm, bright scarlet flowers with yellow throat borne in 15–45cm drooping racemes through autumn and winter. Only for sunny, frost free locations. Coccinea — scarlet.

Thunbergia gregorii
Golden Glory Vine

Showy creeper from tropical Africa. Leaves triangular-ovate to 75mm, deep green, soft hairy texture, margins toothed. Dazzling, rich glowing orange, 3–4cm, flared tubular flowers, freely produced through warm summer months, providing a brilliant and colourful display. Excellent over rocks or stumps, easily trained through wire netting or over brushwood in a warm sunny location. Syn T gibsonii. Named for Dr J W Gregory, original collector of the species.

Thunbergia grandiflora
Sky Flower, Bengal Clock Vine

Vigorous twiner from northern India. Leaves ovate-elliptic to 20cm long, deep green, rough-textured, palmately veined, margins toothed or lobed. Bluish violet, 75mm, flaring tubular flowers borne in axillary racemes most of the year, especially spring through autumn. Full sun, frost free. Grandiflora — large flowered.   **335**

Thunbergia mysorensis
Lady's Slipper

Attractive species from India. Vigorous vine to 6m. Leaves narrowly elliptic to 15cm long, deep green, margins toothed. Mahogany-red buds open to 5cm, curved funnel or tube-shaped yellow flowers with reddish brown lobes borne profusely in long pendent racemes to 45cm long. Seen at its best when growing on top of a high pergola, or from the rafters of a large glasshouse when myriads of rich red and yellow blooms hang gracefully from the ceiling. For subtropical climates or glasshouse.   **336**

TRACHELOSPERMUM

A genus of about twenty twining or shrubby vines with milky sap, from India to Japan, named from the Greek, *trachelos*, a neck and *sperma*, a seed. Main feature of the listed species is its dense glossy foliage and masses of fragrant white flowers. Support is essential such as heavy cord or wires to lead the vine in the desired direction and for strong wiry stems to develop. Locate where full advantage may be taken of its delightful fragrance. Useful in containers with small trellis, or as ground cover. Grows in full sun or partial shade in deeply worked, free-draining, fertile soil.

Apocynaceae. *All evergreen.*

Trachelospermum jasminoides
Star Jasmine

Strong growing, evergreen climber from China building up a multitude of slender stems. Leaves oval-lanceolate, to 75 × 25mm, deep green, very glossy, margins entire. Intensely fragrant, pure white, starry, 2cm flowers, profuse in short racemes late spring through summer virtually covering the whole plant. Although unrelated, a resemblance to jasmine blossom has suggested the specific and common names.

Trachelospermum jasminoides 'Variegata'

Attractive variegated cultivar, leaves ovate to nearly linear-lanceolate, with combination of milky-green and darker green, irregularly margined silvery cream. Flowers similar to above. Grows less vigorously.

VIGNA

A genus of about 150 species of creeping or twining herbs from tropical Africa, tropical America and Asia, named for Dominico Vigna, 17th century professor of botany at Pisa. Some species grown for edible seeds used in soups or stews while others are eaten as bean sprouts. Snail Flower is a rampant grower, twining its shoots around the nearest support, soon forming a dense mass or lush foliage. Curious and quite showy flowers appear during the heat of summer. Good summer screen or bank cover. Plant in any reasonable, well-drained soil in a warm location and cut to ground level when tops die down.

Leguminosae.

Vigna caracalla
Snail Flower

Native to tropical South America, a vigorous vine found in thickets, forest borders and river margins. Bean-like leaves, leaflets ovate to 13 × 10cm, deep green, faintly pubescent, margins entire. Curious, fleshy-textured flowers to 5cm across, delicately fragrant, curled sepals creamy white, marked purple or pale purple, the keel coiled to resemble a small snail's shell. Caracalla — of Caracas, Venezuela. Syn Phaseolus caracalla. Deciduous.

VITIS

A genus of about 65 species of rambling vines or shrubs from North America, Asia, Europe and the Middle East, named from the Latin *vitis*, a vine. The genus includes the species from which modern grape cultivars have arisen but featured here is the beautiful ornamental vine valued for picturesque stem patterns and rich autumn colours. They are vigorous growers and can be seen clambering into large trees, scrambling over walls or stumps, or trained to cover posts, walls or pergolas.

Panicles of small insignificant greenish flowers may, after a hot dry summer result in bunches of small grape-like fruit. They're hardy to severe cold and once established, to long periods of drought. Not really for warm-temperate or sub-tropical gardens, preferring cooler, southern regions. Plant in deeply worked, free-draining, organically enriched, moisture-retentive, fertile, alkaline soil. Annual pruning keeps adventurous shoots from straying too far.

Vitaceae.

Vitis amurensis
Scarlet Leafed Vine
Native to Manchuria. Strong growing vine with rose to crimson young shoots. Leaves with 3–5 deeply cut lobes, to 15–25cm, central lobe broadly ovate, leathery textured, prominently veined, margins serrated, glossy and reddish when young, becoming claret red, deepening to brilliant currant red, crimson, orange and purple in autumn. Fruits small, black and bitter. Named from the Amur River on the Manchurian-Russian border. Deciduous.

WISTERIA

A genus of about 10 species of tall-climbing woody vines from eastern USA, China and Japan, named for Caspar Wistar, 18th century Professor of Anatomy at the University of Pennsylvania. Superbly beautiful, long-lived, twining, woody vines with pendulous panicles of flowers borne profusely during spring before leaves appear. One of nature's masterpieces, a plant of bold proportions and spectacular flowers. Wisteria develops a substantial and picturesque trunk.

Use on pergolas or patio roofs, on trellis or espalier, draped along fences or train as a standard shrub. Grow in deeply worked, free-draining, organically enriched, moisture-retentive, acid soil. Mulch freely and keep moist during the growth or bloom periods. Hardy to –15°C, but locate to take advantage of maximum sunlight. After establishing a framework, size may be controlled by pinching and pruning, aiming to encourage flowering spurs close to the main structure.

Leguminosae. *Deciduous.*

Wisteria floribunda
Japanese Wisteria
Native to Japan and northern China. An outstanding species with clockwise-twining stems to 8m or more. Pinnate leaves to 35cm long, with 11–19 ovate-elliptic to oblong leaflets to 8cm, downy at first, later glossy mid-green and glabrous. Fragrant, violet or violet-blue, pea-shaped flowers in pendent, axillary, 40–90cm racemes, appear with new leaves spring and early summer, and open gradually from the base. Locate to allow for the drop of the long flowering 'chains'. Floribunda — free-flowering.

Wisteria floribunda 'Alba'
White Japanese Wisteria
White fragrant flowers, tinted lilac on the keel, borne in pendent, 45–60cm racemes. Syn W 'Snow Showers'.

Wisteria floribunda 'Carnea'
Pale pink buds opening to white, delicately tinted lilac-pink, fragrant flowers in long open racemes. Syn W 'Lipstick'.

Wisteria floribunda 'Lavender Lace'
Lavender Japanese Wisteria
Fragrant pale lavender and white flowers in long slender racemes to 90cm. Beautiful and spectacular.

Wisteria floribunda 'Macrobotrys'
Magnificent form with fragrant, bluish purple, lilac tinged flowers in racemes to 90cm long. Macrobotrys — with large grapelike clusters.

Wisteria floribunda 'Snow Showers'
White fragrant flowers, tinted lilac on the keel, borne in pendent, 45–60cm racemes. Syn W 'Alba'.

Wisteria floribunda 'Violacea Plena'
Unusual and attractive form with violet blue, fully double flowers in long racemes. Syn 'Black Dragon'.

Wisteria × formosa
American hybrid from W floribunda 'Alba' × W sinensis. Attractive climber with stems twining clockwise, young shoots silky downy. Pinnate leaves downy at first, 9–15 leaflets, bright green and glabrous. Very fragrant, pale violet, 2cm flowers with darker wings and keel, opening at the same time in 25cm pendent racemes early summer. Formosa — handsome or beautiful.

Wisteria sinensis
Chinese Wisteria
Extremely vigorous Chinese species which reaches tremendous proportions if left to itself. Stems twine anticlockwise, becoming gnarled and picturesque with age. Pinnate leaves to 30cm long, with 7–13 elliptic or ovate, 5–8cm leaflets, deep green and glabrous above, hairy beneath. Mildly fragrant, mauve to deep lilac, 25mm flowers, densely packed in 15–30cm racemes, appear in great masses together with the leaves, providing a breathtaking spectacle of colour. May flower again but more sparsely midsummer. Sinensis — of China.   **336**

Wisteria sinensis 'Amethyst'
Light rosy purple, strongly fragrant flowers in 25cm racemes.

Wisteria sinensis 'Blue Sapphire'
Elegant cultivar with blue and mauve, sweetly fragrant flowers in pendent 15cm racemes. Smaller grower, but flowers prolifically.

Wisteria sinensis 'Caroline'
Soft lavender-mauve, sweetly fragrant flowers in crowded, compact, 20–30cm racemes. Flowers most prolifically, virtually covering the plant with spectacular bloom.

Wisteria venusta 'White Silk'
Silky Wisteria
Strong growing Japanese climber, anti-clockwise twining stems to about 9m. Pinnate leaves to 35cm long, with 9–13 elliptic or ovate leaflets to 10cm covered with conspicuous silky hairs. Highly fragrant, 25mm creamy white flowers with a touch of yellow, open together in crowded, pendent, 15cm racemes as new leaves appear in spring. Venusta — meaning handsome or charming.

YOUR GUIDE TO PLANT SELECTION

Use this guide when you need subjects for specific purposes. It may be flowering shrubs of a particular colour, plants for ground cover, perhaps winter flowering trees or a plant for a container. Under the following headings you'll find varieties to cover many of the situations arising in average gardens.

The lists refer to a genus under which you will find the specific plant required. Often, one genus falls under numerous classifications. Grevillea is a good example where there are plants for ground cover, dwarf, medium and tall shrubs and sizeable trees.

CONIFERS

Abies	Ginkgo	Podocarpus
Agathis	Halocarpus	Prumnopitys
Araucaria	Juniperus	Pseudotsuga
Cedrus	Larix	Sequoia
Chamaecyparis	Lepidothamnus	Sequoiadendron
Cryptomeria	Libocedrus	Taxodium
Cupressocyparis	Metasequoia	Taxus
Cupressus	Picea	Thuja
Dacrycarpus	Pinus	Thujopsis
Dacrydium		

FERNS AND PALMS

Asparagus	Cyathea	Phoenix
Asplenium	Cycas	Platycerium
Carpentaria	Dicksonia	Rhopalostylis
Chamaerops	Howea	Trachycarpus

SWORD LEAF PLANTS

Acorus	Beaucarnea	Libertia
Agapanthus	Clivia	Phormium
Agave	Cordyline	Puya
Anigozanthus	Cyperus	Xeronema
Arthropodium	Dracaena	Yucca
Astelia		

STANDARD OR WEEPING TREES

Acer
Cotoneaster
Fagus
Fraxinus
Prunus
Salix
Ulmus

BAMBOOS & GRASSES

Bambusa	Festuca
Carex	Helictotrichon
Chinochloa	Ophiopogon
Cortaderia	Pennisetum
Cyperus	Restio

COLOURFUL LEAVES – DECIDUOUS

Acer	Franklinia	Robinia
Ailanthus	Fraxinus	Salix
Amelanchier	Ginkgo	Sambucus
Berberis	Gleditsia	Sorbus
Carpinus	Glyptostrobus	Spiraea
Carya	Gymnocladus	Stewartia
Catalpa	Koelreuteria	Styrax
Cedrela	Liquidambar	Taxodium
Cercidiphyllum	Liriodendron	Tilia
Chionanthus	Malus	Toxicodendron
Cladrastis	Nyssa	Ulmus
Cornus	Parrotia	Viburnum
Corylus	Phellodendron	Vitis
Cotinus	Pistacia	Weigela
Enkianthus	Populus	Zelkova
Fagus	Prunus	

COLOURFUL LEAVES – EVERGREEN

Abelia	Euonymus	Myrtus
Agonis	Eurya	Nandina
Aucuba	Ficus	Phebalium
Azara	Griselinia	Phormium
Brachyglottis	Hakea	Phormium
Chamaecyparis	Hoheria	Pittosporum
Cleyera	Leucadendron	Pseudowintera
Coprosma	Leucothoe	Rhamnus
Cordyline	Ligustrum	Royena
Coronilla	Lophostemon	Santolina
Dodonaea	Meryta	Strobilanthes
Elaeagnus	Metrosideros	Weinmannia

DRAMATIC FOLIAGE

Agave	Ficus	Monstera
Aucuba	Gunnera	Philodendron
Baccharis	Gymnocladus	Phormium
Bambusa	Harpephyllum	Pisonia
Cedrela	Hosta	Pseudopanax
Cycas	Howea	Puya
Ensete	Lomartia	Radermachera
Fatshedera	Mahonia	Schefflera
Fatsia	Meryta	Stenocarpus

FRAGRANT FLOWERS OR LEAVES

Adenandra
Akebia
Aloysia
Azara
Backhousia
Boronia
Bouvardia
Brunfelsia
Buddleia
Carmichaelia
Chimonanthus
Cinnamomum
Clematis
Coleonema

Coronilla
Corylopsis
Cytisus
Daphne
Eucryphia
Gardenia
Genista
Hamamelis
Helipterum
Hymenosporum
Jasminum
Laurus
Lonicera
Luculia

Magnolia
Malus
Mandevilla
Osmanthus
Plumeria
Podalyria
Prostanthera
Prunus
Pseudowintera
Psoralea
Ptelea
Rhododendron
Rondeletia
Rosmarinus

Solandra
Stauntonia
Stephanotis
Styrax

Trachelospermum
Viburnum
Vigna
Wisteria

ATTRACTIVE TO BIRDS

Acmena
Actinidia
Albizzia
Alnus
Amelanchier
Arbutus
Arctostaphylos
Banksia
Berberis
Betula
Callistemon
Chaenomeles
Clianthus
Cornus
Cotoneaster
Elaeocarpus
Erythrina
Eucalyptus
Fuchsia
Gautheria
Grevillea
Hedera
Hedycarya

Ilex
Juniperus
Knightia
Lonicera
Mahonia
Malus
Melia
Melicope
Metrosideros
Morus
Parthenocissus
Phormium
Pittosporum
Platanus
Podocarpus

Protea
Prunus
Pseudopanax
Pyracantha
Ribes
Sambucus
Schefflera
Sophora
Sorbus
Sorbus
Symphoricarpus
Syzygium
Viburnum
Virgilia
Vitex

SLENDER OR COLUMNAR

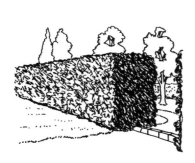

Astartea
Buxus
Chamaecyparis
Cupressus
Juniperus
Libocedrus
Phebalium

Picea
Podocarpus
Populus
Pseudopanax
Salix
Taxus
Thuja

HEDGES, SCREENS AND WINDBREAKS

Abelia
Acmena
Agonis
Araucaria
Bambusa
Buddleia
Callistemon
Casuarina
Corokia
Cortaderia
Cryptomeria
Cupressocyparis
Cupressus
Dodonaea

Escallonia
Euonymus
Feijoa
Griselinia
Hoheria
Juniperus
Laurus
Ligustrum
Lonicera
Metrosideros
Myoporum
Myrtus
Nerium

Phebalium
Phormium
Pinus
Pittosporum
Podocarpus
Populus
Pseudopanax
Pyracantha
Salix
Syzygium
Tecomaria
Thuja
Virgilia

FEATURE OR ROCK GARDENS

Abies
Acer
Agapanthus
Agave
Anigozanthus
Asparagus
Asplenium
Astelia
Asteriscus
Aucuba
Azaleas
Baccharis
Bambusa
Beaucarnea
Brachyglottis
Calluna
Carex
Cedrus
Chamaecyparis

Chamaerops
Chinochloa
Clivia
Coleonema
Coprosma

Cordyline
Cotoneaster
Cryptomeria
Cupressus
Cyathea

Cycas
Cyperus
Dicksonia
Dracaena
Ensete
Euphorbia
Evolvulus
Fatshedera
Fatsia
Festuca
Ficus
Gardenia
Gunnera
Halimium
Hebe
Helichrysum
Helictotrichon
Hibiscus
Lepidothamnus
Leptospermum
Libertia
Libocedrus

Loropetalum
Mahonia
Monstera
Nandina
Nymphaea
Ophiopogon
Othonna
Pennisetum
Philodendron
Phoenix
Phormium
Pseudopanax
Puya
Restio
Rhopalostylis
Schefflera
Sciadopitys
Strelitzia
Taxus
Thuja
Xeronema
Yucca

PLANTS FOR CONTAINERS

Abies
Acer
Agave
Araucaria
Ardisia
Aucuba
Azaleas
Bambusa
Beaucarnea
Camellia
Carpentaria
Cedrus
Chamaecyparis
Clivia
Cordyline
Corynocarpus
Cryptomeria
Cupressocyparis
Cupressus

Cycas
Dacrydium
Ensete
Euonymus
Fatsia
Griselinia
Harpephyllum
Helichrysum
Hibiscus
Howea
Hydrangea
Ilex
Juniperus
Laurus
Libocedrus
Ligustrum
Lomartia
Mahonia
Melicope

Meryta
Metrosideros
Myrtus
Nandina
Nerium
Ophiopogon
Philodendron
Phoenix
Phormium
Photinia
Picea
Pinus
Pittosporum
Plumeria
Podocarpus
Prumnopitys
Pseudopanax
Pseudotsuga
Puya

Pyracantha
Radermachera
Rhododendron vireya
Schefflera
Sciadopitys
Stenocarpus
Strelitzia

Taxus
Thuja
Trachycarpus
Tristaniopsis
Xeronema
Yucca

GROUND COVERS

Agapanthus
Asparagus
Azaleas
Baccharis
Calluna
Camellia
Carex
Ceanothus
Chamaecyparis
Convolvulus
Convolvulus
Coprosma
Cotoneaster
Cytisus

Dampiera
Euonymus
Evolvulus
Festuca
Grevillea
Hebe
Hedera
Helichrysum
Heterocentron
Hypericum
Jasminum
Juniperus
Lantana

Lepidothamnus
Leptospermum
Lotus
Lysimachia
Metrosideros
Muehlenbeckia
Myoporum
Ophiopogon
Parahebe
Podocarpus
Rosmarinus
Rulingia
Santolina

BERRIES OR FRUIT

Chionanthus
Cleyera
Coprosma
Cornus
Corokia
Correa
Corynocarpus
Cotoneaster
Crataegus
Duranta
Elaeocarpus
Elingamita
Euonymus
Feijoa
Gautheria
Gymnocladus
Harpephyllum
Hedycarya
Idesia
Ilex
Juniperus
Lepidothamnus

Macropiper
Mahonia
Malus
Melastoma
Melia
Melicytus
Meryta
Monstera
Morus
Muehlenbeckia
Myrtus
Nandina
Ochna
Ophiopogon
Ostrya
Parthenocissus
Passiflora
Paulownia
Phoenix
Prunus
Pseudowintera
Pterocarya

Pterostyrax
Punica
Pyracantha
Pyrus
Quercus
Rhamnus
Rhopalostylis
Royena
Ruscus
Sambucus
Sarcococca
Schefflera
Schinus
Sorbus
Stauntonia
Symphoricarpus
Syzygium
Tasmannia
Ugni
Viburnum
Vitex
Vitis

Acmena
Actinidia
Ailanthus
Akebia
Albizzia
Amelanchier
Arbutus
Arctostaphylos
Ardisia
Aristotelia

Asparagus
Aucuba
Beilschmiedia
Berberis
Billardiera
Callicarpa
Carpentaria
Carpinus
Castanea
Celastrus

HOT AND DRY PLACES

Acacia
Adenandra
Agapanthus
Agave
Ailanthus
Anigozanthus
Asteriscus
Aulux
Baccharis
Banksia
Calliandra
Callistemon
Carex
Cassinia
Casuarina
Ceanothus
Celtis

Cistus
Convolvulus
Cortaderia
Dryandra
Echium
Elaeagnus
Eucalyptus
Grevillea
Halimium
Hibbertia
Juniperus
Juniperus
Kunzea
Lagerstroemia
Lantana
Lavendula
Leucadendron

Leucospermum
Mahonia
Melaleuca
Metrosideros
Myoporum
Myrtus
Parrotia
Phylica
Pimelia
Pinus
Podalyria
Prostanthera
Protea
Pseudopanax
Psoralea
Punica
Puya

Pyracantha
Raphiolepis
Rosmarinus
Royena
Rulingia

Santolina
Tamarix
Teucrium
Vitex
Yucca

WET OR BOGGY PLACES

Acorus
Alnus
Betula
Chaenomeles
Cordyline
Cortaderia
Cyperus
Dacrycarpus
Fraxinus

Glyptostrobus
Gunnera
Hoheria
Laurelia
Ligustrum
Metrosideros
Myrtus
Nyssa

Phormium
Podocarpus
Populus
Pseudopanax
Salix
Sophora
Taxodium
Ulmus

COASTAL OR SEASIDE

Acacia
Adenandra
Agapanthus
Agave
Araucaria
Arthropodium
Baccharis
Bambusa
Banksia
Beaufortia
Buddleia
Callistemon
Campsis
Casuarina
Ceanothus

Cistus
Convolvulus
Coprosma
Cordyline
Corokia
Cortaderia
Corynocarpus
Cotoneaster
Cupressocyparis
Cupressus
Cytisus
Dryandra
Echium
Euryops
Griselinia

Harpephyllum
Hebe
Helichrysum
Hibbertia
Knightia
Lagunaria
Lantana
Lavendula
Leucadendron
Leucospermum
Melaleuca
Melia
Melicope
Meryta

Metrosideros
Myoporum
Nerium
Olearia
Paulownia
Phebalium
Phoenix
Phormium
Phylica
Pimelia
Pinus
Podalyria
Protea
Pseudopanax

Psoralea
Raphiolepis
Santolina
Solandra
Strelitzia
Tamarix
Taxus
Tecomaria
Teucrium
Trachycarpus
Vitex
Westringia
Xeronema
Yucca

SHADE TREES FOR LAWN OR PATIO

Acacia
Acer
Aesculus
Agonis
Ailanthus
Albizzia
Alnus
Azara
Brachychiton
Catalpa
Cordyline
Davidia
Fraxinus

Gleditsia
Harpephyllum
Hymenosporum
Jacaranda
Koelreuteria
Liquidambar
Liriodendron
Lophostemon
Magnolia
Maytenus
Melia
Meryta

Paulownia
Phellodendron
Prunus
Rhodoleia
Robinia
Schefflera
Schinus
Sorbus
Stenocarpus
Styrax
Tristaniopsis
Ulmus

TREES FOR THE SMALLER GARDEN

Acacia
Acer
Ackama
Acmena
Agonis
Albizzia
Alectryon
Arbutus
Aristotelia
Backhousia
Banksia
Betula
Brachychiton
Camellia
Carpodetus
Cedrela
Celtis
Chionanthus
Clethra

Cornus
Elingamita
Embothrium
Eucryphia
Glyptostrobus
Hedycarya
Hoheria
Knightia
Laburnum
Lagerstroemia
Lagunaria
Leucadendron
Magnolia
Malus
Maytenus
Melaleuca
Melicytus
Meryta
Metrosideros

Michelia
Morus
Myoporum
Nothofagus
Nyssa
Phebalium
Phoenix
Photinia
Phyllocladus
Picea
Pinus
Plagianthus
Planchonella
Podocarpus
Populus
Prumnopitys
Prunus
Rhododendron
Rhodoleia

Robinia
Salix
Sambucus
Sophora

Stewartia
Toxicodendron
Virgilia

FLOWERING OR FOLIAGE TREES

Acer
Aesculus
Albizzia
Arbutus

Betula
Carpinus
Carya
Castanea

Catalpa
Celtis
Cercidiphyllum
Cercis
Chorisia
Cinnamomum
Cladrastis
Cornus
Crataegus
Dacrycarpus
Davidia
Eucalyptus
Fagus
Fraxinus
Ginkgo
Gleditsia

Grevillea
Gymnocladus
Idesia
Jacaranda
Lagunaria
Liquidambar
Liriodendron
Lyonothamnus
Magnolia
Melia
Metasequoia
Metrosideros
Nyssa
Ostrya
Paulownia

Phellodendron
Pistacia
Plagianthus
Platanus
Populus
Pterocarya
Pterostyrax
Quercus
Sequoia
Sequoiadendron
Taxodium
Tilia
Ulmus
Vitex
Zelkova

NEW ZEALAND TREES AND SHRUBS

Ackama
Agathis
Alectryon
Aristotelia
Arthropodium
Ascarina
Astelia
Beilschmiedia
Brachyglottis
Carex
Carpodetus
Cassinia
Chordospartium
Clematis
Clianthus
Coprosma
Cordyline
Corokia
Cortaderia

Corynocarpus
Cyathea
Dacrycarpus
Dacrydium
Dicksonia
Dodonaea
Elaeocarpus
Elingamita
Entelea
Griselinia
Hebe
Hedycarya
Hoheria
Knightia
Laurelia
Lepidothamnus
Leptospermum
Libertia
Libocedrus

Macropiper
Melicope
Melicytus
Meryta
Metrosideros
Muehlenbeckia
Myoporum
Myrsine
Myrtus
Nothofagus
Olearia
Parahebe
Phormium
Phyllocladus
Pisonia
Pittosporum
Plagianthus
Planchonella
Podocarpus

Pomaderris
Prumnopitys
Pseudopanax
Pseudowintera
Quintinia
Rhabdothamnus
Rhopalostylis

Schefflera
Sophora
Tecomanthe
Vitex
Vitex
Weinmannia
Xeronema

AUSTRALIAN TREES AND SHRUBS

Acacia
Acmena
Agonis
Anigozanthus
Asplenium
Astartea
Backhousia

Banksia
Beaufortia
Boronia
Brachychiton
Brachyscome
Callistemon

Calytrix
Carex
Carpentaria
Cassia
Casuarina
Chamelaucium
Correa
Crotalaria
Crowea
Cyathea
Dampiera
Dicksonia
Dodonaea
Dryandra
Epacris
Eriostemon
Eucalyptus
Eucryphia

Eutaxia
Ficus
Grevillea
Hakea
Helichrysum
Helipterum
Hibbertia
Howea
Hymenosporum
Hypocalymma
Indigofera
Kunzea
Lagunaria
Lechenaultia
Leptospermum
Lophostemon
Maytenus
Melaleuca

Muehlenbeckia
Myoporum
Olearia
Phebalium
Pimelia
Platycerium
Prostanthera
Restio
Rulingia
Schefflera
Stenocarpus
Syzygium
Tasmannia
Telopea
Tetratheca
Thryptomene
Tristaniopsis
Westringia

DWARF SHRUBS LESS THAN 1m

Actinodium	Ceratostigma	Eriostemon	Lantana	Puya
Adenandra	Chaenomeles	Euryops	Lavendula	Raphiolepis
Agapetes	Chamaecyparis	Eutaxia	Lechenaultia	Reinwardtia
Arctostaphylos	Chrysocoma	Evolvulus	Leptospermum	Rhododendron
Ardisia	Cistus	Felicia	Leucothoe	Rosmarinus
Arthropodium	Coleonema	Forsythia	Linum	Ruscus
Asclepias	Convolvulus	Gardenia	Lithodora	Russelia
Astartea	Coprosma	Gautheria	Lonicera	Ruta
Astelia	Coronilla	Genista	Loropetalum	Santolina
Asteriscus	Correa	Grevillea	Nandina	Sarcococca
Azaleas	Cotoneaster	Halimium	Parahebe	Serissa
Baeckea	Crowea	Hebe	Phylica	Sophora
Bauera	Cryptomeria	Helichrysum	Picea	Spiraea
Boronia	Cuphea	Helipterum	Pieris	Strobilanthes
Bouvardia	Cytisus	Hibbertia	Pimelia	Taxus
Brachyscome	Daboecia	Hibiscus	Pinus	Tetratheca
Brunfelsia	Dampiera	Hosta	Podalyria	Teucrium
Buxus	Daphne	Hydrangea	Potentilla	Thryptomene
Calluna	Deutzia	Hypericum	Prostanthera	Thuja
Calytrix	Echium	Hypocalymma	Protea	Westringia
Cassinia	Epacris	Juniperus	Punica	Xeronema
Ceanothus	Erica	Justicia		

MEDIUM SHRUBS 1-2m

Abelia	Caryopteris	Euonymus	Melastoma	Punica
Abutilon	Cavendishia	Eurya	Mimetes	Pyracantha
Acacia	Ceanothus	Fuchsia	Muehlenbeckia	Raphiolepis
Acer	Chaenomeles	Grevillea	Myrtus	Restio
Aloysia	Chamaecyparis	Grewia	Nandina	Rhabdothamnus
Alyogyne	Chamelaucium	Gunnera	Nerium	Rhododendron
Aucuba	Choisya	Hibiscus	Ochna	Ribes
Aulux	Clerodendrum	Hydrangea	Olearia	Rondeletia
Azaleas	Cleyera	Indigofera	Osmanthus	Royena
Azaleas — deciduous	Clianthus	Isopogon	Ostrya	Sciadopitys
Azara	Coleonema	Juniperus	Paranomus	Strelitzia
Banksia	Coprosma	Justicia	Philadelphus	Streptosolen
Beaucarnea	Corokia	Kerria	Philodendron	Symphoricarpus
Beaufortia	Cytisus	Kolkwitzia	Phormium	Tasmannia
Berberis	Desfontainea	Kunzea	Photinia	Taxus
Berzelia	Deutzia	Lantana	Physocarpus	Thryptomene
Calliandra	Dodonaea	Leptospermum	Pieris	Thuja
Callicarpa	Edgeworthia	Leucadendron	Plumbago	Tibouchina
Callistemon	Elaeagnus	Leucospermum	Pomaderris	Ugni
Camellia	Enkianthus	Luculia	Prostanthera	Viburnum
Cantua	Erica	Mahonia	Protea	Westringia
Carmichaelia	Escallonia			

TALLER SHRUBS 2-4m

Acacia	Buddleia	Chamaecyparis	Cotinus	Dombeya
Acer	Caesalpinia	Chimonanthus	Cotoneaster	Dryandra
Anopteris	Calliandra	Chordospartium	Crinodendron	Duranta
Ascarina	Callistemon	Cordyline	Crotalaria	Elaeocarpus
Astartea	Camellia	Cornus	Cunonia	Entelea
Banksia	Cassia	Corokia	Cyperus	Erythrina
Brachyglottis	Ceanothus	Corylopsis	Daubentonia	Euonymus
Brunfelsia	Ceratopetalum	Corylus	Dodonaea	Euphorbia

Fatsia
Feijoa
Forsythia
Garrya
Genista
Gordonia
Grevillea
Griselinia
Hakea
Halocarpus
Hamamelis
Hibiscus
Hoheria
Hydrangea
Ilex

Iochroma
Itea
Juniperus
Kalmia
Koelreuteria
Laburnocytisus
Laburnum
Lagerstroemia
Laurus
Leonotis
Leptospermum
Leucadendron
Leucospermum
Libocedrus
Ligustrum

Macropiper
Magnolia
Malus
Melaleuca
Metrosideros
Michelia
Myrsine
Nerium
Phebalium
Photinia
Picea
Pisonia
Pittosporum
Plumeria
Podalyria

Podocarpus
Polygala
Protea
Prumnopitys
Prunus
Pseudopanax
Pseudowintera
Psoralea
Ptelea
Pyracantha
Quintinia
Radermachera
Rhamnus
Rhododendron
Rhopalostylis

Schefflera
Spiraea
Stachyurus
Styrax
Syringa
Tamarix
Taxus
Telopea
Thuja
Thujopsis
Tibouchina
Trachycarpus
Viburnum
Vitex
Weinmannia

MAIN FLOWERING PERIODS: SPRING-SUMMER

Ackama
Acorus
Actinodium
Adenandra
Aesculus
Agapanthus
Agapetes
Akebia
Aloysia
Alyogyne
Anopteris
Arctostaphylos
Aristotelia
Ascarina
Asteriscus
Azaleas
Azaleas — deciduous
Bauera
Beilschmiedia
Berzelia
Billardiera
Boronia
Bougainvillea
Brachychiton
Brachyscome
Brunfelsia
Calliandra
Callistemon
Calluna
Camellia
Cantua
Carpinus
Catalpa
Cavendishia
Ceanothus
Ceratopetalum
Cercis

Chaenomeles
Chamelaucium
Chionanthus
Choisya
Chordospartium
Cistus
Cladrastis
Clematis
Clianthus
Coleonema
Convolvulus
Cornus
Corokia
Coronilla
Corylopsis
Cotoneaster
Crataegus
Crinodendron
Crowea
Cytisus
Dampiera
Daphne
Daubentonia
Davidia
Deutzia
Dombeya
Dryandra
Edgeworthia
Embothrium
Enkianthus
Entelea
Epacris
Erica
Eriostemon
Erythrina
Eucalyptus
Euryops

Euryops
Eutaxia
Evolvulus
Forsythia
Fuchsia
Genista
Grevillea
Grewia
Halimium
Hardenbergia
Hebe
Helichrysum
Helipterum
Hibbertia
Hibiscus
Hydrangea
Hymenosporum
Hypocalymma
Isopogon
Jacaranda
Jasminum
Kalmia
Kerria
Knightia
Kolkwitzia
Kunzea
Laburnum
Lantana
Lavendula
Leptospermum
Leucadendron
Leucospermum
Leucothoe
Linum
Lithodora
Loropetalum
Lotus

Lysimachia
Macfadyena
Magnolia
Malus
Manettia
Melaleuca
Michelia
Mimetes
Nerium
Olearia
Osmanthus
Ostrya
Othonna
Parrotia
Paulownia
Pennisetum
Petrea
Phebalium
Phellodendron
Philadelphus
Phormium
Pieris
Pittosporum
Plagianthus
Plumeria
Podalyria
Polygala
Potentilla
Prostanthera
Protea
Prunus
Psoralea
Ptelea
Pterostyrax
Pyracantha
Pyrus
Radermachera

Raphiolepis
Rhabdothamnus
Rhamnus
Rhodochiton
Rhododendron
Ribes
Rondeletia
Rosmarinus
Rulingia
Ruta
Schizophragma
Serissa
Solandra
Sophora
Spiraea
Stachyurus
Stephanotis
Strelitzia
Streptosolen
Styrax
Syringa
Telopea
Tetratheca
Teucrium
Thunbergia
Tilia
Trachelospermum
Viburnum
Vigna
Virgilia
Weigela
Weinmannia
Westringia
Wisteria
Xeronema
Yucca

MAIN FLOWERING PERIODS: SUMMER-AUTUMN

Agapanthus
Albizzia
Alectryon
Alyogyne
Anigozanthus
Astartea
Asteriscus
Beaufortia
Berberidopsis
Bougainvillea
Bouvardia
Brachychiton
Brunfelsia
Buddleia
Caesalpinia
Calliandra
Callistemon
Calluna
Campsis
Cantua
Carmichaelia
Carpodetus
Caryopteris

Cavendishia
Ceanothus
Ceratopetalum
Ceratostigma
Clerodendrum
Clethra
Cleyera
Convolvulus
Cordyline
Cortaderia
Crotalaria
Cunonia
Cuphea
Cyperus
Daboecia
Daubentonia
Desfontainea
Distictis
Dombeya
Duranta
Elaeocarpus
Elingamita
Epacris

Erica
Erythrina
Eucalyptus
Eucryphia
Evolvulus
Felicia
Fuchsia
Grevillea
Grewia
Heterocentron
Hibbertia
Hibiscus
Hoheria
Hosta
Hydrangea
Hypericum
Iochroma
Itea
Jacaranda
Jasminum
Justicia
Koelreuteria
Lagerstroemia

Lagunaria
Lantana
Lapageria
Leonotis
Lonicera
Mandevilla
Melastoma
Melia
Metrosideros
Nerium
Nymphaea
Othonna
Pandorea
Parahebe
Passiflora
Pennisetum
Pimelia
Planchonella
Plumbago
Plumeria
Podranea
Potentilla

Punica
Quintinia
Raphiolepis
Rhabdothamnus
Rhodochiton
Russelia
Ruta
Santolina
Schefflera
Schinus
Sequoia
Serissa
Solanum
Sollya
Spiraea
Strelitzia
Strobilanthes
Symphoricarpus
Tamarix
Tristaniopsis
Vitex
Yucca

MAIN FLOWERING PERIODS: AUTUMN-WINTER

Acacia
Adenandra
Agonis
Alyogyne
Arbutus
Asclepias
Azara
Banksia
Bauera
Camellia
Cassia
Celastrus

Chaenomeles
Chimonanthus
Choisya
Chorisia
Clivia
Coleonema
Echium
Edgeworthia
Epacris
Erica
Eriostemon
Eucalyptus

Euphorbia
Eurya
Franklinia
Garrya
Gautheria
Gelsemium
Gordonia
Grevillea
Hakea
Hamamelis
Hardenbergia
Hebe

Helipterum
Indigofera
Kunzea
Luculia
Magnolia
Mahonia
Manettia
Paranomus
Phylica
Polygala
Protea

Pyrostegia
Reinwardtia
Rhodoleia
Stenocarpus
Streptosolen
Tecomanthe
Tecomaria
Thryptomene
Thunbergia
Tibouchina
Viburnum

FLOWER COLOURS — RED

Abutilon
Aesculus
Agapetes
Anigozanthus
Aristotelia
Asclepias
Azaleas
Azaleas — deciduous
Beaufortia
Berberidopsis
Boronia
Bougainvillea
Bouvardia
Brachychiton
Calliandra

Callistemon
Camellia
Cavendishia
Ceratopetalum
Chaenomeles
Clematis
Clianthus
Cornus
Crataegus
Crinodendron
Cuphea
Cytisus
Desfontainea
Dodonaea
Embothrium

Epacris
Erica
Erythrina
Escallonia
Eucalyptus
Euphorbia
Fuchsia
Grevillea
Hakea
Hamamelis
Hebe
Hibiscus
Hydrangea
Justicia
Kunzea

Lagerstroemia
Lantana
Lapageria
Leptospermum
Lotus
Malus
Mandevilla
Manettia
Melaleuca
Metrosideros
Nerium
Nymphaea
Parrotia
Passiflora
Protea

Prunus
Punica
Rhododendron
Ribes
Russelia
Schefflera
Spiraea
Stenocarpus
Syringa
Tecomaria
Telopea
Thunbergia
Weigela
Xeronema

FLOWER COLOURS — PINK

Abelia	Chorisia	Grevillea	Leptospermum	Prunus
Abutilon	Cistus	Hardenbergia	Leucospermum	Raphiolepis
Adenandra	Clematis	Hebe	Luculia	Rhodochiton
Aesculus	Clianthus	Helichrysum	Magnolia	Rhododendron
Albizzia	Coleonema	Heterocentron	Malus	Rhodoleia
Astartea	Cornus	Hibiscus	Mandevilla	Ribes
Azaleas	Crataegus	Hydrangea	Nerium	Rondeletia
Boronia	Crowea	Hypocalymma	Nymphaea	Rulingia
Bougainvillea	Cytisus	Indigofera	Olearia	Symphoricarpus
Bouvardia	Daphne	Jasminum	Passiflora	Syringa
Brachychiton	Deutzia	Justicia	Pennisetum	Tamarix
Calluna	Dombeya	Kalmia	Pimelia	Tetratheca
Calytrix	Erica	Kolkwitzia	Podalyria	Thryptomene
Camellia	Escallonia	Lagerstroemia	Podranea	Viburnum
Cantua	Eucalyptus	Lagunaria	Prostanthera	Virgilia
Chaenomeles	Fuchsia	Lantana	Protea	Weigela
Chamelaucium				

FLOWER COLOURS — WHITE

Abutilon	Ceanothus	Erica	Lantana	Potentilla
Adenandra	Chaenomeles	Eriostemon	Leptospermum	Prunus
Agapanthus	Chionanthus	Eucalyptus	Leucothoe	Pterostyrax
Agonis	Choisya	Eucryphia	Linum	Pyracantha
Ailanthus	Cistus	Eurya	Luculia	Quintinia
Amelanchier	Cladrastis	Fatsia	Magnolia	Raphiolepis
Anopteris	Clematis	Fuchsia	Malus	Rhododendron
Arbutus	Clethra	Gardenia	Mandevilla	Sambucus
Arctostaphylos	Clianthus	Genista	Monstera	Schizophragma
Arthropodium	Coleonema	Grevillea	Myoporum	Serissa
Astartea	Convolvulus	Hardenbergia	Nerium	Spiraea
Azaleas	Cordyline	Hebe	Nymphaea	Stephanotis
Backhousia	Cornus	Helichrysum	Olearia	Stewartia
Baeckea	Cortaderia	Helipterum	Osmanthus	Styrax
Beilschmiedia	Cotoneaster	Hibiscus	Parahebe	Syringa
Bouvardia	Crinodendron	Hoheria	Phebalium	Thryptomene
Buddleia	Cunonia	Hosta	Philadelphus	Trachelospermum
Calliandra	Cytisus	Hydrangea	Philodendron	Viburnum
Calluna	Daboecia	Hydrangea	Physocarpus	Weinmannia
Calytrix	Davidia	Itea	Pieris	Westringia
Camellia	Deutzia	Jasminum	Pimelia	Wisteria
Carpodetus	Elaeocarpus	Lagerstroemia	Plumeria	Yucca
Cassinia	Entelea			

FLOWER COLOURS — CREAM

Acacia	Camellia	Franklinia	Leucothoe	Plumeria
Ackama	Catalpa	Gordonia	Loropetalum	Potentilla
Agave	Cytisus	Helichrysum	Magnolia	Pyrus
Azara	Elingamita	Hibiscus	Michelia	Rhododendron
Berzelia	Enkianthus	Hymenosporum	Myrtus	Tasmannia
Billardiera	Eucalyptus	Lantana	Nerium	Tecomanthe
			Pandorea	Tristaniopsis

FLOWER COLOURS — YELLOW

Abutilon
Acacia
Anigozanthus
Asteriscus
Azaleas Deciduous
Azara
Banksia
Berberis
Boronia
Bougainvillea
Buddleia
Callistemon
Carmichaelia
Cassia

Chimonanthus
Chrysocoma
Clematis
Cleyera
Corokia
Corylopsis
Crotalaria
Cytisus
Dryandra
Edgeworthia
Erica
Euphorbia
Euryops
Eutaxia

Forsythia
Garrya
Gelsemium
Genista
Grevillea
Halimium
Hamamelis
Helichrysum
Hibbertia
Hibiscus
Hymenosporum
Hypericum
Isopogon
Jasminum

Kerria
Koelreuteria
Laburnum
Lantana
Leucadendron
Leucospermum
Lomartia
Lonicera
Lysimachia
Macfadyena
Mahonia
Metrosideros
Nymphaea

Ochna
Othonna
Phellodendron
Pomaderris
Potentilla
Radermachera
Reinwardtia
Rhamnus
Rhododendron
Ruta
Santolina
Solandra
Stachyurus

FLOWER COLOURS — ORANGE

Abutilon
Azaleas Deciduous
Banksia
Bougainvillea
Caesalpinia
Campsis

Chaenomeles
Clivia
Daubentonia
Distictis
Dryandra
Erica

Eucalyptus
Grevillea
Hamamelis
Hibiscus
Lantana
Leonotis

Leucospermum
Lonicera
Punica
Pyrostegia
Rhabdothamnus

Rhododendron
Rhododendron vireya
Strelitzia
Streptosolen
Thunbergia

FLOWER COLOURS — BROWN

Alectryon
Banksia

Boronia
Cytisus

Hibiscus
Knightia

FLOWER COLOURS — MAUVE

Alyogyne
Azaleas
Boronia
Brunfelsia
Buddleia
Calluna
Clematis

Cuphea
Cytisus
Daphne
Erica
Grewia
Hebe

Hibiscus
Hosta
Indigofera
Isopogon
Jacaranda
Lagerstroemia

Lantana
Leptospermum
Melastoma
Melia
Podalyria
Prostanthera

Rhododendron
Rosmarinus
Stauntonia
Strobilanthes
Syringa
Virgilia

FLOWER COLOURS — BLUE

Agapanthus
Brachyscome
Caryopteris
Ceanothus
Ceratostigma
Clematis
Clerodendrum

Convolvulus
Dampiera
Duranta
Evolvulus
Hebe
Hydrangea

Iochroma
Lavendula
Lithodora
Nymphaea
Olearia
Paulownia

Plumbago
Prostanthera
Psoralea
Puya
Rhododendron
Rosmarinus

Solanum
Sollya
Teucrium
Thunbergia
Vitex
Wisteria

FLOWER COLOURS — PURPLE

Abutilon	Buddleia	Cytisus	Hardenbergia	Prostanthera
Akebia	Calluna	Daboecia	Hebe	Rhododendron
Aloysia	Cercis	Daphne	Kunzea	Syringa
Bauera	Chordospartium	Echium	Magnolia	Tibouchina
Beaufortia	Clematis	Erica	Petrea	Vigna
Bougainvillea	Cotinus	Felicia	Polygala	

FLOWER COLOURS — GREEN

Acorus	Callistemon	Liriodendron	Plagianthus	Pseudowintera
Alnus	Cyperus	Muehlenbeckia	Planchonella	Ptelea
Anigozanthus	Erica	Paranomus	Protea	Puya
Ascarina	Euphorbia	Phylica	Prunus	Tilia

GLOSSARY OF BOTANICAL TERMS

acuminate — tapering to a point

acute — sharply pointed but not drawn out

adpressed — where an organ lies flat or close to the stem

aerial roots — roots borne wholly above ground

alternate — arranged in two alternating ranks

anther — pollen-bearing tip of stamen

apetalous — without petals

apex — growing point of stem, root or leaf

arboreus — tree-like

aril — fleshy appendage of the hilum in which the seed is embedded

attenuate — tapering concavely to a fine, long drawn out point

auriculate — with two protruding ear-shaped lobes

awn — sharp point or bristle-like appendage on the glumes of grasses

axil — the point above a leaf where it rises from the stem

axillary — in, arising from or pertaining to an axil

basal — the base from which stems, leaves or flowers arise

bifid — deeply cleft into two points or lobes

bifoliate — with two leaves

bifurcate — twice forked

bipinnate — with both primary and secondary pinnate leaflets

biserrate — with a double row of saw teeth

bisexual — flowers with both stamens and pistils (hermaphrodite)

blade — the expanded portion of a leaf excluding the petiole

bloom — the waxy, powdery covering of some fruit, stems or leaves

bract — modified leaf, seen in the inflorescence of Euphorbia pulcherrima

bristly — with long stiff hairs or bristles

bulbil — small bulb-like growth arising from a leaf or inflorescence

bullate — blistered or puckered

caespitose — growing in small dense matted or tufted clumps

calcareous — chalky, alkaline or with high levels of calcium carbonate

calyptra — hood or cap-like structure

calyx — outer whorl of envelopes which protect the unopened flower

campanulate — bell-shaped flower, terminating in flared lobes

catkin — scaly-bracted, flexuous, pendent inflorescence

cauliflorous — flowers produced directly from older trunk or branches

chimaera — a plant created of tissues of various genetic composition

chlorophyll — green coloured substance of photosynthetic plants

ciliate — marginal fringe of fine hairs resembling eyelashes

cirrhous — coiled or spiralling continuation of the midrib

cladode — a stem-leaf, branches simulating or functioning as a leaf

cladophyll — stem-leaf, branchlets simulating or functioning as a leaf

clasping — partially or wholly surround, ie leaf base clasping a stem

cleft — where an organ such as a leaf is cut almost to the centre

clone — asexual, genetically identical offspring of a single parent

compound leaf — usually one of two or more leaflets

compound — comprising two or more similar parts

concave — hollowed out

connate — united, applied to similar structures fused together as one

cordate — heart-shaped, usually applied to leaves

coriaceous — tough and leathery but smooth and pliable

corolla — inner circle or whorl of petals

corymb — short flat-topped inflorescence, outer flowers opening first

crenate — with rounded teeth or scalloped

culm — stem of grasses or bamboos, usually hollow except at nodes

cultivar — hybrid form originating in cultivation

cuneate — inversely triangular or wedge-shaped

cupule — cup-shaped structure subtending fruit as in an acorn

cuspidate — terminating in a sharp, stiff inflexible point

cyme — flat-topped inflorescence with central flower opening first

deciduous — plant which sheds its leaves annually usually over winter

decumbent — reclining or lying stem with apex rising almost vertically

decurved — curved downwards

deltoid — equilateral triangle attached by the broad end

dentate — with shallow teeth, usually directed straight outward

dichotomous — regularly branching by repeated forking into two

digitate — palmately arranged as with the 'fingers' of a compound leaf

dimorphic — two dissimilar forms or shapes, at one or various stages

dioecious — male and female reproductive organs on different plants

dissected — leaf blades cleft several times into small segments

divaricate — branching outwards from main stem at angles of 70–90°

downy — covered with short soft hairs — see pubescent

drupe — one or multi-seeded, soft fleshy fruit, e.g pecan or plum

elliptic — oblong, narrowed at each, widest at the centre

elongate — lengthened or stretched out

endemic — native to or confined to a particular region

entire — margins without being toothed or lobed

epiphyte — dwells on a host tree without deriving nourishment from it

falcate — strongly curved sideways as in a scythe or sickle

fastigiate — branches erect and parallel with the main stem

fertile — producing viable seed

fibrous — woody textured threads

filament — thread-like organ, or stalk carrying staminal anthers

filiform — threadlike, long and slender

floccose — with dense woolly hairs which falls off easily in tufts

funnelform — of a corolla tube which widens towards spreading lobes

glabrous — smooth, not hairy or rough-textured

glaucous — coated with fine grey or blue-green bloom or powder

glume — small dry membranous bract in the inflorescence of grasses

glutinous — sticky

herb — without woody stems or with medicinal or aromatic qualities

herbaceous — non-woody plants

hermaphrodite — bisexual, having stamens and pistil in the same flower

hilum — the scar on a seed at the point where it was attached

hirsute — with long rather distinct and coarse hairs

hybrid — a plant arising from a cross between two dissimilar parents

imbricated — where leaves or bracts overlap as in roof tiles

inflorescence — flowering part or the mode of floral arrangement

internode — part of a stem between two nodes

involucre — a bract or whorl of bracts surrounding flowers

laciniate — irregularly or finely cut as if slashed

lanceolate — lance-shaped, 3–6 times longer than broad

lateral — on or at the side

latex — milky sap secreted from plants such as Asclepias and Euphorbia

lenticel — elliptical pores on young bark through which gas penetrates

lepidote — covered with minute, scurfy scales

liana or liane — woody climbing vine

lignotuber — woody, tuber-like basal structure containing dormant buds

ligulate — strap-shaped

linear — slender, elongated, margins parallel or nearly so

lobe — rounded or pointed part cut less than halfway to the base

marginal — at the edge

membranous — thin-textured, semi-transparent, soft and flexible

monoecious — stamens and pistils in separate flowers on the same plant

monotypic — of one component, as in a genus of one species

mutant — variant differing genetically from its parent or parents

node — point where leaves, shoots, branches or flowers are attached

obcordate — inversely heart-shaped, with the notch at the apex

oblanceolate — as lanceolate but with broadest part above the centre

oblique — sides with unequal angles and dimensions

oblong — with almost parallel sides, 2–3 times longer than wide.

obovate — as ovate but with broadest end above centre

obovoid — ovoid shaped, broadest part below centre

obtuse — blunt or rounded at the end

opposite — usually used of two ranks of leaves positioned opposite

orbicular — circular outline or nearly so

ovary — basal part of the pistil containing future seed

ovate — egg-shaped, rounded at both ends, broadest below centre

palmate — three or more finger-like lobes or segments

panicle — an open and branched inflorescence

papilionaceous — with five petals shaped like a butterfly, pea-shaped

pappus — tuft of delicate bristles or scales in place of the calyx

parasite — an organism living off or at the expense of another

paripinnate — pinnately compound leaf without single terminal leaflet

pectinate — pinnately divided, with long slender comb-like segments

pedicel — stalk of individual flowers or fruit in an inflorescence

peduncle — primary stalk of an individual flower or inflorescence

peltate — where the stalk is attached to an organ inside its margin

pendent — hanging downwards, but not from weight or weakness of stem

pendulous — hanging downwards as a result of weight or weak stem

perianth — collective term for floral envelopes, corolla and calyx

petal — brightly coloured part of the corolla designed to attract

petiole — the stalk of a leaf

phylloclade — flattened stem or branch functioning as a leaf

phyllode — expanded petiole functioning as a leaf as in Acacia

pilose — covered with soft slender shaggy hairs

pinna or pinnae — divisions or leaflets in a pinnate leaf

pinnate — feather-like compound leaf, leaflets each side of a rachis

pinnatifid — pinnately cleft almost to the midrib

pinnule — a secondary segment of a pinna

pistil — female floral organ consisting of ovary, style and stigma

pistillate — unisexual female flower with pistil but without stamens

plantlet — small plant developing on a larger parent plant

plicate — pleated or folded lengthwise like a fan

pollarding — cutting all branches back to the main trunk

pollen — spores or grains containing the male element of fertilization

pollination — transferral of pollen from anther to receptive stigma

pollinator — agent by which pollination is effected

polymorphic — bearing various shaped leaves, growing in varying forms

procumbent — trailing or lying on the ground without rooting

prostrate — lying flat on the ground

pruinose — thickly frosted with white bloom rather than blue-grey

pubescent — covered with short, soft, fine hairs

punctate — dotted with tiny translucent glands as if done with a pin

pyramidal — conical form but with more angular sides

raceme — simple elongated inflorescence with pedicelled flowers

rachis — the axis or midrib of a compound leaf or inflorescence

ray — outer or marginal portion of a daisy or Compositae flower

recurved — curved downward or backward

reflexed — abruptly deflexed at more than 90°

reniform — kidney-shaped

resinous — containing or exuding resin

revolute — margins rolled under

rhizome — creeping underground rootstock

rhomboid — diamond-shaped

rosette — cluster of leaves radiating in a circle from a central point

rugose — irregularly lined or wrinkled

sagittate — arrow-shaped with basal triangular lobes pointing downward

samara — one-seeded, winged fruit as in maple or ash

sanguine — crimson or blood-coloured

saxicolous — inhabiting rocks or rocky places

scabrous — rough or harsh to the touch

scandent — climbing

scape — leafless stalk from ground-level bearing an inflorescence

segment — leaflet of a pinnate leaf

sepal — one of the separate units of a calyx

sericeous — covered with fine, soft, adpressed hair

serrate — finely toothed or notched like a saw

sessile — apparently without a petiole or stalk, sitting close

setose — covered with sharply pointed bristles

simple — as pertaining to leaves, not compound or divided

sinuate — wavy outline of a leaf

sorus — spore clusters seen on the underside of fern leaves

spadix — fleshy axis of a spike bearing minute flowers

spathe — conspicuous leaf or bract surrounding an inflorescence

spathulate — spatula-shaped with base attenuated axis rounded

spicule — tiny, needle-like crystal of oxalic acid

stamen — pollen-bearing male floral organ

stellate — hairs which radiate in star-like manner from a common point

stigma — the part of the pistil which receives pollen

stipule — leaf-like appendage at the base of a petiole

stolon — prostrate stem taking root at nodes and producing plantlets

stomata — pores or apertures in leaf or stem

style — slender part of the pistil between ovary and stigma

subsp — or subspp, abbreviation for sub-species

subulate — awl-shaped, tapering to a narrow point

synonym — a name rejected in favour of another

tendril — modified branch used by climbing plants for attachment

terete — circular or rounded in cross-section

terminal — tip or apex of a stem or branch

terrestrial — growing in the soil

tomentum — dense covering of matted, woolly, short, rigid hairs

topiary — art of clipping or training shrubs in various forms

trifoliolate — with three leaflets

tubular — form resembling a cylinder

umbel — flat-topped inflorescence, pedicels arising from same point

unarmed — devoid of spines

undulate — waved or wavy margins

velutinous — coated with fine soft hairs with texture of velvet

whorl — three or more organs arranged in a circle at one node

xeromorphic — adaptation to water storage or limiting moisture loss

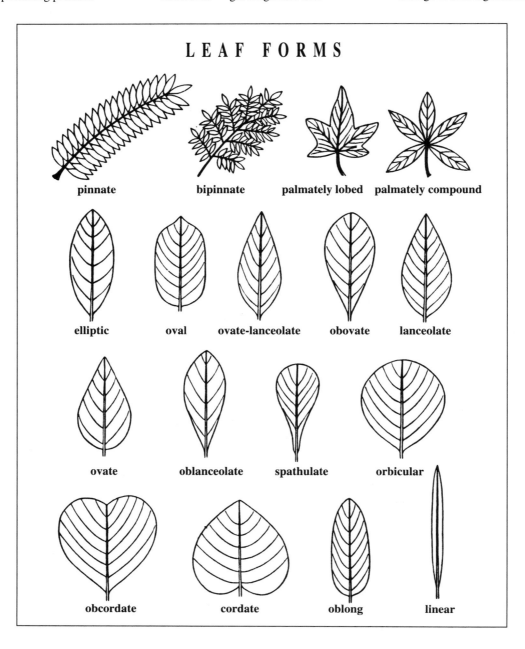

LEAF FORMS

pinnate bipinnate palmately lobed palmately compound

elliptic oval ovate-lanceolate obovate lanceolate

ovate oblanceolate spathulate orbicular

obcordate cordate oblong linear

INDEX OF COMMON NAMES

NOMENCLATURE — SYNONYMS AND ALTERATIONS